Unity AR & VR by Tutorials

By Jimmy Alamparambil, Matt Larson, Eric Van de Kerckhove

& Jonathan Ogle-Barrington

Unity AR & VR by Tutorials

By Jimmy Alamparambil, Matt Larson, Jonathan Ogle-Barrington & Eric Van de Kerckhove

Notice of Rights

Notice of Liability

Trademarks

ISBN: 978-1-942878-64-3

Dedications

"A big thank you to my darlings Lidia, Jasmine and Catherine for their patience during all those times I had to sacrifice my playtime with them. Love you, dears. Also, shout-outs to my colleagues at Unity and at other companies I have worked with, who have helped in various ways for me to be here now. Finally, my sincere gratitude to my relatives and friends who have given me lots of encouragement and love."

— *Jimmy Alamparambil*

"To Camilla, my wife, who has supported me throughout my very varied career and always pushed me to achieve my dream. I'd also like to thank my boss, Ryan Bousfield who gave me the opportunities and has helped me to become the VR Developer I am now. Finally my mother for getting me my first computers and supporting me."

— *Jonathan Ogle-Barrington*

"To Bonnie, who has supported me in my game development endeavors throughout the years. I'd also like to thank the raywenderlich.com team for helping me grow and give back what I've learnt."

— *Eric Van de Kerckhove*

"To my son Felix, I look forward to playing with you in a new world of augmented reality as you grow up. And to my wife Eppie who shares my love for creating and exploring in this world."

— *Matt Larson*

About the Authors

Jimmy Alamparambil is an author on this book. He is a veteran of the game industry, having worked for companies like EA, Ubisoft. Jam City and others on franchises as varied as Medal of Honor, Spyro, GoldenEye, CSI, Spartacus, Petz, Just Dance, Rocksmith, etc. More recently, he has worked on the well received Unity ARKit Plugin, which has been used to create the vast majority of ARKit apps on the AppStore. He currently works in the XR team at Unity, where he is helping to architect and develop the latest AR APIs.

Matt Larson is an author of this book. He is a lifelong gamer and developer of scientific visualization software. He is also the creator of the mixed-reality app, Titan MR, which allows users to explore the surface of Saturn's moon, Titan, and was a finalist for the 2018 Windows Developer Reality Mixer of the Year award and the featured in the Unity HoloLens Contest.

Jonathan Ogle-Barrington is an author on this book. Jonathan has been programming since he was 8 years old when he received his first BBC Master. Starting off in large scale intranet development, he pursued his love of games by starting his own mobile game and app company before taking the role of Lead VR Game Developer at Wolf & Wood. In his role he has worked on the release of 3 multi-award winning VR games including A chair in a Room and The Exorcist: Legion VR on Oculus, SteamVR and PlayStation VR.

Eric Van de Kerckhove is an author and final pass editor of this book. Eric is a Belgian hobbyist game developer and has been so for more than 15 years. He has made a fair share of games over the years, mostly free ones for fun and as learning experiences. Eric is leading the Unity team for raywenderlich.com.

About the Editors

Ben MacKinnon is a tech editor of this book. He has been augmenting Architecture for Soluis since 2013. His work ranges from b2b enterprise apps for Football Stadiums, to interactive art installations, such as the Scottish entry to the 2016 Venice Biennale. In his spare time he is a Tech Editor for the Unity team at raywenderlich.com, and Editor in Chief for games review site and podcast, Glitch Free Gaming.

Sean Duffy is a tech editor of this book. He is a software engineer by day, and hobbyist game and tools developer by night. He loves working with Unity, and is also a Unity Asset Store developer with a special focus on 2D tools to help other game developers. Some of Sean's more popular Unity Assets include his 2D Shooter Bullet and Weapon System and 2D Homing Missiles assets. You can find Sean on Twitter at @shogan85.

Tammy Coron is an editor for this book. She is an independent creative professional and the host of Roundabout: Creative Chaos. She's also the founder of Just Write Code. Find out more at tammycoron.com.

About the Artists

Mike Berg is the designer of the Virtual Pet game art in this book. He is a full-time game artist who is fortunate enough to work with many indie game developers from all over the world. When he's not manipulating pixel colors, he loves to eat good food, spend time with his family, play games and be happy. You can check out his work at www.weheartgames.com

Vicki Wenderlich is the designer and artist of the cover of this book. She is Ray's wife and business partner. She is a digital artist who creates illustrations, game art and a lot of other art or design work for the tutorials and books on raywenderlich.com. When she's not making art, she loves hiking, a good glass of wine and attempting to create the perfect cheese plate.

Table of Contents

Book License

What You Need

To follow along with **everything** in this book, you'll need the following:

- A PC running **Windows 10** with VR capability. This means having a decent CPU and a Geforce GTX 970 or better GPU.
- A Mac running **High Sierra** (10.13) or later. Earlier versions might work, but they're untested.
- **Xcode 9.3 or later.** Xcode is the main development tool for iOS. You'll need Xcode 9.3 or later for some of the tasks in this book. You can download the latest version of Xcode from Apple's developer site here: apple.co/2asi58y
- **One or more devices (iPhone, iPad) running iOS 11 or later.** The device must have an A9 processor or better to support ARKit.
- **One or more Android devices running Android 7 or later that support ARCore.** Here's a full list of supported devices: https://developers.google.com/ar/discover/supported-devices
- An **Oculus Rift** with the Touch controllers.
- An **HTC Vive**.
- A **Microsoft HoloLens**.

If you haven't installed the latest stable version of Unity, be sure to do that before continuing with the book. The instructions and code have been written and tested with that version in mind, using an older version may result in unexpected behavior. You can download the latest version here: https://unity3d.com/get-unity/download

Book Source Code & Forums

You can get the source code for the book, here: https://store.raywenderlich.com/products/unity-ar-and-vr-by-tutorials-source-code

There, you'll find all the code from the chapters for your use.

We've also set up an official forum for the book at forums.raywenderlich.com. This is a great place to ask questions about the book or to submit any errors you may find.

Section I: Introduction to VR

Welcome to the first section of the book where you'll get your feet wet by learning all about the amazing features of virtual reality.

This section act as an introduction to VR and its many use cases. It also covers the history of VR and compares the VR hardware we have available to us today.

These chapters are the start of your virtual reality adventures:

- **Chapter 1: New Realities**: Before diving off the deep end, take a moment to reflect on how we got to these exciting times for virtual reality. Learn about the history of VR and its humble beginnings.
- **Chapter 2: Platforms & Experiences**: Explore the different virtual reality platforms and learn about what sets them apart from each other. If you're not sure what hardware to get, this will make your decision a lot easier.

Chapter 1: New Realities

Jonathan Ogle-Barrington

There's a lot of talk and excitement around the topic of **virtual reality**, also known as **VR**. If you're reading this book, chances are you're at least familiar with some aspects of VR. That's great! However, before jumping in and creating your first VR experience, it's important to understand the history of virtual reality, along with some basic terminology and hardware options. If you'd rather skip to the lengthy discussion, jump to the "TL;DR" section in this chapter for a summary — either is fine.

What is virtual reality?

VR simulates a user's physical presence inside a 3D computer-generated environment. With VR, users can experience and manipulate things within this environment as if they were real. This is done using interactive devices such as a headset, gloves or even full body suits.

History of virtual reality

When talking about the history of VR, most people think about the iconic science fiction films of the 1980's and the promise of living in an immersive virtual world. However, VR has been around longer than that. In fact, it theoretically dates back to the early 1800's, with the first practical applications showing up in the late 1950's.

The 1800's

In 1838, English scientist and inventor Charles Wheatstone's research identified that the brain is capable of binocular vision; that is to say, the brain can process two separate 2D images, one from each eye, and render it into a single 3D scene.

By viewing two side-by-side stereoscopic images through a stereoscope, you can experience depth and immersion. This idea was the basis behind a popular toy called The View-Master.

The View-Master

Not long after that, in the 1860's, French playwright, Antonin Artaud, argued that illusion was not distinct from reality. He further went on to say that the attendees of his plays should consider what's happening on the stage not as *drama*, but as *reality* instead.

The 1900's

In the 1930's, Laurence Manning wrote short stories in which he described a time where people were voluntarily connected to machines that replaced their human sensory input with electrical charges and impulses. For those of you who are fans of the movie, "The Matrix" by the Wachowski Siblings, it might seem like Manning predicted future.

Roughly twenty years later, in the late 1950's, a genius by the name of Morton Heilig started working on what would become the first VR device. Later, in 1962, he developed the Sensorama Simulator, accompanied by five 3D films that Heilig and his wife Marianne produced. The Sensorama's feature list was impressive, even by today's standards, boasting the ability to display stereoscopic 3D images in a wide-angle view, along with body tilting, stereo sound and even the ability to trigger additional sensory functions for wind and aroma. Not bad, eh?

Heilig tried many routes to market his Sensorama device and looked for investors to help. At one point the Sensorama made a brief appearance as a coin-operated device at Universal Studios. Later, it found its way to into arcades. Unfortunately, due to the custom nature of the device, and how difficult it was to replace parts and handle mass production, it didn't get far. In many circumstances, the device flat out broke in the arcades.

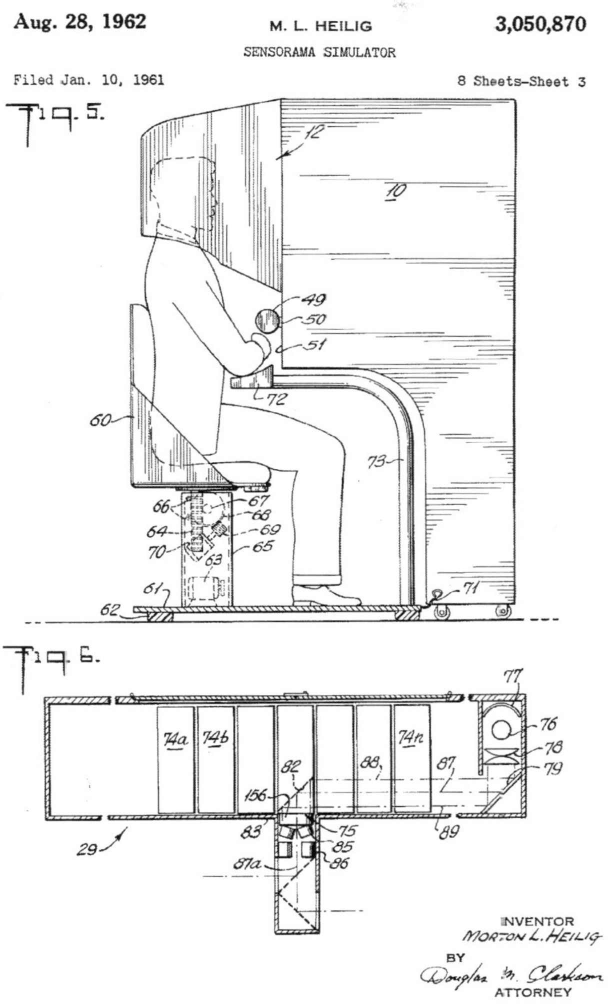

The patent for the Sensorama, filled in 1962

However, it wasn't all bad for Heilig; because of his accomplishments, he secured his place in history as The Father of Virtual Reality.

But Heilig wasn't the only one working on immersive technology. In 1968, Ivan Sutherland, a computer scientist with a strong background in computer graphics, along with Bob Sproull, created what many consider the first Head Mounted Display (HMD), known as "The Sword of Damocles".

Although primitive by today's standards concerning resolution and quality, The Sword of Damocles was capable of displaying output directly to the stereoscopic display based on the direction of the user's gaze. This was possible by using a VR application running on a computer — a set up which is similar to today.

The Samsung Gear VR

Although Ivan Sutherland and Bob Sproull developed the first HMD, it's worth noting that 8 years earlier, Heilig had patented the "Telesphere Mask". Described as "a telescopic television for individual use", this device used miniature television tubes to display stereoscopic 3D images in a wide-angle view.

In addition, it had stereo sound and nozzles capable of discharging aromas similar to the Sensorama. All this tech was packaged into a small form factor resembling the Samsung Gear VR available today.

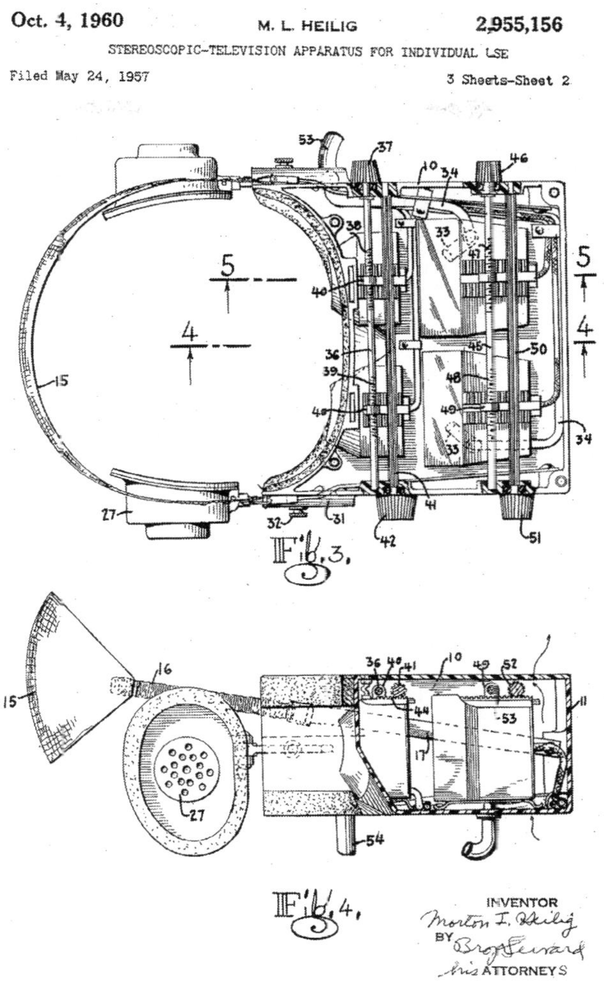

The Telesphere Mask patent from 1960

Things didn't stop there. In 1987, Jaron Lanier, founder of the visual programming lab, (VPL) coined the term "Virtual Reality" and began work on a wide range of VR devices, including the Dataglove and EyePhone HMD.

By the time the 1990's rolled around, VR headsets aimed at the general consumer started becoming a thing. In 1991, Sega announced they planned to release a VR headset for their home consoles, the Sega Genesis and Saturn. This idea was based on an existing design Sega was already using in arcades.

However, due to development difficulties, which included motion sickness and headaches amongst testers, the headset remained a prototype only.

Nintendo also entered the VR market in 1995 with the release of the Virtual Boy. The Virtual Boy was marketed as the first table-top console capable of displaying stereoscopic 3D graphics. It wasn't a head-mounted device; instead, the user was required to place their head against the eyepieces where a red monochrome display used a parallax effect to create the illusion of depth.

Although the Virtual Boy released to the consumer, it didn't have the success Nintendo hoped it would have; many speculated this was due to the shift in focus to the N64 project, and in 1996, Nintendo pulled the Virtual Boy from the market.

Nintendo's Virtual Boy

The early 2000's

Thankfully, VR didn't die with the Virtual Boy. In the early 21st century, changes in the technology world helped pave the way to overcome the technical limitations of virtual reality, these include:

- **Bluetooth/Wireless data transmission**: A key component in almost every modern VR setup, specifically in the transmission of data from peripherals like the Oculus Touch or Vive Controllers.
- **Dedicated GPU's**: The GPU (Graphics Processing Unit) plays a crucial part in the rendering or drawing of 3D scenes to the display. Although the GPU has been around since the 1970's, it wasn't until the early 21st century that personal computers shipped with dedicated GPU's capable of rendering complex 3D scenes. Nowadays, especially with the release of commercial VR headsets, many GPU's are listed as VR ready. In fact, even some lightweight laptops are capable of running full VR experiences.

- **Faster CPU's**: Although the GPU handles the majority of the VR-related work, the CPU performance is still important as it's needed to process the massive amounts of data the headset and its peripherals produce. The CPU is also heavily utilized for the computation of physics interactions within virtual reality; for example, when you pick up an item and throw it in VR, the CPU computes the interactions that item has on the surrounding virtual environment.
- **Broadband/4G**: The introduction of Broadband and high-speed mobile data opened up the digital distribution market — commonly utilized by content providers such as Oculus and Valve in the distribution of their VR content.
- **Digital distribution platforms**: The development of digital distribution platforms revolutionized the way content is consumed, and its estimated that 90% of VR content is delivered digitally via platforms such as Steam, Viveports and the Oculus Store.
- **LCD displays**: LCD displays have been around since the 1970's, but they weren't always this nice. Somewhere in the early 21st century, the quality and resolution surpassed that of conventional cathode-ray-tube (CRT) based displays, and the quality of their output continues to improve.
- **Smartphones**: With the introduction of high-end smartphones with dedicated GPU's, virtual reality has gone mobile. It started with Google Cardboard, and then later, the Samsung Gear VR in 2015. Thanks to devices like this, mobile VR has drastically reduced the barrier to entry for the consumer by allowing them to utilize their existing smartphone to replace an expensive VR-ready computer.

The Oculus Kickstarter to present day

One of the biggest stories to come out of the VR world is about a young man named Palmer Luckey. In 2011, Luckey was working in his parent's garage, trying to produce a new VR headset. At the same time, other industry professionals were looking into VR. That's when John Carmack, from Id Software, came across Palmer's work on a forum they both frequented. After testing an early prototype, Carmack favored Palmer's approach over other devices. Not only that, but there was a promise that the Oculus Rift would be compatible with "Doom 3: BFG Edition".

On August 1, 2012, Palmer Luckey and his company, Oculus, launched the Kickstarter for the Oculus Rift. This allowed consumers to get their hands on an early development kit, the Oculus Rift DK1, in exchange for a pledge of $300.

The Rift DK1 released on March 29, 2013, and just over a year later, the DK2 hit the shelves selling almost 100,000 units before it was replaced by the final prototype, codenamed Crescent Bay.

The Oculus Rift DK1

Finally, on May 6, 2015, they announced that pre-orders for the Oculus Rift CV1 (Consumer Version) would be available in early January 2016; and on March 25, 2016, the first batch of pre-orders shipped!

But Oculus wasn't the only company making waves in the VR world. A partnership between HTC and Valve emerged. Not long after that, they announced their plans to produce a virtual reality system that would integrate into the gaming platform known as Steam.

During a keynote at HTC's Mobile World Congress in March 2015, they unveiled the HTC Vive, with development kits released 6 months later; the first consumer edition released 6 months after that.

The HTC Vive

Since then, a multitude of headsets have been announced and released, including the Sony PSVR — the first VR headset for a console since the failed Virtual Boy. With countless headsets now in the hands of consumers, this certainly isn't where the history of VR will end.

TL;DR

If you didn't manage to get through the sticky details of the history of VR, here's the TL;DR version for you:

Year	Developments
1800's	Panoramic paintings: These paintings filled the viewer's entire field of vision making it an immersive scene.
1838	Stereoscopic photos and viewers: Charles Wheatstone's research identified that the brain is capable of processing two separate 2D images, one from each eye, into one single 3D scene.
1960's	Morton Heilig began working on the first VR device. In 1962, his Sensorama Simulator was born.
1960's	Ivan Sutherland created the first VR Head Mounted Device.
1987	The term "Virtual Reality" was coined by Jaron Lanier, founder of Visual Programming Lab (VPL).
1992	The Lawnmower Man movie introduced the concept of virtual reality to consumers and filmgoers.
1993	At the Consumer Electronics Show, the Sega VR headset was announced for the Sega Genesis console, but it was never released.
1995	The Nintendo Virtual Boy: The first-ever portable VR console capable of displaying 3D graphics in virtual reality.
1999	"The Matrix", a film by the Wachowski siblings, featured characters forcefully living in VR.
2010	The Oculus Kickstarter.
2014	Facebook bought Oculus VR and developed VR chat rooms.
2016	The HTC Vive and Oculus Consumer devices are released.
2017	A multitude of different VR devices are available on the commercial market.

With the history out of the way, it's time to jump into some of the tech behind VR.

The technology behind VR

A virtual reality headset can make you believe that you're walking on the surface of Mars or exorcising a demon in the fictional world of William Peter Blatty; in reality, however, you're in your living room surrounded by family and friends (who are probably trying to trip you). So how does it all work?

Current devices on the market all share a similar form-factor but differ slightly in the way they deliver the content to the HMD. Devices like the HTC Vive, Oculus Rift and Sony's PSVR are known as tethered systems. Tethered systems require wires that attach the headset to a desktop, laptop or console responsible for delivering VR content.

In contrast, headsets from Google and Samsung are known as mobile or standalone VR headsets. Mobile headsets make use of the user's mobile phone to deliver VR content to the headset; whereas standalone headsets make use of internal hardware to deliver content, and therefore do not require a high-end computer or smartphone. As you might have guessed, standalone VR is poised to grow in the market in 2018.

Whether the HMD is tethered, mobile or standalone, the concepts for displaying VR content are similar: two streams of content are sent to the headset, regardless of whether it's to one display or two. A set of lenses inside the headset focus and reshape the content for each eye creating a stereoscopic 3D image. This is done by adjusting the 2D images to mimic how our eyes view the world in real life.

When creating an immersive experience, it's important to remember that the human brain is extraordinarily perceptive and able to consume data in vast quantities. Maintaining a high FPS (Frames Per Second), along with the field of view, is one way to increase the realism and prevent users from noticing stuttering which can lead to VR sickness.

Head tracking

Head tracking is an essential part of the technology that makes VR function. Head tracking refers to adjusting the images rendered to the HMD based on a system called 6DoF (6 degrees of freedom). This system plots the position of the HMD regarding x, y and z and allows the game to react to the players head movements, whether that's forward and backward, side to side or shoulder to shoulder.

A set of internal components are vital to providing 6Dof tracking; these include a gyroscope, accelerometer and magnetometer. These components can be found in most modern day mobile phones, which has led to the increase of mobile VR solutions such as the Samsung Gear VR and the Google Daydream. Both of these devices are little more than a headset with special lenses in which you insert your phone.

Higher end systems such as the Oculus Rift and Sony's PSVR make use of these components, but they also make use of additional tracking via a combination of LEDs and sensors that provide 360-degree tracking. The HTC Vive, for example, uses a set ofbase stations that sweep the area with lasers to detect the precise location of the headset within a defined space.

Peripherals

Although the headset is the main component of a VR system, additional peripherals are needed to deliver full immersion to the user; these can take the form of controllers, gloves or even full body suits.

High-end headsets such as the HTC Vive, Oculus Rift and Sony's PSVR have specialist controllers that are also tracked by the same sensors that track the HMD. These controllers allow you to use your hands within VR through a combination of buttons triggers and thumbsticks.

Oculus Touch hand tracking

Where to go from here?

Well done! You made it through the history of virtual reality and you learned about the main components of VR. In the next chapter, you'll look at the various platforms, headsets and input devices available for VR. You'll also examine what sets them apart from each other as well as the key experiences and games that have helped shape the VR industry.

Chapter 2: Platforms & Experiences

Jonathan Ogle-Barrington

As you read in Chapter 1, "New Realities," the VR market is growing; and with that growth comes a large assortment of headsets, peripherals and platforms. In this chapter, you'll examine what's available, along with the individual strengths and weaknesses of each.

Tethered VR

When considering tethered VR, there are a few options that stand out.

Oculus Rift

Despite its rocky start, the **Oculus Rift** is one of the most popular VR headsets. When the Rift first launched, it came equipped with a single tracking sensor, a small remote for interacting with the home menu and a Microsoft Xbox controller for controlling the game or experience. These days, however, the Oculus Rift ships with two sensors and two **Oculus Touch** controllers, significantly improving the user's overall experience.

The headset itself features twin OLED displays with a resolution of **1080×1200 pixels**, a field of view (FOV) of **110°** and a refresh rate of **90 Hz**.

You can purchase an additional third sensor to enable **360° tracking**; however, despite the extra money needed for that feature, it still falls short of the HTC Vive's room scale tracking.

Pros	Cons
Facebook backing	Does not support 360° tracking out of the box
Superior controller	An immature store compared to other platforms
Built-in audio system	N/A

HTC Vive

When the **HTC Vive** was first released, it was light years ahead of its competitors. Out-of-the-box, the HTC Vive supported **360° room scale tracking** and came with two motion controllers. Not to mention, it was backed by one of the biggest digital distribution platforms, **Steam**.

Although the gap has been significantly reduced with the release of the **Oculus Touch** controllers and the ability of the Oculus Rift to support additional sensors, the HTC Vive offers full room scale tracking and a mature platform. It has also got an update that added a motion interpolation technique known as **asynchronous reprojection**, which lets the refresh rate fall back to **45 Hz** while injecting frames inbetween to simulate fluid movement.

Pros	Cons
Full 360° tracking	Most expensive on the market
Full room scale support	No built-in audio system
Mature platform	N/A

Windows Mixed Reality

Microsoft expanded the options for desktop VR with a line of third-party **Windows Mixed Reality** headsets in 2017 from Acer, ASUS, HP, Lenovo, and Samsung. A notable feature of these headsets was the reuse of **inside-out tracking** developed with the **Microsoft HoloLens** that avoids the requirement to setup **base stations** in the room like the Vive or Oculus systems. Additionally, these headsets featured higher resolution screens with resolution up to **1440x1600** per eye and **90 Hz** refresh rates via LCD or AMOLED screens.

The increased resolution leads to better clarity for text and reduced screen door effects on these headsets. These have slightly worse tracking for controllers and smaller 'sweet' spots for visibility through their lenses than the HTC or Oculus systems. They are low-cost entry points for desktop VR.

Playstation VR

The **PlayStation VR** (PSVR) is the only headset on the market designed to work with a game console. Despite the differences in performance between a high-end PC and the PlayStation 4, the PSVR delivers almost PC-quality virtual reality.

The PSVR is also the only tethered VR system to utilize a single OLED screen with a resolution of **1920×1080 pixels** (960×1080 per eye). Compared to the Oculus Rift and HTC Vive, the PSVR has a slightly smaller field of view — only **100°** as opposed to 110°.

The PSVR is capable of two refresh rates, **90 Hz** and **120 Hz**, along with asynchronous reprojection.

Pros	Cons
Does not require a high-end PC	Poor motion controller tracking
Near PC-quality experience	Ineffective sealing around the headset causes light leaking
Mature platform	N/A

Upcoming Devices

Pimax is an ambitious company looking to launch the first **8K** resolution headset with a whopping **200°** field of view, which closely matches the 220° field of view of the human eye. When this device releases, it'll be light-years ahead of any device on the market by almost doubling the FOV and tripling the resolution. It is likely to also challenge the desktop GPUs to match the capabilities of these displays.

Standalone VR

Now for a look at the standalone VR options. These HMDs are less powerful than their tethered counterparts, but they're cheaper, lighter and you can bring them with you as they are relatively portable.

Google Cardboard

Google Cardboard was Google's first offering in the standalone VR market. Intended as a cheap introduction to VR, its primary focus was to encourage interest in and development of VR games and experiences. Google Cardboard is compatible with both **iOS** and **Android**-based smartphones and is incredibly accessible; however, it's also extremely limited due to the lack of input devices and crude design.

Pros	Cons
Extremely cheap	Crude design
Multi-platform	No controller or input support

Samsung Gear VR

The **Samsung Gear VR**, developed in conjunction with **Oculus**, was released in November 2015 and was the first high-end standalone device on the market. To use the Gear VR, you need a compatible mobile phone which gets inserted into the device. The phone acts as the headset's display and processor, while the device itself acts as a controller and sends telemetry data to the phone.

As with all standalone VR devices that use a mobile phone, the Samsung Gear VR is limited by the processor and graphical capabilities of the phone being used.

Since its release in 2015, the device has been redesigned to support larger mobile phones. Samsung also added a motion controller with a trackpad and trigger, making it easier to interact with the VR content and experience.

Pros	Cons
Lightweight and mobile	Only supports Samsung mobile phones
Cheap and sometimes free with specific phones	Limited by the power of the mobile phone
Has controller support	Limited experience length based on the mobile phones battery life

Google Daydream

Google Daydream, released in 2016, is the successor to Google Cardboard. Sporting a similar form factor to the Samsung Gear VR, the Google Daydream is used by placing a compatible device into the VR headset. A motion controller is provided in the package for input, this allows for richer experiences than its cardboard counterpart.

Pros	Cons
Lightweight and mobile	Only support newer android phones with specific components
The cheapest headset on the market	Lacks content
Has controller support	Limited experience length based on the mobile phone's battery life
N/A	Limited by the power of the mobile phone

Oculus Go

Developed by **Oculus**, the **Oculus Go** is an upcoming standalone VR headset. Unlike the current market offerings, the Go does not require a mobile device; instead, it uses built-in components. The hardware inside is comparable to a mid to high end smartphone. Boasting a resolution of **2560×1440 pixels** (1280×1440 per eye), **3DoF**, **32/64 GB** of internal storage, improved optics, integrated **spatial audio speakers** and a motion controller, the Oculus Go can provide near PC-quality VR at an affordable price — without the need of being tethered to an expensive PC.

Pros	Cons
Lightweight and mobile	Limited motion tracking compared to tethered systems
Does not require a mobile phone	Poor battery-to-charge ratio
Has controller support	Does not sit well on the face; as a result, leaks light
Reasonably priced	Quite a heavy headset

Upcoming Devices

The **HTC Vive Focus** is an upcoming standalone headset already available in China. It has an impressive **3K** resolution, **6DoF Tracking**, **110° FOV**, built-in **spatial audio system**, expandable memory and rapid charging.

The **Oculus Quest** (previously called **Oculus Santa Cruz**) is the latest offering from **Oculus** slated for release in **Q1 2019**. It is positioned to be a standalone headset with more power than the **Oculus Go** and include **6DoF** inside-out tracking and dual displays each with a resolution of **1440×1600 pixels** matching the best VR desktop displays available. It's announcement caused a large excitement at the Connect 5 conference as it will offer the first high-quality standalone VR system allowing free, 6DoF movement around large room environments and provide some aspects of **Mixed Reality** such as seeing borders of obstacles within the room.

Practical VR applications and usage

You may think VR is only good for entertainment or gaming, but the truth is, other industries are starting to take note of its potential and popularity.

Medical

The medical industry has always been at the forefront of technological advancements, and it's no surprise that VR has been applied to a variety of situations that benefit healthcare professionals and patients across a multitude of disciplines.

The use of 3D visualization isn't new to the medical industry — the advances in technology have lead to faster and more precise imaging, surgeons are now able to use X-rays, CT scans and MRI scans to build realistic virtual models of patients (and their ailments) before carrying out risky, and sometimes fatal, exploratory surgery.

In 2017, a medical team partnered with scientists at the University of Minnesota to create a VR model of the hearts of two conjoined twins. By combining MRI and CT scans from both infants, the four surgeons were able to carry out the procedure — inside VR — and explore the walnut-sized organ as if it had been blown up to the size of an operating theater.

Not only was the procedure a success, but within minutes of being inside the simulation, the surgeons noticed some *undiscovered issues*, causing them to change the way they performed the surgery, saving the procedure and the lives of both children.

While it's clear that virtual reality can have some profound effects on medical procedures and training, other areas, including cognitive rehabilitation, treating PTSD, fears and phobias, pain management and even in the treatment of Bipolar Disorder, are seeing its benefits.

Automotive

The automotive industry has used 3D technology in the pre-production of automobiles for a while now, but it has recently adopted VR to help visualize products before physical prototypes are made. However, VR isn't just helping with pre-production. **Ford**, for example, uses virtual reality to help its customers get a sense of how their car will look and feel before they even order it.

Tourism

British Columbia was one of the first to use VR to encourage tourists to visit their region when they released a VR experience named "**The Wild Within**". This experience features two 360° videos: a virtual boat ride and a hike in the mountains of British Columbia.

The hospitality company **Marriott** has also released a similar experience allowing users to "teleport" to different locations around the globe and visit Marriott hotels and their surroundings.

Military

The British government recently announced it would be using the **Oculus Rift** to train trauma medics for real-world battle scenarios. They've also provided the military with virtual reality training simulations that teach different techniques for handling the disposal of IEDs, potentially saving lives in the real-world.

The **Arizona police** department uses virtual reality in a 300°, five-screen setup to train police officers how to react to certain situations. The simulation involves a man with a gun or a woman with a knife. These simulations can have multiple outcomes depending on how the police officer reacts.

Construction

The construction industry is one of the most profitable industries in the world. Unfortunately, it often suffers setbacks during construction because of the inability of its designers, engineers and architect have in seeing a project's complexities — before going into the construction phase.

Traditional construction designs make use of flat technical drawings and 3D models to try to visualize the early concepts; however, with the use of virtual reality, technical drawings and 3D models can be built into a VR experience, where designers, architects and engineers to explore every inch of the proposed project and identify any issues before construction begins. Issues that were difficult to identify or visualize on flat technical drawings and even 3D models can now be caught and dealt with before driving that first nail, potentially avoiding delays and saving thousands in the process.

Entertainment

Entertainment is undoubtedly one of the areas where VR is making the most waves, especially in the gaming industry. However, there are other entertainment areas, such as cinema and music, where VR is making an impact. Both Paul McCartney and Coldplay released VR experiences that allow the user to sit front-and-center at concerts without the need to queue or push through thousands of fans to reach the front. Moreover, Oculus and Netflix also released their own twist on the cinema experience, allowing people to watch films in a deserted movie theatre or in front of a cozy log fire.

Gaming

The area most talked about when discussing virtual reality is gaming. It's no secret that virtual reality has radically changed the way people interact with games and the overall gaming experience.

Virtual reality doesn't just show you the game as you play it, it brings you into the scene; it lets you become the protagonist; it allows you to experience things as if you were *really* there; it draws you into what's happening around you.

Examples of VR

Have you ever wanted to fly a spaceship to the edge of space or draw and paint a picture in 3D space? With virtual reality, you can stop staring at a flat screen and jump into the cockpit. You can look around and see worlds go by; you can grab the control stick or the paintbrush with your own hand and feel what it's *really* like.

Let's take a look at some of the VR experiences already on the market from both indie and AAA studios alike, starting with games.

Games

- **Robo Recall**: One of the most polished VR games to date. In this Oculus exclusive, developed by Epic Games, you're tasked with recalling malfunctioning robots or destroying them with a plethora of weapons. (https://www.oculus.com/experiences/rift/1081190428622821/)
- **Skyrim VR**: An epic game developed by Bethesda that's been re-imagined in virtual reality. (https://store.steampowered.com/app/611670/The_Elder_Scrolls_V_Skyrim_VR/)

- **Job Simulator**: One of the most talked about virtual reality games, released in early 2016. In this game, you're tasked with reviving the careers of the early 21st century. Sound fun, right? (https://store.steampowered.com/app/448280/Job_Simulator/)
- **Virtual Rick-ality**: Based on the popular TV show, Rick and Morty, this game is similar to Job Simulator: you're thrown into the crazy world of Rick and Morty and tasked with solving puzzles and fixing various malfunctions in Rick's workshop. (https://store.steampowered.com/app/469610/Rick_and_Morty_Virtual_Rickality/)
- **Resident Evil 7**: A popular horror series that received a VR makeover. One of the more extended VR experiences on the market, you're thrown into a first-person perspective horror environment guaranteed to disturb even the diehard horror fans. (http://residentevil7.com/)
- **A Chair in a Room:** Initially released on Google Cardboard and the Oculus DK1 in 2014 — and later in 2016 on the HTC Vive — a psychological horror set in America's Deep South. Navigate your way through your memories, piecing together the clues and puzzles, to solve the mystery of how you have awoken in the sinister Greenwater Institute, known only as patient no.6079. Developed by Wolf & Wood, A Chair in a Room went on to win UploadVR's award for horror in 2016, and later, the HTC Vive Community Choice Award. (http://www.achairinaroom.com/)
- **SportsBar VR**: If you have ever fancied a game of pool or darts with friends, but not fancied leaving the house, this could be the game for you! (https://store.steampowered.com/app/269170/Sports_Bar_VR/)
- **Superhot VR**: This popular game made its way to virtual reality and is well worth experiencing. (https://store.steampowered.com/app/617830/SUPERHOT_VR/)

Other experiences

Every day more and more amazing VR experiences are getting released, and it's impossible to cover all of them, but here are a few key experiences that have received a lot of media attention and praise.

- **Allumette**: Tells the story of a young orphan who lives in a city in the cloud. Based loosely on "The Little Match Girl" by Hans Christian Andersen, Allumette is an account of the love between a mother and her daughter, and the sacrifices she makes for the greater good. (https://store.steampowered.com/app/460850/Allumette/)
- **Tilt Brush**: Offers users the ability to draw in a three-dimensional space. (https://www.tiltbrush.com/)
- **theBlu**: Experience the wonder and majesty of the ocean through a series of habitats and come face to face with some of the most awe-inspiring species on the planet. (https://store.steampowered.com/app/451520/theBlu/)

- **Netflix VR**: The Netflix VR app allows you to watch Netflix in the virtual living room of a mansion or enter the "Void Theatre" mode that allows you to expand the screen larger than your FoV giving the impression. (https://www.oculus.com/experiences/go/890562797701371/)
- **Home - A VR Spacewalk** Inspired by real-life NASA training simulations, you can now experience taking a spacewalk 250 miles above the earth. (https://store.steampowered.com/app/512270/Home_A_VR_Spacewalk/)

The difficulties of VR

Like any other tech, the first generations are always the hardest to develop for and around. Whether it's due to lack of documentation, lack of support or a lack of APIs and SDKs, it's important to remember that not everything may exist or work as you expect or desire.

When the **Samsung Gear VR** launched, it didn't have a motion controller; you had to control games using a small trackpad on the side of the device. A setup like that can lead to either very restrictive gameplay or complicated controls. However, eight months later, a motion controller was released that significantly improved the experience of many games and apps on the platform.

To complicate things further, certain techniques and functionality simply do not exist; and it's you're responsible to design things with that in mind. For example, an inventory system in an RPG game: in a standard game, you can display a 2D screen with the player's items; but in VR, a 2D screen won't work. It's up to you to implement a design that does!

Latency and framerates are also things to consider. The key to tricking the human brain into thinking what it's seeing is real is to make sure your game or app runs fast. The minimum frame rate for most VR platforms is 60 frames per second (FPS) which means it takes 16 ms from one frame being displayed to the next. When your game runs, you need to account for the delay in receiving data from your motion controllers and headset, which can range from a few milliseconds up to 10 milliseconds on some headsets. Once you receive the data, then you can carry out the rest of computation, letting your engine render the images for both the left and the right eye.

Later in the book, you'll learn more about the difficulties and pitfalls of VR development. You'll also discover how to overcome VR motion sickness, as well as how to optimize your game to provide the best experience.

Where to go from here?

In the last two chapters, you dove deep into the history of VR. You learned about the underlying technology, platforms, headsets, and input devices currently available (and even some that are soon-to-be released!). You also discovered a range of experiences that are available on the market and what to look out for when developing your own VR apps and games... so what are you waiting for? It's time to get started!

Section II: Beginning VR

Congratulations for making it through the first section. Now it's time to put that basic knowledge you learned to work.

In this section, you'll set up everything for VR and learn about VRTK and its advantages over using the standard plugins provided by the headset developers. You'll also implement some very interesting mechanics that you can easily use in your own games and experiences. To top it all off, learn all about increasing performance and the dangers of virtual movement and its effect on the human body.

Specifically, these aspects of VR are covered:

- **Chapter 3: VRTK Setup**: In this chapter you'll learn about VRTK and its alternatives. You'll also set up the needed devices and your development environment.
- **Chapter 4: VR Movement**: Moving around in VR is lots of fun, but you'll need to keep some things in mind to prevent you and your players from getting sick. This chapter explains how to get around in a virtual space using different types of input and covers what to watch out for.
- **Chapter 5: Interactions**: A game or experience wouldn't be worth its salt without allowing the player to interact with its surroundings in immersive ways. In this chapter, you'll learn about implementing basic interactions.
- **Chapter 6: User Interfaces for VR**: Most games need some sort of user interface, whether it's to keep score or show a health bar. Learn how to create a world space UI in this chapter.
- **Chapter 7: Optimization & Motion Sickness**: This chapter explains how to make your games and experiences nice and snappy while avoiding motion that affects the player negatively.

Chapter 3: VRTK Setup

Jonathan Ogle-Barrington

Now that you know the history, platforms, headsets, uses and difficulties behind virtual reality, it's time to get started with some development. You'll start by looking at **VRTK** (Virtual Reality Toolkit), its features and its alternatives.

In this chapter, you'll also learn about:

- VRTK requirements.
- Cross-platform setup.
- Building for Desktop use.
- Device setup.

What is VRTK and its alternatives

VRTK is a collection of scripts for Unity that aid in prototyping and developing virtual reality applications and games. While Unity provides support for virtual reality out-of-the-box, VRTK builds upon this and provides common solutions such as:

- Locomotion.
- Interacting with 3D objects.
- Interacting with UI elements.
- Body physics.
- 2D and 3D controls like buttons, levers, doors and drawers.

The biggest advantage perhaps of VRTK is the fact that you can use a single project across multiple platforms:

- SteamVR.
- Oculus.
- Ximmerse.
- Google Daydream.
- Windows Mixed Reality.

This reduces the amount of code you need to write just to get started in virtual reality development. Now you can concentrate on developing the parts of the game or app in the same way Unity allows developers to start creating the game — without having to worry about rendering pipelines, input management or other fundamentals of a game engine.

VRTK is not the only solution available for getting started in virtual reality development. Both Oculus and SteamVR provide basic examples. It's also possible to build your own bespoke system or pick up assets from the asset store to provide the specific functionality you need. Where VRTK really shines is its ability to provide a simple, yet extensible framework that works across multiple platforms and is used in many commercial projects. To top it all off, it's also both free and open source.

One alternative worth mentioning is **NewtonVR**. While VRTK and NewtonVR have both been available for roughly the same amount of time as open source solutions, they slightly differ in their support and aim, and therefore offer different levels of complexity for different solutions.

VRTK aims to provide a toolkit for virtual reality development as a whole, hence its broad appeal amongst developers, providing a wide range of support and examples across the core components in virtual reality such as locomotion, interacting with 3D objects, 2D and 3D controls.

NewtonVR, on the other hand, has chosen to focus primarily on a few specific core components that it feels are crucial to providing a realistic virtual reality experience, the major component being physics driven interactions. This means that NewtonVR has tried to create a framework for interacting with objects in virtual reality that closely mimics that of real life.

Here are some of the features of NewtonVR that make it a worthwhile alternative, depending on the desired effect you want within your application or game:

- Objects can be picked up, dropped, thrown, held and interacted with.
- Objects held in the users' hand cannot pass through other objects in the virtual world.

- Objects can have a specific mass. For example, two objects with the same mass can push each other equally. However, an object with considerably less mass, such as a balloon, cannot push something like a concrete block.
- Objects can be configured for pick up at any point, or they can rotate and position themselves to match a predefined orientation.

While these features make NewtonVR an impressive solution, its lack of basic support for locomotion means that its not a complete package. For this reason, the focus going forward is VRTK.

VRTK requirements

There is only one requirement for VRTK itself: a version of Unity greater than 5.5. However, you'll also need to follow the basic system requirements for Oculus and SteamVR. If you're in any doubt, both SteamVR and Oculus provide a system tool to check whether your computer is VR ready.

There are the minimum requirements for you to get started with development with the Oculus Rift and the HTC Vive:

Oculus

- OS: Windows 10 or newer.
- Video Card: NVIDIA GTX 1050 Ti/AMD Radeon RX 470 or greater.
- CPU: Intel i3-6100/AMD Ryzen 3 1200, FX4350 or greater.
- Memory: 8GB+ RAM.
- Video Output: Compatible HDMI 1.3 video output.
- USB Ports: 1x USB 3.0 port, plus 2x USB 2.0 ports.

SteamVR

- OS: Windows 7 SP1, Windows 8.1, or Windows 10.
- Video Card: NVIDIA GTX 970 / AMD R9 290 equivalent or greater.
- CPU: Intel i5-4590 / AMD FX 8350 equivalent or greater.
- Memory: 4GB RAM.
- Video Output: 1x HDMI 1.4 port, or DisplayPort 1.2 or newer.

- USB Ports: 1x USB 3.0 port.
- For room scale VR you'll need a minimum of 2 meters (6.5ft) by 1.5 meters (5ft) of free space.

In order to follow along with the rest of this chapter, make sure you have finished the hardware and driver setup of the VR platform you own first. ea

Setup

Before you get started with setting up VRTK, you'll need to ensure you're using the appropriate version of Unity to maximize the support for XR. For the duration of the book, the projects covered will use the most recent stable version of Unity 2018.2. This is currently available for download at the following URL: https://unity3d.com/get-unity/download.

Project overview

Now, it's time to get up and running with VRTK.

Open the starter project for this chapter in Unity, and take a few moments to familiarize yourself with the folder structure. As you'll see in the Project window, the project comes pre-loaded with a folder named **Razeware**.

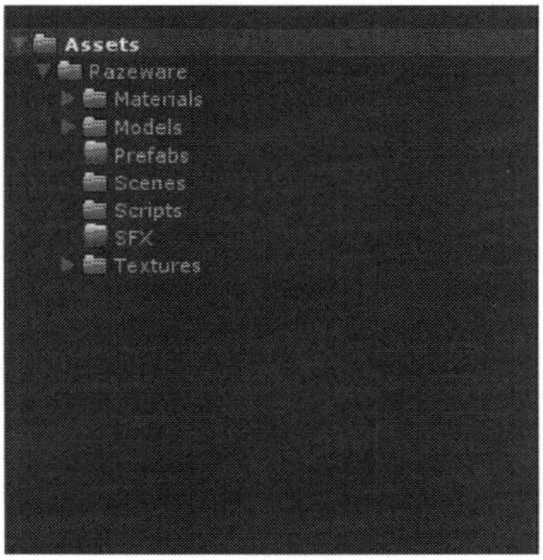

Here's an overview of what's inside:

- **Materials**: All materials used in this chapter.
- **Models**: The models for this chapter.
- **Prefabs**: This is where you'll put all prefabs. It's currently empty.

- **Scenes**: Contains the starting scene.
- **Scripts**: This is where you'll create all custom scripts used in this chapter. To start, it contains a bunch of pre-supplied utility scripts.
- **SFX**: Contains some sound effects to bring the guns to life.
- **Textures**: All textures used in the scene are in here.

With the project open, download the following packages, and import them into the project.

> **Note**: The version dependencies between VRTK and Oculus/SteamVR SDKs are quite picky, so specific versions that work together are referenced below. As VRTK is currently only supplying updates directly in their master branch (and not as releases), the version of VRTK tested and downloaded from the master branch is supplied with the materials for this chapter.

- **Oculus Utilities** - (Current version used is 1.25.2). This Unity package includes scripts, prefabs and other resources to supplement Unity's built-in support for Oculus. Download here: https://developer.oculus.com/downloads/package/oculus-utilities-for-unity-5/1.25.2/
- **Oculus Avatar** - (Version used is 1.24.0): The Oculus Avatar SDK assists developers with implementing social and hand presence for Gear VR, Oculus Go, Oculus Rift and Touch controllers. With the Avatar SDK, it's easy to bring the avatar appearance that users create in Oculus Home into your own applications and make them viewable by other users. Once extracted, you'll find the Unity Package to import under **OVRAvatarSDK/Unity/OvrAvatar.unityPackage**. Get it here: https://developer.oculus.com/downloads/package/oculus-avatar-sdk/1.24.0/
- **Oculus Platform SDK** - (Version used is 1.24.0): The Oculus Platform SDK gives access to some of the core Oculus APIs for commerce, matchmaking, cloud storage, voice chat and achievements. Download this from https://developer.oculus.com/downloads/package/oculus-platform-sdk/1.24.0/
- **Steam VR SDK**: (Version used is 1.2.3): This is Steam's equivalent to the Oculus Platform SDK. It provides access to core APIs such as OpenVR, Chaperone, Compositor and Lighthouse tracking. Get it here: https://github.com/ValveSoftware/steamvr_unity_plugin/releases/tag/1.2.3

Note: Valve recently released version 2.0 of Steam VR SDK which is the current version on the Unity Asset Store, however VRTK does not currently support this version due to some large, non-backward compatible updates. Please ensure you use version 1.2.3 from the above link. Using version 1.2.3 of the SDK wont effect the end result and will run on all platforms regardless of what version of SteamVR they are running.

Note: After importing Steam VR SDK, you may get a warning in Unity about the scripts requiring updating. Simply choose **I made a backup, go ahead** when prompted to have Unity upgrade the scripts.

- **VRTK**: The glue that holds all of the plugins together and allows you to leverage them simply and easily.

Note: Currently the VRTK GitHub Releases page is out of date. Instead, you should use the version of VRTK included in this chapter's materials. Extract it from **projects/starter/VRTK.zip** and copy in only the **Assets** folder to your project under **Assets \ VRTK**.

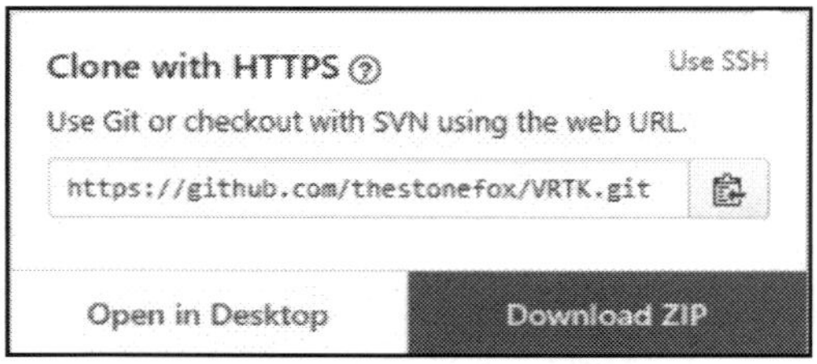

After importing the Oculus Utilities package, you might be prompted to update. Stick to the version referenced in this chapter, and decline the update:

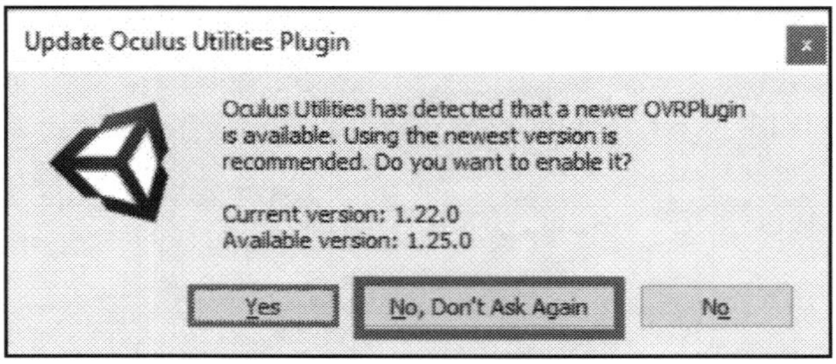

After importing all of the packages, you'll have a folder structure that looks similar to the one below. Please note, the editor may seem unresponsive for some time while importing some of these packages, especially Oculus Avatar, but given enough time, the Unity editor will become responsive again.

For the SteamVR SDK import, after it is done, you'll get a prompt to set up recommended settings. When this appears, select **Accept All**.

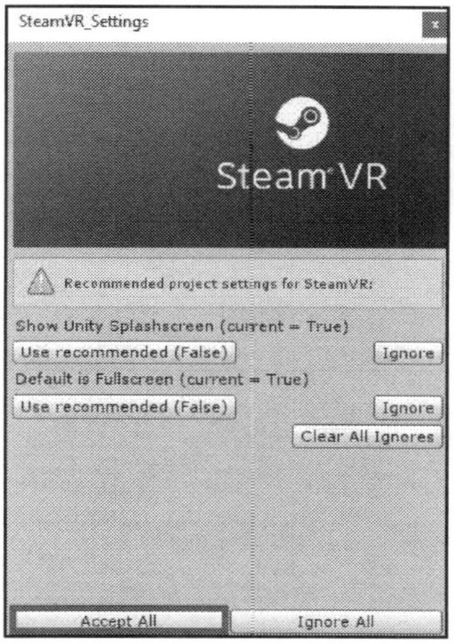

Your **Assets** folder structure will now look like this:

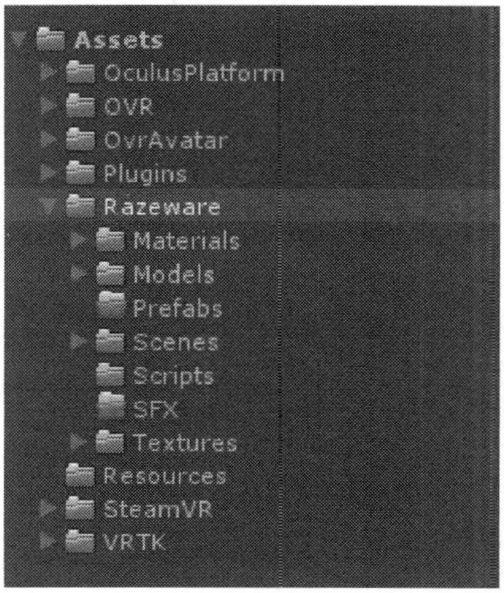

To get things started, open the **Chapter 3 - Setup** scene from the **Razeware \ Scenes** folder and review the scene in the editor.

The scene comes with a few things already set up:

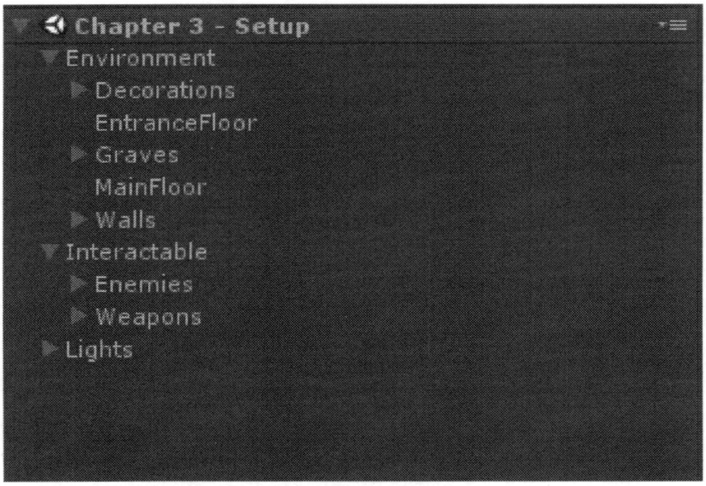

Here's the breakdown of the root GameObjects:

- **Environment**: Contains all of the basic static meshes for the scene.
- **Lights**: The lighting components for the scene.
- **Interactables**: Contains the weapons and enemies that are intractable in the scene.

Creating the VRTK setup

Now that you've imported the required packages and are comfortable with the scene, it's time to set up VRTK.

Begin by creating a new GameObject at the root of the scene, name it **[VRTK_SDK_MANAGER]** and reset its Transform.

Add a **VRTK_SDK Manager** component to the newly created GameObject, and check the **SDK_OCULUS_AVATAR** checkbox for Standalone and Android if available.

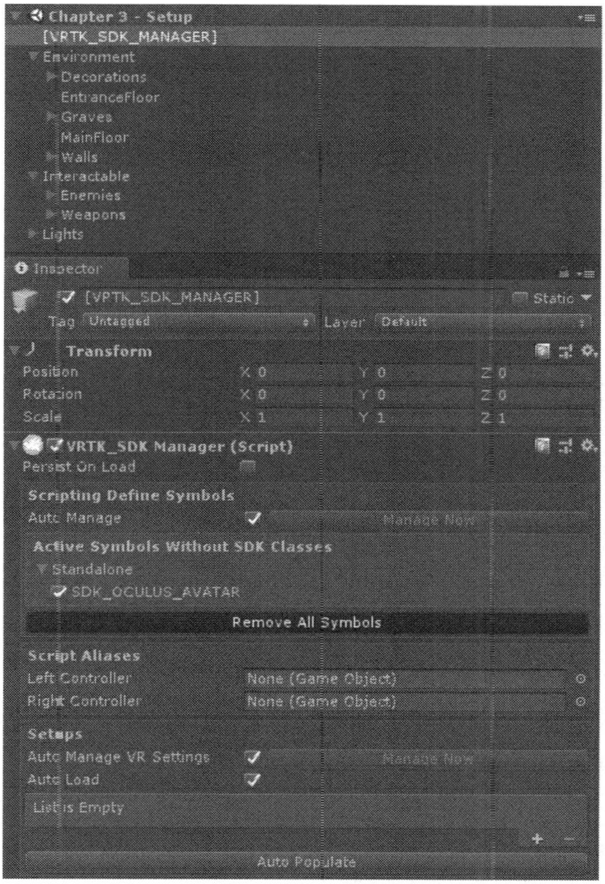

Add another empty GameObject as a child of **[VRTK_SDK_MANAGER]**, name it **[VRTK_SDK_SETUPS]**, and reset its Transform.

Now, create the following empty GameObjects, reset their **Transform** and parent them to **[VRTK_SDK_SETUPS]**:

- SteamVR
- Oculus
- Simulator

Notice that you're creating three GameObjects: one for SteamVR, one for Oculus and another for a Simulator. VRTK comes complete with a system for simulating virtual reality interaction using a mouse and keyboard. This can be extremely useful to get started with, but testing with a headset is recommended.

Your Hierarchy will now look like this:

Next, you'll add the components needed for each SDK to function correctly. Start by dragging the **[CameraRig]** and **[SteamVR]** prefabs from the **SteamVR \ Prefabs** folder onto the SteamVR GameObject you just created.

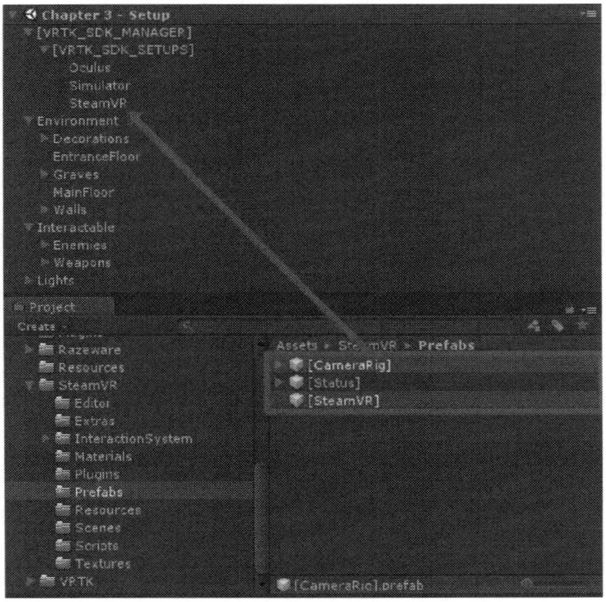

That's all you need for SteamVR, so drag an **OVRCameraRig** prefab from the **Oculus \ VR \ Prefabs** folder and a **LocalAvatar** prefab from the **Oculus \ Avatar \ Content \ Prefabs** onto the **Oculus** GameObject you created.

Select **OVRCameraRig** and change the value of **Tracking Origin Type** to **Floor Level**. This helps position the virtual reality camera correctly within the scene.

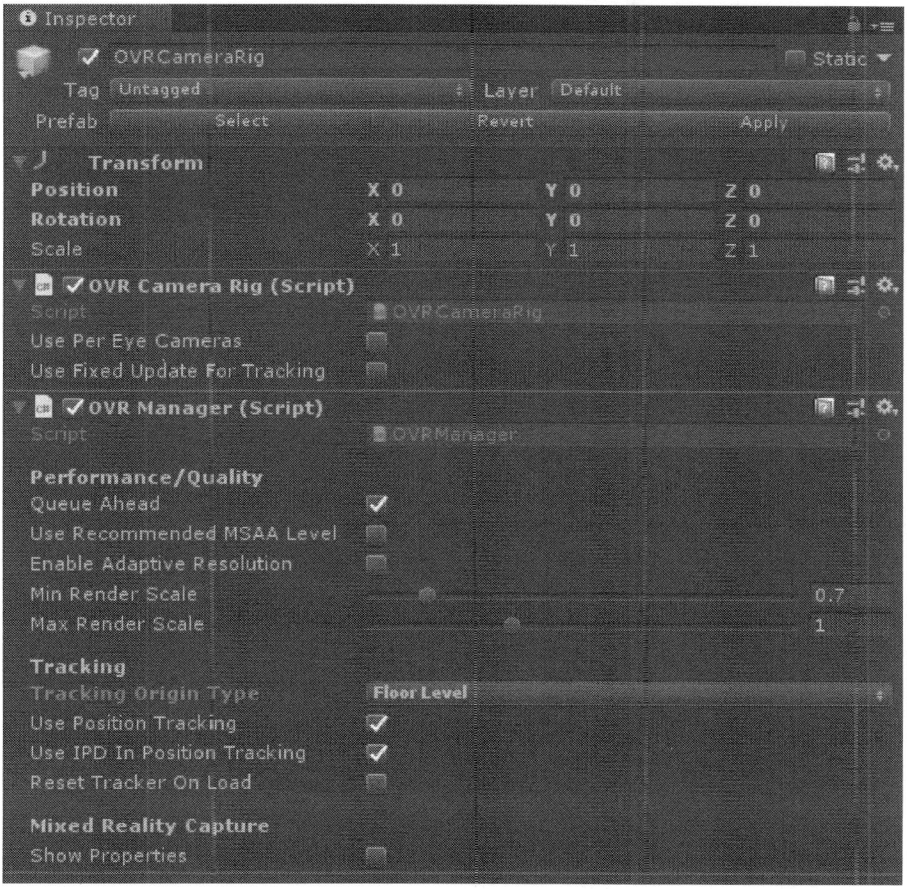

Finally, drag the **[VRSimulator_CameraRig]** prefab from **VRTK \ Assets \ VRTK \ Source \ SDK \ Simulator** folder onto the **Simulator**. Your Hierarchy will now look like this:

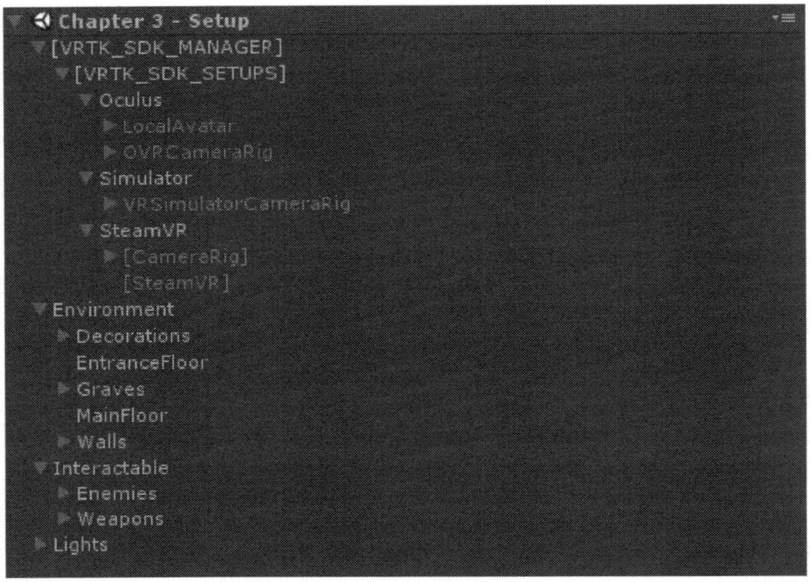

Select the three SDK GameObjects you've just added, and add a **VRTK_SDK Setup** component to all three of them. Select them separately and assign the appropriate value to **Quick Select** for each one:

- **SteamVR**: SteamVR
- **Oculus**: Oculus (Rift)
- **Simulator**: Simulator

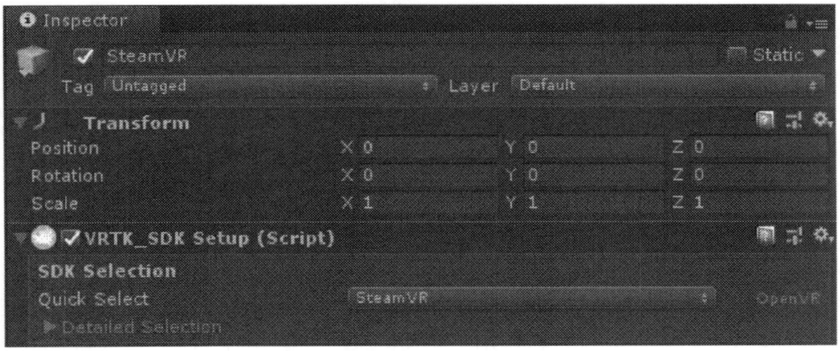

You've just set up all of the SDKs you'll need to create cross-platform apps and games. Go back to the **[VRTK_SDK_MANAGER]** and click the **Auto Populate** button. Your setup section of the **[VRTK_SDK_MANAGER]** will now look like this:

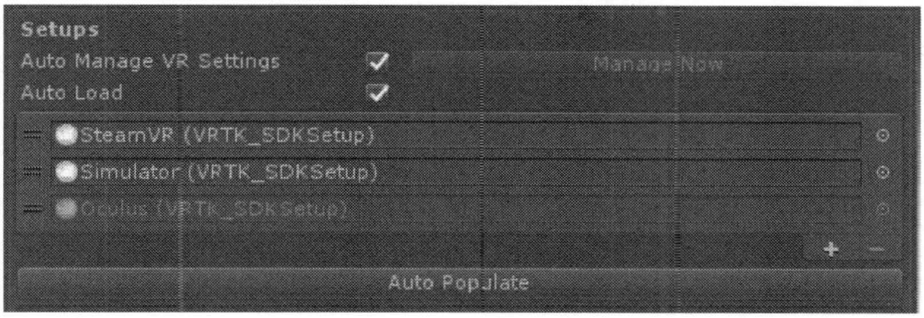

Controller setup

With the SDK setup complete, you now need to set up the users' play area and controllers. The play area will map to SteamVR's Chaperone system and Oculus's Guardian system. These systems ensure that the player knows when he/she is near the bounds of their play space by showing a virtual wall.

The player controller GameObjects that you'll soon create will map to the transform of the Vive wands or Oculus Touch controllers. This will mimic the users' movement in the real world and allow them to interact within the virtual world.

Create an empty GameObject as a child of **[VRTK_SDK_MANAGER]**, reset its Transform and name it **[VRTK_SETUP]**. Create the following empty GameObjects, and add them as children of **[VRTK_SETUP]**:

- **Play Area**
- **Left Controller**
- **Right Controller**

Add a **VRTK_Adaptive Quality** component to **Play Area**, set its **Msaa** (Multisample Anti-aliasing) Level to **2**, and set **Scale Render Viewport** between **0.5** & **2.5**.

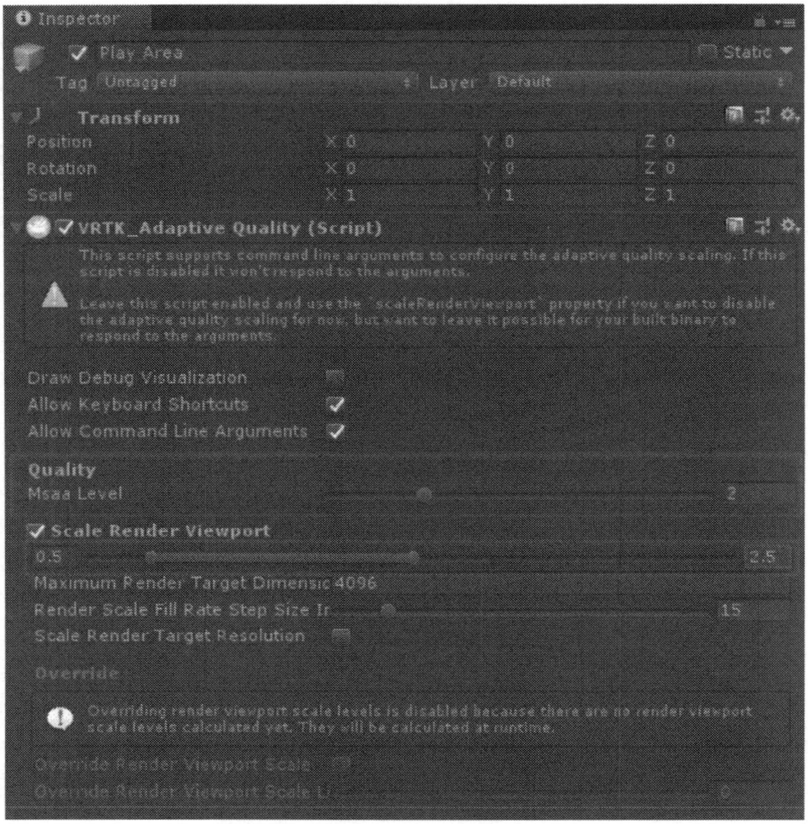

Setting the Msaa to Level 2 prevents jagged images and improves image quality without compromising on speed and performance. Setting the Scale Renderer Viewport allows your game or app to adjust the resolution it's rendered at to maintain a stable frame rate. If this is unchecked, the things are rendered at the resolution recommended by the current VR device you're using.

Next, add the following components to both **Left Controller** and **Right Controller**:

- **VRTK_Controller Events**
- **VRTK_Interact Touch**
- **VRTK_Interact Grab**

Leave the components set to their default values as you'll be reading how to set up and use these in a later chapter. Finally, select **[VRTK_SDK_MANAGER]**, and hook up the controller aliases by dragging **Left Controller** and **Right Controller** to their respective slots.

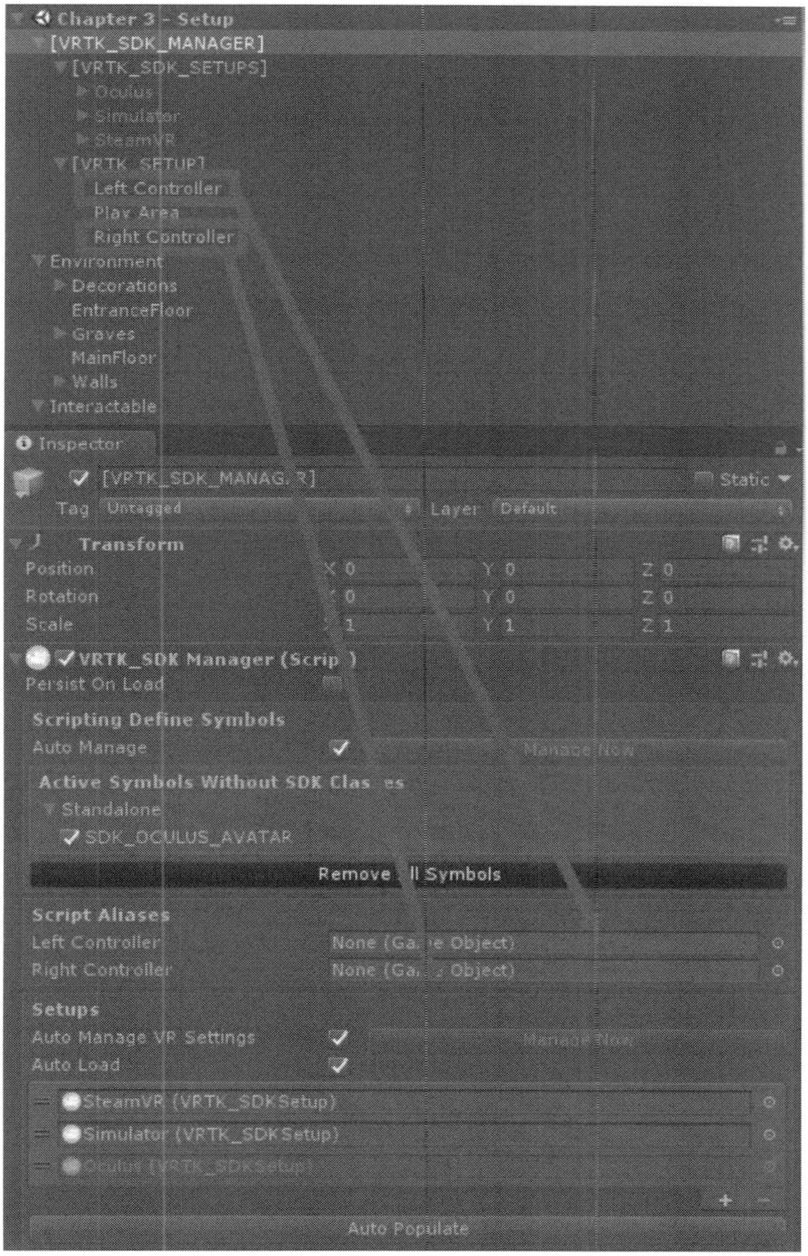

Press the Play button and check that everything works correctly by looking around the scene and swinging around your controllers. If you have any issues, backtrack through this section and verify you set up the **[VRTK_SDK_MANAGER]** correctly.

Building for desktop use

Building a virtual reality game or app is almost identical as building any other game or app from Unity. Head to **Player Settings** and expand the **XR Settings** section. Verify that **Virtual Reality Supported** is checked and your chosen platform is at the top of the **Virtual Reality SDKs**.

It's also worth switching **Stereo Rendering Method** to **Single Pass** to optimize performance. You'll discover why this is a good idea in the VR optimization chapter.

With those options set, you're ready to build for desktop use. Bring up the project **Build Settings**. Verify the **Chapter 3 - Setup** scene from **Razeware \ Scenes** has been added to the **Scenes In Build** section, and click **Build**. Once complete, navigate to the folder you chose and run the compiled executable.

Device setup

If you've followed the setup guide for SteamVR or Oculus, you should already be prepared to run the example you've just built. Although, if you're running on Oculus, there's one additional step.

Open the Oculus app and verify you're signed in. Head to the **Settings** tab and select the **General** options. Then, toggle **on** the **Unknown Source** option.

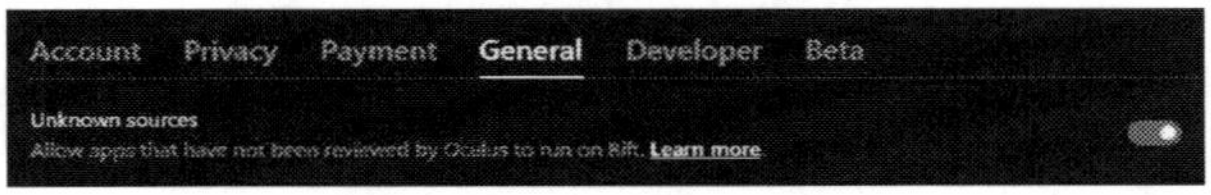

Where to go from here?

Well done! You now know how to set up VRTK to work with Oculus and SteamVR, and you can compile a virtual reality game that runs across both. If you had any problems with the setup process, please compare your version with the final project included with this chapter's resources.

In the next chapter, you'll look at adding a variety of locomotion options that allow you to move around in the scene.

Chapter 4: VR Movement

Jonathan Ogle-Barrington

Movement and interactions are the two common and most essential parts of any VR experience. VR movement — or locomotion as its commonly referred to — can take many forms in games and experiences. Often the user is presented with different locomotion options such as teleportation, free movement, or in some cases, when utilizing SteamVR room-scale they're simply allowed to walk to where they need to be physically. If you've played any VR games or experiences you may have seen some of these options, but have you ever asked yourself why?

In this chapter, you'll look at implementing some of the more popular locomotion options, assess their advantages and disadvantages and see what effect they can have on the player. You'll also get to answer the question of why VR games and experiences need different options for movement.

> **Note:** This chapter contains different ways of moving around, some of which may cause nausea and disorientation for some people. The section on free movement and rotation may especially cause discomfort if you're not used to it inside a VR experience. If you start to feel sick, take a break and get some fresh air.

VR sickness and what to avoid

VR sickness is a condition that manifests when a mismatch of information occurs between the vestibular system (inner ear and brain) and ocular system (eyes and brain). The vestibular system is one of the sensory systems in the human body and contributes to a sense of balance and orientation.

When visual data through the ocular system insinuates you are moving, but you're actually standing still; the mismatch of data processed by the brain can lead to conflicts, and ultimately symptoms similar to kinetosis (motion sickness) resulting in feelings of nausea, postural instability, headaches, sweating and fatigue.

You can find a perfect example of what to avoid when developing a VR experience in the numerous roller coaster games out there. In general, it's best to avoid any experience that can cause motion sickness in real life such as roller coasters, boats, skydiving and so forth.

In reality, a roller coaster can cause kinetosis due to overexcitement of the vestibular system when the rider — who's used to a stable position in which they can determine up from down, floor from ceiling or earth from sky — undergoes rapid movement. The vestibular system undergoes intense stimulation, triggering kinetosis.

Basic teleportation

Teleportation is one of the most common forms of locomotion in virtual reality. Before you start setting up basic teleportation in the project, look at how teleportation works in VRTK.

When you press the teleportation button, a raycast is fired from the hand/head until it collides or reaches its limited length. If the layer is set up for teleportation, the VRTK pointer line renderer turns green. It'll stay red if no area for teleportation is found. On release of the button, if a teleportable area is found, the player is repositioned where the raycast collided.

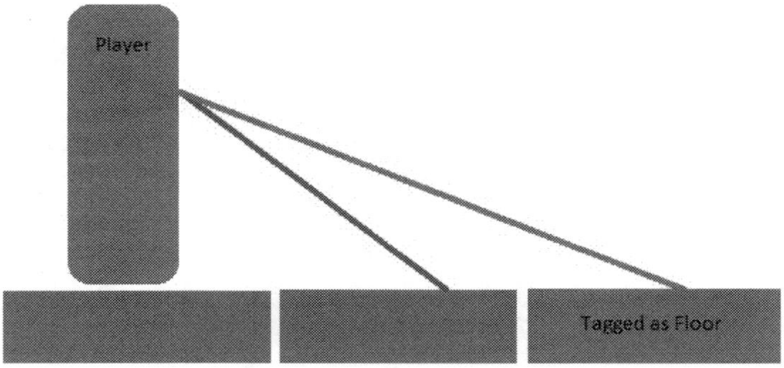

Open the project for this chapter in Unity. Then, open the **Chapter 4 Locomotion (Starter)** scene in the **Assets \ Razeware \ Scenes** project folder.

Select **Play Area** (under **[VRTK_SDK_MANAGER] > [VRTK SETUP]**) and add a **VRTK_BodyPhysics** component to it. This adds a RigidBody and associated colliders to prevent the player from walking through walls and snaps them to the nearest floor when moving. Leave the component set with its default values.

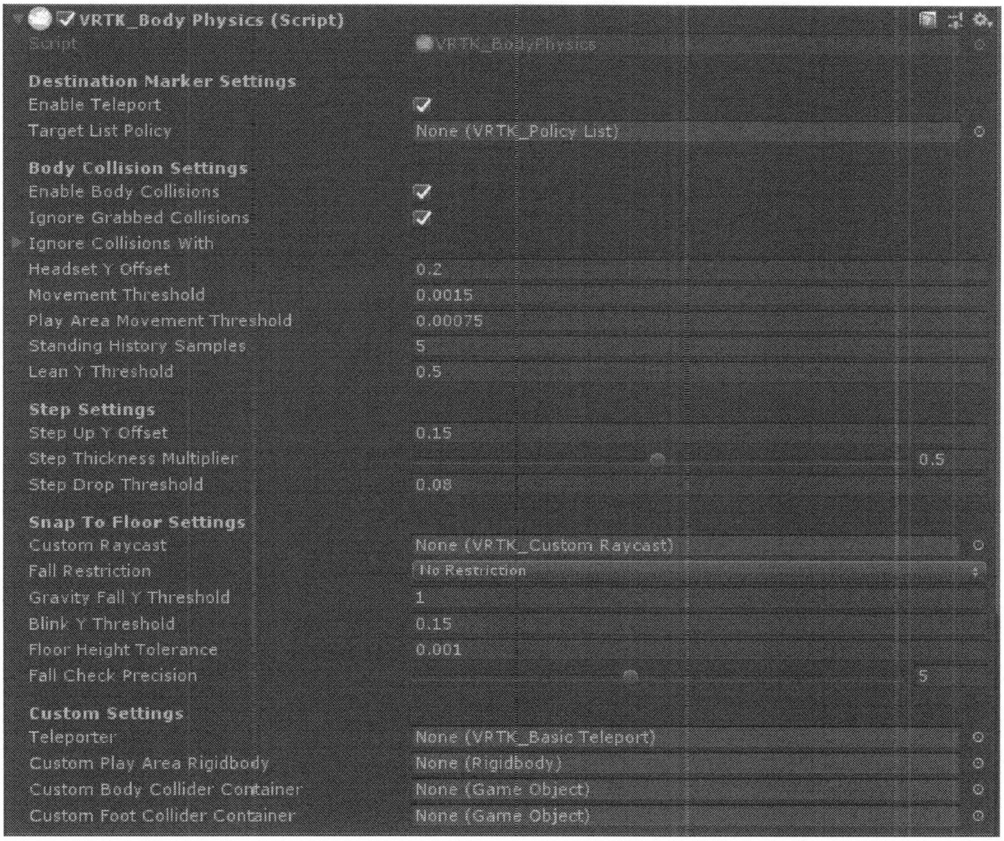

Next, add a **VRTK_HeightAdjustTeleport** component to **Play Area**. The height adjust teleporter script extends the basic teleporter functionality and allows for the height of the of the player to be altered based on whether the teleport location is on top of another object.

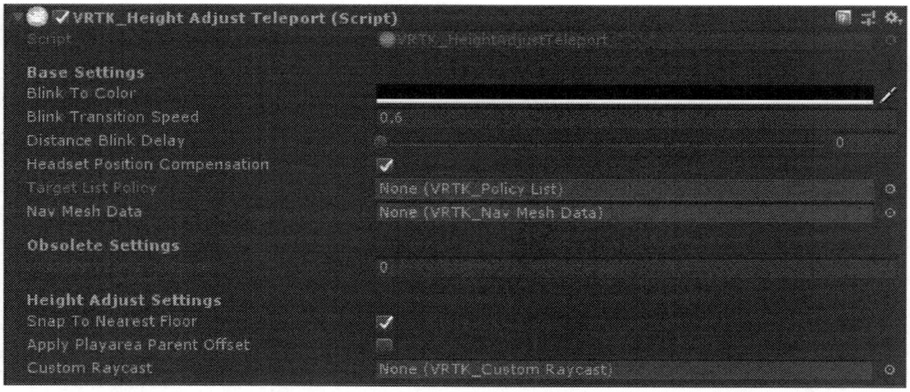

Finally, add a **VRTK_PolicyList** component to **Play Area**. You can use the **Policy List** to create a list of tag, component or layer names that can be checked against to see if another operation is permitted; in this case, you'll set the options to only allow teleportation on a specific game tag (Floor).

Set the **Element 0** value to **Floor**, and change the **Operation** to **Include**. Make sure the **Check Types** drop-down is set to **Tag**.

Set the **Target List Policy** inspector value to the component you just created. This ensures that the teleporter raycast only returns successful if it hits a GameObject that's been tagged as **Floor**.

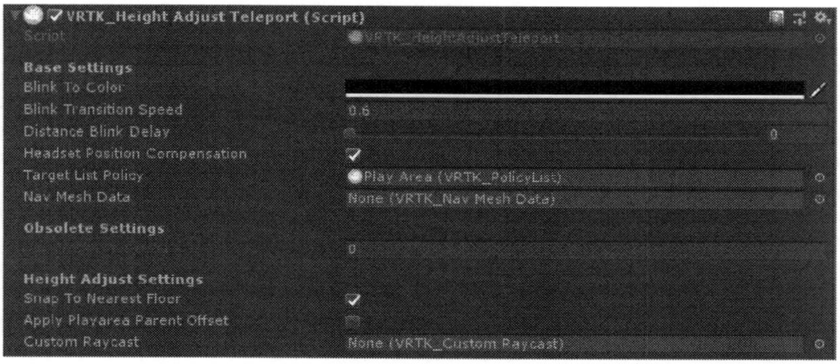

With the play area set up for teleportation, you now need to add some components to emit a pointer and raycast from a tracked GameObject. This is typically carried out on the hands or the head in VR experiences.

Add a **VRTK_Pointer** and a **VRTK_StraightPointerRenderer** component to **Left Controller**.

The pointer is used to emit a pointer and raycast from the GameObject that it's been added to, and the pointer renderer visualizes the pointer in the scene producing the red or green lines, which indicate where — and if — you can teleport.

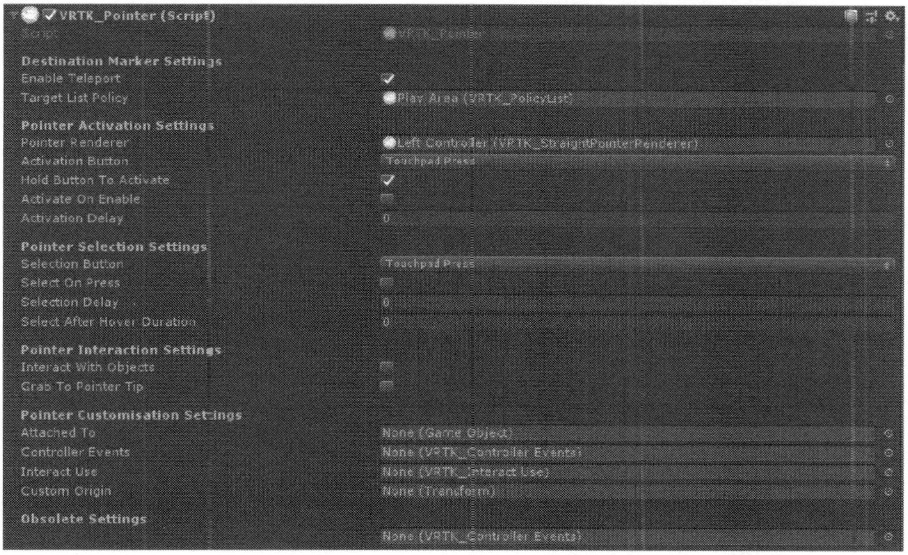

Tick the **Enable Teleport** checkbox on **VRTK_Pointer**, so the system knows this pointer is used for teleportation rather than object interactions.

Point the **Target List Policy** to the policy list you created on the **Play Area** by clicking the circular selection button. This way you can only teleport onto the correctly tagged areas.

Set the **Activation Button** to **Touchpad Press** and change the **Pointer Renderer** to the **VRTK_StraightPointerRenderer** component that you added to the **Left Controller** in the previous step.

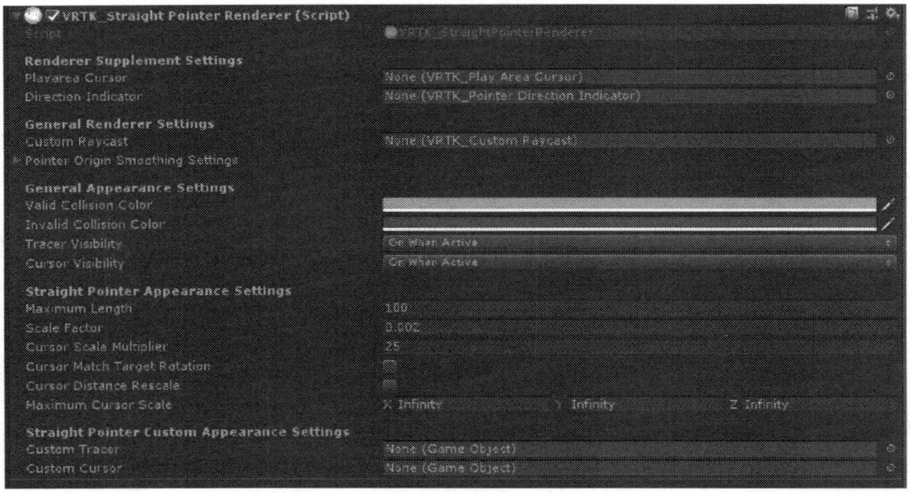

Leave the default settings for the pointer renderer as they are, but feel free to set the **Valid Collision Color** and **Invalid Collision Color** to something more appealing than green and red.

The last thing that needs to be done to enable teleportation in the game is to set the tag to **Floor** on **MainFloor** and **EntranceFloor** found in the scene hierarchy under the **Environment**.

Open the Tag editor under **Edit > Project Settings > Tags and Layers**, and add a new tag named **Floor**.

Select **MainFloor** and **EntranceFloor** in the Hierarchy, and change their **Tag** value to **Floor** using the dropdown at the top left.

Play the scene and teleport around; try untagging the **MainFloor** or **EntranceFloor** to see what effect it has on teleportation.

NavMesh-based teleportation

If you tested out the scene with basic teleportation setup, you might have noticed that although you can teleport around the scene, you can also manage to teleport into objects and enemies. This happens because you allowed teleportation on anything tagged **Floor**, and the **MainFloor** and **EntranceFloor** stretch the full length under the scene.

To get around this problem, you could add colliders to the game objects you want to prevent the player from teleporting into, or you could set up the teleportation system to teleport onto a **NavMesh**.

A navigation mesh is an abstract data structure used in pathfinding to aid in moving through complex spaces. It's especially useful as dynamic obstacles allow the navigation mesh to be modified at runtime.

This means that if you have a car in the scene for example, you can set up a navigation mesh for teleportation but avoid teleporting into the car as its moving around the scene.

Because the basics of teleportation are already set up in VRTK, very little needs to be added to enable NavMesh teleportation. However, you do need to set up the scene for the process of NavMesh baking.

Select **MainFloor** and click the arrow next to the static checkbox above the **Transform** component. Select **Navigation Static**. Do the same to **EntranceFloor**.

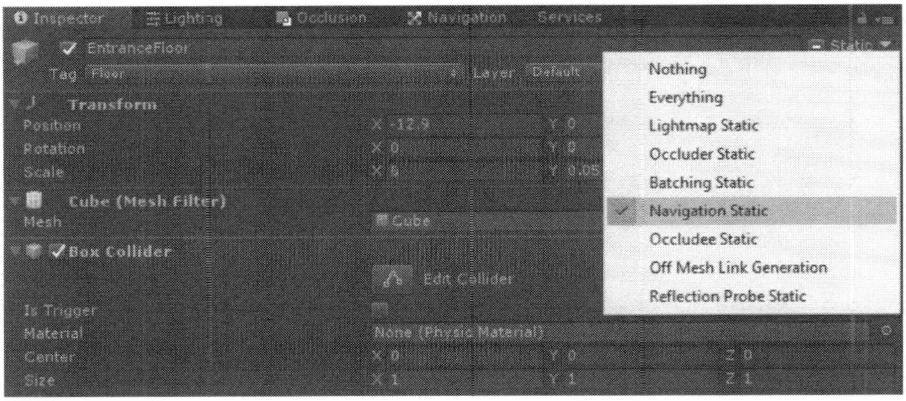

Open a **Navigation** window. If you don't have a navigation window visible, select **Window > AI > Navigation** in the top menu.

Select **MainFloor** and **EntranceFloor** in the Hierarchy and back in the **Navigation** window's Object tab, verify that **Navigation Area** is set to **Walkable**

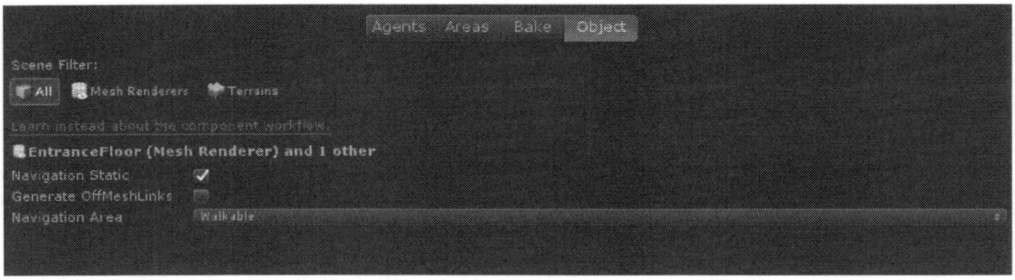

You're now ready to bake the navigation mesh, so switch to the **Bake** tab and click the **Bake** button to do so.

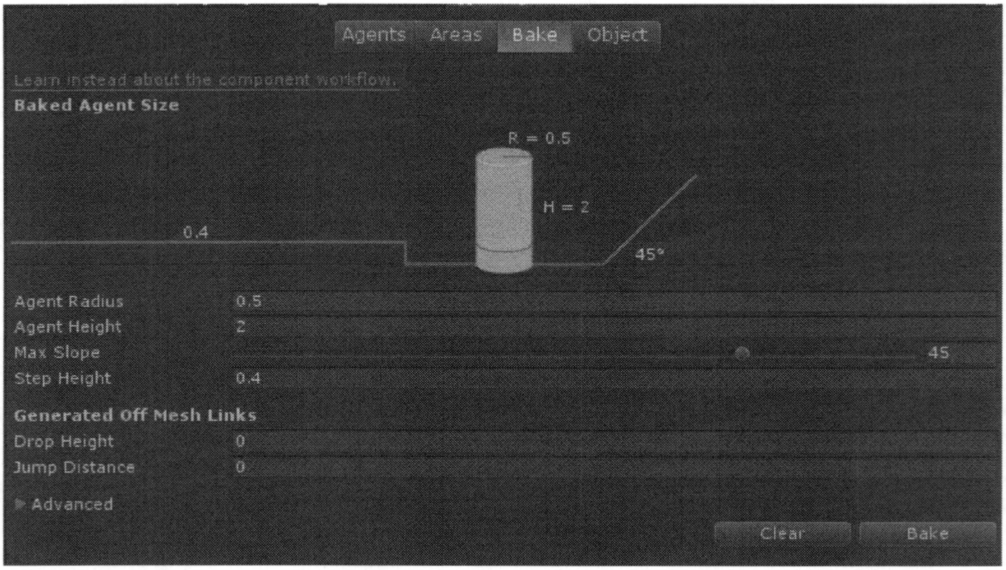

If the set up was a success, your scene will look like the image below. If not, cycle back through the points above to resolve any issues.

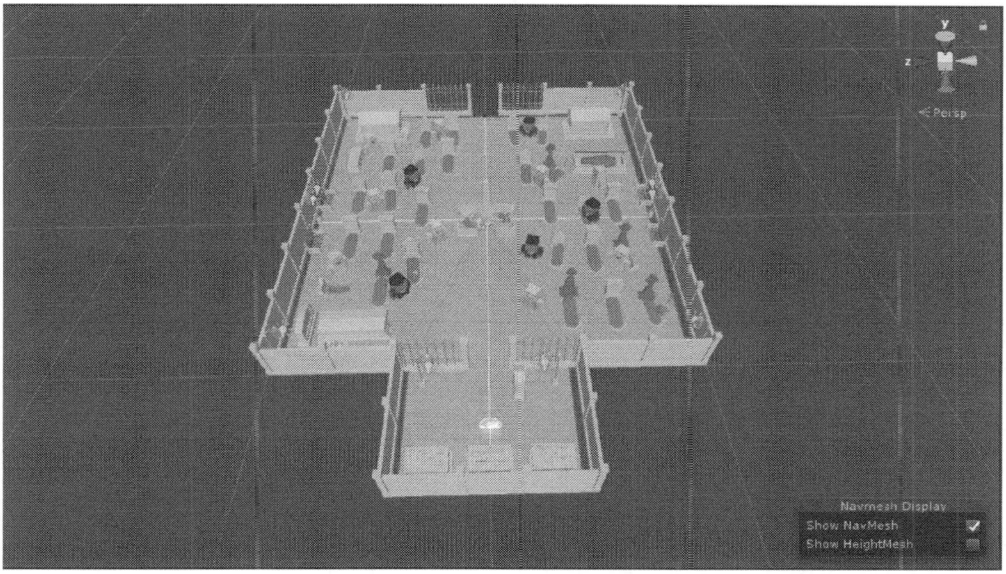

Finally, you need to make a few changes to **Play Area**.First, remove the **VRTK_PolicyList** component and replace it with a **VRTK_NavMeshData** component. Next, set the **Valid Areas** to **Walkable** only.

Next, set the **Nav Mesh Data** field on the **VRTK_HeightAdjustTeleport** component to point to the **VRTK_NavMeshData** script you just added.

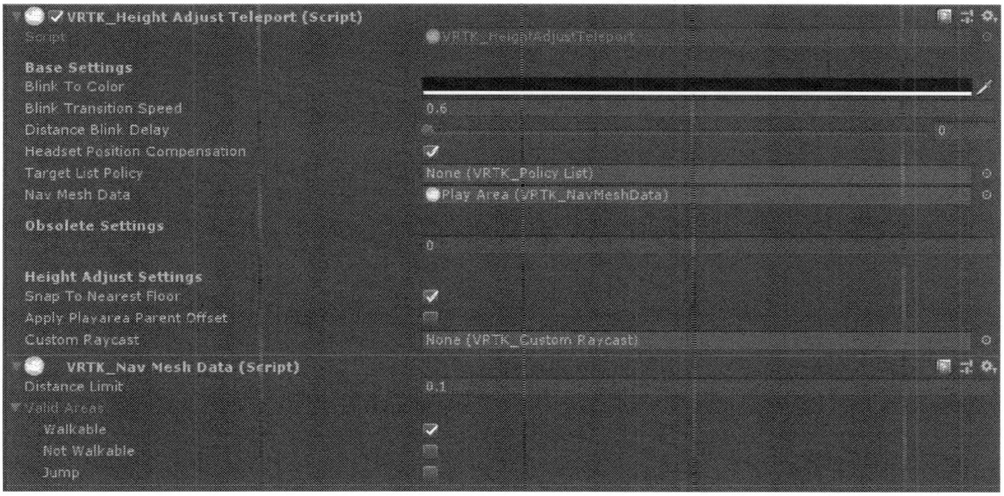

Run the scene, and you'll notice you're able to teleport around as before. However, you may want to have some areas to which the player isn't allowed to teleport.

Stop playing and select **PillarObelisk** found under **Environment \ Graves** in the Hierarchy. Add a **NavMesh Obstacle** component, set its **Shape** to **Box** and tick the **Carve** checkbox. Adjust the **Center** to **(X:0.309 , Y:1.568, Z:0.37)** and set the **Size** to **(X:2.18 , Y:3.136, Z:2.74)** to ensure it stretches across the whole of the central mausoleum.

With the **Carve** check-box ticked, the Nav Mesh Obstacle creates a hole in NavMesh so that the player cannot teleport in that area.

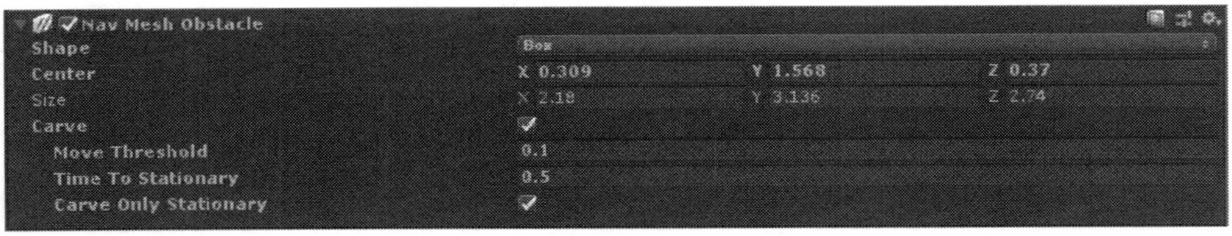

Your NavMesh will now look similar to the following image:

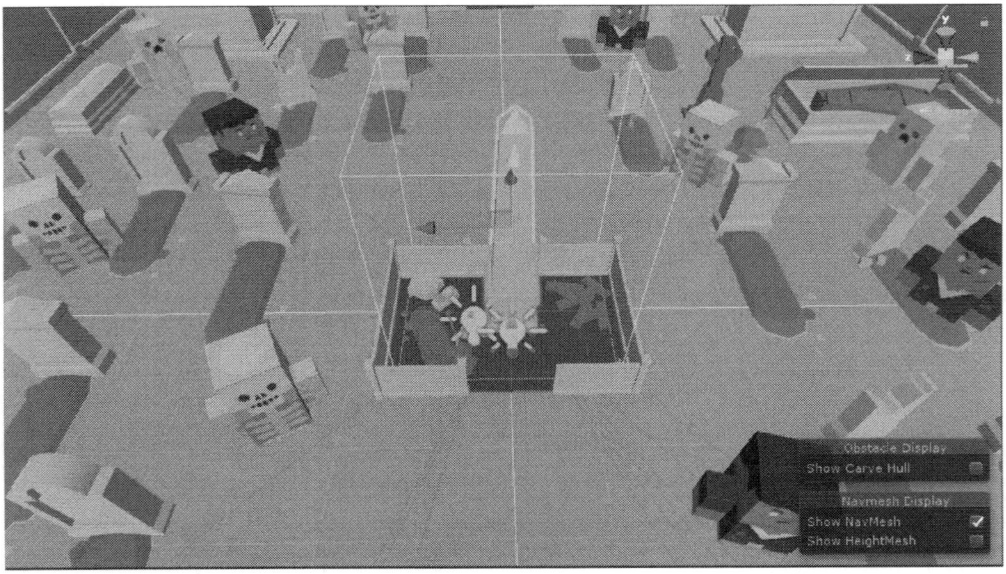

Notice that the central mausoleum area does not have the blue overlay that represents the NavMesh area (you'll need to be on the Navigation window again to show the blue navigation mesh overlay). If your scene does not look correct, check your NavMesh and NavMesh Obstacle setup based on the steps above and re-bake the NavMesh.

You can now add more NavMesh Obstacles to areas in the scene that you don't want the player to be able to navigate like the gravestones for example.

Play the scene again, and try to teleport to a newly configured NavMesh Obstacle area. You'll notice you now cannot teleport to the floor area in these zones.

Head-based teleportation

Now that you have basic teleportation working on the controller, you'll look at adding it to the player's head. In certain scenarios, it may be preferable to allow the player to set the area to teleport to using his/her head rather than their hands. For example, in a first person shooter when you are dual-wielding guns, you wouldn't want to have to aim the gun at the floor to teleport.

First, remove all of the components you just added to the **Left Controller** leaving only the **VRTK_ControllerEvents**, **VRTK_InteractTouch** and **VRTK_InteractGrab** components behind.

Create two new GameObjects underneath **[VRTK_SDK_MANAGER]/[VRTK_SETUP]**: **Headset** and **HeadsetFollower**. On **HeadsetFollower**, add a **VRTK_SDKObjectAlias** component and set its **Sdk Object** value to **Headset**.

This script sets **HeadsetFollower** as a child of the selected SDK Object — in this case, the **Headset**.

Now add a **VRTK_Pointer** and a **VRTK_BezierPointerRenderer** component to **Headset**. As with the previous example, tick the **Enable Teleport** checkbox, set the **Activation Button** to **Touchpad Press** (or a button of your choosing) and point the **Pointer Renderer** to the **VRTK_BezierPointerRenderer** component.

To make it easier to identify the area to which the player will teleport, add a **VRTK_PlayAreaCursor** component. When activated, a rectangular box will display on the floor in the valid/invalid collision color of the **VRTK_BezierPointer** to indicate a valid teleport area. Point the **Playarea Cursor** value on the **VRTK_BezierPointerRenderer** component you just added to reference the new **VRTK_PlayAreaCursor** component.

Finally, add a **VRTK_TransformFollow** component. This will change one GameObject's transform to follow another GameObject's transform; in this case, the **HeadsetFollower** will follow the **Headset** you created previously.

Next, point **Game Object To Follow** to **HeadsetFollower** and change **Game Object To Change** to **Headset**.

Lastly, on the **Headset** for the **VRTK_Pointer** component, make sure **Controller** is set to **Left Controller**, which references the **VRTK_ControllerEvents** component accordingly.

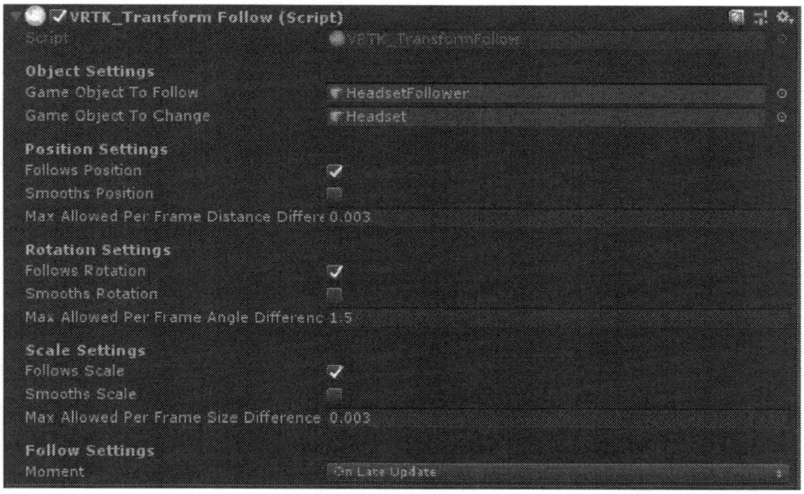

Click the Play button and press the button you assigned to **Activation Button** on the **VRTK_BezierPointer** script. If everything is set up correctly, you'll notice a **VRTK_PlayAreaCursor** displayed on the floor, similar to the image below:

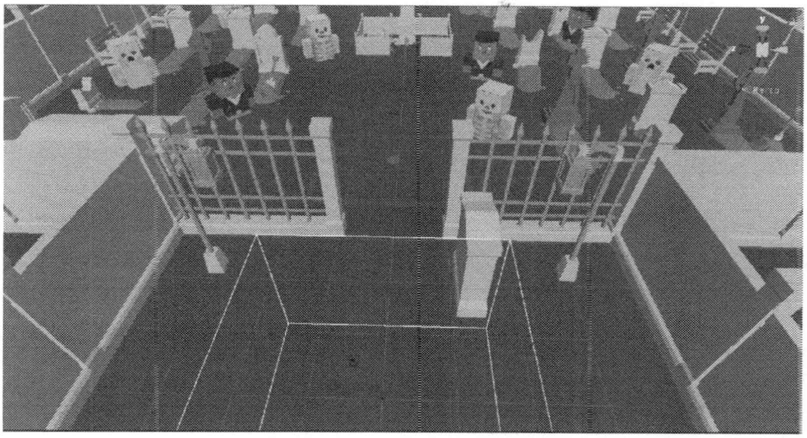

Stepped rotation

Now that you can teleport around the scene, you'll look at rotating the players view so they can look at what they want to shoot rather than always facing forward.

Since you haven't used the **Right Controller** yet, you'll set up rotation on the right hand.

Currently, the **Right Controller** should only have **VRTK_ControllerEvents**, **VRTK_InteractTouch** and **VRTK_InteractGrab** components attached (you'll put these to good use in the next chapter).

On the **Right Controller**, add a **VRTK_SnapRotateObjectControlAction** component. Make sure **Listen on Axis Change** is set to **X Axis Changed** and set **Angle per Snap** to the degree of rotation you want to happen each time the player rotates; a value between **30** and **45** degrees should prevent any disorientation; leave all other values at their default.

Finally, you need to add a **VRTK_TouchpadControl** component. This fires an event each time the X axis and Y axis on the touchpad changes values. Since you set **Listen on Axis Change** to listen for "X Axis Changed", the **VRTK_SnapRotateObjectControlAction** script will be listening for the event fired by the **VRTK_TouchpadControl** and rotate the player the specified angle.

Change the **Object Control Script** on the **Snap Rotate** component to reference the **VRTK_TouchpadControl** component you just added.

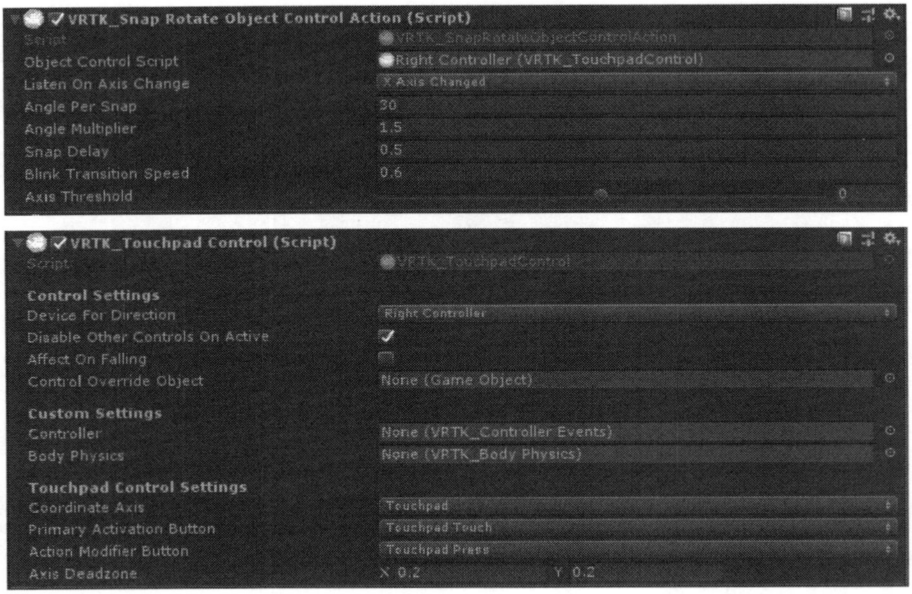

Press the **Play** button and test to see if rotation is working correctly, modify the values of the **VRTK_SnapRotateObjectControlAction** until you find a setting that's comfortable for you.

Free movement and free rotation

The last form of locomotion you'll look at in this chapter is free movement and rotation. It's worth noting this form is not for everyone and can cause nausea. If at any time you feel uncomfortable take a break and get some fresh air.

To get started, remove all of the components from both the left and right controllers apart from **VRTK_ControllerEvents**, **VRTK_InteractTouch** and **VRTK_InteractGrab**.

Add a **VRTK_TouchpadControl** component to each controller and set **Device for Direction** to the corresponding controller on each. Make sure to untick the **Disable Other Controls on Active** so that you can use the left hand for movement and right hand for rotation.

For movement, add a **VRTK_SlideObjectControlAction** to the left controller GameObject. Set the **Object Control Script** to the left controllers **VRTK_TouchpadControl**, and set it to listen to changes on **Y Axis Changed** so that you can control the players forward and backward movement.

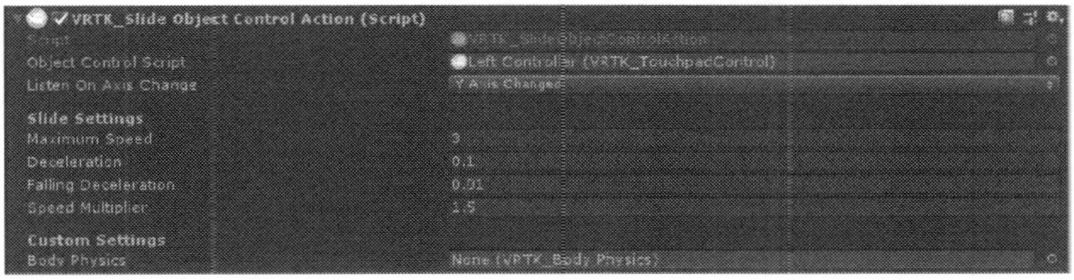

For rotation, add a **VRTK_RotateObjectControlAction** component to the right controller. As before, set the object control script to the corresponding **VRTK_TouchpadControl**, but this time, set it to listen for changes on the **X Axis Changed**.

If you want faster rotation, try altering the **Maximum Rotation Speed** — but be careful not to induce nausea. A high rotation speed can be disorientating.

Run the scene, and try moving around by using the left controller's touchpad and rotating with the right controller's touchpad; you should find the controls similar to a first person shooter style game.

Where to go from here?

Hopefully, without feeling too nauseated. If you had trouble following along, you can review the final project for this chapter. To recap, in this chapter you learned:

- The basics of VR sickness.
- Basic hand and head-based teleportation.
- How to teleport on a NavMesh.
- How to add Stepped Rotation
- How to add Free Movement and Rotation.

In the next chapter, you'll be looking at how to interact with objects in VR, and you'll build on the project so that you can interact with objects in the scene.

Chapter 5: VR Interactions

Jonathan Ogle-Barrington

Now that you've mastered the basics of implementing locomotion in virtual reality using VRTK, it's time to dive into interactions with items in the virtual world.

In this chapter, you'll learn how to:

- Replace the controller models with physical looking hands.
- Highlight objects.
- Pick up objects.
- Set up custom pickup placements on objects.
- Add secondary actions to objects.
- Use an object in-hand.

Open the starter project for this chapter in the Unity editor. Then, open the **Chapter 5 - VR Interactions** scene from the **Razeware \ Scenes** project folder.

There's a small area toward the back of the scene containing a few tables with weapons laid out. You'll spend most of your time learning about VR interactions using this scene.

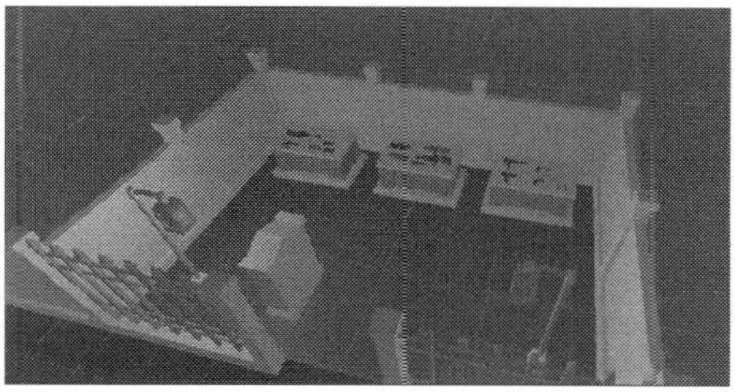

Are you ready for some VR action?

Replacing controller models with hands

To increase the immersion in virtual reality, you can replace the controllers with virtual hands.

Drag an instance of **VRTK_BasicHand** from **VRTK \ Assets \ VRTK \ Prefabs \ AvatarHands \ BasicHands** onto both **Left Controller** and **Right Controller**. You can find these Controller GameObjects in the Hierarchy under **[VRTK_SDK_MANAGER] \ [VRTK_SETUP]**.

Next, add a **VRTK_SDKTransformModify** component to each **VRTK_BasicHand**.

For each **VRTK_BasicHand**, set the size of **Sdk Overrides** to **2**. Then, expand the elements and set one of the **Controller Type** fields to **Steam VR_Vive Wand** and the other element to **Oculus_Oculus Touch**.

For the Left Controller's **VRTK_BasicHand**, set the position, rotation and scale so they match these settings:

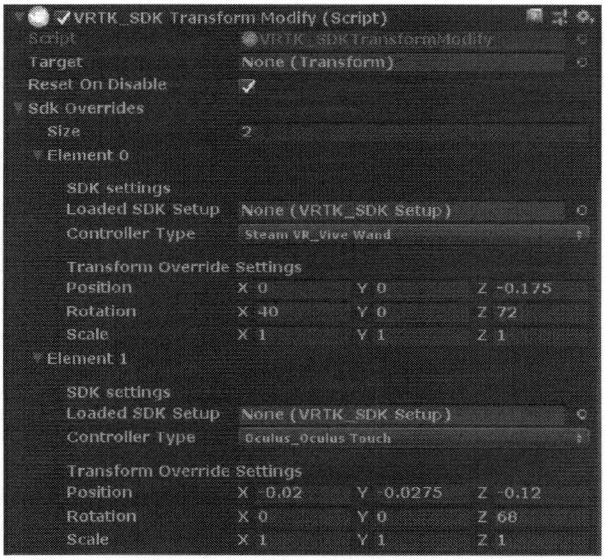

And now for the Right Controller:

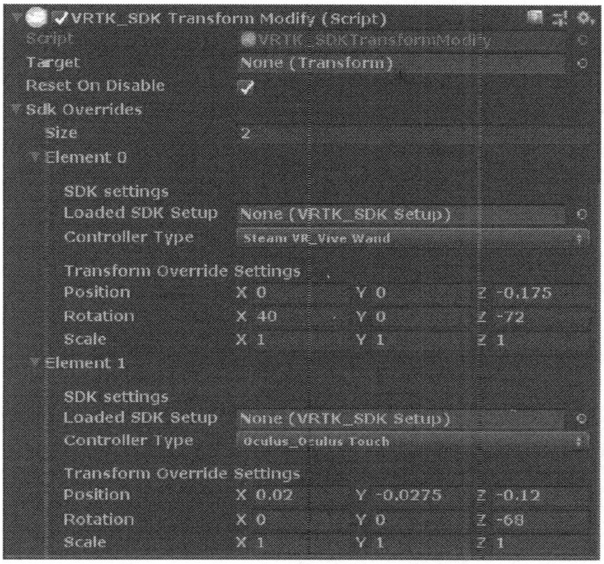

On the Left Controller, set the **Custom Collider Container** field on **VRTK_InteractTouch** component to **HandColliders** found under **LeftController \ VRTK_BasicHand**.

Also on the Left Controller, set the **Controller Attach Point** field on **VRTK_InteractGrab** to **GrabAttachPoint** found under **LeftController \ VRTK_BasicHand**.

Now, do the same for the Right Controller. **VRTK_InteractTouch** and **VRTK_InteractGrab** should look like the following image:

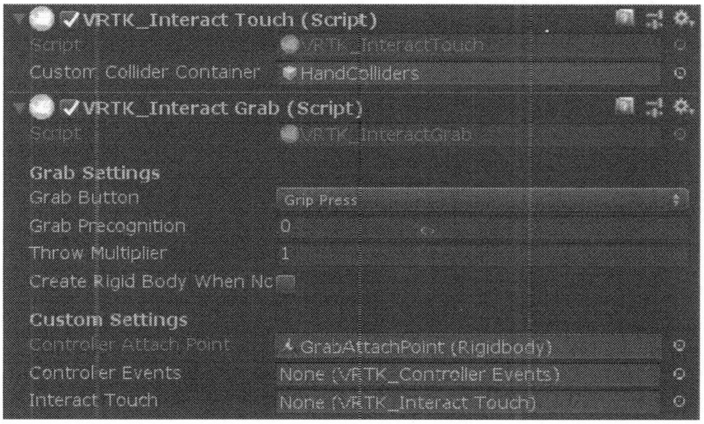

Modify the three platform GameObjects under **[VRTK_SDK_SETUPS]**. For each platform, uncheck the **Auto Populate** checkbox on **VRTK_SDKSetup**.

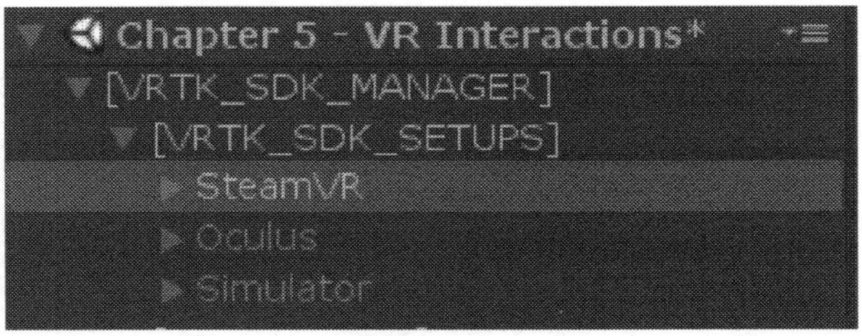

With the platform GameObjects selected in the Inspector, assign the **Model Aliases** field for both **Left Controller** and **Right Controller** to **VRTK_BasicHand**. Your setup for each platform should now match these images:

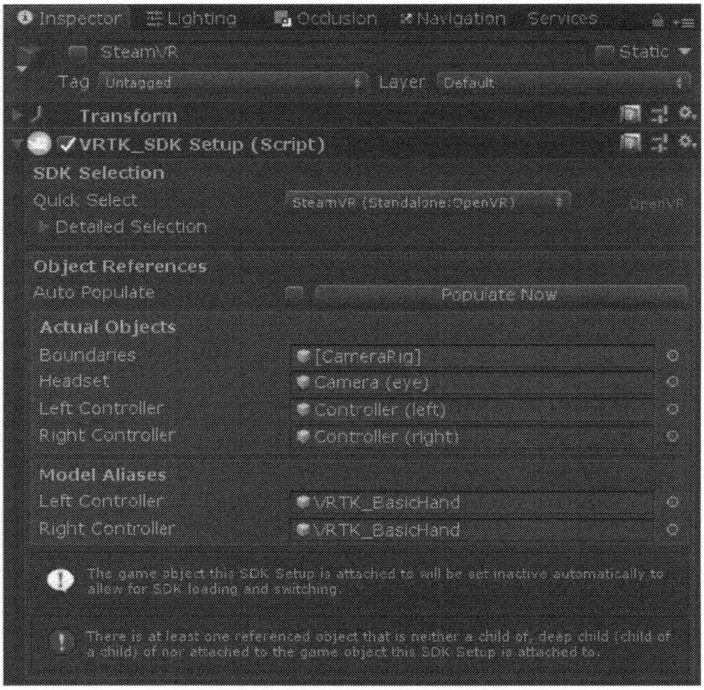

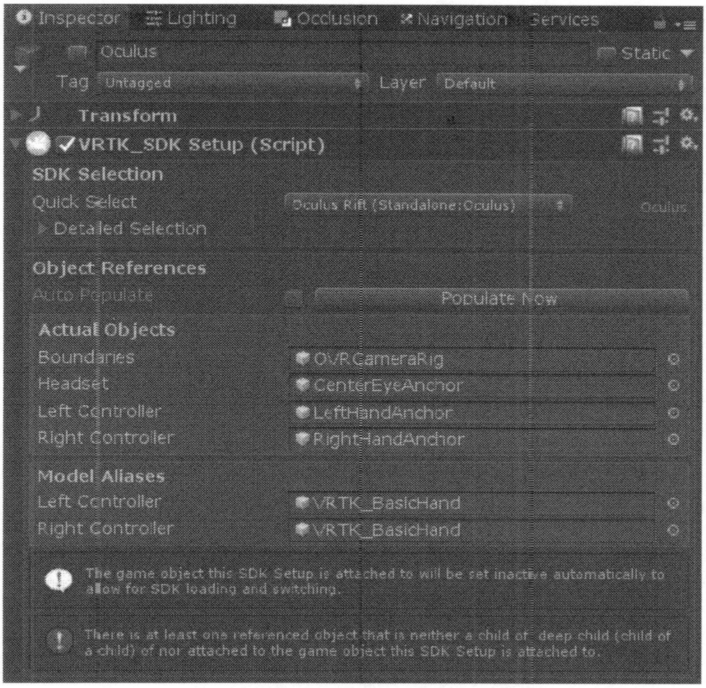

Finally, delete **LocalAvatar** from **[VRTK_SDK_MANAGER] \ [VRTK_SDK_SETUPS] \ Oculus** as you are now using your own hands system and you won't need to use the avatar system provided by Oculus.

Click Play to try things out, and you'll see hands instead of controllers.

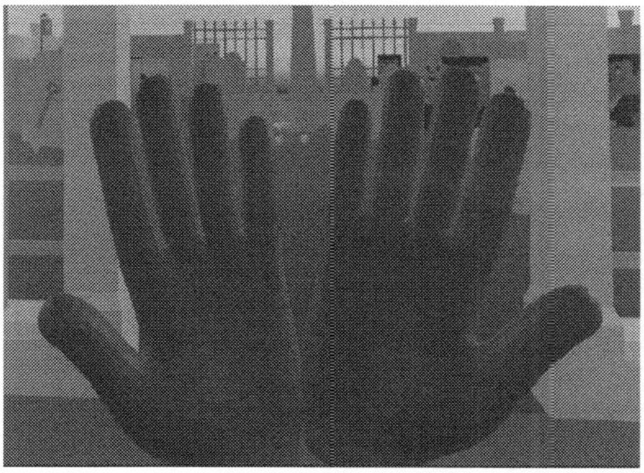

Object highlighting

To make it easier to determine what objects you can interact with in virtual reality, you can add highlights.

Locate **knifeRound_smooth** and select the child mesh GameObject underneath it named **Mesh1_Group1_Model**. Add a **Rigidbody** to **knifeRound_smooth** and a **Box Collider** to the child **Mesh1_Group1_Model**, keeping the default options.

Add a **VRTK_InteractableObject** script to **knifeRound_smooth**. Right now, you don't need to change any values as you're just setting it up for highlighting.

Add a **VRTK_InteractObjectHighlighter** script and set the color of the **Touch Highlight** inspector value to a color of your choice. Don't forget to set up the alpha color value otherwise your highlight will be invisible.

Run the scene and move to the Knife. Place either hand over the object. Notice that it changes color.

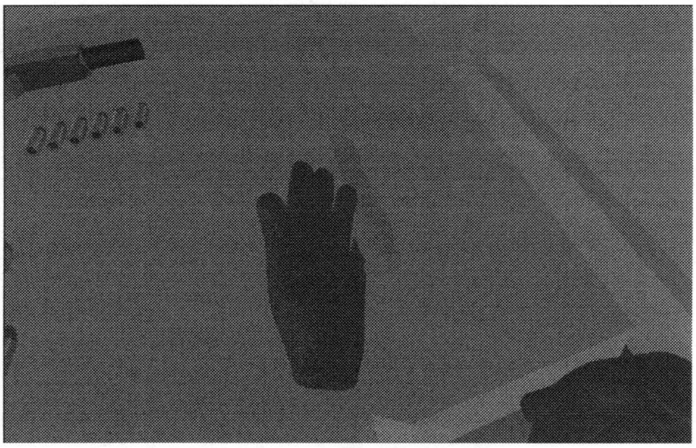

While this works, it doesn't look great — nobody wants to run around playing a game with a bright yellow knife, so try something a bit more subtle.

Add a **VRTK_OutlineObjectCopyHighlighter** component to **knifeRound_smooth**. Make sure the **Active** checkbox is ticked and set the **Thickness** to **0.4**. Under **Custom Outline Models**, set the size to **1**. Then, add in the child object of **knifeRound_smooth** named **Mesh1_Group1_Model**.

When you're done, it'll look like this:

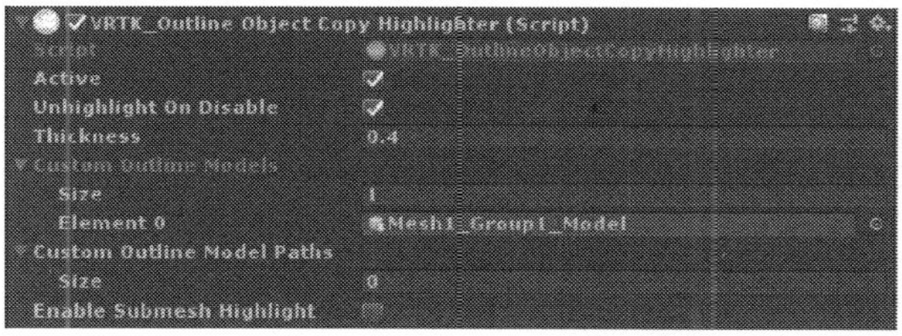

Run the scene. Notice how the knife now has a nice outline around it. Much better!

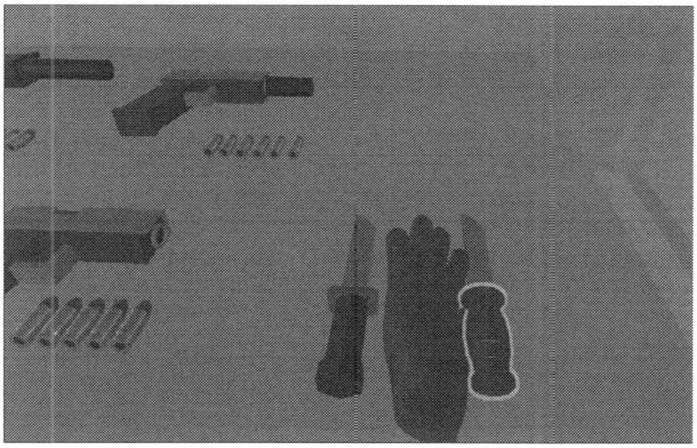

Picking up items

In the previous section, you added a **VRTK_InteractableObject** to the knife. This is the main component that deals with how you interact with objects. It handles all of the boilerplate code needed so you can focus on adding more interesting features.

First, check the box on the **knifeRound_smooth** titled **Is Grabbable**; since this item is a knife, and you might want to throw it, tick the box titled **Hold Button To Grab** and make sure **Stay Grabbed On Teleport** is also checked.

The following chart explains what each of these options means and how they affect interactions when picked up:

Option	Effect
Is Grabbable	Determines if the object can be grabbed.
Hold Button To Grab	If this is checked then the grab button on the controller needs to be continually held down to keep grabbing. If this is unchecked the grab button toggles the grab action with one button press to grab and another to release.
Stay Grabbed On Teleport	If this is checked then the object will stay grabbed to the controller when a teleport occurs. If it is unchecked then the object will be released when a teleport occurs.
Is Usable	Determines if the object can be used.
Hold Button To Use	If this is checked then the use button on the controller needs to be continually held down to keep using. If this is unchecked the the use button toggles the use action with one button press to start using and another to stop using.
Use Only If Grabbed	If this is checked the object can be used only if it is currently being grabbed.

Run the scene and use the **Grip** button on your controller to pick up the knife and swing it around a bit. Next, release the grip button and it should drop to the floor.

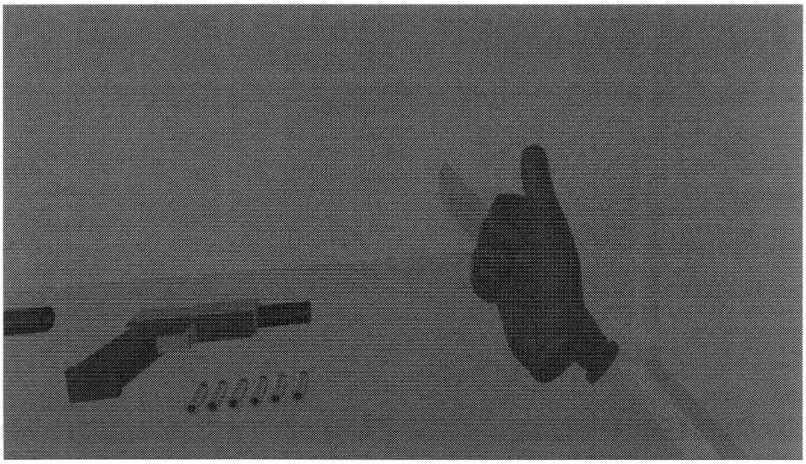

Although what you have is working, the placement of the knife is not ideal.

Add a **VRTK_InteractObjectAppearance** component to **knifeRound_smooth**.

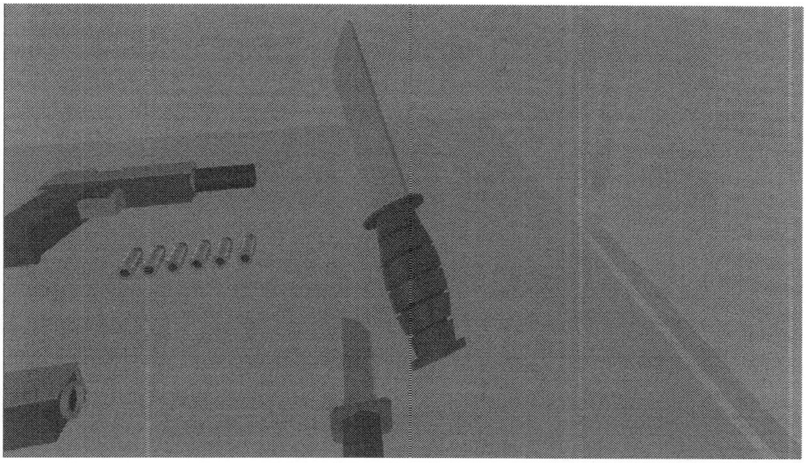

While this gives you the desired effect, it might not work for every object; a better solution is to add a custom pickup placement to position and orientate the object in the player's hand.

Custom pick up placements

To make it easier to use and interact with items — and also make them feel more realistic — you can set up custom pick up placements that alter the position and rotation when the item is picked up.

To get started, add a **Rigidbody** with default values to **Pistol**. Then, add a **Box Collider** to **Handle** found below **Pistol**, and set the size and center position so it matches the following:

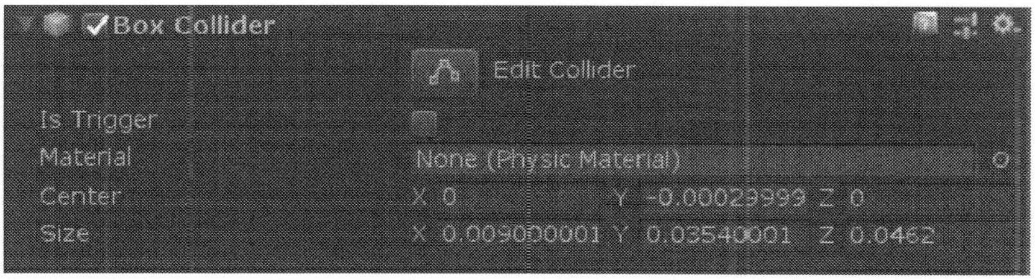

Next, add a **Pistol** component to **Pistol** and check the box for **Is Grabbable**; this script is derived from **VRTK_InteractableObject**, so it implements all of the standard functionality required for an object to allow interactions along with some custom functions for shooting.

To have the pistol snap to the correct position, you need to create two new GameObjects as children of **Pistol** found under **Interactable \ Weapons**. Name one **SnapHandleLeft** and the other **SnapHandleRight** and reset both their Transforms.

On each, add a **VRTK_SDKTransformModify** and set the size of the **Sdk Overrides** to **2**. Set the **Controller Type** for one to **Oculus_Oculus Touch** and the other to **Steam VR_Vive Wand**.

For the **SnapHandleLeft Transform Override Settings**, set the position and rotation to match the following:

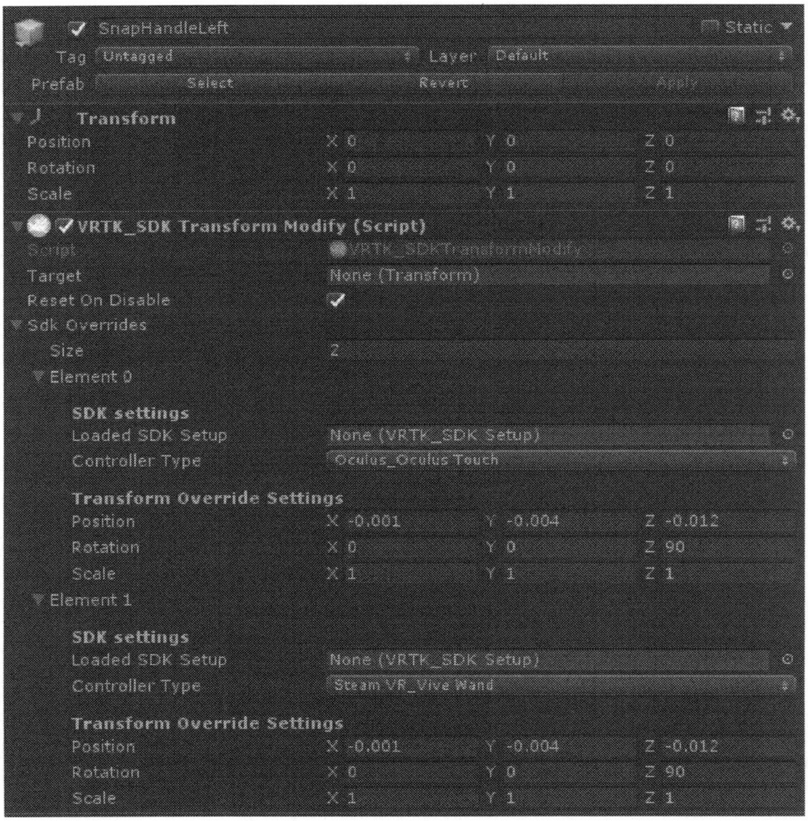

Then, do the same for **SnapHandleRight**:

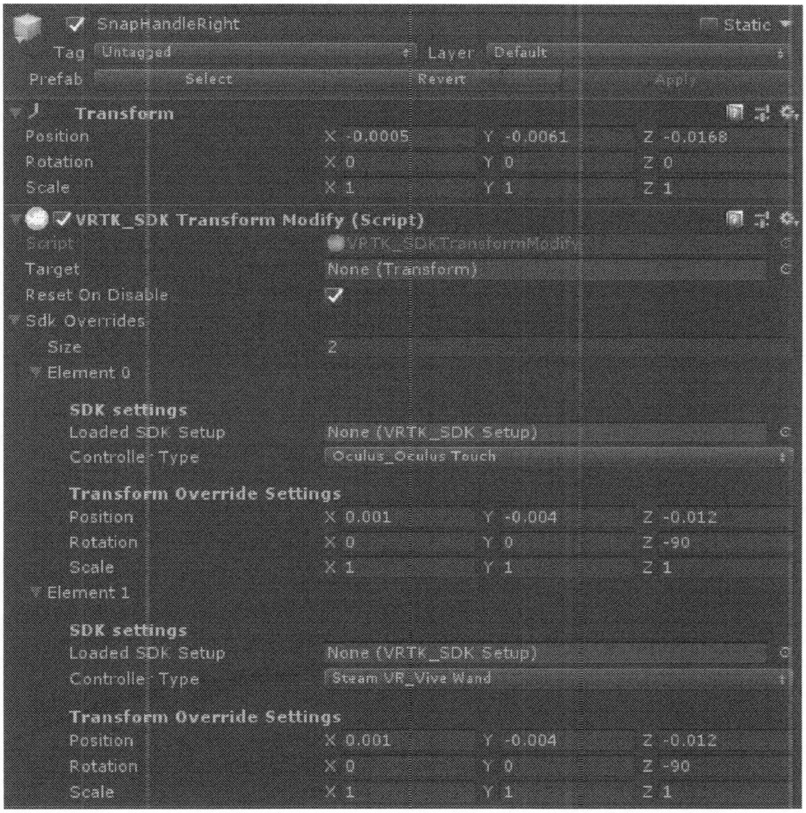

Add a **VRTK_ChildOfControllerGrabAttach** script to **Pistol** and set the Right and Left Snap Handles to the corresponding GameObjects created in the previous steps.

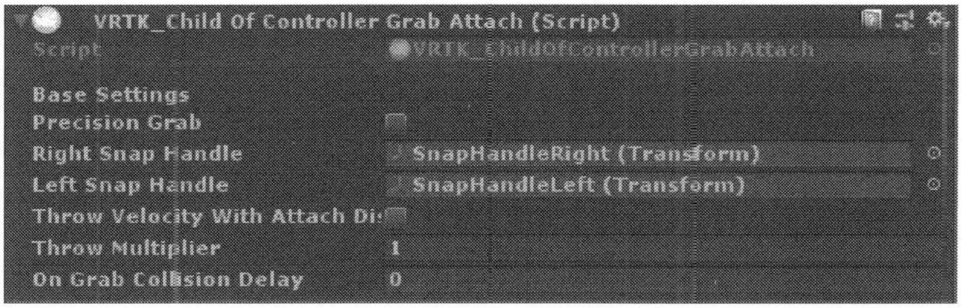

Now add a **VRTK_SwapControllerGrabAction** script to **Pistol**. This allows you to swap the pistol between the left and right hands when grabbing while holding the pistol.

Set the **Grab Attach Mechanim Script** inspector value on the **Pistol** script to the **VRTK_ChildOfControllerGrabAttach** and the **Secondary Grab Action Script** inspector value to the **VRTK_SwapControllerGrabAction** component you just added.

Now, add the necessary scripts to highlight the pistol like you did with the knife:

- Select the child mesh.
- Add a **Rigidbody**, **Box Collider** and a **VRTK_InteractableObject** component and leave their values at the defaults.

- Add a **VRTK_InteractObjectHighlighter** component and set the color of **Touch Highlight** to a color of your choice.

Jump into the scene and try grabbing the pistol in the left and right hand. Make sure it looks like it's in the correct position. Depending on whether you are using an Oculus or a Vive you may need to tweak the values on the **SnapHandleRight** and **SnapHandleLeft** components.

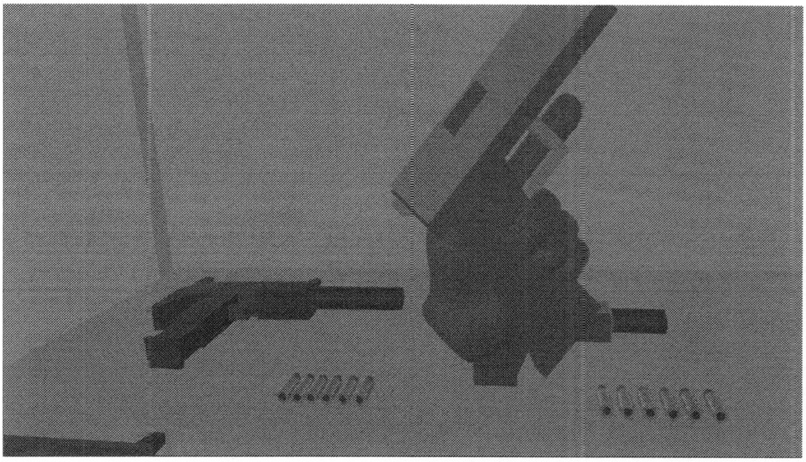

Secondary actions

With the pistol in your hand, you can now add the ability to rack the weapon by pulling back on the top of the gun, just like every good action hero does before running into a gunfight. :]

To get started, add a **Rigidbody** with default values and a **BoxCollider** to **Slider** found under **Pistol**, set the **BoxCollider** value as per the following:

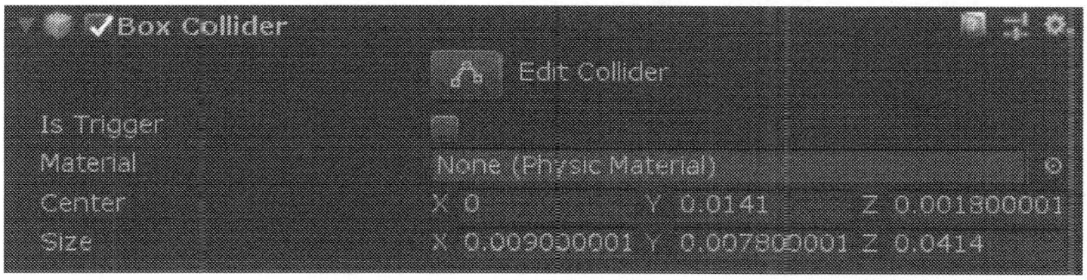

As **Slider** is designed to only move on one axis rather than all three, you need to add a joint to restrict movement.

Add a **Configurable Joint** to **Slider**, set the **Connected Body** to the **Rigidbody** of **Pistol** and set the Y-Axis **Anchor** value to **0.5**. Then, set the **Connected Anchor** XYZ values to: **(X:-5.684342, Y:0.5000001, Z:0)**. The reason why these last values need to be so precise is because of the small scale of the part you're manipulating, every millimeter (Unity uses the metric system) counts.

Now, set the Y-Axis value of the **Secondary Axis** inspector value to **-1**.

To ensure the joint only moves on one axis for a specific distance, you need to lock and limit motion. Set **X Motion** to **Limited**, **Y Motion** and **Z Motion** to **Locked**, and all **Angular Motion** values to **Locked** as you don't want the slider to rotate on any axes.

Expand **Linear Limit** and set the **Limit** inspector value to **0.05** to restrict the movement of the slider. Then, scroll down and expand the **X Drive** inspector field and set the values to the following:

- **Position Spring** = 1000
- **Position Dampner** = 100
- **Maximum Force** = 100

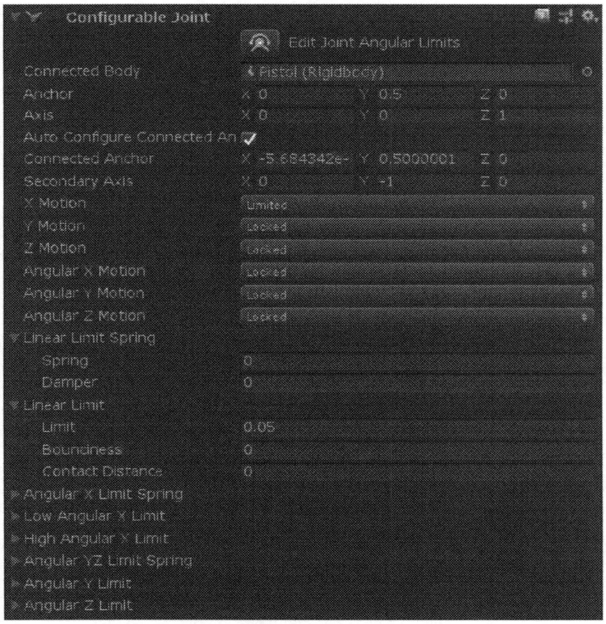

This controls the driving force that moves the joint linearly along its local X-axis.

With the Rigidbody, BoxCollider and joint configured, add the **PistolRack** script from **Assets \ Razeware \ Scripts** to **Slider**, which is a child of **Pistol**. Like the **Pistol** script you added earlier, the **PistolRack** script is derived from **VRTK_InteractableObject**.

Add a **VRTK_TrackObjectGrabAttach** component to **Slider** and set it as the **Grab Attach Mechanim Script** inspector value on the **PistolRack** script. The **Track Object Grab Attach** component doesn't directly attach the object to the controller. Rather, via a joint, it ensures the object tracks the direction of the controller. This means when you grab the top of the gun and pull back, the slider moves with the hand but not attach to the hand.

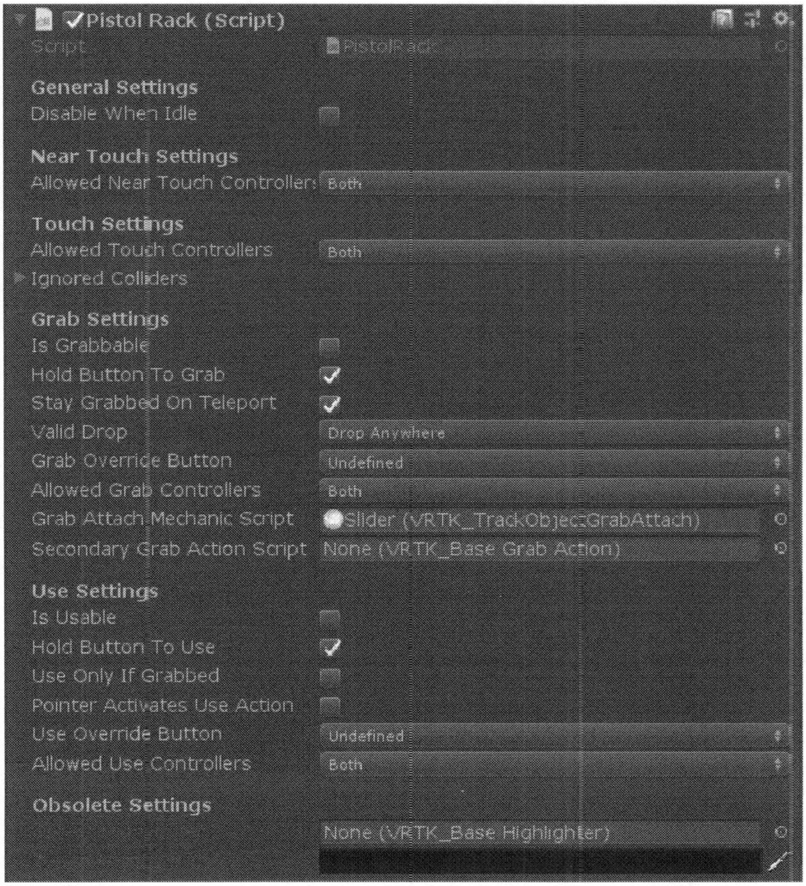

Finally, add **VRTK_InteractObjectHighliighter** and **VRTK_OutlineObjectCopyHighlighter** from the previous section, so the top of the gun is also highlighted when the hand comes in to contact with it. As you are applying the highlighting to the current GameObject you do not need to add any values to the **Custom Outline Models**

Run the scene and pick up the gun. The gun body is highlighted, and you can pull back on the top of the gun to rack it.

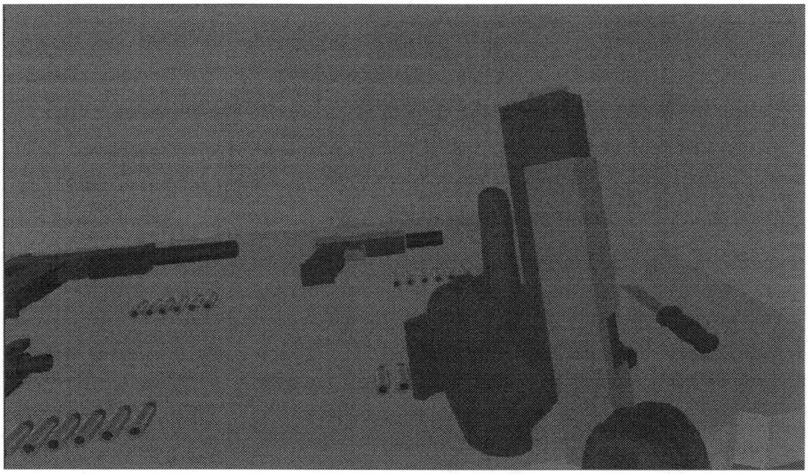

Using items in-hand

Now that you can pick up the pistol with one hand and rack it with the other, the final part is to make the pistol fire a bullet.

First, set up the bullet by adding a **RigidBody** to the top-level **Bullet** found below the main **Pistol**. Set the **Mass** to **0.1**.

Below **Bullet** are two child GameObjects. One represents the bullet casing and the other the actual round. Add a **Capsule Collider** to **Round** and set the values like so:

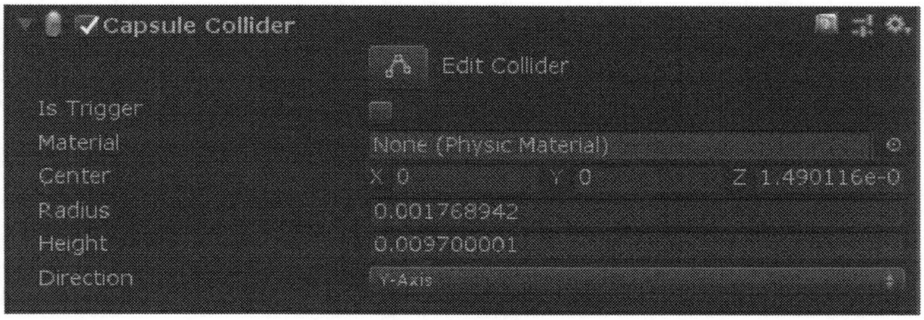

Select **Pistol** and check the checkbox for **Is Usable** and **Use Only If Grabbed** on the **Pistol** script. This ensures that when you pull the trigger, the **Pistol** script receives a notification of that event so you can tell the script to fire the bullet.

Set the **Gun End** value in the inspector to **Forward Position** found under the main **Pistol**; this gives the script the transform and direction from which to shoot the bullet.

Next, change the **Bullet Speed** to **100**. You can increase or decrease this to see the effect — it might be useful to set it to a lower value when testing so you can clearly see the bullet and the direction it's moving.

Now set the **Bullet Life** to **5**; this determines how many seconds the bullet is left active in the scene before being destroyed.

Drag the **Bullet** GameObject from under the main **Pistol** to the **Bullet** inspector value on the **Pistol** script; this is the GameObject that is instantiated each time the trigger is pulled.

Finally, drag **Slider** to the **Slide**, **Slide Rigidbody** and **Slide Collider** inspector values of the **Pistol** script; this allows the slider to move back and forward when the gun is fired.

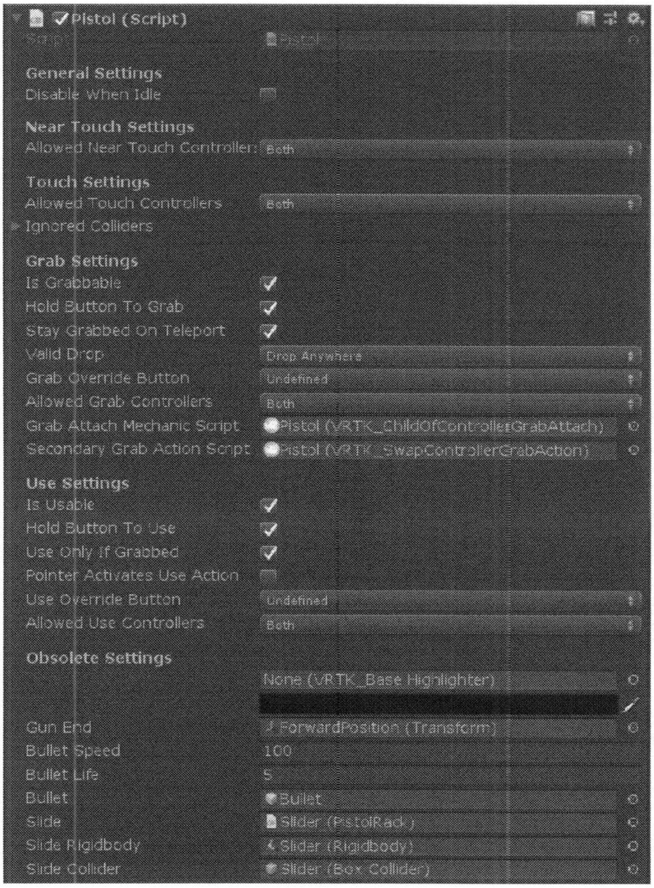

Click Play in the scene. You can highlight the gun body and top with both hands, pick up the pistol and switch hands, rack the pistol and shoot the pistol.

Where to go from here?

Congratulations, you made it to the end of this chapter! Grab the gun and fire some celebratory shots into the air. If you had trouble following along, you can review the final project for this chapter.

To recap, in this chapter you learned how to:

- Replace the controller models with physical looking hands.
- Highlight objects.
- Pick up objects.
- Set up custom pickup placements on objects.
- Add secondary actions to objects.
- Use an object in-hand.

In the next chapter, you'll look at adding user interface (UI) elements. You'll also learn where and how to display information within VR.

Chapter 6: VR User Interface

Jonathan Ogle-Barrington

The user interface (UI) is an important part of any video game. It's used to inform the user of their health and score, instruct a user how to play the game, and most importantly, it helps to control the flow of the game through the use of menus and pause screens.

In a non-VR game or application, a Heads Up Display or HUD is typically placed over top of the main screen and shows information to the user. This type of UI is known as **non-diegetic UI**, meaning it doesn't exist in the world of the game, but it directly relates to what the user is seeing or interacting with inside the game.

In Unity, you can add a HUD-style, non-diegetic UI by using a **Screen Space - Overlay** or **Screen Space - Camera** UI Canvas. Unfortunately, this approach doesn't work well with VR because the user is unable to focus on something so close to their eyes — it's incredibly distracting and uncomfortable as it moves with the user's head as if it was glued on.

A better, more intuitive and less distracting option for VR is to position the UI within the environment using a **World Space** UI Canvas. This approach is known as **Spatial UI**.

In this chapter, you're going to explore various ways of using UI within an existing project. Specifically, you'll learn how to:

- Create a standard UI.
- Add a spatial UI.
- Fabricate a game menu.
- Implement pointer interactions.
- Add 3D user controls

Standard UI

To help you understand why you need to use spatial UI, you'll start by adding a standard (non-diegetic) UI that displays the frame rate of the game.

Open the starter project for this chapter. Next, open the **Assets \ Razeware \ Chapter 6 - VR User Interface** scene.

In the hierarchy, create a new **UI > Canvas** and name it **FramerateUI**. Set its **Render Mode** to **Screen Space - Camera**.

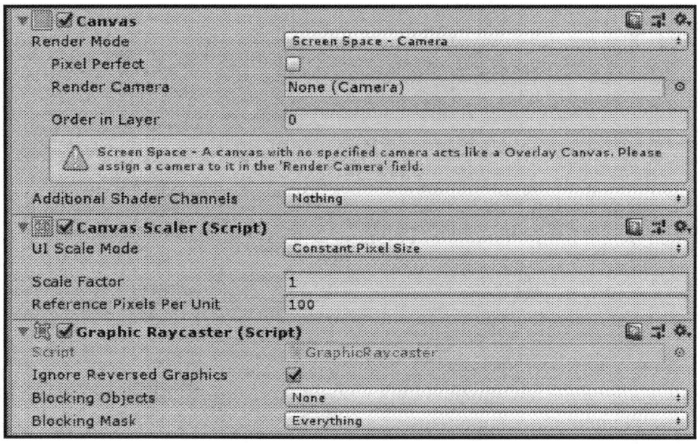

> **Note**: It's ok to ignore the warning about the **Render Camera**. This field gets set during runtime, but since VRTK supports multiple setups, it's inadvisable to set it to a specific camera until the platform is detected.

Next, create a new **UI > Text** as a child of **FramerateUI** and name it **FramesPerSecondText**. Set its **Font Size** to **50**, **Horizontal Overflow** to **Overflow** and **Vertical Overflow** to **Overflow**. This means you won't need to worry about the size and positioning of the UI. It also ensures that you display all of the content.

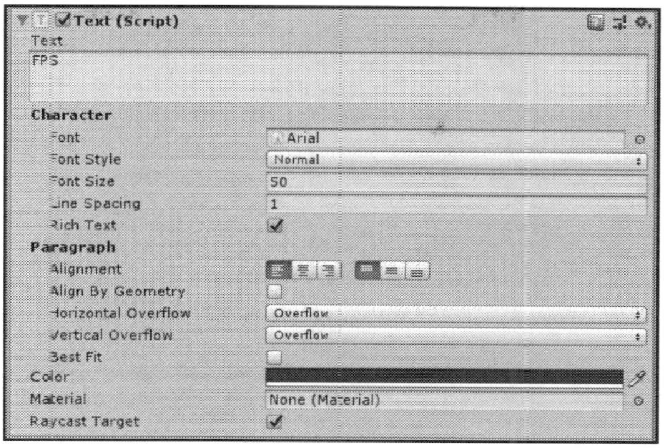

Finally, add a **VRTK_FramesPerSecondViewer** component to **FramesPerSecondText** and keep the default values.

Click play, and notice how the frame rate is displayed directly in front of you and attached to your head. Whenever you move, the UI moves and follows the tracking of the headset. As you can see, this is quite distracting and can ruin immersion, which is why Spatial UI is favored over the standard UI setup in VR.

Spatial UI

In most shooting games, there's a piece of UI to indicate the current ammo count of the weapon. As you've seen, it's not practical to add an ammo count to the screen. Instead, you're going to attach a **VRTK_ObjectTooltip** to the pistol and display the ammo count there.

Start by creating an empty GameObject named **Tooltips**. Make it a child of **Pistol** found under **Interactables \ Weapons** and set the transform's position, rotation and scale to **(X: -0.0184, Y: 0.016, Z: -0.02)**, **(X: 0, Y: 0, Z: 0)** and **(X: 0.2, Y: 0.2, Z: 0.2)** respectively.

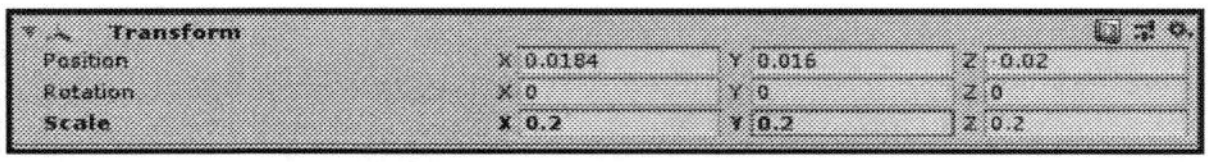

On **Tooltips**, add a **VRTK_ObjectTooltip** component. Next, create two empty GameObjects as its children.

Name the first GameObject **Line** and reset its **Transform** component. Now add a **Line Renderer** component; you'll use this to draw a line from the pistol to the tooltip.

On **Line Renderer**, set **Cast Shadows** to **Off** and uncheck **Receive Shadows**. Next, switch **Motion Vectors** to **Per Object Motion** and set the position, width and color to **(X: 0, Y: 0, Z: 0)**, **1.0** and **pure black** respectively.

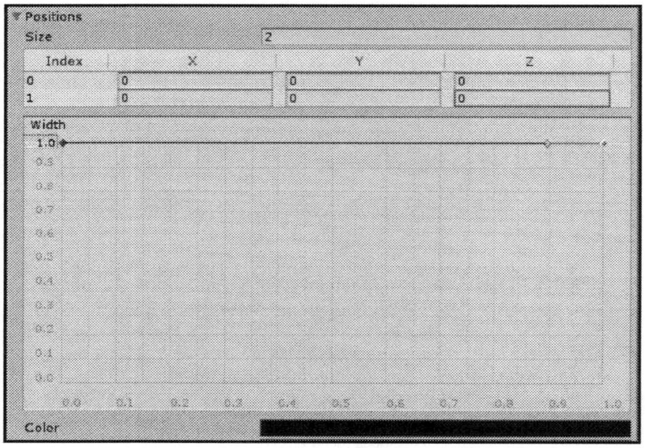

Name the second GameObject **LineStart**. This serves as the start position for the **Line Renderer**. Set its position to **(X: -0.05, Y: 0, Z: 0)**.

Inside **Assets \ Razeware \ Prefabs**, drag the **TooltipCanvas** onto **Tooltips**. This forms the canvas where you'll display the text for the ammo count.

Now, create one more empty GameObject named **LineEnd**, and place it under **Pistol \ Slider**. To position the **Line Renderer** in the correct spot on the pistol, set its position to **(X: 0.0035, Y: 0.0114, Z: -0.0129)** and set its scale to **(X: 0.2, Y: 0.2, Z: 0.2)**.

Returning to **Tooltips**, change **Draw Line From** to **LineStart** and set **Draw Line To** to **LineEnd**. Also, set the **Container Size** to **(X: 100, Y: 30)** and the **Font Color** to **pure white**.

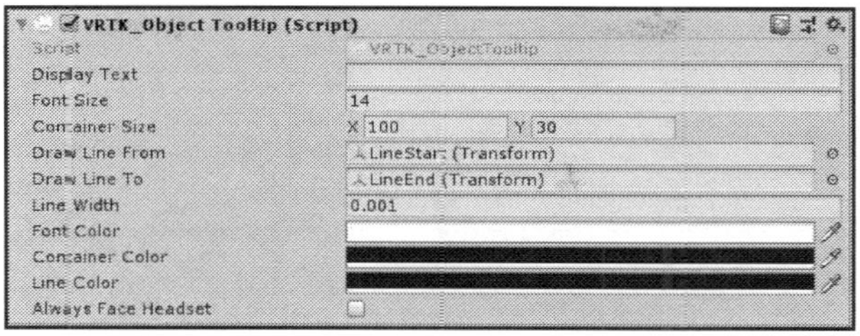

The final step is to set the **Ammo Tooltip Game Object** inspector value of the **Pistol** script to **Tooltips**.

Jump into the scene and pick up the pistol. Notice the tooltip, which is similar to the image below. It displays your current ammo count and lets you know when it's time to reload.

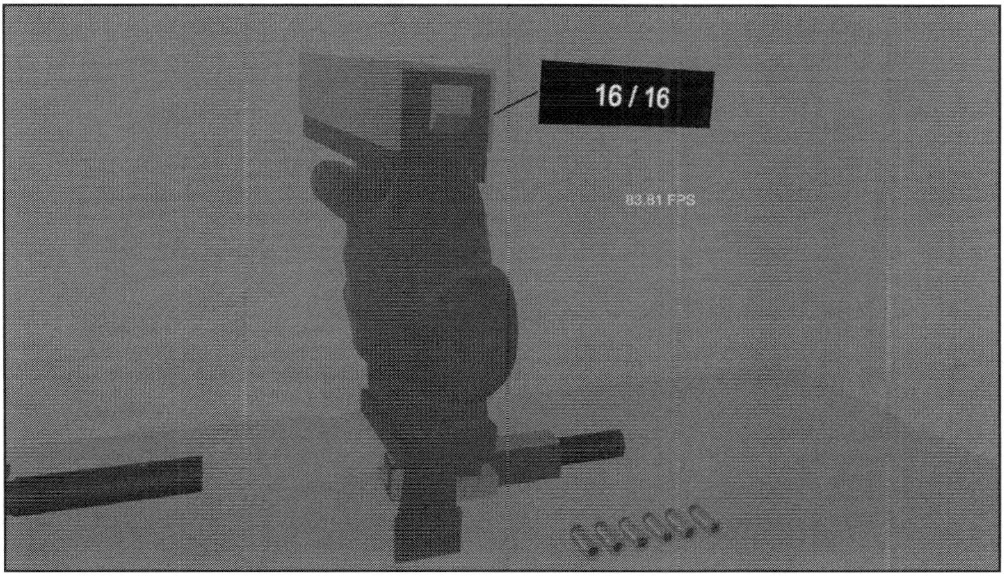

Menus

In a non-VR game, you can use a 2D or 3D interface with a menu to walk the user through starting a new game or resuming an earlier one. As you saw in the previous section, adding a standard menu system is not practical or even usable.

If you looked around the scene, you probably noticed that the tombstone at the entrance now has a UI attached to it.

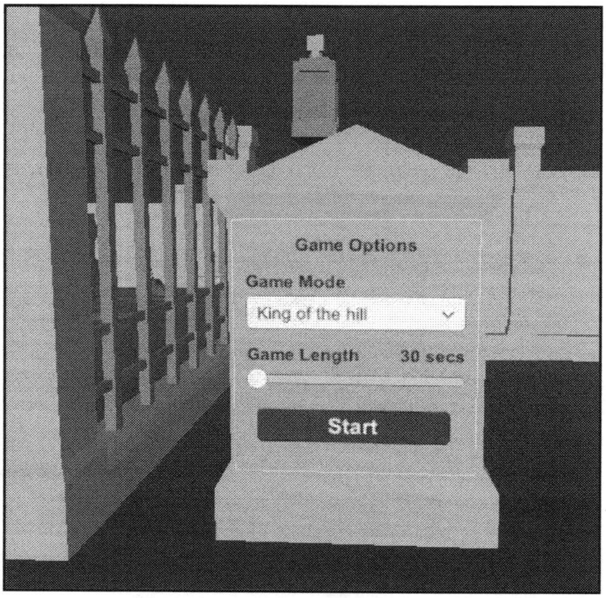

Start by selecting **Menu UI** in the hierarchy, which is a child of **Interactable**, and add a **VRTK_UICanvas** and a **Menu Controller** component to it.

Set the value of **Game Time Text** to **Value** in the Inspector, this GameObject is a child of **Interactables \ MenuUI \ GameTime**. Next, set **Enemy Game Object** to the top-level **Enemies** located inside **Interactables** in the Hierarchy.

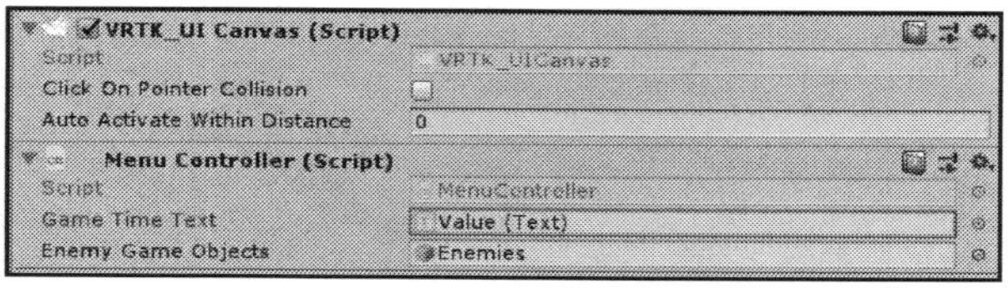

Next, under **Interactables**, select **StartButton** and set the **On Click** event object to **MenuUI**. Now select **MenuController**, followed by the **StartTheGame** function. This calls the **StartTheGame()** method of the **Menu Controller** component when the user "clicks" the **StartButton**

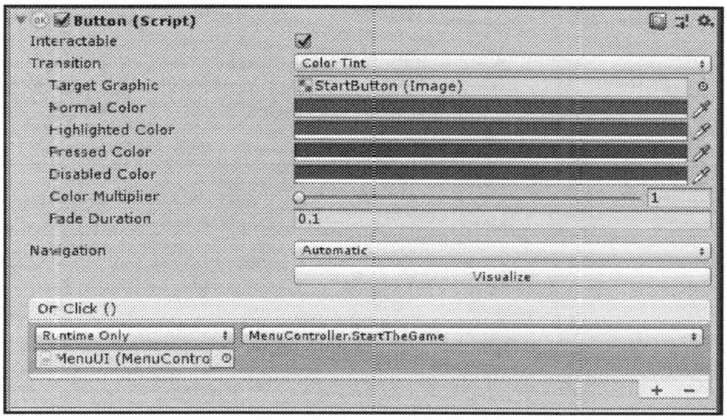

Finally, select **GameTime** and set the **On Value Changed** event object to **MenuUI**; this time, however, set the method call to **UpdateGameTime** under **MenuController**

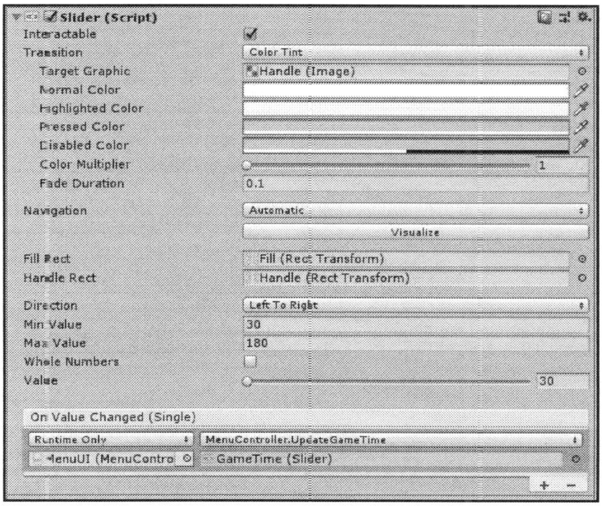

These are all of the changes you need to make to the UI elements for them to function properly in VR. However, if you click play and run the game, you'll notice that you have no way to interact with the UI elements. That's because by default, they're only interactable with a mouse-click event.

In the next section, you'll learn how you can use a virtual laser pointer to interact with UI elements instead.

Pointer Interactions

To interact with UI elements on a world canvas you need to make use of the **VRTK_UIPointer**. The **VRTK_UIPointer** works in a similar manner to the pointers used in the previous sections on locomotion: It displays a colored line straight out from the point or origin, but rather than allowing teleportation, it allows you to select and interact with the UI object its end point touches. It's basically a laser, but you can point this one to your eyes without any danger. :]

To get started with pointer interactions, inside **[VRTK_SDK_MANAGER] \ [VRTK_SETUP]**, select **Right Controller** and add a **VRTK_UIPointer**, a **VRTK_Pointer** and a **VRTK_StraightPointRenderer** component.

On **VRTK_Pointer**, set **Pointer Renderer** to the **Right Controller** and uncheck **Enable Teleport**. All of the other default settings are fine.

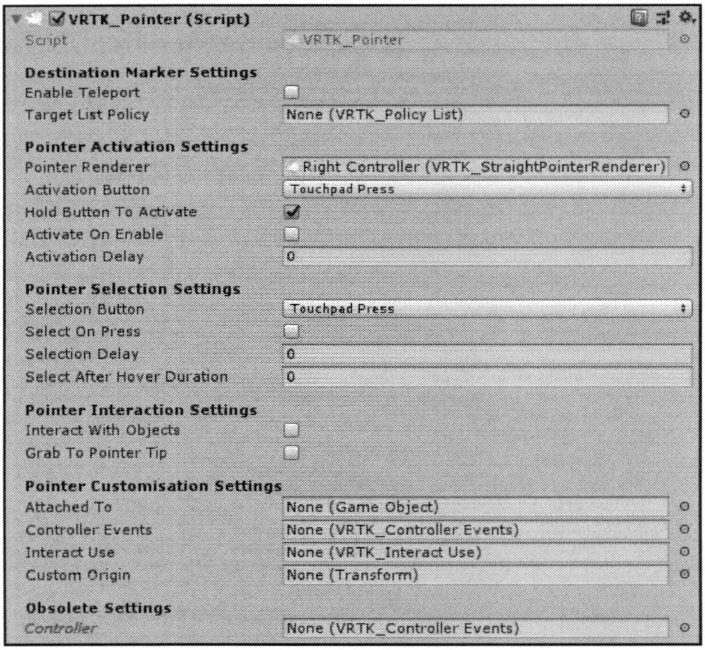

Click Play, and with the right hand, hold the grip button and press down on the touchpad or analog stick to display the pointer.

Using the trigger, you can interact with the UI elements on the tombstone such as the drop-down for changing the game mode, the slider for setting the game length and the Start button to start the game.

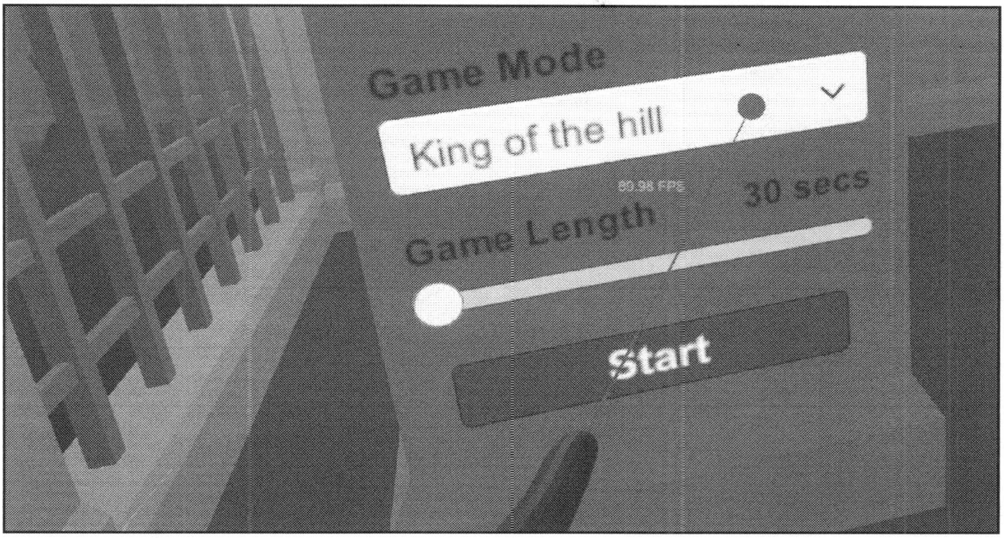

3D Controls

You're almost done! You have a game where you can move around the scene, interact with weapons and interact with UI to start the game, but you still need a simple mechanism for restarting the game.

On the back wall of the scene, you may have noticed a lever. Pulling this should restart the level.Select **LevelControl** inside **Interactables \ RestartLevel \ LevelContainer** and add a **VRTK_Artifical_Rotator** component to it; this limits the axis and degrees in which the level can rotate.

Change the **Operate Axis** to the **Z Axis** and set **Hinge Point** to **HingePoint** found under **LevelControl**. Also, set the **Angle Limits** to **(Min: 0, Max: 90)** and change the **Force Resting Angle Threshold** to **0**.

Continuing with the **VRTK_Artifical Rotator**, update the **Step Size** to **1** and check the **Use Step As Value** checkbox. Next, set the **Snap Force** to **10** and check the **Snap To Step** checkbox.

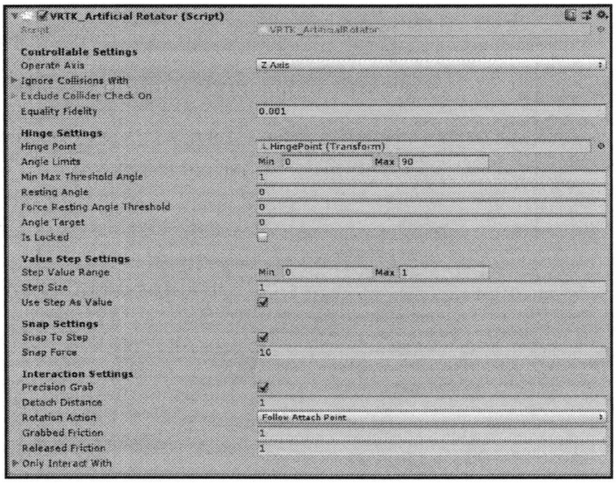

Finally, add a **Reset Level** component to **LevelControl**. This simple script waits for the level to reach its maximum limit and then restarts the scene.

Click play and grab your pistol. Press the start button to shoot the hordes of zombies, ghosts and skeletons. When it's all over, grab the lever to restart the level.

Where to go from here?

Well done! You now know how to set up the basics of a cross-platform VR game that includes locomotion, virtual world interactions and UI interactions.

If you want to continue to work on this project and add more functionality, you can start by:

- Adding the ability to use other weapons.
- Setting up a system to track the time it takes to kill all the enemies.
- Adding different scoring zones to the enemy, e.g. 50 points for shooting in the head and 10 for the body.
- Creating different game modes that can be attached to the tombstone UI.

In the next and final chapter of the beginner's section, you'll look at Optimization and Motion Sickness in VR.

Chapter 7: Optimization & Motion Sickness

Eric Van de Kerckhove

A stable frame rate is essential for any game, but especially in VR — even the smallest hiccup can cause an uncomfortable feeling for the player. VR content is rendered twice and needs to run at 90 frames per second instead of 60. That means you have double the amount of stuff to render, 150% faster than that of traditional PC games. Sounds like a challenge!

But don't worry, there are many ways to make your games and experiences run at their fullest potential while keeping things looking beautiful and stylish.

In this chapter, you'll learn how to:

- Use the profiler and frame debugger.
- Change the render scale at runtime.
- Use single pass stereo rendering.
- Optimize the geometry, textures and materials.
- Avoid VR sickness.

Getting started

Open the starter project for this chapter and open the **Desert** scene from the **Razeware \ Scenes** folder.

> **Note**: You may get prompted to update to the included Oculus Utilities plugin. For now, decline the update as this chapter's project files are configured with **version 1.24.0** in mind.

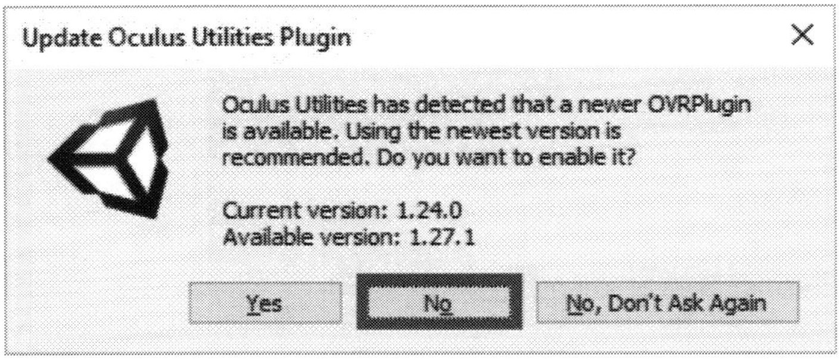

Look around the scene. It's a small chunk of desert with objects — like cacti and rocks — scattered around with colliders attached.

Play the scene to get a feel for how the level is laid out. The **VRTK SDK Manager** and controller aliases are already set up, so you can teleport around using the touchpad of any of the controllers.

After verifying that everything works, check out the Project view:

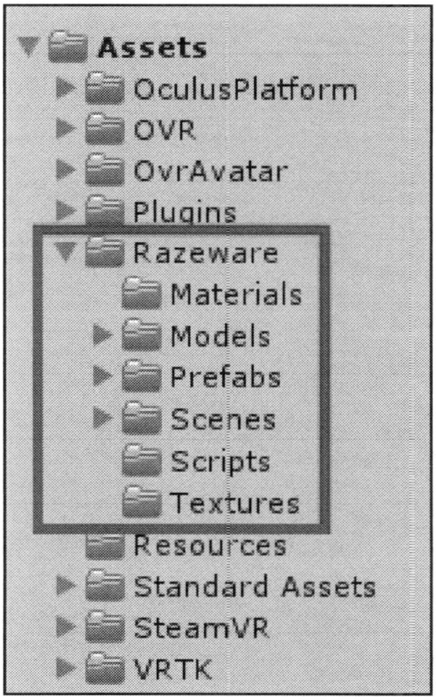

The custom-made assets for this chapter are all contained in the Razeware folder. Here's a close look:

- **Materials**: The materials for the desert.
- **Models**: This contains all of the models.
- **Prefabs**: All of the world objects in the scene are prefabs from this folder.
- **Scenes**: The desert scene.

- **Scripts**: Empty for now; you'll place all of the scripts here.
- **Textures**: Two textures for the desert models.

With that out of the way, it's time to dive right in!

Using the Profiler and the Frame Debugger

Before performing optimization on your projects, it's important to know where to apply it. Unity comes with some excellent analysis tools built-in for figuring out why your game or experience is running too slow or has hitches now and then.

The profiler

The profiler helps you understand how much time is spent rendering each frame of your game. It shows a detailed overview of the calculations that happen throughout a game session, and it allows you to inspect every frame.

Open the Profiler window by selecting **Window > Analysis > Profiler** in the top menu. Press the **Record** button on the top left and play the scene for a few seconds. Look around a bit and do some teleporting. Now, look at the Profiler again and notice it's filled with all sorts of data.

The Profiler is divided into two different sections. The top part is a timeline with colored graphs showing how much each process is taxing the CPU, GPU and RAM.

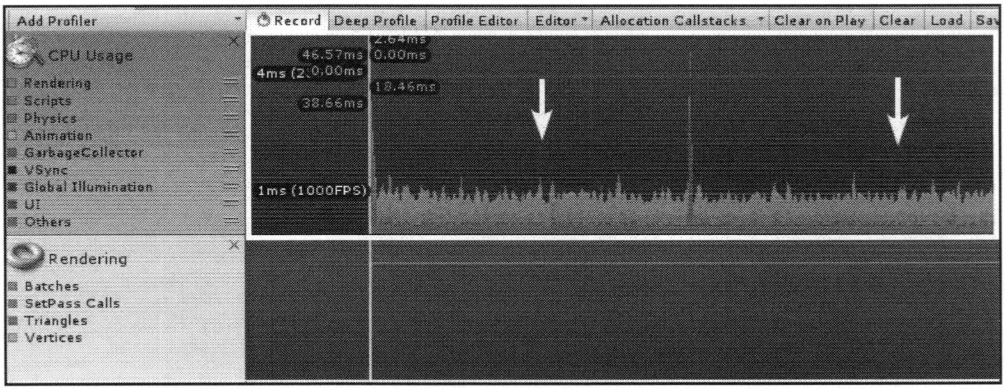

The default view of the bottom part of the Profiler is another timeline, this one showing what goes on in a single frame, and for how long in chronological order.

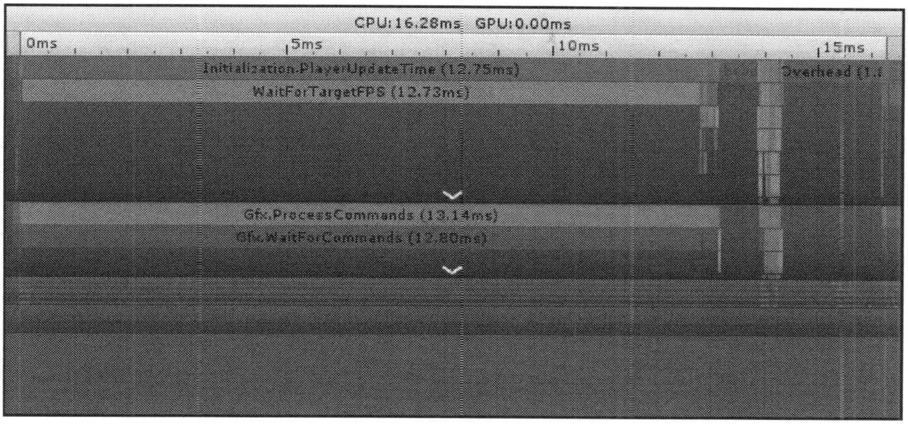

Change the view to **Hierarchy** at the top-left of the bottom part by selecting its entry in the drop-down.

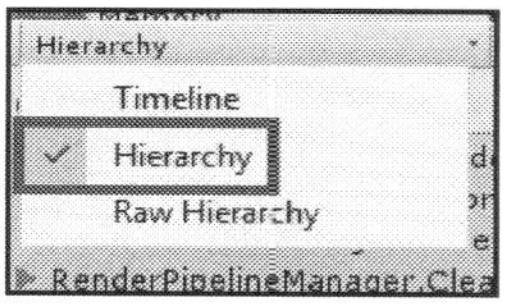

The Hierarchy view shows the same data as the Timeline, but in a table that you can sort by frame time, calls and garbage collection allocations.

Click the graph area to select a specific point in time where some of your recorded session captured a bit of activity.

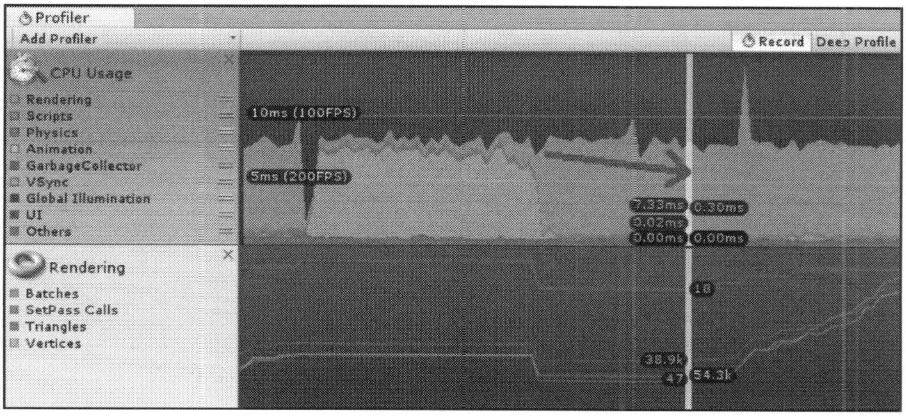

To get an optimal view of what's going on, maximize the Profiler window so that it fills the screen, and click on the **Total** header of the table until it sorts in **descending** order (from big to small) — when done correctly, an arrow pointing down appears:

To get even more information on what's eating precious CPU cycles, click the drop-down on the top-right of the bottom section that reads **No Details** and select **Show Related Objects**.

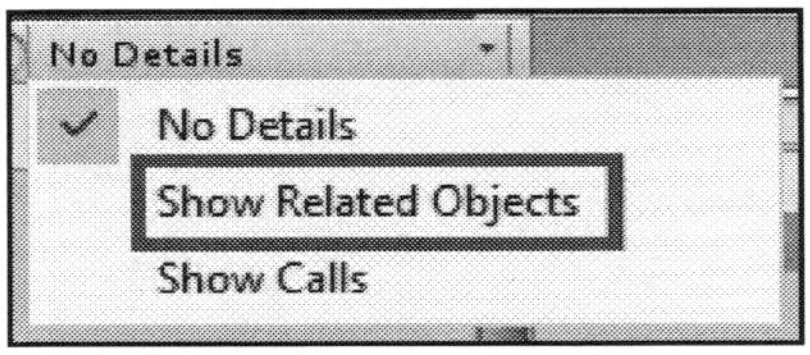

You'll now see the GameObjects that are related to the selected call. For example, select **VRTK_ControllerEvents.Update()** on the left, and you'll see that both controller objects show up in the list:

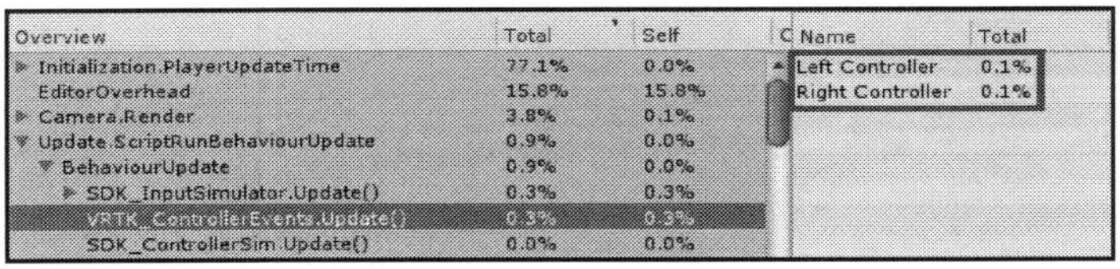

Explaining how to use the Profiler in detail is outside the scope of this chapter, but here's a typical workflow:

- Clear the Profiler and press the record button.
- Play a short section of your game where the FPS drops suddenly or where you notice other hiccups.
- Look at the Profiler. Search for spikes in the top timeline and select one of them.
- Use the bottom section to find out what caused the spike in CPU usage or GC allocation.
- Come up with a fix and implement it such as moving heavy calculations out of the main thread.
- Rinse and repeat until satisfied.

To find out more about the Profiler, check out these resources:

- **Profiler overview for beginners**: https://unity3d.com/learn/tutorials/topics/interface-essentials/profiler-overview-beginners
- **Profiler window documentation**: https://docs.unity3d.com/Manual/ProfilerWindow.html

Frame debugger

Draw calls hold information telling the GPU about textures, states, shaders and objects to render among others. These are put together by the CPU in a 'draw call package' to ship over to the GPU for processing.

An important performance tuning task is optimizing your game to make these as efficient to send along the pipeline as possible — and the Frame Debugger can help you with this task. The Frame Debugger window shows all of the draw calls and lets you cycle through each call in chronological order to see how a single frame is built.

Open the Frame Debugger window by selecting **Window > Analysis > Frame Debugger** in the top menu.

Next, start the game by pressing the **Play** button at the top of the editor's main window. Now press the **Enable** button at the top-left of the Frame Debugger window to capture a single frame.

The game is paused, and the list on the left is filled with draw calls and other events like framebuffer clears.

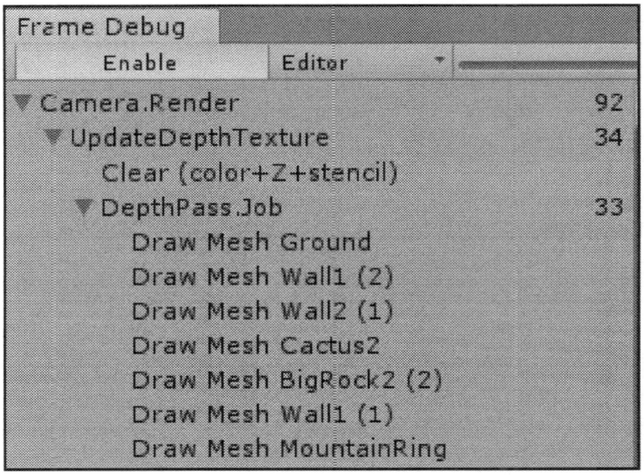

The panel on the right shows detailed information about the draw call or event like the shader, material and texture.

> **Note**: If the Frame Debugger doesn't show details after capture, ensure you start the scene from the **Game** window, not the **Scene** window. Then, click **Enable** to capture the frame details once the game is running in the editor.

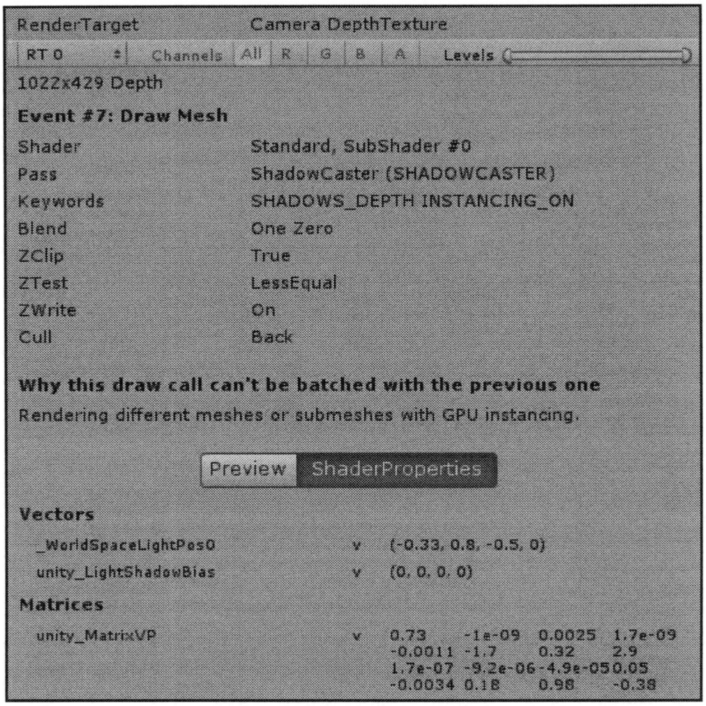

By default the **ShaderProperties** tab is shown, this contains lots of details about the draw call. Perhaps the most crucial piece of info, though, when looking to optimize a game is the "Why this draw call can't be batched with the previous one" section. This explains why this draw call couldn't be combined with the previous one.

For a full list of the possible reasons, see this blog post by Unity:https://blogs.unity3d.com/2017/04/03/how-to-see-why-your-draw-calls-are-not-batched-in-5-6/

You want to render as many meshes as possible in a single draw call for maximum performance, so fix as many of these reasons as possible in your projects. Use shared materials, texture atlases and mark non-moving objects as static.

Next, switch to the **Preview** tab by pressing the **Preview** button.

Select one of the **Draw Mesh** draw calls on the left. You'll get a 3D preview of the mesh with some extra information like its name and the number of vertices it has.

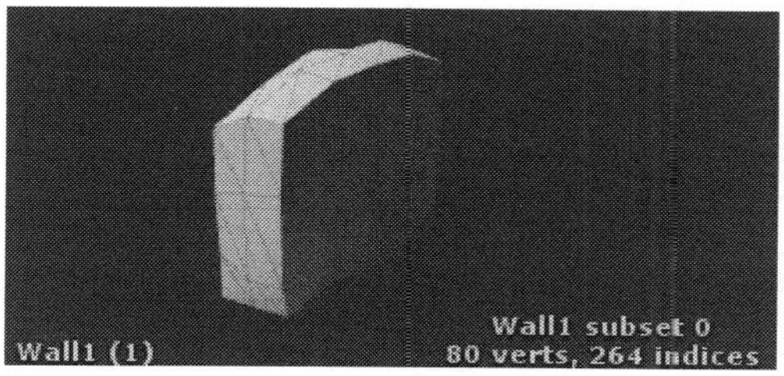

Finally, you can see the total amount of draw calls at the top of the window. You can use the slider to scrub through the draw calls in this frame capture.

You can find more information about the Frame Debugger here:

- **Frame Debugger manual**: https://docs.unity3d.com/Manual/FrameDebugger.html
- **Frame Debugger tutorial:** https://unity3d.com/learn/tutorials/topics/graphics/frame-debugger

Render scale

Changing the render scale is a good way to increase performance or quality. Downscaling the final render resolution makes the image appear fuzzier but speeds up rendering as the fill rate is much lower. Upscaling the resolution above the native resolution makes everything appear crisp and detailed.

Here are some of the ways you can change the render scale.

> **Note**: Changing the render scale only works with actual hardware, it won't have any effect when running the simulator in the editor.

Eye texture resolution scale

First, you can change the size of the render texture itself and discard the previous one. To do this, you change the `XRSettings.eyeTextureResolutionScale` variable in any script.

The scale is applied to both dimensions (width & height), so a value of **0.5**, for example, gives you an image that's **25%** the size of the original. The scaling of the render texture is computationally heavy, so don't change this value mid-game as that can cause a short freeze. It's useful to change if you detected a low-end device for example.

Render viewport scale

Instead of scaling the whole render texture, you can scale the render viewport. This way, the image only gets rendered on part of the render texture. You can change this in realtime without a problem, although not all XR platforms will make the change instantly.

Create a new C# script in **Razeware \ Scripts** and name it **AdjustViewportScale**. Open the newly created file in a code editor and remove the `Start` method.

Add the following `using` statement at the top of the file:

```
using UnityEngine.XR;
```

You need the XR namespace to use the XRSettings class.

Add the following `if` statements inside `Update()`:

```
if (Input.GetKeyDown(KeyCode.LeftArrow))
{
    XRSettings.renderViewportScale -= 0.1f; // 1
}

if (Input.GetKeyDown(KeyCode.RightArrow))
{
    XRSettings.renderViewportScale += 0.1f; // 2
}
```

Here's what these do:

1. Decrease the render viewport scale by 10% when the left arrow key is pressed.
2. Increase the render viewport scale by 10% when the right arrow key is pressed.

Save this script and return to the editor.

Create a new empty GameObject in the Hierarchy and name it **AdjustViewportScale**. Then, add an **Adjust Viewport Scale** component to it.

Now, run the scene, put on your HMD and keep your fingers on the arrow keys of your keyboard. Try pressing the left arrow key a few times; you should see the resolution visually decrease.

All the magic happens with the `XRSettings.renderViewportScale` variable. Instead of scaling the entire render texture, this value controls what percent of the texture is used. You can change this in real-time without a problem, although not all XR platforms will make the change instantly. This also only works with forward rendering.

Disable the **Adjust Viewport Scale** component on **AdjustViewportScale**; there's a better option when using VRTK.

VRTK Adaptive Quality component

VRTK comes with a nice component that automatically scales the viewport based on the level of performance. If things are running slowly, it'll decrease the resolution to a given point. Alternatively, it'll increase the resolution if your machine has enough power to process it.

Unfold **[VRTK_SDK_MANAGER]** and **[VRTK_SETUP]**, and select **Play Area**. Add a **VRTK_Adaptive Quality** component to it.

The default values on this component are OK out-of-the-box, but you can widen the minimum and maximum viewport scale to allow for both weaker and beefier specs.

Set the minimum of **Scale Render Viewport** to **0.5** and the maximum to **4**.

The viewport will now automatically render between half and up to 4x the native resolution for a nice bump in performance or a free increase in quality.

Single Pass Stereo rendering

By default, Unity renders VR content using a technique called **multi pass rendering**; this renders the full view once for every eye. However, drawing everything twice comes with a severe performance cost as it doubles the number of vertices the device needs to process. Luckily, since version 5.6, Unity has added other, more efficient techniques to use in VR.

Single Pass Stereo rendering, also known as double-wide rendering, is a rendering technique that allows Unity to render both the left and right eye images at the same time into one packed Render Texture that's twice the width of a single eye texture. This allows the GPU to share culling for both eyes.

The GPU only needs to iterate through the GameObjects in the scene once to calculate what objects are visible and where the shadows should appear.Using this technique gives a considerable boost in performance: About 20% less CPU time and around 10% GPU time is utilized.

Another rendering technique that's available is **single pass stereo instancing**. This technique improves upon the regular single pass rendering by using **GPU Instancing** to halve the number of draw calls needed.This feature is still in preview, though, and only works on Windows 10 for now, but according to Unity, support for the PS4 is coming soon.

The performance gains are only marginally better than using regular single pass rendering since the bulk of the CPU overhead is already taken care of by simply switching to single pass rendering. However, it's still faster, so if you meet the requirements, be sure to take advantage of it. Single pass stereo instancing is also the only single pass rendering technique available on the HoloLens.

In the case of this chapter, since you're already using a PC VR headset, it's assumed you're on Windows 10, so you can make use of the most efficient technique.

Open the **Player Settings** by selecting **Edit > Project Settings > Player** in the top menu and unfold the **XR Settings**. Select **Single Pass Instanced (Preview)** in the **Stereo Rendering Method** drop-down to switch rendering techniques.

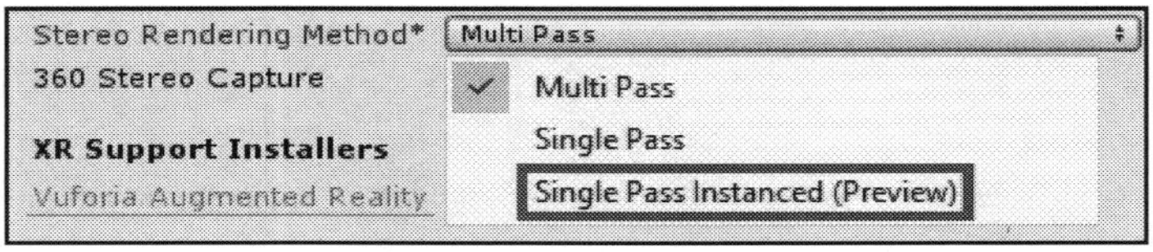

That's all you have to do for a massive performance boost. If this is giving you any trouble, switch to the regular **Single Pass** rendering method.

Find out more about these techniques here:

- https://docs.unity3d.com/Manual/SinglePassStereoRendering.html
- https://docs.unity3d.com/Manual/SinglePassInstancing.html
- https://blogs.unity3d.com/2017/11/21/how-to-maximize-ar-and-vr-performance-with-advanced-stereo-rendering
- https://www.youtube.com/watch?v=datOOos-944

Optimizing geometry

When developing for VR, it's important to be conscious of how expensive your models are to render and what the player will and won't be seeing.

After creating a model (or downloading/getting one), check how many vertices it has. Do you really need that much detail to have a simple silhouette?

Decimating meshes

An easy way to decrease the amount of vertices of **static** models is using a **Decimate** modifier on it in Blender. Note that this only works for static models; never use a Decimate modifier on meshes that you need to deform and animate.

After adding the modifier, you'll have to play around with the ratio until the number of vertices is reduced to your liking, while the model still looks good. Keep decreasing the ratio until it looks too bad to use, then bump it up a bit again.

If you don't have Blender, here's an example when applied to one of the cactus meshes:

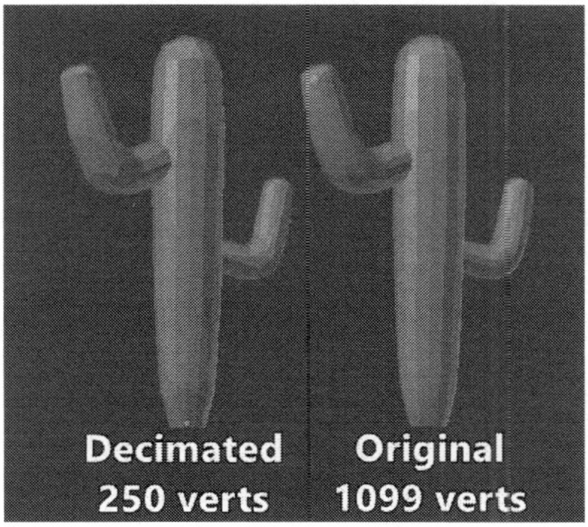

The silhouettes for both look almost identical, while the version on the left contains less than a fourth of the vertices of the original mesh. The fewer vertices the GPU has to process, the faster it can work on other tasks, so simplify your geometry as much as you can.

Cutting away unseen faces

Another important aspect of optimizing the geometry is deleting all faces that the player won't see. An excellent example of this is the ring of mountains around the scene. Since the player will always be at ground level, you can make some assumptions on what parts of the mesh they won't ever see, such as:

- All back-facing faces.
- Any part of the mesh occluded by another part when looking from the ground.

Here's a comparison of the big mesh surrounding the scene before and after cutting away all unneeded faces:

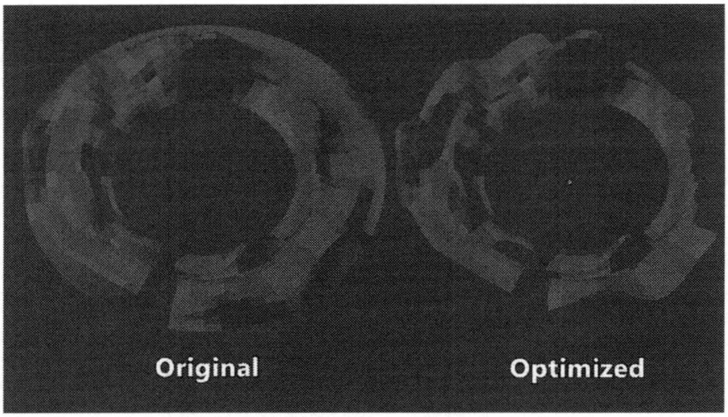

Here's what that looks like up close from the back of the ring:

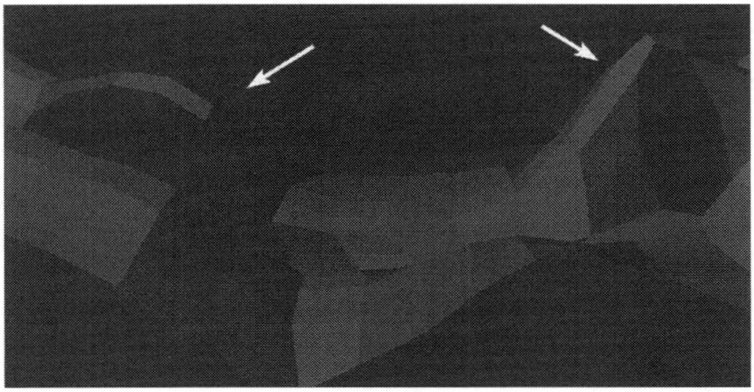

The backside of those humps were removed since the player can't reach those spots anyway. While the savings of this technique are minor, every little bit counts. When you apply this strategy to large surfaces, the number of vertices that don't need rendering can quickly add up.

Static batching

The best way to batch your **non-moving** models together is by marking them **static**. Doing so allows Unity to combine all of these models into big, combined meshes which reduces the draw calls by quite a bit.

Select **World** in the Hierarchy and check the **Static** box. When prompted to enable the static flags for all child objects as well, select **Yes, change children**.

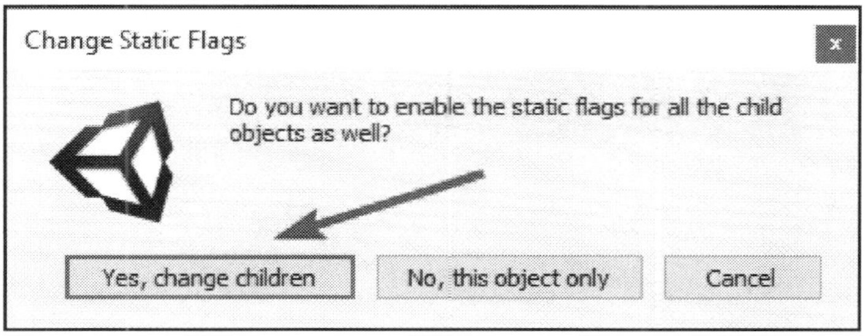

All of the world objects are now marked completely static. Usually, when you'd check the **Static** checkbox, a lightmap automatically gets baked. However, this is disabled in the **Lighting** window for this project, so you don't have to wait for the baking to finish:

You can enable this again by selecting **Window > Rendering > Lighting settings** in the top menu and checking the checkbox on the bottom.The difference after marking the objects static is staggering:

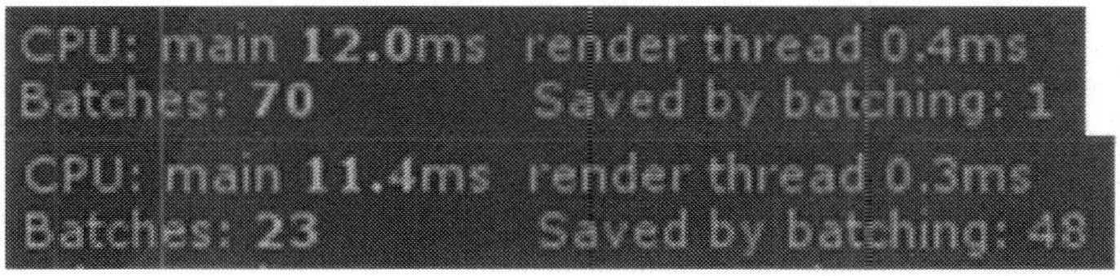

The top information is without static batching while the bottom numbers show the massive gains by enabling it. From 70 to just 23 batches with a single checkbox, now that's efficiency!

Occlusion culling

On the same note as optimizing geometry, why even bother rendering objects that the player can't see? By default, Unity uses a technique called **frustum culling** to disable objects that aren't inside the **frustum** (the pyramid-shaped field of view) and the **clipping planes** of the camera.

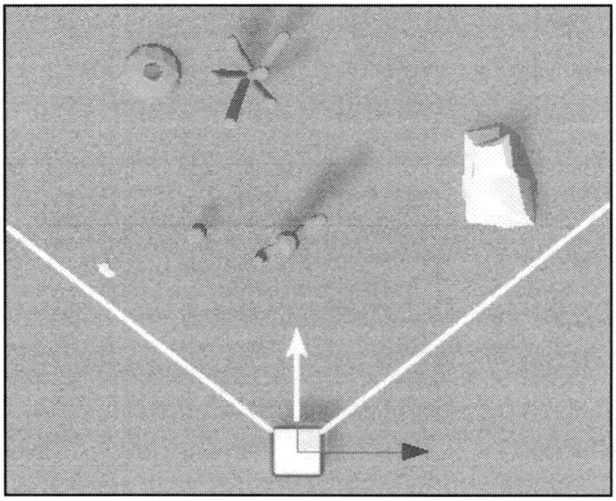

What frustum culling doesn't do, however, is cull objects that are behind other objects like walls and big rocks. Below you can see the player's camera looking toward the bottom of the view. Any objects inside the frustum are rendered, even though the player is staring at a wall.

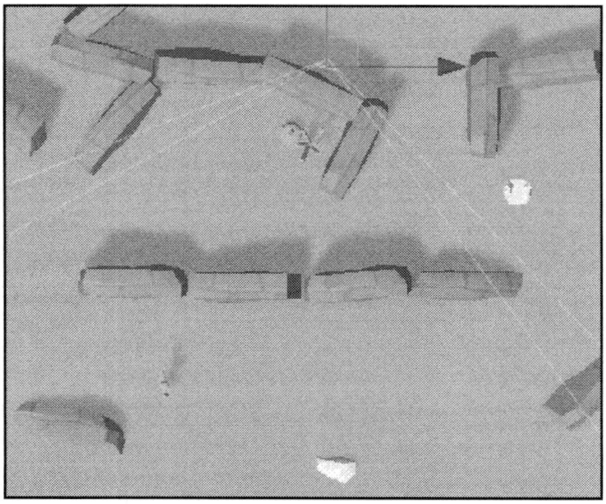

Culling objects behind others is called **occlusion culling** and thus requires you to bake in some extra data into the scene. To have optimal culling, you need small, **static** level geometry in separate GameObjects. You also need large objects like mountains or buildings to create level sections. The desert scene might not be ideal as it's mostly one big space with objects of all sizes scattered around, but it can still benefit from occlusion culling.

Open the Occlusion window by selecting **Window > Rendering > Occlusion Culling** from the top menu. Open the **Bake** tab and change the value of **Smallest Occluder** to **2**.

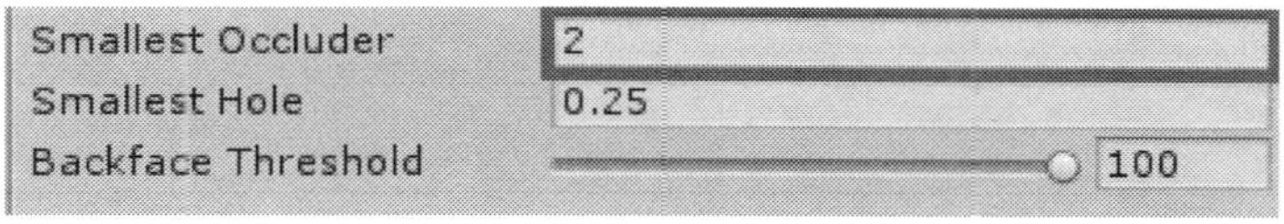

The default value of 4 meters is way too large for the desert scene. The small walls in the center of the scene should act as occluders, for example, and they are only about 2-3 meters in length.

Now, click the Bake button on the lower right to bake the occlusion data in the scene. This might take a few minutes depending on your hardware. You'll see the scene getting split into small cells that form a binary tree in the end.

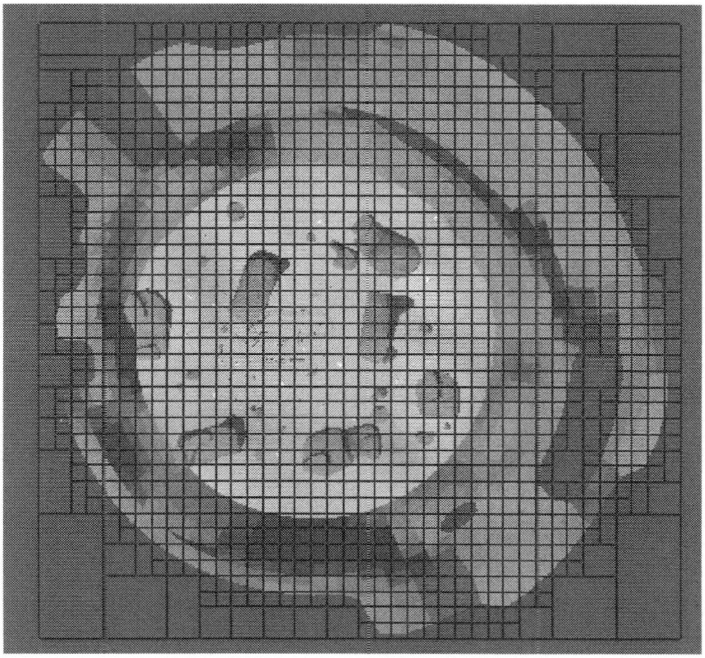

Click the Visualization tab and play the scene. Keep looking at the Scene view while moving around with either the simulator or actual hardware — you'll see that the objects appear and disappear depending on where you're looking.

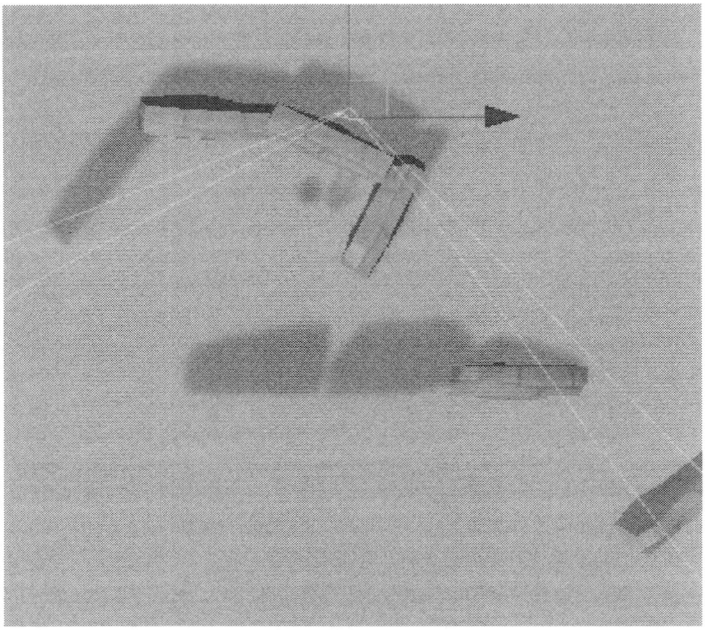

This saves another good chunk of performance, and it only required the press of a button and a few minutes of your time!

For more information about occlusion culling, check out https://docs.unity3d.com/Manual/OcclusionCulling.html

Textures and materials

Getting your textures and materials correct is essential for achieving a high framerate. This section discusses how to set up your textures, map materials to models and optimize the materials for maximum performance.

Textures

In VR, texture quality is more important than the number of polygons displayed. Players tend to stand still more in VR to look at their near surroundings and might even inspect objects up close. That said, throwing dozens of 2K textures in the scene is a terrible idea, especially when it comes to mobile VR.

Use **texture atlases** whenever possible. Either combine the textures yourself, ask your artist to do this or use a tool from the Asset Store like **Mesh Baker** to automate the process. The only disadvantage of texture atlases is that they can't have repeating patterns, so you might have to adjust your art process.

All of the models in the **Desert** scene — except for the ground — use a single texture to decrease the load on the GPU drastically. You can find the **DesertShared** texture in **Razeware \ Textures**.

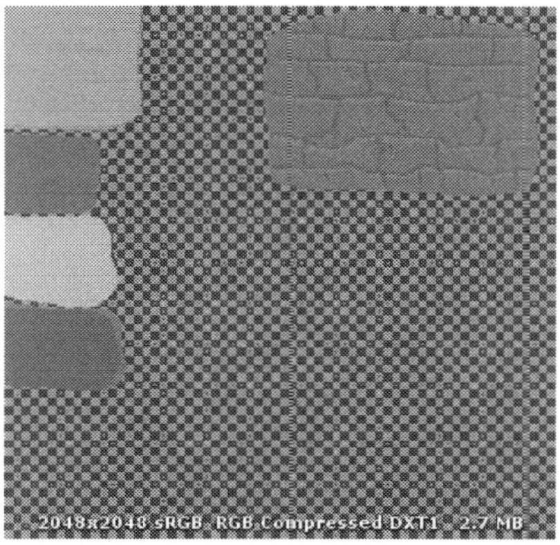

This texture was made with expandability in mind, allowing you to paint on more colors and textures. If the scene was to contain only the current objects, a final texture might look like this:

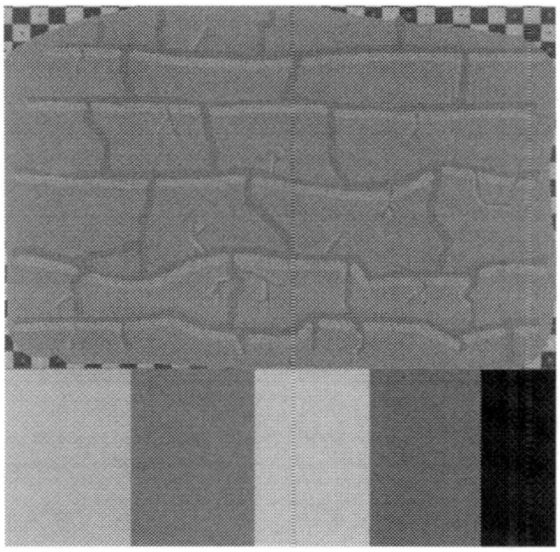

Also, note that textures should always be a **power of two** in size (like 512x512 or 128x256), this size allows Unity to more effectively compress the texture. Another critical thing to note about textures is that you should store them in a **lossless format** like PNG or BMP since Unity takes care of the compression for you for the output platform of your game builds.

Material remapping

Since Unity 2017.1, any models you import into a project use the embedded materials instead of extracting them to a folder. While this makes it easy to use a model and drag it straight into a scene with the correct texture applied automatically, it comes with some significant disadvantages:

- You can't adjust the material at all, so tweaking the smoothness, adding a normal map or enabling **GPU Instancing**, for example, is impossible.
- If you have a bunch of models all using the same material and texture, you'd expect them to be batched together in a single draw call, but this won't work with embedded materials.

Select the **Cactus2** model in **Razeware \ Models \ World Models** and open its Materials tab in the Inspector, you'll notice it's using the material embedded within:

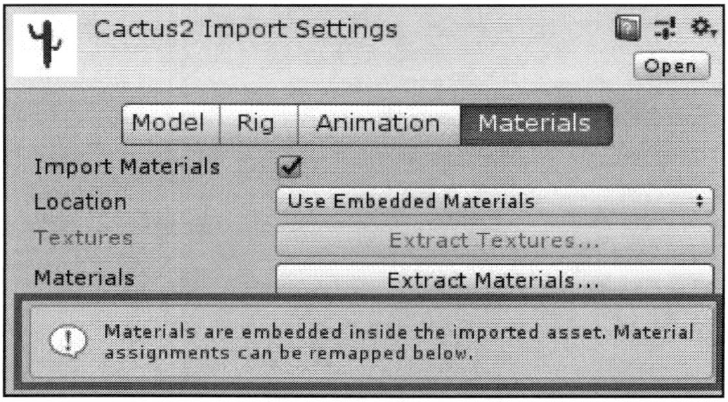

You can remap (a non-destructive replace) the material used by using the **Remapped Materials** section below. Expand the On Demand Remap sub-section to open a small remap helper tool.

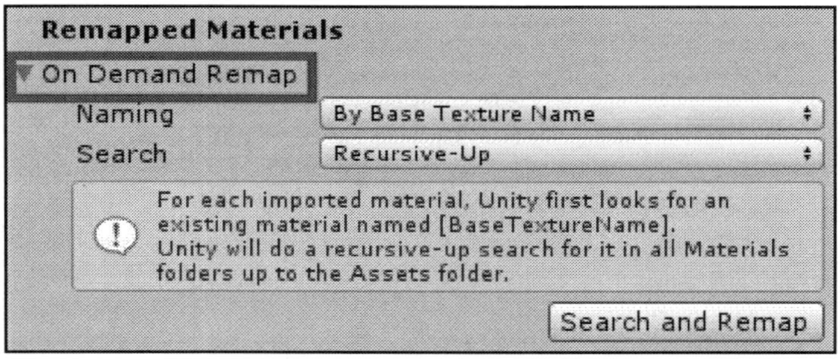

There's a material you can use in **Razeware \ Materials** named **DesertSharedMaterial**. While you could just select the material manually, it's often easier to automatically find the needed material. That's where the tool comes in. It searches in the Assets folder for a material with a specific name and then assigns it to the model.

Select **From Model's Material** in the **Naming** drop-down and **Recursive-Up** in the **Search** drop-down so that the tool tries to find a material named **DesertSharedMaterial**.

The default value in the drop-down searches for the texture name, which is **DesertShared**, so the correct material won't be found otherwise.

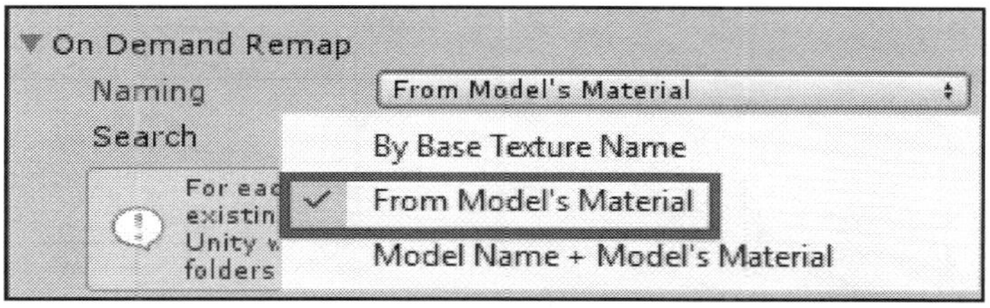

Now, click the **Search and Remap** button. You'll notice the material is found in an instant and assigned to the material field below.

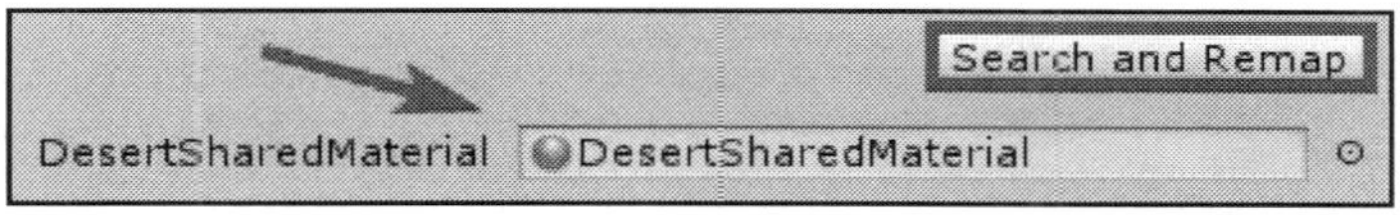

That's it! The **Cactus2** model now uses the external material.

For more information on the model importer's Material settings, check out Unity's documentation here: https://docs.unity3d.com/Manual/FBXImporter-Materials.html

Material optimizing

As discussed before, most of the models in the scene are using the same material, namely **DesertSharedMaterial**. Select this material in **Razeware \ Assets \ Materials** and look at the Inspector.

Any changes you make to this material applies to everything visible in the scene except the ground. The material is using the **Standard** shader by default, this shader performs sufficiently for PC hardware, but on lower end hardware like mobile, you might want to consider other shaders.

The fastest shader to use — if your art style allows it — is an unlit shader. Switch **DesertSharedMaterial**'s shader by selecting **Mobile > Unlit (Supports Lightmap)** in the **Shader** drop-down at the top.

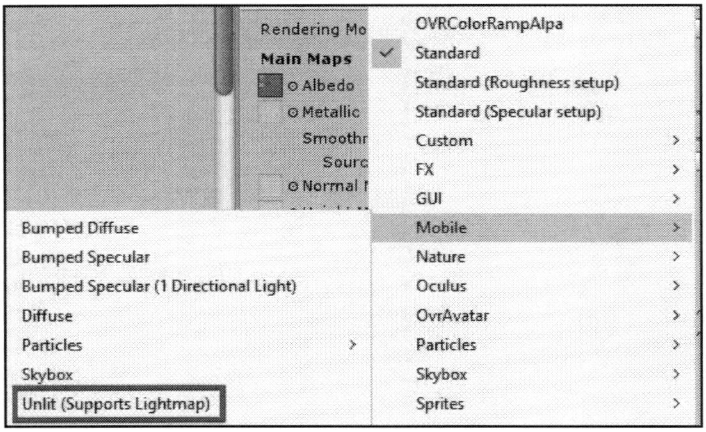

If you look at the Scene view now, you'll see that most of the models are reduced to colored silhouettes. The stone wall in the middle there still looks decent, though, because it has a texture painted on it instead of flat colors like the other objects.

While this makes for a cool art style if you're going for a *Proteus* vibe in VR, the scene is a lot more readable with some lightning information. Switch the Shader to **Mobile > Diffuse** this time.

That looks a lot better once again, right? This shader is an excellent option if you don't need any of the fancy features of the Standard shader, but you still want the lighting and shadows to be automatically calculated.

The last interesting option for more performance is **GPU Instancing**. Enabling this on your materials allows Unity to render multiple copies of the same mesh at once at runtime. In ideal circumstances, this can bring a fantastic boost to performance, potentially saving thousands of draw calls.

However, there are lots of restrictions and requirements for the instancing to work optimally:

- **The mesh needs to have 300 vertices or less.**
- Only one material may be present on the mesh.
- All of the meshes need to be the same for a single batch.
- Instancing can't be combined with static batching.
- Colors can vary, but you need to write a custom shader or modify an existing one for this to batch correctly.
- **Real-time Global Illumination breaks batching.**

Especially the points in bold (above) limit the usefulness of GPU instancing. Most models, even simple ones will likely exceed 300 vertices, and almost any modern game uses real-time GI nowadays.Since the models are already statically batched and you're using real-time GI, leave GPU instancing off.

For more information on GPU instancing, check out the official documentation: https://docs.unity3d.com/Manual/GPUInstancing.html

How to avoid VR sickness

Virtual reality sickness occurs when exposed to certain triggers in a virtual environment. The symptoms are similar to those of motion sickness and include general discomfort, headache, nausea, vomiting, sweating and retching. Pretty bad stuff indeed! However, there are several ways to avoid the worst VR sickness triggers.

Here are some things to avoid in VR:

- **Fast movement** in any direction can suddenly trigger the player and take them out of the experience in an instant. Limit the movement speed or use teleportation instead.
- Letting the player **free fall** after they've walked off a ledge. Not only is falling in VR a scary experience, but it also makes even the most hardened VR veterans sick. Instead of showing the fall to the player, fade to black and teleport them to the ground.
- Giving the player **direct control** of their movement using a joystick for example. It's easy for the player to get nauseous by moving around in unnatural ways. Diagonal movement is especially a bad idea. Opt for other ways of locomotion instead, like hand swinging or teleportation.
- A **low framerate**, hiccups and other performance problems. Fix these problems as soon as possible and add a system that automatically adjusts the resolution and effects as a safeguard.

You can still use some of these if you combine them with the right techniques. Here are some things that can help to make the player feel comfortable:

- **Optimize the performance** of your game or experience! Squeeze out every last drop of wasted CPU and GPU cycles. Seeing as you're reading this chapter, you've already made a step in the right direction.
- When moving the player instantly (like teleporting), always use some sort of **fade** or **cut** to black in between.
- Add a **vignette** around the corners of the player's view when moving fast. This takes the focus away from the edges of the field of view and avoids sickness.
- Put the player inside of the **cockpit** of a vehicle for truly high-speed locomotion. Like vignette, this takes the focus away from the edges. However, because of the way human brains work, it's also far more accepted to move and rotate quickly when you're inside of a vehicle, and you can allow direct movement.

Where to go from here?

Congrats on finishing this chapter! Hopefully, you've learned a thing or two about how to improve the performance of your games and experiences.

To recap, in this chapter you learned how to:

- Use the profiler and frame debugger.
- Change the render scale at runtime.
- Use single pass stereo rendering.
- Optimize the geometry, textures and materials.
- Avoid VR sickness.

Be sure to check out these articles by Unity for even more optimization tips:

- Optimization in VR: https://unity3d.com/learn/tutorials/topics/virtual-reality/optimisation-vr-unity
- Getting started with VR development: https://unity3d.com/learn/tutorials/topics/xr/getting-started-vr-development

In the next chapter, you'll learn about implementing advanced interactions using VRTK.

Section III: Advanced VR

If you want to take your VR skills even further, this section is for you. Delve into advanced topics like special interactions and interesting ways of getting around in the virtual space. Create natural feeling user interfaces around the player and their virtual hands. Lastly, explore how VR goes further than just entertainment.

This advanced VR section explains the following topics:

- **Chapter 8: Advanced VR Interactions**: Take your VR skills to the next level by using VRTK to create satisfying interactions with objects in the virtual world. In this chapter, you'll dive deeper into VRTK and the tools it provides.
- **Chapter 9: Advanced VR Movement**: Now that you've mastered basic movement, it's time to take a look at some other options. This chapter delves into several ways of locomotion and shows how to use them in practice.
- **Chapter 10: Advanced VR User Interfaces**: This chapter explores more advanced ways of showing user interface elements with a curved canvas and a menu that's attached to the controller.
- **Chapter 11: VR in Interactive Media**: VR is used in more than just games; there's a wide range of industries out there utilizing virtual worlds and objects to save time and express concepts and ideas. In this chapter, you'll get an introduction to different ways of using VR.

Chapter 8: Advanced VR Interactions

Eric Van de Kerckhove

Now that you've mastered the basics of implementing gameplay in virtual reality using VRTK, it's time to dive into some advanced topics. You'll start by exploring some of the components that make interacting with the virtual world more interesting.

In this chapter, you'll learn how to:

- Create tooltips for objects and controllers.
- Fix objects to your controllers.
- Use joints to accurately pick up objects.
- Snap objects into place.
- Use haptic feedback.

It's time for some VR action!

Getting started

Before diving straight into the deep end, take a moment to get familiar with the project.

Project overview

In Unity, open the starter project for this chapter and look at the Project window. As you can see, this project comes pre-loaded with many assets:

Here's an overview of what's inside:

- **OculusPlatform, OVR & OvrAvatar**: The APIs for the Oculus Rift.
- **Plugins**: Code libraries for the Oculus Rift.
- **Resources**: Contains the settings file for Oculus Avatar.
- **Standard Assets:** Unity's standard character controllers and physics materials.
- **SteamVR**: The SteamVR plugin, along with its scripts and prefabs.
- **VRTK**: The Virtual Reality Toolkit plugin.

To get things started, open the **Chapter 8 - Advanced Interactions** scene from the **Razeware \ Scenes** folder, and review the scene in the editor.

The scene comes with a few things already set up:

Here's the breakdown:

- **AdvancedFullChapter8**: Contains all of the basic static meshes for the scene.
- **BasicLight & ExtraLights**: Various lights for the scene. **ExtraLights** is disabled by default.
- **RW Props**: Contains the statues in the scene and is the parent GameObject for the interactables.
- **Chapter8 BGM**: A simple GameObject with an **Audio Source** attached that plays classical music in the background. If that's not your style, feel free to replace the music with some funky beats!

Now that you know this project inside and out, it's time to get cracking.

Creating the VRTK setup

By now, you may know how to prepare everything for **VRTK**, but to make it easier on yourself, you're going to create a template setup which you can reuse.

SDK Manager

Create a new GameObject, name it **[VRTK_SDK_MANAGER]**, and reset its **Transform** component. This will serve as the parent for the different SDK setups.

Add a **VRTK_SDK Manager** component to the newly created GameObject, and check any of the **SDK_OCULUS_AVATAR** checkboxes; the other one will get checked automatically.

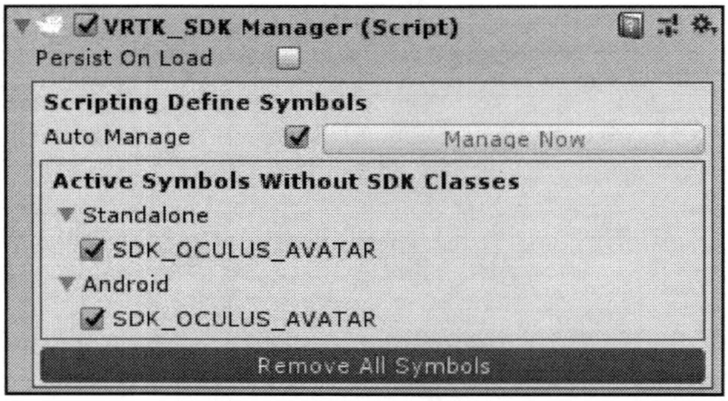

Add another empty GameObject as a child of **[VRTK_SDK_MANAGER]**, name it **[VRTK_SDK_SETUPS]**, and reset its **Transform**.

Now create the following GameObjects, reset their **Transform**, and parent them to **[VRTK_SDK_SETUPS]**:

- SteamVR
- Oculus
- Simulator

When you're done, the hierarchy in the SDK Manager will look like this:

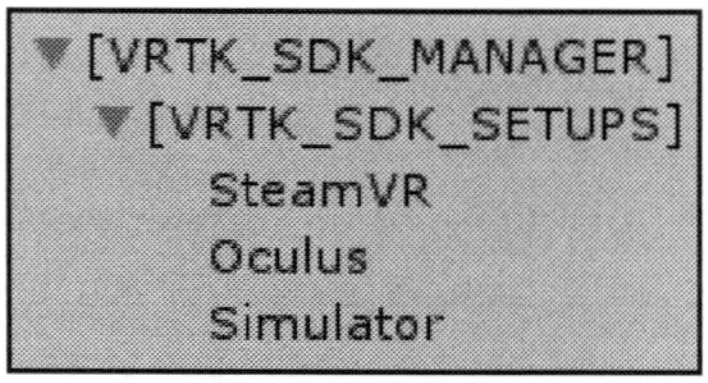

To create parented instances, drag the **[CameraRig]** and **[SteamVR]** prefabs from the **SteamVR \ Prefabs** folder onto the **SteamVR** GameObject.

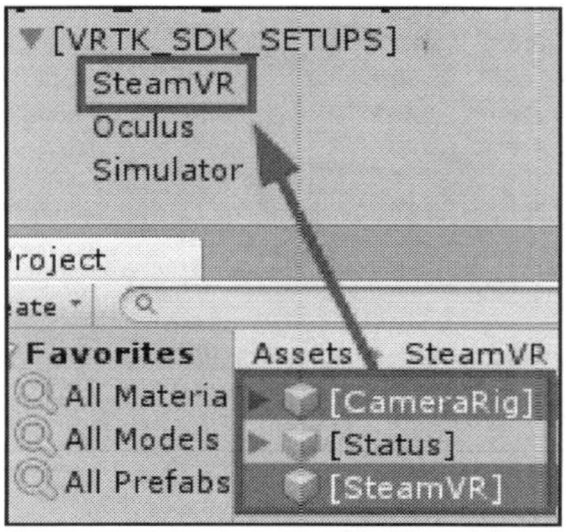

Drag the **OVRCameraRig** prefab from the **OVR \ Prefabs** folder onto **Oculus** to parent the prefab. Do the same for the **LocalAvatar** prefab from the **OvrAvatar \ Content \ Prefabs** folder.

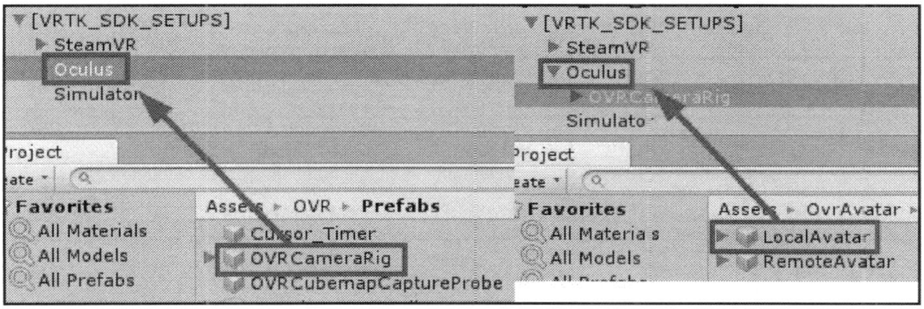

Select **OVRCameraRig** and change the value of **Tracking Origin Type** to **Floor Level**. This helps position the camera correctly.

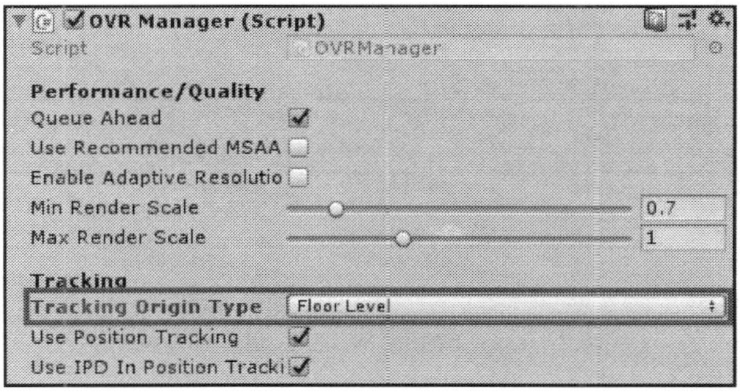

Now drag the **VRSimulatorCameraRig** prefab from the **VRTK \ Prefabs** folder onto the **Simulator** GameObject.

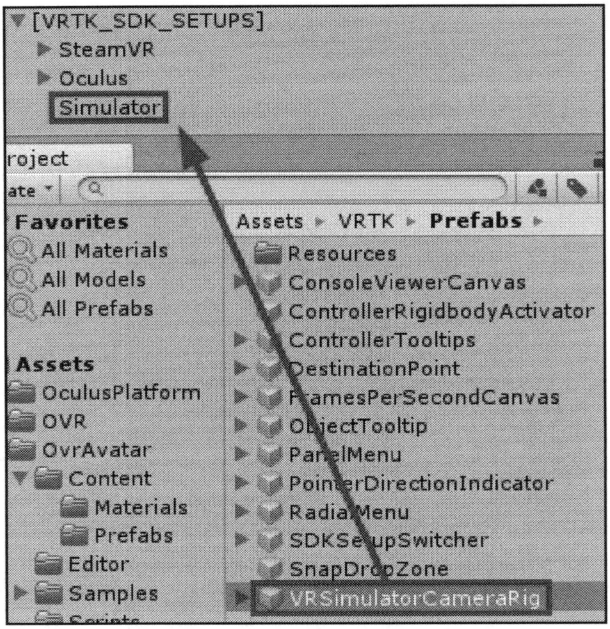

Select the three SDK GameObjects you've just added, and add a **VRTK_SDK Setup** component to all of them. Select them all separately and assign the appropriate value to **Quick Select** for each one:

- SteamVR: SteamVR
- Oculus: Oculus (Rift)
- Simulator: Simulator

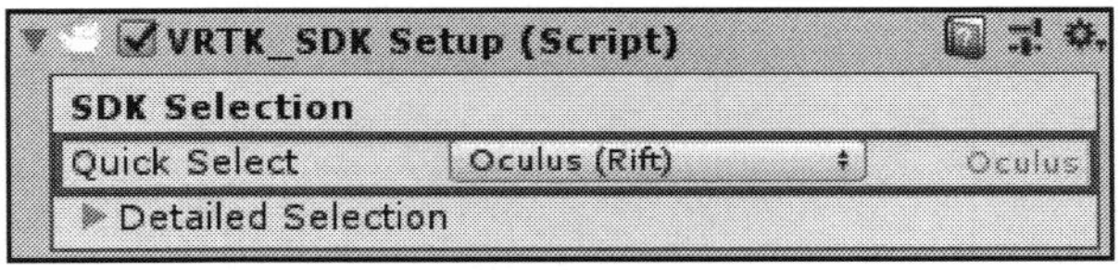

Now that you've added all of the SDK setups, let the SDK Manager auto populate its setup list by selecting **[VRTK_SDK_MANAGER]** and clicking on the **Auto Populate** button at the bottom.

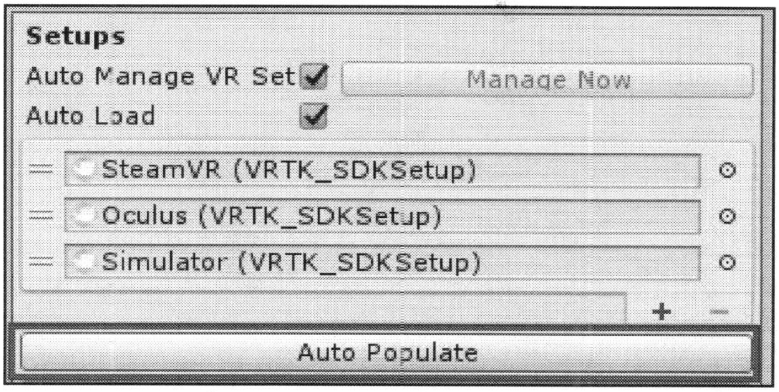

That's it for the SDK Manager. You're ready to move on to the play area and controller aliases.

Play area and controller aliases

As a child of **[VRTK_SDK_MANAGER]**, create an empty GameObject. Reset its **Transform** and name it **[VRTK_SETUP]**. Create the following empty GameObjects and add them as children of **[VRTK_SETUP]**:

- **Play Area**
- **Left Controller**
- **Right Controller**

When you're done, the resulting hierarchy will look like this:

Add a **VRTK_Adaptive Quality** component to **Play Area**, set its **Msaa Level** to **2**, and set **Scale Render Viewport** between **0.5** & **2.5**.

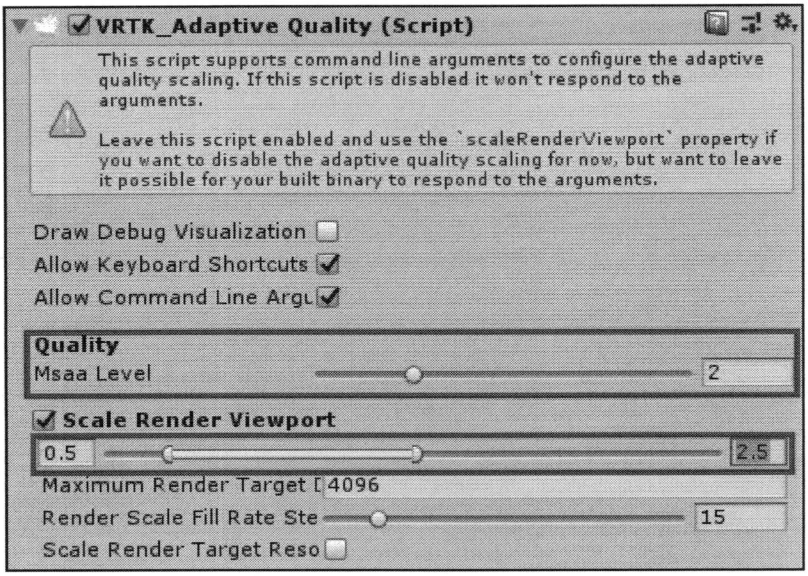

This adjusts the render resolution depending on the performance; it can both upscale and downscale, so you'll always use the optimal resolution.

Now add a **VRTK_Height Adjust Teleport** component to the **Play Area**. This serves as the base teleport method for all scenes unless specified otherwise. You can leave the variables at their defaults.

Add the following components to both **Left Controller** and **Right Controller**:

- **VRTK_Controller Events**
- **VRTK_Interact Touch**
- **VRTK_Interact Grab**

Leave all of these components at their default values.

Add a **VRTK_Pointer** and a **VRTK_StraightPointerRenderer** component to **Left Controller**. This will add a straight pointer to your left controller which you can use to teleport.

Finally, click the selection button next to **VRTK_Pointer**'s **Pointer Renderer** slot, and select **Left Controller**.

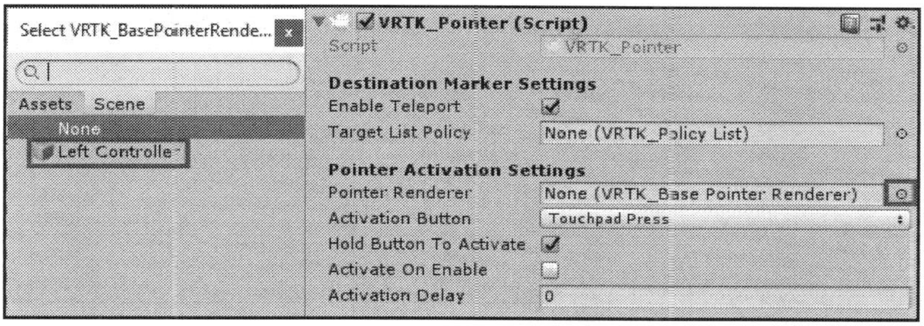

Select **VRTK_SDK_MANAGER**, and hook up the controller aliases by dragging **Left Controller** and **Right Controller** to their respective slots.

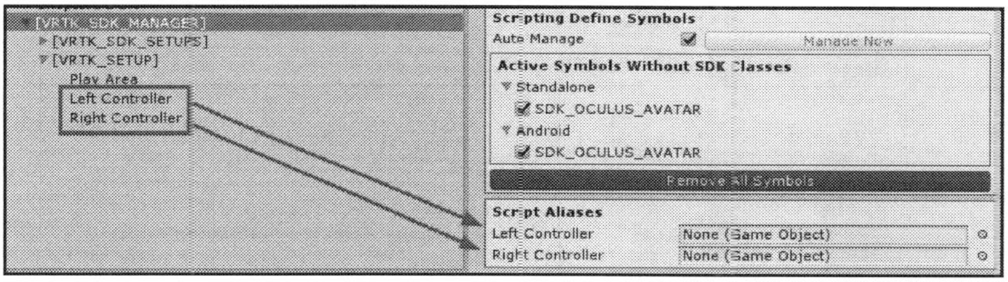

Now that the SDK Manager is ready, create a new folder under **Razeware** named **Prefabs**. To turn the manager into a prefab, drag **[VRTK_SDK_MANAGER]** to the newly created **Razeware \ Prefabs** folder.

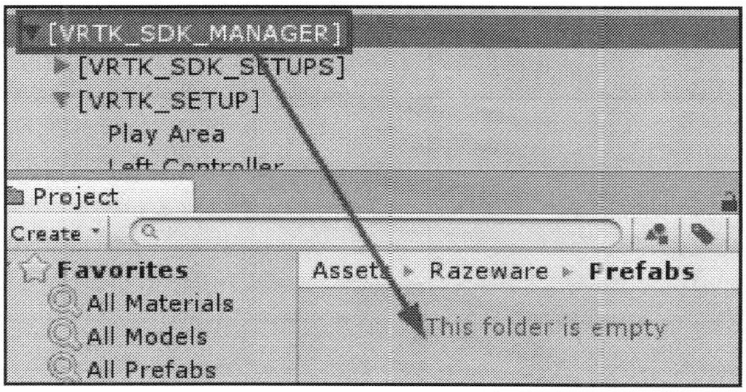

Test if everything works correctly by taking a look around the scene with your preferred headset. If you find any issues, backtrack through this section and compare the steps with what you have.

The work you've done will prove to be a considerable time saver later on, but now it's time to move on.

In the next section, you'll learn how to add tooltips to GameObjects.

Object tooltips

Tooltips are like small 3D signs you can use to label objects.

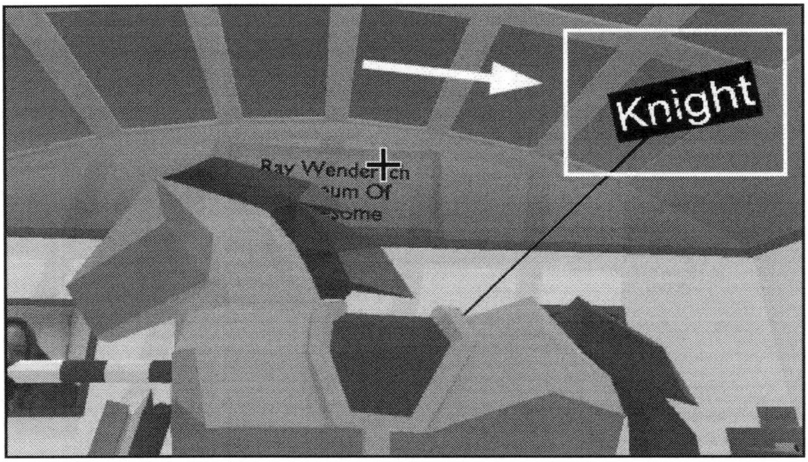

For this book, you'll be adding a name label to the armored horse, named "Knight", in the middle of the museum. (You may remember him from the previous book!)

To make a tooltip, you need two GameObjects: a **root GameObject** that will act as the target and the actual **ObjectTooltip** that's provided by VRTK.

Start off by creating a container for tooltips; this helps to keep the scene nice and tidy.

Create a new GameObject, name it **Object Tooltips**, and reset its **Transform** component.

Now create the target for the knight by adding a new, empty GameObject as a child of **Object Tooltips**. Name it **KnightTip** and change its **Position** to **(X:0, Y:1.8, Z:0)**.

Drag an **ObjectTooltip** prefab from the **VRTK \ Prefabs** folder onto **KnightTip** to make it a child.

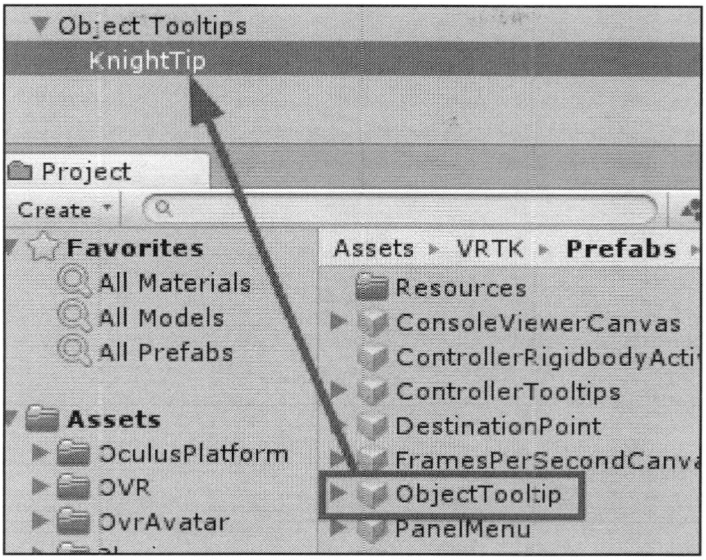

Change the **Position** of **ObjectTooltip** to **(X:1.35, Y:1.3, Z:-0.5)**, and change the following properties of its **VRTK_Object Tooltip** component:

- **Display Text**: Knight
- **Font Size**: 200
- **Container Size**: (X:600, Y:250)
- **Line Width**: 0.01
- **Font Color**: Pure White (R:255, G:255, B:255)
- **Container Color**: Pure Black (R:0, G:0, B:0)
- **Always Face Headset**: Checked

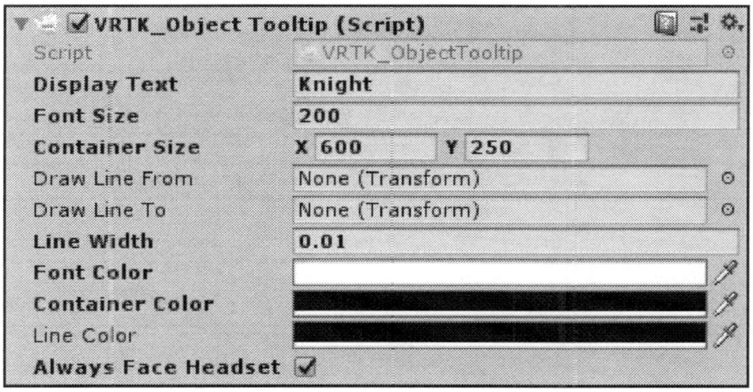

All of these, except the last one, change the visuals of the tooltip.

Always Face Headset causes the tooltip to look at the player's headset at all times so they will never be looking at the text sideways or from the back. The reason why **Draw Line From & Draw Line To** isn't being set is because you're using a parent GameObject, and the tooltip *knows* to draw the line from that position to itself.

All of these changes alter the look from this tiny tooltip for ants:

To this hulking, beefy powerhouse of a tooltip:

Well at least it's easy to see, right?

To test if it's working correctly, play the scene and look at the knight from different angles; the tooltip should always be visible!

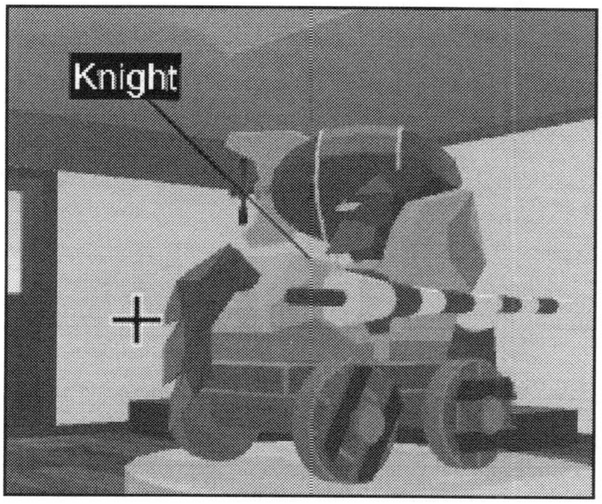

That's it for object tooltips, be sure to experiment with different styles in your projects.

Next up, the controller, which can also have tooltips!

Controller tooltips

When you start playing a new game, learning the controls can get confusing, especially with VR — a developing platform that doesn't yet have a lot of standard controls schemes like PCs and consoles. In this section, you'll create a set of tooltips like this one:

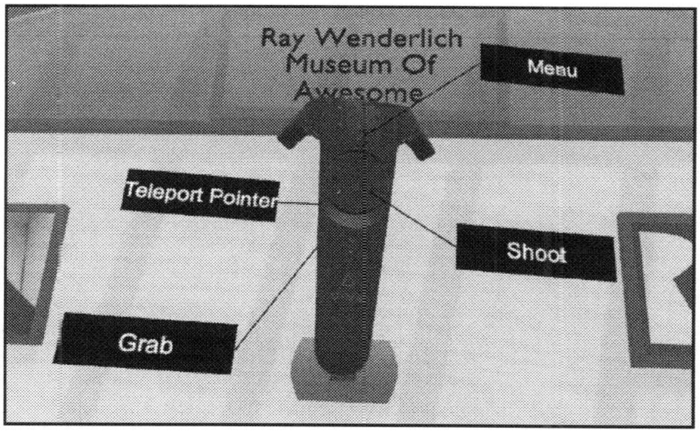

Creating these is ridiculously simple, all you need to do is drag a **ControllerTooltips** prefab from the **VRTK \ Prefabs** folder onto **Left Controller**.

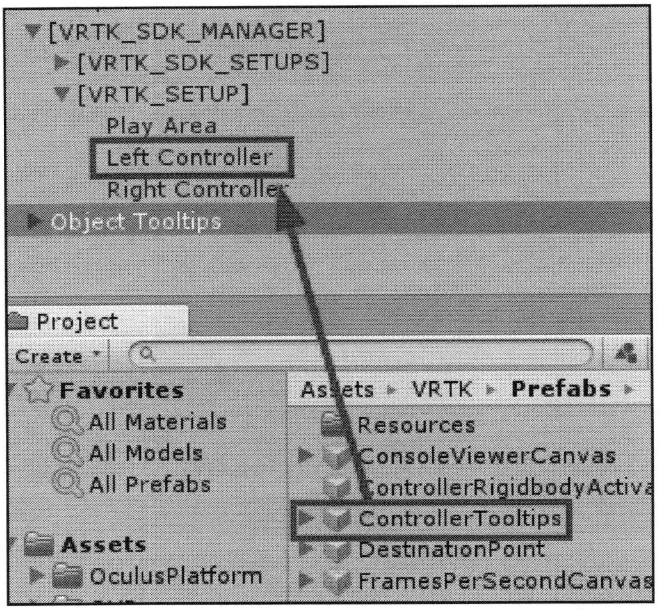

This adds a bunch of pre-configured tooltips — like you added in the previous section — and the **VRTK_Controller Tooltips** component acts as a manager for these.

Look at the **Button Text Settings** on the newly added **ControllerTooltips**. These correspond to all possible buttons on the HTC Vive and Oculus Rift. The names don't necessarily match that of the controller, however, here's an overview of the **HTC Vive controller** and an **Oculus Touch controller**:

- **Trigger**: Hair Trigger on Vive, Trigger on Rift
- **Grip**: Grip on Vive, Grip on Rift
- **Touchpad**: Touchpad on Vive, Analog Stick on Rift
- **Button One**: N/A on Vive, Bottom Button on Rift
- **Button Two**: Menu Button on Vive, Top Button on Rift
- **Start Menu**: N/A on Vive, Start Button on Rift

Notice the last three differ between the Vive and the Rift. In this case, you'll be targeting the HTC Vive setup as an example. If you're using an Oculus Rift, switch around the **Button Two** and **Start Menu Text**.

Change the **Button Text Settings** to the following:

- **Trigger Text**: Teleport Pointer
- **Grip Text**: Grab
- **Touchpad Text**: Shoot
- **Button One Text**: (empty)
- **Button Two Text**: Menu
- **Start Menu Text**: (empty)

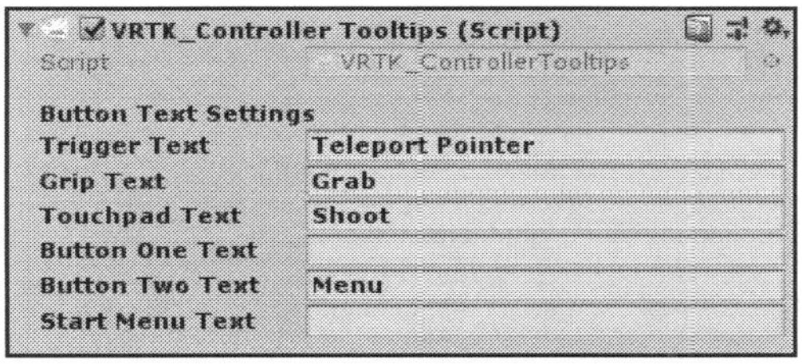

The **Object Tooltips** are hidden for all empty text fields. That means, if you only want to label just one or two inputs, that's not a problem! Now that tooltips are done, save the scene so you don't lose any work. Then, run the scene, look at your controller, and you'll see the tooltips spread all around it.

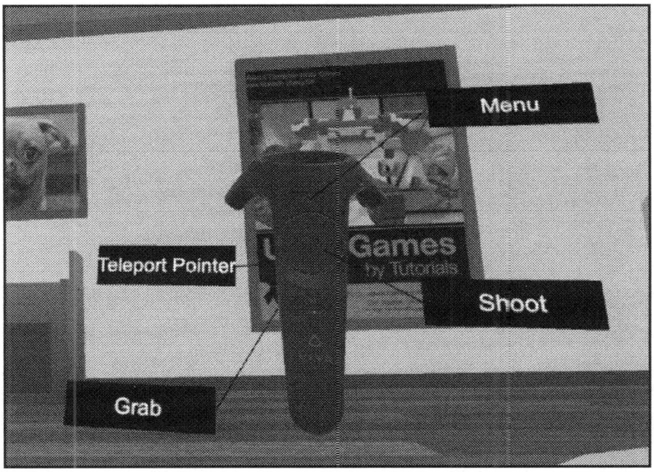

Adding tooltips was fun, right?

In the next sections, you'll explore how to add some specific functionality to pick up objects.

Fixing objects to your hands

In some cases, you might want an object to be fixed to a controller. Or you might want to replace an object with another one after you grab it. Think guns, swords and boxing gloves, for example. You can even automatically grab a GameObject or cloned prefab right at the start of the scene.

For now, though, you'll start off with creating a basic example: a tank figurine that attaches to your controller permanently once you grab it. This is what happens when you spill a bottle of glue on your tank! :]

Simple fixing

Create a new empty GameObject, name it **TankFigure**, and set its **Position** to **(X:8, Y: 1.115, Z:3.5)**. Then, drag **Tank** from the **Razeware \ Models** folder and drop it onto **TankFigure**, making **Tank** a child of **TankFigure**.

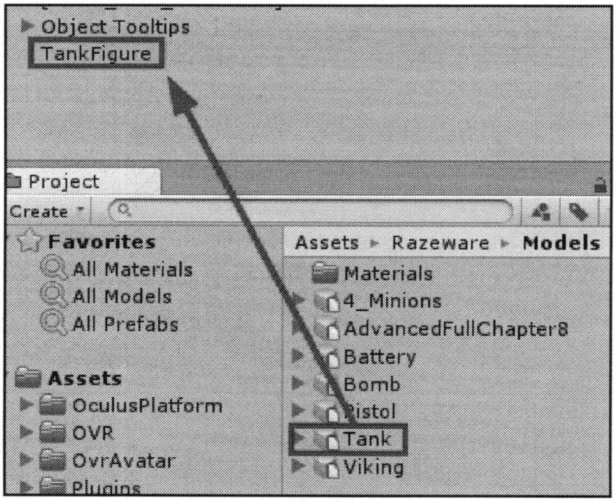

Change the newly added model's **Scale** to **(X:0.21, Y:0.21, Z:0.21)**, and drag **TankFigure** onto **RW Props** to parent it.

When you're done, the new hierarchy will look like this:

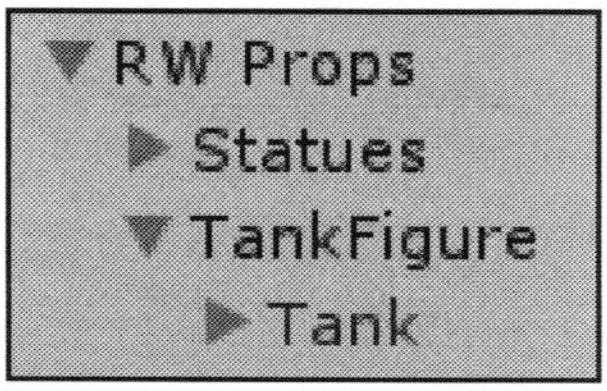

Create a new folder inside the **Razeware \ Prefabs** folder and name it **Grab**. Drag the **TankFigure** onto the new folder to turn it into a prefab.

You'll now have a little tank sitting on the table.

This is cool, but you need a way to interact with it.

The easiest and fastest way to add the components you'll need for this interaction is to use VRTK's interactable setup wizard.

With TankFigure still selected, open the setup by selecting **Window ▸ VRTK ▸ Setup Interactable Object** in the top menu.

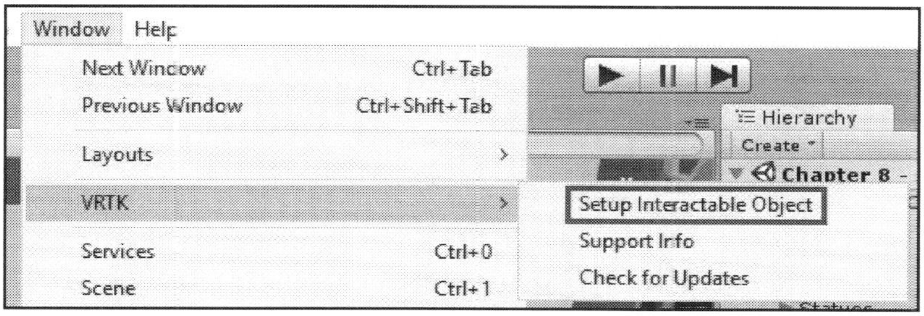

Leave everything at their default values and press the **Setup selected object(s)** button at the bottom.

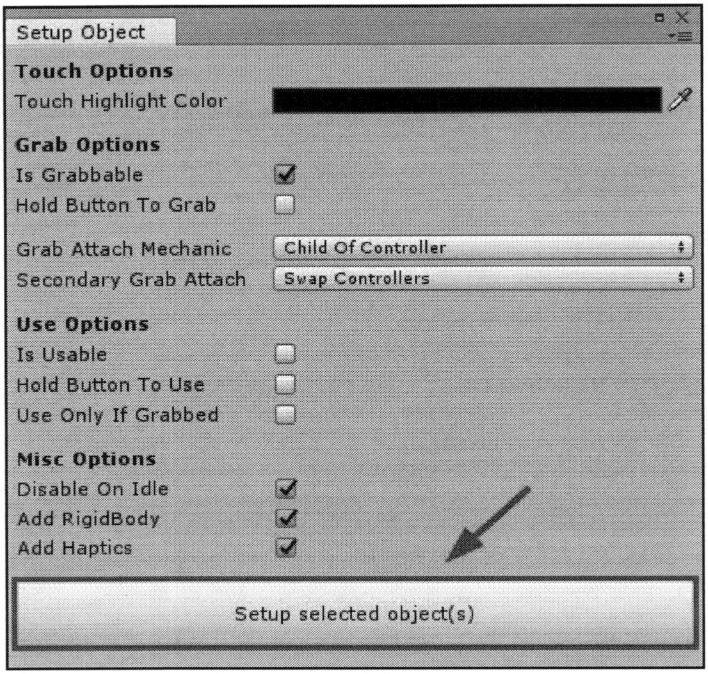

Close the setup window and remove the **VRTK_Interact Haptics** component from **TankFigure**.

Under the **Grab Options** in the **VRTK_Interactable Object**, set **Valid Drop** to **No Drop**; this setting makes it so the player can't drop the tank after grabbing it.

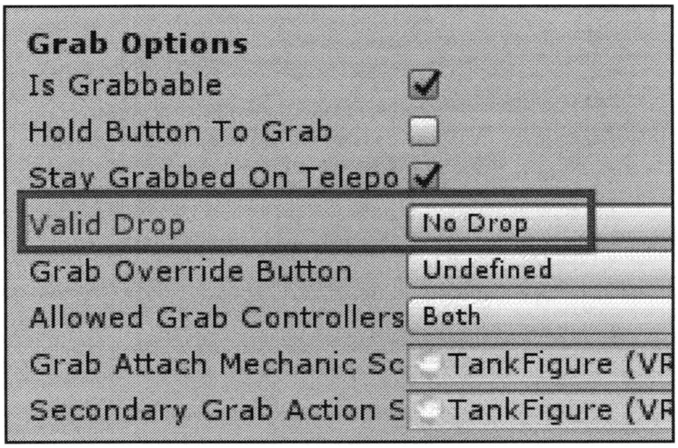

Before testing if it all works, add a **Box Collider** component to **TankFigure**, set its **Center** to **(X:0, Y:0.06, Z:0)** and its **Size** to **(X:0.3, Y:0.23, Z:0.3)**.

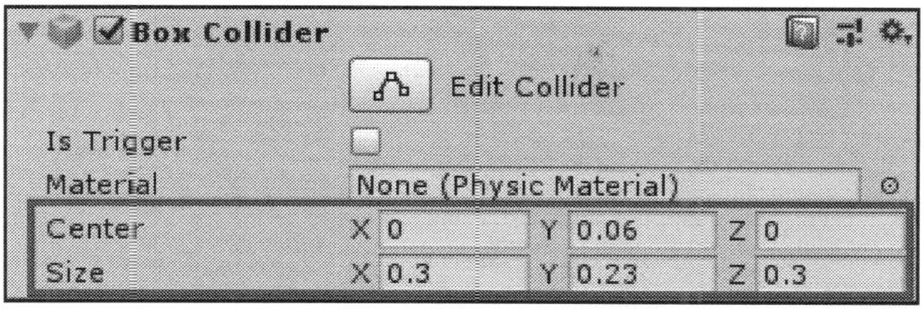

This surrounds the small tank. To test it out, dive into VR and try to pick up the sticky tank.

> **Note**: If you can't find the figurine anywhere, you may have skipped this step, which causes the tank to drop through the floor.

No matter how hard to try, this tank won't come off! If you don't want your players to drop something important, or if you want to attach silly stuff to their controllers, this works out nicely.

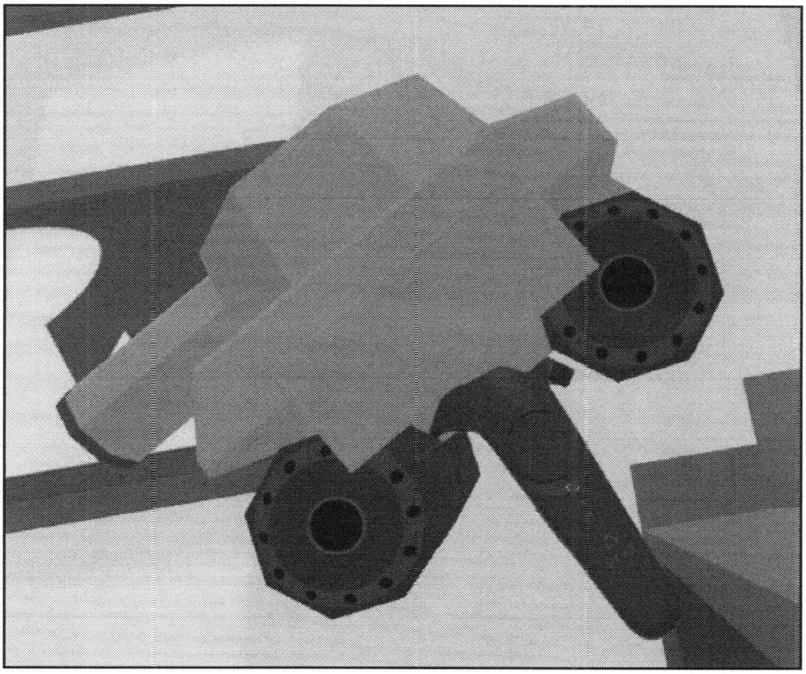

Next, you're going to add a pistol that replaces the controller.

Custom fixing

Add a new empty GameObject to the scene as a parent of **RW Props**, and name it **Pistol**. Change its **Position** to **(X:8, Y:1.15, Z:4.5)**, and drag the **Pistol** model from the **Razeware \ Models** folder onto **Pistol** to create a child.

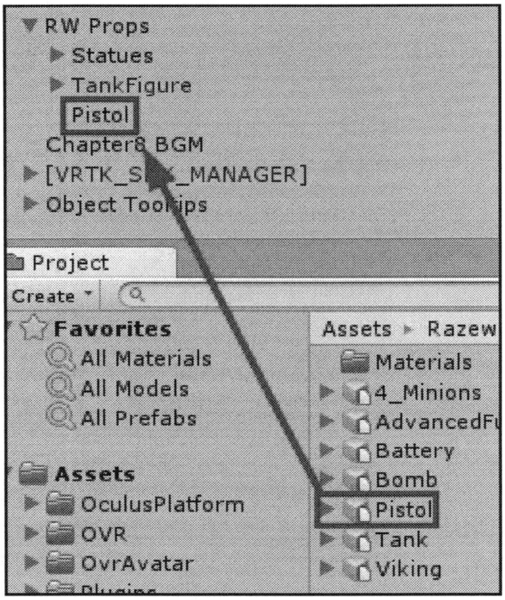

At the moment, the pistol is a tad too big and not positioned correctly. To fix this, change its Position to **(X:0, Y:0, Z:0)**, its Rotation to **(X:-90, Y:90, Z:-90)**, and its Scale to **(X:23, Y:23, Z:23)**.

There, all better:

Select the **Pistol** parent and open the VRTK setup wizard (**Window ▸ VRTK ▸ Setup Interactable Object**). Leave everything at their default values and hit the **Setup selected object(s)** button.

Close the window and remove the **VRTK_Interact Haptics** component from **Pistol**.

Add a **Box Collider** and set its **Center** and **Size** to **(X:0, Y:-0.018, Z:0.065)** and **(X: 0.11, Y:0.24, Z:0.37)** respectively.

Change **Valid Drop** on the **VRTK_Interactable Object** component to **No Drop**. Right now, it behaves exactly like the tank. To hide the controller when the pistol is grabbed, add a **VRTK_Interact Controller Appearance** component to the **Pistol**, and enable the **Hide Controller On Grab** checkbox.

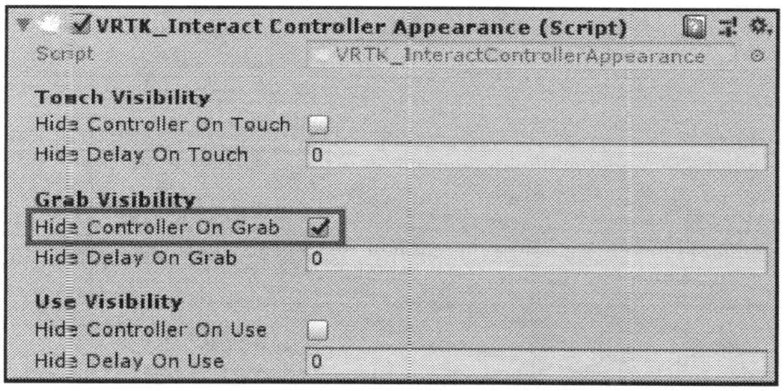

Test out the scene and see if the controller disappears when you grab the pistol. Well, the controller disappears, but you're stuck with a gun that's at an awkward angle:

The reason for this is because GameObjects are attached to your controller at the angle you started grabbing them. To fix this, you'll need to add a **snap handle** so the position and rotation of the pistol are always the same relative to the controller.

To create the snap handle, create a new empty GameObject as a child of the parent **Pistol** GameObject and name it **SnapHandle**.

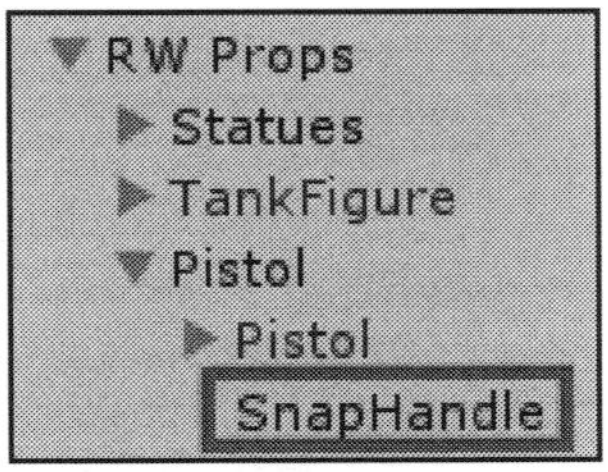

Set its Position to **(X:0, Y:0.015, Z:0.015)** and its Rotation to **(X:75, Y:0, Z:0)**; this will orient the handle like this:

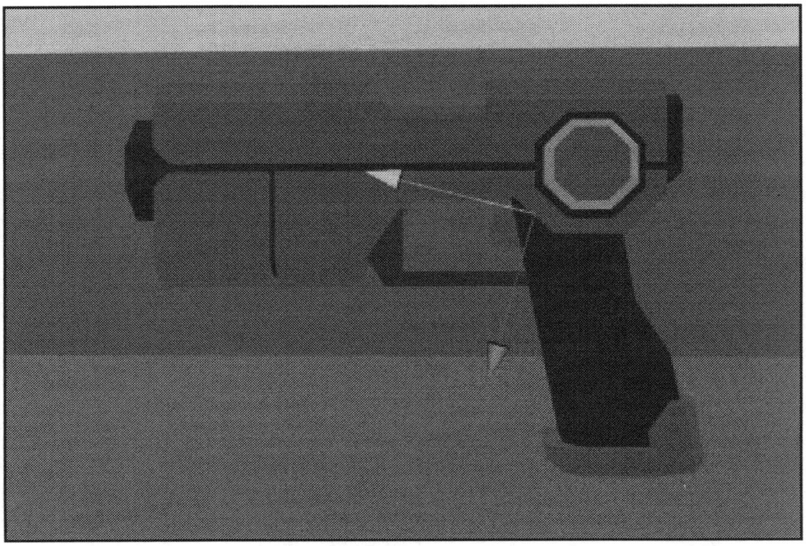

Notice how the handle is rotated 75 degrees on the x-axis? This is important to remember if you want to position snap handles correctly for objects with a grip like guns, swords and other objects.

Here's how the snap handle will affect how the controller grabs the pistol:

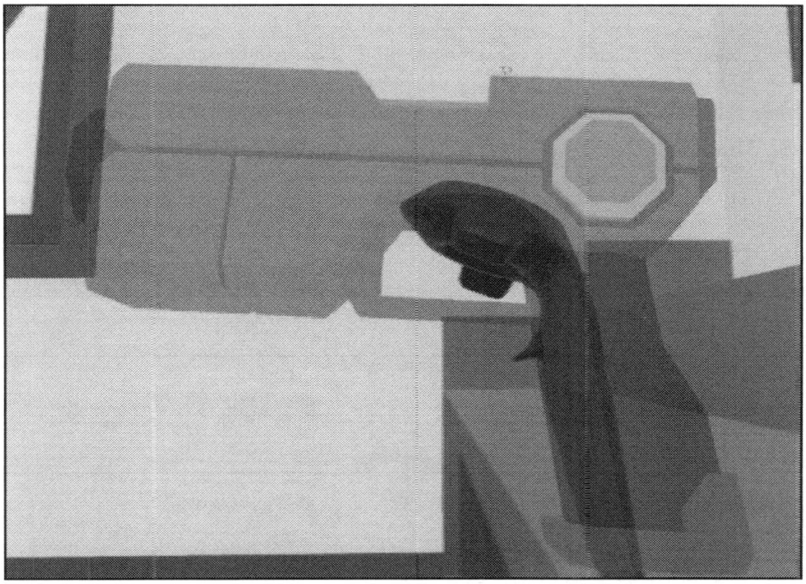

Now drag the **SnapHandle** to the **Right** and **Left Snap Handle** slots in **Pistol**'s **VRTK_Child Of Controller Grab Attach** component.

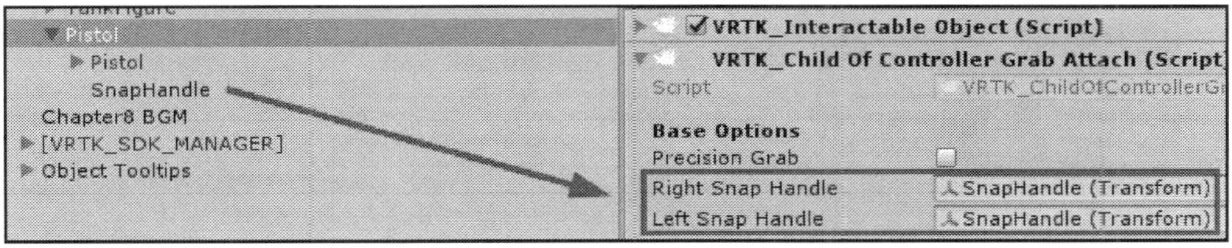

Make the **Pistol** into a prefab by dragging it into the **Razeware \ Prefabs \ Grab** folder, then play the scene again.

The pistol is now aligned to your hand in a more natural position and will follow your hand rotation. The controller itself is also hidden.

This what the developers of **Job Simulator** have dubbed **Tomato presence**:

> Tomato presence is the concept that hand presence can be maintained using a stand-in object in VR and that the brain will intuitively accept it.

Before moving on to the next section, there's one more related mechanic you need to work out: automatically grabbing a GameObject.

Auto grabbing

To automatically grab an object at the start of the scene, you *could* write a script, but as it turns out, VRTK has a handy component you can add to a controller alias called **VRTK_Object Auto Grab**. This can automatically grab any interactable objects from the scene or an instantiated prefeb.

Select the **Right Controller** under **[VRTK_SDK_MANAGER] \ [VRTK_SETUP]**, and add a **VRTK_Object Auto Grab** component to it.

Then, drag the **Pistol** to the **Object To Grab** field.

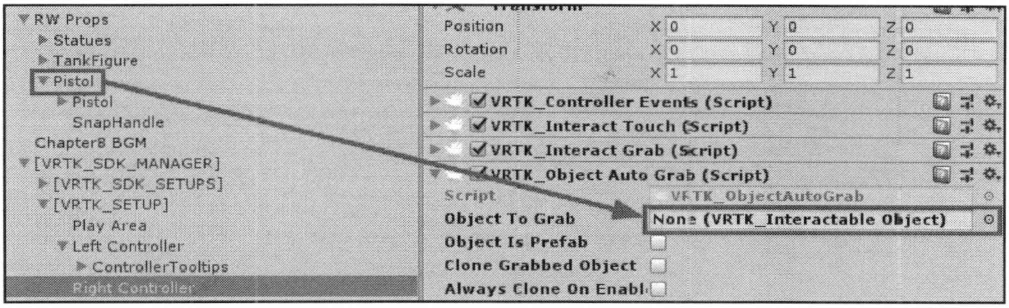

That's it! Try the scene again, and the pistol will automagically replace your right controller.

Hand attachments with joints

There are other methods of attaching objects to controllers besides just parenting them.

If you played around in the scene a bit, you might have noticed you can move the objects right through other objects as soon as you're holding them. It's almost as if you're holding a ghost object. Spooky!

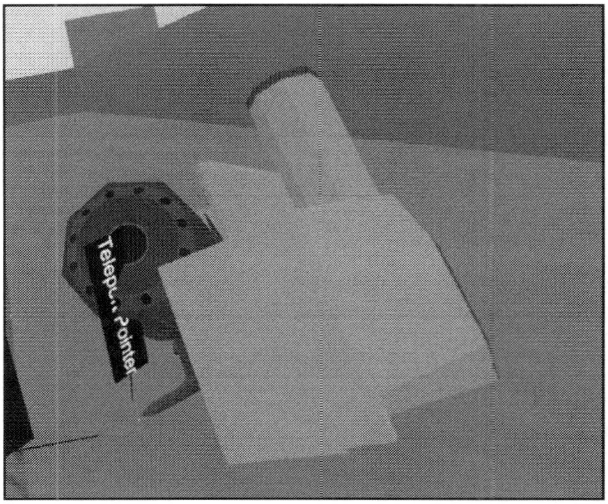

This is because the rigidbody gets set to kinematic if you're using the **VRTK_Child Of Controller Grab Attach** component.

For the next object, you'll use a **fixed joint** to attach the object to the controller, giving it some realistic behavior.

Create a new empty GameObject as a child of **RW Props**. Name it **VikingDoll**, and set its **Position** and **Rotation** to **(X:8, Y:1.04, Z:5.5)** and **(X:0, Y:-90, Z:0)** respectively.

Drag the **Viking** model from the **Razeware \ Models** folder onto **VikingDoll** in the Hierarchy to parent an instance of the model, and set its Scale to **(X:0.16, Y:0.16, Z: 0.16)**.

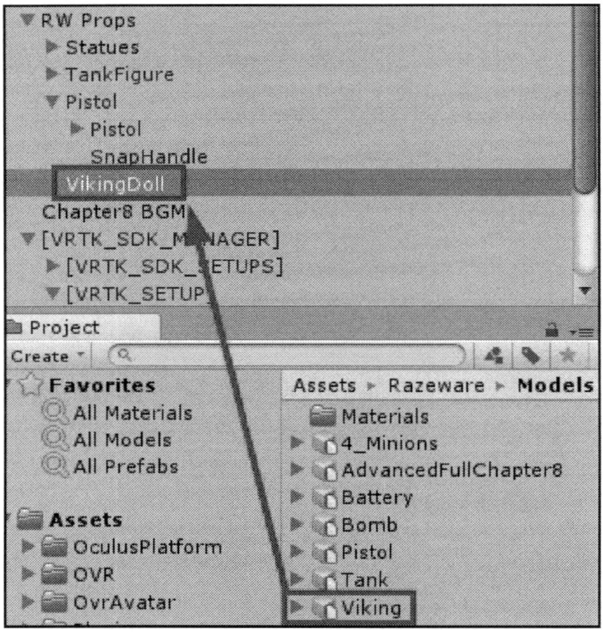

Now, to add a basic VRTK setup.

Select **VikingDoll** and open the VRTK setup wizard (**Window ▸ VRTK ▸ Setup Interactable Object**).

Leave everything at their default values except for **Grab Attach Mechanic**; set this to **Fixed Joint** and hit the **Setup selected object(s)** button.

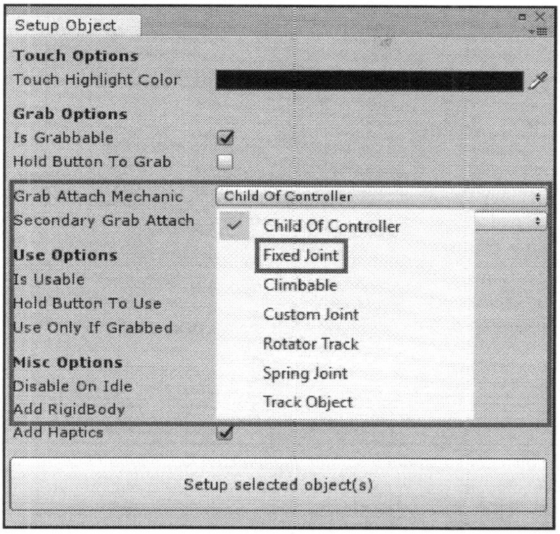

Close the window and remove the **VRTK_Interact Haptics** component and enable **Precision Grab** on the **VRTK_Fixed Joint Grab Attach** component.

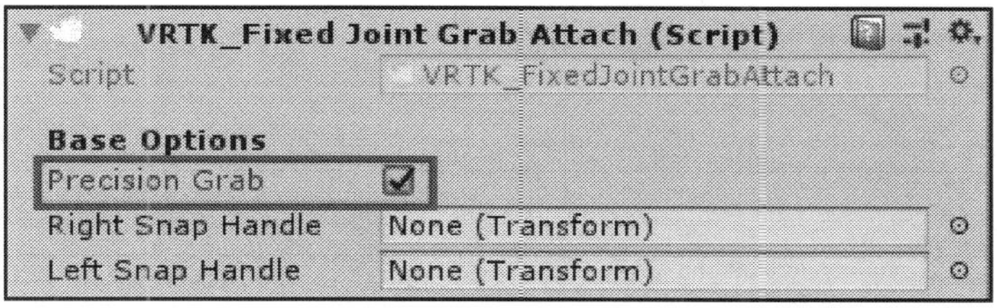

Add a **Box Collider** to the **VikingDoll**, and set the Center to **(X:0, Y:0.2, Z:0.02)** and the Size to **(X:0.2, Y:0.4, Z:0.18)**.

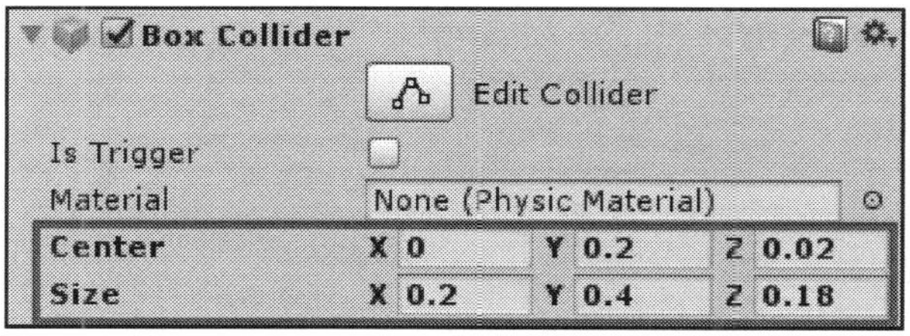

That's all you have to change to get fixed joint attaching working!

The precision grab allows you to grab the object at the particular point where the controller is colliding with the object.

Try the scene again and grab the viking doll. If you attempt to move the doll through the table, you'll "lose grip", and you'll drop the doll.

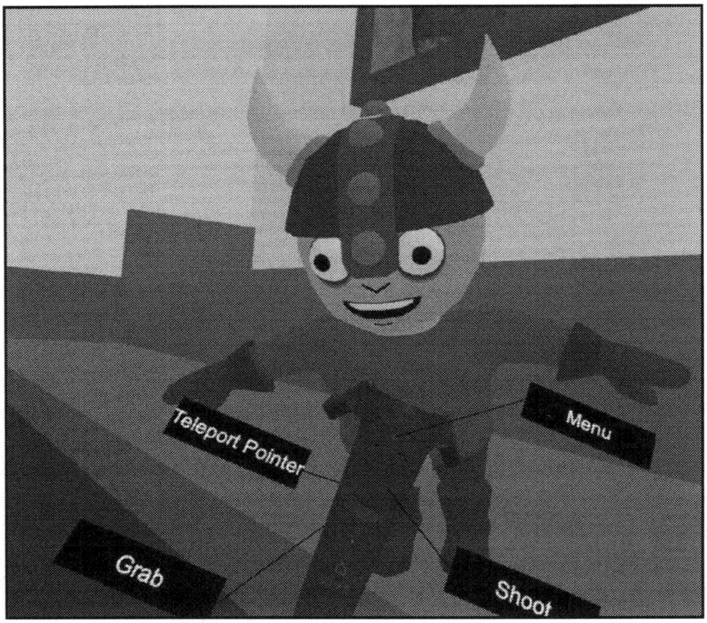

The joint breaks because the force between the controller and the doll is too great. The controller can move around freely, but the doll can't enter solid objects, so it's as if you pull a string from both ends until it snaps.

The force needed to snap this imaginary string is set by the **Break Force** field on the **VRTK_Fixed Joint Grab Attach** component.

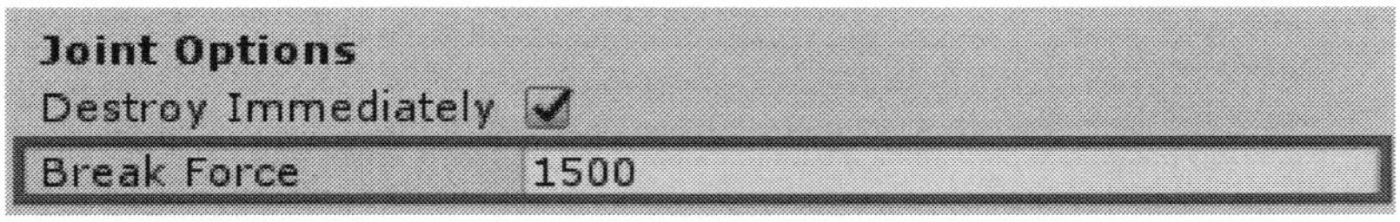

If you don't want to break the link between the controller and the object at all, but still want to avoid objects going through each other, there's also the **Track Object** grab attach mechanic.

This attachment method applies the velocity of the controller to the grabbed object. It's less accurate than the methods previously discussed, but it may help you in certain scenarios.

You'll see more grab attach mechanics in the next chapter. For now, it's time to move on to object snapping.

Object snapping

You can create a lot of different behaviors by snapping objects together. Snapping objects together means that you can insert one object into another object. For example, a USB stick in a USB port, a wheel on a car, and so on.

In this section, you'll create a battery and a battery holder which provides the museum with some extra juice to power an extra set of lights.

First, create the battery:

Add a new empty GameObject to the scene, name it **Battery**, and set its **Position** and **Rotation** to **(X:8, Y:1.08, Z:8)** and **(X:0, Y:-120, Z:0)** respectively.

Drag the **Battery** model from the **Razeware \ Models** folder onto the GameObject you just created, so it has some visuals.

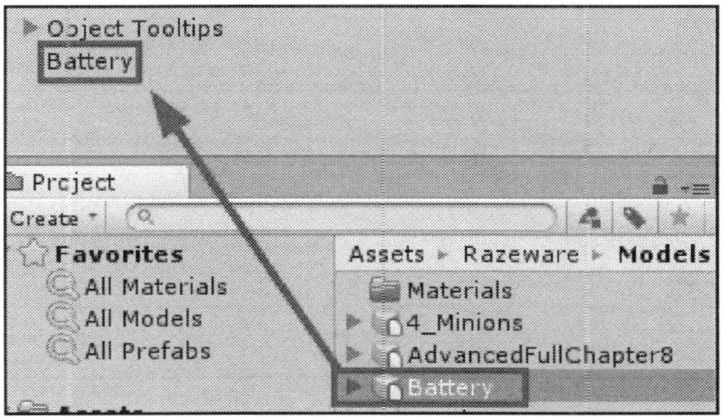

The **Battery** model is composed of two parts: the battery and the battery holder:

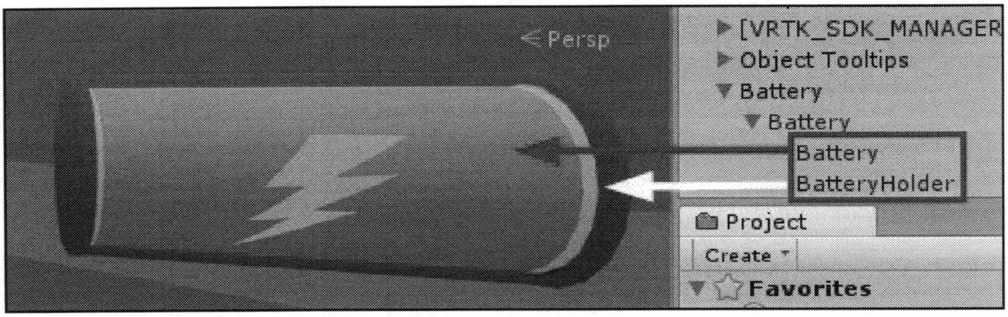

Separate **BatteryHolder** by dragging it between **Object Tooltips** and **Battery** in the **Hierarchy**. You'll be asked to break the prefab instance. When prompted, select OK.

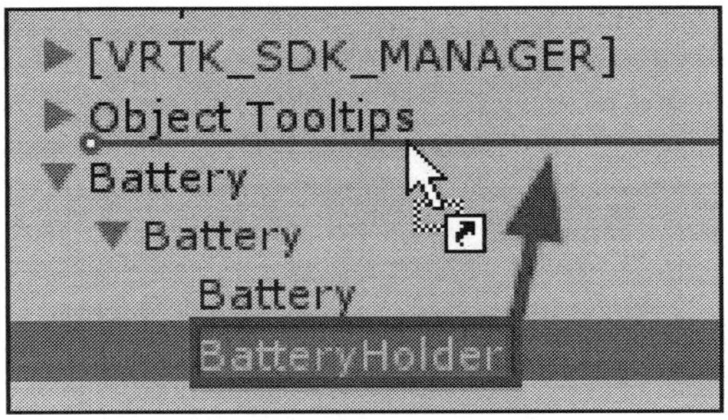

To make things a bit less confusing moving on, rename it to **BatteryHolderModel**, and reset its **Position** to **(X:0, Y:0, Z:0)** so it's out of the way.

To add basic functionality to the battery, select the **Battery** parent GameObject and open the Interactable Object wizard.

Set the **Touch Highlight Color** to a solid yellow **(R:255, G:255, B:0)**, uncheck **Add Haptics**, and click the **Setup selected object(s)** button.

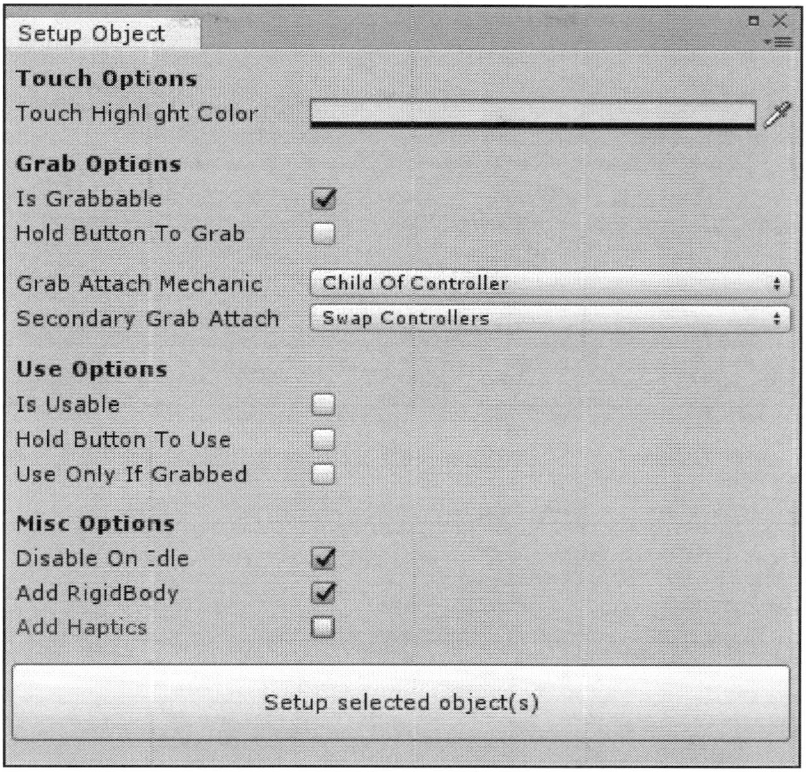

Add a **Capsule Collider** component to the **Battery**. Set its **Radius** to **0.08**, its **Height** to **0.4**, and enable **Is Trigger**. Also, set the **Direction** to **X-Axis**.

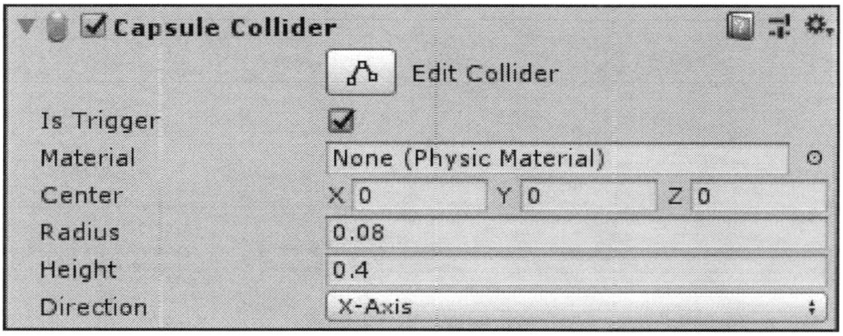

Finally, drag the parent **Battery** GameObject to the** Razeware \ Prefabs \ Grab** folder to turn it into a prefab.

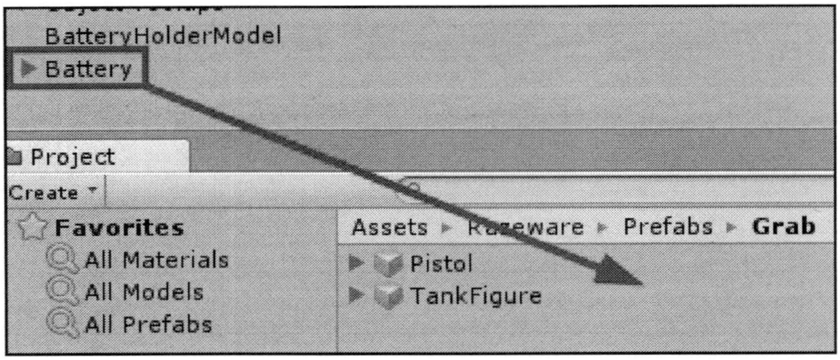

You can now pick up the battery and throw it around, but there's still nowhere to plug it in. This is where the **BatteryHolder** comes into play!

Create a new empty GameObject, name it **BatteryHolder**, and set its **Position** to **(X:0, Y:1.35, Z:9.2)**.

Drag **BatteryHolderModel** onto **BatteryHolder** to parent it, and set its **Position** and **Rotation** to **(X:0, Y:0, Z:0)** and **(X:-90, Y:180, Z:0)** respectively. The result will look like this:

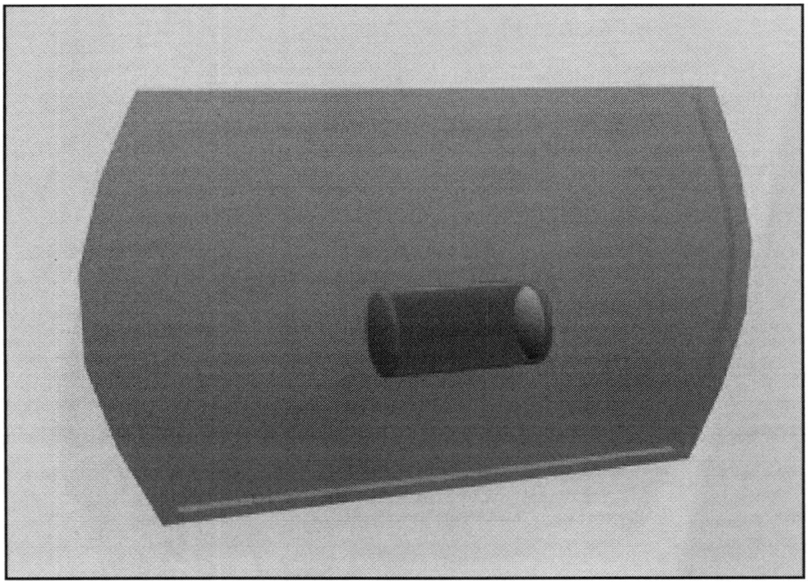

To allow objects to accept other objects to snap onto them, you need a **Snap Drop Zone** — this component filters out the objects that can be attached to it and handles the movement, rotation and scale transition.

Add a **VRTK_Snap Drop Zone** component to the **BatteryHolder**. Assign the **Battery** prefab to the **Highlight Object Prefab** field, and set **Snap Duration** to **0.2**. Set the **Highlight Color** to a bright green color **(X:40, Y:255, Z:0)**.

You'll now see a pink transparent copy of the battery inside the holder:

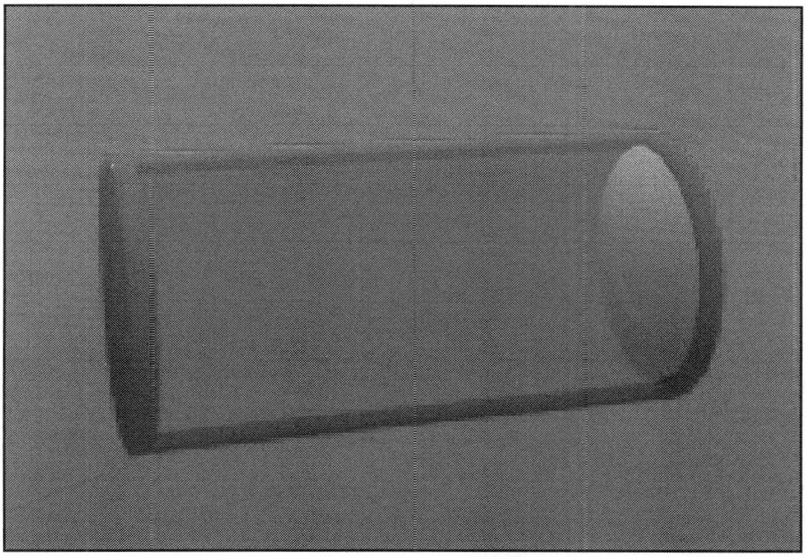

Right now, most of the snap drop zone settings are ready, except it won't accept any objects as-is. To add valid objects, you need to add a **Policy List**; this is a handy way of filtering based on several requirements. It can filter by tag, script or layer, and can even accept or reject everything if you wish.

Add a **VRTK_Policy List** component to the **BatteryHolder**, set its **Operation** to **Include**, and fill in **Battery** in **Element 0** of the list.

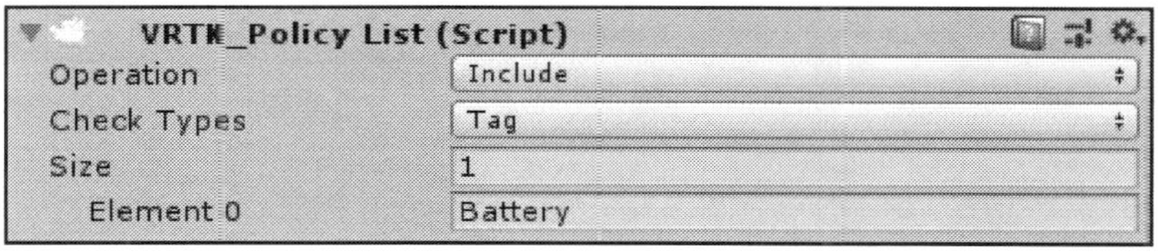

Now all of the objects with the **Battery** tag are allowed to snap into this object. Assign the **Battery** tag to the **Battery** by selecting the **Battery** GameObject and choosing **Battery** from the **Tag** dropdown. Click the **Apply** button afterward, so the prefab gets saved too.

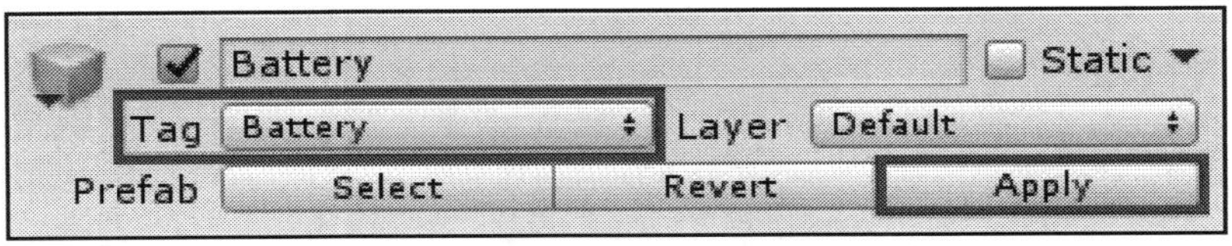

Select **BatteryHolder** and drag the **VRTK_Policy List** component onto the **VRTK_Snap Drop Zone** component's **Valid Object List Policy** field to set up the reference to the policy list that should be used for objects allowed to be snapped into place on the battery holder.

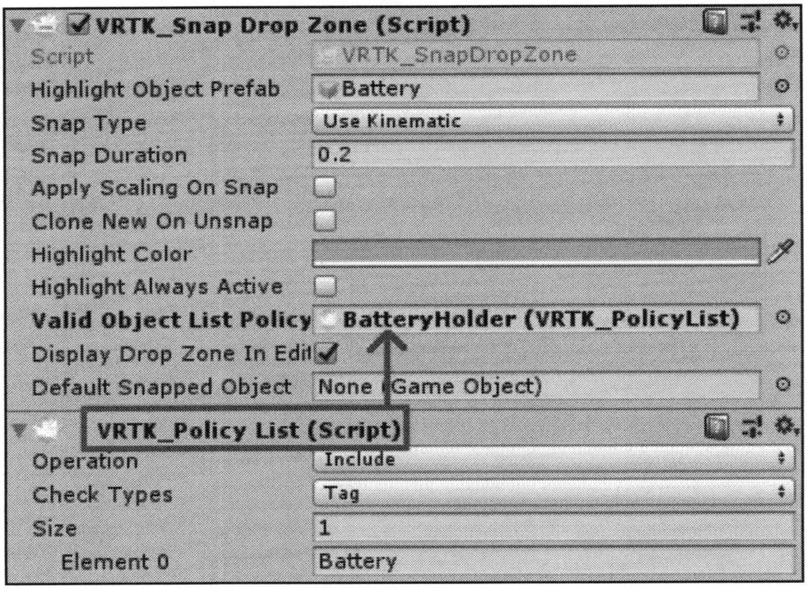

The drop zone needs a collider and a rigidbody so it can detect when an object enters in range. Select **BatteryHolder** and add a **Rigidbody** and a **Capsule Collider** component. Disable the gravity on the rigidbody and make it kinematic, you don't want it falling on the floor.

Set the **Radius** on the collider to **0.1**, set **Height** to **0.5**, and change the **Direction** to **X-Axis**.

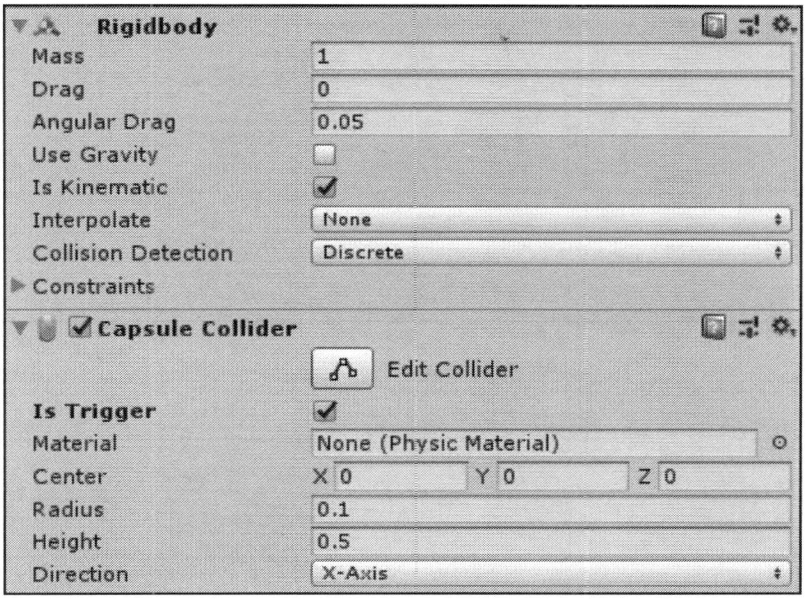

There's one final part missing to complete the **BatteryHolder**: you need a way of making stuff happen when the battery is put inside the batter holder. For this, you'll need another component: a **Snap Drop Zone Unity Events**. This lets you visually link the events.

Add a **VRTK_Snap Drop Zone_Unity Events** component to **BatteryHolder**, and add a new event to both **On Object Snapped To Drop Zone** and **On Object Unsnapped From Drop Zone**. Drag **ExtraLights** to both **Object** slots and select **GameObject ▸ SetActive**. For the snap event, check the box so it'll become active.

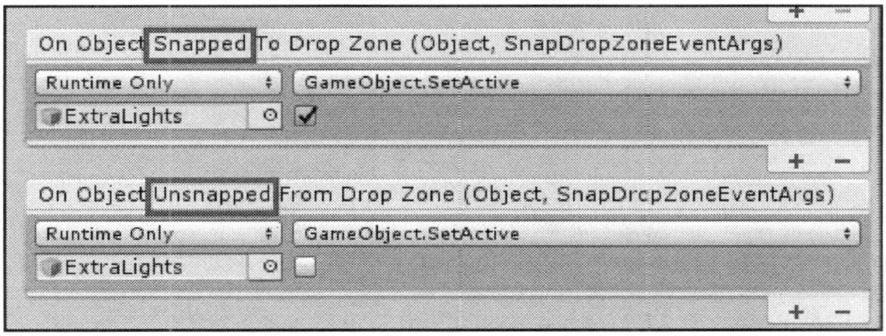

Create a new folder in the **Razeware \ Prefabs** folder named **DropZone**. Drag the **BatteryHolder** to the newly created folder to turn **BatteryHolder** into a prefab.

Everything is ready for snapping now. Run the scene and try to pick up the battery; teleport to the battery holder and snap the battery into place.

If everything works correctly, you'll see an extra set of lights switch on.

Haptic feedback

There are a few ways to add haptic feedback (or vibration) to interactions, such as adding a component that handles the haptics.

Add a new empty GameObject to the **Hierarchy**, name it **BombToy**, and parent it to **RW Props**. Set its **Position** to **(X:8, Y:1.11, Z:6.5)**, and drag the **Bomb** model from the **Razeware \ Models** folder onto the newly made GameObject to give it some visuals.

Reset the **Bomb Position** to **(X:0, Y:0, Z:0)**; and to size it down a bit, set its scale to **(X: 18.5, Y:18.5, Z:18.5)**. You'll now have a bomb sitting on the table:

Don't worry; it's safe!

Select **BombToy** and open the **VRTK setup wizard** (via **Window > VRTK**); leave everything at their default values and click the **Setup selected object(s)** button.

Add a **Sphere Collider** component to the **BombToy** with a **Radius** of **0.105** to prevent it from dropping through the floor.

The component you're interested in is **VRTK_Interact Haptics**. Until now, you've removed this as it wasn't needed for the other objects.

To get it to work, you'll need to tweak its variables.

Set **Strength On Touch** to **0.2**, **Duration On Touch** to **0.1** and **Interval On Touch** to **0.1** as well in the **Haptics On Touch** section.

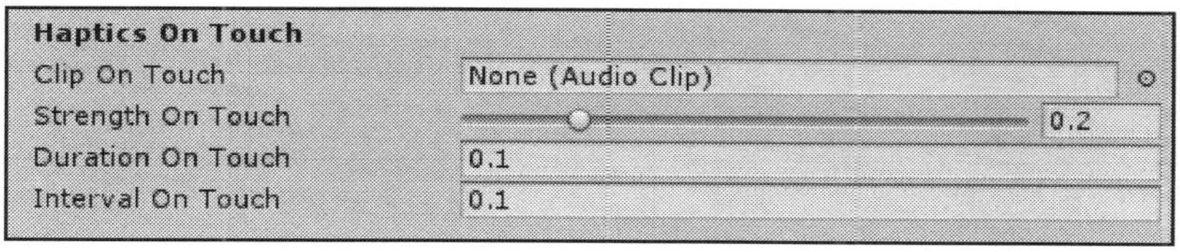

This gives a light and short vibration when you touch the bomb with your controller.

To make it vibrate when you grab it, change the following:

Set **Strength On Grab** to **0.4**, **Duration On Grab** to **0.2** and **Interval On Grab** to **0.05** as well in the **Haptics On Grab** section. This causes the controller to vibrate a bit more violently, letting you know you've successfully grabbed the object.

Drag the **BombToy** to the **Razeware \ Prefabs \ Grab** folder to turn it into a prefab. Test if the bomb works as intended by running the scene then touching and grabbing the bomb.

You can also create more interesting effects by creating your own scripts to handle the haptics. To demonstrate, you'll add a pulse-effect to the battery while you hold it.

Create a new C# script in the **Razeware \ Scripts** folder, name it **PulseOnHold**, and open it in your code editor.

Remove the `Start()` and `Update()` methods, and add the following line below the other `using` statements:

```
using VRTK;
```

Now replace this line:

```
public class PulseOnHold : MonoBehaviour {
```

With this one:

```
public class PulseOnHold : VRTK_InteractableObject {
```

This causes the script to derive from **InteractableObject**, which includes some essential functionality.

Now, add the following variables below the class declaration:

```
public float pulseInterval = 2f; // 1
public float pulseDuration = .2f; // 2

private VRTK_ControllerReference controllerReference; // 3
private IEnumerator pulseRoutine; // 4
```

Here's what they're used for:

1. The time between every pulse.
2. The amount of time the pulse lasts.
3. A reference to the controller that receives the vibration.
4. A cached coroutine for correctly starting and stopping the haptic feedback.

Add the following coroutine to do the vibrating:

```
IEnumerator DoPulsing()
{
    while (gameObject.activeSelf)
    {
VRTK_ControllerHaptics.TriggerHapticPulse(controllerReference,
0.5f, pulseDuration, 0.01f);
        yield return new WaitForSeconds(pulseInterval);
    }
}
```

This keeps vibrating the controller at the specified interval until the GameObject gets deactivated or the coroutine is stopped.

Next, add the following methods:

```
private void OnEnable() // 1
{
    base.OnEnable();
```

```
        pulseRoutine = DoPulsing();
    }

    public override void Grabbed(VRTK_InteractGrab
    grabbingObject) // 2
    {
        base.Grabbed(grabbingObject);
        controllerReference =

    VRTK_ControllerReference.GetControllerReference(grabbingObject.c
    ontrollerEvents.gameObject);
        StartCoroutine(pulseRoutine);
    }

    public override void Ungrabbed(VRTK_InteractGrab grabbingObject)
    // 3
    {
        base.Ungrabbed(grabbingObject);
        controllerReference = null;
        StopCoroutine(pulseRoutine);
    }
```

Here's the breakdown:

1. Call the base class `OnEnable()` method and cache a reference to the `DoPulsing()` coroutine.
2. This method gets called when a controller grabs the GameObject to which this script is attached. The `grabbingObject` is stored as the controller, and the pulse routine is started.
3. This method gets called when a controller releases the GameObject to which this script is attached. The controller is cleared, and the pulse routine is stopped.

Save the script and return to the Unity editor.

Add the **Pulse On Hold** component to the **Battery**, and remove the **VRTK_Interactable Object** component. Your custom component replaces its functionality.

Next, you'll take a look at the **Pulse On Hold** component.

Change the **Touch Highlight Color** to Pure Yellow **(R:255, G:255, B:0)** and check **Is Grabbable**.

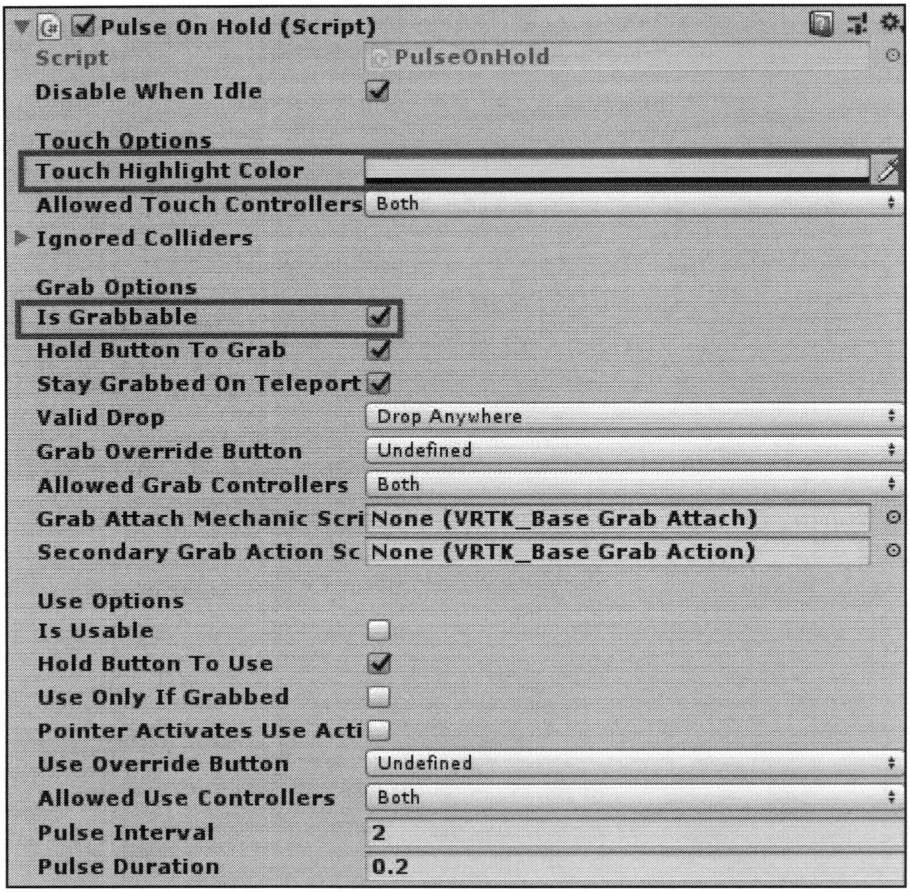

Don't forget to update the base battery prefab by clicking **Apply** on the **Battery** GameObject in the Hierarchy.

That's it! Run the scene and grab the battery. You should feel a pulse as long as you've got the battery in your hand. Can you feel the force flow with all that energy?

Where to go from here?

Well done! You now know how to add exciting mechanics to your own VR games.

If you had trouble following along, or you want to compare your project to the sample one, you can find the final project included with this chapter's resources files.

Here's a quick recap of what you did. In this chapter, you learned how to:

- Create tooltips for objects and controllers.
- Fix objects to your controllers.
- Use joints to accurately pick up objects.
- Snap objects into place.
- Use haptic feedback.

In the next chapter, you'll look at some advanced ways of moving around within a scene.

Chapter 9: Advanced VR Movement

Eric Van de Kerckhove

Movement is an essential part of any VR experience, and the most common way to move a player is with teleportation. One of the reasons teleportation is so popular in VR is because it helps to avoid motion sickness — the human body doesn't like it when there's a mismatch between what it sees and what it feels.

However, there are other ways to move besides teleportation, and this chapter will not only cover the basics of teleportation, but also those other modes of transportation.

> **Note**: This chapter contains different ways of moving around, some of which may cause nausea and disorientation for some people. The body physics, climbing and arm swinging sections may especially cause discomfort if you're not used to falling or forced movement inside a VR experience. If you start to feel sick, take a break and get some fresh air.

In this chapter, you'll learn how to:

- Teleport on terrain.
- Use destination points to cover large distances.
- Use fixed positions for teleport locations.
- Dash teleport.
- Use body physics.
- Climb objects.
- Move around using an arm swinging movement.

Getting started

To begin, open the starter project for this chapter in Unity and look around the scene.

This scene consists of two sections: the obstacle field and the terrain. In this chapter, you'll only need to add GameObjects and components to the terrain.

Now, look at the assets:

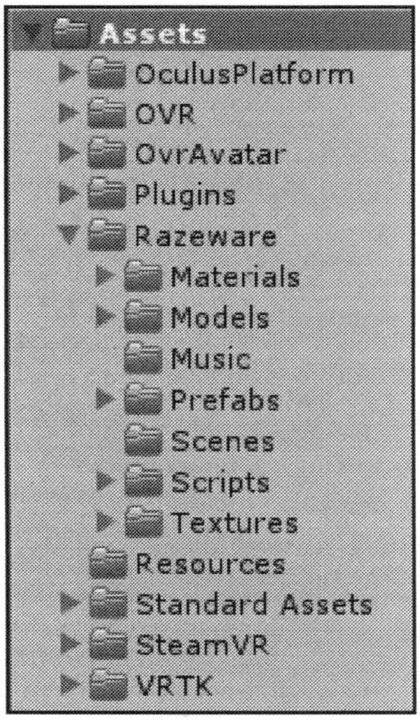

These are the same as in the previous chapter, except for the terrain asset in the root of the **Assets** folder.

The scene doesn't contain a VRTK SDK Manager so you won't be able to look around the world for yourself just yet. To remedy this, drag the **[VRTK_SDK_MANAGER]** prefab from the **Razeware\Prefabs** folder into the root of the **Hierarchy**.

Get your VR headset and controllers ready, then press the Play button to get a good look at everything from the ground level.

To teleport, use the left controller.

Not sure how teleportation works? No worries, because next up is a quick introduction to how teleporting works.

Terrain teleportation

Before adding any components, you should first understand how the **VRTK_Height Adjust Teleport** component that's attached to the **Play Area** works. When you point the laser pointer at a collider and let go, a raycast is shot toward the endpoint. Both the play area and the player within get transported to the position of that point.

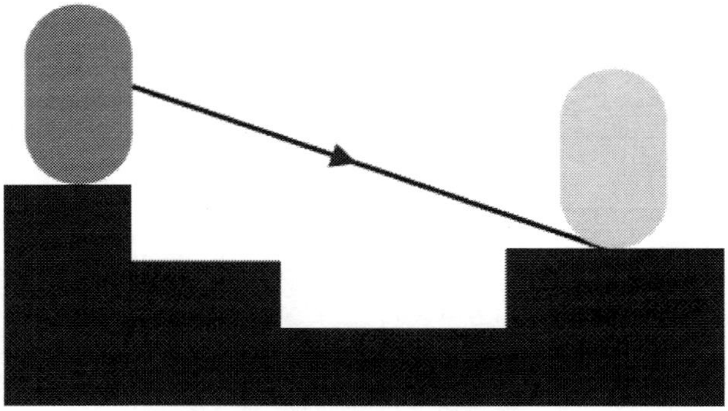

This also means it can adapt to any type of collider, including terrain colliders. You can try this out by playing the scene and teleporting onto the green terrain.

Perfect! With that out of the way, it's time to explore some exciting ways of extending and replacing the movement system.

Destination points

While you were playing with teleportation, you may have realized that you can't move to locations you can't see. For example, if you wanted to teleport to the top of the tower from the ground, you won't be able to because you can't see it from the ground.

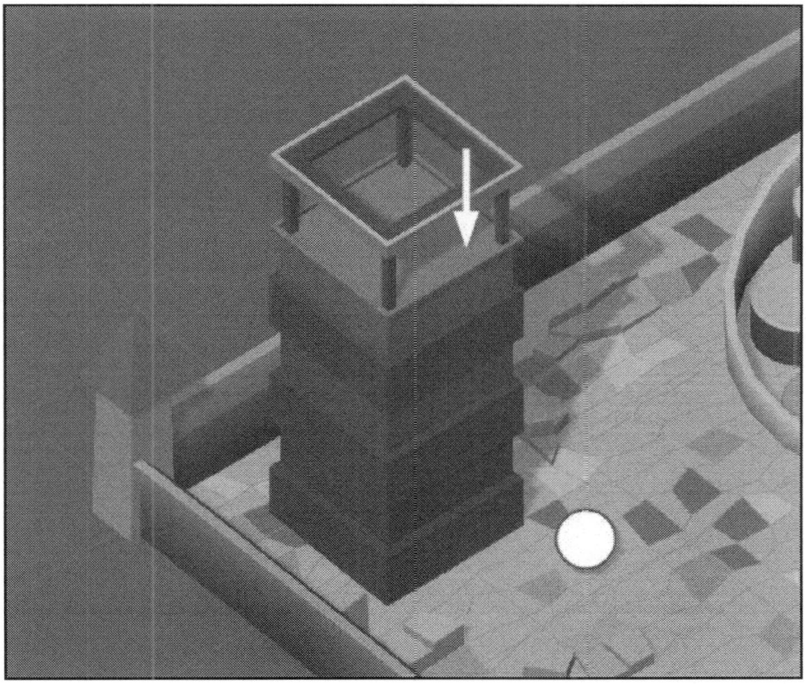

However, there's a way to set up "portals" between two points using **destination points**.

Add a new empty GameObject to the Hierarchy, name it **Destination Points** and reset its **Transform**. This acts as a folder for all of the destination points.

Now, create another empty GameObject, parent it to **Destination Points** and name it **Teleport**. Reset its **Transform** as well. This holds the destination points to teleport up and down the tower.

Drag a **DestinationPoint** prefab from the **VRTK\Prefabs** folder onto **Teleport** to parent it. Set its **Position** to **(X:-15, Y:0, Z:-16)**, and double-click the **DestinationPoint** in the Hierarchy to get a better look at it.

Unlike in *The Matrix*, this blue pill can take you wherever you desire.

If this blue pill looks yellow in your editor, that's because a destination point has three child GameObjects:

- **defaultCursor**: Blue, shown by default.
- **hoverCursor**: Green, gets shown when you hover over it with a laser pointer.
- **lockedCursor**: Yellow, shown if **Enable Teleport** is turned off on the main destination point component.

These are all placed at **(X:0, Y:0, Z:0)** by default, so they overlap. Here's a blown out view of all three:

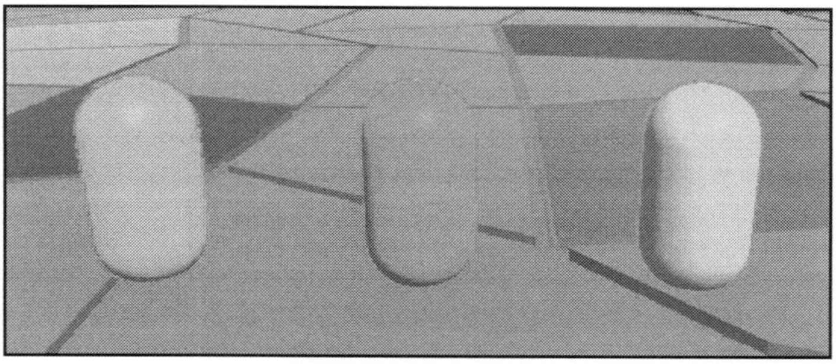

Having just one of these won't do you any good though. Duplicate **DestinationPoint**, name it **High Point**, and move it to **(X:-20, Y:21.5, Z:-17.5)**. This positions it at the top of the tower:

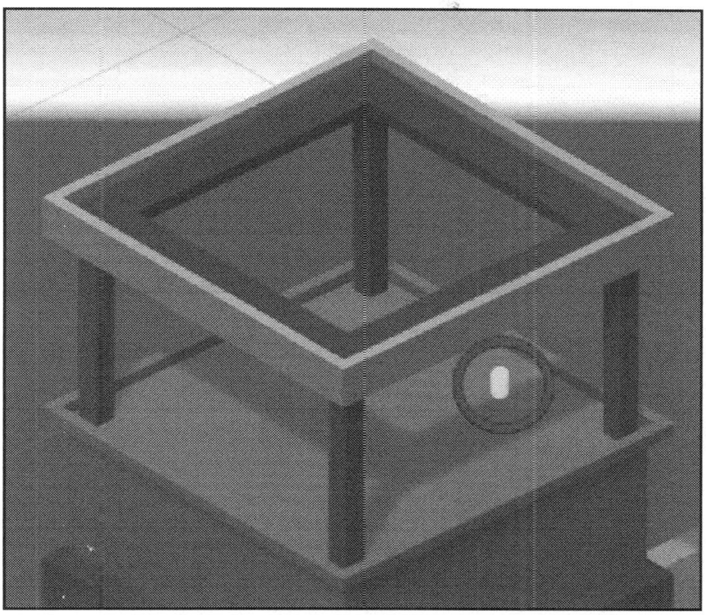

It's time to link them up: select **DestinationPoint** and drag **High Point** onto the **Destination Location** slot.

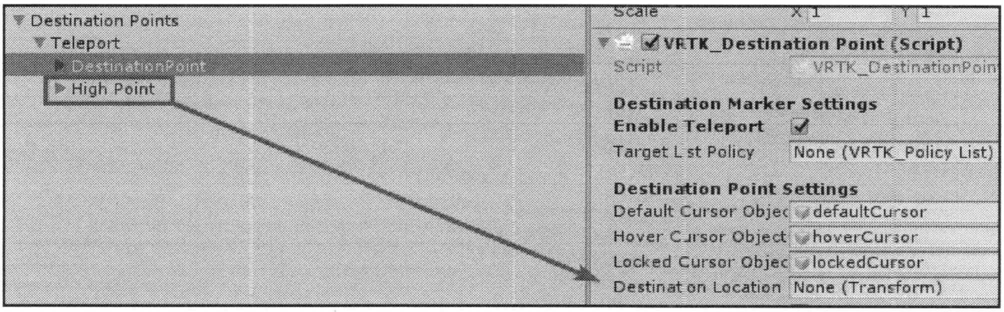

Now select **High Point** and drag **DestinationPoint** to its **Destination Location**. This creates a connection between them in two directions so that you can teleport freely between them.

Play the scene and try it out. Point the teleport line toward the bottom destination point and let go like you'd do on the floor. If all goes well, you'll teleport to the top of the tower. While you're up there, enjoy the view.

Fixed teleportation

Some VR games don't allow you to teleport everywhere. Instead, they rely on fixed hotspots to limit the player's movement. This is ideal for creating immersive experiences and puzzle games like *Myst* and *Riven*. To create this behavior, you'll need to use destination points again.

Create an empty GameObject and name it **Fixed**. Parent it to **Destination Points** and reset its **Transform**.

This serves as the root for the teleport hotspots. Now drag an instance of **DestinationPoint** from the **VRTK\Prefabs** folder onto **Fixed** to parent it. Name it **Fixed Point** and change its **Position** to **(X:-22, Y:1.5, Z:-10.5)**.

This positions it on top of one of the rocks next to the tower:

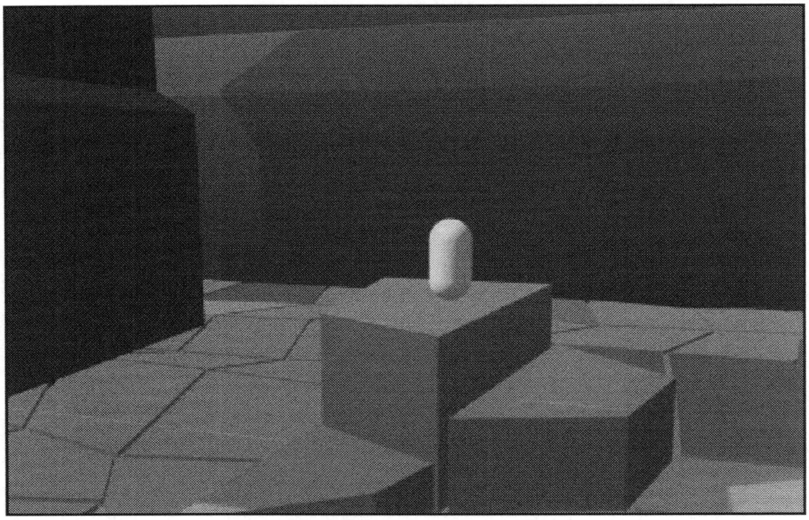

This destination point doesn't need a **Destination Location** as the destination is the object itself. Create another eleven **Fixed Point** GameObjects, parenting them to **Fixed**, and setting them up with the following positions:

- **(X:-27, Y:1.4, Z:-3.6)**
- **(X:1.4, Y:1.2, Z:6.6)**
- **(X:-13, Y:0.6, Z:2.6)**
- **(X:-18, Y:2.7, Z:4.9)**
- **(X:-21, Y:4.7, Z:10)**
- **(X:-20, Y:5.8, Z:15.6)**
- **(X:-15, Y:7.8, Z:18.6)**
- **(X:-9, Y:9.2, Z:18.5)**
- **(X:11, Y:1, Z:-4.2)**
- **(X:-11.5, Y:10, Z:15)**
- **(X:-11, Y:10, Z:7)**

You should now have a group of destination points spread all over the scene:

Everything is now in place for fixed teleportation, except one crucial detail: the player can still teleport around freely, so there's no reason to the use the fixed points yet.

To limit the places the player is allowed to teleport, add a **VRTK_PolicyList** component to the **Play Area** under **[VRTK_SETUP]**.

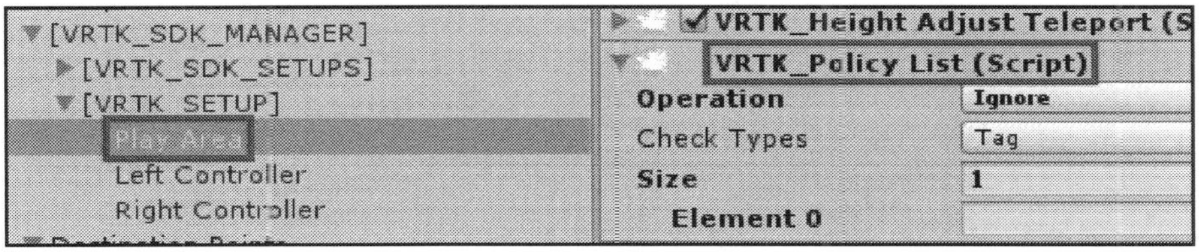

Because you're limiting teleportation to only the destination points, set the **Operation** on the policy list to **Include**, set **Check Types** to **Script** only, and enter **VRTK_DestinationPoint** in **Element 0**.

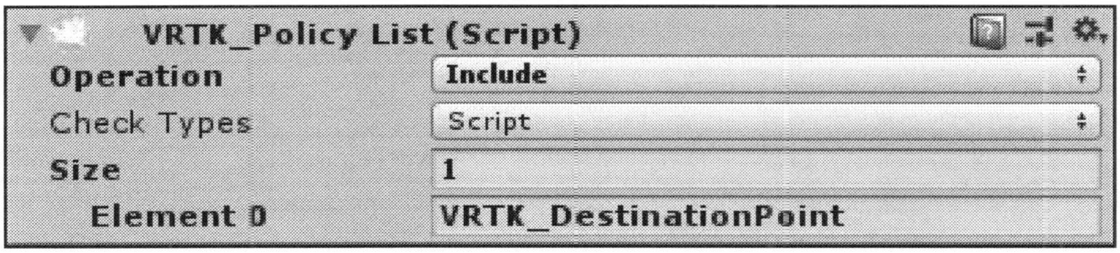

Drag the policy list component to the **Target List Policy** slot on the **VRTK_Height Adjust Teleport** component to make it use the list.

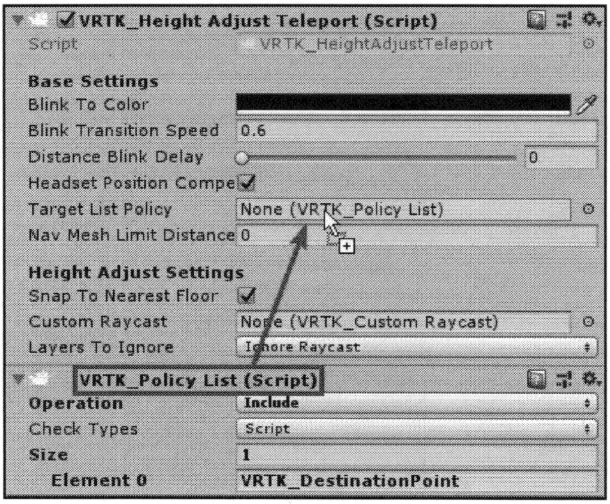

That's it. Play the scene and teleport around. As you do, notice how you can only use the destination points to move around.

You can scatter more fixed points around and create a "scenic" route around the level by duplicating the existing ones and moving them to the terrain, for example. In a full game, you'd likely place them next to things like machines and other objects the player can manipulate.

Before moving on to the next section, remove the **Target List Policy** from the **VRTK_Height Adjust Teleport** component by setting it to **None**.

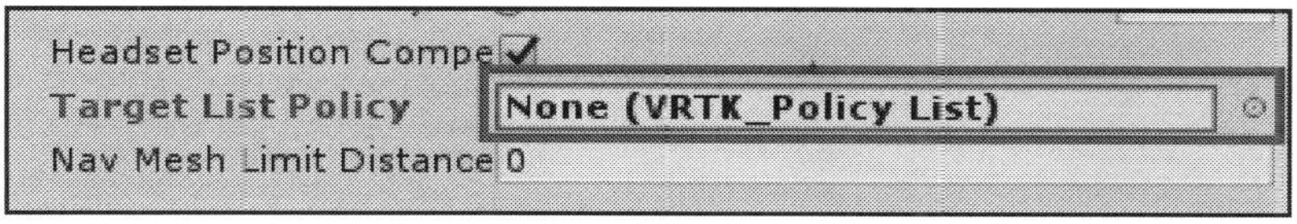

You'll need free movement for the next mechanics to work correctly.

Dash teleport

Until now, you've been teleporting instantly to your destination. There's another way to move around though: using dash teleporting. Dash teleporting means that you "dash" to the final position, which makes the camera smoothly move towards the destination.

Remove the **VRTK_Height Adjust Teleport** component from **Play Area** and replace it with the **VRTK_DashTeleport** component.

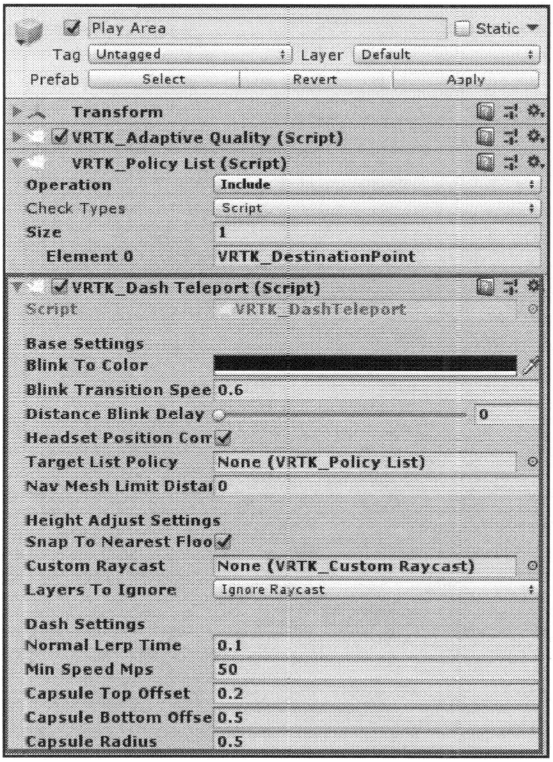

This component is derived from the **Height Adjust Teleport**, so teleporting will behave the same as before except for the dash movement. The replacement was all you needed.

Play the scene and teleport around; you'll notice you'll be jolted forward after confirming the teleport destination.

> **Note**: After adding dash teleporting, you might notice that after teleporting to destination points, they disappear. This seems to be a bug with the current version of VRTK and will hopefully be fixed soon.

Body physics

> **Important Note:** This section can make you sick. Simulated falling in VR can cause severe nausea and a feeling like the floor is being pulled away from under you. If you're not used to VR or are sensitive to this, please sit down while testing.

Time to take a leap of faith. Play the scene, get to the top of the tower and try walking over the edge. Once you're there, look down.

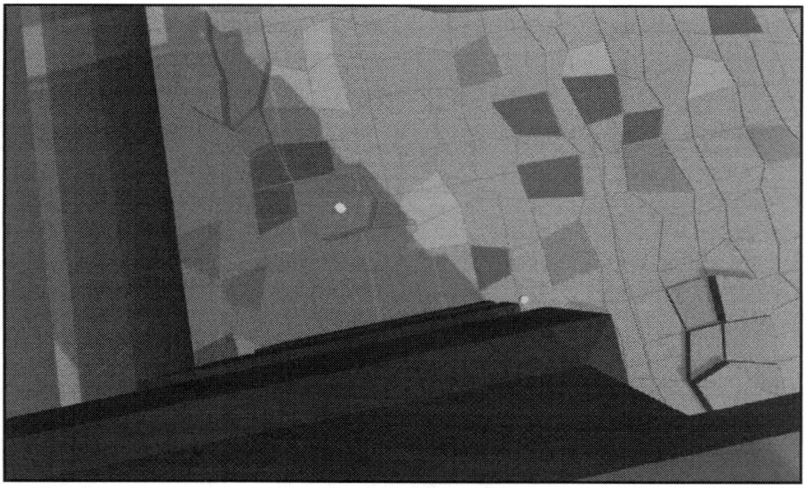

Nothing happens. This is the default behavior for the VRTK setup — the height adjustment only happens after teleporting, not when walking around.

To add gravity and ground collision, add a **VRTK_BodPyhysics** component to **Play Area**.

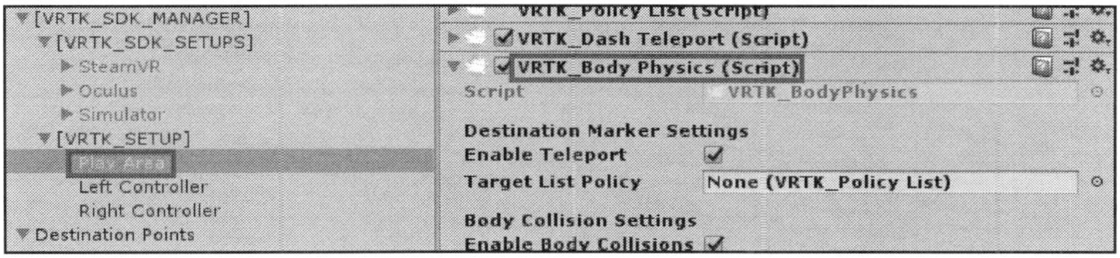

The default values are great for semi-realistic falling and stepping on things like slopes. Try it out in play mode: teleport to the small blue tower first and step over the edge; you'll drop down to the ground.

If you're comfortable with that, try the big tower next.

Another good reason to add body physics to your setup is that it allows you to add **climbing**, which you'll look at next.

Climbing

One of most fun things to do in VR is to climb around *Tomb Raider* style toward your objective. With the help of VRTK, you can make almost any surface climbable. Need a fence to climb, a ladder or a wall of jello-o? No problem, because in this section, you'll prepare a ladder for climbing.

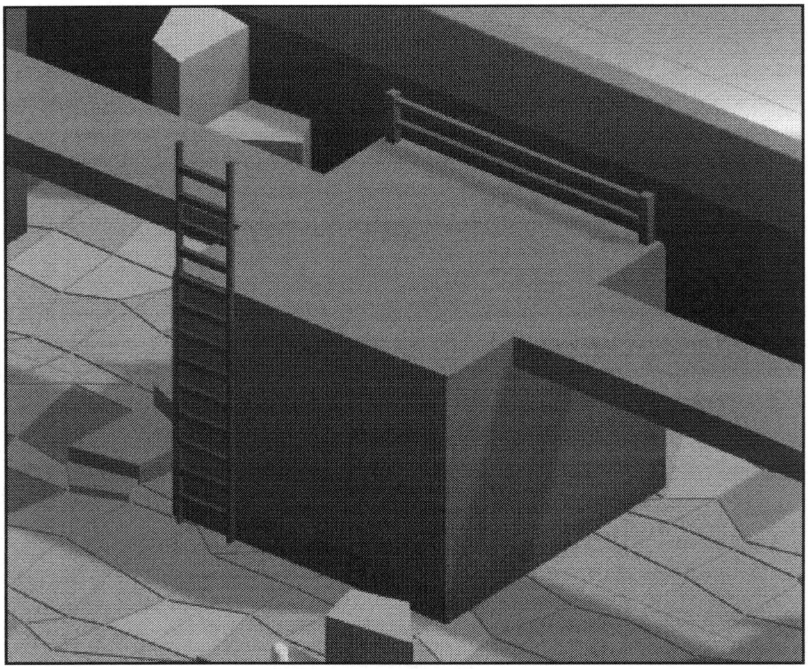

Find the ladder under the **AdvancedFullChapter9** GameObject and select it.

You'll notice it has a convex mesh collider attached to it, but you can use any kind of collider for the climbing to work.

Open the VRTK setup wizard by selecting **Window ▸ VRTK ▸ Setup Interactable Object** in the top menu.

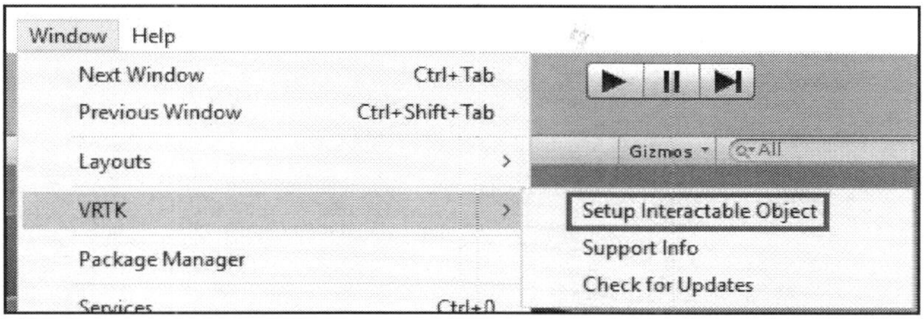

While you *could* add the needed components manually, it's usually much faster to use the setup wizard.

Check the **Hold Button To Grab** toggle, and set the **Grab Attach Mechanic** to **Climbable**. Uncheck **Add RigidBody** and **Add Haptics**.

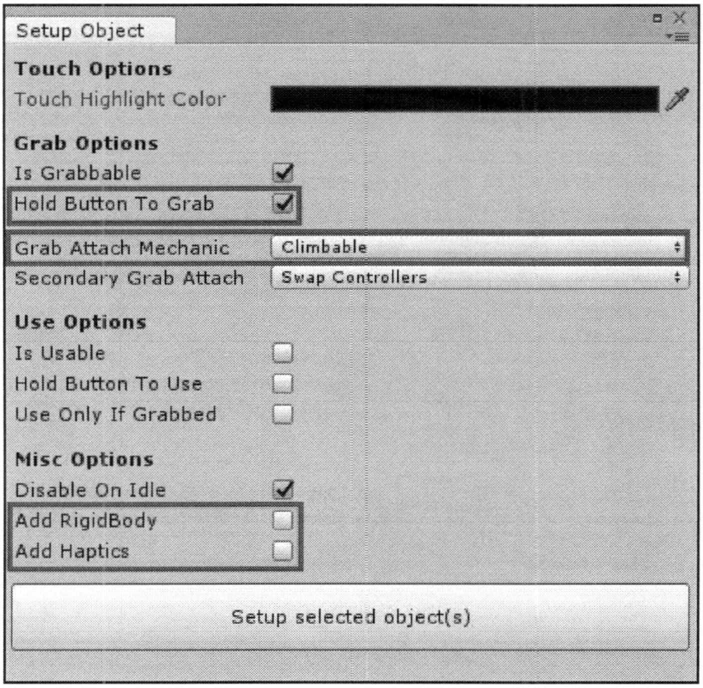

Click the **Setup selected object(s)** button to apply the changes. This adds a few new components to the ladder, including **VRTK_Climbable Grab Attach**.

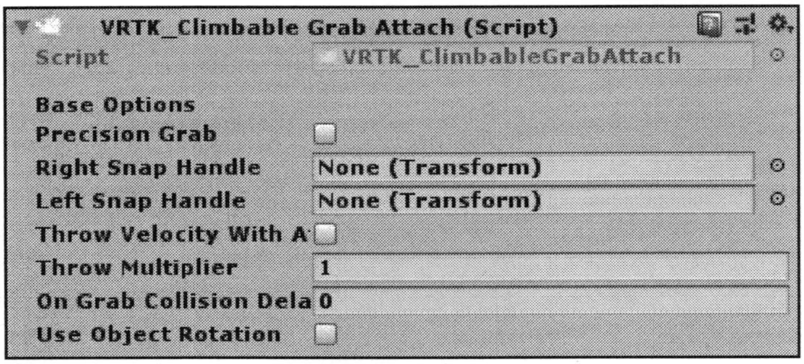

This is a special kind of grab component that communicates with the Play Area. Only objects with this component attached are climbable. You generally don't want players to climb up all the walls unless they're *Spiderman* or something.

For climbing to fully function, you'll also need to add a new component to the **Play Area**. Select **Play Area** and add a **VRTK_PlayerClimb** component to it.

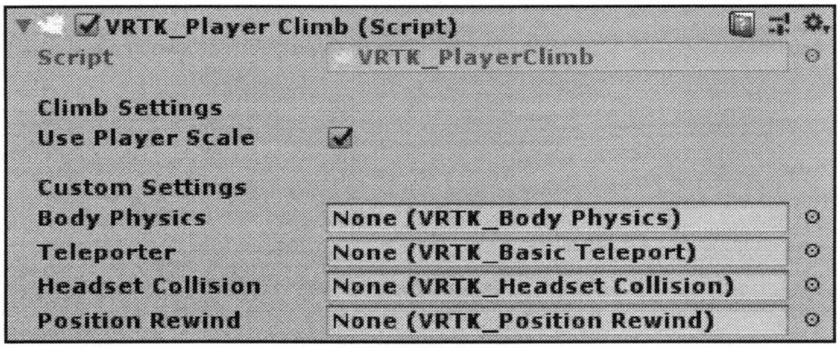

This is the crucial part that allows climbing to work; it manipulates the position of your virtual body when you grab a climbable object. For example, if you grab the ladder and move the controller that grabbed it downwards, you'll pull yourself up and vice-versa.

The custom settings are linked automatically if the components are present on the same GameObject, or any of its children, and the last two are optional.

To deal with players putting their head into objects like walls and seeing straight through (instantly breaking all immersion in the progress), you can add a fade to black effect. To do this, you need two things: a way to know when the player's head collides with a solid object, and a script that can fade the headset view to black and back again.

Once again, VRTK has you covered.

Add both a **VRTK_HeadsetCollision** and a **VRTK_HeadsetCollisionFade** component to the **Play Area**. After adding the latter, you'll notice the **VRTK_HeadsetFade** component was automatically added.

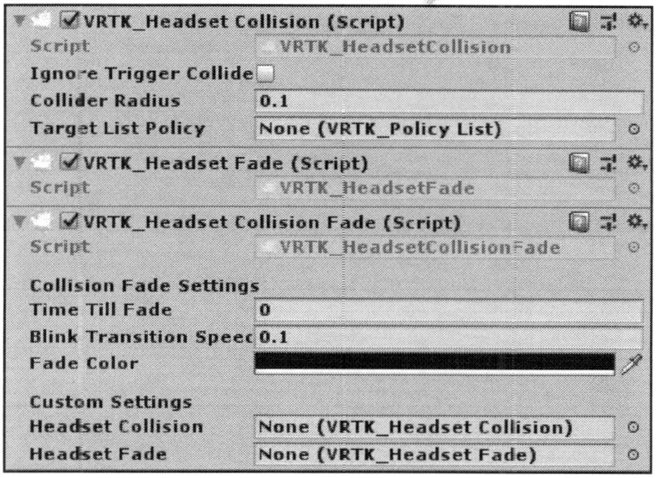

VRTK_HeadsetCollision reports to **VRTK_HeadsetCollisionFade** when the player's head hits an object, which in turn calls **VRTK_HeadsetFade** to fade the player's view to black.

The final pieces of the puzzle are the **VRTK_InteractGrab** and **VRTK_InteractTouch** components that you added to both controllers when creating the VRTK Setup prefab in Chapter 8, "Advanced VR Interactions". These are used by the climbing components to locate and use the controllers.

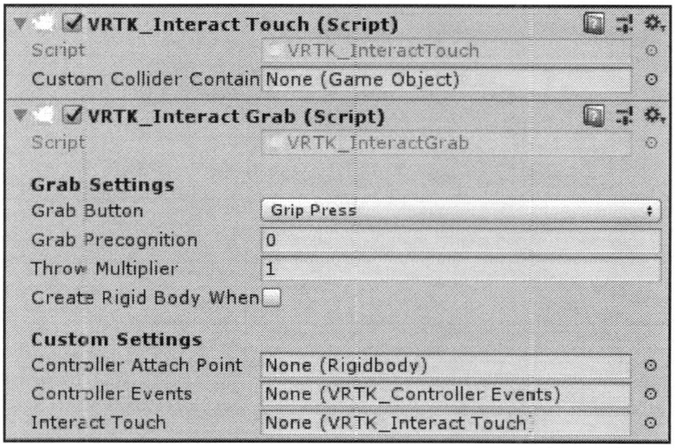

That all that's needed to implement climbing.

Play the scene and teleport next to the ladder. Squeeze the controller while hovering over the ladder to grab it and pull yourself up. You can alternate between the controllers to climb all the way up like you would in real life.

Any object can be made climbable. For example, climbing the huge tower instead of teleporting to the top would make for an exciting challenge. You're welcome! :]

Arm swinging movement

Teleporting is cool, but in some cases, letting the player swing his or her arms to move can increase immersion. This enables them to decide how fast they want to move and allows for small, accurate movements.

To add this type of movement, you need to add another component to the Play Area.

Select **Play Area**, and add a **VRTK_MoveInPlace** component to it.

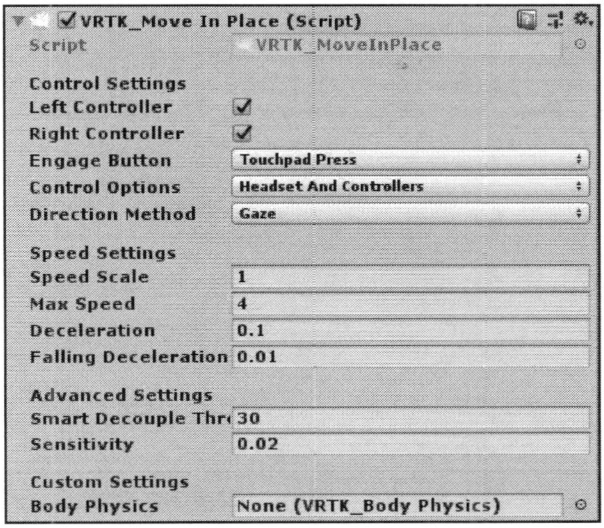

By default, you need to press the touchpad for the swing movement to work, but because this input is already used to teleport, you need to change the **Engage Button** to **Trigger Press**.

There's also no need to allow both controllers to activate the swing movement, so uncheck **Left Controller**.

The setup will look like this when you're done:

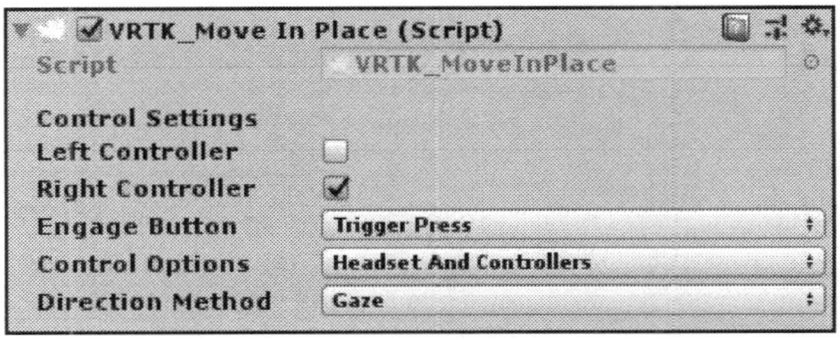

That's it. Enter play mode and give it a try. Hold down the right trigger and swing your arms back and forth like you'd do when walking. The faster you do this, the faster you'll move forward. Look at where you want to go, and the movement direction will change accordingly.

Where to go from here?

Congratulations, you made it to the end of this chapter. If you had trouble following along, you can always review the final project for this chapter.

To recap, in this chapter you learned how to:

- Teleport on terrain.
- Use destination points to cover large distances.
- Use fixed positions for teleport locations.
- Dash teleport.
- Use body physics.
- Climb objects.
- Move around using arm swinging movement.

This was just the tip of the iceberg. There are many more ways of changing and enhancing the movement in VR. For example, vehicles like cars, boats and planes are an excellent way to avoid motion sickness and let the player move around quickly. Grappling hooks are also a neat option for movement.

In the next chapter, you'll learn about advanced user interfaces and how to let non-VR players participate.

Chapter 10: Advanced VR User Interfaces

Eric Van de Kerckhove

Most games use a user interface (UI) to convey information like lives, health and score, and also to register the player's input with controls like buttons and checkboxes.

When it comes to VR, you can't just use the same UI you'd use for regular games and applications because it can feel flat and not intuitive. Interfaces have to be 3D objects or at least rounded when using traditional UI elements to keep everything easy to navigate.

For this project, you'll learn how to let non-VR players participate in the game. While it can be fun to watch your friends do all kinds of cool stuff, joining them — or even working against them — makes for far more memorable moments.

In this chapter, you'll learn how to:

- Create a curved UI.
- Add a controller menu.
- Create an overhead map.
- Let non-VR players interact with the game.

Getting started

Open the starter project that corresponds to this chapter and look at the **Project** view. The **Razeware** folder contains the custom assets:

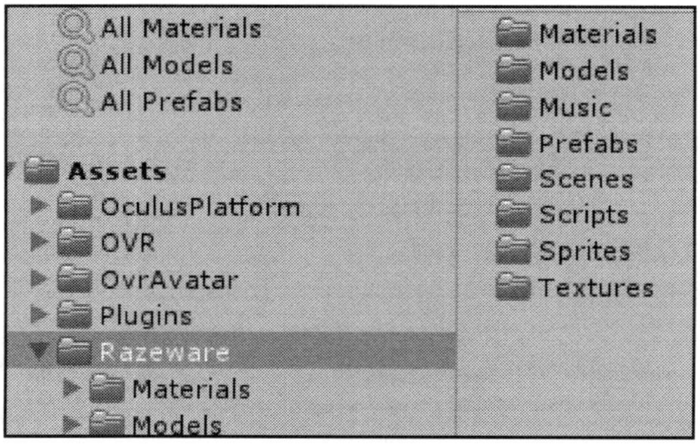

Most of the assets are the same as the previous chapters, except for the following:

- **Models**: A curved plane model was added to use for the curved user interface.
- **Scripts**: New **Shared** folder to store the utility scripts, which you'll take care of later.
- **Sprites**: Some sprites that will be used for the map and controller menu.

Open the **Chapter 10 - Advanced UI** scene under the **Razeware \ Scenes** project folder.

Play the scene and teleport around; the scene is composed out of several rooms that are linked together in a maze-like fashion.

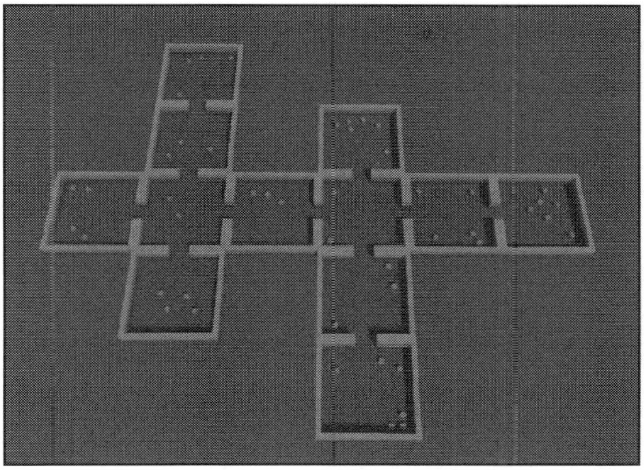

Time to get down to business!

Curved UI

To start off, you'll be creating a curved world space canvas that you can use for displaying game info or briefings, for example.

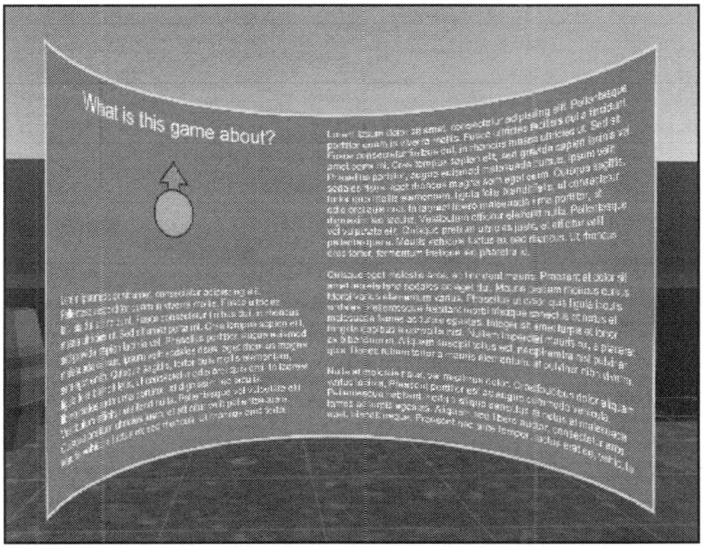

Setting up the curved plane

The first part of creating a curved user interface is preparing a curved plane where you can project the 2D UI. Luckily, you won't need to create one yourself; it's already prepared for you. It's a simple model:

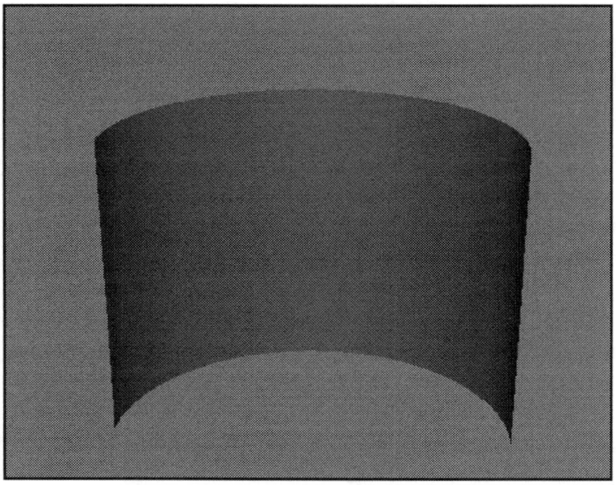

Create a new empty GameObject, name it **CurvedUI** and reset its **Transform** component. To parent the **CurvedPlane** model, drag it from the **Razeware \ Models** folder onto the GameObject you just created. Set its **Position** and **Rotation** to **(X:3, Y: 1.6, Z:1)** and **(X:-90, Y:180, Z:90)** respectively. This adds the model to the scene in all its beautiful, gray glory.

The next step is to create a new material for this plane to use. Create a new material in the **Razeware \ Materials** folder, name it **Curved UI Material** and set its shader to **Unlit/Transparent**.

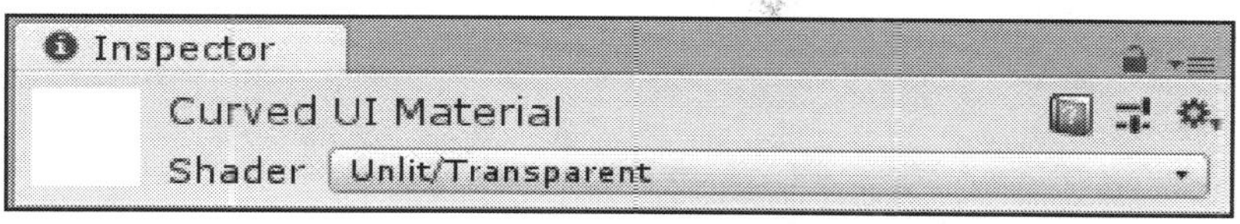

Drag the material onto **CurvedPlane** in the Hierarchy to apply it to the plane.

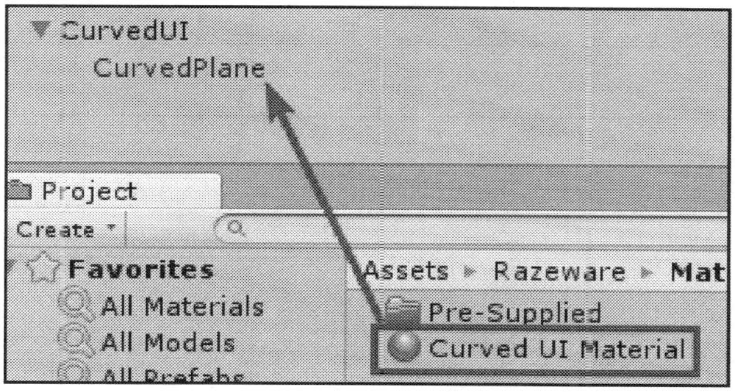

The plane now looks pure white without any lightning or shadows affecting it. This is ideal to display UI controls, like text and buttons, as each element will look as bright as the others.

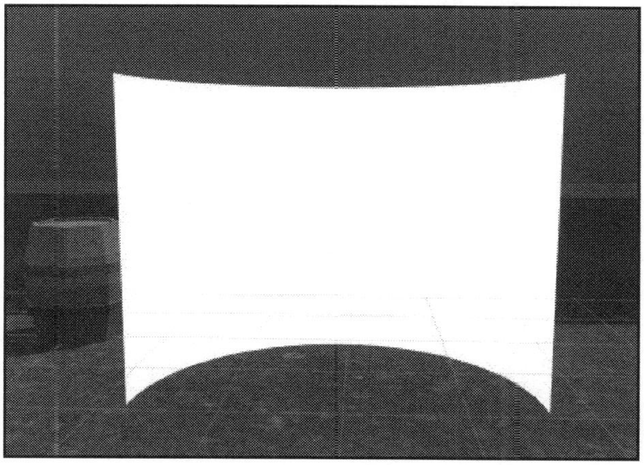

The next step is projecting a regular 2D UI onto the surface of the plane.

Curved UI camera set up

One of the easiest ways of rendering the input from a view onto a 3D model is by using a **Render Texture**. This special texture can be continuously filled in while the game is running.

Create a new folder named **Render Textures** inside of the **Razeware** folder, and create a new **Render Texture** in it.

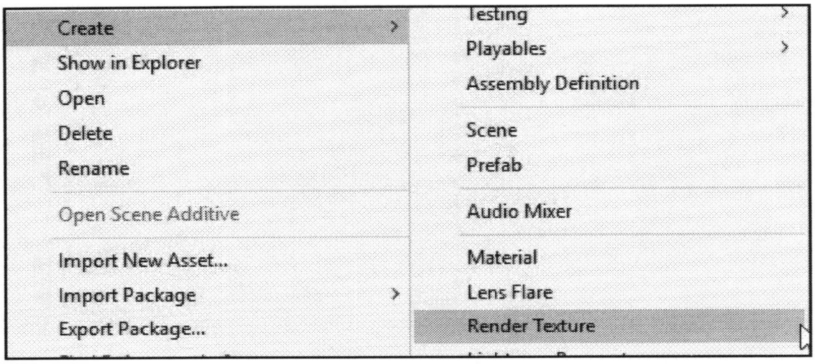

Name it **Curved UI Render Texture**, change its **Size** to **2048 x 1024** and set its **Depth Buffer** to **No depth buffer**.

The size is the most crucial variable here as that will change how crisp the final result looks. The higher it is, the more pixels it takes into account, however, more memory and processing power will need to be used as well. The **aspect ratio** of the size (width divided by height) needs to match the final model the texture will be projected on or the image will appear stretched.

In the case of the curved plane, the **width** of the surface of the plane is **twice** as large as its **height**.

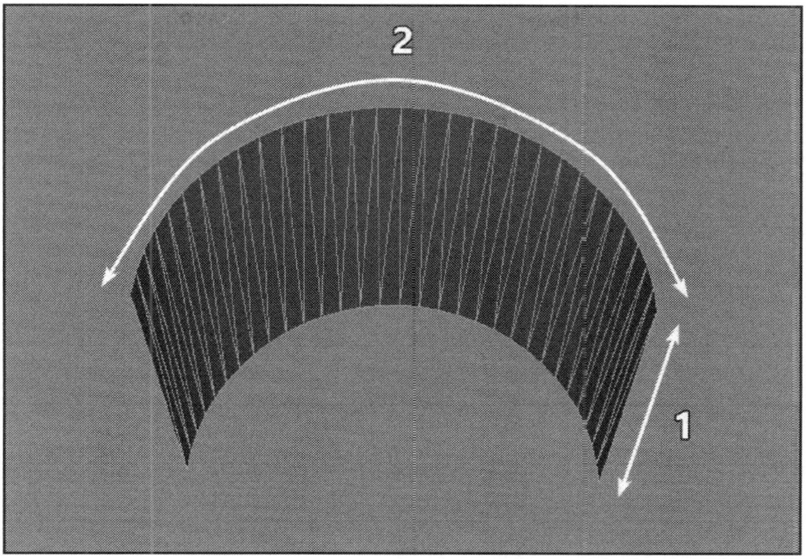

That explains where the **2048 x 1024** size comes from. If you decide to use another model to show the UI on something like a hemisphere, for example, you'll need to adjust the size accordingly.

Now drag the render texture onto **CurvedPlane** so it gets used as the texture for the unlit material.

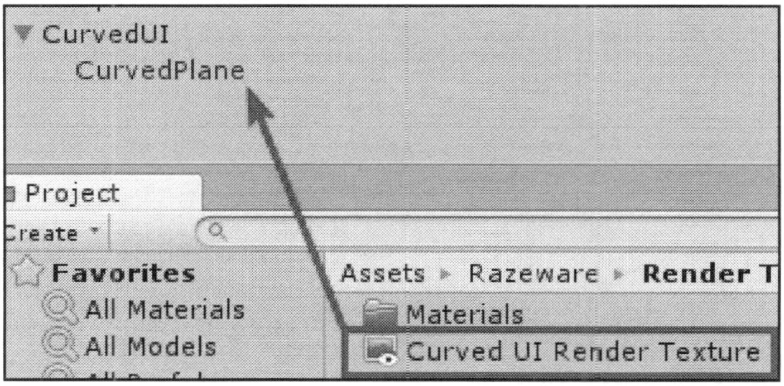

After doing this, you'll notice the curved plane has become invisible — this is to be expected as the render texture isn't receiving any input yet. For that, you'll need a camera.

Create a new camera, parent it to **CurvedUI** and name it **Curved UI Camera**. Set its **Position** to **(X:0, Y:50, Z:0)**, this positions the camera far above the rest of the level.

Change the following properties of its Camera component to:

- **Clear Flags**: Solid Color
- **Background**: Pure Black (**(R:0, G:0, B:0)**)
- **Culling Mask**: Only UI
- **Projection**: Orthographic
- **Size**: 5
- **Depth**: 1

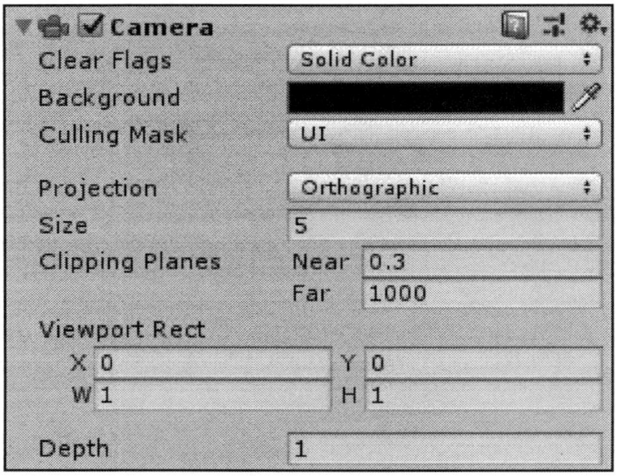

Now drag **Curved UI Render Texture** onto the **Target Texture** slot of the camera.

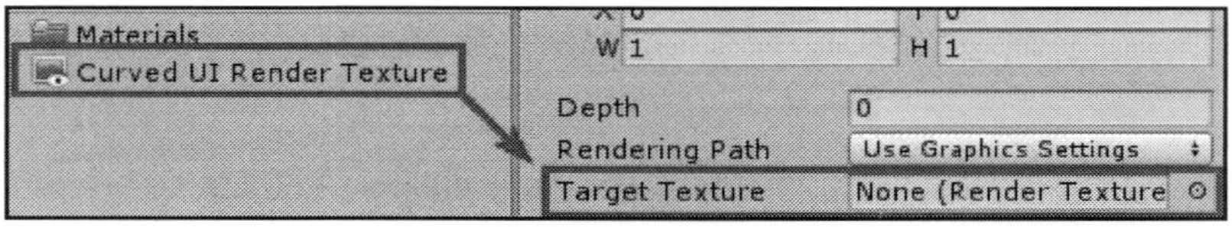

Finally, change **Target Eye** to **None (Main Display)**. This makes sure the camera view won't be rendered inside the HMD.

Time to render something to the curved plane! This can be anything, really. You could even display 3D models or a view of the gameplay at an angle — similar to a security camera. However, in this case, you're going to display a user interface.

Add a new Canvas as a child of **Curved UI Camera** and name it **Curved UI Canvas**.

Change the canvas' layer to **UI**, set its **Render Mode** to **Screen Space - Camera** and drag the **Curved UI Camera** onto its **Render Camera** slot.

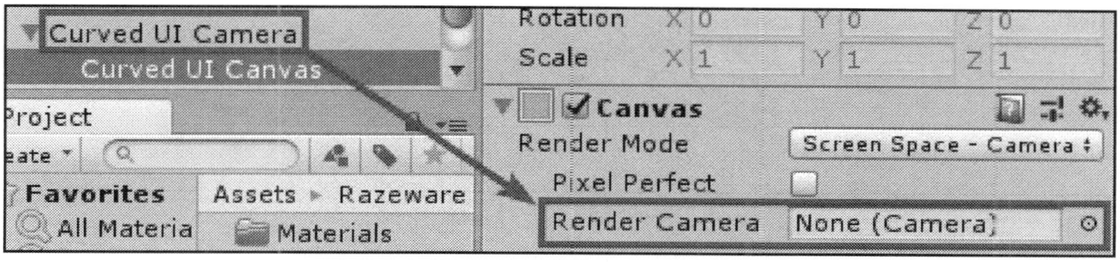

Anything you add to this canvas now will be shown on the curved plane. Add a new Image to the canvas, name it **BackgroundImage** and change its **Source Image** to **HintBackground**.

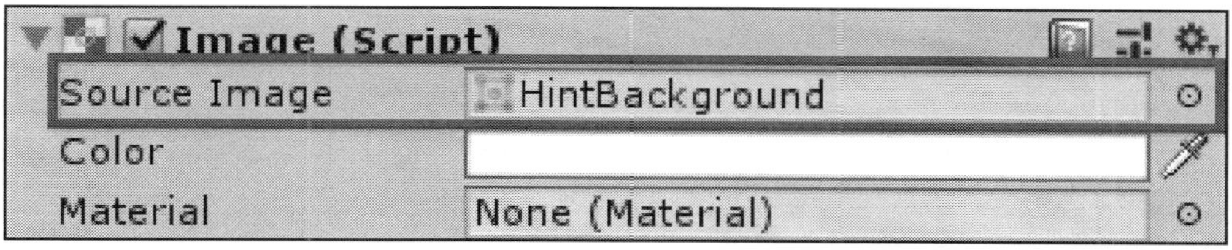

Make its **Rect Transform** fill the entire canvas by opening the **Anchor Presets** panel and clicking the bottom right option while holding **ALT**.

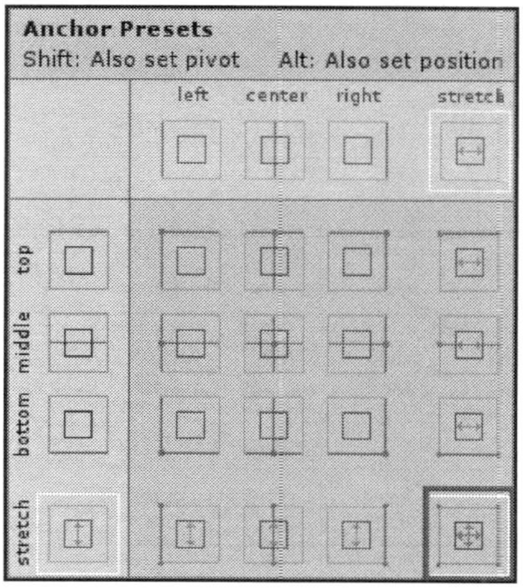

Now look at the curved UI model in the Scene view, notice how the image you just added to the canvas is projected onto it.

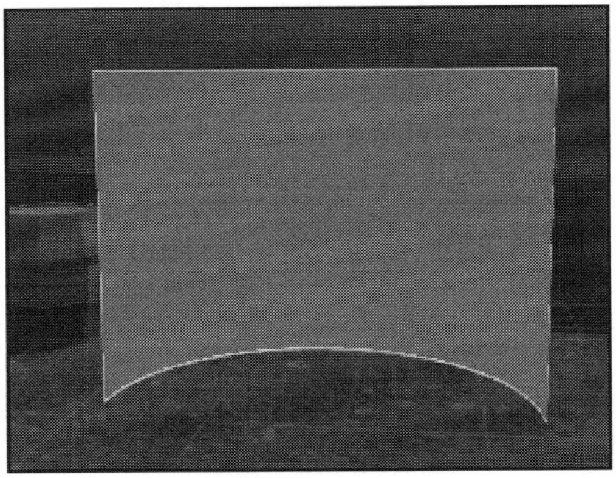

After you add some UI elements, you can use the canvas to show a briefing to the player, for example:

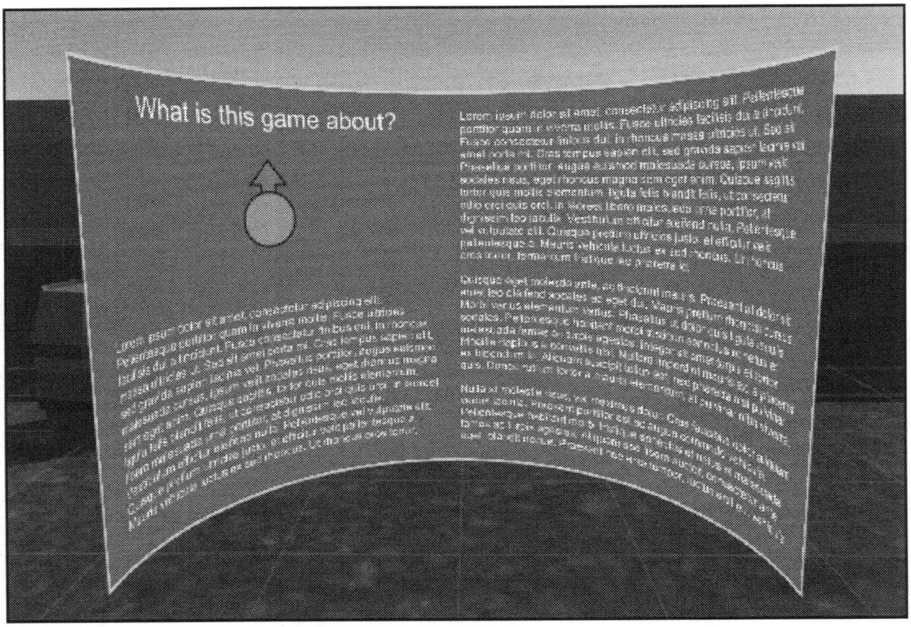

Because the focus of this chapter isn't to teach you how to use Unity's UI system, you won't go into any detail on how to add these elements. Check out the **Introduction to Unity UI** tutorial series in the Unity section on raywenderlich.com for more info on how to do that.

Play the scene and teleport over to the curved plane; if you look around, you'll notice it's much easier to see and read everything.

> **Note**: This way of showing a curved UI is only for non-interactable user interfaces like showing status or simple text. There are other solutions available for integrating interactions, for example, **Curved UI** by **chisley** on the Unity Asset Store.

In the next section, you'll get to see how to add a menu to one of your controllers easily.

Controller menu

Most VR controllers have only a small selection of buttons you can use. One of the ways to counter this is to add a set of virtual buttons you can use with either the touchpad on the HTC Vive or the analog stick on the Oculus Rift.

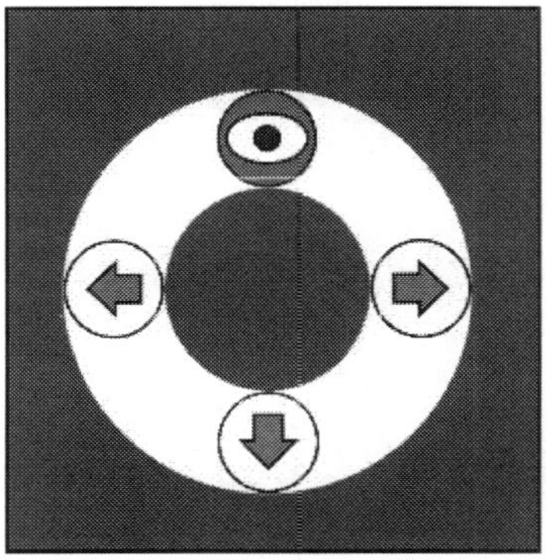

VRTK has a handy prefab that you can use to create a controller menu automatically. Drag the **RadialMenu** prefab from the **VRTK \ Prefabs** folder onto the **Left Controller** in the Hierarchy to parent it.

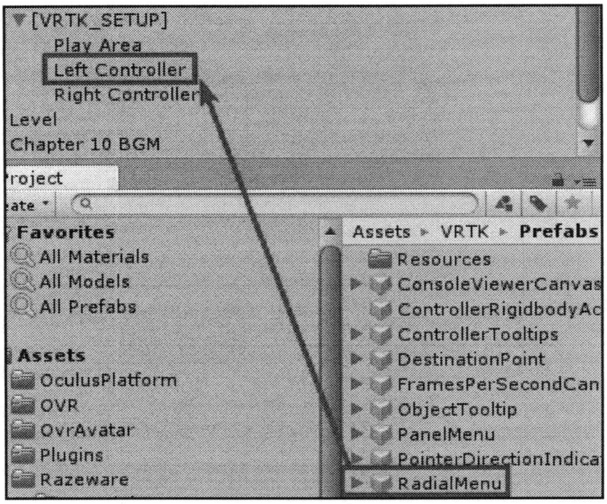

This creates a default radial menu at the scene root **(X:0, Y:0, Z:0)**.

To change the buttons' appearance, you can change the properties of the **VRTK_Radial Menu** component on the **Panel**, which is the grandchild of **RadialMenu**.

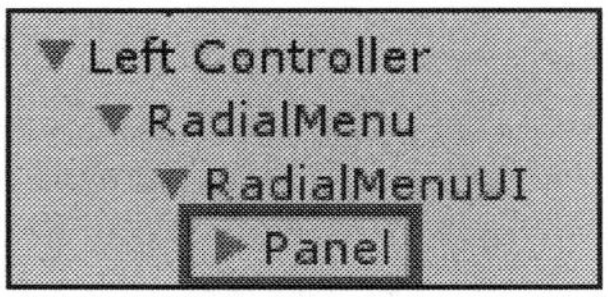

Unfold the **Buttons** list and set up the following **Button Icon** for each element:

- **Element 0**: IconSee
- **Element 1**: IconLeft
- **Element 2**: IconDown
- **Element 3**: IconRight

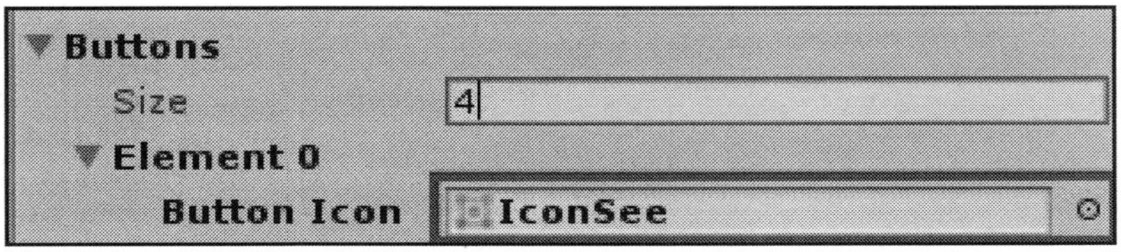

The arrow buttons are used to rotate the player around in-place. This makes it easier for people playing your game in a small space.

For this, you'll need to do some scripting. Create a new C# script in the **Razeware \ Scripts \ Shared **folder and name it **RotatePlayAreaAroundPlayer**.

Open the script in your favorite editor and remove both the `Start()` and `Update()` methods.

Add the following line to the top of the script, below the other using directives:

```
using VRTK;
```

This line is needed to call some VRTK specific methods.

Add the following variables below the class declaration:

```
public float RotationPerSwipe = 45f; // 1
public float FadeDuration = 0.2f; // 2
```

1. The amount of **rotation** to perform in **degrees** per swipe (or press of a button).
2. Time in seconds to fade the screen to black inside the HMD. This helps to avoid motion sickness.

Add the following coroutine below the variables:

```
IEnumerator RotatePlayArea(float rotation) // 1
{
    VRTK_SDK_Bridge.HeadsetFade(Color.black, FadeDuration); // 2
    yield return new WaitForSeconds(FadeDuration); // 3

VRTK_DeviceFinder.PlayAreaTransform().RotateAround(VRTK_DeviceFi
nder.HeadsetTransform().position, Vector3.up, rotation); // 4
    VRTK_SDK_Bridge.HeadsetFade(Color.clear, FadeDuration); // 5
}
```

Here's what this coroutine does:

1. Accept a `float` as a parameter to use as the **rotation**.
2. Fade the headset to black.
3. Wait for the fade to end.
4. **Rotate** the play area around the position of the headset by the **rotation** that was given as a parameter.
5. Fade the headset back to a clear view.

Now, add these methods below `RotatePlayArea()`:

```
public void RotateLeft()
{
    StartCoroutine(RotatePlayArea(-RotationPerSwipe));
}

public void RotateRight()
{
    StartCoroutine(RotatePlayArea(RotationPerSwipe));
}

public void Rotate180()
{
    StartCoroutine(RotatePlayArea(180f));
}
```

These three methods call `RotatePlayArea()` with different rotation values. `RotateLeft()` and `RotateRight()` use the **RotationPerSwipe** variable to dictate the rotation, while `Rotate180()` passes **180** to face the player backwards.

Save this script and return to the editor.

Then, add the **Rotate Play Area Around Player** component to the **Play Area**.

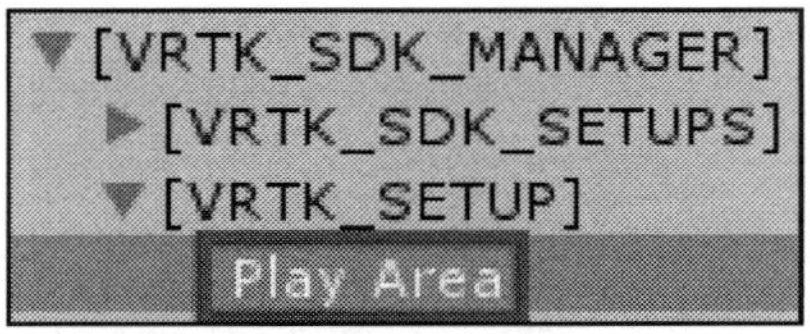

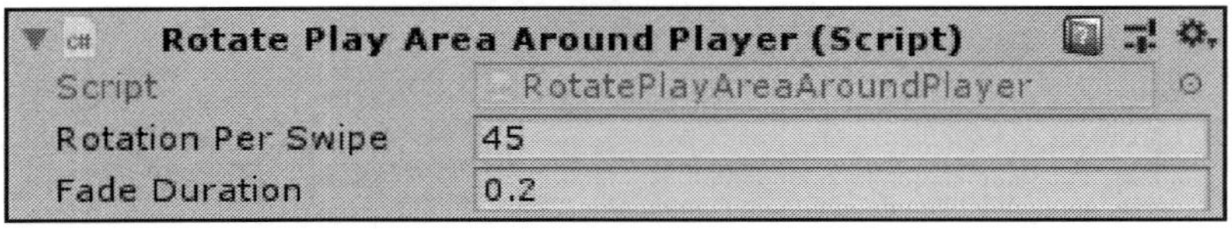

Select the **Panel** grandchild of **RadialMenu** again and add the following to the **On Click ()** events of the buttons:

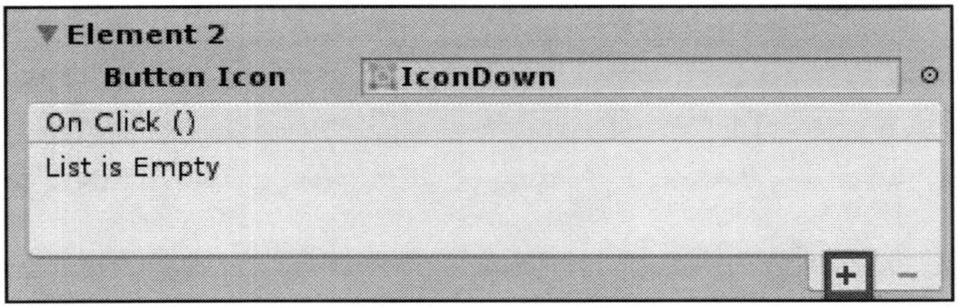

- **Element 1 (IconLeft):** Drag the **Play Area** to the object field and select **PlayAreaAroundPlayer > RotateLeft** () as the method in the dropdown.
- **Element 2 (IconDown)**: Drag the **Play Area** to the object field and select **PlayAreaAroundPlayer > Rotate180** () as the method in the dropdown.
- **Element 3 (IconRight)**: Drag the **Play Area** to the object field and select **PlayAreaAroundPlayer > RotateRight** () as the method in the dropdown.

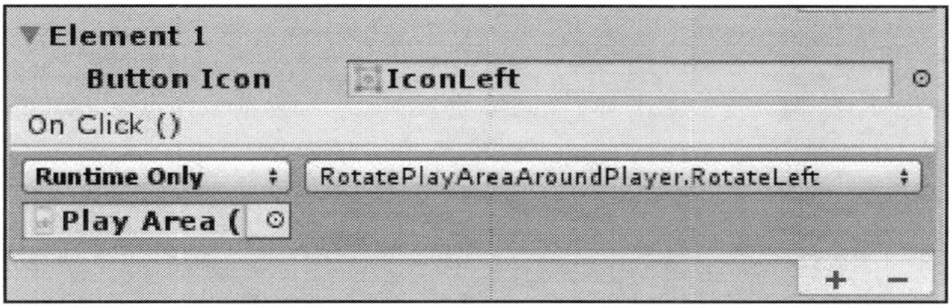

The buttons are now linked to the rotation script. Play the scene and touch the touchpad or analog stick on the left controller — a menu will pop up. Select a direction by moving your thumb around and click down to confirm an option. This is an excellent method of giving the player an easy way to rotate around in-place.

In the next section, you'll learn how to create an external mini-map and get a non-VR player to interact with the game.

External camera view set up

Being a simple spectator when a friend is playing a VR game can be pretty fun, but the gameplay on the screen will always look a bit off because of the player's micro-movements. Being able to get a tactical view of the level and even interacting with it can make for some awesome moments. Whether you help your friend by pointing them in the right direction or you put down some extra obstacles to increase the challenge, just joining the game is satisfying.

In these last sections, you'll be adding an overhead map for spectators — you'll even add some functionality so players can interact with it, affecting the gameplay for the VR player.

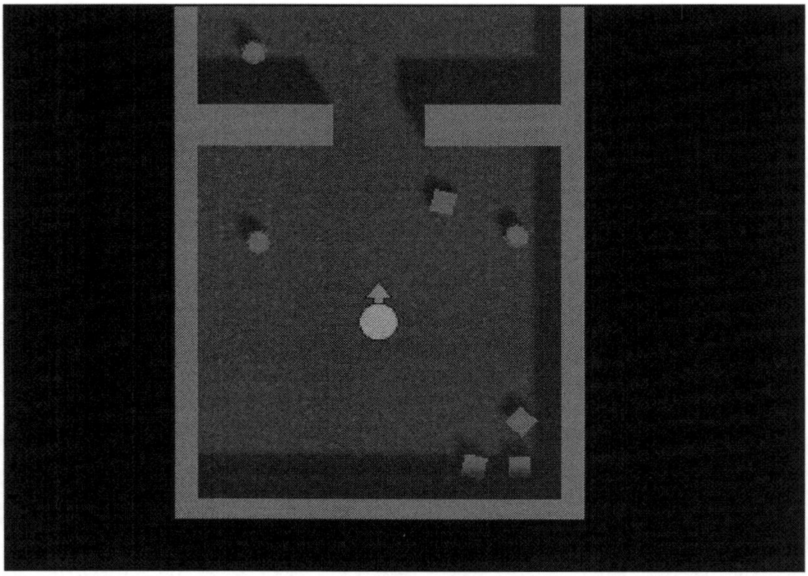

Create a new empty GameObject, name it **PlayerScreen** and reset its **Transform**. This serves as the root for all of the elements of the "spectator" view. Move it to the top of the Hierarchy, so it's easy to locate.

Add a new camera as a child of **PlayerScreen** and name it **ScreenCamera**. Set its Position and Rotation to **(X:0, Y:30, Z:0)** and **(X:90, Y:0, Z:0)** respectively. Change the following properties of the **Camera** component to make it 2D:

- **Clear Flags**: Solid Color
- **Background**: Pure Black **(R:0, G:0, B:0)**
- **Projection**: Orthographic
- **Size**: 25
- **Depth**: 10
- **Target Eye**: None (Main Display)

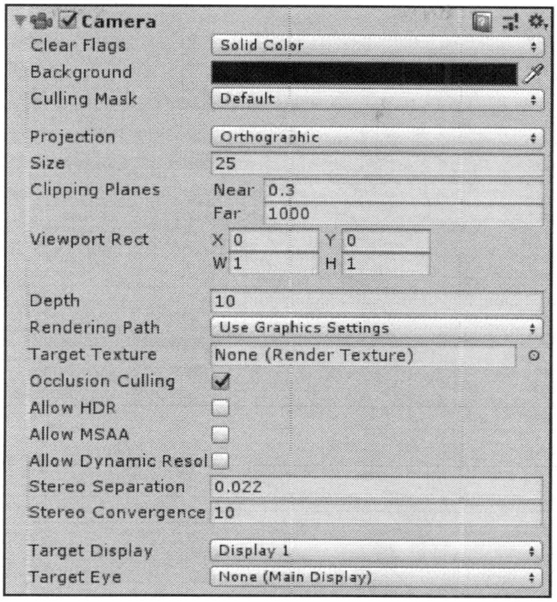

If you take a look at the Game view now, this is what you should see:

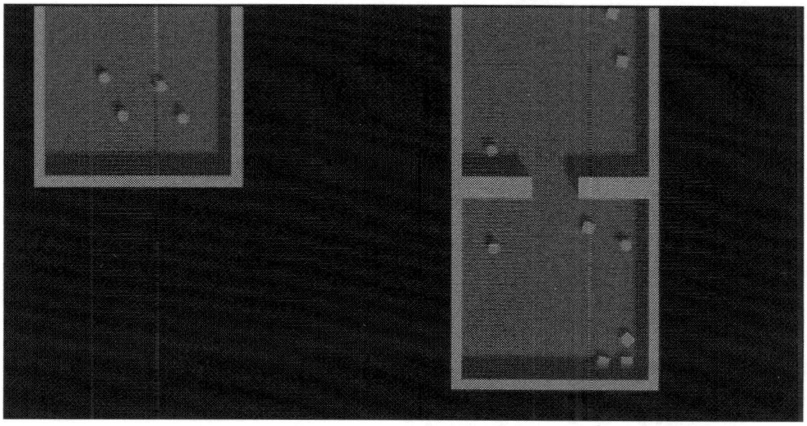

This is already cool, but there's no way to tell where the player is and where they are facing. To fix that, you can add a marker on the map.

Add a new Sprite as a child of **PlayerScreen** and name it **PlayerMapSprite**.

Set its Position, Rotation and Scale to **(X:0, Y:20, Z:0)**, **(X:90, Y:0, Z:0)** and **(X:3, Y:3, Z:3)** respectively. Change its **Sprite** to **PlayerIcon**.

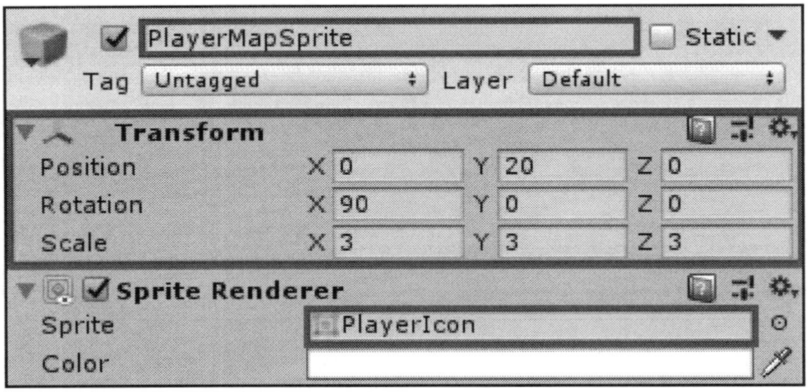

The result in the Game view should look like this:

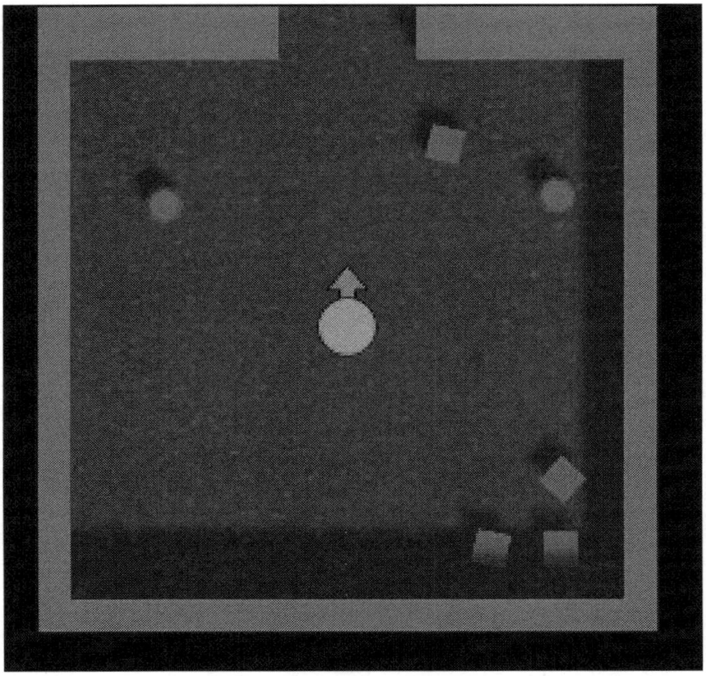

It's a lot clearer now where the player is situated. However, the icon doesn't move or rotate with the player — at least not yet. For that, you'll need to do some more scripting!

Create a new C# script in the **Razeware \ Scripts \ Shared** folder and name it **FollowGameObject**. Open it in a code editor and remove the `Start` and `Update` methods.

This will become a utility script to make a GameObject follow another easily. It's tiny but helpful.

Add the following variables below the class declaration:

```
public Transform TransformToFollow; // 1
public float MoveSpeed = 20; // 2
public Vector3 Offset; // 3

// 4
public bool FollowX = true;
public bool FollowY = true;
public bool FollowZ = true;
```

Here's what these are used for:

1. The Transform of the GameObject to follow.
2. The speed at which to follow the object.
3. An offset from the position of the object this script is following. This is especially useful for leaving space between the objects and to zoom in and out.
4. Following can be enabled separately on each of the axes, making it possible to lock some of them to avoid movement on the Y-axis for example.

Now, add the following method below the variables:

```
public void LateUpdate()
{
    // 1
    Vector3 positionNextFrame =
Vector3.MoveTowards(transform.position,
TransformToFollow.position + Offset, MoveSpeed *
Time.fixedDeltaTime);
    // 2
    if (!FollowX)
    {
        positionNextFrame.x = transform.position.x;
    }

    if (!FollowY)
    {
        positionNextFrame.y = transform.position.y;
    }

    if (!FollowZ)
    {
        positionNextFrame.z = transform.position.z;
    }

    //3
```

```
    transform.position = positionNextFrame;
}
```

Here's what's happening:

1. Calculate the position that this GameObject should potentially be at and store it in `positionNextFrame`.
2. For each of the axes, if this GameObject should **not** be following along the axis, reset the position and the axis.
3. Apply the new position.

Save this script and return to the editor. Select **PlayerMapSprite** and add a **Follow Game Object** component to it. Set its **Move Speed** to **200** and uncheck **Follow Y**.

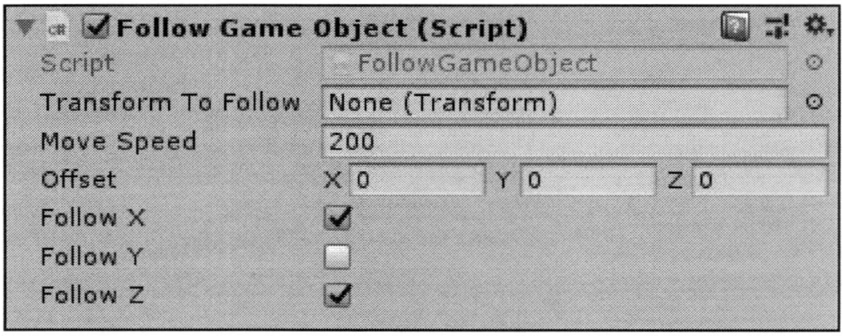

In most games, you could just assign a GameObject to the **Transform To Follow** slot and be done with it — but as you're using VRTK, and you want to follow the player's headset, there's a bit more work to be done. The active headset is enabled and set up dynamically by VRTK at runtime so you can't assign it in the editor.

Disable the **Follow Game Object** component by unchecking the checkbox next to its name. It will be re-enabled at runtime by another script.

To make the follow script find the player's headset, you'll need to create a small helper script.

Create a new folder named **Chapter 10** in the **Razeware \ Scripts** folder and add a new C# script in there. Name it **ApplyHeadsetToFollow**, open it in a code editor and remove the `Start` method.

Add the following line below the other `using` directives:

```
using VRTK;
```

To get a reference to the headset, you'll need to use some of VRTK's methods.

Add the following attribute right above the class declaration:

```
[RequireComponent(typeof(FollowGameObject))]
```

This script is useless without the **FollowGameObject** attached to the same GameObject, so it's best to enforce it using the attribute above.

Add this variable below the class declaration:

```
private FollowGameObject followGameObject;
```

This variable is used to cache the `FollowGameObject` component.

Add the following method below the variable you just added

```
void Awake()
{
    followGameObject = GetComponent<FollowGameObject>();
}
```

This caches the `FollowGameObject` component.

Finally, add the following inside of the `Update` method:

```
if (VRTK_DeviceFinder.HeadsetTransform() != null &&
followGameObject.TransformToFollow == null) // 1
{
    followGameObject.TransformToFollow =
VRTK_DeviceFinder.HeadsetTransform(); // 2
    followGameObject.enabled = true; // 3
}
```

This part waits until there's a headset available and then assigns it to `FollowGameObject` component:

1. Only execute the next code if there's a headset available and it wasn't assigned to the `FollowGameObject` component yet.
2. Set the object to follow on the `FollowGameObject` component to the transform of the player's headset.
3. Enable the `FollowGameObject` component.

Save this script and return to the editor.

Select **PlayerMapSprite** and add a **Apply Headset To Follow** component to it.

Now play the scene and teleport around a bit, take the headset off every once and a while, and you should see the icon has moved with you in the Game view.

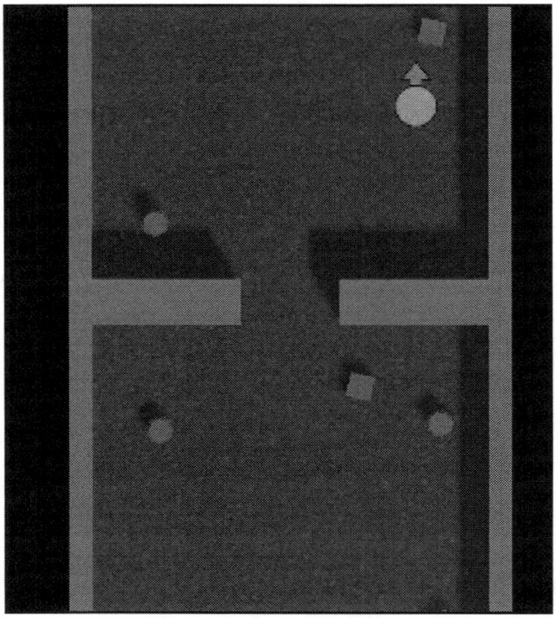

There's another problem now you may have noticed already — the camera isn't moving along with the player. Luckily you already have all needed components ready to be added.

Select **ScreenCamera** and add a **Follow Game Object** component to it. Change the Offset to **(X:0, Y:25, Z:0)**, uncheck **Follow Y** and disable the component.

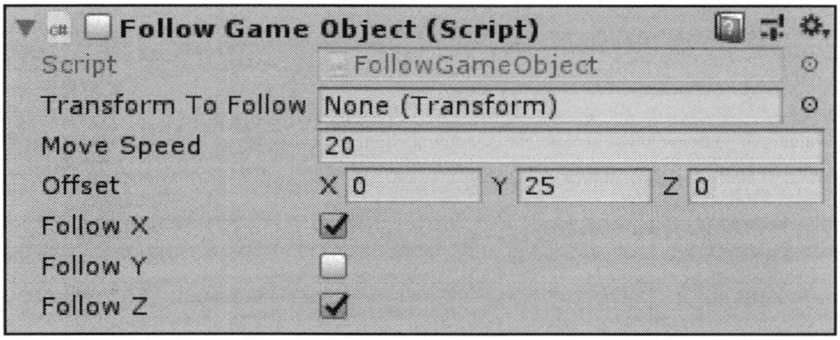

Next, add a **Apply Headset To Follow** component. This makes the camera follow the player's headset like the icon does.

Now play the scene again and teleport some distance forwards. The camera will now follow the player around, so the level can be made as big as you want.

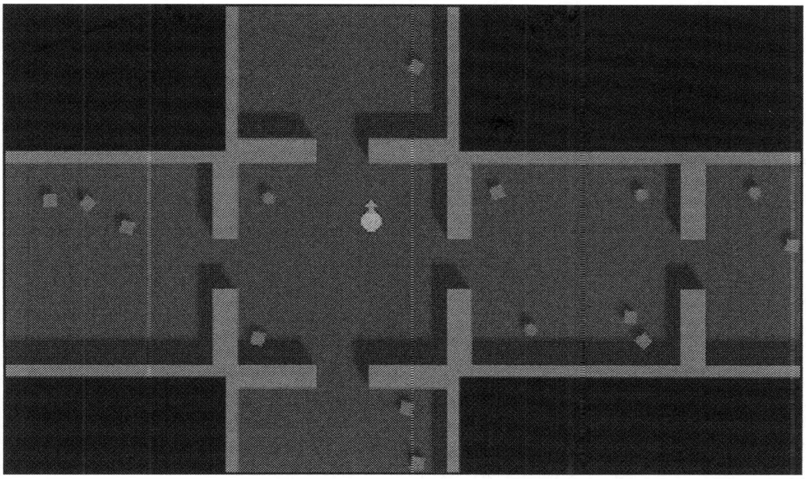

All that's left is to make the icon rotate. Scripting time!

Create a new C# script named **SyncWithHeadsetYRotation** in the **Razeware \ Scripts \ Chapter 10** folder. Open in it in your favorite IDE and remove the `Start()` method.

Add the following using directive below the others:

```
using VRTK;
```

You'll need this to be able to call some VRTK methods.

Next, add the following variable just below the class declaration:

```
private Transform headsetTransform;
```

This variable holds a reference to the player's headset.

Now, add this block of code to the `Update` method:

```
if (!headsetTransform &&
VRTK_DeviceFinder.HeadsetTransform()) // 1
{
    headsetTransform = VRTK_DeviceFinder.HeadsetTransform();
}

if (headsetTransform) // 2
{
    Vector3 rotation = transform.rotation.eulerAngles;
    rotation.y = headsetTransform.rotation.eulerAngles.y;
    transform.rotation = Quaternion.Euler(rotation);
}
```

Here's what this does:

1. If the headset's transform isn't cached yet, and a headset is available, cache the headset's transform.
2. If there's a reference to the headset cached, rotate its Y axis to the same rotation as the player's headset.

That concludes this simple script. Save it and return to the editor.

Now select the **PlayerMapSprite** and add the **Sync With Headset Y Rotation** component. Hit the play button and test out the new script by rotating the headset and looking at the Game view.

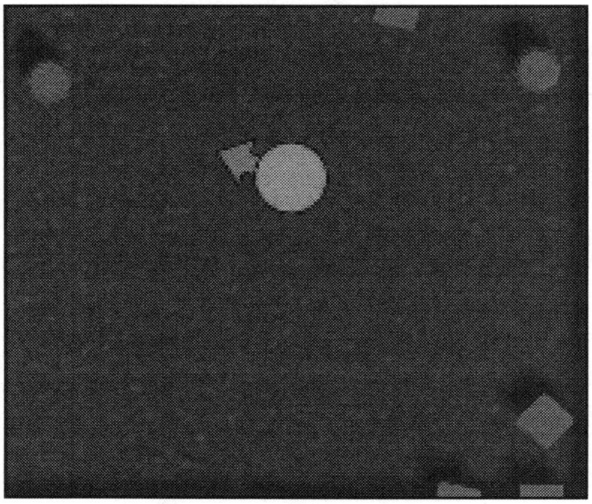

External view: keyboard and mouse input

Having a bird's view of the level is handy for the second player as they can play a supporting role for the VR player. Wouldn't it be nice to have more impact on the gameplay though?

You'll be adding a final script to let the second player place objects in the level like barrels and boxes.

Create a new C# script in the **Razeware \ Scripts \ Chapter 10** folder and name it **ExternalCameraInput**. Open it in an editor and remove the **Start** method.

Add the following variables below the class declaration:

```
// 1
public GameObject barrelPrefab;
public GameObject cratePrefab;
// 2
private Camera screenCam;
```

Here's what they're for:

1. References to the barrel and crate prefab that will be spawned.
2. A reference to the non-VR camera.

Add the following method below the variables:

```
void Awake()
{
    screenCam = GetComponent<Camera>();
}
```

This finds the **Camera** component that's attached to this GameObject and caches it into the `screenCam` variable for later use.

Next, add this helper method:

```
private bool MouseRayHitsGround(out RaycastHit hit) // 1
{
    Ray ray =
screenCam.ScreenPointToRay(Input.mousePosition); // 2
    if (Physics.Raycast(ray, out hit, 100)) // 3
    {
        return true;
    }

    return false; // 4
}
```

1. This method checks whether there's an object under the mouse pointer with a collider. It accepts a `RaycastHit` as a parameter, which gets filled in with the raycast result.
2. Create a new ray pointing toward the screen at the mouse's position.
3. Shoot the ray and collect its hit in the `hit` parameter. If anything was hit, return `true`.
4. Nothing was hit so return `false`.

Now, add this method to spawn new GameObjects:

```
private void CreateNewObject(Vector3 position, GameObject
prefab) // 1
{
    Vector3 objectPosition = position; // 2
    objectPosition.y += prefab.transform.position.y; // 3
    // 4
    Instantiate(prefab, objectPosition,
prefab.transform.rotation);
}
```

This is how it works:

1. Pass the `position` of the spawned prefab and the `prefab` itself as parameters.
2. Create a temporary variable named `objectPosition` and put the value of `position` in it.
3. Move the `objectPosition` up by the Y position of the prefab. This moves the object up a bit so its bottom will hit the top of the collider below it.
4. Spawn the prefab at the `objectPosition`, with the same rotation as the prefab.

Lastly, add this code block to the `Update()` method:

```
RaycastHit hit; // 1

// 2
if (Input.GetMouseButtonDown(0) && MouseRayHitsGround(out hit))
{
    CreateNewObject(hit.point, barrelPrefab);

}

// 3
if (Input.GetMouseButtonDown(1) && MouseRayHitsGround(out hit))
{
    CreateNewObject(hit.point, cratePrefab);
}
```

Here's what this does:

1. Create a `RaycastHit` to be used below.
2. If the **left mouse button** was clicked and the cursor is over a solid collider (preferably the ground) spawn a new **barrel**.
3. If the **right mouse button** was clicked and the cursor is over a solid collider (preferably the ground) spawn a new **crate**.

That's it, save the script and return to the editor.

Select **ScreenCamera** (child of **PlayerScreen**) and add a **External Camera Input** component to it. Drag the **Barrel** and **Crate** prefabs from the **Razeware \ Prefabs \ Props** folder to the corresponding **Prefab** slots.

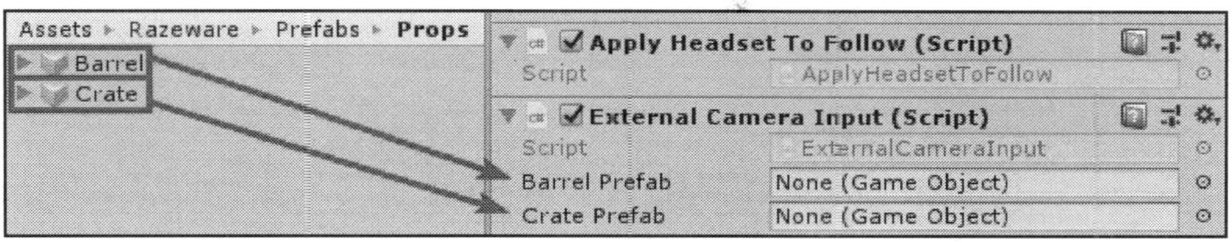

Now play the scene again and click around on the map with both left and right mouse clicks. You'll see a bunch of barrels and crates appear.

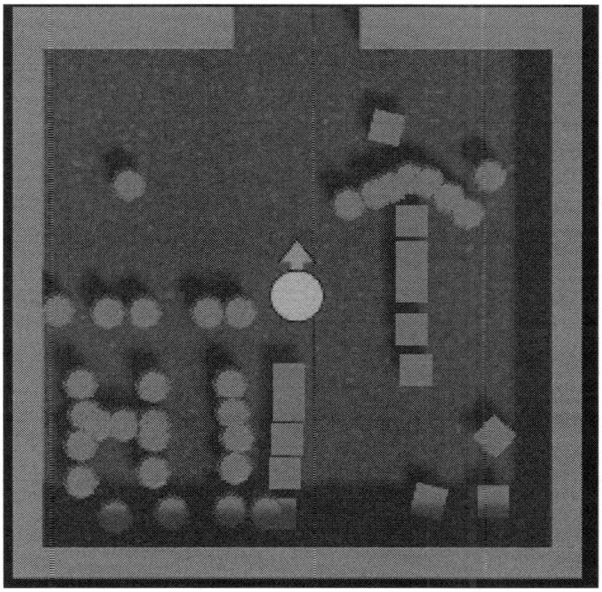

This was just a small example of how to add some interaction, but you can use the same systems to add enemies, build walls, or anything else you can dream up. If you add another camera with a first person controller attached to it, you can even make a full-on co-op game!

Where to go from here?

Congratulations on finishing this chapter. Check out the final project if there's anything you missed.

To summarize, in this chapter you learned how to:

- Create a curved UI.
- Add a controller menu.
- Create an overhead map.
- Let non-VR players interact with the game.

In the next chapter, you'll learn how to use VR in interactive media.

Chapter 11: VR in Interactive Media

Eric Van de Kerckhove

The world of VR is broad and diverse. Besides games, there are many experiences out there — 360-degree videos, architecture, medical use and education are just the tip of the iceberg. In this final VR chapter, you'll see that you can not only use Unity to make games with VR functionality but also to create interactive media.

In this chapter, you'll learn about: Displaying 360° videos; simulating scary situations in VR to overcome them; leveraging VR for virtual museums; using VR in architecture; and telling stories in VR.

Getting started

Open the starter project for this chapter in Unity and look at the Project window. A few new files were added to the Razeware folder.

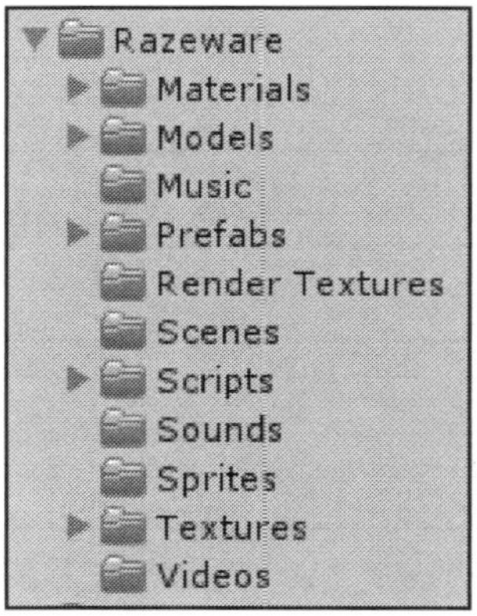

- **Scenes**: The starter scenes for this chapter.
- **Sounds**: An ambient wind sound.
- **Videos**: Contains a 360-degree video.

Open the **Interactive Media A** scene from the **Razeware\Scenes** folder and look at the Hierarchy.

The scene contains a single directional light and a minimal VRTK setup. The controllers don't have any extra functionality. You'll be adding a 360-degree video to this next, and you'll be amazed at how easy it is.

Displaying 360 video

A 360-degree video is an immersive, 3D video that's projected onto a sphere. They're usually recorded using a single omnidirectional camera or a group of cameras. They rose in popularity the last couple of years; you can even watch 360-degree videos on websites like YouTube using a regular flat-display like a monitor or a smartphone.

In the case of this project, the player is placed inside the sphere on which the video is projected. Since all Unity scenes come with a skybox by default (which is just a large sphere basically), you'll be using that since it's efficient and easy to set up.

To start, look at the video you'll be using in the **Razeware\Videos** folder. It's called **360_BavarianAlps**. Open it in a video player, and you'll see something like this:

The reason why the video looks a bit weird is that it's not flatly projected like regular videos, it uses **equirectangular** projection. This is the same kind of projection that modern world maps use.

Time to get it working in Unity!

Add a new **Video Player** to the Hierarchy, and then add an **Audio Source** component to it. Drag the **360_BavarianAlps** video from the **Razeware\Videos** folder onto the **Video Player**'s **Video Clip** slot.

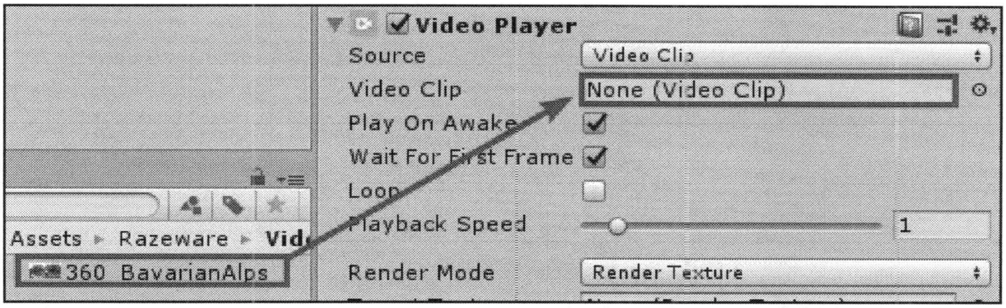

Next, drag the **Audio Source** component onto the **Video Player** component's **Audio Source** slot; this redirects the sound of the video to the Audio Source.

This GameObject does most of the hard work — it'll load and play the video with sound.Playing the scene right away won't do anything yet, you need to add a few more parts.

Create a new **Render Texture** in the **Razeware\Render Textures** folder, and name it **360 Render Texture**. The most important property to change is the **Size**, which needs to be the same width and height as the source video. In this case, the video's dimensions are **4096×2048** as you can see by selecting it and looking at the Inspector:

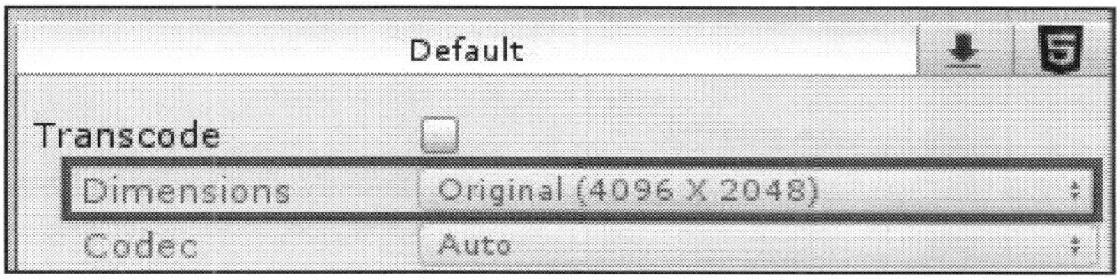

Select the render texture again and set its Size to **4096×2048**. Change the **Depth Buffer** to **No depth buffer**, you don't need to use any depth data and disabling it halves the amount of memory the render texture will need (from 64 MB to 32 MB).Select the **Video Player** again and drag **360 Render Texture** onto its **Target Texture** slot. This makes the video player render the video to the render texture.

The render texture needs a way to be displayed on the skybox, for this you'll need to create a new material. Create a new material in the **Razeware\Materials** folder, and name it **360 Skybox Material**.

Change its **Shader** to **Skybox/Panoramic**, and drag the **360 Render Texture** from the **Razeware\Render Textures** folder onto the **Spherical (HDR)** slot.

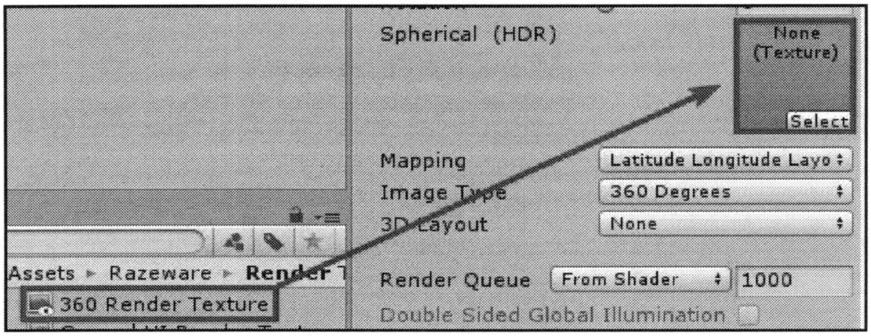

The final step is to assign the new skybox material. Open the **Lightning Settings** window (**Window ▸ Lightning ▸ Settings**) and drag the **360 Skybox Material** from the **Razeware\Materials** folder onto the **Skybox Material** slot. Finally, close the lightning window.

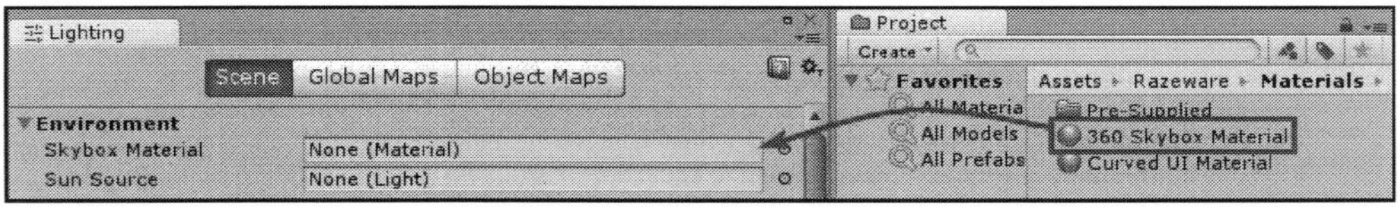

With everything set up, play the scene. Put on your headset, and take a good look around.

Breathe in that fresh air. Doesn't the water vapor feel cool on your skin? Well, not really, but it's still a pretty relaxing scene!

You can use videos like these in your own games and experiences. For example, a common technique for mobile VR is pre-rendering a beautifully detailed environment into a 360-degree video and using that as the skybox as you did here.

Another use is giving you the general feel of a real-world place — you could be sitting at a bar in Ireland, standing on top of Mount Fuji or looking at the salt flats of Bolivia, all in a matter of minutes. This particular use has gained popularity with vacation agencies.

No matter how you use 360-degree videos, they're a valuable tool for sure.

Next up is a height simulator. I hope you're not afraid of heights!

Height simulator

Everyone is afraid of something. Some people are afraid of spiders, while others are afraid of small spaces or germs.

Most phobias are challenging to conquer. To do so usually involves a confrontation with the thing that scares you. One way of helping with this process is by using VR. Studies show that exposure to the things that scare people in a virtual environment can help a lot in their treatment.

There are already quite a few therapy-related VR applications floating around on the internet. There are apps for overcoming the fear of heights, public speaking, spiders, live burials, snakes and ocean creatures.

If you have one of these phobias and try one of these apps, don't push yourself. You have to take it slow to reap the benefits.

Now that you have some context, it's time to show how you can make a simple big height simulator in Unity.

To start off, open the **Chapter 11 - Interactive Media B** scene, and look around.

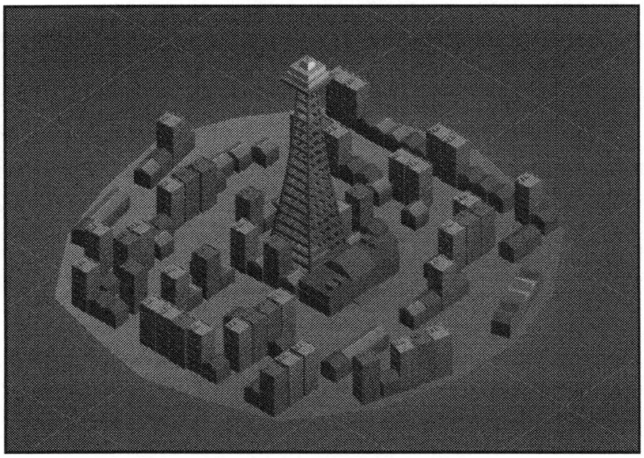

The scene is made to simulate a small island city with a massive tower in the middle. The player is placed near the top of the tower, looking down on the city.

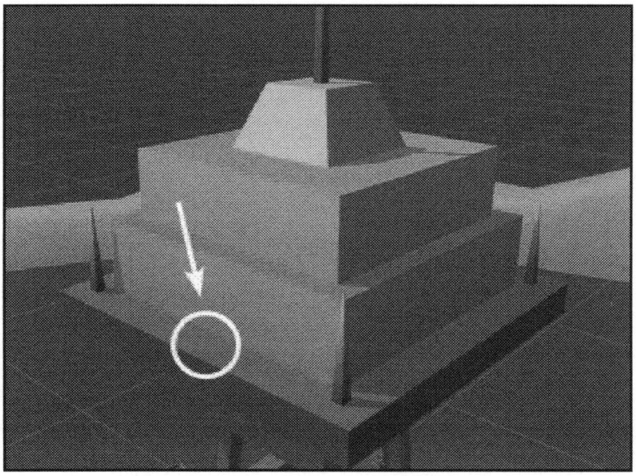

To give a sense of scale, the player starts on the ground level and then teleports to the top. A simple VRTK setup is provided and positioned at the bottom of the tower.

To get the player to the top, you'll need some familiar friends: **Destination Points**! Drag a copy of the **DestinationPoint** prefab from the **VRTK\Prefabs** folder to the Hierarchy and set its **Position** to **(X:0, Y:0.32, Z:-3)**.

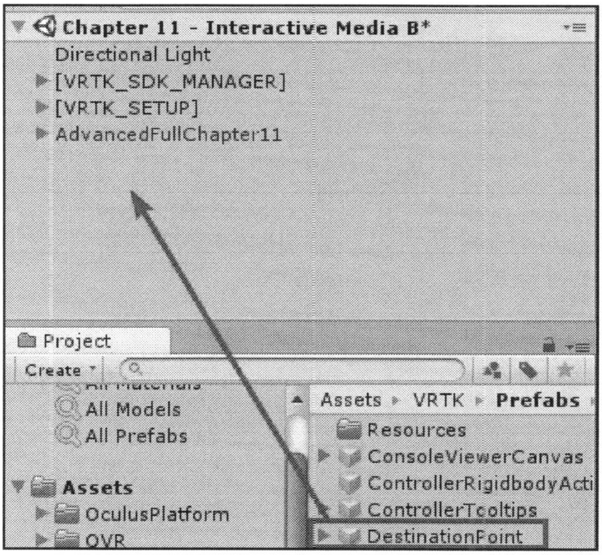

The teleport "pill" is now added to the ground level.

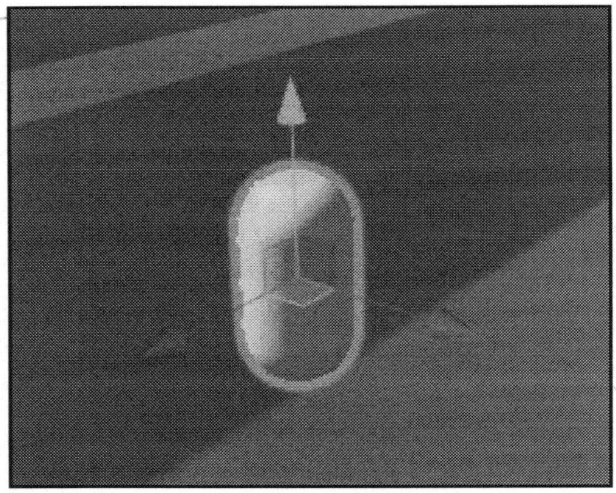

To get the player to the tower, you'll need a new GameObject to mark the location to teleport to. Create a new GameObject, name it **High Point**, and change its **Position** to **(X:10.5, Y:144, Z:-2)**.

Select **DestinationPoint**, and drag **High Point** onto its **Destination Location** slot.

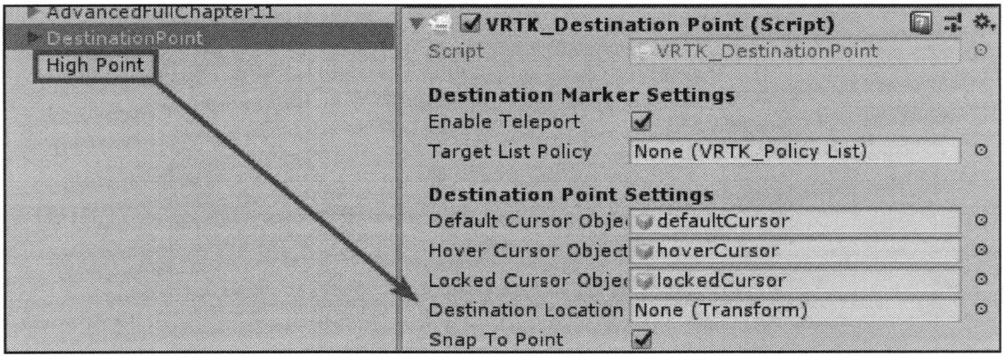

This creates a one-way connection to the position on top of the tower. No escape!

To create a truly immersive experience, there needs to be some noise when the player arrives at the top of the tower. An audio loop for that has been provided for you to use.

Create a new Audio Source, name it **AmbientWind**, and change its **Position** to **(X:0, Y: 144, Z:0)**. Now drag the **AmbientWind** sound from the **Razeware\Sounds** folder onto the **AudioClip** slot. Finally, check the **Loop** checkbox, so the sound keeps looping.

That's all you need! Run the game and try teleporting to the top of the tower. Step up to the border and carefully take a look down.

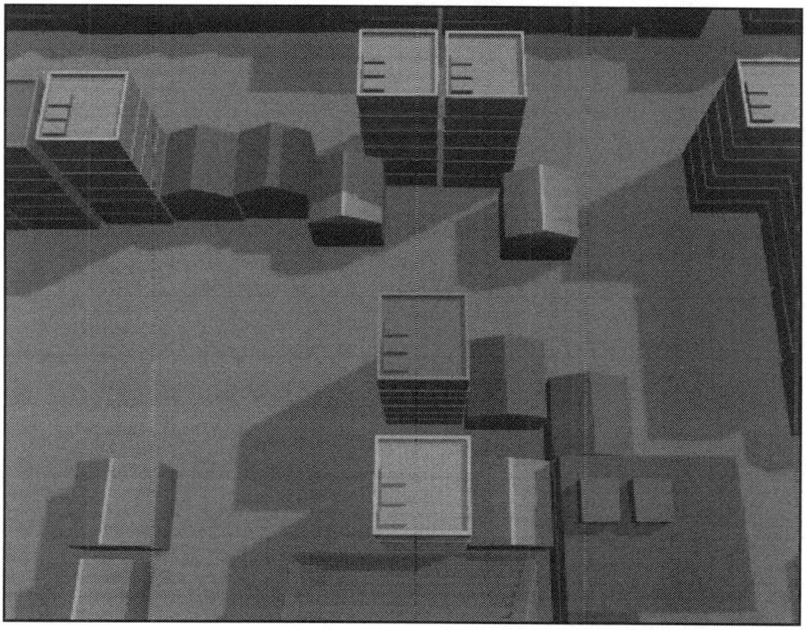

You can build upon the scene by adding more realistic models and adding weather effects to enhance the overall feel. In the next sections, you'll see some examples of how you can use VR to create powerful experiences.

VR museum

There are museums out there for just about anything, from history to fashion and electronics. Whatever you're interested in, they can serve as a source of inspiration on top of playing games, reading books and taking walks.

A regular museum has limitations. You need to go there physically, and some things just can't be explained with objects, images and videos alone. That's where VR comes in!

Virtual museum

The first way of translating a museum into a VR experience is to create the museum itself (or a part of it) in a 3D modeling package, like Blender or Maya, and import that into Unity.

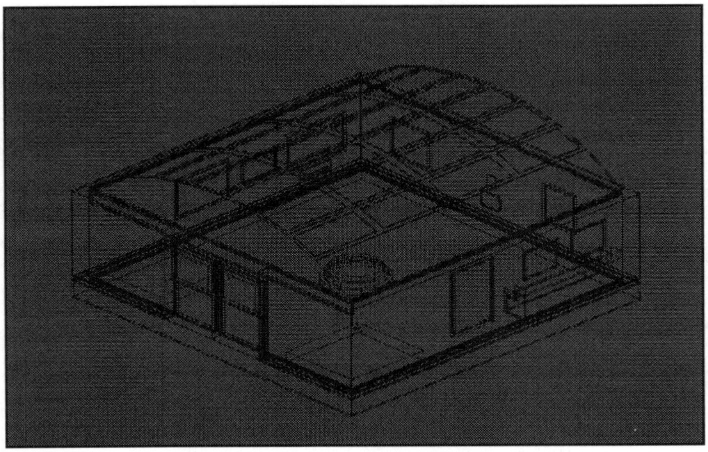

Using this, you can add things like paintings, statues, images and videos to the virtual museum. Now your visitors won't have to travel to appreciate the beauty.

You can also add non-realistic objects and materials to add to the experience. For example, let's say your museum has an exhibition about a certain young wizard — you can add talking paintings and stairs that magically rotate.

Another good use of the model might be to show off your ideas to potential investors. It's easy to add new objects and move, rotate and scale them any way you want in the available space; this makes generating previews for people a relatively straightforward process.

Places and events

Another method of transferring the thought behind museums to virtual reality is by recreating locations and events in a virtual space. For example, imagine getting transported onto the Titanic or inside the courtyard of a medieval castle. You can convey history exceptionally well with VR by placing yourself among the people of the past, like Einstein or Tesla. The educational value of this is enormous — you can get an actual feel of a place if done well, and it's much more immersive than reading a textbook.

Architecture

In the past, architects had to rely on blueprints and 3D renders. Those are hopelessly static though; customers have no clue how it will look in real life. VR is changing the way architects design buildings. Never before was it this easy to preview designs with a real sense of scale, depth and spatial awareness.

Creating everything in a virtual space also allows for easy modifications. If a room is too large, move the walls! How would a window look in that corner? Time to find out. :]

Enscape, for example, is a real-time visualization tool that works together with Revit, the architectural suite by AutoDesk.

It lets you walk through the designs created in Revit while wearing an HMD. It supports the Oculus Rift, the HTC Vive and Windows Mixed Reality.

Clients and designers can also explore designs together using **Prospect** by Iris VR. Up to 12 people can join up and make decisions together.

The new generation of architects will make extensive use of VR to create the perfect match between designer and client.

Storytelling

Since the humble beginnings of VR, it's been used for telling stories. The *View-Master*, for example, showed stereoscopic images that could tell small stories purely through these simple visuals. A more modern example of the same concept is a short story named *Pearl*. *Pearl* is a 360-degree video that tells the story of a girl and her father chasing their dreams. If you have five minutes, check it out.

Some even more recent examples:

- **Allumette**: A free stop-motion VR movie about a young girl that lives in a village on top of the clouds.
- **Colosse**: A polished story with a unique art style and excellent sound design.
- **A Chair in a Room**: A game with a very creepy atmosphere.
- **The Gallery**: An adventure game with an intriguing story that combines classic point-n-click mechanics with full 3D exploration.

There are many ways to tell stories. Some of the best games combine great gameplay with an interesting story. Games like Skyrim VR, Rick and Morty: Virtual Rick-ality and Resident Evil 7 all provide immersive worlds and their own stories. If you're aiming for immersion, you might want to include objects the player can pick up or add a few small easter eggs. With VR, these things are possible.

Where to go from here?

In this chapter you learned about:

- Displaying 360° Videos.
- Simulating scary situations in VR to overcome them.
- Leveraging VR for virtual museums.
- Using VR in architecture.
- Telling stories in VR.

In the next chapter, you'll get introduced to Augmented Reality with Unity!

Section IV: Introduction to AR

Get up to speed with the current AR technology in this section. Learn about the history of AR from its humble beginnings up to the current day and compare the available hardware so you can make a concise decision on what to use for your next project.

This sections includes:

- **Chapter 12: Augmented Reality**: Explore the history of augmented reality, and learn about the fundamental technology behind it. Find out what makes AR different from VR, and learn about some examples of AR being used currently in this enlightening chapter.
- **Chapter 13: Augmented Reality Platforms**: This chapter delves into the various AR platforms that are commonly being used at this time: ARKit, ARCore, Hololens, and Magic Leap. If you're wondering what AR hardware to get, this chapter will get you up to speed on the current options and summarizes the pros and cons for each.

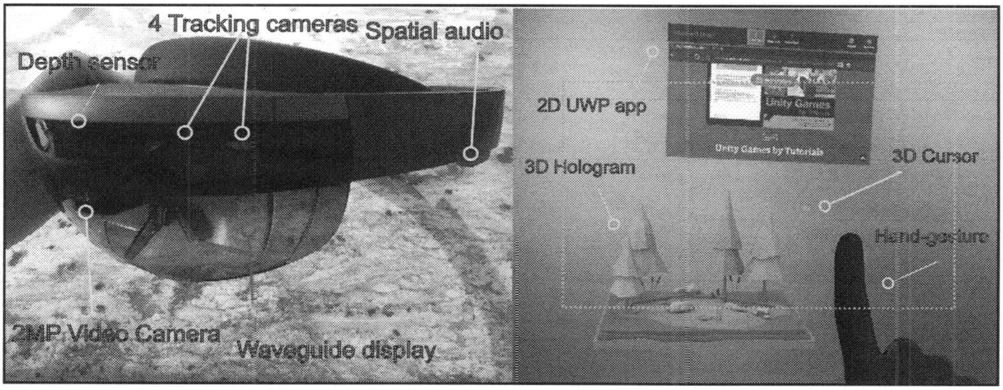

Chapter 12: Augmented Reality

Jimmy Alamparambil

There's been much excitement recently around the subject of **Augmented Reality** (AR), and it's likely that you're familiar with some aspects of the technology — especially since you're reading this book. However, before creating your own AR experiences, it's a good idea to understand what augmented reality is and from where it originated.

What is augmented reality?

Augmented reality is the enhancement of the real-world environment using virtual objects and information. With AR, you can alter the physical environment with visual, auditory, haptic, touch, olfactory and other sensory additions. Most people are familiar with the visual enhancements, like placing virtual objects on a real table or watching an animated character walk across your desk.

Most people understand the concept of AR because of popular culture. For example, Hollywood blockbuster movies like *Star Wars*, *Minority Report* and *Iron Man* all featured AR technology. But it's not just in the movies; TV programs, books, and other media use AR as an essential driver of the story's narrative.

But where did it all start?

History of augmented reality

Believe it or not, augmented reality has been around since the 1970s. In fact, it was in 1968 that **Ivan Sutherland** and **Bob Sproull** created what many consider to be the first augmented reality display. Their device — known as the *Sword of Damocles* because of the sizeable ceiling-mounted equipment connected to the computer providing the optics — was a primitive **head mounted display** (HMD), yet it was capable of displaying a virtual wireframe cube in which the user could move around to view the different sides of the cube.

From that initial spark, various projects explored the possibilities of AR. Unfortunately, progress was slow, and the computing power of the time was limited. However, in the 1990s, better hardware and software brought about significant improvements to AR. Research facilities in academia, government and enterprise fields paved the way.

Here are just a few notable milestones from that decade:

- **1992**: Caudell and Mizell worked on an AR HMD to guide the assembly of wire bundles in Boeing's airplane factories. The first appearance of the term **augmented reality** appeared in their work.
- **1994**: State et al. at UNC Chapel Hill showed a medical AR application that could observe a virtual representation of a fetus within a living pregnant patient.
- **1996**: Schmalstieg et al. developed a collaborative AR system that allowed multiple users with HMDs to experience virtual objects in a shared space.
- **1998**: Thomas et al. published work on the creation of an outdoor AR navigation system. This system was used for 3D surveying and most famously for the first outdoor AR game, *ARQuake*.
- **1998**: Sportvision used their AR system to display a virtual yellow first down marker during a live NFL game broadcast.

The 1990s were great for AR, but mainly in specialized research labs. But this changed in 1999 when Kato and Billinghurst released **ARToolkit**, the first open source AR software platform. ARToolkit allowed AR to flourish outside of the labs.The thing that set ARToolkit apart from the competition besides its availability was that it implemented a method that allowed to detect and track "fiducial" markers, which were images consisting of unique patterns contained inside a squared frame.

Not long after that, experimenters played around with AR on their desktops using their webcams.

In the new millennium, cell phones and mobile computing evolved rapidly and allowed the AR software to run on mobile chipsets. It also allowed more portable experiences. Within three years, AR systems were running autonomously on PDAs as the first handheld AR system.

Evolution of this technology made AR available to consumers on smartphones. After that, things moved quickly.

- **2005**: Thousands of attendees at SIGGRAPH got to experience *The Invisible Train*, a multiplayer handheld AR game
- **2008**: An ad for BMW Mini could be held against a webcam on their website to see a virtual Mini appear on the ad.
- **2009**: ARToolkit for Flash was released, allowing web developers to get in on the AR craze.
- **2012**: Google Glass was introduced. But it didn't fare well with consumers (remember the stigma of Glassholes?). It's still used in enterprise applications, however.
- **2013**: Magic Leap received the most considerable AR investment ($55 million) to date. Magic Leap has gone on to secure multiple rounds, totaling close to $2 billion.
- **2015**: Hololens was released, but it was too expensive for consumers. It is, however, widely used in enterprise applications.
- **2016**: Pokemon Go was released and became popular with a peak daily active users (DAU) of 45 million. This was *the major title* that made consumers aware of AR (although the AR mode in the game is optional and gives no advantage in gameplay).
- **2017**: ARKit and ARCore were announced; ARKit 1.0 was released, allowing stable consumer-level AR on a massive scale for the first time.
- **2018**: ARCore 1.0 was released; ARKit 1.5 and ARKit 2 were released.

Fundamental technology behind AR

ARKit on iOS and ARCore on Android are two of the most popular AR platforms available. Both are referred to as **mobile markerless AR**. Mobile markerless AR works by using various technologies to help "understand" the real world so you can enhance it with virtual objects.

Many of the technologies used for mobile markerless AR came from other fields that needed to understand the real environment better, for example, robotics. Most mobile devices have a camera and an IMU (Inertial Measurement Unit), which are the two hardware components needed to achieve this.

Camera images are run through some computer vision algorithms to get a sense of how fast pixels are moving around with the movement of the camera lenses.

This is achieved by the fact that the camera intrinsics (i.e., the camera's physical characteristics) are well-known by the computer vision algorithms, and it can determine how pixels will change based on its distance from the lens. The movement and orientation of the camera are detected by the IMU as well.

Each of these methods by itself is error-prone, but when the IMU and camera are both calibrated well against each other, and there is an overarching algorithm that checks one against the other, the error is surprisingly minimal, and the results are impressively accurate and stable.

This method of combining data from different sensory sources so that the resulting information is more accurate is referred to as **sensor fusion**. Thus allowing you to keep track of the position and orientation of the device camera in the real world - this is called world tracking in AR parlance.

As part of **visual inertial odometry** (the algorithm described above for world tracking), **feature points** are detected in 3D space within the scene. These are determined from the moving points in the scene, so usually, this means there's a way of distinguishing them from the surrounding pixels.

For example, if you have a blank white wall, adjacent pixels on the wall all look the same, so it's hard for computer vision algorithms to detect any movement by looking at that wall, even if the camera is moving. However, if there's patterned wallpaper on the wall, the pixels adjacent to each other will be distinguishably moving. These **feature points** have a 3D position in the scene and are the building blocks of understanding the environment around you.

The most basic scene understanding that mobile AR has introduced is a way to determine where there are flat surfaces in the scene. This is called **plane detection** and estimates the presence of a plane by figuring out that there are many coplanar feature points within a particular area. Plane detection is important because flat surfaces are one place that you can attach or **anchor** virtual content so that they look grounded to the real scene.

This is the central technology behind modern mobile markerless AR. Each platform, of course, adds on its own interesting enhancements and utilities, which you'll discover later in the book.

The differences between VR and AR

In the previous chapters, you learned about VR and its various applications, along with some examples. It's time to look at some differences between VR and AR to help you understand both better.

Reality replacement

In VR, you *replace reality* in its entirety with a virtual one; in AR, you add *virtual enhancements* to specific parts of reality. Think of it as different points on the **reality-virtuality continuum**, as proposed by Milgram et al. (http://etclab.mie.utoronto.ca/publication/1994/Milgram_Takemura_SPIE1994.pdf).

Immersion

In one sense, you're fully immersed in a virtual world when you use VR, and since you use an HMD, you cannot perceive anything else. Whereas in mobile AR, you're usually looking at the virtual enhancements through a phone, and so the immersion might not be as noticeable since the enhancements only exist within a window of your perspective.

On the other hand, it looks like mobile AR is soon going to be implemented as AR glasses (e.g., see Magic Leap, https://www.polygon.com/2017/12/20/16800626/magic-leap-one-first-hardware-reveal) so everything you see could be enhanced virtually. Besides, since the virtual enhancements are couched in reality and appear anchored to your real surroundings, the immersion will be palpable.

VR sickness

Some people have a hard time spending any amount of time using VR HMDs. They end up with motion sickness symptoms. This tends to occur because there's a mismatch in sensory perception of self-motion as compared to the incongruent sensory inputs from the visual system, the vestibular system and other systems within the user's body.

This is one of the reasons why VR experiences have to maintain a high frame rate to reduce any lag between head motion and the rendering of the world according to the new position of the eyes.

Equipment availability

Most VR HMDs are expensive and need to be connected to expensive computers to run correctly. This means that there are not many people who can access VR experiences.

Mobile markerless AR, in comparison, came out of the gate able to run on a large number of existing mobile devices (currently around 500 million) and required no extra hardware to use. This made it available to a broader consumer audience and resulted in more awareness of the technology.

Equipment portability

Most VR hardware currently available needs to be connected to a computer or game console, so the amount of movement is limited to a single room. With mobile markerless AR, all devices are mobile, and the experiences can happen anywhere indoors or outdoors. This allows greater freedom of movement as well as differentiation in the types of content possible.

These are the main points of difference, although many of these may change over time and make these technologies closer together. Mobile standalone VR headsets like the Oculus Go and the Oculus Quest for example.

Examples of AR

Although AR seems like a gimmick, it's truly revolutionary and useful in many industries and applications. AR can help save lives or make business more efficient. Some applications emphasize user efficiency while others focus on the quality of the experience. There are also other applications of AR that embrace the "gimmickiness" of the technology.

In the following paragraphs are a few interesting examples that have been around. Many of these examples may not be using mobile markerless AR but can point the way to some exciting applications of the technology you're learning about.

Retail

In retail, AR has been around for a while to help sell all kinds of things to consumers.

- ***IKEA Place***: Lets you place furniture in your rooms to see whether they'll match the decor and fit where you want them. (https://itunes.apple.com/us/app/ikea-place/id1279244498?mt=8)

- ***Modiface***: Uses AR and face tracking to let you see what you'd look like with beauty products, helping you to purchase online with confidence. (http://modiface.com/)
- ***Lego AR Studio***: Mix virtual and physical Lego sets together to play and encourage the consumer to buy more Lego sets. (https://www.lego.com/en-us/aboutus/news-room/2017/december/lego-ar-studio)
- ***Various fitting room apps***: Virtually try on clothing and shoes before buying them. (https://apparelmag.com/using-virtual-and-augmented-reality-bridge-digital-divide)

Manufacturing

Manufacturing has a lot of processes and needs for human interaction with machine parts or other real objects. There are some exciting applications of AR in this field.

- ***DHL***: Is working with others to implement *vision picking* in warehousing operations to reduce error and increase productivity. (http://www.supplychain247.com/article/vision_picking_in_the_warehouse_augmented_reality_in_logistics)
- ***Boeing***: Uses AR on assembly lines to allow more accessible and more accurate production pipelines. (https://www.engineering.com/DesignSoftware/DesignSoftwareArticles/ArticleID/10069/Boeings-AR-Tablet-Tool-for-Assembly-Lines.aspx)
- ***Vital Enterprises***: Uses AR to provide an efficient method to maintain various machinery and equipment used in manufacturing and factory floors. (https://www.vital.enterprises/)

Construction

AR is used in construction to *overlay blueprints* over actual construction to identify planning problems before they affect the building. (https://www.autodesk.com/redshift/augmented-reality-in-construction/)

- ***Bentley***: Uses Hololens with its software and data from cities to render where subsurface utility pipes might be to avoid damaging them during excavation. (https://communities.bentley.com/other/old_site_member_blogs/bentley_employees/b/stephanecotes_blog/posts/using-the-hololens-for-accurate-subsurface-utility-pipes-augmented-reality)

Games

As far as consumers go, games are the most demonstrative of an AR experience. There are lots of games which have either a component that works in AR or a complete experience that's tuned to AR.

- ***Pokemon Go***: This game was a phenomenon when it was released — and it still is. Although the AR mode is not central to the game, whenever someone talks about AR gaming, this game is always mentioned. The interactions in the game, where you travel to real-world locations seem to cement the sense of it being couched in reality. (https://www.pokemongo.com/)
- ***Star Wars Jedi Challenge***: Uses a combination of a headset by Lenovo with a conventional mobile markerless AR device to give a more immersive AR experience. There are three experiences built in to enjoy this hardware combination. (https://www3.lenovo.com/us/en/jedichallenges/)
- ***ARise***: An app that leverages on the fact that you can move around the environment to see different perspectives to create puzzles based on perspective. (https://itunes.apple.com/us/app/arise/id1281550152?mt=8)

Medical

- ***Accuvein***: Uses AR to show doctors and nurses where the veins are in your body to avoid what is usually a 40% miss rate when trying to draw blood. (http://www.accuvein.com/2015/11/accuvein-cited-as-a-premier-augmented-reality-application/)
- ***CAMDASS***: Has an AR system that can provide 3D guidance in diagnosing problems and performing surgery. (https://scitechdaily.com/researchers-at-esa-develop-augmented-reality-headset-for-medical-diagnosis/)

Training

AR used in training can help remote workers to get knowledge that exists in a knowledge base or with an expert in the area. We can also make this training available just when needed by using *see-what-i-see* (SWIS) capabilities.

- ***Aero Glass***: Provides AR aerial navigation training by overlaying flight path information on to pilots HMD. (https://glass.aero/)
- ***Jigspace***: Uses interactions in true 3D to teach you about almost anything you want to learn about. AR allows you to move around your subject matter to give you a better understanding of the lessons. (https://jig.space/)

Automotive

As the automotive industry adopts many of the new technologies available like AI and machine learning for autonomous cars, they also use AR for various enhancements.

- ***BMW***: Has a car configurator that will let you choose interiors, exteriors and wheels and let you see the virtual car in your real garage. (https://itunes.apple.com/us/app/bmw-i-visualizer/id1319928768?mt=8)
- ***Jaguar Land Rover***: Allows you to test out their vehicles in AR by placing you in a virtual car in your real environment. (https://www.mobilemarketer.com/news/jaguar-land-rover-links-banner-ads-to-ar-test-drive/444199/)
- ***Porsche Tech Live Look***: Allows Porsche service centers to solve problems with your vehicle faster and get help from experts at other locations. (https://www.cnet.com/roadshow/news/porsche-tech-live-look-brings-ar-to-dealerships/)
- ***MARTA***: Does something similar for Volkswagen. (https://www.volkswagenag.com/en/group/research/virtual-technologies.html)
- ***Wayray***: Produces an AR navigation overlay that helps people drive better. (https://wayray.com/navion)

Education

- ***InsightHeart***: Teaches you everything you might want to know about the human heart in great detail, with the models appearing in your current environment so that you can examine them. (https://itunes.apple.com/us/app/insight-heart/id1280845473?mt=8)
- ***Sky Guide AR***: Overlays data about the heavenly bodies that you are looking at in the night sky. (https://itunes.apple.com/us/app/sky-guide-ar/id576588894?mt=8)
- ***My Very Hungry Caterpillar AR***: An interactive kid's storybook but allows kids to place the story on a surface and focus on the view of the story that they prefer. (https://itunes.apple.com/us/app/my-very-hungry-caterpillar-ar/id1277085142?mt=8

There are various other examples in the different industries enumerated above and in other industries as well. In fact, AR is going to be ubiquitous in our future.

Where to go from here?

That concludes this chapter. I hope you enjoyed learning about how augmented reality came to be as we know it today.

Now that you're up to speed with the history of AR, how it differs from VR and learned about some of the applications, you're ready to dive deeper into the hardware.In the next chapter, you'll discover the differences between the most prominent AR solutions available at the time of writing.

Chapter 13: Augmented Reality Platforms

Jimmy Alamparambil & Matt Larson

Augmented reality has been around for a while, and there are many platforms used to create AR experiences. In this chapter, you'll focus on some of the more popular ones currently available.

ARKit

In 2015, Apple acquired Metaio, an augmented reality startup and spinoff from another project created at Volkswagen. Metaio, which launched in 2003, released an SDK that worked with multiple platforms and allowed for markerless AR. Some speculated that Apple wanted to use the resources they acquired from Metaio to create their own AR platform.

At WWDC 2017, Apple announced ARKit, an augmented reality platform for iOS. The initial ARKit beta was included with the iOS 11 beta. Although an A9 chip or newer is required to run the high number of computations needed for world-tracking, Apple made sure that even phones bought two years earlier would display AR content. With this inclusion of its older devices, it was projected that the total number of devices capable of working with ARKit would be roughly 400 million by the end of 2017 — a staggering number not previously seen by AR developers. Not only this, but the AR demos at WWDC 2017 looked to be the most stable and accurate thus far. Plus, ARKit didn't require markers.

Unity was one of the first to release an ARKit plugin. This plugin lets developers access the functionality of the ARKit SDK while working within Unity. This integration made it easier for developers to experiment with AR, and videos soon started surfacing on social media showcasing their app ideas.

However, it wasn't until September 2017 that ARKit 1.0 was officially released with iOS 11. Almost immediately, developers published their ARKit apps on the App Store, and many were rewarded as early adopters of the technology.

The primary features of ARKit 1.0 include:

- **World-tracking**: Receive updated position and orientation data as the device (iPhone or iPad) moves around within the real-world environment.
- **Feature points** : A list of points in 3D that show the important, detected points within a view.
- **Plane detection**: The ability to detect horizontal flat surfaces and update its understanding of these flat surfaces as it gathers more information.
- **Camera feed**: The camera feed is passed through so that you can see the real-world on which you're going to add virtual content.
- **Light estimation**: Provides an approximation of the lighting in an environment by estimating intensity from the camera feed.
- **Hit test**: Find how far out from a point on the screen the closest plane or feature point is.
- **Tracking quality**: A measurement of how well the world-tracking and other features are working. The tracking quality is affected by things like low light, lack of discernible features and excessive motion.

In January 2018, Apple announced their plans to update ARKit 1.0. A few months later in the Spring of 2018, ARKit 1.5 was released and included the following *additional* features:

- **Image detection**: Recognize the location and orientation of a preset fiducial marker. Developers could then use this marker as the origin for an AR experience.
- **Vertical planes**: Detect vertical surfaces, making it easier to add virtual doors and windows to the walls.
- **Detailed mesh for planes**: Instead of the previous rectangular definition of planes, this feature gives you more detailed shapes when describing the detected surfaces.
- **Other additive features**: Re-localization, autofocus, video formats and additional hit test result types.

These features weren't haphazardly added, though. Apple identified them as the minimal set of features required to stir interest in the mainstream AR development community. As it turns out, AR developers were quick to adopt this SDK and started creating experiences that showcased their talents; and since ARKit is *just another Apple API*, iOS developers picked it up fairly quickly.

Perhaps the biggest push in making ARKit so popular is how well it performs and how straight forward it is to use. Because Apple controls both the hardware and software, there's built-in AR support at the hardware level, and developers don't need to worry about complex algorithms to get things to work. This makes the initial experience of world-tracking — although still sometimes unpredictable — stable, accurate and enjoyable.

Apple also used its marketing muscles to encourage non-developers to give ARKit-created content a try. They had big names demonstrate their ARKit apps at their developer and press events — names like Disney, Lego, IKEA and Porsche.

Of course, as with anything else, there's a downside: the older devices don't have specialized hardware, like depth cameras, and therefore it lacks the sophisticated algorithms needed for more advanced AR experiences. Despite this shortcoming, ARKit allows a whole mass of people to get a taste for AR.

ARCore

Google has been working with AR in their Advanced Technology And Projects (ATAP) group project, Project Tango. Project Tango uses a depth camera on an Android phone to help the computer vision algorithms determine the phone's position and orientation in the world. Because Tango requires a depth camera, it was limited to some of the most expensive Android phones. Fortunately, it wasn't long before Google realized they needed a cheaper alternative.

In 2017, Google announced ARCore and released a Developer Preview. Although the Developer Preview only supported three kinds of devices, Google promised additional device support for nearly one hundred million units sold by the time its release rolled around.

At this same time, Google provided the ARCore plugin for Unity. Like the Unity ARKit plugin, the ARCore plugin lets developers create ARCore apps from within the Unity Editor; and it wasn't long before videos began to surface on social media showing the power of ARCore.

Finally, on February 23, 2018, Google announced and released ARCore 1.0. As promised, this release worked with thirteen different devices that altogether accounted for one hundred million units sold. They also added more support and a better experience within the Play Store for users when they had to install ARCore.

The ARCore 1.0 feature set includes:

- **World-tracking**: Receive updated position and orientation data as the device moves around within the real-world environment.
- **Oriented feature points**: A list of points in 3D that show the important, detected points within a view; each point has an orientation in the world deciphered from its neighbors.
- **Plane detection**: The ability to detect horizontal flat surfaces and update its understanding of these flat surfaces as it gathers more information.
- **Camera feed**: The camera feed is passed through so that you can see the real-world on which you're going to add virtual content.
- **Light estimation**: Provides an approximation of the lighting in an environment by estimating intensity from the camera feed.
- **Hit test**: Find how far out from a point on the screen the closest plane or feature point is.

> **Note:** The features are similar to the ones in ARKit, and because the fundamental AR interactions are similar on the two major mobile platforms, it's possible to expose them under a common API. More about that later!

Google gave quite a marketing push to ARCore and showed some exciting applications of AR that could be pursued. They worked with recognizable brands — like Weta Digital and Disney Star Wars — to show the advantages of using ARCore. In the Google Play Store, they published an app named "AR Stickers" that lets you place 3D characters into your environment and take photos and videos with these characters.

When comparing Google's Project Tango to ARCore, two things stand out:

- ARCore targets the mainstream mobile audience making it easier for Google to get buy-in from developers who may want a broader consumer base for their products.
- Because ARCore doesn't include the depth data of the scene anymore, it's challenging to do world-tracking based on computer vision algorithms. As a result, stability and performance will suffer.

Nonetheless, ARCore apps are impressive and comparable to mobile AR apps on the other big platforms.

Microsoft HoloLens

In March 2016, Microsoft took a massive step into hardware development with the release of the HoloLens. This augmented reality headset contains an entirely independent Windows 10 computer and dual waveguide displays to render 3D objects realistically at distances of 1 meter or further from the user. As a natural descendant of the Microsoft Kinect platform, this device re-uses that sensor technology to provide real-time scans of the depth in the room. Although now more than two years old, the accurate depth tracking provides exceptional stability to the virtual content and exceeds other commercial augmented reality headsets and mobile-based augmented reality systems.

> **Note:** A consumer-level release of the HoloLens is still in the future; this hardware targets enterprise and industrial customers.

The Hololens headset has an adjustable band that secures to the user's head. This helps to keep the waveguide displays in-view at all times. Four microphones around the adjustable band provide accurate voice recording which provides another mechanism for user interaction. Speakers above each ear provide spatial audio, and a front-facing video camera can record video while an application is running — something that can be used in the application itself.

The processor on the HoloLens is an Intel Atom Central Processing Unit (CPU) accompanied by a Holographic Processing Unit (HPU) that handles the major processing of raw depth data from the forward-facing depth sensors.

The system is powered like that of modern mobile hardware, and the GPU is slightly less powerful than modern iPhone technology. It has 64 gigabytes of SSD space for applications and 2 GB of RAM that's divided between the CPU and HPU.

It contains a full-fledged Windows 10 operating system and can run most Windows Universal Platform (UWP) apps as 2D Window panes. Multiple 2D applications can be placed simultaneously in the room and visible at the same time.

However, fully immersive 3D applications require the full processing of the device and cannot be multitasked with 2D or other 3D applications.

The dominant development platform for the HoloLens is Unity, the first game engine to support the Microsoft HoloLens and the easiest way to start building apps for the device.

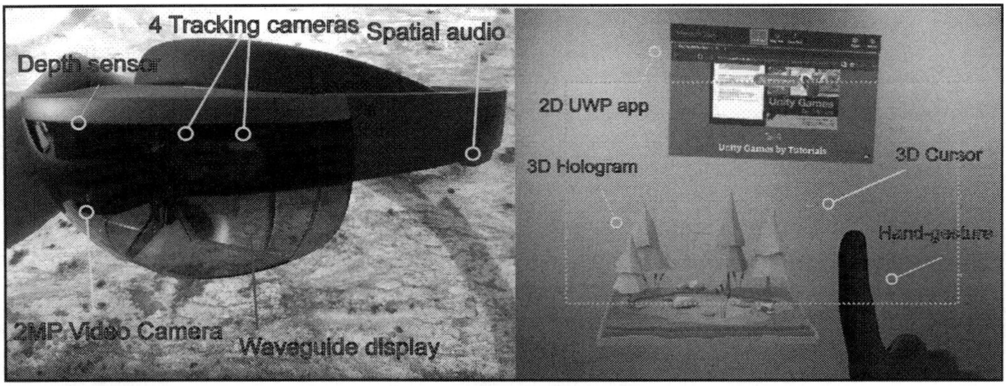

The significant characteristics of the HoloLens platform include:

- **Room mapping**: 3D mesh generation from the forward sensors allows the Holographic models to exist anywhere within the room including walls, tables, floors and furniture. The models can interact with real-world objects using anchors and Unity Physics.
- **Anchoring of objects**: The HoloLens has exceptionally stable object positioning that enhances the presence of 3D models in the room. This exceeds the current mobile-based AR systems for stability. The HoloLens also upscales the frames per second to 240 FPS (though divided between displaying four individual colors as separate frames) to enhance the stability of objects.
- **Standalone**: The device is entirely standalone and cordless. It features WiFi and Bluetooth connectivity allowing for network applications.
- **Hands-free**: Users can interact using hand-gestures such as the 'Air-tap' which behaves like a mouse-click, and a 'Bloom' gesture to exit a scene. Drag and scaling gestures are also available.
- **Limited Field-of-View**: Represented by the green box in the right-side image, a field-of-view where models are displayed is a smaller horizontal rectangular space than the total view-space. To provide an immersive experience, you need to use small Holograms or position Holograms farther away, such as on a wall.
- **A large platform with a Shared API**: HoloLens applications can also easily work as Windows Mixed Reality applications for the immersive VR headsets available from several other companies including Samsung, Acer, Asus, HP, and Dell.

The updated HoloLens 2 will be available in late June 2019 as announced at the Mobile World Conference 2019. The next version addresses the major limitation of the small Field-of-View by projecting lasers on the waveguide display to double the Field-of-View area while maintaining crisp 47 pixels per degree resolution.

The major enhancement may be 25-point hand tracking to create user interfaces where its possible to press a virtual button or even play a virtual piano with both hands. The HoloLens 2 will incorporate eye tracking, iris recognition technologies, and an ARM architecture.

Magic Leap and Lumin OS

After much anticipation, the first Magic Leap headsets started shipping on August 8, 2018, with hand-delivered units arriving at customer locations in a limited number of cities within the United States. This device includes a Lightwear headset with a permanently attached cable to a Lightpack that contains the processing hardware and battery. Like the HoloLens, it uses a waveguide display to create the illusions of 3D objects overlaid through transparent lenses on the real world. The developer SDK was released earlier in 2018 and includes a simulator Magic Leap Remote to allow testing applications without the device.

Lumin OS is a custom OS derived from Linux and Android. Lumin Runtime provides APIs for video, graphics and audio for multiple concurrent client applications. The Lumin SDK provides toolkits for interacting with the mixed reality capabilities of the Magic Leap and is integrated into both Unity and Unreal game engines.

A comparison between the Magic Leap One and the HoloLens platforms indicate that many competitive improvements are present in this device and will likely become a strong platform for augmented reality development.

- **Room mapping**: Like the HoloLens, it has fast room mapping and voxel-based mesh creation to make solid surfaces that game objects can collide or hit via raycasts.
- **Anchoring of objects**: The Magic Leap One can maintain objects firmly positioned in real-world locations.
- **Larger Field-of-View**: Developer specifications for the field-of-view measure the horizontal FoV at 40 degrees width and vertical FoV span of 30 degrees. This doubles the HoloLens 1 FoV height and is overall 45% larger. The displays have reduced clarity when using text in applications and reduced brightness compared with the HoloLens.

- **Eye-tracking**: Like the upcoming HoloLens 2, the Magic Leap One features eye-tracking for user interaction. This is featured in the OS where the tracking can change focus between multiple windows.
- **Gesture control for menus**: The Magic Leap One has hand-tracking, letting the developer write applications with near real-time interactions with fingers and hands such as tapping directly on a menu.
- **6-degree of freedom controller**: this controller is required to interact with the Lumin OS Shell. The controller offers greater precision than gesture-based interactions.

The Magic Leap developer kit costs a $2,295 and is hand delivered by an employee to introduce and adjust the headset to the customer. This device is largely aimed at entertainment and audio-visual markets.

Where to go from here?

In this chapter you learned about the most popular AR platforms that are currently available to create experiences on. You also learned about some of the features that each of the platforms provided.

In the following chapters, you will learn more about the mobile handheld AR platforms **ARKit** and **ARCore**. You will learn how to create AR experiences on these two platforms in a cross-platform way using Unity: arrange components and write code that will build your experience for both platforms in one shot.

Later on in the book, you will learn more about the **HoloLens** and how to build your AR experiences to take advantage of that platform's set of features.

But first you will look at setting up for development on AR devices that support either ARKit or ARCore.

Section V: ARKit & ARCore Basics

In this section you'll discover what ARKit and ARCore have to offer in the AR landscape. Learn about ARFoundation, a cross-platform framework that will simplify your life when creating apps for both platforms.

Get to grips with using ARFoundation to create virtual objects right in your living room. And learn how to create a dynamic user interface in AR and how to detect the physical space around you and use that in your games and experiences.

Specifically, you'll learn the following:

- **Chapter 14: Platform Setup**: Learn what the requirements are for ARKit and ARCore and how to set it all up. You will also be introduced to ARFoundation. In this chapter, you'll find out what you need exactly for a smooth start with AR.
- **Chapter 15: Adding Virtual Objects**: Create virtual objects and spawn them to augment a real space for your players to interact with. You'll learn all about placing objects and interacting with them in this chapter.

- **Chapter 16: User Interface & Interactions**: Discover how to display text and other UI elements in AR. In this chapter you'll be shown how to handle user interfaces elegantly in augmented reality.
- **Chapter 17: Anchors & Planes in AR**: Map out the world around you with planes and anchor game objects to them in realtime. This chapter covers world tracking and goes over the concept of planes in AR.

As you work through these chapters, you will learn by creating examples that use AR features to enhance your reality:

Chapter 14: Platform Setup

Jimmy Alamparambil

In this chapter, you'll use **ARKit** and **ARCore** to develop augmented reality apps for both iOS and Android. If you only have one type of device (an iPhone or an Android device), you can skip to the relevant section.

You'll also learn how to use the **AR Foundation** package which provides higher-level functionality and works with the low-level **XR Subsystems API**.

XR Subsystems

At GDC 2018, Unity revealed their multi-platform API for XR (AR and VR) with the announcement of the **XR Subsystems**. The XR Subsystems work with multiple AR SDKs — including ARKit and ARCore — and has been available since Unity 2018.1.

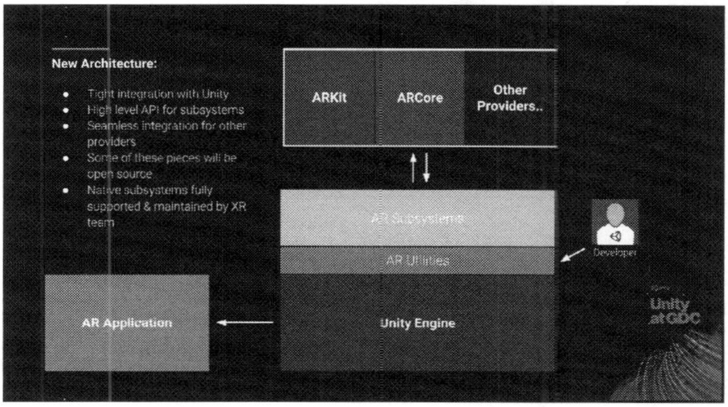

Using Unity's integrated AR plugins offers several advantages:

- When learning, you don't have to refer to the individual platform because common functionalities exist within both ARKit and ARCore.
- When creating apps, you can target a broader audience by creating a single app targeted for both platforms.
- You can abstract the AR specific development making it easier to include more platforms as they're released.

You can use the **Package Manager** which comes with Unity to download and update the subsystems for ARKit and ARCore.

Are you ready to augment some reality?

In the next two sections, you will get an opportunity to setup the two target platforms **ARKit** and **ARCore** for use with **AR Foundation**. You may select either one of the platforms to start with and you can skip the section for the other one since there are a lot of similarities. In case you have devices for both mobile AR platforms, you may come back to the section you skipped and set up the development environment for the other device when you reach the end of the chapter.

ARKit

With ARKit and Unity, you can develop AR apps for iOS devices. However, there are some requirements you'll need to meet before you can begin:

- **Apple Mac** (Macbook, iMac, Mac Pro or Mac Mini) development machine.
- **macOS 10.13 (High Sierra)** or above.
- **Unity Editor 2018.1** or later with iOS support.
- **Xcode 9.3** or later.
- **iOS device** that supports ARKit (iPhone 6S or later, iPad (2017) or later).
- **iOS 11.3** or later.

If you meet these requirements, you're ready to get started with ARKit and Unity.

Open the starter project for this chapter in the Unity Editor.

To use Unity as a creation platform for ARKit, and to access the native ARKit SDK via the XR Subsystems API, you need the **ARKit XR Plugin** package. This package is included in the starter project, but it's important to verify things are set up correctly within the project.

Go to the top menu and select **Window > Package Manager** to open.

You'll see a window like this:

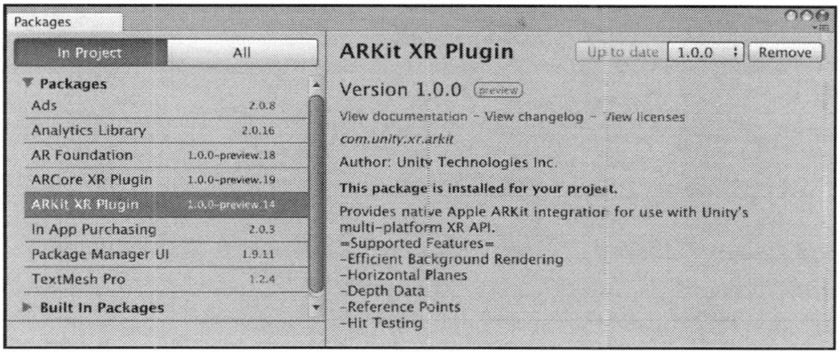

The **ARKit XR Plugin** package is included in the package list. You can update it to the latest version if a newer one exists.You'll also need to use the **AR Foundation** package for the higher-level functionality; this is also already included in the list of packages within this project.

If everything looks good, you're ready to add some content to the project. If you look at the project window, you'll see the following folders:

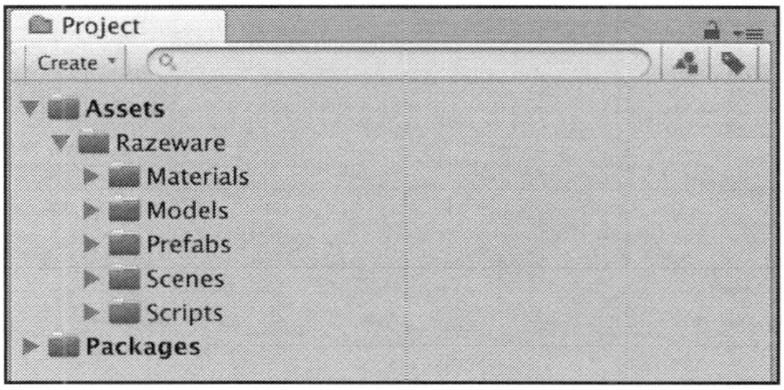

Create a new scene and save it in the **Assets \ Razeware \ Scenes** folder as **ARKitSetup**. Like any default scene, it has a **Directional Light**, a **Main Camera** and nothing else.

Now, make the following modifications to the **Main Camera**:

1. Select **Main Camera** and change its position to **(X:0, Y:0, Z:0)**. When you initialize ARKit, it automatically resets the world tracking position to **(X:0, Y:0, Z:0)**, and you want the camera in the scene to track the device in the real world.
2. In the **Camera** component of the **Main Camera**, modify the **Clear Flags** to use **Depth only** so the background is the live video feed from ARKit instead of the skybox or a screen clear.

3. Add a **Tracked Pose Driver** component to the **Main Camera**. The ARKit device automatically updates this component; it moves and rotates (or "poses") the **Main Camera** in the Unity scene the same way the device moves in the real world.

Set up the following on the **Tracked Pose Driver** component:

- Set **Device** to Generic XR Device.
- Change **Pose Source** to Color Camera.
- Set **Tracking Type** to Rotation and Position.
- Change **Update Type** to Update And Before Render.
- Check the box for **Use Relative Transform**.
- Leave **Use Pose Provider** empty.

4. Add a **ARCameraBackground** component to the **Main Camera**, and leave the checkboxes unchecked. The **ARKit XR Plugin** will select a material for you. This component renders the live feed from the device's camera to the background of this camera.

The **Main Camera** should now look like this in the Inspector:

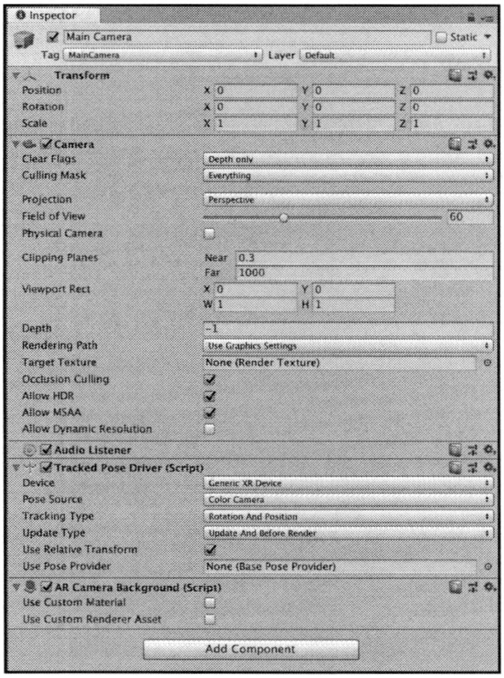

Note: The **ARCameraBackground** component is part of the **ARFoundation** package and is documented as part of that package.

Now, create an empty GameObject to the root of the Hierarchy and name it **AR Session**. Next, add a **ARSession** component to the newly created GameObject.Select **AR Session** , and in the **AR Session** component, leave the **Light Estimation** box unchecked and the **Attempt Update** box checked.

AR Session will now look like this in the Inspector:

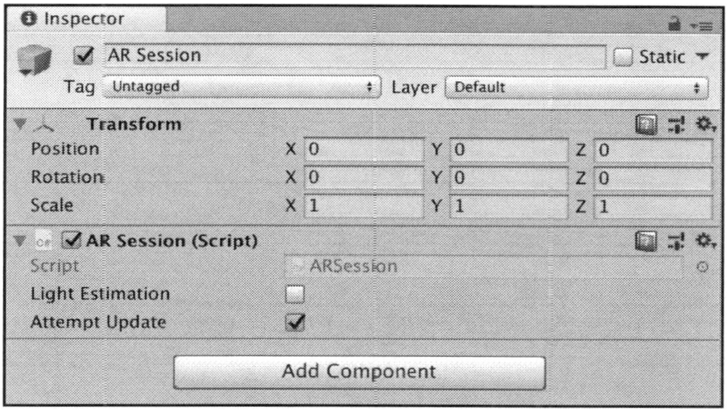

AR Session does the initialization of the AR Session for ARKit.

Note: The **AR Session** component is also part of the **ARFoundation** package.

If you run this scene on the device right now, it'll be working with world tracking enabled, but since you don't have any virtual objects in the scene, you won't be able to tell whether it's working or not. Time to fix that by adding a single virtual object to the scene.

Drag the **PlayerRobotPrefab** prefab from the **Assets \ Razeware \ Prefabs** folder into the root of the Hierarchy. Set the position to **(X:0, Y:0, Z:1)** so it'll appear 1 meter in front of the camera. The camera is facing forward (positive on the Z-axis) and is placed at the origin when the app starts.

This scene is now ready for testing.

Building to the device and testing the scene

From the Unity top menu, select **File > Build Settings...**. In the dialog box presented, select the **iOS** platform and click **Switch Platform**. This will take some time, so be patient.

The **Build Settings** dialog box will look like this after changing platforms:

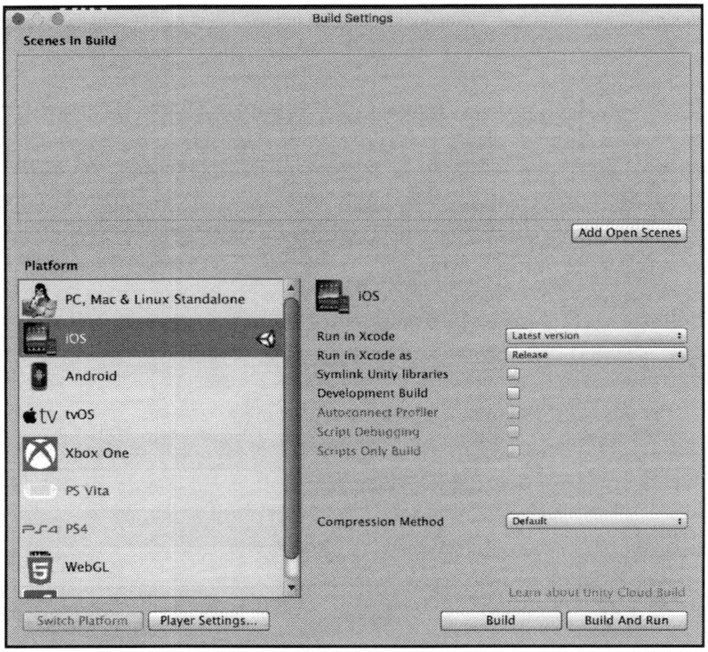

Click the **Add Open Scenes** button to add the current scene to the build.

From the same dialog box, select **Player Settings** and look at the contents of the Inspector. In the first section, change the **Product Name** to **My Awesome AR Game** for example. The name has no impact on the rest of the app so feel free to change it to whatever you like.

In the **Other Settings** section, make sure **Metal** is selected as the Graphics API. Also, make sure there's some text in the **Camera Usage Description** field otherwise ARKit will throw an exception error at build time. This field is required on iOS apps that use the camera to specify what the app is using the camera for.

Click **Build** on the **Build Settings** dialog to export an Xcode project. You'll be prompted for a folder in which to save the project.

Once exported, open the Xcode project in the latest version of Xcode, connect a supported iOS device, and select that device as the target for your app.

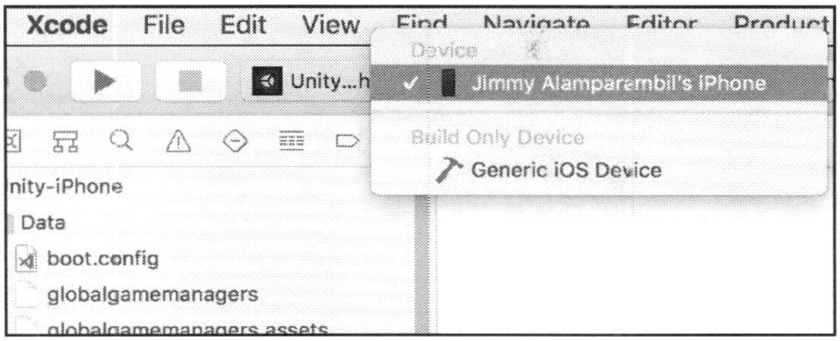

Before you can build to the device, you need to configure code-signing in Xcode. Check the **Automatically manage signing** box in the **Signing** section of the project settings and select your personal team from the list.

You're ready to build and run the app. Press the button that looks like a **Play** button on the top left side of the Xcode UI.

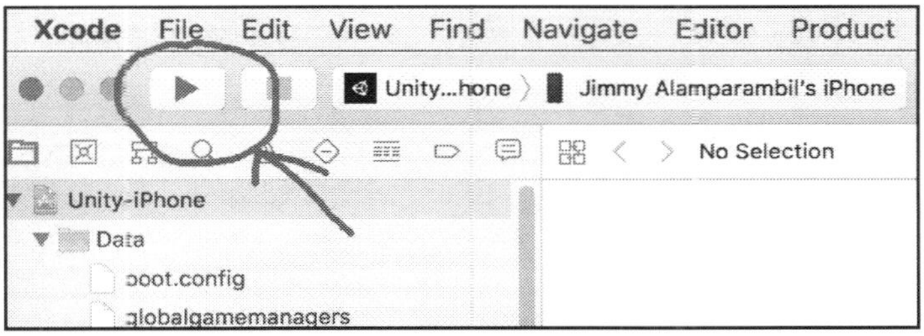

If all goes well, the scene runs in ARKit on the iOS device. Here's a screenshot of what it looks like on my phone:

Congratulations! You just created an ARKit app for iOS in Unity.

ARCore

ARCore lets you develop AR apps for the Android ecosystem. When combined with Unity, you can supercharge your AR development. However, there are some requirements you need to meet first:

- **Unity 2018.1** or later with Android support.
- **Android Studio 3.1** or later.
- **Android SDK version 7.0 (API Level 24)** or higher — usually installed by Android Studio.
- **Android device** that supports ARCore. See the growing list of supported devices at https://developers.google.com/ar/discover/#supported_devices

If you meet all of the requirements, you're ready to get started with ARCore.Open the starter project for this chapter in the Unity Editor.

To use Unity as a creation platform for ARCore, and to access the native ARCore SDK via the XR Subsystems API, you need the **ARCore XR Plugin** package. This package is included in the starter project; however, you need to verify it's set up correctly within the project.

Go to the top menu and select **Window > Package Manager**.A window that looks like this will pop up:

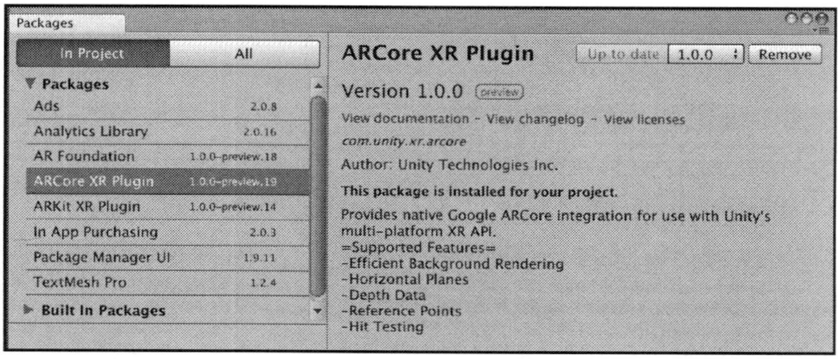

The **ARCore XR Plugin** package is included in the package list. You can update to the latest version of the **ARCore XR Plugin** if a newer one exists.You'll also need the **AR Foundation** package for the higher-level functionality; this is also already included in the list of packages within this project.

If everything looks good, it's time to add some content to the project. Look at the Project window, and you'll see the following folders:

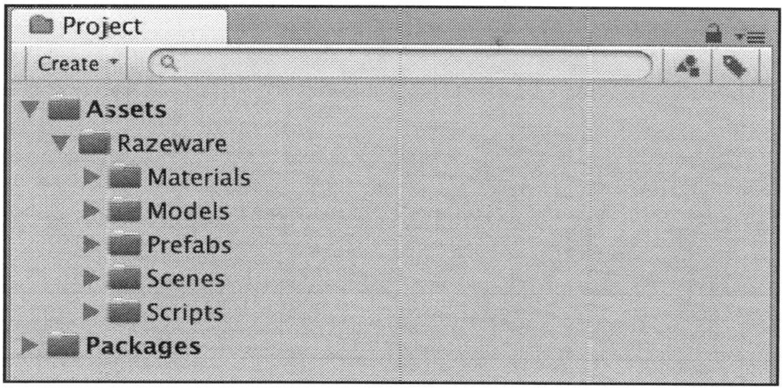

Create a new scene and save it in the **Assets \ Razeware \ Scenes** folder as **ARCoreSetup**. Like any default scene, it should have only a **Directional light** and a **Main Camera** in the scene and nothing else.

Now make the following modifications to the camera:

1. Select **Main Camera** and change its position to **(X:0, Y:0, Z:0)**. When you initialize ARCore, it automatically resets the world tracking position to **(X:0, Y:0, Z:0)**, and you want the camera in your scene to track the device in the real world.
2. In the **Camera** component of the **Main Camera**, modify the **Clear Flags** to use **Depth only**. This sets the background as the live video feed from ARCore instead of using the skybox or a screen clear.
3. Add a **Tracked Pose Driver** component to the **Main Camera**. The ARCore device automatically updates this component; it moves and rotates (or "poses") the **Main Camera** in the Unity scene the same way the device moves in the real world.

Change the following on the **Tracked Pose Driver** component:

- Change **Device** to Generic XR Device.
- Set **Pose Source** to Color Camera.
- Adjust **Tracking Type** to Rotation and Position.
- Change **Update Type** to Update And Before Render.
- Check the box for **Use Relative Transform**.
- Leave **Use Pose Provider** empty.

4. Add a **ARCameraBackground** component to the **Main Camera** and leave the checkboxes unchecked — the **ARKit XR Plugin** will select a material for you. This component renders the live feed from the device's camera to the background of this camera.

The **Main Camera** should look like this in the Inspector:

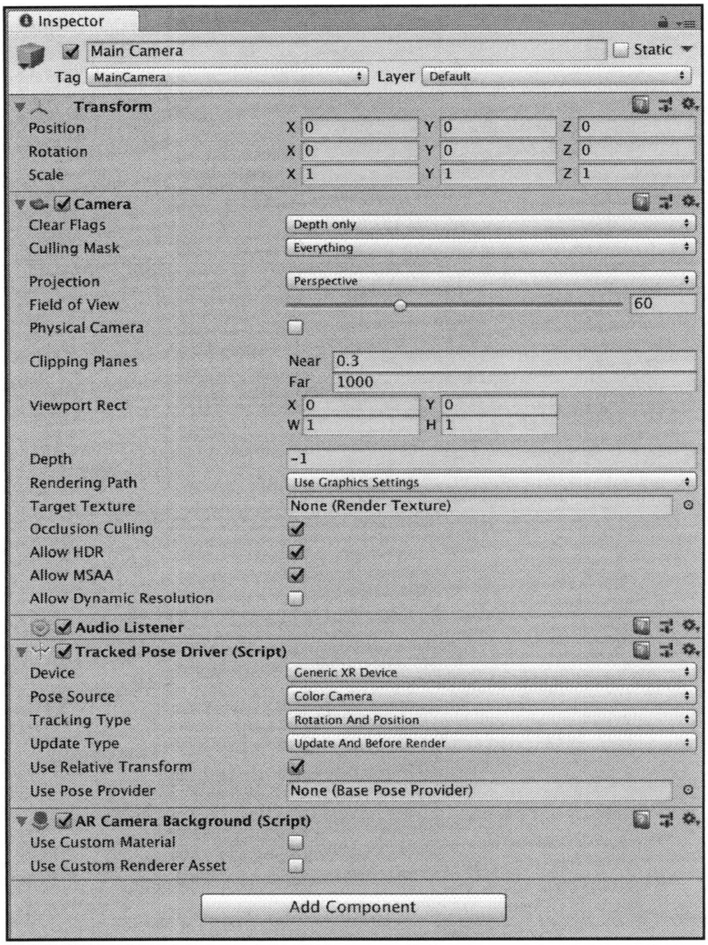

Note: The **ARCameraBackground** component is part of the **ARFoundation** package and is documented as part of that package.

Now, add a new empty GameObject to the root of the Hierarchy, name it **AR Session** and add a **ARSession** to the GameObject.

Select the **AR Session** and in the **AR Session** component, ensure the **Light Estimation** box is unchecked and the **Attempt Update** box is checked.

The **AR Session** should now look like this:

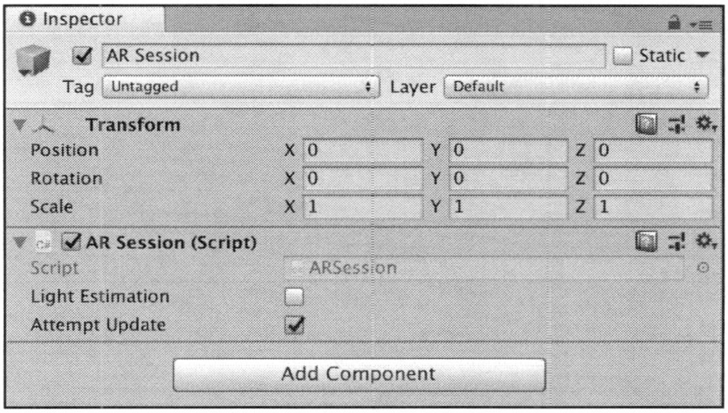

The **AR Session** GameObject does the initialization of the AR Session for ARCore.

> **Note:** The **AR Session** component is also part of the **ARFoundation** package and is documented as part of that package.

If you run this scene on the device, it'll be working with world tracking enabled, but since you do not have any virtual objects in the scene, you won't be able to tell whether it's working or not. Time to fix that by adding a single virtual object to the scene:

Drag the **PlayerRobotPrefab** prefab from the **Assets \ Razeware \ Prefabs** folder into the root of the Hierarchy. Set its position to **(X:0, Y:0, Z:1)** so it'll appear 1 meter in front of the camera. The camera is facing forward (positive on the Z-axis) and is placed at the origin when the app starts.

The scene is now ready for testing!

Building to the device and testing the scene

If you haven't already, you need to enable developer options and USB debugging on your ARCore-compatible Android device following the directions on this webpage: https://developer.android.com/studio/debug/dev-options.html#enable

With your Android device connected, select **File > Build Settings...** in the top menu. In the Build Settings window, select the **Android platform** and click the **Switch Platform** button. This process will take some time.

After changing platforms, the **Build Settings** dialog box will look like this:

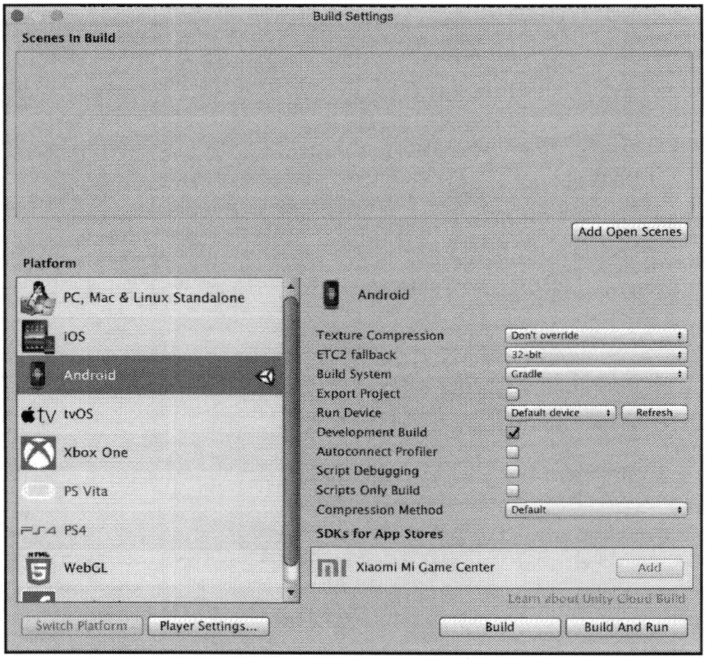

Click **Add Open Scenes** to add the current scene to the build.

In the same window, select **Player Settings** and look at the Inspector. Change the **Product Name** in the first section to **My Awesome AR App** for example. The name doesn't have any impact on the rest of the app, so feel free to choose anything you like here.

Uncheck the **Multithreaded Rendering** box in **Other Settings**. Also, uncheck the **ARCore Supported** box in the **XR Settings** - that option is there for supporting an older version of the ARCore plugin.

Click the **Build And Run** button in the **Build Settings** window and provide an APK name and location for the build (to store the built APK). This action also installs and runs the app on the connected device.

> **Note:** If this is the first AR Core app you have run on the device, you will get a pop up asking you to install AR Core from the Play Store.

Here's the result:

Congratulations! You built an ARCore app using Unity.

ARFoundation

The XR Subsystems APIs mentioned above provide the raw AR data from the mobile AR SDKs like ARKit and ARCore to higher level frameworks. **AR Foundation** is one such framework that provides higher level functionality including GameObject components, convenience methods and optimal workflows to make the life of a Unity AR developer that much easier.

Using **ARFoundation** has several advantages:

- It allows you to write higher-level code for AR development instead of targeting the low-level XRSubsystems API.
- You don't have to write a lot of boilerplate code or utilitarian functionality since it's provided for you.

Technically, you've already been using some of the **AR Foundation** APIs. In the previous sections of this chapter, you used the **ARSession** and **ARCameraBackground** components. Now it's time to create another AR app using more components of **ARFoundation**, which you'll soon see is much shorter.

First, create a new scene and save it in the **Assets \ Razeware \ Scenes** folder as **ARFoundationSetup**.

ARFoundation provides a key component named **AR Session Origin**. When you create a new scene in Unity, the camera is typically placed at **(X:0, Y:1, Z:-10)** so that you can look at any GameObject that has been created at the origin.

ARFoundation provides a shortcut to create and set up the **AR Camera**.

Delete the **Main Camera** in the scene and select **GameObject/XR/AR Session Origin** in the **Create** menu to create a new **AR Session Origin**.

The **AR Session Origin** also creates a child named **AR Camera** which contains the **ARCameraBackground** and **Tracked Pose Driver** components that are needed to make it work in AR.

> **Note:** When a **ARSession** begins, the **AR Camera** transform gets reset to the origin **(X:0, Y:0, Z:0)** before it starts updating that transform according to the movement of the AR device.

Any offset or rotation of the **AR Camera** that existed to make you look at a place of interest would get wiped out. One use of **AR Session Origin** is to position the **AR Camera** without changing the local transform on it.

You can now move **AR Session Origin** around the scene and rotate it until the **AR Camera** is pointing at where you would like the experience to begin. Because the **AR Camera** is a child of **AR Session Origin** it's transform remains **(X:0, Y:0, Z:0)**.

Next, drag the **PlayerRobotPrefab** from the **Assets \ Razeware \ Prefabs** folder into the root of the Hierarchy like you did with the previous setup.

Leave the position of **PlayerRobotPrefab** at **(X:0, Y:0, Z:0)** and move **AR Session Origin** to **(X:0, Y:0, Z:-1)** so the robot prefab will appear 1 meter in front of the camera.

This is different from the previous setup in that you're moving the camera to point at the object you want instead of moving the object to the right position for the camera.

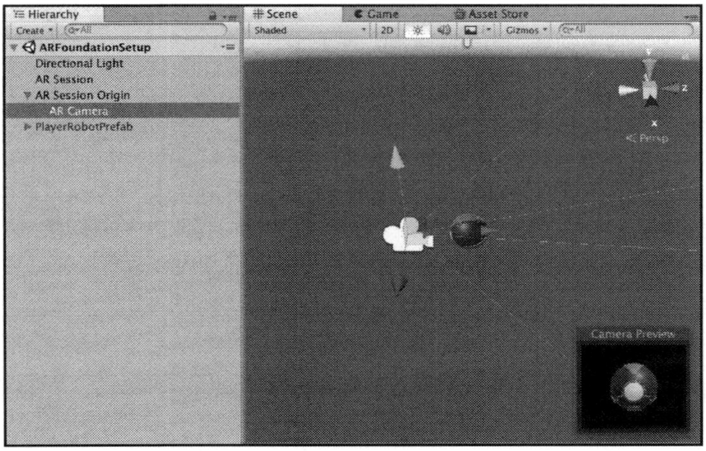

Add an empty **GameObject** called **AR Session** and add the **AR Session** component as you have done before. You now have all of the elements in the scene that were there in the previous setup scenes.

To show how easy it is to add some extra elements with **ARFoundation**, you're going to add a component to visualize the feature points detected by the AR SDK. You'll use one of the standard components available with **ARFoundation** named **ARPointCloudManager**.

Select **AR Session Origin** and add a **ARPointCloudManager** component. In the Inspector, you'll see the **AR Point Cloud Manager** component has an empty reference to a **Point Cloud Prefab**; this prefab provides the implementation of the visualization of the point cloud.

For this component, select the **Assets \ Razeware \ Prefabs \ RazewarePointCloudVisualizer** prefab for the **Point Cloud Prefab** slot.

When you're done, the **AR Session Origin** will look like this in the Inspector:

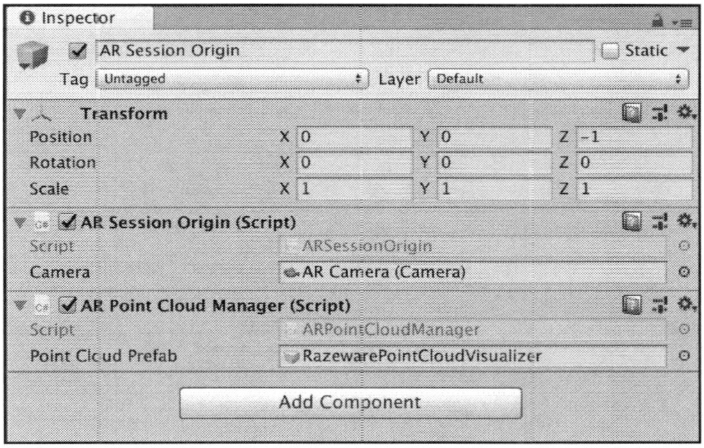

Note: Like **AR Session** and **ARCameraBackground**, **AR Session Origin** and **ARPointCloudManager** components are part of the **ARFoundation** package and are documented as part of that package.

Ready to build? Depending on your device, using either the ARKit or ARCore methods described earlier, build and run the project.

Running it on your device will look almost identical to the platform-specific scenes with one key difference: you'll see the feature points:

If you feel adventurous and have devices that support both mobile AR platforms, you can create and test the same app for each platform. It's best to download a separate copy of the project for the two platform versions and put them in different folders on your hard-drive as it saves a lot of time by not having to switch platforms.

Where to go from here?

In this chapter you learned how to make your AR device and development machine ready to create AR apps. You also learned how to setup **ARFoundation** to start developing cross-platform AR apps in Unity. For good measure, you built a couple of AR examples on to your AR device to try out.

In the next chapter, you will learn how to create virtual objects to enhance the real world, the first step in creating your very own augmented reality experience.

Chapter 15: Adding Virtual Objects

Jimmy Alamparambil

In the last chapter, you got your feet wet making an AR app. In this chapter, you'll look at virtual objects and the different ways you can make them appear in the real world either statically at the start position, or dynamically by detecting the context of the world around you and placing them into the scene.

Placing virtual objects in AR

With augmented reality, you place virtual objects into the real world and make these virtual objects appear as if they were real too. Within Unity, you have a virtual world where you can add virtual objects; this is known as the **scene**. With the help of world tracking and other features of AR, you can align the virtual world (the Unity scene) with the real world (the scene in front of the device's camera). Because Unity uses a virtual *Camera* to view the virtual world created within the Unity scene, you can use that abstraction to align the device camera with Unity's virtual camera.

When you initialize the **ARSession**, the position and orientation of the device camera are used to set the origin of the virtual scene. The position is used as-is, but the orientation is adjusted, so the "up" vector is always the opposite of the direction of gravity, and the forward direction (the direction the device camera is facing) is always the positive Z-axis in the virtual world.

For the real world scene, you can use the video feed from the device camera and set it as the background clear texture for the virtual camera. You can also use a projection matrix for the virtual camera that's obtained from the AR SDKs; this causes the virtual camera to have the same perspective as the device camera.

Unity and the AR SDKs all use meters as the basic unit of distance measurement. So in Unity, if you place a virtual object at **(X:0 ,Y:0, Z:1)**, it'll be one meter away from the origin in the positive Z direction. That means that anything you place there should be visible (if it's large enough) from the origin when you start the **ARSession**. From the example scene in the previous chapter, notice how you're able to see the **PlayerRobot** when you start up the AR scene.

Open the starter project for this chapter, and open the **Chapter15Startup** scene. This scene already has an **ARSession** included, so you don't need to add it. However, you're going to change this scene, so save it as **PlacingVirtualObjects** in the same folder using the **/File/Save As..** menu item.

Time to place some virtual objects in the scene to see how they'll appear when you navigate through the world!

In the Project window, navigate to **Assets \ Razeware \ Prefabs** and drag the **goldCollectible** prefab onto the root of the Hierarchy. You should now have a copy of the **goldCollectible** prefab in your scene at **(X:0 ,Y:0 ,Z:0)**.

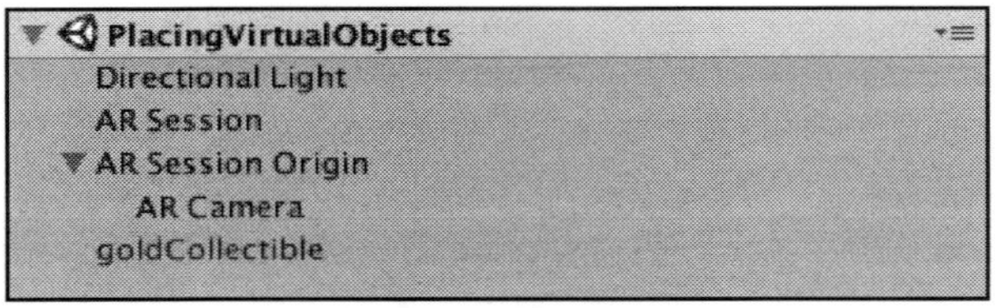

Select this new object and move it to **(X:0 ,Y:0, Z:1)**, so the transform looks like the following in the Inspector:

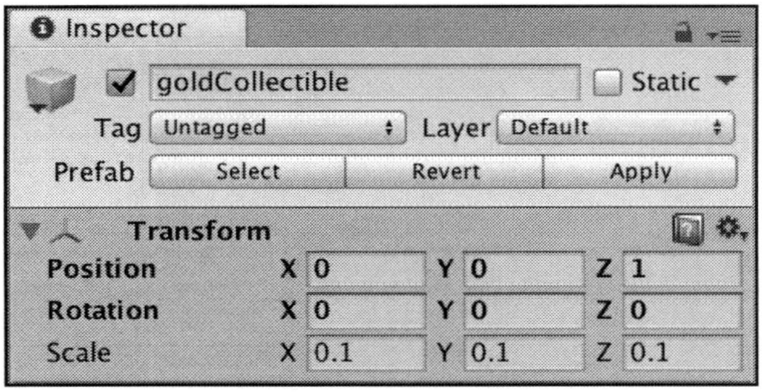

Now build to the device and start the app. Look toward the middle of the room, and you'll see a gold ball floating in the air around 1 meter in front of you. You can move forward through the world, and the ball will move toward you as if you're getting closer to it — just as you'd expect if the ball was real.

When you're close enough to the gold ball, move around it and view it from all angles. It still looks like it's floating in a fixed point in the air and you're moving around it. This is the basic notion of world tracking; the AR SDK detects where in the real world the device camera is in relation to the start position. It then transmits that information to the Unity camera which updates its position and orientation in the same way. Thus the Unity camera moves through the virtual scene as the device camera moves through the real world. The virtual and real worlds appear aligned in their movement.

Time to put a few more balls into the scene.

Go back to the scene in the editor and select **goldCollectible** in the Hierarchy. Now, duplicate it (**Cmd+D/Ctrl+D**) and set the duplicate at **(X:0 ,Y:0, Z:1.5)**. Repeat this action a few times, and position the gold balls, so they look like the following (from above):

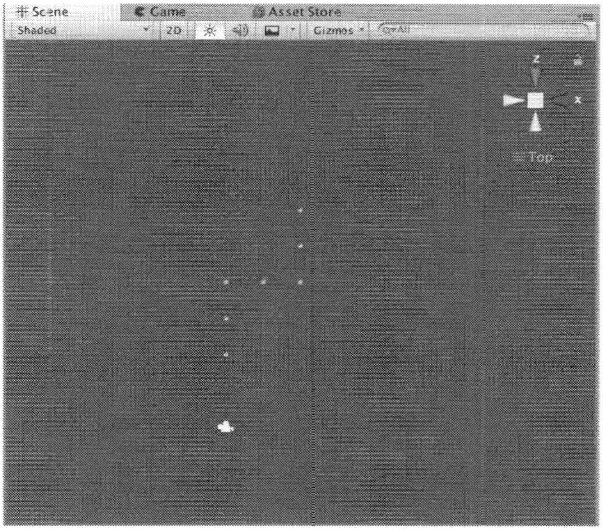

Build this scene to the device. Before starting the app, find an ample space in which you can move around. When you're ready and have enough room to move around, start the app.

You'll see the pattern of gold balls stretching out in front of you like it was laid out in the virtual scene. You can also walk along the line of balls. Notice the distance between them is about **50cm**, just like it was in the scene.

While you're walking along the path of gold balls, look behind you, and you'll continue to see the ones you've passed.

Save the scene so you can play with it later.

Creating virtual objects in AR

You learned how to place objects in the virtual scene, so they appear to augment the real world. But in many cases, you don't want to navigate through a prepared set of objects or a pre-existing map of sorts. Instead, you might want to see what's currently in the scene and create virtual objects in specific places, oriented in specific ways, so they appear correctly in a particular context.

In later chapters, you'll learn how to determine the context of the real world, but for now, you'll dynamically add content to a virtual scene while navigating in AR.

First, you need a way to determine where in the virtual scene you want to create the object before placing it. You can use the position of the device camera to determine a location in the real world. From there, you can detect a tap on the touchscreen to create a copy of an object in the virtual world at the position where the camera is currently located.

Open the **Chapter15Startup** scene, and this time, save it as **CreatingVirtualObjects**. Add a new GameObject to the root of the Hierarchy and name it **TapAddsGameObject**. Once again, save the scene.

Now, navigate to the **Assets \ Razeware \ Scripts folder** in the Project view, **right-click** an empty space and select **Create \ C# Script**. Name this new script **TapAddsGameObject.cs** and open it in a code editor.

At the top of the file, make sure you have the following `using` statements to import the classes you'll need:

```
using UnityEngine;
using UnityEngine.XR.ARFoundation;
```

You need two references on this component when it's run, so put these lines at the top of the class in the script:

```
public ARSessionOrigin arSessionOrigin; //1
public GameObject virtualObjectPrefab; //2
```

1. This is a reference to the ARSessionOrigin, from which you will get a reference to the camera in the scene to determine *where* to create the GameObject.
2. Reference to the prefab that you're going to instantiate whenever the screen is tapped.

Now for some validation of the references at startup:

```
void Start()
{
    if (virtualObjectPrefab == null || arSessionOrigin == null)
    {
        Debug.LogError ("GameObject references missing - needed
            for the functionality of this script!");
    }
}
```

If either the prefab or the camera that is needed for the script has a missing reference, print out an error message on the console.

All the magic happens in the **Update** function of the script:

```
void Update()
{
    if (Input.GetMouseButtonDown(0)) //1
    {
        //user tapped the screen this frame (or clicked mouse)
        //create an object from prefab and parent to the
        // GameObject that this script is attached to
        GameObject virtualObj =
            Instantiate<GameObject>(virtualObjectPrefab,
                gameObject.transform); //2

        //move the virtual object to where the camera is located
        //make it appear a bit in front of camera
        Camera trackedCamera = arSessionOrigin.camera; //3
        virtualObj.transform.position =
            trackedCamera.transform.position +
            trackedCamera.transform.forward * 0.4f; //4

        virtualObj.transform.rotation =
            trackedCamera.transform.rotation; //5
    }
}
```

1. This checks whether the screen was touched on this frame and if so runs the rest of the code.
2. A copy of the prefab is instantiated and made a child of the GameObject this script is on.
3. Get a reference to the AR camera that mimics the position and rotation of the AR device.
4. Get a position that is 40cm in front of the AR camera and set that as the position of the virtual object that is in the scene.
5. Set the rotation of the virtual object to be the same as the AR camera.

The code includes comments explaining what's happening in more detail, but basically, it waits for a tap on the screen — **Input.GetMouseButtonDown** gets translated to tap on touchscreen — and when it detects a tap, it instantiates a copy of the prefab you referenced at the top, and then moves the generated virtual object a small distance in front of the camera, so it appears on the next frame.

Save the script, and return to the scene in the Unity. Select **TapAddsGameObject** in the hierarchy view. Next, in the bottom of the Inspector, press the **Add Component** button and add a **TapAddsGameObject.cs** component onto this GameObject.

You need to set the references on this component to get it to work correctly.

First, drag the **goldCollectible** prefab from **Assets \ Razeware \ Prefabs** folder to the **Virtual Object Prefab** field of the component. Then, from the Hierarchy, drag the **AR Session Origin** reference to the **AR Session Origin** field of the component.

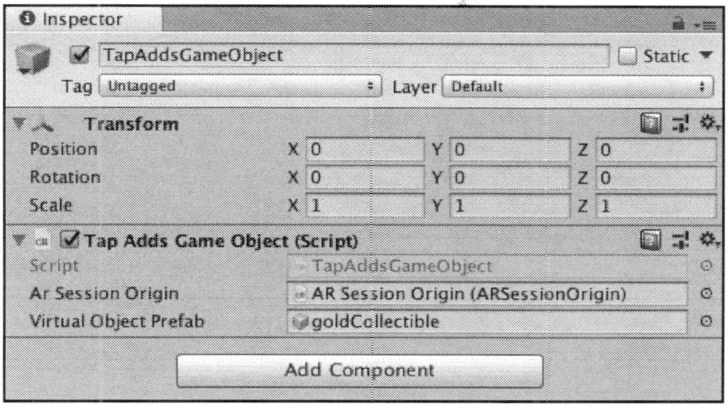

Now you're all set to try out the scene on the device.

Build to the device and run the app. Walk around and tap on the screen whenever (and wherever) you want to create a gold ball. After a while, look around, and you'll see all of the gold balls you added.

Here's an example of a smiley face I drew by tapping a few times:

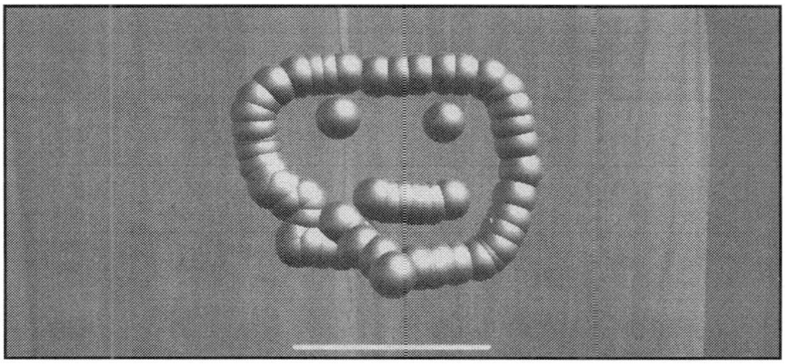

For this project, you used a sphere mesh as the virtual object, but that's the beauty of using Unity for a creation tool — anything that Unity supports can be a virtual object in an AR scene. That means you can have skinned meshes, animations, sprites or any number of other rendering primitives.

For example, if you used particles in a particle system in place of the gold ball, and added a color picker, and a method to turn on and off drawing, you would have a particle painter.

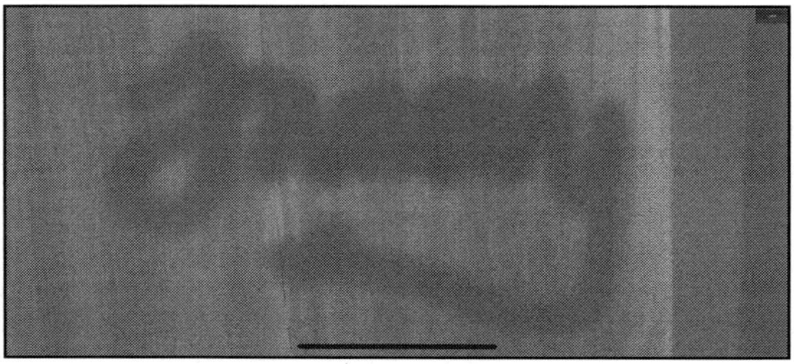

Raycast subsystem

A standard feature on the mobile AR platforms is a **Hit Test**. The Hit Test feature allows the user to make a raycast into the AR SDK's understanding of the current environment and will return any surfaces or feature points that were hit by the ray that was cast.

The Hit Test feature is exposed to the user through the AR SDK API. This uses a different API than a `Physics.Raycast` since the surfaces and feature points do not exist in the Unity scene, but will still get hit by the Hit Test. You'll read in Chapter 18 how to use Unity's Physics system to carry out collision detection.

In the meantime, these Hit Tests can be used to find points on surfaces or near feature points that you can place some virtual objects on. The `Raycast` subsystem is part of the `XRSubsystems` in the Unity XR API, but **ARFoundation** provides a simpler API to use. To do a Hit Test, call this method on the **AR Session Origin** in the scene:

```
public bool Raycast(Vector3 screenPoint,
    List<ARRaycastHit> hitResults,
    TrackableType trackableTypeMask = TrackableType.All)
```

You will use this API in the next section.

This API is documented in the **ARFoundation** docs. It lets you specify a number of flags which can be used in combination with each other to detect hits on planes, infinite planes, plane boundary meshes, feature points and other AR environment features.

Adding tap gestures

You can now use the `Raycast` API described earlier to place a virtual object on a real surface detected by this API. For example, you can use this API to only place content on a flat surface you point at on the screen.

Open the **Chapter15Startup** scene, and this time, save it as **CreatingHitTestObjects**. Add a new GameObject to the root of the Hierarchy and name it **HitTestAddsGameObject**. Once again, save the scene.

Now, create a new C# script named **HitTestAddsGameObject.cs** in the **Assets \ Razeware \ Scripts** folder. Right-click that folder in the project view and select to **Create \ C# Script**.

Start with the listing of the assemblies you'll use in your script:

```
using System.Collections.Generic;
using UnityEngine;
using UnityEngine.Experimental.XR;
using UnityEngine.XR.ARFoundation;
```

You need two references on this component when it's run. You want the reference to a prefab of the GameObject that you're going to create whenever the screen is tapped when pointing to a flat surface, and you want to keep a reference to the **AR Session Origin** in the scene so you can call the `Raycast` API from it.

Put this at the top of the script **MonoBehaviour** class:

```
public ARSessionOrigin arSessionOrigin; //1
public GameObject virtualObjectPrefab; //2
```

1. This is a reference to the **AR Session Origin**, from which you invoke the `Raycast` API.

2. Reference to the prefab that you're going to instantiate whenever the screen is tapped.

Now for some validation of the references at startup:

```
void Start()
{
    if (virtualObjectPrefab == null || arSessionOrigin == null)
    {
        Debug.LogError("GameObject references missing - needed
            for the functionality of this script!");
    }
}
```

Same as before, if either the prefab or the **AR Session Origin** that is needed for the script has a missing reference, print out an error message on the console.

Now to create a couple of helper methods. First, create a method in the class that can create the virtual object in the right position and orientation:

```
void CreateVirtualObjectWithTransform(Pose hitPose)
{
    //create an object and parent to the AR Session Origin
    GameObject virtualObj =
Instantiate<GameObject>(virtualObjectPrefab,
            arSessionOrigin.transform); //1

    //move the virtual object to where the hit is located
    virtualObj.transform.position = hitPose.position; //2
    virtualObj.transform.rotation = hitPose.rotation; //3
}
```

1. A copy of the prefab is instantiated and made a child of the **AR Session Origin**.
2. Set the position of the virtual object to be the same as the position of the `Pose` that is passed into this method.
3. Set the rotation of the virtual object to be the same as the rotation of the `Pose` that is passed into this method.

Next, create a method that calls the `Raycast` API with the trackable type passed in, and call the method you just wrote above to create a virtual object if there's a hit:

```
bool HitTestWithTrackableType(Vector3 screenPositon,
    TrackableType trackableTypeMask)
{
    List<ARRaycastHit> hitResults = new List<ARRaycastHit>(); //
1

    if (arSessionOrigin.Raycast(screenPositon, hitResults,
                                trackableTypeMask)) //2
    {
        foreach (var hitResult in hitResults) //3
        {
            CreateVirtualObjectWithTransform(
                hitResult.sessionRelativePose); //4
            return true; //5
        }
    }
    return false; //6
}
```

1. Create an empty list of raycast hit results.
2. Call the `Raycast` API to cast a ray using the screen position and the trackable types that are passed into this method to collide against. The return from the API will be a boolean that is true only if there is at least one hit. The hitResults list will contain all the resulting collisions.
3. Iterate though all the collisions of the raycast on relevant trackable types.
4. For each of the collisions, create a virtual object at the position and rotation of the collision.
5. Return true from the method after handling the first collision.
6. If no collision was detected, return false.

Finally, in the update method of the class, whenever you get a tap, check whether the player tapped one of the trackable types in order of priority, and create a virtual object whenever there's a hit on any of the trackables listed:

```
void Update()
{
    if (Input.GetMouseButtonDown(0)) //1
    {
        //user tapped the screen this frame (or clicked mouse)

        // prioritize trackable types to hit test against
        TrackableType[] trackableTypes =
            {
                TrackableType.PlaneWithinPolygon,
                TrackableType.PlaneWithinBounds,
                TrackableType.PlaneEstimated,
                TrackableType.FeaturePoint
            }; //2

        //check for each trackable types in order
        foreach (TrackableType trackableType in
trackableTypes) //3
        {
            if (HitTestWithTrackableType(Input.mousePosition,
                trackableType)) //4
            {
                return; //5
            }
        }
    }
}
```

1. This checks whether the screen was touched on this frame and if so runs the rest of the code.
2. An array of trackable types in the order in which you want to check collisions against. In this case it will first check whether you have tapped within the boundary polygon of a plane that has been detected.
3. Iterate through the members of the array above in the order listed.
4. For each trackable type, call the method we created above with tapped screen position and trackable type as parameters.
5. If any call to that method returns true, that means a collision was detected and virtual object was created in that spot, so you can exit out of the update method.

Save the script, and go back to the scene in the Unity Editor. Select **HitTestAddsGameObject** in the Hierarchy. Then, in the bottom of the Inspector, press **Add Component** and select the **Hit Test Adds GameObject** component.

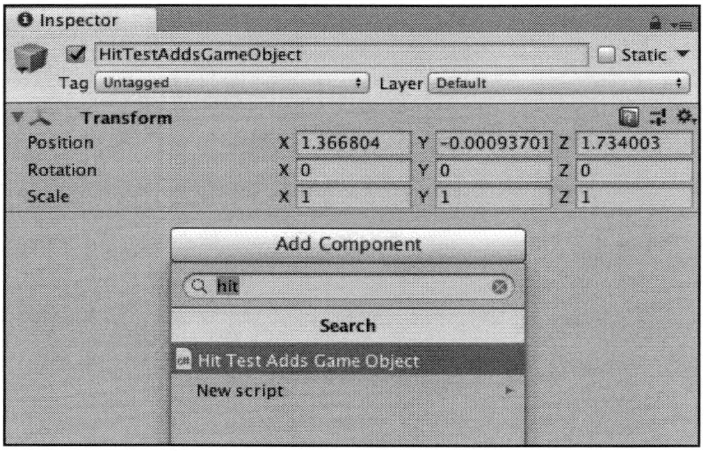

Next, you need to set the references on this component so that it works correctly. First, drag the **goldCollectible** prefab from the **Assets \ Razeware \ Prefabs** folder onto the **Virtual Object Prefab** field.

Then, drag the **AR Session Origin** to the **AR Session Origin** field.

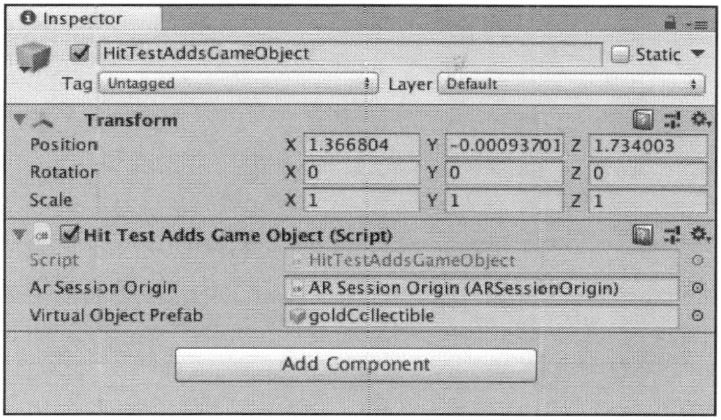

You're now ready to test this masterpiece of interactive AR virtual object generation.

Build the scene to the device and run it. You'll see the video from the real environment around you. Find a flat surface — like a table or wall — with lots of texture on it.

Center the surface on the device's screen, and tap on the screen where the surface is located — a gold ball will appear on that surface.

Fantastic! You are now an expert in creating virtual objects on real world surfaces!

Where to go from here?

In this chapter, you learned how to create virtual objects to augment the real environment. You added virtual objects placed a certain offset from the start position, and you placed virtual objects dynamically based on the current position of the device, or more contextually, based on surfaces or other environmental features.

Next you will learn how to interact with the virtual objects that you have created to augment your world. You will see various forms of user interfaces both screen based as well as environment based. You will also learn to provide a good user experience for AR even when there are issues with the data returned by the AR platform. Read on!

Chapter 16: User Interface & Interactions

Jimmy Alamparambil

When creating AR content, you need to consider the way users will interact with your content. This helps you determine how to present these interactions to the user, and how to get user input into the system in such a way that the user experience is immersive, intuitive and enjoyable. Both Apple and Google offer some advice on how to accomplish this in their respective guidelines and best practices:

- **Apple**: https://developer.apple.com/ios/human-interface-guidelines/technologies/augmented-reality
- **Google**: https://blog.google/products/google-vr/best-practices-mobile-ar-design

In this chapter, you'll learn how to implement some of these guidelines.

Displaying text and images in AR

As a starting point, you can use regular mobile app UI (user interface) components that frame the experience. You can use both text and image components as usual. In most situations however, this isn't ideal because the user interface elements cover part of the viewing area which reduces the amount of space available to see the augmented world as intended. This, by itself, is enough to take the user out of the experience and immediately makes it less immersive as there's no context associated with the elements. However, there are some advantages to placing user interface elements like this: they're easy to make, readable and understandable.

So, with that in mind, it's time to create some of these UI elements. To achieve this, you'll make use of Unity's UI system. For reference, you can look at the Unity manual section on the UI system: https://docs.unity3d.com/Manual/UISystem.html

Text

You'll start with a text status bar that lets you know the position of the device camera in the world and whether or not tracking is working.

Start by opening the existing starter project for this chapter included within the scenes folder. Open the **Chapter16Startup** scene. Notice that both the **AR Session** and **AR Session Origin** are already set up.

You're going to alter this scene, so save it as **TextAndUI** in the same folder using **File > Save As..** from the top menu.

Next, drag the **StatusBarUI** prefab into the Hierarchy from the **Assets \ Razeware \ Prefabs** folder. This prefab, which has already been created for you, implements the status bar UI canvas using the standard Unity UI elements.

The text of this status bar needs to change based on the state of the AR app, so you'll need to write a new script to handle this. Create a new C# script in the **Assets \ Razeware \ Scripts** folder and name it **WorldPositionTracker.cs**.

Open it in a code editor and edit the contents of the script to match this:

```
using UnityEngine;
using UnityEngine.UI;
using UnityEngine.XR.ARFoundation;
using UnityEngine.Experimental.XR; //1

namespace Razeware.ARBook
{
    //2
    public class WorldPositionTracker : MonoBehaviour
    {
        /// <summary>
        /// The first-person camera being used to render the
passthrough
        /// camera image (i.e. AR background).
        /// </summary>

        public Camera FirstPersonCamera; //3

        /// <summary>
        /// A gameobject parenting UI for displaying the
messages.
        /// </summary>

        public Text messagesUI; //4


        //5
        void Update ()
```

```
        {
            //6
            if
(ARSubsystemManager.sessionSubsystem.TrackingState ==
                TrackingState.Tracking)
            {
                string message = "Current world position of
camera is ";
                message +=

FirstPersonCamera.transform.position.ToString();
                messagesUI.text = message; //7
            }
            //8
            else if
(ARSubsystemManager.sessionSubsystem.TrackingState
                == TrackingState.Unavailable)
            {
                messagesUI.text = "Session lost tracking..."; //
9
            }
            else
            {
                messagesUI.text = "AR systems
initializing..."; //10
            }
        }
    }
}
```

1. Declare all the namespaces used in this class.
2. Declare the class derived from Monobehaviour.
3. Reference to `Camera` that is driven by the AR device. This will be set in the Editor.
4. Reference to `Text` component that will be used to show the UI message text. Also set in the Editor.
5. Main logic lives in the `Update` method of the Monobehaviour.
6. If the **Session Subsystem TrackingState** is **Tracking** then everything is currently working as expected.
7. Output a message in the UI that shows the current world position of the tracked **AR Camera**.
8. If the **Session Subsystem TrackingState** is **Unavailable** then the AR device has lost tracking.

9. Output a message in the UI showing that tracking has been lost.
10. If neither of the above is true, tracking has not been initialized yet, so output a message to that effect.

First, you get the reference to the AR Camera that you're using so you can get its position to put into the status bar text. This means you'll need a reference to the `Text` component that displays the message as well. Those are the references specified at the top of the file.

The functionality of this script is mostly in the `Update` function. This is where you check to see if the AR session has a tracking state that's normal; if so, you display the position of the AR camera. Otherwise, you try to determine whether the session has lost tracking or is initializing, and you present the appropriate information.

Save the script and return to the editor. Create a new empty GameObject in the Hierarchy and name it **WorldPositionTracker**. Next, add a **World Position Tracker** component to it.

Now drag the **AR Camera** to the **FirstPersonCamera** field and drag **Text** to the **MessagesUI** field to set up the references.

The result should look like this:

You're now ready to build this scene to a device and test it out. Your screen will look something like this:

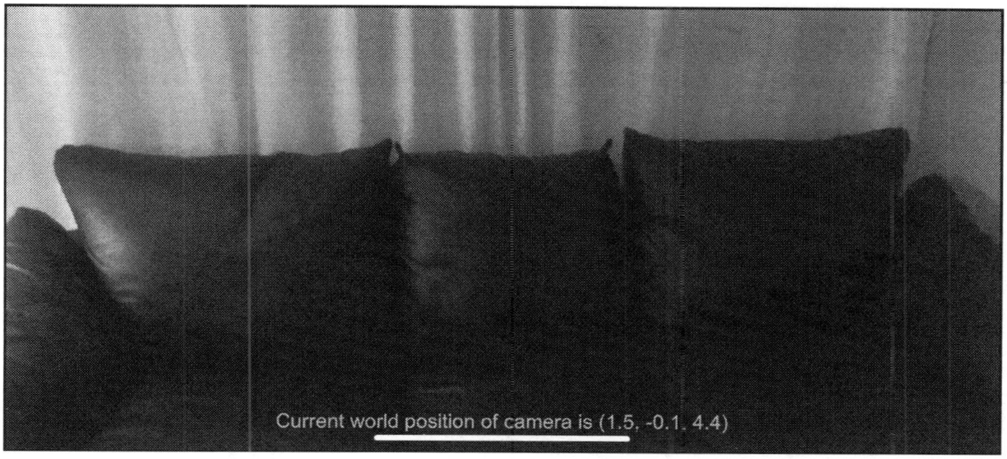

Images and buttons

Similar to the text status UI created in the previous section, you can also create images and buttons in the regular UI that can affect your AR experience. These can provide a little more interactivity than the plain text, but the level of immersion is still lacking due to its static appearance in relation to the window into the AR world.

Start again by opening the starter scene named **Chapter16Startup** for this chapter included within the **Scenes** folder. Open the scene, and save it as **ImageAndButton** in the same folder. Finally, open this new scene.

Drag the **ImageAndButtonUI** prefab from the **Prefabs** folder into Hierarchy. This has all of the UI elements ready to implement the functionality.

At this point, you'll need to create a new script to create a virtual object when the user presses a button.Create a new C# script in the **Assets \ Razeware \ Scripts** folder and name it **VirtualObjectCreator.cs**. Open it in your favorite code editor and replace its contents with:

```
using UnityEngine;

namespace Razeware.ARBook
{
    //1
    public class VirtualObjectCreator : MonoBehaviour
    {

        public Camera trackedCamera; //2
```

```
        public GameObject virtualObjectPrefab; //3

        void Start()
        {
            if (virtualObjectPrefab == null || trackedCamera ==
null) //4
            {
                Debug.LogError ("GameObject references missing
                    - needed for the functionality of this
script!");
            }
        }

        //5
        public void CreateVirtualObject()
        {
            //user clicked the button
            //create an object from prefab and parent to the
            //GameObject that this script is attached to
            GameObject virtualObj = Instantiate<GameObject>
                (virtualObjectPrefab, gameObject.transform); //6

            //move the virtual object to where the camera is
located
            //make it appear a bit in front of camera
            virtualObj.transform.position =
                trackedCamera.transform.position +
                trackedCamera.transform.forward * 0.4f; //7

            virtualObj.transform.rotation =
                trackedCamera.transform.rotation; //8
        }
    }
}
```

1. Declare a class that derives from Monobehaviour.
2. Reference to a `Camera` that is driven by the AR device. This will be set in the Editor.
3. Reference to a prefab that will be instantiated to form our virtual object in the scene. Set in the Editor.
4. On startup, check that the two references above have been setup in the Editor, otherwise print an error message.
5. `CreateVirtualObject` method will be called from a UI button to carry out the main task of this GameObject.
6. Instantiate the referenced prefab and parent it to the transform of this `VirtualObjectCreator`.

7. Set the position of the instanced virtual object to be 40cm in front of the **AR Camera** at the time of instantiation.
8. Set the rotation of the instanced virtual object to mimic that of the **AR Camera**.

This script has references to the **AR Camera** and a virtual object prefab. It also has a public function, when called, that creates a copy of the virtual object at the position of the tracked camera. You'll call this public function when the UI button is clicked.

Save this script and return to the editor. Create a new empty GameObject and name it **VirtualObjectCreator**. Next, add a **Virtual Object Creator** component to it.

Drag **AR Camera** to the **Tracked Camera** field and drag the **GoldCollectible** prefab from the **Assets \ Razeware \ Prefabs** folder onto the **Virtual Object Prefab** slot to set up the needed references.

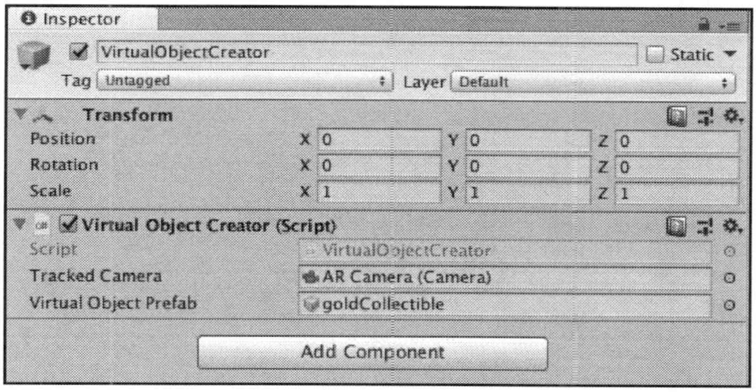

To hook **VirtualObjectCreator** up to the UI, select **CreateButton** in the Hierarchy, it's a child of **ImageAndButtonUI**.

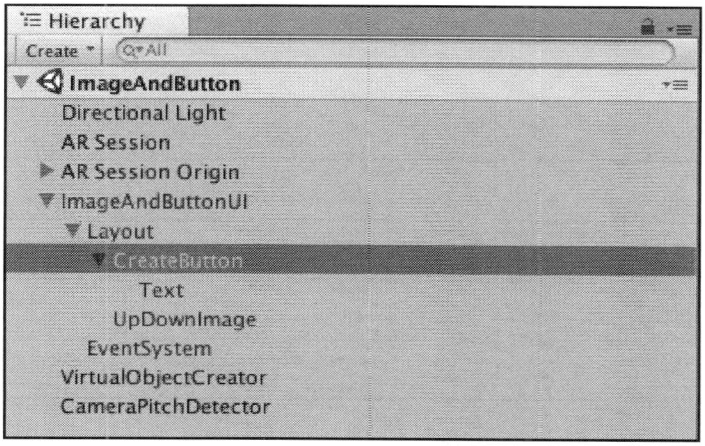

In the Inspector, locate the **Button** component and add an element to the `On Click ()` list at the bottom.

Drag **VirtualObjectCreator** to the **GameObject** slot and select `VirtualObjectCreator.CreateVirtualObject()` from the dropdown as the method to execute when the button is clicked.

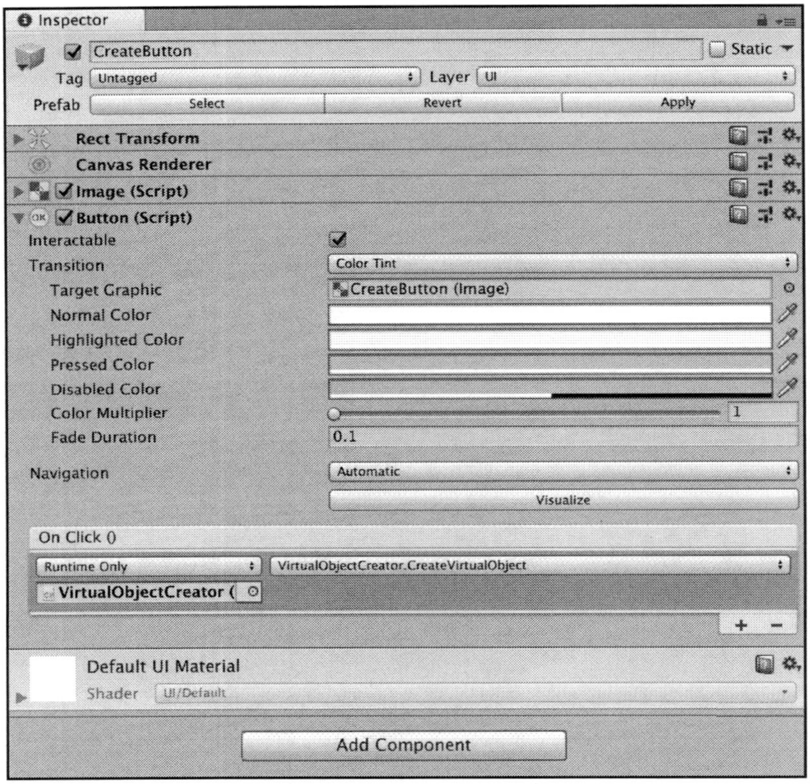

Next, you'll add an image to the UI that corresponds to the pitch of the camera (whether it's facing above or below the horizon). For this, create a new C# script in the **Scripts** folder and name it **CameraPitchDetector.cs**. Open it in a code editor and replace the content with the following :

```
using UnityEngine;
using UnityEngine.UI;

namespace Razeware.ARBook
{
    //1
    public class CameraPitchDetector : MonoBehaviour
    {
        public Camera trackedCamera; //2
```

```
        public Sprite upArrow; //3

        public Sprite downArrow; //4

        public Sprite circle; //5

        public Image pitchIndicator; //6

        void Start()
        {
            //7
            if (trackedCamera == null || upArrow == null ||
                downArrow == null || circle == null ||
                pitchIndicator == null)
            {
                Debug.LogError ("GameObject references missing -
                    needed for the functionality of this
script!");
            }
        }

        //8
        void Update()
        {
            // check whether the forward vector of the camera
projects
            // a positive or negative amount on to up vector
            float dotProd = Vector3.Dot
(trackedCamera.transform.forward,
                                                Vector3.up); //9

            pitchIndicator.sprite = (dotProd > 0.01f) ?
upArrow :
                (dotProd < -0.01f) ? downArrow : circle; //10
        }
    }
}
```

1. Declare the class derived from Monobehaviour.
2. Reference to a `Camera` that is driven by the AR device. This will be set in the Editor.
3. Reference to a `Sprite` that will represent an upwards arrow icon. Set in the Editor.
4. Reference to a `Sprite` that will represent a downwards arrow icon. Set in the Editor.
5. Reference to a `Sprite` that will represent an circle icon. Set in the Editor.
6. Reference to an `Image` that will show one of the `Sprites` above on a UI to indicate the pitch of the camera. Set in the Editor.

7. If any of the references above is missing, this script will not work, so print out an error message.
8. Logic for this component all happens in the `Update` method.
9. Calculate the dot product of the up vector and the forward transform of the **AR Camera**.
10. Based on the dot product, choose the `Sprite` to set on the pitchIndicator. Positive dot product means the camera is pointing above the horizon, negative below the horizon and zero means it is level.

Save the script and return to the editor.Now, create a new empty GameObject in the Hierarchy, name it **CameraPitchDetector** and select it.

Add a **Camera Pitch Detector** component and drag **AR Camera** to the **Tracked Camera** field.

The next three fields are expecting sprites. Drag these in from the **Assets \ Razeware \ Sprites** folder to their respective fields:

- **arrow_up**
- **arrow_down**
- **Circle**

Finally, drag **UpDownImage** from the UI to the **Pitch Indicator** slot.

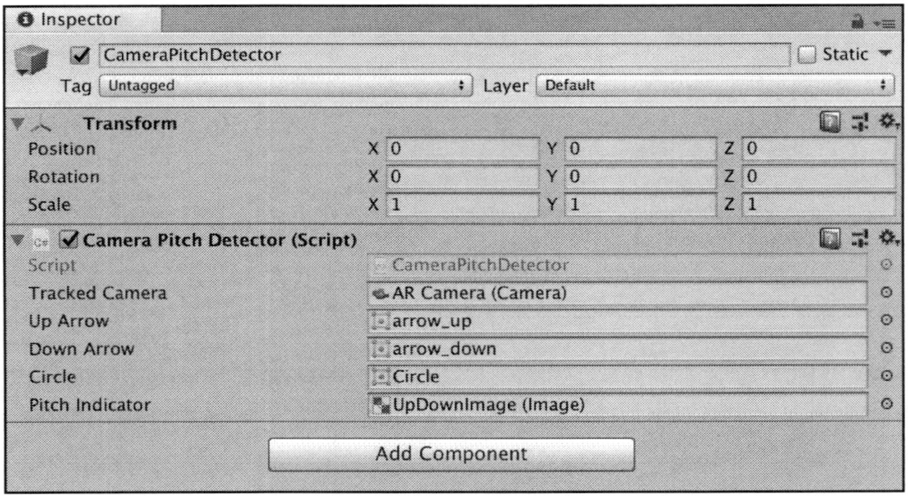

Now save the scene, build it and test it on your device. Notice how the arrow image indicates whether the camera points above or below the horizon and pressing the button creates a virtual object a few centimeters in front of the camera.

Text and objects in 3D

You can be more immersive in AR by creating UI elements in the scene instead of on the window into your scene. Because your scene is in 3D, the UI shouldn't be limited to a 2D plane, but anchored to the world itself.

Next, you'll create a scene where you can tap on a virtual object and display some text in a world-space UI billboard.

Start by opening the starter scene named **Chapter16Startup** for this chapter included within the **Scenes** folder. Save it as **WorldUI** in the same folder using **File > Save As..** from the top menu.

Now, drag in the **WorldUI** prefab from the **Assets \ Razeware \Prefabs** folder into the Hierarchy. This GameObject contains a sphere and a world-space UI canvas that displays a text message. You'll be adding some extra functionality to this to make the message change whenever you tap the sphere.

Create a new C# script, name it **KillerSphereLogic.cs** and save it in the **Assets \ Razeware \ Scripts** folder. Open it in a code editor and replace its contents with:

```
using UnityEngine;
using UnityEngine.UI;

namespace Razeware.ARBook
{
```

```
    //1
    public class KillerSphereLogic : MonoBehaviour
    {
        public Material redMaterial; //2

        public Material greenMaterial; //3

        public Camera trackedCamera; //4

        public Text sphereMessage; //5

        public LayerMask sphereCollMask; //6

        private MeshRenderer meshRenderer; //7

        private bool killmode = false; //8

        void Start()
        {
            meshRenderer = GetComponent<MeshRenderer>(); //9
            ToggleKillMode(); //10
        }
    }
}
```

1. Declare the class derived from Monobehaviour.
2. Reference to a `Material` to set on the sphere when it is in kill mode. Set in the Editor.
3. Reference to a `Material` to set on the sphere when it is not in kill mode. Set in the Editor.
4. Reference to a `Camera` that is driven by the AR device. Set in the Editor.
5. Reference to a `Text` component that will be used to show the UI message text for the sphere. Set in the Editor.
6. `LayerMask` that is set on the sphere's GameObject used to filter Physics raycast hits.
7. Reference to `MeshRenderer` component that is on the current GameObject. Set in script code (see 9).
8. Boolean to keep track of the "killmode" state of this script. Starts as `false`.
9. On startup, store the reference to the `MeshRenderer` component that is on the current GameObject. Saves on calling expensive `GetComponent` method every time you need this.
10. Call the method `ToggleKillMode` (defined below) on startup to initialize the state.

In the same script add two more methods to the `KillerSphereLogic` class.

```
//1
void ToggleKillMode()
{
    killmode = !killmode; //2

    sphereMessage.text = killmode ?
            "Please keep away" : "Come closer here"; //3

    meshRenderer.material = killmode ?
            redMaterial : greenMaterial; //4
}

void Update()
{
    transform.LookAt (trackedCamera.transform); //5

    //6
    if (Input.GetMouseButtonDown (0))
    {
        //tapped on screen - check if you touched sphere
        Ray ray =
trackedCamera.ScreenPointToRay(Input.mousePosition);//7


        RaycastHit rayHit; //8
        if (Physics.Raycast(ray, out rayHit, float.MaxValue,
                            sphereCollMask)) //9
        {
            if (rayHit.collider.gameObject == gameObject) //10
            {
                ToggleKillMode(); //11
            }
        }
    }
}
```

1. Define the method `ToggleKillMode` that is used to toggle the mode and adjust the appearance of the new mode.
2. The actual toggle of the boolean that represents the "killmode" state of this script.
3. Change the message on the UI on top of the sphere to correspond to current state of the script.
4. Change the material on the sphere based on the current state of the script.
5. In the`Update` method, always face this sphere to the **AR Camera** so that the text UI appears correctly to the user.
6. Check if the user tapped the screen.

7. Create a ray from the tapped position in relation to the **AR Camera**.
8. Storage for the result of the raycast if there was a collision.
9. Check if the raycast of the ray hits any collider with the layer mask. Returns true if there is a hit.
10. Check that the collider that was hit belongs to this sphere GameObject.
11. If the sphere collider was tapped, call the `ToggleKillMode` method to change state and appearance.

This script checks if you've tapped on the sphere; if so, it toggles the message in the UI and the material used to render the sphere. Save the script and return to the editor. Select the top GameObject in the **WorldUI** hierarchy in the scene (which contains the `MeshRenderer` for the sphere) and add this script as a new component to it. Set the following references in the **KillerSphereLogic** component in the Inspector:

First, drag the **RedMaterial** and **GreenMaterial** from the **Assets \ Razeware \ Materials** folder to the first two slots in this component respectively. Next, drag **AR Camera** to the **Tracked Camera** slot and drag the **WorldUI**'s child **Text** to the **SphereMessage** slot.

Finally, set **SphereCollMask** to **ARGameObject**, which is an existing collision layer in the project.

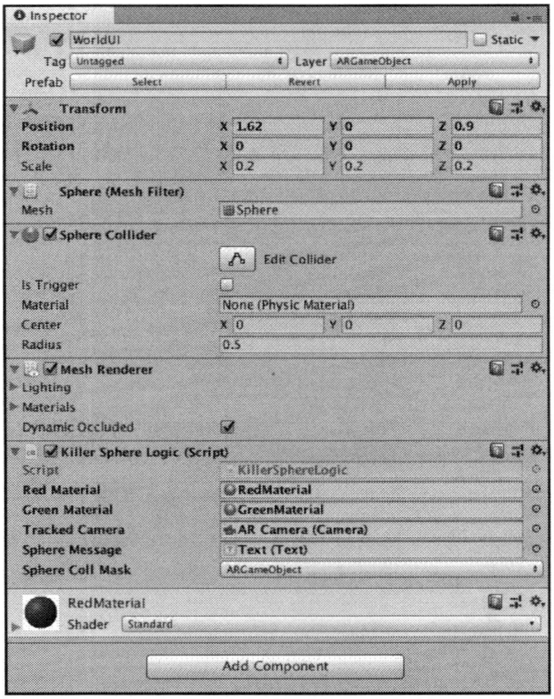

Now build and run this on a device to see if everything is working correctly.

Notice the difference between this and the previous UI efforts. The text message is positioned in the world and is pinned to the virtual sphere object — not to the window of the device. You only see it when you look in the direction of the sphere.

Also, instead of a button on the window of the device, you interact directly with the virtual sphere object by tapping it to change some state in the experience.

Handling UI interactions in AR

There are two types of UI interactions you're interested in when dealing with mobile AR: direct and indirect interactions:

Direct interactions are when the user touches the screen to specify what element of the UI they want to interact with. This might be a screen space UI element or a UI element that is in the world space and accessible via a raycast on the touchscreen. This is the most common type of interaction you'll see in current iterations of AR software. In fact, you already used it in the **TapAddsGameObject.cs** and other similar scripts in previous chapters.

Indirect interactions are when the user points the device at an object they want to select in the 3D environment and it's selected for them automatically. Think of it as a raycast from the center of the device screen into the scene. This is the technique used by the **FocusTarget** script introduced later in this chapter to help with UI for object placement.

Each of these techniques has advantages and disadvantages in different circumstances. As you design your AR experiences, keep this in mind and decide which to use depending on the situation.

User experience for AR

When everything works correctly in AR, the experience and the level of immersion is amazing. However, with this first iteration of AR SDKs we currently have, there are occasions where things fall apart. In these situations, you want to make sure the user is aware of the limitations and is guided and directed to make the experience as enjoyable as possible.

Initial AR experience

When AR SDKs initialize, there's a bit of a delay to get started. They require some movement on the user's part to begin detecting feature points and get world tracking to be more accurate. You need to guide the user during this start-up phase, so they're not left wondering what's going on.

First, as things are getting initialized, you can display something to inform the user about the progress being made to initialize the SDK. One way to do this is to provide a UI with text and graphics that tell the user of any delays.

Next, you can prompt the user to move the device around to enable the AR SDK to detect feature points and planes more easily. For this, you can provide more text and animated graphics on how to move the device to get the best experience.

There are other ways to provide feedback to the user; you can provide a contextual hint rather than general text and graphics. For example, in a fairytale experience, you might have a fairy move around the scene and request the user to follow the fairy, providing the movement needed to calibrate the device. Little tricks like these are common in a lot of games to guide the attention of players and AR is no exception.

Object placement UI

One of the common interactions in AR is to place a virtual object into the scene. For example, placing a mug on a flat horizontal surface like a table.Because the location of suitable placement areas is not always obvious, you should provide a way for your users to visualize where they can place virtual objects in their environment. For this, you usually use a UI element near the center of the device screen that changes shape or color based on how suitable a position is for object placement.

Time to try this out!

Open up the **Chapter16Startup** scene from the **Scenes** folder and save it as **FocusTarget** in the same folder using the **File > Save As..** top menu option.

Open up the **FocusTarget** scene, select **ARSessionOrigin** and add an **ARPlaneManager** component to it. This causes the session to start looking for planes. You do not need to populate the **PlanePrefab** field of this component because you don't need to visualize the planes themselves. In this case, you only need to detect them so your UI can raycast against them and locate viable placement sites.

Now create a new empty GameObject and name it **FocusTarget**. This is going to keep track of where to place the object placement UI and what the UI should look like.

Create a new C# script named **FocusTarget.cs** and save it in the **Assets \ Razeware \ Scripts** folder. Open it up in a code editor and add the following code:

```
using System.Collections.Generic;
using UnityEngine;
using UnityEngine.Experimental.XR;
using UnityEngine.XR.ARFoundation;

namespace Razeware.ARBook
{
    //1
    public class FocusTarget : MonoBehaviour
    {
        //2
        public enum FocusState
        {
            Initializing,
            Finding,
            Found
        }

        public ARSessionOrigin arSessionOrigin; //3
        public GameObject findingTarget; //4
        public GameObject foundTarget; //5

        public float findingTargetDist = 1.0f; //6
        bool trackingInitialized; //7
    }
}
```

1. Declare the class derived from Monobehaviour.
2. Declare an `enum` to list all the different states that this script could be in.
3. Reference to `ARSessionOrigin` for raycast and camera functionality. Set in Editor.
4. Reference to GameObject to be displayed when in finding state. Set in Editor.
5. Reference to GameObject to be displayed when in found state. Set in Editor.
6. Distance to cast ray to check if there is a surface nearby.
7. Boolean to keep track if tracking has been initialized.

Next add a `FocusState` field and a property in this class that activates the correct GameObject

```
private FocusState targetState; //1

public FocusState TargetState //2
{
    get { return targetState; } //3
    set
    {
        targetState = value; //4
        foundTarget.SetActive(targetState ==
FocusState.Found); //5
        findingTarget.SetActive(targetState !=
FocusState.Found); //6
    }
}
```

1. Private backing field that keeps track of current `FocusState`.
2. Public property that uses the backing field above.
3. Getter for property just returns the current value of the backing field.
4. Set the new value of the property.
5. If the newly set **targetState** is `FocusState.Found`, set the **foundTarget** to be active.
6. If the newly set **targetState** is not `FocusState.Found`, set the **findingTarget** to be active.

Now add these methods to the `FocusTarget` class:

```
// Use this for initialization
void Start()
{
    TargetState = FocusState.Initializing; //1
    trackingInitialized = true; //2
}


private void TransformFocusTarget(Pose hitPose) //3
{
    //move the focus target to where the hit is located
    foundTarget.transform.position = hitPose.position; //4
    foundTarget.transform.rotation = hitPose.rotation; //5
}


private bool HitTestWithTrackableType(Vector3 screenPositon,
                    TrackableType trackableTypeMask).     //6
{
```

```
    List<ARRaycastHit> hitResults = new List<ARRaycastHit>(); //
7
    if (arSessionOrigin.Raycast(screenPositon,
                hitResults, trackableTypeMask)) //8
    {
        foreach (var hitResult in hitResults) //9
        {
            //session relative pose
            TransformFocusTarget(hitResult.sessionRelativePose);
//10
            return true;
        }
    }
    return false; //11
}
```

1. On startup, set the target state to be Initializing.
2. Set `trackingInitialized` boolean to `true`.
3. Method to call to move the **foundTarget** based on the `Pose` passed in as a parameter.
4. Set new position of the **foundTarget** to be the position of the Pose.
5. Set new rotation of the foundTarget to be the rotation of the Pose.
6. Method to do a hit test from a screen position against a trackable type.
7. Start with an empty list of hit results.
8. Use the **AR Session Origin** raycast to get all the hits against the trackable type passed in.
9. Iterate over all the hit results (although you exit from this method after processing the first one).
10. For each hit result, call the `TransformFocusTarget` method above (3) with the `Pose` from the hit result. Return true to indicate that you got a hit.
11. If there was no hit, return false.

Finally, add an `Update` method to the class:

```
void Update()
{
    //use center of screen for focusing
    Vector3 center = new Vector3(Screen.width / 2,
                        Screen.height / 2,
findingTargetDist); //1

    // prioritize trackable types to hit test against
    //2
```

```
    TrackableType[] trackableTypes =
{ TrackableType.PlaneWithinPolygon };

    //check for each trackable types in order
    foreach (TrackableType trackableType in trackableTypes) //3
    {
        if (HitTestWithTrackableType(center, trackableType)) //4
        {
            TargetState = FocusState.Found; //5
            return;
        }
    }

    if (trackingInitialized) //6
    {
        TargetState = FocusState.Finding; //7

        //check camera forward is facing downward
        if
(Vector3.Dot(arSessionOrigin.camera.transform.forward,
                        Vector3.down) > 0.1f) //8
        {
            //position the focus finding target a distance from
camera
            //and facing up
            findingTarget.transform.position =

arSessionOrigin.camera.ScreenToWorldPoint(center); //9

            //vector from camera to focustarget
            Vector3 vecToCamera =
findingTarget.transform.position -
                arSessionOrigin.camera.transform.position; //10

            //find vector that is orthogonal to camera vector
            //and up vector
            Vector3 vecOrthogonal =
                Vector3.Cross(vecToCamera, Vector3.up); //11

            //find vector orthogonal to both above and up vector
            Vector3 vecForward =
                Vector3.Cross(vecOrthogonal, Vector3.up); //12

            findingTarget.transform.rotation =
                    Quaternion.LookRotation(vecForward,
Vector3.up); //13
        }
        else
        {
            //don't display finding target if camera
            //is not facing below horizon
            findingTarget.SetActive(false); //14
        }
```

```
        }
    }
```

1. Create a `Vector` from the center of the screen as x and y values and the `findingTargetDist` as the z value.
2. List all the trackable types that you want the focus target to appear on in this array in order of priority.
3. Iterate over all the elements of the array in (2) in order.
4. For each trackable type call `HitTestWithTrackableType` method with the center screen vector and this trackable type as parameters.
5. If there was a hit, set the `TargetState` property to `FocusState.Found` and exit from the method.
6. When you reach this spot in the script, you have not found any hits on the hit test, so you are likely going to show the **findingTarget**.
7. Set the `TargetState` property to `FocusState.Finding`.
8. Check the dot product of the **AR Camera** forward vector and the world down vector to see if the camera is facing below the horizon.
9. Set the position of **findingTarget** to be the position `findingTargetDist` away in the camera forward direction.
10. Find the vector from the **AR Camera** to the **findingTarget**.
11. Find a vector orthogonal to the vector above (10) and the up vector. This will be the left vector of the **findingTarget**.
12. Find a vector orthogonal to the vector above (11) and the up vector. This will be the forward vector of the **findingTarget**.
13. Set the **findingTarget** rotation using the vector calculated in (12) and the up vector.
14. If the camera was facing the horizon or above, set the **findingTarget** to inactive so that it doesn't render.

The script keeps track of two states of the interaction: the first is where you're trying to find a good spot; the second is when you've found one. Each transition into a state enables the specific GameObject for that state and disables the GameObject for the other state.

A viable spot is considered found when a ray through the center of the screen gets a `RaycastHit` against a plane in the scene. When that happens, you take the position and orientation of the hit and set the "found" GameObject at that pose and activate it.

If a hit is not found in the update loop, you consider this as still searching and activate the "finding" GameObject which animates automatically to show that placement has not been found.

The display of the "finding" GameObject is always a certain distance away along the ray through the center of the screen, except if that ray is pointing above the horizon, in which case the GameObject is invisible.

Save the script and return to the editor.

Select **FocusTarget** and add a **Focus Target** component to it. It's time to add the two kinds of UI that can appear during this interaction: one for the "searching" UI; and one for the "found a good place" UI. Drag both the **FocusTargetFinding** and **FocusTargetFocused** from the **Prefabs** folder into the Hierarchy. Next, select **FocusTarget** and drag the instances you've just added to their corresponding slots on the **Focus Target** component.

Finally, drag **AR Session Origin** to the **Ar Session Origin** field. The **FocusTarget** will now look like this in the Inspector:

When you run this on the device, you'll be able to look around your environment and see the "focus target" flash bigger and smaller as it searches for good placement sites.

When it finds a suitable flat surface to place your content, it'll change into a crosshair. Pretty cool, right?

Tracking state

Considering the algorithms and computations based on the video feed from the camera and IMU data are used for the world tracking; there are occasions when the quality of the tracking can be lower than normal. Some common reasons include:

- Low light
- Fast movement
- Not enough distinguishable features, like a plain wall with no textures, for example

Since these states are specific to the environment and lighting conditions of the individual devices, it makes sense to treat them dynamically and inform the user when one of these situations arise.

You can detect when tracking isn't working correctly by hooking the event `TrackingChanged` and checking when its value becomes `TrackingStateLimited`.

You can inform the user what they need to do to correct the situation by looking at the `TrackingStateReason` which lets you know *why* the tracking is limited in each particular case.

You can then translate that into actions the user can take to remedy the situation and get back to the full AR experience.

Future of interaction

The AR SDKs that are currently available are still in their initial phases. But things are changing rapidly — even this year you'll see some significant developments in the field of AR. That said, you can expect many other types of interactions that will be possible in AR. Here are some of them enumerated in no particular order:

Hand tracking

At the moment, the most common AR devices are handheld, but you can expect AR devices in the future to be eye-worn like Magic Leap, Hololens and others. With this kind of hardware and technology, you can get more immersive with your experiences, reduce hand fatigue and free up your hands so you can interact more directly with AR elements.

LeapMotion recently showed off a set of reference AR glasses design with their hand tracking hardware used for gesture recognition. They showed manipulation of virtual objects and their occlusion against the hand, as well as having regular UI attached to the hand. The interactions shown gave us a glimpse of what will be possible using hand tracking.

Eye gaze tracking

For eye-worn AR glasses, the detection of the specific direction that the wearer is looking at can provide cues for interaction. One way it might work is to narrow down what the wearer is interested in by following the wearer's gaze. Another approach might be to use indirect manipulation as described before but using the eye gaze direction as the vector which is used for pinpointing the interaction element.

Brain-Computer Interface (BCI)

This describes an interface where the user only has to *think* of a specific interaction, and the AR system recognizes the user's intent from the sensor that detects the user's brain activity. This has a lot of potential — if it works well — but it's also the one that needs a lot of research and development to get right and is probably the furthest out regarding stable implementation.

These are just a few of the possible future ways to interact with AR SDKs. There may be other interesting ways for interaction yet to be discovered or invented as the AR SDKs become more mature.

Where to go from here?

In this chapter you learned about creating user interfaces for your AR experience so that you can interact with your users in an intuitive manner. You learned how different user interaction models can make your app more immersive and intuitive to use.

In the next chapter, you will learn how to detect flat surfaces in the world to place your AR content on, using plane anchors. You will also learn about other kinds of anchors and how they can help place your virtual content appropriately in the real environment around you.

Chapter 17: Anchors & Planes in AR

Jimmy Alamparambil

Using computer vision algorithms and data from the gyroscopes and accelerometers (also known as the Intertial Measurement Unit or IMU for short), the AR SDKs can determine where a device is currently located in relation to the original starting point of the AR experience. Using world tracking and feature point detection, along with another key feature known as **anchors**, you can create some amazing augmented reality experiences.

In this chapter, you'll learn about the different types of anchors and how you can use them to place virtual objects within real-world environments.

Anchors

Think of anchors as locations relative to the real world environment to which virtual objects can be attached.

As time goes by, the AR SDKs gain a better understanding of the real world by detecting various feature points. As more feature points are detected, the existing anchors update their positions, orientations and other parameters. In most cases, as the real-world is analyzed and understood, more anchors get added.

There are different types of anchors in AR, but for now, you'll focus on the most basic type of anchors that both ARKit and ARCore support: **Plane Anchors**.

Plane anchors

The simplest type of anchor used for object placement is the **plane anchor**. With plane anchors, you can place virtual content on a flat surface — usually a horizontal surface like a table or the floor — or a vertical surface like a wall.

When a flat surface is first detected, the understanding of the plane that describes the surface is based on the limited number of feature points that have been detected on the surface. As more feature points are detected along the surface, the approximation of the plane gets more accurate and closer to the actual surface.

Imagine there's a table in the room. When the plane anchor for this table is initially detected, it might only cover a small portion of the table. As you move the device over the rest of the table, the plane anchor gets larger until it covers the entire table.

Now, imagine you place a virtual object at the center of a table. At first, it may look as if the object is floating slightly above the table. However, as tracking improves, and the table's surface is better understood, the object will look as if it is now resting on the table — provided you placed the virtual object as a child of a plane anchor.

Plane anchors contain a few parameters, such as a position and orientation for the plane which is the origin of the coordinate system for the plane. They also contain center and rectangular extents that get updated as the AR SDK gets more information about the plane.

Plane anchors also have a boundary mesh that more accurately describes the shape of the surface it's approximating. For instance, a round table will have a boundary mesh that's circular. But what good are plane anchors if you can't see or update them as the environment changes?

Plane visualization

Load the starter project for this chapter and open up the scene named **Chapter17Startup**. This scene contains the basic setup for an AR app, with the **ARSession** and **ARSessionOrigin** already populated in the Hierarchy. Make a copy of this scene by saving it as **PlaneVisualizer.unity** in the **Assets \ Razeware \ Scenes** folder.

Now, select **ARSessionOrigin** and press **Add Component** at the bottom of the Inspector. Next, select **AR Plane Manager** to add it as a component to **ARSessionOrigin**.

Here's the final result:

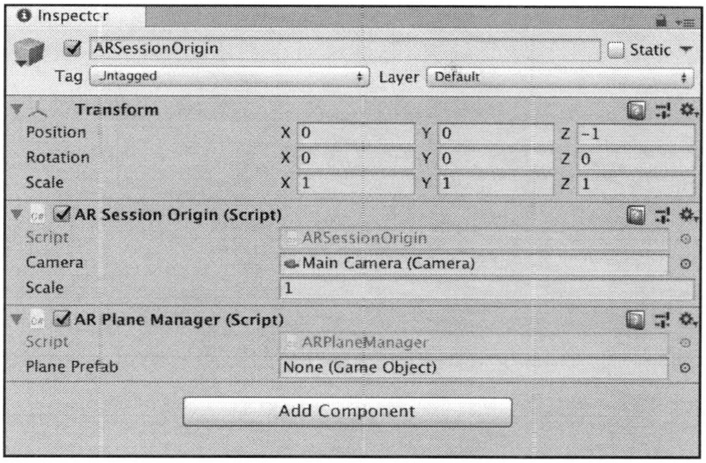

The **AR Plane Manager** component keeps track of every plane anchor that's been detected by the AR SDK, and it updates each plane anchor's position and orientation based on the events it receives from the AR SDK. If the AR SDK removes its understanding of a plane anchor, the **AR Plane Manager** component also removes it from its managed list of plane anchors.

Did you notice the **Plane Prefab** parameter slot on the **AR Plane Manager** component? It takes a Prefab GameObject. For each new plane anchor detected, the **AR Plane Manager** component creates a GameObject out of this prefab and keeps track of it, updating it and removing it when needed. This lets you relate a GameObject in Unity to each of the plane anchors as they're detected and updated.

You can use the GameObject it creates to do various things, such as use it for visualizing the detected planes. For that, you'll need to add a prefab that will create a good visualization of the planes as they're detected and use that prefab in the **Plane Prefab** parameter slot.

Create a C# script named **RazewarePlaneVisualizer.cs** and save it in the **Assets \ Razeware \ Scripts** folder. Open it in a code editor and add the following code at the top:

```
using UnityEngine;
using UnityEngine.XR.ARFoundation; //1

[RequireComponent(typeof(ARPlane))] //2
public class RazewarePlaneVisualizer : MonoBehaviour //3
{

}
```

1. First specify all the namespaces that you will be using in this script.
2. This attribute specifies that this script requires a component of type **ARPlane** to also be on the same GameObject in order to work properly.
3. The declaration of the class that derives from **Monobehaviour** that you are creating.

Here, you start with two `using` statements and a `RequireComponent` for **ARPlane** — a component you need on the GameObject to get the position, orientation and size of the plane you want to visualize. **ARPlane** is the AR SDK understanding of the detected plane anchor.

To keep track of the **ARPlane** component, you'll need some private variables. You'll also need a `bool` so you'll know when to update the plane.

Initialize these properties in the `Awake` method:

```
ARPlane arPlane; //1
bool needsUpdate; //2

void Awake ()
{
    arPlane = GetComponent<ARPlane>(); //3
    needsUpdate = false; //4
}
```

1. Store a reference to the **ARPlane** component on this GameObject to avoid calling `GetComponent` every time you need it.
2. Boolean to keep track of when the plane parameters need to be updated.
3. When the script starts, find the **ARPlane** component and store a reference to it in a private field.
4. Set the `needsUpdate` field to false;

```
private void OnEnable()
{
    arPlane.updated += ArPlane_Updated; //1
    needsUpdate = true; //2
}

private void OnDisable()
{
    arPlane.updated -= ArPlane_Updated; //3
    needsUpdate = false;
}

void ArPlane_Updated(ARPlane obj) //4
{
    //If our plane is updated, then update its dimensions in
```

```
        //the Update() method
        if (arPlane == obj) //5
        {
            needsUpdate = true;
        }
    }
```

1. When this GameObject is enabled, add a listener to the `updated` event on the **ARPlane** component. This listener method will get called whenever the AR SDK determines a plane has changed in some way.
2. When the GameObject is enabled, initial values for the plane parameters need to be obtained, so `needsUpdate` should be set to `true`.
3. When the GameObject is disabled, remove the listener to the `updated` event and set `needsUpdate` to `false`.
4. This is the listener method declared in step 1 above - it will get called with an updated `ARPlane` object whenever the AR SDK determines a plane has changed.
5. In the listener method, check that the event that has occured belongs to the **ARPlane** component that is on this GameObject. If so, set `needsUpdate` to `true` so the update method can handle the change.

Once you know you have to update the plane, you need to update its local position, orientation and size based on the properties set on the `ARPlane` component:

```
    void Update()
    {
        if (needsUpdate) //1
        {
            transform.localRotation =
                arPlane.boundedPlane.Pose.rotation; //2
            transform.localPosition =
                arPlane.boundedPlane.Center; //3
            transform.localScale =
                new Vector3(arPlane.boundedPlane.Size.x, 1.0f,
                    arPlane.boundedPlane.Size.y); //4
            needsUpdate = false; //5
        }
    }
```

1. Checks the `needsUpdate` boolean to see if anything has changed with the plane represented by this GameObject in order to update it.
2. Update the rotation of this GameObject to match the pose rotation of the **ARPlane** associated with it.

3. Update the position of this GameObject to be at the coordinates of the center of the **ARPlane** associated with it.
4. Update the scale of this GameObject to match the extents of the **ARPlane** associated with it.
5. Set `needsUpdate` to be false to avoid updates until the next time the AR SDK raises an event to say something has changed with the plane.

With the rest of the code added, save the script and return to the editor.

Create a new GameObject in the Hierarchy and name it **RazewarePlaneVisualizer**. Remember, the script requires an **ARPlane** component, so add it to this newly made GameObject. While you're there, also add the **Razeware Plane Visualizer** component you just created.

When you're done, this is what it should look like in the Inspector:

As it is, a copy of this GameObject will be created for every plane detected, and its transform will be moved, rotated and sized according to the plane anchor updates. However, since this GameObject does not currently have anything that renders, you won't be able to visualize what those planes look like in the scene.

The Plane Visiualizer expects a plane mesh that's 1 meter by 1 meter in size. Create a new **Plane** by clicking the **Create** dropdown at the top left of the Hierarchy and selecting **3D Object ▸ Plane**. Drag the new plane onto **RazewarePlaneVisualizer** to it a child and set its scale to **(X:0.1, Y:0.1, Z:0.1)** to make it a single unit sized plane. With this, any alteration on the parent transform will be acting on the plane, and everything will work out as expected.

Rename the plane to **UnitPlane**, remove the **Mesh Collider** component and choose **Assets \ Razeware \ Materials \ PlaneMaterial** as its material. When you're done, it should look like this in the Hierarchy and the Inspector:

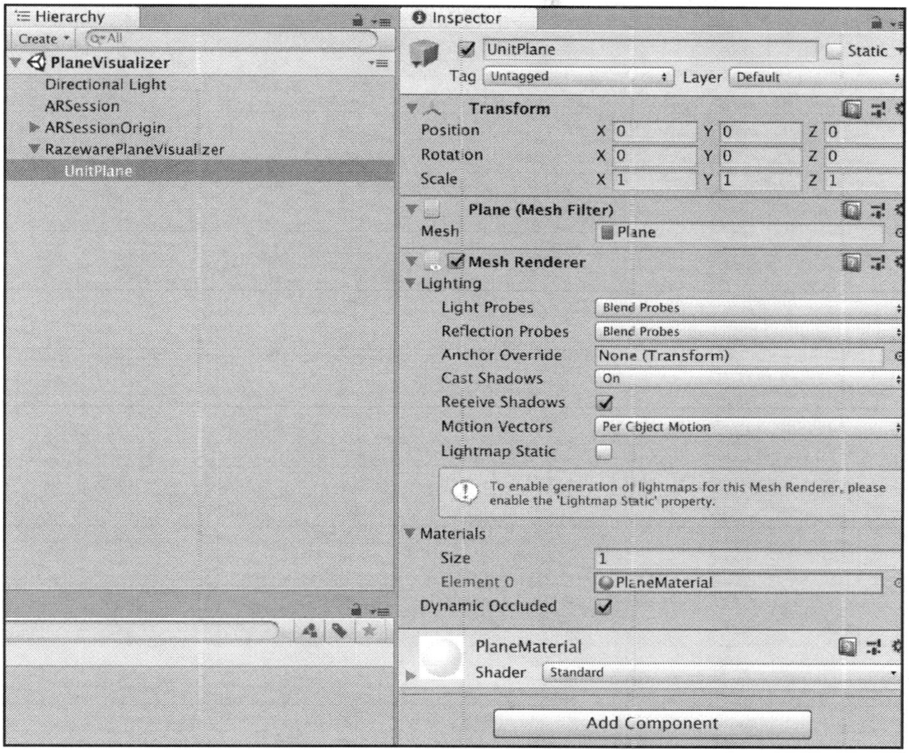

Create a new prefab in the **Assets \ Razeware \ Prefabs** folder named **RazewarePlaneVisualizer** by dragging the **RazewarePlaneVisualizer** from the Hierarchy to that folder in the project view. Now you can delete the **RazewarePlaneVisualizer** from the scene since you have saved the template you need.

Now, select **ARSessionOrigin**, drag the **RazewarePlaneVisualizer** prefab you just made onto the **Plane Prefab** slot of the **AR Plane Manager** component and save the scene.

Open the **Build Settings**, choose your primary deployment platform (iOS for ARKit or Android for ARCore) and add the current scene to the build by clicking the **Add Open Scenes** button.

Now press the **Build And Run** button to build and run this to your device. Time to harvest the fruits of your labor!

With the app running, look around your room with the device. As planes get detected, your app will show some virtual transparent green planes that correspond to the visualization of the detected planes in the real world.

> **Note**: You may need to adjust the **AR Camera Clipping Planes** `near` parameter in the Inspector to correctly visualize planes that are too close to you.

Virtual object placement

In Chapter 15, you learned about the **Raycast Subsystem** and using the AR SDKs understanding of the world to place objects. That system used a mechanism native to the AR SDKs called Hit Test to cast a ray against the detected surfaces and return positions in the world where hits occurred.

Unity already has a collision system and physics raycasts that you could use to interact with your virtual objects like you would in any regular Unity app. You can leverage these systems to create a more flexible way to place virtual objects and interact with them in AR.

The way you'll do this is by creating a collision plane for every plane anchor that is detected in the real world. Then, you'll do a regular physics raycast to check where there is an intersection with a collision plane in Unity and place the virtual object there.

This is distinctly different from the Raycast Subsystem in that you're using Unity's Physics module to find the collision instead of the AR SDK Hit Test. In this case, the advantage is not apparent, but as you create representations of your AR side objects on the Unity side, you get to use the power of all the Unity features to interact and animate the virtual objects in the scene. Time to get down to it!

Open the **PlaneVisualizer.unity** scene. Create a copy of the scene by saving it as **ObjectPlacerScene** in the **Assets \ Razeware \ Scenes** folder.

You'll need to modify the **RazewarePlaneVisualizer** prefab so that it has a collision mesh and it is in the right layer for you to detect collisions on it.

Drag the prefab into the Hierarchy and select the **UnitPlane**. In the Inspector, add a **Mesh Collider** component to this GameObject and select the **ARGameObject** layer (Layer 11) in the top right of the Inspector. Click the **Apply** button so your changes get applied to the prefab in the project. The **UnitPlane** should now look like this in the Inspector:

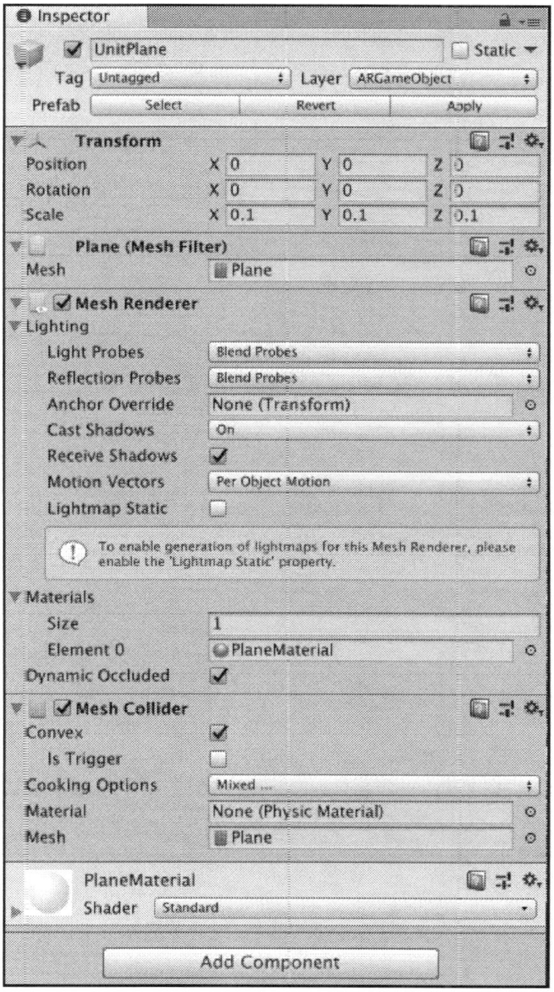

Now delete the **UnitPlane** in the Hierarchy since you're referring to it from **ARPlaneManager**. This means every time a plane is generated, you'll now have a mesh collider with the **ARGameObject** layer on it.

Now, create a new empty GameObject in the root of the Hierarchy and name it **EggParent**. This is going to be the root of the virtual object you're going to place on the planes.

Now drag the **EggPrefab** prefab from the **Assets \ Razeware \ Prefabs** folder to the Hierarchy and parent it to the **EggParent**.

Next, you're going to create the script needed to check for the mesh collision on the planes and place the virtual object at the collision point. Create a new C# script named **PutObjectOnPlane.cs** in the **Assets \ Razeware \ Scripts** folder and open it in a code editor.In this script, you'll first add references to the GameObject you want to place and the **Main Camera**.

```
using System.Collections;
using System.Collections.Generic;
using UnityEngine; //1

public class PutObjectOnPlane : MonoBehaviour //2
{

    public Transform m_ObjectToPlace; //3

    public Camera ARCamera; //4
}
```

1. Declare namespaces that will be used in this script.
2. Declare the class derived from Monobehaviour.
3. Reference of a `Transform` that will be set in the Editor which will be the root of the GameObject to place.
4. Reference of a `Camera` that represents the position and rotation of the AR device.

On startup, you need to hide the virtual object, so it does not appear on the scene. It should only appear when you tap on a plane, so put this code in the script:

```
void Start()
{
    m_ObjectToPlace.gameObject.SetActive (false);
}
```

This disables the GameObject that you want place on starting up this script so that it does not render or update.

Next, you need to check if the user has tapped on the screen, and if so, perform a Physics Raycast into the scene from the point-of-view of the camera to see if it hits any collisions in the **ARGameObject** layer. If it does, you need to move the virtual object to the collision point, parent it to the plane and enable it.

Add the following code:

```
void Update() //1
{
    if (Input.GetMouseButton(0)) //2
    {

        Ray ray =
            ARCamera.ScreenPointToRay(Input.mousePosition); //3

        // Planes are in layer ARGameObject
        int layerMask =
            1 << LayerMask.NameToLayer("ARGameObject"); //4

        RaycastHit rayHit; //5
        if (Physics.Raycast(ray, out rayHit,
            float.MaxValue, layerMask)) //6
        {
            m_ObjectToPlace.gameObject.SetActive(true); //7
            m_ObjectToPlace.transform.position =
rayHit.point; //8
            //we rotate our origin to match the plane we are put
on
            m_ObjectToPlace.transform.rotation =
                rayHit.transform.rotation; //9
            //we also parent it to the plane so that any
            //plane updates will propagate to us
            m_ObjectToPlace.transform.parent = rayHit.transform;
//10
        }
    }
}
```

1. Update method of the script which is called every frame
2. Check whether there was a tap on the screen of the AR device.
3. If there was a tap, calculate the ray that corresponds to the tapped screen position on the view of the camera.
4. Get the layer mask to use for the raycast. The generated planes will use the "ARGameObject" layer.
5. `rayHit` will contain the raycast result if the ray collided with anything.
6. Call the `Physics.Raycast` method with the parameters from above, and make sure to test all the way to the furthest extent of the ray. If there was a hit that method will return `true`.
7. If there was a hit, enable the rendering and update of the GameObject you want to place.

8. Place the GameObject at the position of the hit.
9. Rotate the GameObject so that it is aligned with the plane that was hit.
10. Set the parent of the GameObject to be the transform of the collision plane GameObject.

Great! Save this script and return to the editor.

Now create a new empty GameObject in the root of the Hierarchy and name it **ObjectPlacer**. This is what the Hierarchy will look like when you're done:

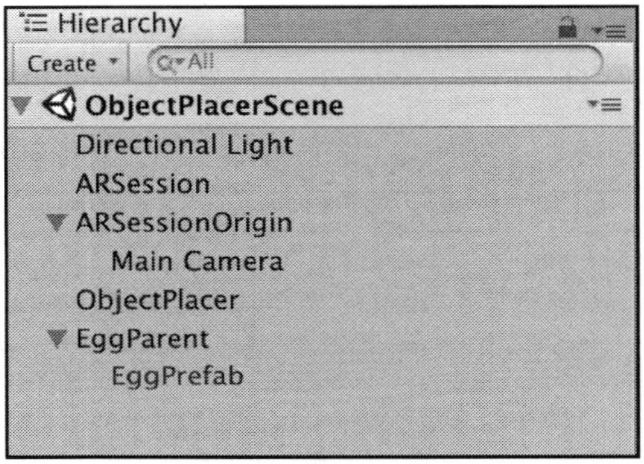

Select **ObjectPlacer** and add the **PutObjectPlane** script component on to it. Drag the **EggParent** transform from the hierarchy view into the **Object To Place** parameter on the component in the Inspector. Drag the **Main Camera** into the **AR Camera** parameter. The Inspector of **ObjectPlacer** will now look like this:

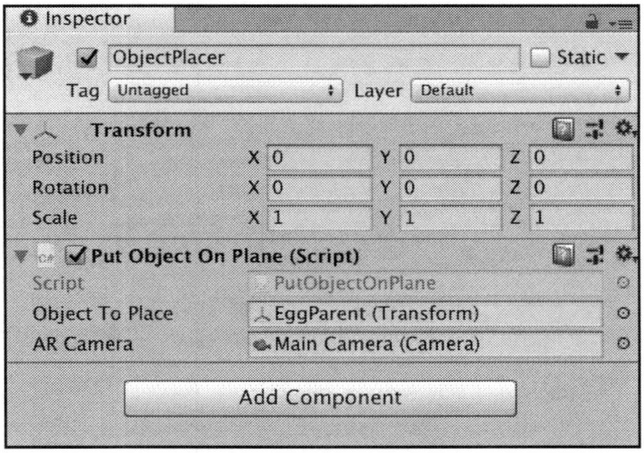

You're now ready to test this out. Build this scene to the device and look around. You'll see plane visualizations like last time.

Now, point your device at one of the planes that have been detected and touch the screen on some part of the plane. You'll see the yellow egg appear on that spot:

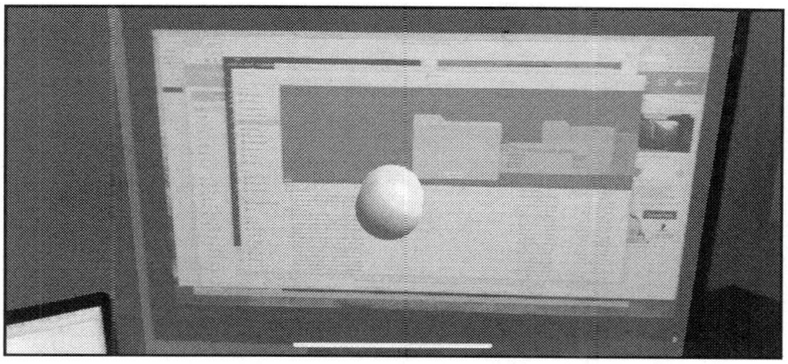

Since you parented the virtual object to the plane GameObject, any updates to the plane anchor will mean your virtual object will move along with it and be able to settle to the new, more accurate approximation of the plane that the AR SDK has found.

Reference points (user anchors)

Suppose you have somehow found an arbitrary point in your real environment (not necessarily on an existing flat surface) that you want to use as a place to attach your virtual content. Imagine that you want to use that point and still get the benefits of the AR SDK updating the position and orientation of the anchor as its understanding of the environment gets better.

For this case, you'd create a **Reference Point** (or **User Anchor** as it's sometimes referred to by the AR SDKs) and inform the AR SDK of its existence The AR SDK would then send back updates of the anchor position and orientation as its understanding improves.

You can use the same project with a new scene to show how reference points are created and removed.

Load up the **Chapter17Startup** scene. It contains the basic setup for AR apps, with **ARSession** and **ARSessionOrigin** already add to the Hierarchy. Save a copy of this scene in the **Assets \ Razeware \ Scenes** folder and name it **ReferencePoints**.

Open this newly created scene, select **ARSessionOrigin** and look at it in the Inspector. Click **Add Component** at the bottom of the Inspector, and add an **AR Reference Point Manager** component.

The **ARSessionOrigin** will now look like this:

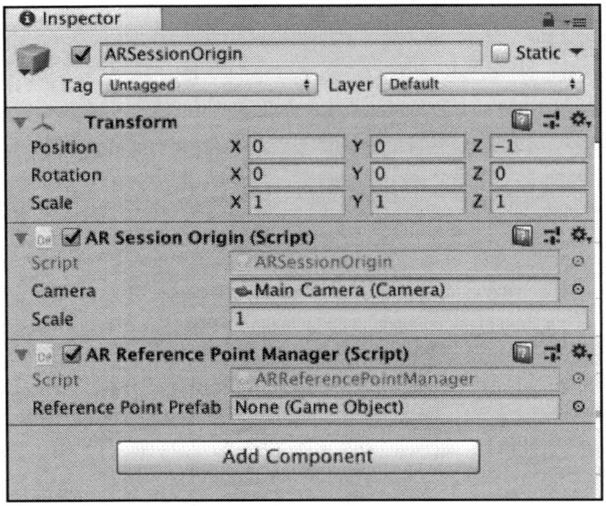

The **AR Reference Point Manager** component allows you to create or remove a reference point (or user anchor) in the AR SDK. Once a reference point is created in the AR SDK, it gets updated whenever the environmental understanding of the AR SDK improves.

You would usually parent a virtual object to the reference point you created so that the virtual object is automatically updated when the environment is better understood. In this case, you'll add a reference point and a virtual object that's attached to it when you tap on the screen.

Time to create the prefab that will be created every time you add a reference point in the scene.

First, create a new empty GameObject in the Hierarchy, name it **ReferencePointPrefab** and select it. Press the **Add Component** button in the Inspector and add a **AR Reference Point** component. Now you need a visual appearance for the virtual object, so create a capsule as a child of the **ReferencePointPrefab** and set its scale to **(X:0.05, Y: 0.05, Z:0.05)**.

Select **EggMaterial** as its Material on the **Mesh Renderer**. The capsule should now appear like this in the Inspector and the Hierarchy:

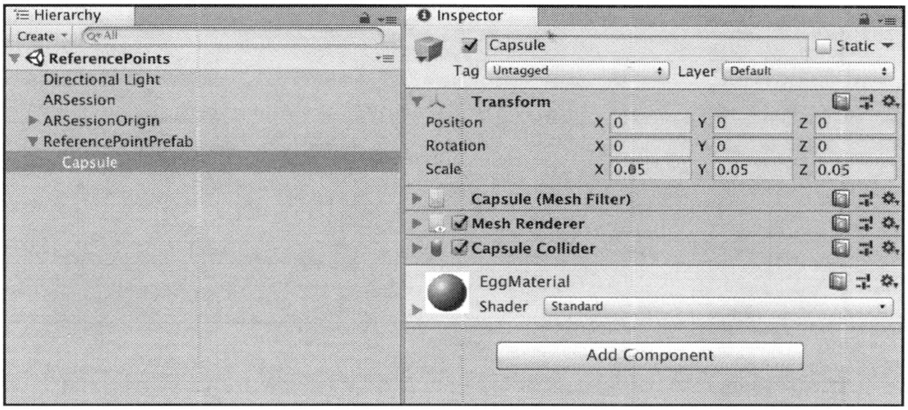

Drag **ReferencePointPrefab** to the **Prefabs** folder in the Project view to create a prefab with the same name. You can now delete the original from the Hierarchy. Select **ARSessionOrigin** and in the Inspector, drag the reference of the prefab from the **Prefabs** folder onto the **Reference Point Prefab** field of the **AR Reference Point Manager** component.

Next, you'll create a script that will add and remove these reference points.

Create a new script in the **Scripts** folder and name it **RazewareRPSpawner**. Op it in a code editor and edit the script so it matches the following:

```
using System.Collections;
using System.Collections.Generic;
using UnityEngine;
using UnityEngine.XR.ARFoundation;
using UnityEngine.SpatialTracking; //1

[RequireComponent(typeof(ARReferencePointManager))] //2
public class RazewareRPSpawner : MonoBehaviour //3
{
    public Camera camera; //4

    ARReferencePointManager referencePointManager; //5
    List<ARReferencePoint> arReferencePoints; //6

    void Start()
    {
        referencePointManager =
            GetComponent<ARReferencePointManager>(); //7
        arReferencePoints = new List<ARReferencePoint>(); //8
    }
}
```

1. Declare namespaces that this class will use.
2. **AR Reference Point Manager** component must be present on GameObject for this script to work.
3. Declare class that derives from Monobehaviour.
4. Reference to `Camera` that corresponds to AR device position and rotation.
5. Field to store reference to the required **AR Reference Point Manager** component to avoid calling `GetComponent` all the time.
6. List to store created reference points.
7. On startup, store the reference of the **AR Reference Point Manager** component that is on this GameObject.
8. Initialize the list of reference points to an empty list.

You start off by requiring the **AR Reference Point Manager** component in the same GameObject which gives you the ability to add and remove reference points. You also create a public reference to the **Camera** being controlled by the device, which you'll set in the Editor. You also need to create a list of reference points to keep track of the ones you created.

Then you make two public functions which will be called via button presses.

```
public void CreateReferencePoint() //1
{
    ARReferencePoint arrp =
        referencePointManager.TryAddReferencePoint(
            camera.transform.position +
            (camera.transform.forward * 0.5f),
            camera.transform.rotation); //2

    arReferencePoints.Add(arrp); //3
}

public void RemoveFirstReferencePoint() //4
{
    if (arReferencePoints.Count > 0) //5
    {
        ARReferencePoint arrp = arReferencePoints[0]; //6
        //7
        if
(referencePointManager.TryRemoveReferencePoint(arrp.data.Id))
        {
            arReferencePoints.Remove(arrp); //8
        }
    }
}
```

1. Method to create a reference point. This will be called directly from a UI button press.
2. Use a method on the **AR Reference Point Manager** component to try and add a reference point at a point slightly in front of the camera position.
3. Add the reference point created to the list of reference points.
4. Method to remove the first reference point in the list. This will be called directly from a UI button press.
5. This method only works if there is at least one reference point in the list.
6. Get a reference to the first reference point in the list.
7. Try and remove that reference point from the **AR Reference Point Manager** component. This method returns true if the reference point was successfully removed.
8. When reference point is removed from the component, it should also be removed from the list.

CreateReferencePoint will create a new reference point 0.5 meters in front of the camera with the same rotation as the camera. It will add the newly created reference point to our list. **RemoveFirstReferencePoint** will see if you have any reference points in our list, and if so, will remove the first one from it. Save the script and return to the editor. Now select **ARSessionOrigin** and look at the Inspector. Add a **Razeware RP Spawner** component and drag the **Main Camera** from the Hierarchy onto the **Camera** field.

This is the result in the Inspector:

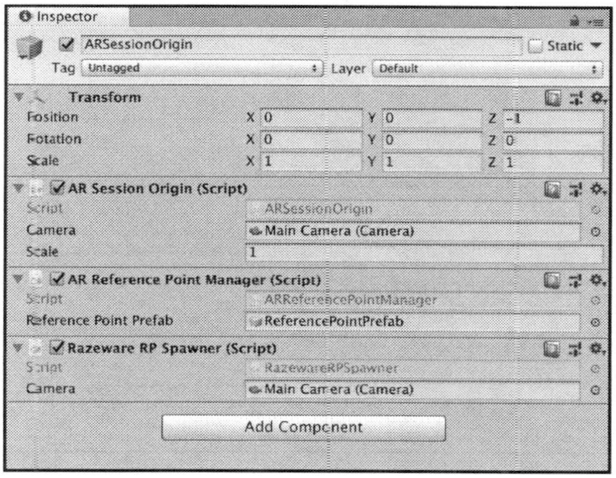

You're all set to make the UI. There's a prefab in the **Prefabs** folder named **SpawnerUI**. Drag it to the Hierarchy view to create a canvas with two buttons.

Locate the GameObject named **Create RP** that's a child of the newly created UI. This GameObject has a **Button** component. Add a new entry in its **On Click ()** list. Drag **ARSessionOrigin** to to the field of the GameObject to call in case a click on the left. Next, open the method dropdown and select the **RazewareRPSpawner.CreateReferencePoint** method.

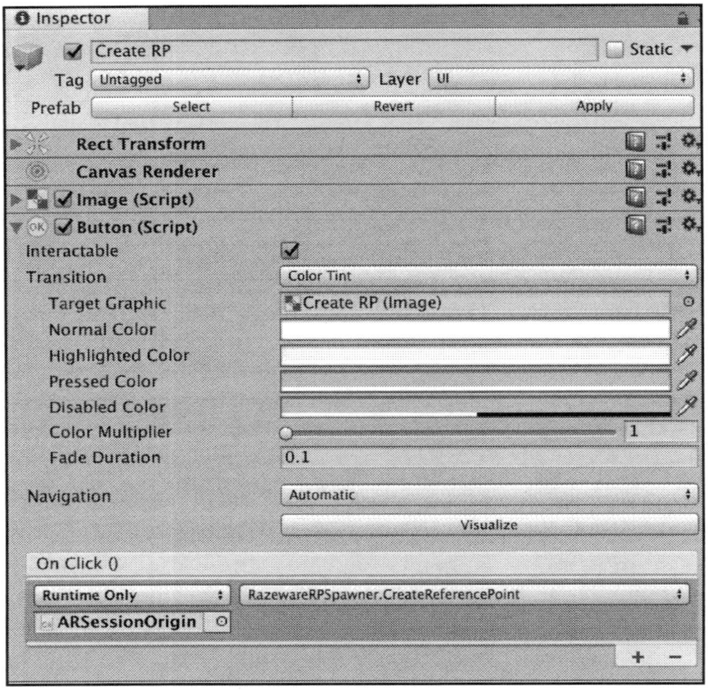

Similarly, locate **Remove RP** in the Hierarchy and repeat the same steps as just described, but this time, use **RazewareRPSpawner.RemoveFirstReferencePoint** as the method name. You're now ready to build this scene to the device and try it out. Open the **Build Settings**, choose your primary deployment platform (iOS for ARKit or Android for ARCore) and press the **Build And Run** button.

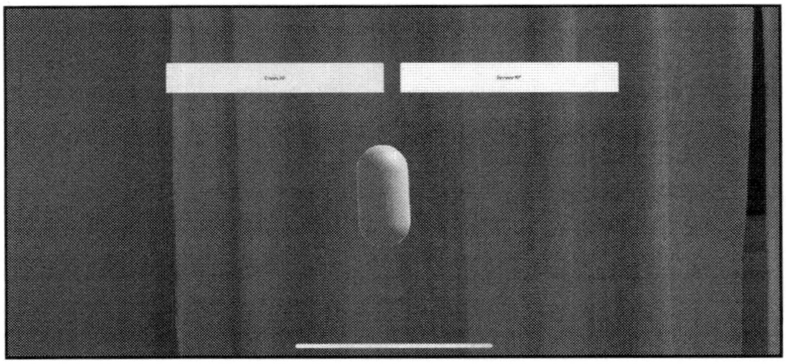

More anchors

In this chapter, you examined the two main types of anchors that you can use to attach your virtual content to. There are other types of anchors that are supported by either one of the platforms or the other. There's a good chance these other anchor types will become standard across all of the AR SDKs at some point, so it's useful to know about them.

Face anchors

With the iPhone X and iOS 11.2, ARKit introduced Face Tracking. An AR app that initializes the configuration for face tracking is informed when a face is detected on the front camera of the iPhone X. This will be detected in the form of a face anchor, and as the face moves, the anchor will update with the new position and orientation. You can treat this anchor similar to other anchors in case you want to attach virtual ornaments or masks to the face in question.

Image anchors

Before ARKit and ARCore were released, the most common type of AR SDKs would use marker-based or image-based AR. They would use an image as a marker that would establish the origin of the world tracking done by the device, and provide an anchor on which you could put virtual content. ARKit and ARCore both recently introduced a similar concept in Image anchors.

You can specify certain images in your app and configure the AR SDKs to try and detect those images in your real-world environment. When one of the images are detected, there will be an image anchor added to the scene at that spot.

This can be used to synchronize experiences across multiple players, but also as markers for specific types of AR content.

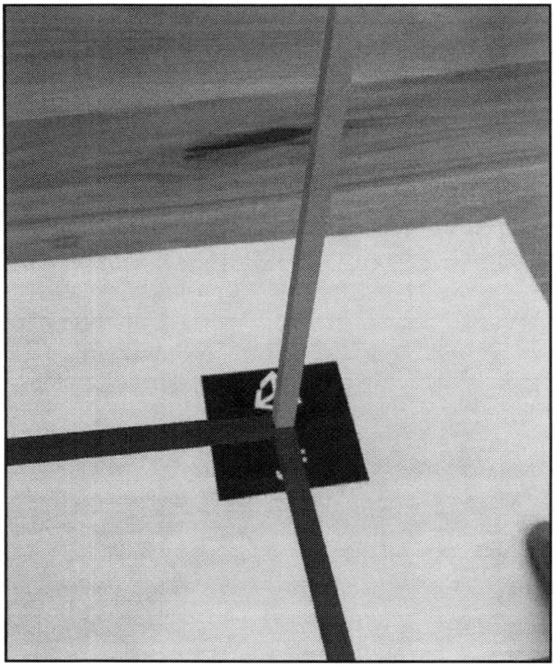

Object anchors

In ARKit version 2.0, Apple introduced the concept of reference objects which are akin to markers mentioned above, except they are full 3D. You would scan an object like a coke can and use that scan to detect any instances of coke cans in your environment. ARKit would then create an object anchor at the spot where it detected the coke can.

For example, you might want a virtual butterfly to sit on top of the coke can on your table.

Environment probe anchors

Also in ARKit 2.0, Apple introduced environment probe anchors that will create and update a reflected environment map of the surrounding area so that you can improve the immersiveness of your virtual objects in this area by using the environment map for lighting your virtual objects.

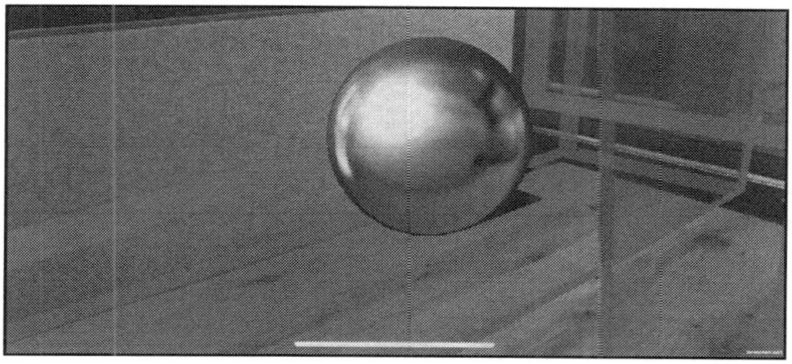

Oriented feature points

Feature points are 3D positions where the AR SDK was able to determine from the camera feed that something existed in the real environment. ARCore introduced the concept of oriented feature points in the 1.0 release. These were less like feature points and more like anchors because they had the concept of orientation (or surface normals). You could use these oriented feature points to place virtual objects in the scene so that they believably stuck to the surface where the feature point was detected.

Where to go from here?

In this chapter you learned about how to place virtual objects on flat surfaces in the real world. You also learned about other types of anchors that you could use to augment your world.

In the next chapter, you will learn how to use Unity features to enhance the AR experience you are creating. You will learn how to use Unity Physics to simulate real time interactions between the virtual objects and the real environment. You will also learn how to use rendering techniques to make the virtual objects appear more part of the environment.

Section VI: ARKit & ARCore Advanced

Explore more advanced AR topics in this section. Insert physics and lighting in your scene to add some polish. Find out how to use ARFoundation to scale your virtual content if the situation calls for it. As a cherry on top, learn how to create a multiplayer AR experience that you can play with up three of your friends.

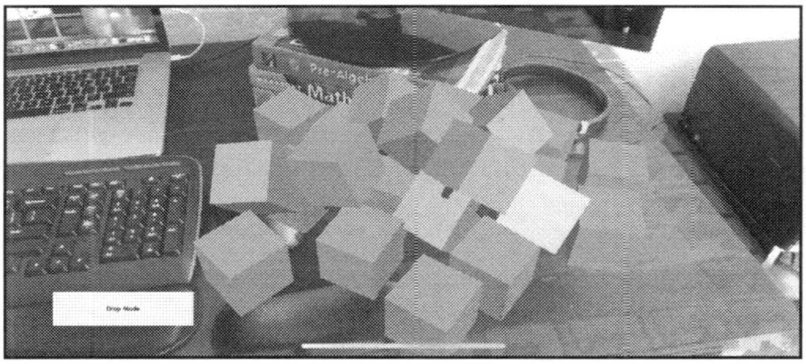

This section covers these topics:

- **Chapter 18: Physics & Rendering**: Ground your objects in the world with physics and lighting. This chapter covers how to use physics and how to add lighting and shadows in augmented reality.
- **Chapter 19: Scaled Content**: This chapter discusses the advantages and disadvantages of scaling content in augmented reality. It also shows you how to make your virtual content appear to be a different size or orientation when augmenting the real world.
- **Chapter 20: Multiplayer AR**: Getting your games connected and playing with others is a wonderful experience. Doing this in AR is even more exciting as you and your friends share the space in which the game appears. In this chapter, you will create an exciting multiplayer AR game using most of the techniques learnt in the previous chapters.

Chapter 18: Physics & Rendering

Jimmy Alamparambil

To deliver the most immersive augmented reality experiences, the virtual objects you place within the scene need to look and behave like real-world objects. In other words, they need to react realistically to the shapes and surface edges of the real environment. In this chapter, you'll look at some of the ways to achieve this believably with your own virtual content.

Physics

To mimic realistic behavior on virtual objects, you can make use of **PhysX**, the realistic 3D physics module included with Unity. In case you didn't know, PhysX is what Unity's Physics class uses for all its calculation.

Collision detection

In Chapter 15, you learned about hit-testing and how the AR SDKs use raycasting to detect when surfaces or feature points are hit. In many cases, this works well, but not when you want to use the Unity Physics engine to simulate certain behaviors or reactions to colliding with other objects. Consider how dice might bounce off a table or into each other when you drop them.

To get collision detection working, you need to create a GameObject whose shape matches the shape of the surface; you also need to add a Physics Collider component to that GameObject. By doing so, you bring the real surface into the Unity physics simulation world. With the surface now available, you can raycast against it and add virtual content where the physics raycast hits the virtual collision prefab.

If you recall, you did this in Chapter 17 in the **ObjectPlacerScene** scene. To recap:

- You created a GameObject with a mesh collider for each plane anchor you found.
- You used a Unity Physics raycast to get hits on that collider where you touched it on the screen.
- You placed a virtual object into the scene at the location of the hit point.

In the following sections, you're going to build on this collision detection ability.

Adding physics to virtual objects

If you want to use Unity's Physics system to simulate the realistic behavior that results from the interaction of virtual objects, you'll need to add Physics components to each of your virtual objects. You'll also need to create GameObjects with Physics components that are representative of the real objects, but only if you want the virtual objects to interact with the real scene.

For example, let's say you have a flat surface in the real world, and you want to throw a few virtual cubes on top of it and have them react as if they were real. In this case, you would detect the plane anchor that represents that flat surface, and then create a GameObject from a plane prefab that has a Physics Collider component attached. Time to build a scene to demonstrate things.

Open the **Chapter18Startup** scene from the **Assets \ Razeware \ Scenes** folder and save it as **Physics** in the same folder.The first thing is to create colliders for the detected surfaces, so the cubes have something on which to land.

Select **ARSessionOrigin** in the Hierarchy. In the Inspector, press **Add Component**, and add an **AR Plane Manager** component. Next, drag the **RazewarePlaneVisualizer** prefab from the **Prefabs** folder into the **Plane Prefab** slot for this component. Now the app will create green-bordered planes with colliders whenever a plane is detected in the real environment.

From there, you can do a raycast to find a spot on the surface, and once detected, drop the virtual objects slightly above it. So now, you need to create a cube prefab that will obey physics; you'll be dropping these onto the planes.To create a cube in the Hierarchy, select **/GameObject/3D Object/Cube** from the menu and rename it to **DropCube**.

Now, for the correct interaction to occur with the table and the other cubes, you'll need two components on the cube Prefab. The first is the box collider that represents the shape of the virtual cube, and since the cube is dynamic and will move based on the Physics components you provide, you'll also need a Rigidbody component to give the cube Physics properties like weight and movement.

Change the scale of **DropCube** to **(X:0.05, Y:0.05, Z:0.05)** since the standard cube is too large to drop onto your table. Note that it already has a **Box Collider** component, which is an essential part of its physics model as mentioned above.

Now add a new **Rigidbody** component and change its **Mass** to **0.01** so the cube interacts physically as if it's 1 gram instead of 1 kilogram. and note that it uses gravity. Change the **Material** of the **Mesh Renderer** to **CubeMaterial**, this give the cube a nice orange color. When you're done, the Inspector for the **DropCube** will look like this:

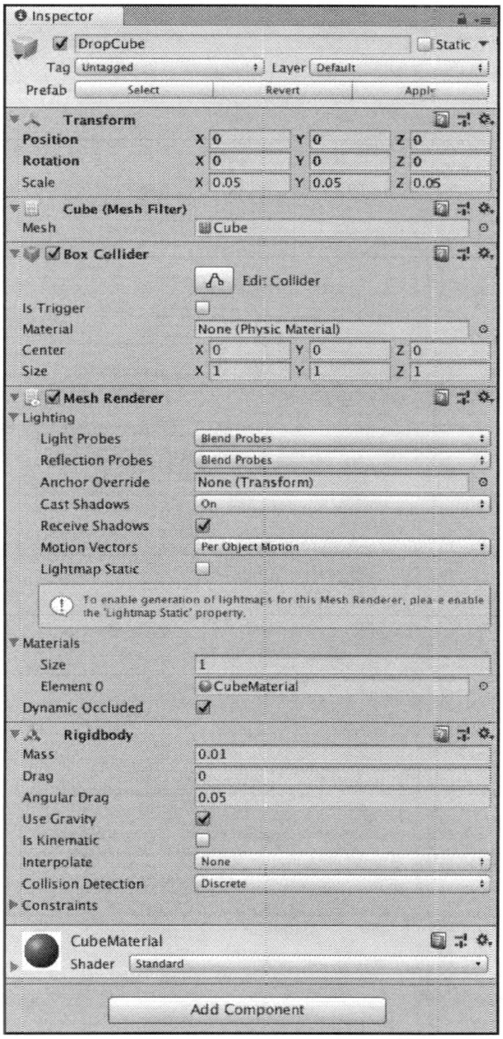

Save **DropCube** as a prefab by dragging it into the **Assets \ Razeware \ Prefabs** folder and delete it from the Hierarchy.

Next, create a script named **Assets \ Razeware \ Scripts \ DropFromAbove.cs**, and add the following code:

```
using UnityEngine;

public class DropFromAbove : MonoBehaviour //1
{
    public GameObject prefabToDrop; //2
    public float createHeight; //3

    private bool firstClick = true; //4
}
```

1. Declare the class derived from Monobehaviour.
2. Reference to a prefab to be instantiated whenever user taps on the screen.
3. Parameter of this script to specify how high off the plane the object should drop from.
4. Boolean to keep track of when tap occurred.

In the class, create an `Update` method:

```
void Update()
{
    if (!isActiveAndEnabled) //1
    {
        return;
    }

    if (Input.GetMouseButton(0)) //2
    {
        if (firstClick) //3
        {
            var camera = Camera.main;
            Ray ray =
camera.ScreenPointToRay(Input.mousePosition); //4

            int layerMask =
                1 << LayerMask.NameToLayer("ARGameObject"); //5

            RaycastHit rayHit;
            if (Physics.Raycast(ray, out rayHit,
                float.MaxValue, layerMask)) //6
            {
                Vector3 position = rayHit.point; //7
                GameObject cubeGO = Instantiate(prefabToDrop,
                                    new Vector3(position.x,
position.y +
                                    createHeight, position.z),
                                    Quaternion.identity); //8
```

```
                Rigidbody rb = cubeGO.GetComponent<Rigidbody>();
//9
                rb.AddTorque(new Vector3(0.5f, 0.0f, 1.0f)); //
10
            }
            firstClick = false; //11
        }
    }
    else
    {
        firstClick = true; //12
    }
}
```

1. Proceed only if the GameObject this script is on is active and enabled.
2. Check if there is a tap on the screen.
3. Check that the tap is not from the last frame.
4. Create a ray based on camera view from the current touch location.
5. Create a layer mask to check for plane colliders created by the **AR Plane Manager**.
6. Do a raycast with the ray calculated to see if we hit any plane colliders.
7. If we hit a collider, keep track of the point where hit occured.
8. Instantiate a GameObject from the prefab referenced and position it `createHeight` meters above the touched point.
9. Get the `Rigidbody` component of the GameObject created.
10. Add some torque to that rigidbody to make it spin as it falls.
11. Set boolean to show that we have handled the first tap on the screen.
12. If there was no touch this frame, the previous touch is now done.

This code is similar to the **PutObjectOnPlane.cs** script from the last chapter, except for three things:

- It takes a prefab reference and instantiates a new GameObject for every touch.
- It creates the GameObject at a height so that it will drop on to the surface below it.
- It gives it a bit of a spin for effect.

Time to put these ingredients together and create the physics cube dropper.

Save the script and return to the editor. Create a new empty GameObject in the Hierarchy and name it **CubeMaker**. In the Inspector for this GameObject, click **Add Component** and add the **Drop From Above** component you just created.

Finally, drag **DropCube** to the **Prefab To Drop** slot and save the scene. You're now ready to build to the device and test it out.

Run the app and scan around your room until the app detects and renders one or two green-bordered planes. Tap on one of the planes via your touchscreen and you should see orange cubes dropping stylishly on to your flat surface, while colliding with each other and the flat surface.

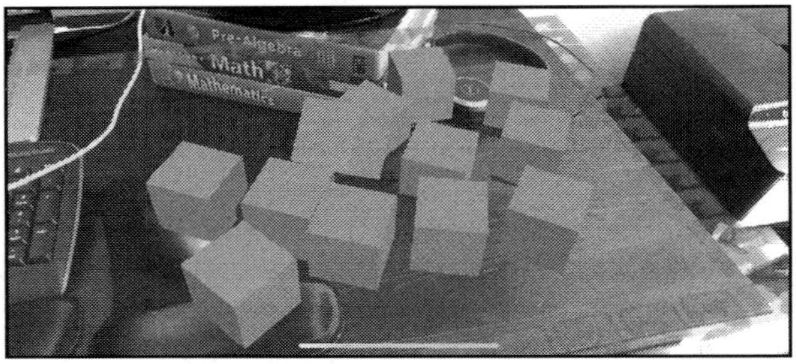

Applying forces and motion

In this section, you'll add two modes to the app: one for creating cubes to drop on the plane and the other to push around the cubes on the planes.

Start by saving the **Physics** scene from the last section as **Physics2** in the **Assets \ Razeware \ Scenes** folder.Next, create a **C#** script named **MoveObject** in the **Assets \ Razeware \ Scripts** folder to create the functionality of pushing GameObjects around. Open the script and replace everything in there with this code:

```
using UnityEngine;

public class MoveObjects : MonoBehaviour //1
{
    public GameObject wreckerGo; //2

    void Update()
    {
        if (!isActiveAndEnabled) //3
        {
            return;
        }

        if (Input.GetMouseButton(0)) //4
        {
            var camera = Camera.main;
```

```
            Ray ray =
camera.ScreenPointToRay(Input.mousePosition); //5

            int layerMask =
                1 << LayerMask.NameToLayer("ARGameObject"); //6

            RaycastHit rayHit;
            if (Physics.Raycast(ray, out rayHit,
                float.MaxValue, layerMask)) //7
            {
                if (wreckerGo.activeSelf)
                {
                    //move it from current position to
                    //where we are leading it
                    wreckerGo.transform.position =

Vector3.MoveTowards(wreckerGo.transform.position,
                        rayHit.point, 0.1f); //8
                }
                else
                {
                    wreckerGo.transform.position = rayHit.point;
                    wreckerGo.SetActive(true); //9
                }
            }
            else
            {
                //we're no longer on the plane
                wreckerGo.SetActive(false); //10
            }
        }
        else
        {
            //we're no longer touching screen
            wreckerGo.SetActive(false); //11
        }
    }
}
```

1. Declare the class derived from Monobehaviour.
2. Reference to GameObject in the scene that will be moved to push other physics objects around.
3. Proceed only if the GameObject this script is on is active and enabled.
4. Check if there is a tap on the screen.t frame.
5. Create a ray based on camera view from the current touch location.
6. Create a layer mask to check for plane colliders created by the **AR Plane Manager**.
7. Do a raycast with the ray calculated to see if we hit any plane colliders.

8. If the referenced **wreckerGO** is already active, move it towards the point tapped on the plane.
9. If it was not active, set its position to the point tapped on the plane, and set it to be active.
10. If the tap or drag is not on a detected plane, deactivate the **wreckerGO**.
11. If there is no touch detected on the screen, deactivate the **wreckerGO**.

This code takes a GameObject with a collider on it and moves it around the scene as you touch and move your finger around on the plane.

Save the script and return to the editor. Create an empty GameObject for running this script, and name it **ObjectMover**. Next, add a **Move Objects** component to the **ObjectMover** via the Inspector.

You now need a GameObject with a collider that the script will use to push other objects around.

Create an empty GameObject on the root of the Hierarchy and name it **Wrecker** and add a **Capsule Collider** to it. Finally, change the transform and capsule sizes so that your capsule has scale of **(X:0.05 , Y:0.05, Z:0.05)**, radius of 1, height of 4, and center at **(X:0 , Y:1, Z:0)**.

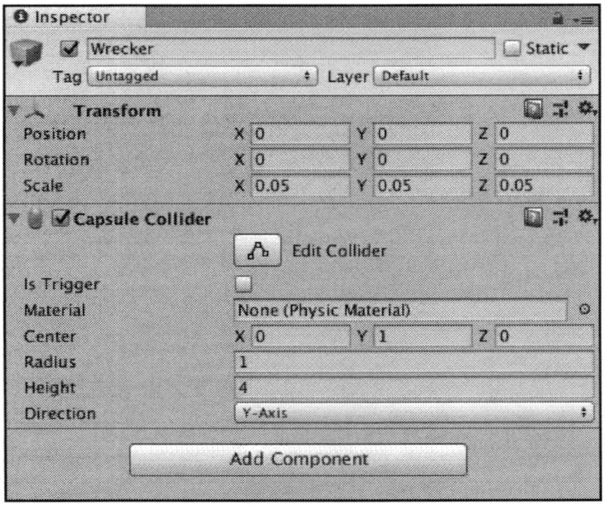

Now, select **ObjectMover** in the Hierarchy once more and drag **Wrecker** to its **Wrecker GO** slot. **ObjectMover** should now look like this:

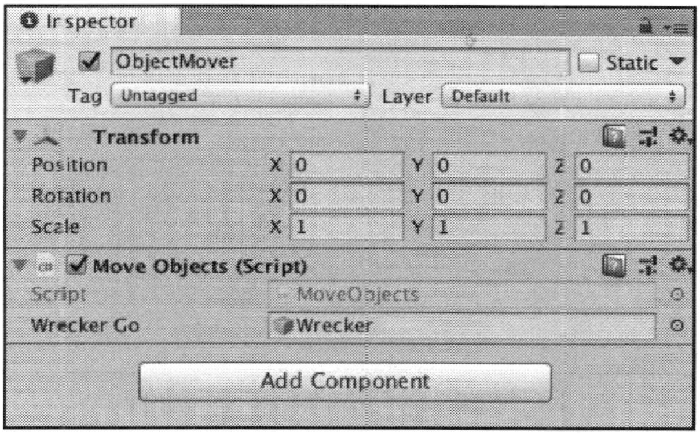

Create a new C# script in the **Assets \ Razeware \ Scripts** folder and name it **ModeSwitcher**. Open the script in a code editor and replace the contents with:

```
using UnityEngine;
using UnityEngine.UI;

public class ModeSwitcher : MonoBehaviour //1
{
    public GameObject dropObjects;
    public GameObject moveObjects; //2

    private int appMode; //3

    void Start()
    {
        appMode = 0; //4
        dropObjects.SetActive(appMode == 0); //5
        moveObjects.SetActive(appMode == 1); //6
    }

    public void ButtonToggle(Text description) //7
    {
        appMode = (appMode + 1) % 2; //8
        description.text =
            (appMode == 0) ? "Drop Mode" : "Push Mode"; //9

        dropObjects.SetActive(appMode == 0); //10
        moveObjects.SetActive(appMode == 1); //11
    }
}
```

1. Declare the class derived from Monobehaviour.
2. References to GameObjects in the scene that control the "drop objects" and the "move objects" behaviours.
3. Field that keeps track of which mode of the app the user is in.
4. Start up with `appMode` set to 0 (drop mode).
5. Activate the GameObject that controls the drop mode.
6. Deactivate the GameObject that controls the move mode.
7. `ButtonToggle` method will be called from a UI button and will pass in a `Text` object.
8. If the button was pressed, toggle the `appMode`.
9. Change the text on the UI button to describe the current `appMode`.
10. If the `appMode` is the drop mode, activate the GameObject that controls the drop mode, otherwise deactivate it.
11. If the `appMode` is the move mode, activate the GameObject that controls the move mode, otherwise deactivate it.

The two GameObjects that are referenced at the top of the script are the ones that provide the functionality for each of the interactions. The script uses a method that toggles between the two modes of the app and enables and disables these GameObjects depending on which functionality is desired for the mode.

Save the script and return to the editor. To make use of this script, create a new empty GameObject in the root of the Hierarchy and name it **ModeSwitcher**. Add a **Mode Switcher** component to the newly made GameObject. Drag **CubeMaker** and **ObjectMover** to the **Drop Objects** and **Move Objects** slots respectively. When you're done, **ModeSwitcher** should look like this in the Inspector:

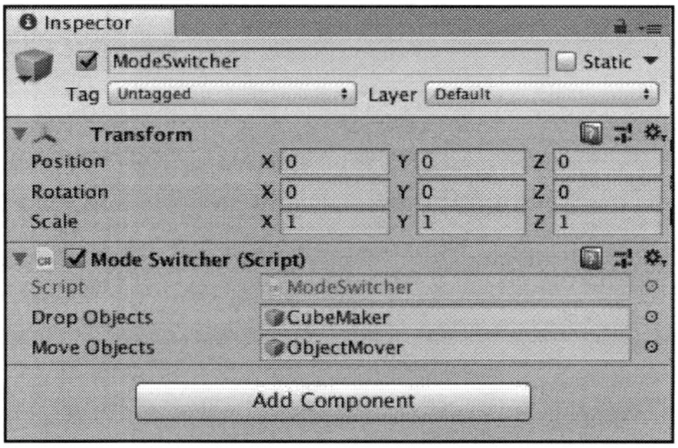

Finally, you need to add the UI which has been created for you as a prefab for this exercise.

Drag the **Physics2UI** prefab from the **Assets \ Razeware \ Prefabs** folder into the root of the Hierarchy.

Unfold the hierarchy of the UI and select **Button** (two levels down from the root). Add an `OnClick` handler to the **Button** component by pressing the + button.

Pressing the button should switch between the two modes, so drag **ModeSwitcher** from the Hierarchy to the `OnClick` GameObject slot.

Select the **/ModeSwitcher/ButtonToggle/** method in the dropdown. For the function parameter, drag **Text** that is under the **Button** as the `Text` parameter.

This last part makes the button text change as the mode of the app changes.

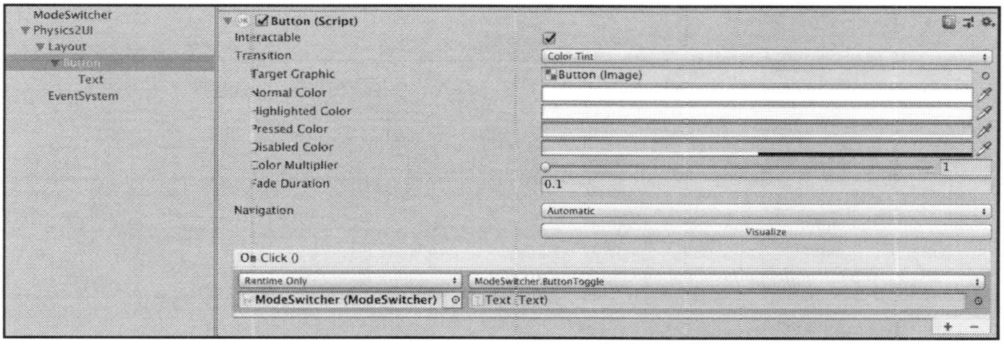

You're now ready to build this to the device and run it. It'll start off the same as the **Physics** scene by being able to drop cubes when a plane is touched. However, now you can press the button on the lower left of the screen and it will toggle the mode so that you can push the existing boxes around by touching the screen near them.

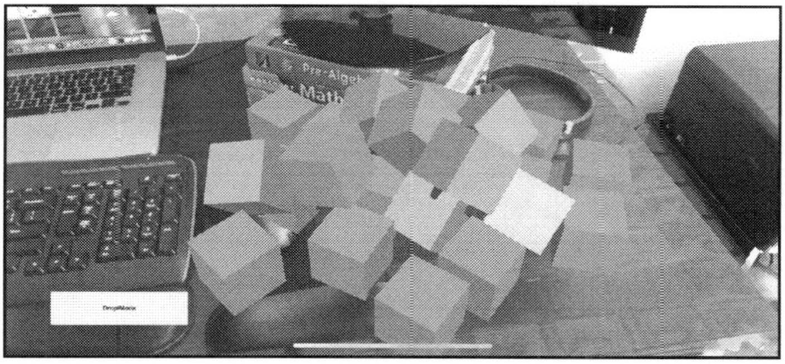

Rendering

Unity has many rendering features that you can use to make your virtual objects appear grounded in the real environment. In this section, you'll discover some features and techniques you can use to achieve this.

Lighting

One of the best ways you can change the appearance of a virtual object is to alter the lighting. Unity provides many tools to light a virtual object realistically — in fact, you could write an entire book on lighting. Until that gets made however, have a look at Unity's "Lighting Overview" section in the docs at https://docs.unity3d.com/Manual/LightingInUnity.html for an overview.

The goal here is to get the lighting to react naturally with your virtual objects. It has to adapt to the real world situation. The AR SDKs provide you with a basic estimation of the brightness and coloration of the scene to help you with this.

Make a copy of the **Chapter18Startup** scene and save it as **Lighting** in the **Assets \ Razeware \ Scenes** folder.

Select **ARSession** in the Hierarchy and make sure that it enables light estimation when the session starts by checking the **Light Estimation** checkbox:

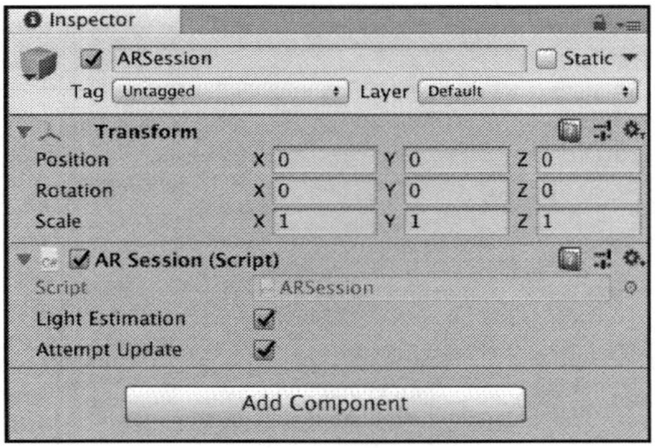

Notice there's already a **Directional Light** in the scene that lights all of the virtual objects. You want this light to be affected by the light estimation of the real scene so your virtual objects appear like they are part of that real scene.

First, you need to add something to be lit by the light to the scene. Drag the **goldball** prefab from the **Assets \ Razeware \ Prefabs** folder to the Hierarchy.

Next, you need to write a script that you'll put on the light so it can change the intensity of the light based on the light estimate you get from the AR SDK.

Create a new C# script file in the **Assets \ Razeware \ Scripts** folder and name it **AmbientLightEstimation.cs**. Open it up in a code editor and replace its contents:

```
using UnityEngine;
using UnityEngine.XR.ARFoundation;

[RequireComponent(typeof(Light))] //1
public class AmbientLightEstimation : MonoBehaviour //2
{
    private Light lightComponent; //3

    void OnEnable()
    {
        lightComponent = GetComponent<Light>(); //4
        ARSubsystemManager.cameraFrameReceived +=
            OnCameraFrameReceived; //5
    }

    void OnCameraFrameReceived(ARCameraFrameEventArgs
camFrameEvent) //6
    {
        LightEstimationData led = camFrameEvent.lightEstimation;
//7

        if (led.averageBrightness.HasValue)
        {
            lightComponent.intensity =
led.averageBrightness.Value; //8
        }

        if (led.averageColorTemperature.HasValue)
        {
            lightComponent.colorTemperature =
                led.averageColorTemperature.Value; //9
        }
    }

    void OnDisable()
    {
        ARSubsystemManager.cameraFrameReceived -=
            OnCameraFrameReceived; //10
    }
}
```

1. **Light** component must be present on GameObject for this script to work.
2. Declare class that derives from Monobehaviour.
3. Storage for the `Light` component on this GameObject to avoid calling `GetComponent` every time you need it.
4. Store the light component whenever this GameObject is enabled.

5. Subscribe to `cameraFrameReceived` events from the underlying system.
6. This delegate method is called whenever a camera frame is received.
7. Store the light estimation data structure for use in this method.
8. If data contains an average brightness value, use that value to affect the intesity of the light component.
9. If the data contains an average color temperature value, use that value on the color temperature of the light component.
10. When this GameObject is disabled, remove the subscription to the `cameraFrameReceived` event.

The script ensures that it's only added to a GameObject that also has a `Light` component on it. When it's first enabled, it gets a reference to the light component that you're going to change the parameters for dynamically. During enabling, you also subscribe to an event that the `ARSubsystemManager` provides to you that will let you know when a new camera frame is received. In your case, you're interested in the lighting estimation which changes with each camera frame.

In the event handler for when a camera frame is received, you get the light estimation data from the event arguments. You then check whether the light estimation provides values for the parameters `intensity` and `colorTemperature`, which can both be changed dynamically on a `Light` component via script. If values are available from the event, you update the values on the light component with these new values.

> **Note**: To test whether the brightness of the real scene affects the lighting of the virtual objects, you can go to a dark room and turn on and off the lights, or you can test in a well-lit area by partly covering the camera lens for a bit with your hands or fingers.

Save the script and return to the editor. Select **Directional Light** and add a **Ambient Light Estimation** component to it. Now build and run the game onto the device to test it.

This is just one of the ways you can attempt to affect the lighting in Unity — and it works well. There are a few other ways to affect lighting with the data you get from the AR SDKs. One is to use a post-process shader that uses the light intensity and color temperature values to affect the final output of the scene. This is the method used by the Google ARCore examples. Another way is to change the global light settings in Unity and set the ambient intensity and temperature there.

In the future, as more hardware and software advances are made, you'll see AR SDKs that support a better estimation of the lighting in the scene. In turn, this will help to model the lighting on virtual objects more accurately.

Shadow casting

One visual way to establish that a virtual object exists in the real scene is when the virtual object casts a shadow on to real surfaces. This has a believable effect if done right. Unity's rendering engine has some decent shadow casting techniques built-in. However, these techniques tend to only work on scenes that are entirely virtual. So, how do you make a virtual shadow appear on a real surface?

The main idea is to create an invisible virtual surface that approximates the real surface in the scene. When you cast a shadow on to this invisible surface, it'll look like the shadow is being cast on to the real surface.

Time to build it!

Save the lighting example scene **Lighting**, as **Shadows** in the **Assets \ Razeware \ Scenes** folder and delete **goldball** from the Hierarchy.

Next, you need a plane prefab that will get instantiated every time AR SDK detects a plane. If you recall, you already created on of these in Chapter 17 and named the prefab **RazewarePlaneVisualizer**. You're going to reuse it with some changes; there's an updated file included it in the starter assets for this chapter. You can find it in **Assets \ Razeware \ Prefabs**. Make a copy of this file, and rename it to **RazewareShadowPlane**.

Drag the **RazewareShadowPlane** prefab to the Hierarchy to instantiate it. There's only one change you'll need to make: this object should not use the **PlaneMaterial**, it should be invisible unless it has a shadow on it. Create a new material named **ShadowPlaneMaterial** in the **Assets \ Razeware \ Materials** folder and select the **Custom \ MobileARShadows** shader.

To make a shadow appear on an invisible surface, you can use the pixel shader. The shadow material has a pixel shader that only works on the shadow pass, so for the times that there are no shadows on it, nothing gets rendered on that plane. When there is a shadow, the pixel shader takes the darkness of the shadow pixel and multiplies it by the existing color in the framebuffer, which in this case is the video feed where the real surface is and darkens it. This gives the desired effect. To understand how it works better, you can view the source for this file, which is in the folder and well commented.

Next, in the Inspector, the **UnitPlane** will look like this:

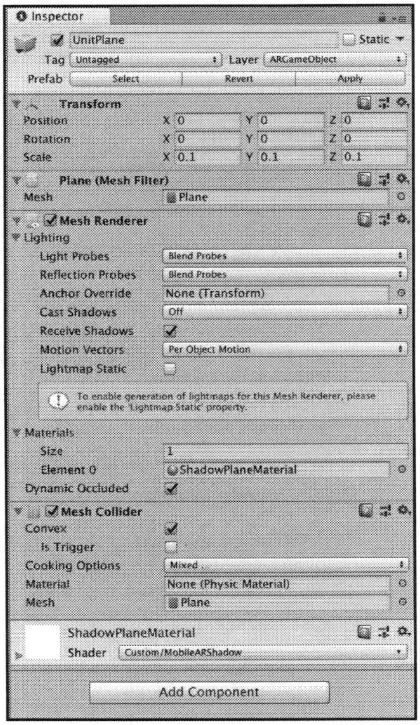

Select **RazewareShadowPlane**'s child **UnitPlane** in the Hierarchy. Change its material to the **ShadowPlaneMaterial**.One other small change is that you want this plane to receive shadows, but should not cast it, so make sure the **Cast Shadows** dropdown is set **Off**.

Click **Apply** on the top right of the Inspector to apply your changes to the prefab that's in the Prefabs folder. Now you can delete **RazewareShadowPlane** in the Hierarchy, as your prefab contains the changes you made.You can use this prefab as a template for the plane visualizer. Select **ARSessionOrigin** in the Hierarchy and a **AR Plane Manager** component to it.

Next, drag the **RazewareShadowPlane** prefab you made earlier into the **Plane Prefab** slot.Excellent, the app will now create invisible shadow-receiving planes whenever a plane is detected in the real environment!

To test the shadowing out, you'll show an object on the plane when you touch it, and that object will cast a shadow on the plane on which it is placed.

Again, from the previous chapter, there's a script that handles this named **PutObjectOnPlane**. It's located in the starter assets for this chapter.

Create a new empty GameObject in the Hierarchy and name it **ObjectPlacer**. Next, add a **PutObjectOnPlane** component to it and drag **Main Camera** to the **AR Camera** slot.

Drag the **PlayerRobotv2** prefab from the **Assets \ Razeware \ Prefabs** folder to the root of the Hierarchy. This is going to be your shadow caster.Next, select **ObjectPlacer** and drag **PlayerRobotv2** onto the **Object To Place** slot of the **PutObjectOnPlane** component.

Save the scene.

You're now all set to build and test the scene on the device, but there are some final settings that you should check. The project settings for the starter project for this chapter already has this set up for you, but it's good to know how to change it for your situation.

The shadow parameters are in the **/Edit/ProjectSettings/Quality** settings for the project. For this project, the set up is as follows:

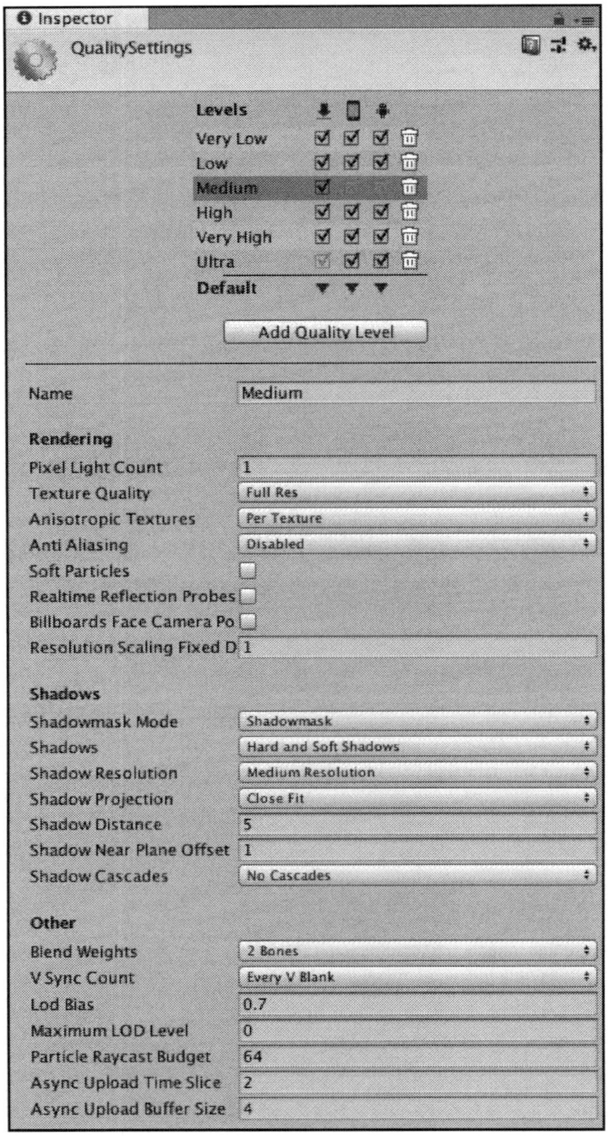

Read up on this page to see how to change these settings for your situation: https://docs.unity3d.com/Manual/class-QualitySettings.html.

Once you build to the device, your scene will look similar to this:

The method above is to create real-time dynamic shadows with interaction with other virtual objects in Unity's rendering system. If you want to have a more optimized but not as high-quality solution, you could use a drop shadow texture underneath your virtual object.

Occlusion

Another interaction between virtual objects and real objects in the scene that establishes a level of believability is occlusion. Imagine you have a table surface, and you place a virtual object on the floor below the table. Once you move the device to be above the table and look down at the table surface, you'll see the virtual object through the table surface. That's to be expected as there is no occlusion of the virtual object. However, if that object were real, you would not be able to see it from above the table.

How do you make it more believable? You can do the same thing you did before for shadow casting and create a plane prefab for every surface that is detected. There will be a plane prefab created for the surface of the table, and this GameObject now uses an Occlusion Material, which is invisible but prevents you from seeing what is behind it. In this case, you'll not be able to see the virtual object through the table surface.

The Occlusion Material does not render anything to the frame buffer, but in a render pass before any other virtual object, it writes the depth of the surface to the depth buffer. When the virtual object is rendered, it is rejected by the z-buffer as its depth is further than the depth of the surface. Thus the effect is that you'll not see the virtual objects rendered behind the table surface.

Time for more scene building!

You can reuse most of the previous scene, so start by making a copy of the **Shadows** scene in the **Assets \ Razeware \ Scenes** folder and naming it **Occlusion**.

The main change to make is to create a new plane prefab for the visualizer to use. Make a copy of the **RenderwareShadowPlane** prefab from the example above, and name it **RazewareOccluderPlane**. Drag this new prefab into the Hierarchyy root to make your changes to it. Select the **UnitPlane** child of the **RazewareOccluderPlane** copy in the scene.

Now, change the material on its **Mesh Renderer** to the provided **OcclusionPlaneMaterial**. If you examine this material in the Inspector, you'll notice that its **Render Queue** is set to **Geometry-10 (1990)**. This means that the plane this material is on will be rendered before any other virtual object. If you examine the shader that this material uses, you'll notice that it writes its depth into the depth buffer and does not alter the framebuffer at all.

Click **Apply** to save the changes to the prefab, and then replace the **RazewareShadowPlane** prefab with the **RazewareOccluderPlane** in the **Plane Prefab** slot of the **AR Plane Manager**. Save the scene, and you'll be ready to build to a device and test this scene. First, find the plane of the table. Then, find the plane of the floor under the table, and place the object on the plane of the floor.

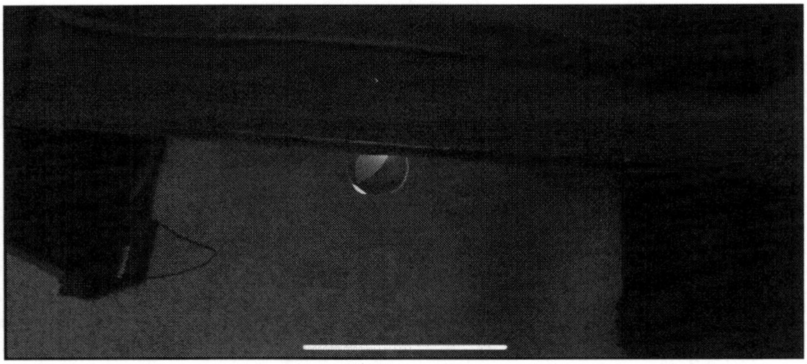

Where to go from here?

Unity has some robust features in the physics and rendering departments. In this chapter, you learned how to make use of some of them to provide basic enhancements to the virtual objects in your scene, and this make them more immersive to your audience. There are many more ways in which you can enhance your virtual objects as you'll discover in later chapters. A common problem encountered in AR is to reconcile the scale of your content with the scale of the real world. For example an AR experience might want to show the top down view of a city on a table. In the next chapter you will learn how to create the illusion of scaling your virtual objects to fit your real world environment.

Chapter 19: Scaled & Transformed Content

Jimmy Alamparambil

A common use case for AR is to present virtual content on top of a table or other small, flat surface. Sometimes this content is sizable — like a city or mountain landscape — and needs to be scaled down to fit comfortably on smaller surfaces.

In this chapter, you'll learn some techniques for scaling as well as what pitfalls to watch out for when doing so.

Why scale content?

In AR, there are many reasons to scale content — sizing things based on the real-world environment is one such reason. Think about it: you don't know where your app or game will be used, so you have no idea what size to scale your content.

Perhaps the user is playing indoors on a coffee table, or maybe they're outdoors on a football field. Only after the experience begins can you determine the proper size.

Another popular reason to scale content is because you've obtained it from other sources and the scale is already established by the creator.

When you use that content for your experience, you may need to change its scale. For instance, you might have a human character with a life-size scale, but you want to animate it on a table with a height of only a few inches instead of six feet tall.

Why scaling content is difficult

So what's the big deal? Doesn't Unity have a scale parameter on all of its transforms? Couldn't you just take the content and scale it up or down dynamically when you establish the proper scale? Sure, that could sometimes; but in many cases, the content may not be scalable. In fact, certain elements within Unity are not easily scaled in this way.

Physics

Physics is particularly susceptible to changes in scale, whether it's in Unity or any other engine.

To generate realistic looking physics, GameObjects must have the correct collision dimensions and corresponding Physics Materials attached. Once you change the dimensions of your objects and try to compensate by adjusting the properties of the Physics Materials like weight and gravity, the physical interactions begin to fall apart. The objects might feel lighter when they collide, or things may look like they're moving slower or faster than they should. With that in mind, you want the Physics interactions to occur at real-world scale, yet display them at an appropriate scale for your particular application.

Baked Lighting

Another aspect of a scene that's difficult to handle when scaling is the baked lighting of the scene. When light is baked, it considers the size of the meshes in real-world scale and uses the properties of the lighting that conforms to how light would interact with world-scale objects. If you then try to scale these objects, the baked lighting looks out of place — even if you adjusted the lighting parameters to try and compensate. Because light is baked beforehand, scaling the pre-lit objects in the scene at runtime results in a scene that looks improperly lit.

Navmeshes

Navmeshes are navigation meshes — an abstract data structure used by artificial intelligent agents to find their path through your level. When a non-player character moves toward you while avoiding the walls, they're most likely using a navmesh added by a level design tool. Navmeshes are dependent on using specific dimensions to create them, as they depend on the width of the pathways for movement as well as the tolerance in the separation between adjacent meshes to still create a path over them. The biggest problem however, is that if you create a navmesh in the editor, you can't scale it at runtime.

Terrain

Terrain is generated in the Unity editor by manipulating brushes to paint landscape features and adding procedural decorations on top of the created landscape. Once created, the terrain is static in world space and can neither be scaled nor moved or rotated. This presents a challenge: getting the content to display in a way that looks as if it fits within the real-world environment.

Particle effects

Particle effects are another rendering feature that doesn't work well with scaling. The main reason being that particle effects are not easily scaled by just changing a value on the parent transform. Instead, the particle system parameters encode the size of the particles over their lifetimes.

Also, a particle effect is rarely just one particle system, but rather a collection of particle systems that work together to achieve the desired effect.

For example, a fire effect might combine blue flame particles, orange flame particles, smoke particles and spark particles. Figuring out how to scale the particles in each system becomes more difficult than just changing the scale in one place.

Location and orientation of content

While scaling may be the most common problem to overcome, sometimes you'll want to focus on a particular part of a large piece of content. This requires the position and the rotation of the camera to be manipulated, but there's no way to take direct control of that, as those values are directly linked to the user's physical camera.

For example, let's say you want to start the player looking at a specific part of your level, a bench in a park overlooking a nice statue. Since there's no way of knowing if the player starts out looking "forward" in the real world, you can't directly control the experience. The player might as well be looking at the garbage bin next to the bench or that tree behind him/her, completely ruining the feel you were going for.

ARSessionOrigin

To solve some of the problems with scaling, **ARFoundation** sets up a Transform named **ARSessionOrigin** in the Hierarchy as a parent of the **ARCamera** . This transform manipulates the location, orientation and scale of the camera based on the needs of the content you're trying to display. You'll see how this works as you go through the rest of this chapter.

Translate content

As discussed before, there's no way of grabbing the device out of the player's hand to move it exactly where you want. What you can do however, is position the objects in the scene.

Whenever you start a **ARSession**, the **ARCamera** always starts at position **(X:0, Y:0, Z: 0)**.Imagine you had a capsule in the scene (this is your virtual content) at **(X:0, Y:0, Z:0)** as well:

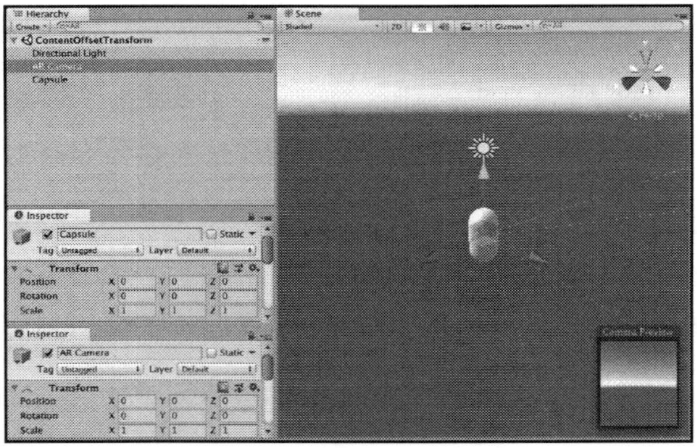

Unfortunately, the camera is inside the capsule, and as you can see from the camera preview window, the capsule cannot be seen by the camera.

Now suppose you always wanted to have the capsule appear 5 meters in front of the camera when you started up. There are two ways you could do this:

1. Move the capsule 5 meters in the forward direction of the camera. Imagine this method is not possible due to one of the reasons given in the previous section.
2. Move the camera back 5 meters. But you cannot directly manipulate the **ARCamera** position, as that is controlled by the AR device.

The solution is to use the second method by introducing a **ContentOffsetTransform** as a parent of the **ARCamera** and have that `Transform`'s position move to **(X:0, Y:0, Z:-5)**:

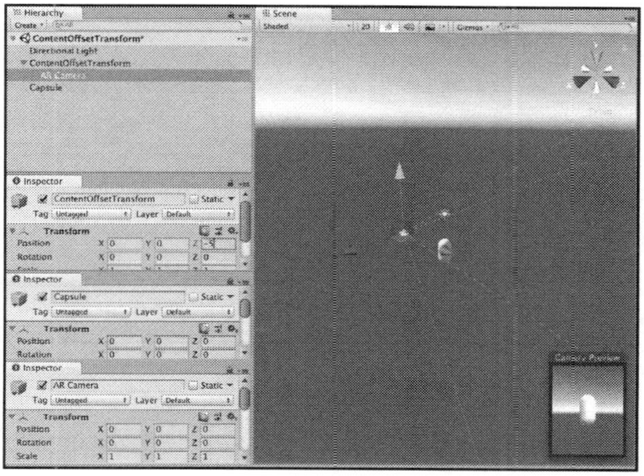

The effect of this is to move your whole scene and the virtual content in it forward by 5 meters *relative* to the **ARCamera**. You can now see the capsule in the camera preview window.

ARSessionOrigin effectively uses this functionality on the method `MakeContentAppearAt` which takes a content root transform and a position in the world that content should appear at, and it will calculate the **ContentOffsetTransform** to apply on to the **ARCamera**.

You can try this out in practice:

Load the **Chapter20Startup** scene from the **Assets \ Razeware \ Scenes** folder and save it as **TranslateMaze** in that same folder.

Next, you'll import some content to play with.

Drag the **MazeParent** prefab from the **Assets \ Razeware \ Prefabs** folder into the root of the Hierarchy. This prefab contains a mesh that's placed away 100 meters from the center of the scene in both the X and Z directions.

Although you can scale and translate this **MazeParent** without issue, imagine if it was a set of meshes that had some of the limitations mentioned earlier — you wouldn't be able to scale or transform it in any way.

Next, you're going to set things up so you can start the experience in a particular spot of the maze, say at the transform named **PlacementNode** within the maze hierarchy. The plan is to make the position of this piece of content the center of attention.

Create a new C# script in the **Assets \ Razeware \ Scripts** folder and name it **TranslateContent**. Open the script in a code editor, and replace the contents with the following code:

```
using System.Collections.Generic;
using UnityEngine;
using UnityEngine.EventSystems;
using UnityEngine.Experimental.XR;
using UnityEngine.XR.ARFoundation;

namespace Razeware.ARBook
{
    [RequireComponent(typeof(ARSessionOrigin))]
    public class TranslateContent : MonoBehaviour                    //1
    {
        public Transform placementTransform;                         //2

        private ARSessionOrigin arSessionOrigin;                     //3

        private static List<ARRaycastHit> RaycastHits = new
List<ARRaycastHit>();

        void Start()                                                 //4
        {
            arSessionOrigin = GetComponent<ARSessionOrigin>();
        }

        void Update()                                               //5
        {
            //if we touched the screen, and that results in a
tap on a detected plane, place content where we tapped
            if (Input.GetMouseButton(0) &&
                !
EventSystem.current.IsPointerOverGameObject(Input.GetTouch(0).fi
ngerId) &&
                arSessionOrigin.Raycast(Input.mousePosition,
RaycastHits, TrackableType.PlaneWithinBounds))
            {

arSessionOrigin.MakeContentAppearAt(placementTransform,
RaycastHits[0].pose.position);
            }
        }
    }
}
```

1. Declare class that derives from MonoBehaviour, and has attribute to require an **ARSessionOrigin** component on the GameObject.
2. Reference to a **Transform** settable from the Editor that denotes the root of the content that should appear where you tap.

3. Field to store reference to **ARSessionOrigin** component to avoid having to call `GetComponent` every time you need it.
4. On startup, store the reference to **ARSessionOrigin**.
5. If you tap the screen and you hit a detected plane, call **ARSessionOrigin.MakeContentAppearAt** with the position of the hit point on the plane.

This script lives on the same GameObject that contains the **ARSessionOrigin** component and references a **Placement Transform** that you populate in the Inspector. You would drag in the reference to the root of your content hierarchy here.

Then, when you tap on a detected plane while running this in AR, the script calls the `MakeContentAppearAt` method which creates a **ContentOffsetTransform** as described before and sets its position in such a way that the content appears at the right place in the world.

Save the script and return to the editor.Select **AR Session Origin** in the Hierarchy and add a **TranslateContent** component to it.Now drag **PlacementNode** (one of children of the maze) into the **Placement Transform** slot. This is what the result should look like:

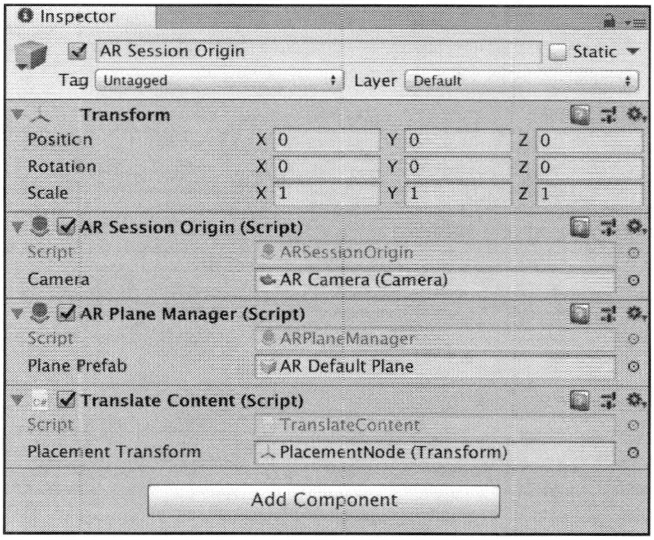

You're now ready to try this out in AR. Build and run this scene on an AR device and look around on the ground until you detect the floor plane.

Next, tap on the floor and you'll see the subsection of the maze appears at that spot.

As described above, this is all an illusion! This version of **MakeContentAppearAt** first creates a transform named **ContentOffsetTransform** below **ARSessionOrigin**, but it contains the camera as a child. It then translates the **ContentOffsetTransform** so that the point on the plane you tapped is coincident with the content transform specified. This moves the camera to the correct position and makes it appear as if the content transform moved to the point on the plane that was tapped.

Rotate content

Great stuff so far! You have now figured out how to move virtual content around to control the user experience. But you are still not satisfied: the virtual object that you are looking at is facing the wrong direction. Imagine you want to align a virtual object in the scene to a real world object in the environment.

This is a typical scenario: you have detected a table in the real world as a plane trackable, and you have placed the capsule and cubes as content on it in the correct position using the method from the last section. But the content is oriented based on the virtual scene in Unity Editor, while the detected table trackable plane could be oriented in some other way:

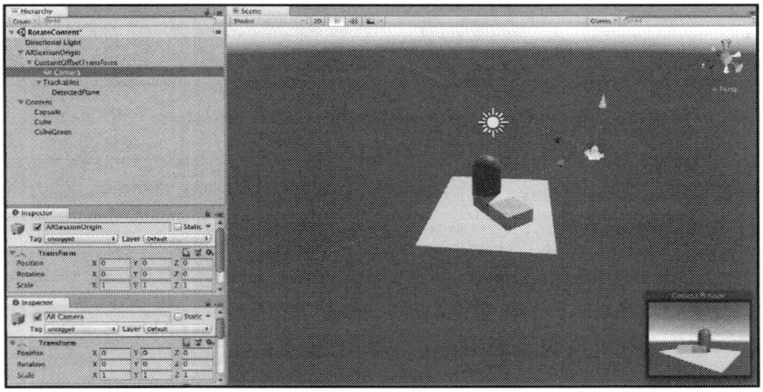

Imagine you wanted to align the content to the edges of the plane. How do you do this?

As before there are two possibilities:

1. Rotate the root of the content hierarchy to make it align. Imagine this is not possible due to reasons given at beginning of this chapter.
2. Rotate the camera and all the trackables, pivoting around the content origin.

You will use the second method, but putting a rotation on the **ContentOffsetTransform** would just turn the camera around in place. You will fix this by using the `Transform` above the **ContentOffsetTransform** called **ARSessionOrigin** and changing the rotation there, which makes the rotation pivot around the position that you placed your content on.

If you look at the Hierarchy in the picture above, it reflects the arrangement used by ARFoundation in an AR app. You will notice the **Trackables** root, under which all the GameObjects representing detected trackables are generated. Just like the **ARCamera**, **Trackables** is also under **ARSessionOrigin** and **ContentOffsetTransform**. This means any transformation would affect the camera and the trackables in the same way (so they would not move or rotate in relation to each other).

For the example above, changing the **Y-axis** rotation on **ARSessionOrigin** (see the Inspector for it right under the Hierarchy) looks like this:

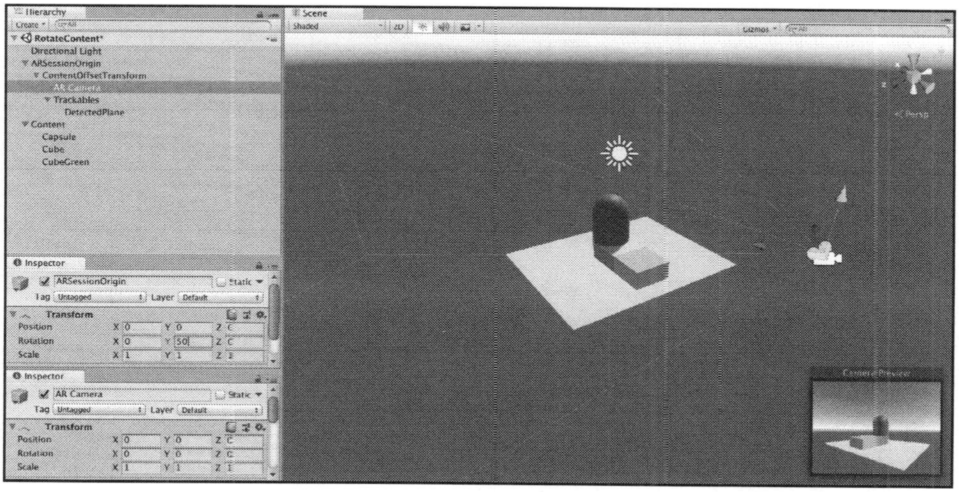

Looking at the camera previews on the two pictures above, you will notice that the **DetectedPlane** does not appear to have moved or rotated *relative* to the **ARCamera**. So in the scene view you can see what actually happens (camera and trackables are rotated around the content placement position), while the camera preview shows what the illusion looks like to the user (the content is rotated so that it is aligned with the plane).

ARSessionOrigin has a version of the `MakeContentAppear` method that will take the content root transform and a rotation and appear to rotate the content by the amount specified.

To try this out in practice and add rotation to the experience, you'll build upon the **TranslateMaze** scene. Save it as a new scene in the **Assets \ Razeware \ Scenes** folder and name it **RotateMaze**.

Now, drag the **Canvas** prefab from the **Assets \ Razeware \ Prefabs** folder into the root of the Hierarchy. This provides your scene with a virtual joystick to control the amount of rotation to carry out on the scene.

Next, create a new C# script in the **Assets \ Razeware \ Scripts** folder and name it **RotateContent**. Open the script in your favorite code editor and replace everything in there with:

```
using UnityEngine;
using UnityEngine.XR.ARFoundation;

namespace Razeware.ARBook
{
    [RequireComponent(typeof(ARSessionOrigin))]
    public class RotateContent : MonoBehaviour          //1
    {
        public Transform pivotTransform;                 //2
        public VirtualJoystick rotateJoystick;
        public float rotationSpeed;

        private float currentAngle;
        private ARSessionOrigin arSessionOrigin;        //3

        void Start()                                     //4
        {
            arSessionOrigin = GetComponent<ARSessionOrigin>();
            currentAngle = 0;
        }

        void Update()                                    //5
        {
            currentAngle += rotateJoystick.Horizontal() *
rotationSpeed * Time.deltaTime;

            arSessionOrigin.MakeContentAppearAt(pivotTransform,
Quaternion.AngleAxis(currentAngle, Vector3.up));
        }
    }
}
```

1. Declare class that derives from MonoBehaviour, and has attribute to require an **ARSessionOrigin** component on the GameObject.

2. Reference to a **Transform**, a **VirtualJoystick** and a float settable from the Editor.
3. Field to store reference to **ARSessionOrigin** component to avoid having to call `GetComponent` every time you need it.
4. On startup, store the reference to **ARSessionOrigin** and set the `currentAngle` field to 0.
5. Change the `currentAngle` using the VirtualJoystick horizontal movement, and call **ARSessionOrigin.MakeContentAppearAt** using the **pivotTransform** and a quaternion based on the `currentAngle`.

This script has a reference to a **Pivot Transform** which is used as the center of rotation of the scene. It uses the referenced **Rotate Joystick** to control how much the scene is rotated; you can also specify its **Rotation Speed**.

The script checks the virtual joystick horizontal axis to determine how much to spin the scene around the content transform. It then gets the resulting rotation and creates a quaternion out of it which is used in the **MakeContentAppearAt** method on the **ARSessionOrigin**.

Save the script and return to the editor.Select **AR Session Origin** and add the **Rotate Content** component you just made to it. Drag **MazeParent**'s child **PlacementNode** to its **Pivot Transform** slot.

Next, drag **VirtualJoystick** in the **Canvas** hierarchy to the **Rotate Joystick** slot and set the **Rotation Speed** to **30**.

This is how the Hierarchy and Inspector for **AR Session Origin** should look like after doing all of this:

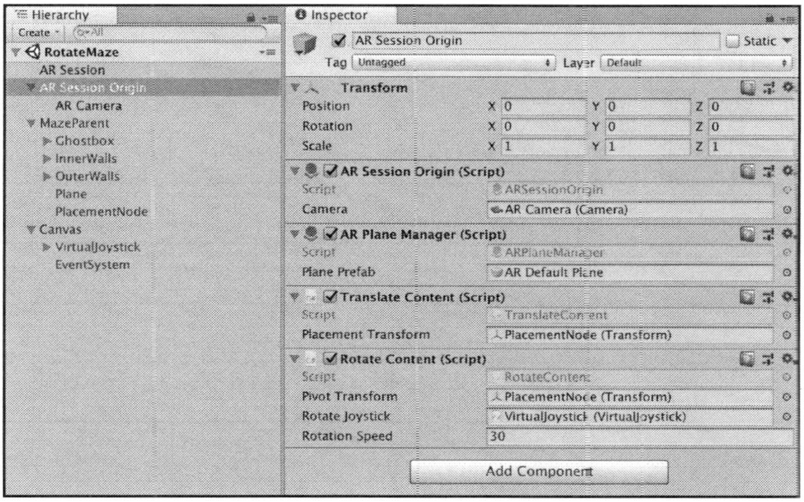

Build the scene to an AR device and run it. Find a floor plane and tap to place the maze. Use the virtual joystick to rotate the mesh around the **PlacementNode** transform. Notice how the mesh rotates around.

In truth, the mesh only appears to rotate; it's the **ContentOffsetTransform** that's actually rotating — along with the camera and all the trackables — in the opposite direction around the chosen transform.

You can use this kind of manipulation of the scene to provide a specific vista for the start of an AR experience, or a direction from which to view the level, despite the direction you're facing in the real world.

Scale content

Now comes the part you've been waiting for! You've managed to translate and rotate your content in relation to the AR device without actually moving or rotating your content. So, how are you going to scale this content without changing its actual scale?

Here's the secret to scaling: instead of making the content smaller, you pull back the camera to a certain distance, this creates the illusion of the content shrinking. To make the content appear larger, you move the camera closer.

Imagine you have a detected plane where you have placed and oriented the content properly, but you now need to scale the content so that it appears to use much less area on the detected plane:

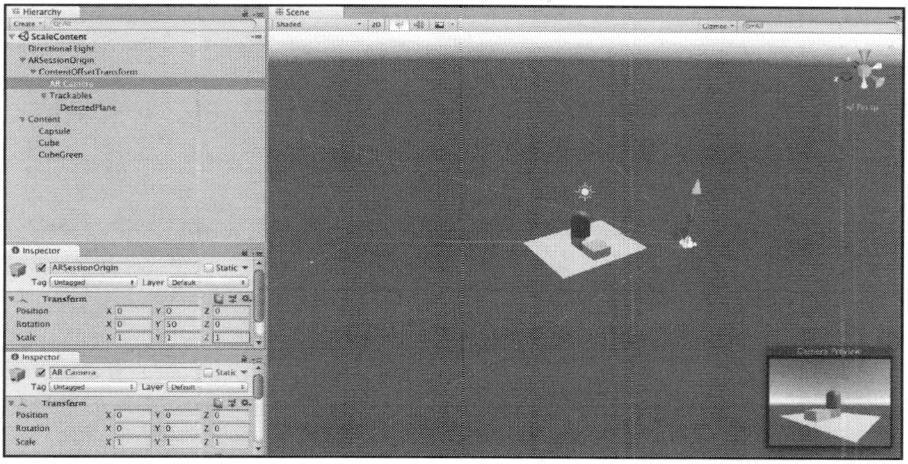

Considering you cannot actually scale the content due to the reasons mentioned at the beginning of the chapter, you can use a scale on the **ARSessionOrigin** to achieve the illusion of scaling the content.

The scale you put on the **ARSessionOrigin** will cause the translation offset on the **ContentOffsetTransform** to be scaled by that amount. So if you want the content to appear half sized, you would put a value of **(X:2, Y:2, Z:2)** on the scale so that the camera moves back to twice the current distance from the content:

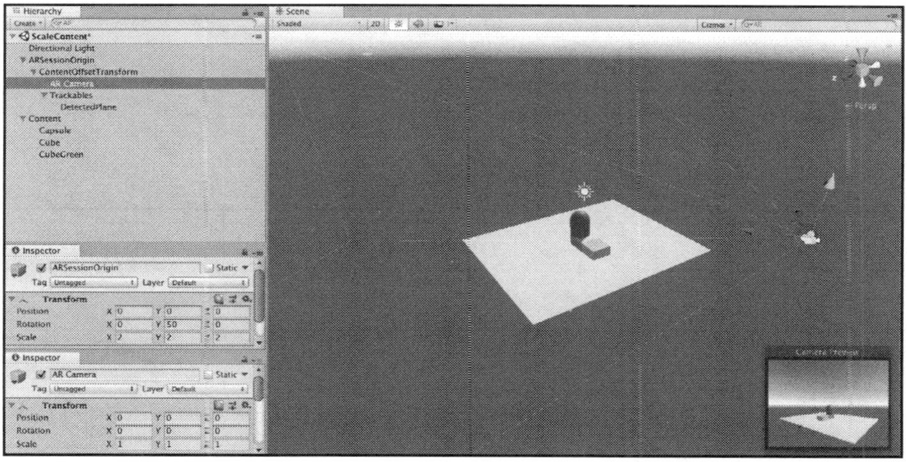

As before, applying a uniform scale of 2 on **ARSessionOrigin** not only moves the **ARCamera** back by that scale, it also scales up the **DetectedPlane** by the same amount, so the plane looks identical in size in the camera previews in both instances.

In the scene view you can see what is actually happening in the Unity coordinate system (camera moves back, plane scales up, content remains unchanged). So do you want to emulate Hank Pym in your AR experience? As before, save the scene from the previous section in the **Assets \ Razeware \ Scenes** and name it **ScaleMaze**. Drag the **LeftJoystick** prefab from the **Assets \ Razeware \ Prefabs** folder onto **Canvas**. This is going to be your way to control the scale of the content.

Create a new script in the **Assets \ Razeware \ Scripts** and name it **ScaleContent**. As always, open it in a code editor and replace it with this code:

```
using UnityEngine;
using UnityEngine.XR.ARFoundation;

namespace Razeware.ARBook
{
    [RequireComponent(typeof(ARSessionOrigin))]
    public class ScaleContent : MonoBehaviour          //1
    {
        public VirtualJoystick scaleJoystick;          //2
        public float scaleSpeed;

        ARSessionOrigin arSessionOrigin;               //3
        float currentScaleNumber;

        void Start()                                   //4
        {
            arSessionOrigin = GetComponent<ARSessionOrigin>();
            currentScaleNumber = 0.0f;
        }

        void Update()                                  //5
        {
            //the vertical axis of the virtual joystick
increases and decreases a number
            currentScaleNumber += scaleJoystick.Vertical() *
scaleSpeed * Time.deltaTime;

            //we need to generate scale from this number (and
invert it so that content appears to scale)
            float scale = currentScaleNumber < 0.0f ? 1.0f -
currentScaleNumber : 1.0f / (1.0f + currentScaleNumber);

            arSessionOrigin.transform.localScale =  Vector3.one
* scale;
        }
    }
}
```

1. Declare a class that derives from MonoBehaviour, and has attribute to require an **ARSessionOrigin** component on the GameObject.
2. Reference to a **VirtualJoystick** and a float settable from the Editor.
3. Field to store reference to **ARSessionOrigin** component to avoid having to call `GetComponent` every time you need it.
4. On startup, store the reference to **ARSessionOrigin** and set the `currentScaleNumber` field to 0.
5. Change the `currentScaleNumber` using the VirtualJoystick movement, calculate a scale from the number and set the **ARSessionOrigin**'s local scale to that value.

This script contains a reference to a **Scale Joystick** whose vertical axis is used to scale up and scale down the presented content. It also contains a reference to **Scale Speed** which is used to change the speed at which you're scaling up or down.

The scale is represented by a "scale number" that ranges between positive and negative values. You convert this number into a scale like so: scale number of zero represents a scale of 1, positive scale numbers represent scales of less than 1, and negative numbers represent scales more than 1.

Finally, the resulting scale is applied to the **ARSessionOrigin** transform and works as described above. Save the script and return to the editor. To make it work, add a **Scale Content** component to the **AR Session Origin**. Next, drag **LeftJoystick** from the Hierarchy onto the **Scale Joystick** slot and and put in a value of **1** for the **Scale Speed**.

This is the result:

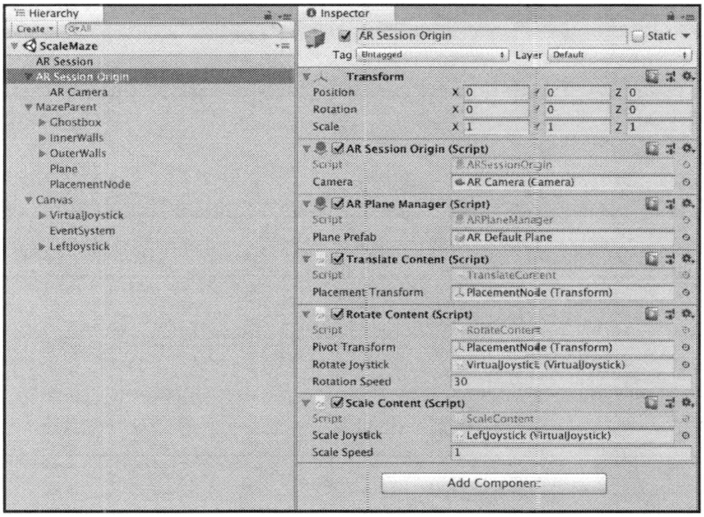

Time to run it on a device! Build and run the scene and give it a try. First, find a floor plane and tap on it to place the maze onto the floor. Now, spin the maze around using the virtual joystick on the right of the screen and increase and decrease the size of the maze on the floor using the virtual joystick on the left of the screen.

Multiple ARSessionOrigin

Now that you know how to make a single piece of content appear in the right place with a proper orientation and scale, you may want to make different pieces of content appear at different scales.

To do this you create multiple **AR Session Origin** hierarchies with their own **ARCamera**. Each piece of content should only be rendered by one of the cameras, so you'll need a shared **RenderLayer** for each of the GameObjects in a piece of content. These are then rendered by the one camera that has the same **RenderLayer** in its **CullingMask**.

Only one camera should render the video feed of the real world background that you're going to augment, so you'll only put the **ARCameraBackground** component on one camera, and you'll make sure the **Depth** parameter on that camera (which specifies its rendering order) is the smallest so it gets rendered first.

You'll also need to watch out for depth buffer rendering issues. When you have multiple pieces of content, all being rendered at different scales, the value in the depth buffer between them is not related.Because the scaling is done by moving the camera instead of scaling the objects, you might have to control the rendering order between the different **ARSessionOrigin** hierarchies manually to make sure they appear right. You can do this by putting in an increasing **Depth** parameter value on the Camera component to denote rendering order.

Other uses of ARSessionOrigin

In this chapter, you saw how to make your AR content appear at the right scale, position and orientation based on the needs of your application. This is important in many AR experience scenarios.

You can also use this method to move the content for other uses where you don't have control of the device's camera movement. One example might be a **screen shake effect**, where your whole scene shakes, as if there was an earthquake going on.

You also learned some reasons why you may not be able to manipulate the content directly in the hierarchy, and how to control the transform hierarchy such that you can create the illusion of making the content move, rotate and scale without actually changing the content.

Where to go from here?

In the next chapter, you will build a whole AR experience based on the things you have learned in this and the last few chapters, including dynamically manipulating the appearance of the content by determining the size of a plane and adjusting the scale and position of your content to match.

Chapter 20: Multiplayer AR

Jimmy Alamparambil

In the last few chapters, you learned about some of the different aspects of creating AR experiences using **ARFoundation** and **Unity**. In this chapter, you'll expand your knowledge, add some new code, and create an AR experience that you can enjoy with up to three of your friends.

The choice of gameplay for this chapter is based on the classic multiplayer arcade game, *Pacman*. In this AR-modified game, every player's mobile device has a view into the gameplay area. Each player controls their own robot that moves toward the point where the player touches the floor of the maze. There are also enemy robots; these chase the player robots. Don't get caught, otherwise you'll lose the game!

There are also orbs the players can collect to earn points and a large golden power orb that briefly gives the player the power to touch the enemy robots and destroy them. When powered up, the player is also able to touch and destroy other player robots.

Sound like fun, right? Time to make it happen! :]

Planning

Since you're concerned mostly with the AR aspects of this experience, you can start with a basic multiplayer demo as the template for this application. By doing so, you'll have most of the networking aspects already set up. The startup project for this chapter is based on the *Network Meteroids* project (https://assetstore.unity.com/packages/essentials/tutorial-projects/network-meteoroid-62227) which gives you a sample game using a Networking Lobby and multiplayer connections via UNET (Unity's built-in Networking solution).

To learn the basics of UNET HLAPI and multiplayer networking, review the Unity documentation at https://docs.unity3d.com/Manual/UNetConcepts.html

In the *Network Meteoroids* project, the game flow is determined by two scenes that are arranged like so:

For this to work with AR, you need a starting scene that establishes the AR session. It needs to start world tracking and find out from the user where they want to place the gameplay area. Your game can then store this information and use it later in the main game scene to help position the gameplay area. The flow, in this case, adds a scene to the beginning of the flow shown above:

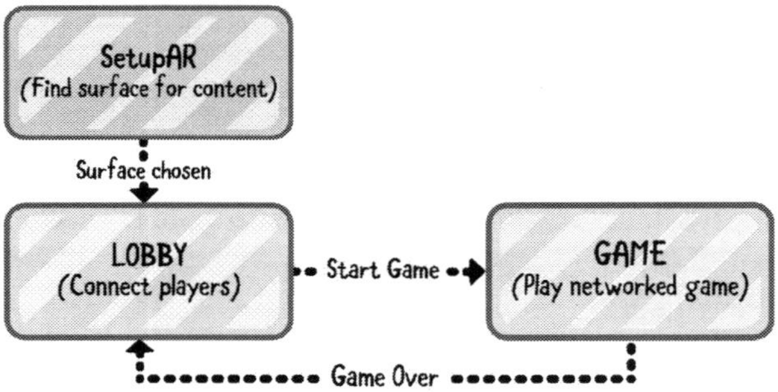

AR Setup

Load the **Assets \ Razeware \ Robot \ Scenes \ Chapter21Startup.unity** scene in the project for this chapter and save the scene as **Assets \ Razeware \ Robot \ Scenes \ NetworkRobotSetupAR.unity**.

Now, create a new C# script named **PlaneChooser** in the **Assets \ Razeware \ Robot \ Scripts** folder and replace its contents with the following code:

```
using System.Collections;
using UnityEngine;
using UnityEngine.Experimental.XR;
using UnityEngine.SceneManagement;
using UnityEngine.XR.ARFoundation;

namespace Razeware.ARBook
{
```

```
    public class PlaneChooser : MonoBehaviour
    {

    }
}
```

This sets up the using statements for later use and declares the class.Next, add these fields inside of the class:

```
public static PlaneChooser Instance;     //1

public string lobbySceneStr;            //2

public ARSessionOrigin ARSessionOrigin;

bool inMouseHandler;                     //3
bool doneChoosingPlane;

//keep some parameters of the plane you found
//so that you can choose where to place your game
Vector3 tappedPosition;                  //4
Quaternion tappedRotation;
float tappedMinDimension;
Camera arCamera;

float savedCameraNear;                   //5
float savedCameraFar;
```

Here's a look at each group of fields and how you'll use them:

1. A static field used to store the only instance of this **PlaneChooser** class.
2. Public fields that you'll set in the editor.
3. Fields to store the current state of this script.
4. Fields to store plane parameters that are used to place content.
5. Fields to store camera parameters that are affected by scale.

Now add the `Awake` and `Start` methods below the fields:

```
//1
void Awake()
{
    Instance = this;
    arCamera = ARSessionOrigin.GetComponentInChildren<Camera>();
    if (arCamera == null)
    {
        arCamera = Camera.main;
    }
```

```
        savedCameraNear = arCamera.nearClipPlane;
        savedCameraFar = arCamera.farClipPlane;
    }

    //2
    void Start()
    {
        inMouseHandler = false;
        doneChoosingPlane = false;
        DontDestroyOnLoad(gameObject);
    }
```

Here's a closer look at each method:

1. On `Awake`, store the instance of the script, a reference to the camera and the camera near and far clip plane values.
2. On `Start`, initialize the state of the script and set it up so it's not destroyed when the next scene is loaded.

The next three methods to add are as follows:

```
    //1
    void Update()
    {
        if (Input.GetMouseButtonDown(0) && !inMouseHandler)
        {
            StartCoroutine(MouseHandler());
        }

        if (doneChoosingPlane)
        {
            LoadLobbyScene();
        }
    }

    //2
    public Camera GetARCamera()
    {
        return arCamera;
    }

    //3
    void LoadLobbyScene()
    {
        SceneManager.LoadScene(lobbySceneStr);
        enabled = false;
    }
```

Looking at these methods, here's what they do:

1. `Update` runs the `MouseHandler` coroutine if there's a tap on the screen; if a plane is chosen, it runs the `LoadLobbyScene` method.
2. This returns a reference to the **ARCamera**.
3. `LoadLobbyScene` loads the lobby scene and disables this script to stop trying to choose planes.

Next, you need to add the `MouseHandler` coroutine:

```
IEnumerator MouseHandler()
{
    inMouseHandler = true;                                   //1

    Ray ray =
        arCamera.ScreenPointToRay(Input.mousePosition); //2

    RaycastHit rayHit;
    if (Physics.Raycast (ray, out rayHit))
    {
        ARPlane arPlane =
            rayHit.collider.gameObject.GetComponent<ARPlane>();

        if (arPlane != null)                                 //3
        {
            bool isHorizontal =
                (arPlane.boundedPlane.Alignment &
                 PlaneAlignment.Horizontal) != 0;

            if (isHorizontal)
            {
                tappedPosition =
                    arPlane.boundedPlane.Pose.position;
                tappedRotation =
                    arPlane.boundedPlane.Pose.rotation;
                tappedMinDimension =
                    Mathf.Min(arPlane.boundedPlane.Width,
                        arPlane.boundedPlane.Height);

                doneChoosingPlane = true;
            }
        }
    }

    inMouseHandler = false;                                  //1
    yield return null;
}
```

Going through this code:

1. Set a boolean to indicate the script is within this coroutine. This gets unset at the end of the script.
2. Do a Physics Raycast from the tapped position on the screen in the camera direction.
3. If a horizontal plane was hit, it's chosen and its configuration is stored. The boolean is then set to go to the lobby scene

Finally, add the last method, `PlaceOnSelectedPlane`, which gets will get called later on to make the content appear on the chosen plane:

```
public void PlaceOnSelectedPlane(Transform contentParent,
                                    float contentDimension)
{
    ARSessionOrigin.MakeContentAppearAt(
        contentParent, tappedPosition,tappedRotation); //1

    ARSessionOrigin.transform.localScale =
        Vector3.one * (contentDimension/tappedMinDimension);
    arCamera.nearClipPlane =
        savedCameraNear * (contentDimension /
tappedMinDimension); //2
    arCamera.farClipPlane =
        savedCameraFar * (contentDimension /
tappedMinDimension);

    ARPlaneManager arPlaneManager =
        ARSessionOrigin.GetComponent<ARPlaneManager>(); //3

    //do not generate any more visible planes
    arPlaneManager.planePrefab = null;

    //turn off existing visible planes

ARSessionOrigin.trackablesParent.gameObject.SetActive(false);
}
```

Here's how it works:

1. Call the **ARSessionOrigin.MakeContentAppearAt** method to position the content using the saved plane position and rotation. Change the local scale of **ARSessionOrigin** to make the content appear to fit on the chosen plane.
2. Scale the camera's `Near` and `Far` parameters so that content is not clipped when the camera moves back.
3. Stop **ARPlaneManager** from generating more planes, and turn off all existing visible planes.

This script does three things:

1. Handles touch input in `MouseHandler` by checking whether you have tapped on any horizontal planes (which implies you have selected that plane for content placement). If this happens, it saves the position, rotation and size of the plane for later use.
2. If a plane is selected, it sends you to the lobby scene as specified in the planned flow.
3. `PlaceOnSelectedPlane` is called once the content is loaded in another scene so you can place that content on the selected plane.

Save the script and return to the editor.Create a new GameObject in the Hierarchy, name it **PlaneChooser** and add a **Place On SelectedPlane** component to it. For the **LobbySceneStr** parameter on this component, type **"NetworkRobotLobby"**, which is what you're going to name the scene for the lobby. For the **ARSesssionOrigin** parameter, drag in a reference to the **ARSessionOrigin** GameObject in the scene.

There's one more thing to do in this scene. You want some of these GameObjects to stay alive when you load new scenes since you're going to use them in the actual game scene that gets loaded after the lobby scene. For example, you want **ARSession** and **ARSessionOrigin** to be present to handle your AR related interactions while in the game. You also want **PlaneChooser** to stick around to help you place your game content correctly in the real environment.

In the `Start` method of the **PlaneChooser** script, you already have a statement that does this:

```
DontDestroyOnLoad(gameObject);
```

However, for the other two GameObjects, you need to create a new script to do this. Create a new script in **Assets \ Razeware \ Robot \ Scripts** and name it **DontDestroyOnLoad** and replace the contents with:

```
using UnityEngine;

namespace Razeware.ARBook
{
    public class DontDestroyOnLoad : MonoBehaviour
    {
        void Awake()
        {
            DontDestroyOnLoad(gameObject);
        }
    }
}
```

This small utility script simply prevents the GameObject it's attached to from being destroyed when a new scene loads. Save it and return to the editor.

Now, add the **Dont Destroy On Load** component you just created to both **ARSession** and **ARSessionOrigin** so they'll survive scene loads. Now save the **NetworkRobotSetupAR** scene.

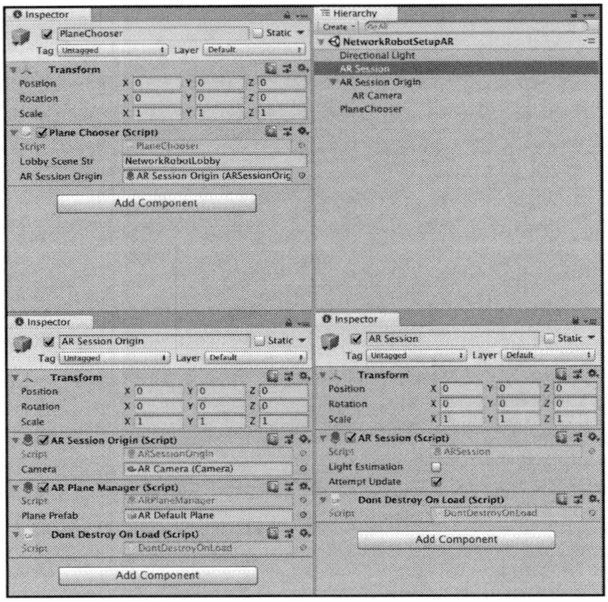

It's time to add this scene to your build settings while you have it open. From the top menu, select **File > BuildSettings...** and click the **Add Open Scenes** button to add this scene to the build at index 0, indicating this scene is going to be the first one loaded as soon as the app starts.

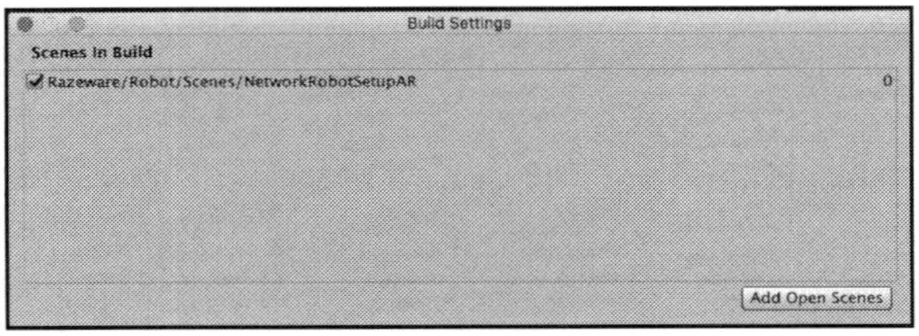

Game Scene

Next in the flow comes the lobby scene, but you'll create the game scene first because you'll need some references from that scene to put into the lobby scene.

Create a new scene in **Assets \ Razeware \ Robot \ Scenes** and name it **NetworkRobotScene**.

Open the scene and make sure there's a **Main Camera** and a **Directional Light**. Since you're going to be using the **ARCamera** that is present in the setup scene, disable the **Main Camera** GameObject. Next, add an **EventSystem** in the root of the hierarchy by selecting **GameObject > UI >EventSystem** in the Create menu. This will be used by your UI canvas later. Speaking of UI, you can now drag **GameCanvas** from **Assets \ Razeware \ Robot \ Prefabs** into the root of the scene hierarchy.

Now you want to import the gameplay maze that you're going to be playing in. Drag **RazemanMaze** from **Assets \ Razeware \ Robot \ Prefabs** into the root of the Hierarchy.

NavMesh

You'll need to do some extra work on this maze: You want to create the navigation mesh that will allow your players and the enemy robots to navigate along the maze. Select the top menu item **Window > AI > Navigation** which opens the **Navigation** window. This is where you can specify parameters for all of your navigation elements.You can leave most things with their default values, but click the **Bake** tab on the top of the window and change the **Agent Radius** to **0.4**. Now, click on the **Bake** button on the bottom of that tab. Your results will look like this:

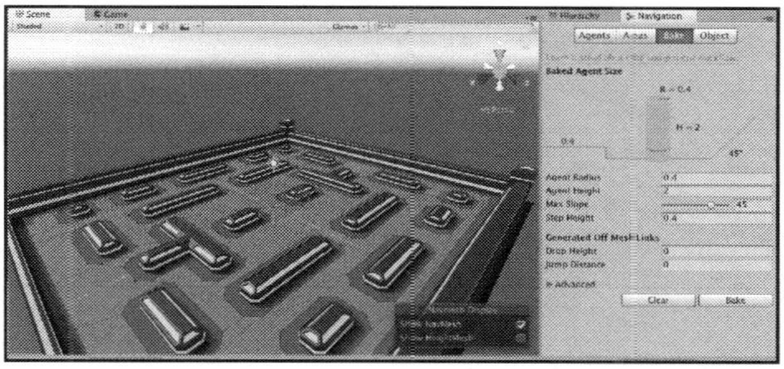

The light blue highlighted portions of the level make up the **NavMesh** for that level. Now is an excellent time to save the scene — and the project as well.

NetworkCollectible

Next, you'll create a script that defines how the collectible objects in the game will work. Create a script named **NetworkCollectible** in the **Assets \ Razeware \ Robot \ Scripts** folder and replace everything in there with:

```
using UnityEngine;
using UnityEngine.Networking;

namespace Razeware.ARBook
{
```

```
    [RequireComponent(typeof(NetworkTransform))]
    public class NetworkCollectible :
NetworkBehaviour          //1
    {
        public int scoreValue =
1;                          //2
        public bool isPowerUp = false;

        protected bool isDestroyed =
false;                 //3
        protected NetworkTransform netTransform;
        protected Collider collectibleCollider;

        void
Start()                                          //4
        {
            netTransform = GetComponent<NetworkTransform>();
            collectibleCollider = GetComponent<Collider>();
        }
    }
}
```

Here's a closer look:

1. Declare a class that derives from `NetworkBehaviour`, using the UNET networking framework to synchronize across devices.
2. Add two public fields that are settable from editor to define the collectibles.
3. Three fields set and used within the script to declare if the object is destroyed, its network transform and its collider respectively.
4. `Start` stores the references to two components to avoid expensive `GetComponent` calls during runtime.

Now, add the following server callback method to the class:

```
[ServerCallback]
void OnTriggerEnter(Collider collider)           //1
{
    if (isDestroyed)
    {
        return;                                  //2
    }

    //we collide so we dirty the
    //NetworkTrasnform to sync it on clients.
    netTransform.SetDirtyBit(1);

    if (collider.gameObject.tag == "Player")     //3
    {
        //we collided with the player,
```

```
        //they have collected me
        NetworkPlayerRobot robot =

collider.gameObject.GetComponent<NetworkPlayerRobot>();
        robot.score += scoreValue;
        if (isPowerUp)                              //4
        {
            robot.ServerPowerUp(true);
        }

        collectibleCollider.enabled = false;        //5
        Collected();
    }
}
```

This is how it works:

1. `OnTriggerEnter` gets called whenever the trigger collider of this collectible is touched by another collider (only on the server side).
2. Check that the collectible has not already been collected and update the clients with the new state.
3. If a player collision triggered the collectible, add the collectible's score value to the player score.
4. If a collectible is a power-up, call the server method to power up the player.
5. Disable the collider and call `Collected()` to handle getting collected.

Finally, to complete this script, add the `Collected()` method to handle getting collected:

```
//1
[Server]
public void Collected()
{
    //if 2 players touch the collectible the same frame,
    //they will both generate the callback before the
collectible
    //get destroyed but we want to destroy it only once.
    if (isDestroyed)
    {
        return;
    }

    isDestroyed = true;

NetworkRobotGameManager.Instance.RpcPlayCollectedSound(); //2

    if (isPowerUp)
```

```
    {
        NetworkRobotGameManager.Instance.numActivePowerPills--;
    }
    else
    {
NetworkRobotGameManager.Instance.numActiveCollectibles--;
    }

    //destroy the collectible
    NetworkServer.Destroy(gameObject);                //3
}
```

Here's a closer look at this method:

1. `Collected()` runs on the server, checks if it has already been destroyed and sets `isDestroyed` otherwise.
2. Play the collected sound and update the counts of active regular and active power-up collectibles in the level.
3. Destroy the `NetworkBehaviour` on all clients.

You now have a class that derives from `NetworkBehaviour` and therefore can use UNET functionality easily to transmit messages to other devices that might be running copies of the game. The way UNET works is that `NetworkBehaviours` can have three ways of calling methods:

- Run on only the server.
- Run on the client side only.
- Run on both sides.

This script works mostly on the server side so that when one of the players collides with the collectible, it will add the score to the player, and if it is a power-up collectible, the player gets powered-up.

The script also plays the collected sound, keeps track of the number of active collectibles on the game manager and destroys itself when collected.

Save the script and return to the editor.This script won't compile yet since it's missing the definition of a couple of types. Fear not! You're going to write those scripts later in this section so that all the scripts will compile.

NetworkEnemy

Create a new C# script named **NetworkEnemy** in the **Assets \ Razeware \ Robot \ Scripts** folder and replace the contents with:

```
using UnityEngine;
using UnityEngine.Networking;
using UnityEngine.AI;

namespace Razeware.ARBook
{
    [RequireComponent(typeof(NetworkTransform))]
    public class NetworkEnemy : NetworkBehaviour    //1
    {
        public Transform target;                    //2
        public float navigationUpdate;
        public float deathDuration;
        public int scoreValue;

        public GameObject normalGO;                 //3
        public GameObject scaredGO;
        public GameObject deadGO;

    }
}
```

Here's a closer look at the code:

1. Declare a class that derives from `NetworkBehaviour`.
2. Public fields to set references and values for this script from the editor.
3. Public fields to set references to parts of the GameObject hierarchy that should be activated for the appearance of the enemy in each of three states.

Now, add the following fields:

```
Transform spawnTransform;                   //1
NavMeshAgent agent;
Collider enemyCollider;

float navigationTime = 0;                   //2
bool isKilled;
float deathTime;

[SyncVar]
protected bool poweredUpPlayerExists;       //3

enum EnemyState                             //4
{
    Hunting,
```

```
    Running,
    Dead,
    ReadyToRespawn
}

EnemyState state;
```

Here's the breakdown:

1. Fields to save a reference to components to avoid having to call `GetComponent` every time you need them.
2. Fields to keep track of the internal script state.
3. A boolean that's synchronized across all of the clients; it keeps track of any powered-up players that exist.
4. An enumeration defining all of the states in which the enemy can be, followed by the current state of the enemy.

Now, write the `Start` method:

```
void Start()
{
    agent = GetComponent<NavMeshAgent>(); //1
    enemyCollider = GetComponent<Collider>();
    GameObject spawnTransformGo =
        new GameObject("SpawnTransform"); //2
    spawnTransform = spawnTransformGo.transform;
    spawnTransform.position = transform.position;
    //cause first frame to navigate.
    navigationTime = navigationUpdate;  //3
    state = EnemyState.Hunting;
    poweredUpPlayerExists = false;
    if (NetworkClient.active)   //4
    {

NetworkRobotGameManager.Instance.EventPoweredUpPlayerExists
            += ChangeScaredState;
        poweredUpPlayerExists =
            NetworkRobotGameManager.Instance.playerPoweredUp;
    }

    ChangeScaredState(poweredUpPlayerExists); //5
}
```

Here's what's happening:

1. Cache the needed components to avoid having to call `GetComponent` every time you need them.
2. Create a new GameObject at the position where this enemy spawns to save the spawn position.
3. Initialize the script variables: set the initial `navigationTime` to equal the `navigationUpdate` so that a navigation update happens right at the start.
4. If there's a network connection, subscribe to an event that will callback `ChangeScaredState` when a powered-up player starts or stops existing. Get the current value of the existence of a powered-up player.
5. Call `ChangeScaredState` and pass in the current value of `poweredUpPlayerExists`.

Next, add the `ChangeScaredState` method:

```
//server has called us to say that a powered up
//player exists, or that none are powered
void ChangeScaredState(bool poweredUpPlayerExists)
{
    if (state == EnemyState.Hunting &&
        poweredUpPlayerExists)          //1
    {
        ChangeState(EnemyState.Running);
    }
    else if (state == EnemyState.Running &&
        !poweredUpPlayerExists)         //2
    {
        ChangeState(EnemyState.Hunting);
    }

    this.poweredUpPlayerExists =
        poweredUpPlayerExists;          //3
}
```

With this code, you:

1. Check if the enemy is hunting and a powered-up player becomes active: change enemy's state to `EnemyState.Running`.
2. Check if the enemy is running and whether or not a player with a power-up exists; if so, change the enemy's state to `EnemyState.Hunting`.
3. Update the local boolean that keeps track of powered up player existing.

Now, add two more methods. One named `ChangeState`, and the other named `ChangeGODisplay`:

```
//1
void ChangeState(EnemyState newState)
{
    if (newState != state)                          //2
    {
        switch (newState)
        {
            case EnemyState.Hunting:                //3
                ChangeGODisplay(normalGO);
                target = NetworkRobotGameManager.Instance.

GetClosestPlayer(transform.position).transform;
                break;
            case EnemyState.Dead:                   //4
                NetworkRobotGameManager.Instance.
                    RpcPlayDeathSound();
                ChangeGODisplay(deadGO);
                target = spawnTransform;
                break;
            case EnemyState.Running:                //5
                ChangeGODisplay(scaredGO);
                target = spawnTransform;
                break;
        }

        navigationTime = navigationUpdate;          //6
        state = newState;
        enemyCollider.enabled = (state != EnemyState.Dead);
    }
}

//7
void ChangeGODisplay(GameObject go)
{
    normalGO.SetActive(go == normalGO);
    scaredGO.SetActive(go == scaredGO);
    deadGO.SetActive(go == deadGO);
}
```

Here's a closer look at the code:

1. `ChangeState` gets called with the new state of the enemy.
2. Check that the state has changed, and handle things according to the new state being set.
3. When the enemy goes to hunting state, change the GameObject to be displayed to show the normal enemy appearance and target the closest player to the enemy to navigate to.

4. When the enemy goes to the dead state, play the enemy dying sound, change the GameObject to be displayed to show the dead enemy appearance and navigate back to its spawn position where it'll resurrect.
5. When the enemy goes to running state, change the GameObject to be displayed to show the running enemy appearance, and navigate back to its spawn position where it is safe.
6. Force a navigation update this frame so that enemy heads towards a new target, store new state and disable the collider if the enemy is dead so that it neither kills or gets killed while navigating to its spawn position.
7. `ChangeGODisplay` changes the appearance of the enemy by activating the GameObject root of the desired appearance and turning all others off.

Next, add the three `ClientRpc` methods, these are called from the server side of the object:

```
[ClientRpc]
void RpcChangeScaredState(bool poweredUpPlayerExists) //1
{
    ChangeScaredState(poweredUpPlayerExists);
}

[ClientRpc]
void RpcChangeState(EnemyState newState)
{
    ChangeState(newState);
}

[ClientRpc]
void RpcFindNewTarget()                                    //2
{
    NetworkPlayerRobot potentialTarget =
        NetworkRobotGameManager.Instance.
            GetClosestPlayer(transform.position);
    if (potentialTarget != null)
    {
        target = potentialTarget.transform;
    }
}
```

Here's how it works:

1. `RpcChangeScaredState` forwards to the client side `ChangeScaredState` method, and `RpcChangeState` forwards to `ChangeState`.
2. `RpcFindNewTarget` finds a potential target by looking for the closest player via the **NetworkRobotGameManager**. If found, it sets the target of this enemy to that player.

Now, you need to write the update method for the server side:

```
[ServerCallback]
void Update()                                          //1
{
    if (target != null)
    {
        navigationTime += Time.deltaTime;
        if (navigationTime > navigationUpdate)         //2
        {
            if (state == EnemyState.Hunting)
            {
                RpcFindNewTarget();
            }

            agent.destination = target.position;      //3
            navigationTime = 0;
        }

        CheckDeathUpdate();                            //4
    }
}
```

Here's how it works:

1. `Update` checks if there is a target for the enemy; if so, it updates the `navigationTime` by adding the current time delta.
2. If the enemy has exceeded the `navigationUpdate` period and is still hunting, it should reacquire a target by calling `RpcFindNewTarget`.
3. Set the **NavMeshAgent** destination to the position of the current target, and since the enemy updated this frame, reset `navigationTime` to **0**.
4. Call `CheckDeathUpdate` to see if an enemy died this frame.

Next, add the `CheckDeathUpdate` server side method:

```
[Server]
void CheckDeathUpdate()
{
    if (state != EnemyState.Dead)              //1
    {
        return;
    }

    deathTime += Time.deltaTime;

    Vector3 currentPos =
        new Vector3(transform.position.x,
            0.0f, transform.position.z);
```

```
        Vector3 targetPos =
            new Vector3(spawnTransform.position.x,
                0.0f, spawnTransform.position.z);

        float dist = Vector3.Distance(currentPos, targetPos);

        if (dist < 0.1f && deathTime > deathDuration) //2
        {
            RpcChargeState(EnemyState.Hunting);
            isKilled = false;

            RpcChargeScaredState(poweredUpPlayerExists); //3
            deathTime = 0.0f;
        }
    }
```

Breaking this method down:

1. If the enemy is dead, update the death timer with the current delta time. Find the distance between current enemy position and enemy spawn position.
2. If the enemy is closer than 0.1 meters to the spawn position, and the enemy has exceeded the `deathDuration` period in the dead state, resurrect it by changing the state to `EnemyState.Hunting` and setting `isKilled` to false.
3. If resurrected, change the state enemy based on the existence of a powered up player in the game and reset `deathTime` to 0 to get ready to die again.

Now add a method on the server side that is called when something enters the enemy trigger volume:

```
    [ServerCallback]
    void OnTriggerEnter(Collider collider)
    {
        if (collider.gameObject.tag == "Player")     //1
        {
            NetworkPlayerRobot robot =

    collider.gameObject.GetComponent<NetworkPlayerRobot>();
            if (robot.poweredUp)                     //2
            {
                Killed();
                robot.score += scoreValue;
            }
            else
            {
                if (state == EnemyState.Hunting)     //3
                {
                    robot.Killed();
                    RpcFindNewTarget();
                }
```

```
        }
    }
}
```

Look at this code, you:

1. Check if the enemy collided with one of the players.
2. If the player is powered-up, kill the enemy by calling `Killed`, and add this enemy's `scoreValue` to the player's score.
3. If the player was not powered-up, and the enemy state was hunting, kill the player and find the next target for the enemy.

Finally, write the `Killed` method:

```
[Server]
public void Killed()                              //1
{
    if (isKilled)
    {
        return;
    }

    isKilled = true;

    RpcChangeState(EnemyState.Dead);    //2
}
```

This code:

1. Checks if this enemy has already been killed, and if not, it sets the boolean to confirm this enemy is killed.
2. It then calls the client to change the enemy state to dead.

Save this script and return to the editor.

NetworkEnemy.cs is a script that you'll place on enemy robots. There are three parameters that you need to populate with references to the GameObjects that will form three different appearances for the enemy robot based on its current state: **normalGO**, **scaredGO** and **deadGO**. The script changes the state of the enemy — it will be *hunting* for the players normally — but if one of the players has powered-up, the enemy will be *running* away. If it's been killed by one of the powered-up players, it will be *dead*, but can be resurrected after a while.

A **NetworkEnemy** will also have the **NavMeshAgent** component that will allow it to navigate the maze via the **NavMesh** that you created above.

Normally, the agent looks for the closest player robot as its destination at each navigation update. But if it's either running away scared or dead, the agent will use its spawn position as its destination.

The one other thing this script does is to detect whether the enemy robot has collided with a player robot, and react to that event. If the player robot is powered-up, the enemy robot is killed, changes its appearance to **deadGO** and heads back to its spawn position to be resurrected sometime later. If the player robot is not powered-up, and the enemy robot is in the *hunting* state, then kill the player robot and look for the next closest player to try and catch.

NetworkPlayerRobot

Next, you'll write the script that gets placed on the player robots. Create a file named **NetworkPlayerRobot** in the **Assets \ Razeware \ Robot \ Scripts** folder and replace everything inside with:

```
using UnityEngine;
using UnityEngine.Networking;
using UnityEngine.UI;

namespace Razeware.ARBook
{
    [RequireComponent(typeof(NetworkTransform))]
    [RequireComponent(typeof(Rigidbody))]
    public class NetworkPlayerRobot : NetworkBehaviour
    {

    }
}
```

The definition of the class has attributes to denote that it requires two other components to make it work: a **NetworkTransform** to make sure the server and other clients are aware of the transform of this player and a **Rigidbody** so that it can bounce off colliders like the walls and other players.

Continue adding some public fields that can be edited in the Inspector later on:

```
public float rotationSpeed = 45.0f;      //1
public float speed = 2.0f;
public float maxSpeed = 3.0f;
public float moveThreshold = 0.1f;
public float slowThreshold = 0.5f;
public float rotateThreshold = 3.0f;

public float powerUpDuration = 7.0f;
public float bounceBackDuration = 1.5f;
```

```
public GameObject normalGO;                 //2
public GameObject poweredGO;
public GameObject scaredGO;

public Renderer[] renderersToColor;        //3

//Network syncvar
[SyncVar(hook = "OnScoreChanged")]         //4
public int score;
[SyncVar]
public Color color;
[SyncVar]
public string playerName;
[SyncVar(hook = "OnLifeChanged")]
public int lifeCount;
[SyncVar(hook = "OnPowerUpChanged")]
public bool poweredUp;
```

Here's what they're for:

1. Initial fields allow you to change some parameters to adjust the movement, physics and gameplay from the editor. Default values have been found to work well, but you can play around with these values later on.
2. References to three GameObjects which would represent the appearance of the player in each of its three states. These can be set up in the editor.
3. References to renderers that need to change color based on the color chosen by the player. These can be set up in editor.
4. Some fields that are synced across all the clients and server version of this player object using **[SyncVar]** attribute. The **hook** parameter references method in this object that will get called when that value changes.

Now, add some protected and private fields:

```
protected Rigidbody playerRigidbody;       //1
protected Collider playerCollider;
protected Text scoreText;

protected float playerRotation = 0;        //2

protected Vector3 targetPosition;

protected bool canControl = true;

[SyncVar] protected float powerDownTimer;

protected float bounceBackTimer;
```

```
//hard to control WHEN Init is called
//(networking make order between object spawning non
deterministic)
//so we call init from multiple location
//(depending on what between playerbehavior & manager is created
first).
protected bool wasInit;                    //3

Camera arCamera;
```

Here's what's happening:

1. Store some references to avoid having to call `GetComponent` multiple times.
2. These variables store the player's rotation,the target position, whether this object can be controller, a power down timer and a bounce back timer respectively.
3. Boolean to keep track of when the player has been initialized since the order of creation of player and game manager could be non-deterministic.

Next, write two utility methods that are used throughout the script:

```
void ChangeGODisplay(GameObject go)                    //1
{
    normalGO.SetActive(go == normalGO);
    poweredGO.SetActive(go == poweredGO);
    scaredGO.SetActive(go == scaredGO);
}

void UpdateScoreLifeText()                             //2
{
    if (scoreText != null)
    {
        scoreText.text = playerName +
            "\nSCORE : " + score + "\nLIFE : ";
        for (int i = 1; i <= lifeCount; ++i)
        {
            scoreText.text += "X";
        }
    }
}
```

Here's what they do:

1. `ChangeGODisplay` selects one of the three GameObject references to activate to show the appearance of the player in that state.
2. `UpdateScoreLifeText` formats the score and number of lives for this player for display on a `Text` UI.

Now add the `Awake` and `Start` methods:

```
void Awake()
{
    //register the spaceship in the gamemanager,
    //that will allow to loop on it.
    NetworkRobotGameManager.Robots.Add(this);          //1

    arCamera = PlaneChooser.Instance.GetARCamera();    //2
}

void Start()
{
    playerRigidbody = GetComponent<Rigidbody>();       //3
    playerCollider = GetComponent<Collider>();

    foreach (Renderer r in renderersToColor)           //4
    {
        r.material.color = color;
    }

    if (NetworkRobotGameManager.Instance != null)
    {
        //we MAY be awake late (see comment on _wasInit above)
        // so if the instance is already there we init
        Init();                                        //5
    }
}
```

With this code, you:

1. Add the player to the **NetworkRobotGameManager** list of players.
2. Get the `Camera` from the **PlaneChooser** which was set up in the **NetworkRobotSetupAR** scene.
3. Store component references for later use.
4. Change the color of the referenced renderers to this player's color.
5. If the **NetworkRobotGameManager** exists, call `Init`.

Add the `Init` method next:

```
public void Init()
{
    if (wasInit)
    {
        return;
    }

    GameObject scoreGO =
```

```
        new GameObject(playerName + "score");    //1
    scoreGO.transform.SetParent(
        NetworkRobotGameManager.Instance.uiScoreZone.transform,
            false);
    scoreText = scoreGO.AddComponent<Text>();
    scoreText.alignment = TextAnchor.MiddleCenter;
    scoreText.font =
        NetworkRobotGameManager.Instance.uiScoreFont;
    scoreText.resizeTextForBestFit = true;
    scoreText.color = color;
    wasInit = true;

    transform.position =

NetworkRobotGameManager.Instance.GetPossibleSpawnPosition(); //2
    targetPosition = transform.position;

    bounceBackTimer = 0.0f;
    powerDownTimer = 0.0f;

    lifeCount = 1;
    ChangeGODisplay(normalGO);           //3
    UpdateScoreLifeText();
}
```

With this method, you:

1. Create a new GameObject to display the score and set it up.
2. Initialize the position from **NetworkRobotGameManager** and start values of other gameplay parameters.
3. Change the appearance of the player to normal, and update the game HUD which contains score and lives.

Next, you'll write four methods that are callbacks from Unity or UNet SyncVar updates:

```
void OnDestroy()
{
    NetworkRobotGameManager.Robots.Remove(this); //1
}

// --- Score & Life management & display
void OnScoreChanged(int newValue)
{
    score = newValue;
    UpdateScoreLifeText(); //2
}

void OnLifeChanged(int newValue)
{
    lifeCount = newValue;
```

```
    UpdateScoreLifeText(); //3
}

void OnPowerUpChanged(bool newValue)
{
    //set value
    poweredUp = newValue;
    if (poweredUp)
    {
NetworkRobotGameManager.Instance.RpcPlayPowerUpSound(); //4

        if (isLocalPlayer)
        {
            //start timer for powerdown
            powerDownTimer = powerUpDuration;
        }
    }
    else
    {
NetworkRobotGameManager.Instance.RpcPlayPowerDownSound(); //5
    }
}
```

Here's how they work:

1. If this **NetworkPlayerRobot** is destroyed, remove it from the list of players on the **NetworkRobotGameManager**.
2. When the score is changed, store the new value and update the scoreboard.
3. When you lose or gain a life, store the new value and update the scoreboard.
4. When you power up, play the power-up sound, and start the `powerDownTimer`.
5. When you power down, play the power down sound.

Next, add these methods to communicate between the server and client sides of the code:

```
[Command]
void CmdPowerUp(bool enablePU)              //1
{
    ServerPowerUp(enablePU);
}

[Server]
public void ServerPowerUp(bool enablePU)    //2
{
    poweredUp = enablePU;
    NetworkRobotGameManager.Instance.CheckPowerUpInfo();
```

```
}

[ClientRpc]
public void RpcPlayerNormalGO()               //3
{
    ChangeGODisplay(normalGO);
}

[ClientRpc]
public void RpcPlayerPoweredGO()
{
    ChangeGODisplay(poweredGO);
}

[ClientRpc]
public void RpcPlayerScaredGO()
{
    ChangeGODisplay(scaredGO);
}
```

Here's a closer look:

1. `CmdPowerUp` is a command. A command allows you to call from the client to the server. This calls a server-only method `ServerPowerUp`.
2. `ServerPowerUp` sets the `poweredUp` boolean and calls the **NetworkRobotGameManager** to check the state of all player power-ups.
3. Define three RPC (from server to client) methods to change the appearance of the player, and delegate that to `ChangeGODisplay`.

Next, write a **[ClientCallback]** method for `Update`:

```
[ClientCallback]
void Update()
{
    playerRotation = 0;

    if (!isLocalPlayer || !canControl)  //1
    {
        return;
    }

    if (powerDownTimer > 0.0f)          //2
    {
        powerDownTimer -= Time.deltaTime;
        if (powerDownTimer <= 0.0f)
        {
            CmdPowerUp(false);
        }
    }
```

```
    if (bounceBackTimer > 0.0f)         //3
    {
        bounceBackTimer -= Time.deltaTime;
        //don't allow user interaction if bouncing
        return;
    }

    if (Input.GetMouseButton(0))        //4
    {
        Ray ray =
            arCamera.ScreenPointToRay(Input.mousePosition);

        // Planes are in layer Floor
        int layerMask =
            1 << LayerMask.NameToLayer("Floor");

        RaycastHit rayHit;
        if (Physics.Raycast(ray, out rayHit, float.MaxValue,
layerMask))
        {
            targetPosition = rayHit.point;
        }
    }
}
```

With this code, you:

1. Only continue with the method if it's the local player (you cannot control other player's robots), and your player is in control.
2. If there's a power down timer, count it down and call the command to power this player down (propagating the information via the server to others as well) if the timer reaches 0.
3. Check if the player has been knocked back and don't give back control until bounce-back is complete.
4. See if the player tapped on the floor collider, and try to move the robot towards the position the player tapped.

Now, add a **[ClientCallback]** method for `FixedUpdate`, usually used for physics based movements:

```
[ClientCallback]
void FixedUpdate()
{
    if (!hasAuthority)
    {
        return;
    }
```

```
    if (!canControl)
    {
        //if we can't control, mean we're destroyed,
        //so make sure the robot stay in spawn place
        playerRigidbody.rotation = Quaternion.identity;
        playerRigidbody.position = Vector3.zero;
        playerRigidbody.velocity = Vector3.zero;
        playerRigidbody.angularVelocity = Vector3.zero;
    }
    else
    {
        Vector3 toTarget = (targetPosition -
transform.position); //1
        toTarget = new Vector3(toTarget.x, 0.0f, toTarget.z);
        if (toTarget.magnitude > moveThreshold)
        {
            //rotate to face target
            float diffAngle =
                Vector3.SignedAngle(transform.forward,
                    toTarget.normalized, Vector3.up);
            float absDiffAngle = Mathf.Abs(diffAngle);
            if (absDiffAngle > rotateThreshold) //2
            {
                float rotAngle = rotationSpeed *
                     Time.fixedDeltaTime;
                rotAngle = absDiffAngle > rotAngle ? rotAngle :
                     absDiffAngle;
                rotAngle = diffAngle > 0.0f ? rotAngle :
                    -rotAngle;
                playerRigidbody.rotation =
                    playerRigidbody.rotation *
Quaternion.Euler(0,
                        rotAngle, 0);
            }

            //slowdown as you get closer
            float slowdownFactor =
                (toTarget.magnitude / slowThreshold); //3
            slowdownFactor = slowdownFactor > 1.0f ? 1.0f :
                 slowdownFactor;

            playerRigidbody.velocity = toTarget.normalized *
                speed * slowdownFactor;

            if (playerRigidbody.velocity.magnitude > maxSpeed)
            {
                playerRigidbody.velocity =
                    playerRigidbody.velocity.normalized *
maxSpeed;
            }
        }
        else
        {
```

```
                playerRigidbody.velocity = Vector3.zero; //4
                playerRigidbody.angularVelocity = Vector3.zero;
            }
        }
    }
```

Here's a look at the code:

1. Check if you are further away than the move threshold from the tapped position on the floor.
2. Rotate to face the target position.
3. Adjust the robot's velocity as it gets closer to the tapped position.
4. If close enough to target, stop moving.

Finally, write some methods to finish off the script:

```
[ServerCallback]
void OnCollisionEnter(Collision coll)
{
    if (coll.gameObject.tag == "Player")     //1
    {
        //we collided with a player, check if
        //they are powered up.
        NetworkPlayerRobot otherRobot =
            coll.gameObject.GetComponent<NetworkPlayerRobot>();
        if (otherRobot.poweredUp && !poweredUp)
        {
            Killed();                          //2
        }
        else
        {
            BounceBack(otherRobot.gameObject.transform); //3
        }
    }
}

[Server]
public void Killed()                           //4
{
    lifeCount = 0;

    NetworkRobotGameManager.Instance.RpcPlayDeathSound();

    NetworkServer.Destroy(gameObject);
}

[Server]
public void BounceBack(Transform otherPlayer) //5
{
```

```
        Vector3 diff = transform.position - otherPlayer.position;

        RpcBounceBackTo(transform.position + (diff * 3.0f));
    }

    [ClientRpc]
    void RpcBounceBackTo(Vector3 newPosition)    //6
    {
        targetPosition = newPosition;
        bounceBackTimer = bounceBackDuration;
    }
```

Here's the breakdown:

1. When the player collides with another player, the following actions happen:
2. If the other player is powered up and this player is not, this player is killed.
3. In all other cases, bounce back from the other player.
4. When killed, play the death sound and destroy the GameObject via the **NetworkServer**.
5. When bouncing back, find the vector between the two player robots and triple it for the bounce back amount.
6. RPC method that gets called on the client to set the player to the new position and starts a timer for the duration the player is not in control because of the knockback.

This script has some functionality that runs on the server to make sure all instances of this player robot, on all devices, have their states synced up. Similar to the enemy robot script, this one uses references to three different GameObjects to display which state the player is in: **normalGO**, **poweredGO** and **scaredGO**.

When initializing, the player robot informs the **NetworkRobotGameManager** of its presence and creates a **scoreText** UI element where it will keep track of this player's stats.

The script has hooks for when various events happen in the game and it provides client-side functions (the ones that have the **[ClientRpc]** and **[ClientCallback]** attributes on them) to react to those events. Examples include when the player gets some points, gets a power-up, gets killed, or has to change its appearance due to some other player powering up.

It has a client-side **Update** function that keeps track of user input on a device and controls the player robot that belongs to the player on that device. The **FixedUpdate** method also helps to animate the rigid body on the client.

In addition, there's a server-side method that checks when player robots collide with other player robots and either bounces back off of them or gets killed if the other robot is powered-up and yours is not.Save the script and return to the editor to create the **Network Robot Game Manager**.

NetworkRobotGameManager

You're ready to create the game manager that's going to orchestrate all of the elements of your game. Create a new C# script named **NetworkRobotGameManager** in the **Assets \ Razeware \ Robot \ Scripts** folder and replace the contents with:

```
using UnityEngine;
using UnityEngine.Networking;
using Razeware.NetworkLobby;
using System.Collections;
using System.Collections.Generic;
using UnityEngine.UI;
using UnityEngine.AI;

namespace Razeware.ARBook
{
    public class NetworkRobotGameManager : NetworkBehaviour
    {

    }
}
```

This creates a base `NetworkBehaviour` manager class.Add the fields that you need for the manager, including public ones that you can set up from the editor:

```
public static List<NetworkPlayerRobot> Robots =
    new List<NetworkPlayerRobot>();  //1
public static NetworkRobotGameManager Instance;

public Transform contentTransform;  //2
public float contentMaxDimension;

public GameObject uiScoreZone;
public Font uiScoreFont;
public Text winnerDisplay;

[Header("Gameplay")] public GameObject[] enemyPrefabs;
public GameObject[] collectiblePrefabs;
// index 0 = normal, index 1 = powerup

public Vector2 collectibleSpawnMinPosition;
public Vector2 collectibleSpawnMaxPosition;
```

```
public List<Transform> spawnPositions;
public List<Transform> enemySpawnPositions;

public AudioClip gameBackgroundMusic;   //3
public AudioClip startRoundSound;
public AudioClip collectedSound;
public AudioClip powerUpSound;
public AudioClip powerDownSound;
public AudioClip deathSound;

public delegate void PoweredUpPlayerExistsDelegate(bool exists);

[SyncEvent]
public event PoweredUpPlayerExistsDelegate
EventPoweredUpPlayerExists; //4

[SyncVar] public bool playerPoweredUp;

[SyncVar] public int numActiveCollectibles;

[SyncVar] public int numActivePowerPills;

[Space]

protected bool spawningCollectibles = true; //5
protected bool spawningPowerPills = true;

protected bool running = false;
protected int regularPillsBatch = 9;
protected AudioSource audioSource;
```

Here's a look at what you added:

1. Some static fields that keep track of players and the manager itself.
2. Some fields to set up references and values in the Inspector for other GameObjects, transforms and parameters needed in the manager script.
3. Collection of audio clips for the sound effects of the game.
4. **SyncEvents** and **SyncVars** which can be invoked or changed on one client or the server, and will be propagated to all the other clients via the server.
5. Fields used within the manager, there hold whether collectibles and power pills will be spawned, whether the game is running, the amount of pills and a reference to the audio source.

Next, add some helper methods. The first one will spawn collectibles:

```
void SpawnCollectible(GameObject prefab, bool isPowerUp = false)
{
    bool positionFound = false;
    Vector3 position;
    NavMeshHit hit;

    do  //1
    {
        float xpos =

Mathf.Round(Random.Range(collectibleSpawnMinPosition.x,
                collectibleSpawnMaxPosition.x));
        float zpos =

Mathf.Round(Random.Range(collectibleSpawnMinPosition.y,
                collectibleSpawnMaxPosition.y));

        if (Mathf.Abs(xpos) < 4.0f && Mathf.Abs(zpos) < 4.0f)
        {
            continue;  //too close to center ghostbox
        }

        position = new Vector3(xpos, 0.0f, zpos);
        positionFound =
            NavMesh.SamplePosition(position,
            out hit, 0.1f, NavMesh.AllAreas);
    } while (!positionFound);

    position =
        new Vector3(hit.position.x, 0.3f, hit.position.z); //2
    GameObject go =
        Instantiate(prefab, position,
        Quaternion.Euler(Random.value * 360.0f,
            Random.value * 360.0f, Random.value * 360.0f))
            as GameObject;
    NetworkServer.Spawn(go);

    if (isPowerUp)  //3
    {
        numActivePowerPills++;
    }
    else
    {
        numActiveCollectibles++;
    }
}
```

With this code, you:

1. Find a random position on the level not too close to the center box where enemies spawn, and where you can access via the **NavMesh** in the level.
2. Instantiate the collectible prefab in the position found, and inform the **NetworkServer** that you spawned it.
3. Depending on whether a collectible is a power-up or not, add one to the number of collectibles in that bucket.

Now add the following coroutines:

```
IEnumerator CollectiblesCoroutine() //1
{
    const float MIN_TIME = 3.0f;
    const float MAX_TIME = 5.0f;

    yield return new WaitForSeconds(
        Random.Range(MIN_TIME, MAX_TIME));

    for (int i = 0; i < regularPillsBatch; i++)
    {
        yield return new WaitForSeconds(0.1f);
        SpawnCollectible(collectiblePrefabs[0]);
    }

    spawningCollectibles = false;
}

IEnumerator PowerPillCoroutine() //2
{
    const float MIN_TIME = 15.0f;
    const float MAX_TIME = 20.0f;

    yield return new WaitForSeconds(
        Random.Range(MIN_TIME, MAX_TIME));

    SpawnCollectible(collectiblePrefabs[1], true);
    spawningPowerPills = false;
}
```

Here's a look at the two coroutines and what they do:

1. Coroutine that spawns a batch of regular collectibles (blue pills) after a delay.
2. Coroutine that spawns a single power-up collectible (gold pill) after a delay.

Now add these two helper methods used for enemy spawning:

```
public Vector3 GetPossibleEnemySpawnPosition() //1
{
    Vector3 retVal = new Vector3(0.0f, 1.0f, 0.0f);
    if (enemySpawnPositions.Count > 0)
    {
        Transform chosen =
            enemySpawnPositions.FindLast(t => t != null);
        if (chosen != null)
        {
            enemySpawnPositions.Remove(chosen);
            retVal = chosen.position;
        }
    }

    return retVal;
}

public NetworkPlayerRobot GetClosestPlayer(Vector3 from) //2
{
    NetworkPlayerRobot result = null;
    float closestDist = float.MaxValue;

    foreach (NetworkPlayerRobot npr in Robots)
    {
        float playerDist =
            Vector3.Distance(from, npr.transform.position);
        if (playerDist < closestDist)
        {
            closestDist = playerDist;
            result = npr;
        }
    }

    return result;
}
```

With this code, you:

1. Find a possible enemy spawn position by choosing one from the list set up in the Editor. Once chosen, that spawn position is removed from the list so that enemies do not spawn in the same spot.
2. Find the closest player to a specific position by calculating the distance of each player to that position and returning the one with minimum distance from the point.

Now, add the enemy spawn coroutine itself:

```
IEnumerator EnemiesCoroutine()
{
    const float MIN_TIME = 5.0f;
    const float MAX_TIME = 10.0f;

    yield return new WaitForSeconds(
        Random.Range(MIN_TIME, MAX_TIME));

    for (int i = 0; i < Robots.Count; i++)
    {

        Vector3 position =
            GetPossibleEnemySpawnPosition(); //1

        GameObject go =
            Instantiate(enemyPrefabs[enemyPrefabs.Length - 1],
                position, Quaternion.Euler(Random.value *
                360.0f, Random.value * 360.0f,
                Random.value * 360.0f)) as GameObject;

        NetworkEnemy enemy = go.GetComponent<NetworkEnemy>();
        NetworkPlayerRobot closest =
            GetClosestPlayer(position); //2
        enemy.target = closest.transform;

        NavMeshAgent agent =
            go.GetComponent<NavMeshAgent>(); //3
        agent.speed = Random.Range(1.5f, 2.0f);
        agent.acceleration = agent.speed * 4.0f;

        NetworkServer.Spawn(go);
    }
}
```

Here's a closer look:

1. This coroutine waits a few seconds, searches for a possible spawn position and instantiates an enemy there.
2. `GetClosestPlayer` from the helper method and set that target on the **NetworkEnemy** component.
3. Set up some random values for the **NavMeshAgent** of the enemy and inform the **NetworkServer** that the enemy was spawned.

Next are some methods to initialize the game:

```
void Awake()                            //1
{
    Instance = this;
```

```
        playerPoweredUp = false;
        winnerDisplay.enabled = false;
        audioSource = GetComponent<AudioSource>();
    }

    void Start()                              //2
    {
        if (isServer)
        {
            StartCoroutine(EnemiesCoroutine());
            StartCoroutine(CollectiblesCoroutine());
            StartCoroutine(PowerPillCoroutine());
        }

        foreach (var robot in Robots)   //3
        {
            robot.Init();
        }
    }

    public override void OnStartClient() //4
    {
        base.OnStartClient();

        PlaneChooser.Instance.PlaceOnSelectedPlane(
            contentTransform, contentMaxDimension);

        foreach (GameObject obj in enemyPrefabs) //5
        {
            ClientScene.RegisterPrefab(obj);
        }

        foreach (GameObject obj in collectiblePrefabs)
        {
            ClientScene.RegisterPrefab(obj);
        }

        audioSource.clip = gameBackgroundMusic;  //6
        audioSource.loop = true;
        //make it 2d
        audioSource.spatialBlend = 0.0f;
        audioSource.Play();
        audioSource.PlayOneShot(startRoundSound);
    }
```

Here's a closer look at the code:

1. On `Awake`, set up some parameters and get the **AudioSource** component for use in playing sound effects.
2. On `Start`, run the coroutines described above to generate enemies, regular collectibles and a power pill.

3. Also, go through all of the players and initialize them if not already done.
4. Method called whenever the network client portion of the object gets started. Use the **PlaneChooser** to make the content transform set up in the editor appear on the selected plane.
5. Register all of the prefabs that are needed and will be spawned in the client scene.
6. Initialize the **AudioSource**, play the background music in a loop and play the round start sound.

Next, add the code to handle the updates as a server callback:

```
[ServerCallback]
void Update()
{
    //our game start check (more than one player has started)
    if (Robots.Count > 1)
    {
        running = true;
    }

    //only check for game end after it has started
    if (!running)
    {
        return;
    }

    int numLivePlayers = 0;
    NetworkPlayerRobot oneLivePlayer = null;
    for (int i = 0; i < Robots.Count; ++i)   //1
    {
        if (Robots[i].lifeCount > 0)
        {
            numLivePlayers++;
            oneLivePlayer = Robots[i];
        }
    }

    if (numLivePlayers == 1)     //2
    {
        RpcDisplayWinner(oneLivePlayer.playerName);

        StartCoroutine(ReturnToLobby());
        return;
    }

    if (!spawningCollectibles &&
        numActiveCollectibles == 0) //3
    {
        spawningCollectibles = true;
        StartCoroutine(CollectiblesCoroutine());
```

```
        }

        if (!spawningPowerPills && numActivePowerPills == 0)
        {
            spawningPowerPills = true;
            StartCoroutine(PowerPillCoroutine());
        }
    }
```

Looking at the code:

1. Iterate over the players and check how many are still alive.
2. If there's only one, display that player as the winner in the HUD, wait a while and go back to the lobby to start the next game.
3. Whenever the regular collectibles or the power-ups are all eaten up, create the next batch.

Next, write the RPC methods used to play some sounds and display the winner on the client devices:

```
// 1
[ClientRpc]
void RpcDisplayWinner(string playerName)
{
    winnerDisplay.enabled = true;
    winnerDisplay.text = playerName + " wins!";
}

// 2
[ClientRpc]
public void RpcPlayDeathSound()
{
    audioSource.PlayOneShot(deathSound);
}

[ClientRpc]
public void RpcPlayPowerUpSound()
{
    audioSource.PlayOneShot(powerUpSound);
}

[ClientRpc]
public void RpcPlayPowerDownSound()
{
    audioSource.PlayOneShot(powerDownSound);
}

[ClientRpc]
public void RpcPlayCollectedSound()
{
```

```
    audioSource.PlayOneShot(collectedSound);
}
```

The first piece of code above displays a piece of text when a player wins. The second part handles playing the different sound effects.Finish this script by writing the following methods in the class:

```
public Vector3 GetPossibleSpawnPosition()    //1
{
    Vector3 retVal = new Vector3(0.0f, 1.0f, 0.0f);
    if (spawnPositions.Count > 0)
    {
        Transform chosen =
            spawnPositions.FindLast(t => t != null);
        if (chosen != null)
        {
            spawnPositions.Remove(chosen);
            retVal = chosen.position;
        }
    }

    return retVal;
}

IEnumerator ReturnToLobby()                      //2
{
    running = false;
    yield return new WaitForSeconds(4.0f);
    LobbyManager.s_Singleton.ServerReturnToLobby();
}

[Server]
public void CheckPowerUpInfo()                   //3
{
    bool poweredUpPlayerExists = false;

    foreach (NetworkPlayerRobot nr in Robots)
    {
        poweredUpPlayerExists |= nr.poweredUp;
    }

    playerPoweredUp = poweredUpPlayerExists;
    EventPoweredUpPlayerExists.Invoke(
        poweredUpPlayerExists); //4

    foreach (NetworkPlayerRobot nr in Robots) //5
    {
        if (nr.poweredUp)
        {
            nr.RpcPlayerPoweredGO();
        }
```

```
            else if (playerPoweredUp)
            {
                nr.RpcPlayerScaredGO();
            }
            else
            {
                nr.RpcPlayerNormalGO();
            }
        }
    }
```

Here's a closer look at the code:

1. Iterates through a list of possible player spawn positions set up in the Editor, and returns one, after removing it from the list. Usually called from **NetworkPlayerRobot** to find a position for spawning.
2. After a delay (for winner display), invoke the **LobbyManager** to return the game to the lobby screen.
3. A server method that iterates through the players to see if any are powered up.
4. Invoke an event to inform all clients whether a power-up player exists or not.
5. Iterate through players and set their appearance based on their power-up state as well as that of any other player that might be powered-up. This last method is called whenever a player powers up by eating a power pill or their power-up state times out.

The game manager calls the **PlaneChooser** instance when it's started on the client side and makes sure the maze play field on this device appears in the correct position, orientation and scale based on the **SetupAR** scene interaction earlier.

During **Update**, it first checks whether there's only one surviving player robot, and if so, display that player as the winner and sends all players back into the lobby after a slight delay for the next round. It also checks whether all of the collectibles are gone, and if so, it creates some more after a slight delay.

It has a method that is called whenever a player robot powers up or down to check what each of the player robots appearance should be at this time. The rest of the methods in the script allows different scripts to play various sound effects on the device.

At this point, you have written all of the scripts for this scene, and all the scripts should compile. You now have to place the script components on the right objects and prefabs and connect up the different references.Save the script and return to the editor, it's time to hook everything up!

Setting up the elements

First, you need to set up the prefabs with their new scripts. Drag a copy of the **Assets \ Razeware \ Robot \ Prefabs \ PlayerRobotv3** prefab into your scene hierarchy and add a **Network Player Robot** component to it. It should automatically add the **NetworkTransform** and **NetworkIdentity** components (which are dependencies) to the prefab as well. Now change the parameters so that the components look like this:

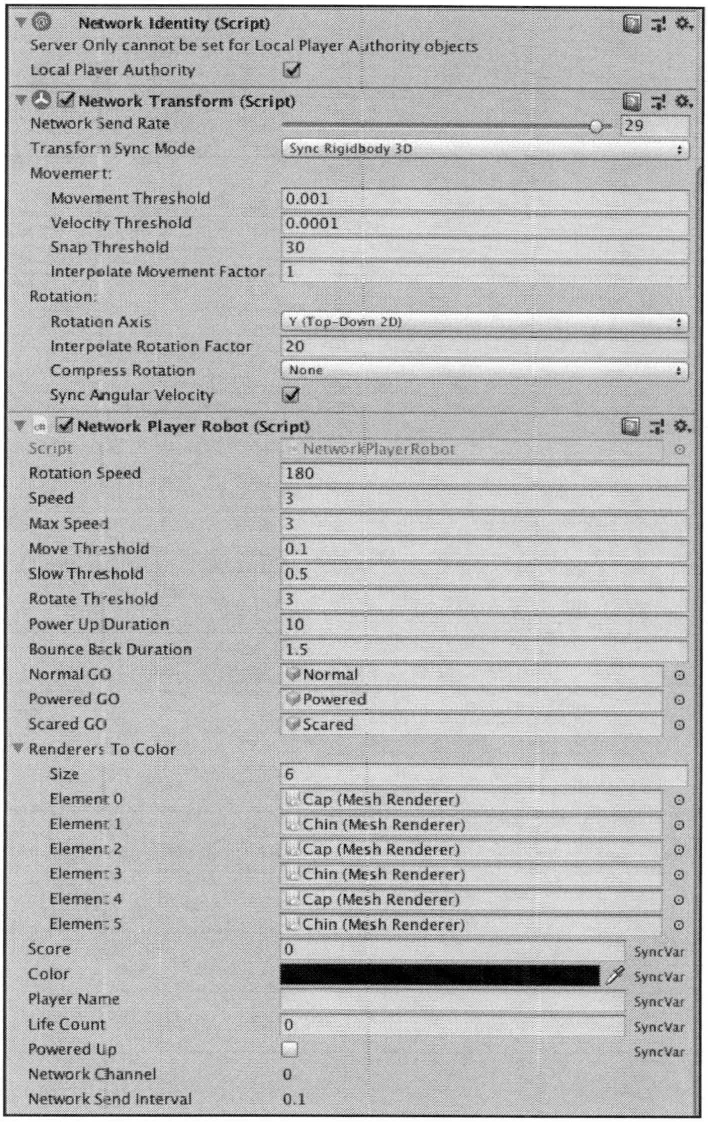

The references to the **GameObjects** and **Renderers** are all the items that exist inside the prefab. The RenderersToColor parameter should include the items named *Cap* and *Chin* that exist within this prefab. Click **Apply** on the top section of the Inspector to save these components and their parameters as part of the prefab. You can then delete the prefab from the scene hierarchy.

Next, drag in **Assets \ Razeware \ Robot \ Prefabs \ EnemyRobot_v1** prefab into the scene hierarchy and add a **Network Enemy** as a component and change the parameters so that the new components look like this:

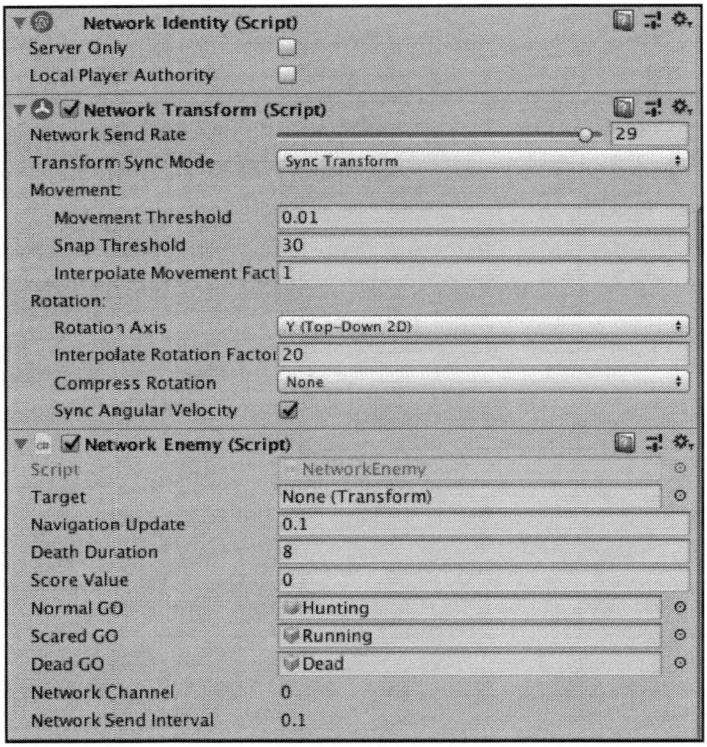

The GameObject references should be set to GameObjects that already exist in the prefab. Click **Apply** to save the prefab and delete it from the scene hierarchy.

You need to add components to the two collectible prefabs as well. Drag **Assets \ Razeware \ Robot \ Prefabs \ GreenCollectible** into the scene hierarchy and add a **Network Collectible** component.

Change the parameters so that the new components look like this:

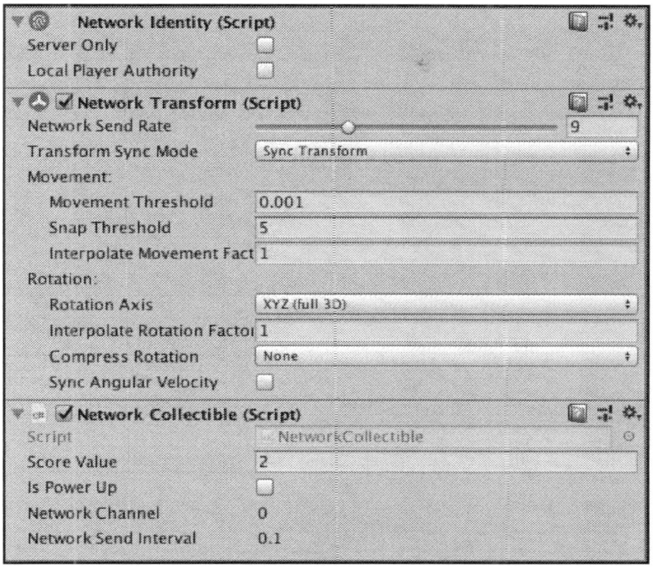

Click **Apply** and delete the prefab from the scene hierarchy. Drag **Assets Razeware \ Robot \ Prefabs \ BlueCollectible** prefab into the scene hierarchy and add a **NetworkCollectible** component. Change the parameters so that the new components look like this:

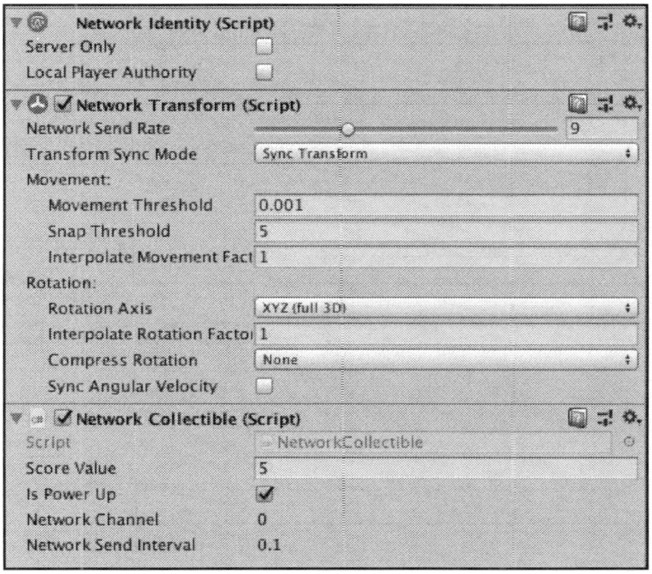

Click **Apply** and delete the prefab from the scene hierarchy.

Next, create a new GameObject in the Hierarchy, name it **RobotGameManager** and add a **Network Robot Game Manager** component to it. This is the component that handles most of the main network game logic.

Now change the parameters so that the new components look like this:

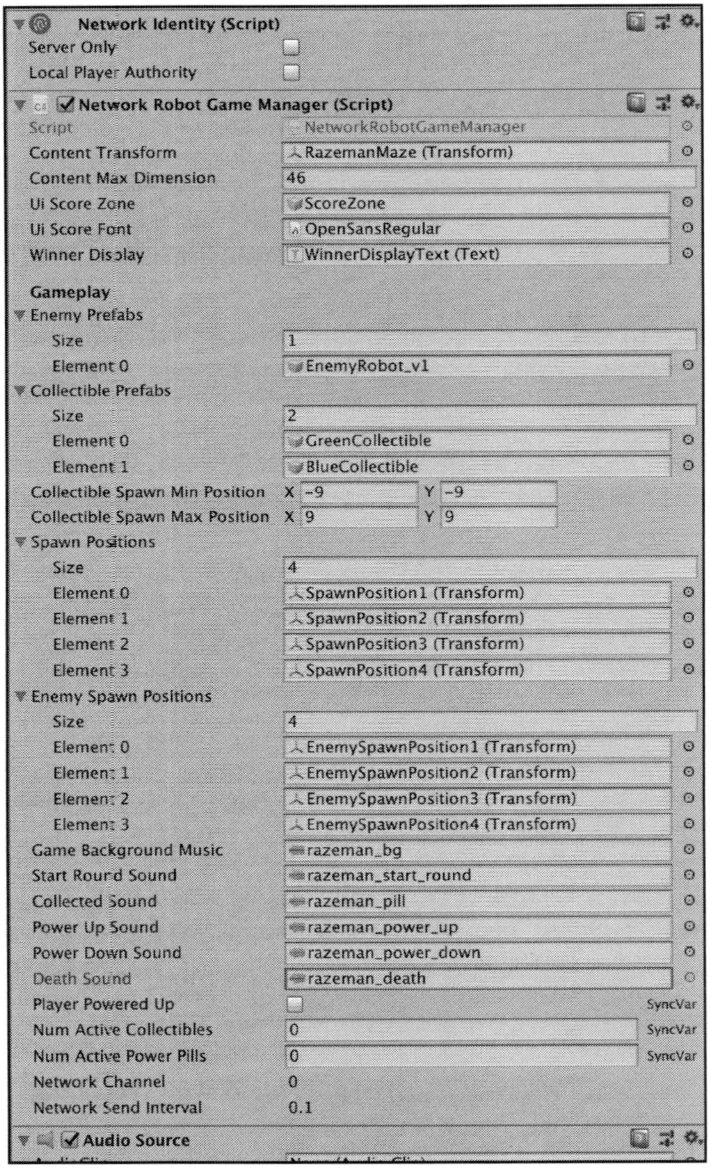

The **UIScoreZone** and **WinnerDisplay** are references to items that live under the **GameCanvas** in the scene. The fonts are referenced from the asset folder **Assets \ Razeware \ Robot \ Fonts \ OpenSans**. There are references to the enemy prefabs and the two types of collectible prefabs that we created above. There are references to transforms under **RazemanMaze** in the scene, including a list of player spawn positions and a list of enemy spawn positions. Finally, the music and sound effects files are found in the assets folder **Assets \ Razeware \ Robot \ Audio**.

Finally, add an **AudioSource** component to this GameObject and save the scene.

Same as with the first scene, add this scene to your build settings while you have it open. From the menu, choose **File/BuildSettings...** and click **Add Open Scene** to add this scene to the build. The order of this scene and the next scene in the build settings list won't matter as they are loaded from other scenes.

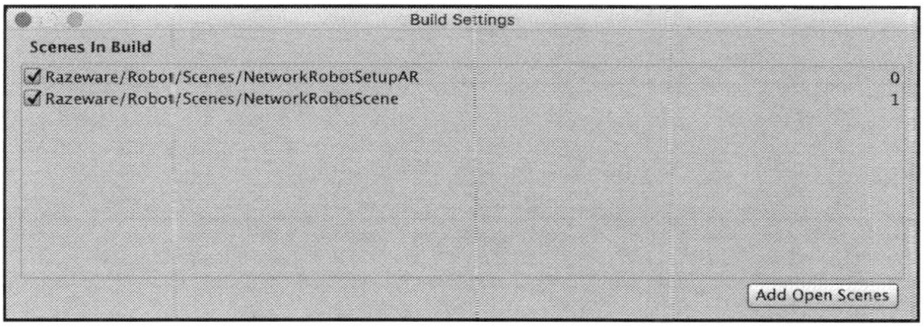

Lobby

The last scene you need to set up for the flow is the lobby scene. Create a new scene and save it as **Assets \ Razeware \ Robot \ Scenes \ NetworkRobotLobby**. Remove any existing GameObjects, but leave the Main Camera in for debugging — just make sure you disable it. Add an EventSystem to the scene hierarchy via **GameObject/UI/EventSystem**. Drag in the **Assets \ Razeware \ Robot \ Prefabs \ LobbyManager** prefab into the scene hierarchy.

Create a script named **NetworkRobotLobbyHook** in the **Assets \ Razeware \ Robot \ Scripts** folder and edit it to add this code:

```
using UnityEngine;
using Razeware.NetworkLobby;
using UnityEngine.Networking;

namespace Razeware.ARBook
{
    public class NetworkRobotLobbyHook : LobbyHook
```

```
    {
        public override void OnLobbyServerSceneLoadedForPlayer(
          NetworkManager manager, GameObject lobbyPlayer,
          GameObject gamePlayer)
        {
            LobbyPlayer lobby =
             lobbyPlayer.GetComponent<LobbyPlayer>();
            NetworkPlayerRobot robot =
             gamePlayer.GetComponent<NetworkPlayerRobot>();

            robot.name = lobby.name;
            robot.playerName = lobby.playerName;
            robot.color = lobby.playerColor;
            robot.score = 0;
            robot.lifeCount = 3;
        }
    }
}
```

This script transfers the information associated with a player in the lobby scene to the **NetworkRobotPlayer** so you can use it within the game scene. Save the script and add it as a component to **LobbyManager** in the scene.

In the Lobby Manager component in LobbyManager, drag a reference to **Assets \ Razeware \ Robot \ Prefabs \ PlayerRobotv3** to the **GamePlayerPrefab** parameter.

Save the scene and add it to the build settings because because it's required for the next step. From the menu, select **File/BuildSettings...** and click **Add Open Scene** to add this scene to the build.

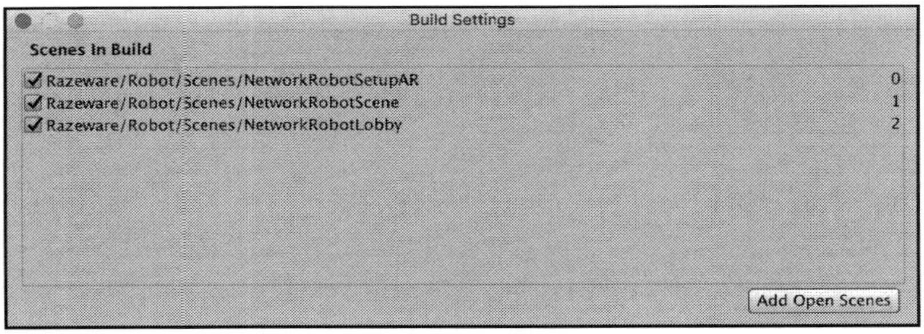

Drag a reference to this lobby scene from **Assets \ Razeware \ Robot \ Scenes \ NetworkRobotLobby** into the **LobbyScene** parameter.

Next, drag a reference to the game scene **Assets \ Razeware \ Robot \ Scenes \ NetworkRobotScene** into the **PlayScene** parameter.

The top part of the **LobbyManager** component will now look like this:

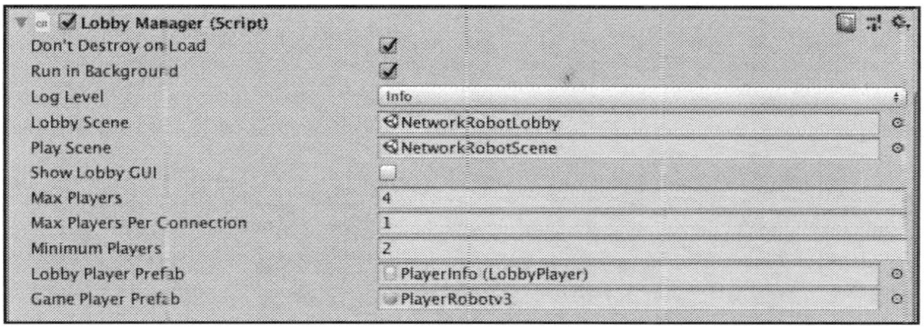

Save the scene again and you're now ready to build this experience to a few devices to test it out!Open the **Build Settings** window and build and run the game on at least two devices and up to four to test if everything works!

Multiplayer experience

Gather up to three of your friends to help you test the multiplayer AR experience that you just created. Give each of them a device with a copy of the app on it. Connect all of the devices to the same WiFi for the best results.

Settings

Once you run this app on an AR device, you'll be in the first part of the experience where you'll need to choose which surface you want to populate the playing field maze on. You'll see blue squares indicating the flat surfaces that are recognized. Find one large enough to put the maze on and tap the touchscreen at that location to select that surface. After doing so, you'll get sent to the network lobby to make the connection with other players.

For the best results, all players should start their app on their devices from the same side of the potential flat surface, and everyone playing should select the same surface. This is because you're using the plane transform as your synchronization point, and you want the plane transform to be oriented in the same direction for all players to share similar coordinates.

Lobby

At this point, you and your friends will be on the lobby screen. Whomever you selected to be the host can start a server by going to the **Create a game** text input box and entering a unique name. When you're ready, press **Create**.

Once the game starts, all of the others can choose to join the game by touching the **List Servers** button and entering the connection screen of the lobby. To change a player's color, tap on it. To change the player's name, tap the text input box. After all of the players have joined, they each need to press **Ready**. Once they do, the game will start a few seconds later.

Main game

The game starts with each of the player's robots in one of the corners of the maze and the enemy robots in the middle. There are regular energy orbs and power-up orbs spread out in the level. You move your robot by touching somewhere on the floor of the maze and your robot attempts to navigate to the place you last touched.

To win the game, you need to be the last player left while collecting as many points as possible. The enemy robots chase the player robots and destroy them on contact. Player robots bounce off each other on contact.

If one of the player robots touches a power orb, it powers up and can destroy the enemies as well as other player robots. At this point, the enemies will be running away and won't be able to destroy other players either. If two player robots collide while they're both powered up, they bounce off each other.

Playing this game can get very frantic as people run around the playing surface trying to keep their robots alive, collecting orbs for points and trying to destroy their opponent's robots. Watch out and have fun!

Where to go from here?

In this chapter, you learned to use the lessons from previous chapters to put together a multiplayer AR game that you could enjoy playing with your friends. You can make improvements to the experience, but you're now armed with the resources to create a full-fledged handheld AR app on your own. Consider some ideas on how to use AR for an exciting experience and take a stab at implementing it using the information from this book. Happy creating!

In the next section of this book, you'll learn about the Hololens and how to create AR experiences on it using Unity.

Section VII: HoloLens

In this section you'll learn how the to develop for the Microsoft HoloLens with the HoloToolkit in Unity. Along the way you will work with gesture input, room mapping, spatial sound, and animated characters as you create a small virtual pet game. The completed project features a cute bear who can walk around your room, place spatially anchored objects, and discover hidden items from under your floor.

In this section you'll get a great explanation for the following:

Chapter 21: Deploying Your First HoloLens Project: Start here with the Microsoft HoloLens and Windows Mixed Reality systems and learn how easy it is to use in your next game. At the end of the chapter you will have created your first project on the HoloLens.

Chapter 22: Navigating Around HoloLens Spatial Maps: Learn about the different ways of handling input with the HoloLens. This chapter explains how to create a user interface with the HoloToolkit. Learn how to interact with gestures and navigate the bear around spatial maps.

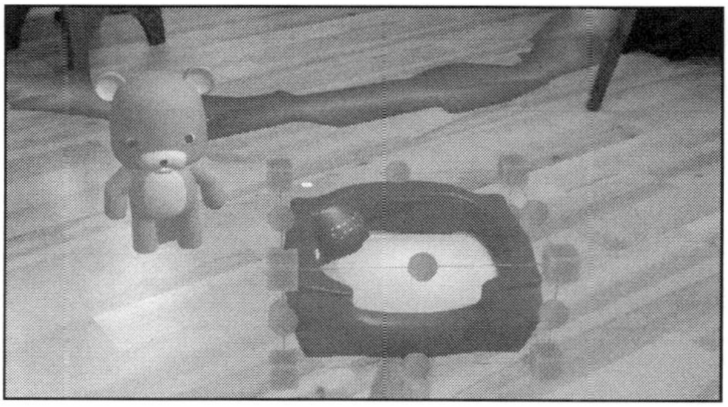

Chapter 23: Persisting Real-World Locations on the HoloLens: Take the experience further by dynamically adding objects to the room, moving them around, and saving spatial anchors.

Chapter 24: Mixing Media: Explore complex character animations and learn how to create windows into 'hidden worlds' in AR. This chapter also covers voice input, cameras and spatial audio for spectacular results.

Chapter 21: Deploying Your First HoloLens Project

Matt Larson

In the next four chapters, you'll learn the essential tools and techniques for development on the Microsoft HoloLens using Unity. You'll start by building a virtual pet game with a rigged and animated 3D model. From there, you'll gain essential skills such as spatial mapping, anchoring holograms in the environment and responding to air-tap user interactions.

You'll also learn advanced concepts:

- Working with NavAgents on dynamically changing meshes (*Chapter 22: Navigating around HoloLens Spatial Maps*).
- Saving spatial anchors and holographic data (*Chapter 23: Persisting Real-World Locations on the HoloLens*).
- Incorporating spatial audio, photo taking, and voice recognition (*Chapter 24: Mixing Media*).

Start by setting up your HoloLens development environment. If you've already set up these tools, you can skip the next section and jump into creating your first scene.

Required software and setup

There are several requirements needed before beginning HoloLens development. Before starting, please install the following:

- **Windows 10** with the Fall Windows Creator Edition update or newer.
- **Visual Studio 2017** (https://www.visualstudio.com/downloads/).

- **Windows 10 SDK** (https://developer.microsoft.com/en-US/windows/downloads/windows-10-sdk).
- **Unity 2018.2.x** (https://unity3d.com/get-unity/download).
- **Mixed Reality Toolkit** (https://github.com/Microsoft/MixedRealityToolkit-Unity).
- Having the **Windows Store .NET Scripting Backend** component for Unity installed.

Once you meet all the requirements, it's time to get started!

Before you go further, you must enable **Developer Mode** on the HoloLens. This mode allows Visual Studio to connect and deploy apps. Turn on the HoloLens, gaze at the Settings tile and air-tap. Open the Settings app by placing the 2D panel in your room. Select the **Update** menu item. Select the **For Developers** menu item and enable **Developer Mode**. Now you should also enable **Device Portal** — this mode lets you connect to the HoloLens from your PC for extra information and diagnostics.

Open Unity and the starter project **FirstHololensProject**. This chapter will also walk through common steps to import a useful HoloLens development toolkit and individual assets.

Importing MRTK and creating your first scene

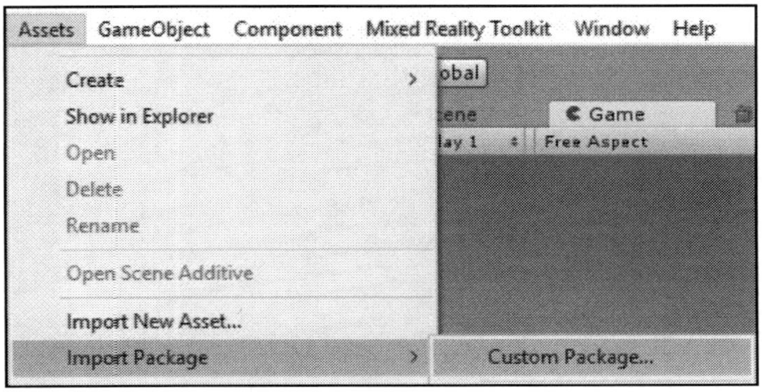

You'll use the Mixed Reality Toolkit (MRTK) extensively to simplify the creation of HoloLens projects. MRTK provides quick menu options that configure the project and scene for a HoloLens target. More importantly, the MRTK provides lots of prefabs and scripts that are essential components for a HoloLens application.

The **HoloTookit for Unity 2017.4.1** or newer is acceptable to work with Unity 2018.2.

Note: The Mixed Reality Toolkit now describes both the HoloToolkit and the Microsoft Mixed Reality Toolkit v2. The following chapters work with the HoloToolkit that is in stable release at the time of writing. The Mixed Reality Toolkit v2.0 is in beta for future support of the HoloLens 2 after June 2019. Major changes in namespaces, managers, and input methods are expected in the final MRTK v2.0 release.

Select **Assets** ▸ **Import Package** ▸ **Custom Package** and select **HoloToolkit-Unity-2017.2.1.4.unitypackage** from this chapter's **starter** folder.

Select all of the components of the MRTK for importing. After the import, there will be a new directory in the **Assets** folder called **HoloToolkit** containing the entire Mixed Reality Toolkit. There's also a new menu option named **Mixed Reality Toolkit** that provides quick helper options.

Now select **Mixed Reality Toolkit** ▸ **Apply Mixed Reality Project Settings** using the new menu in the Unity toolbar.

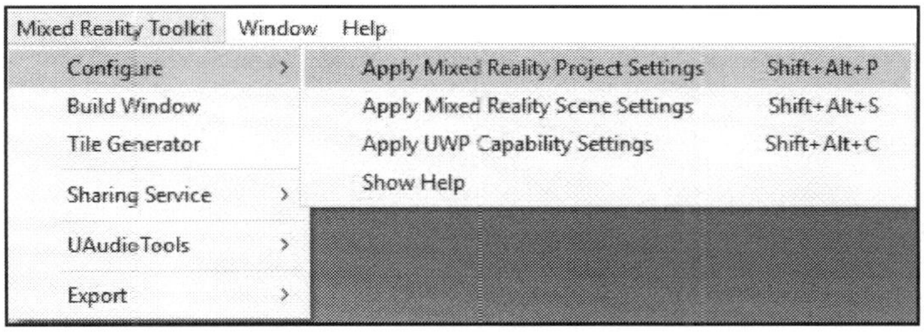

This configures Unity for the HoloLens and other Mixed Reality targets. Common build settings are applied, so you don't need to tweak all of the options yourself.

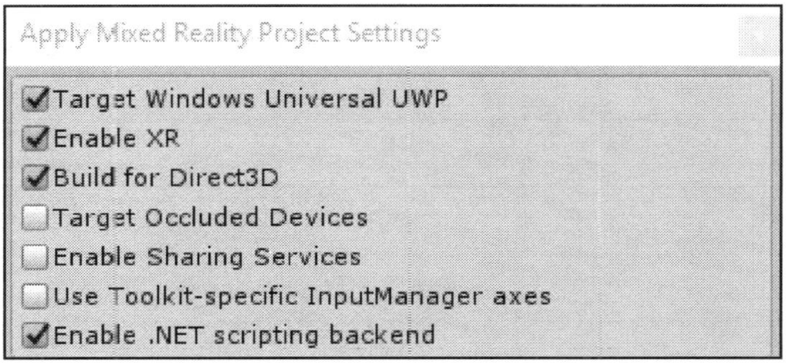

Open the starter scene **Razeware/Scenes/DiveAndDeploy**.

You will now configure this scene for Mixed Reality with the **Mixed Reality Toolkit** menu by selecting **Apply Mixed Reality Scene Settings**.

Leave all of the defaults selected and click **Apply**.

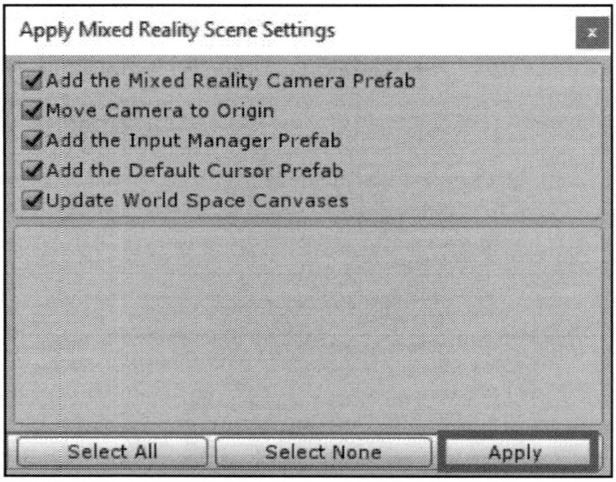

Several new GameObjects were added to the scene including **Default Cursor**, **InputManager**, and **MixedRealityCameraParent**. The Hierarchy should now look like this:

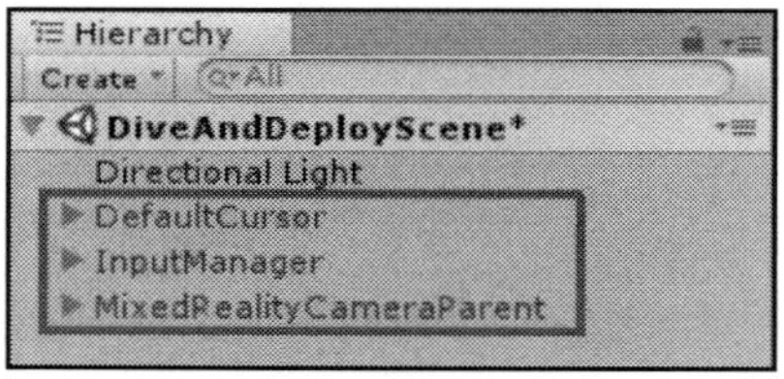

Here's a quick rundown of what each of these objects does:

- **MixedRealityCameraParent** includes a **MixedRealityCamera** prefab, a **MotionControllers** prefab and a **Boundary** prefab. The MotionControllers and Boundary prefabs provide 3D renderings of hand-held Mixed Reality controllers and a visual representation of your boundary when in VR. Neither of these is relevant to a HoloLens application, but you'll leave these as they won't conflict with a HoloLens application and can provide support later for VR applications.
- **MixedRealityCamera** (nested under **MixedRealityCameraParent**) is a stereo camera linked to your head mounted display for either the HoloLens or a Windows Mixed Reality headset. This camera rotates and translates as your head moves.
- **InputManager** handles the mouse, HoloLens gestures, and gamepad input with a custom **EventSystem**.

- **DefaultCursor** is a holographic cursor showing your gaze and is visible on the surface of meshes in front of your headset when running an application.

Import the starter assets

In the Assets folder under **Razeware**, you will find sub-folders for a basic project hierarchy:

- Animations
- Materials
- Models
- Prefabs
- Scenes
- Scripts
- Textures

Import **BearModel.fbx** from the **starter** folder into the project, and place it in the **Razeware/Models** folder. Next, import **BearSkin.png** as a texture in the **Razeware/Textures** folder. Create a new **Material** named **BearMaterial** in the **Razeware/Materials** folder and choose **MixedRealityToolkit/StandardShader** as its shader from the **Shader** dropdown — this is an optimized shader for use on the HoloLens.

Drag the **BearSkin** texture into the **Albedo** field to make it the texture map for the material.

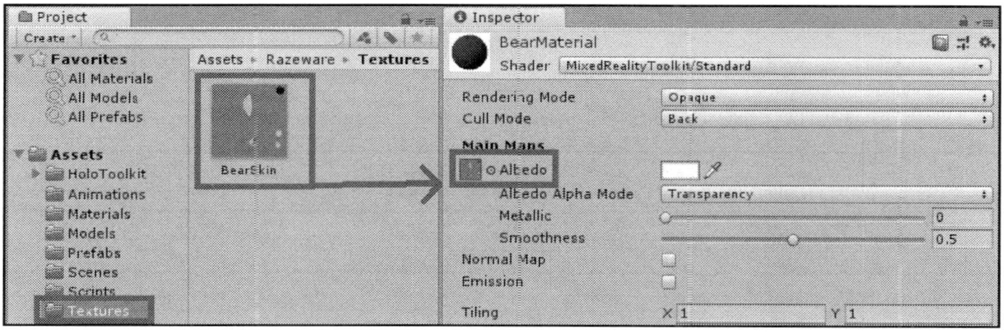

Set the **Albedo** color to pure white so the material looks nice and bright.

If you want, you can use the **Rendering Options** section to create unique and interesting effects. For example, **Rim Light** can be used to create futuristic edge lighting.

Near Plane Fade can be used to make the object disappear when approaching the **Fade Begin** distance.

Additionally, the **Fluent Options** provide interactive elements such as different colored lighting on gaze via **Hover Light**, or options that round corners, provide border lighting, glow, or ambient environmental colors. Tweak these however you want until it looks good to you.

Create an empty GameObject named **Pet** in the Hierarchy. Change its **Position** to (**X:0**, **Y:-0.2**, **Z:2**) to place it 2 meters in front of the camera starting location.

Next, drag the **Razeware/Models/BearModel** into **Pet** to parent it and set its **Rotation** to (**X:0**, **Y:180**, **Z:0**) so that it faces the camera.

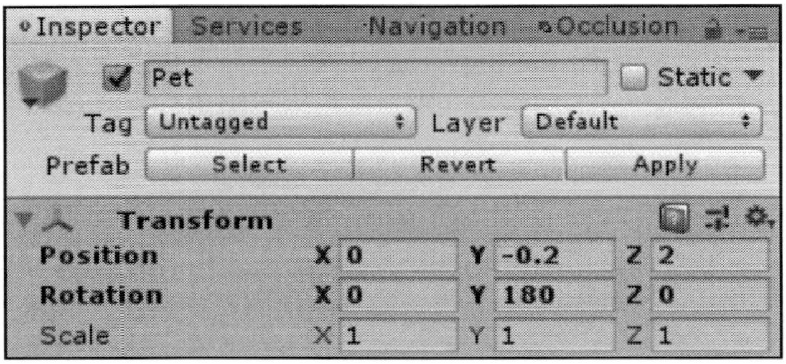

The virtual pet will now be visible in the **Game** scene, but without any coloration.

Expand the hierarchy of **BearModel** to notice it contains an **Armature** and a **CuteCharacter** mesh model. The **Armature** here is a set of 'bones' that are used to animate the pet.

Change the **Material** of **CuteCharacter** to the **BearMaterial** material that you created earlier.

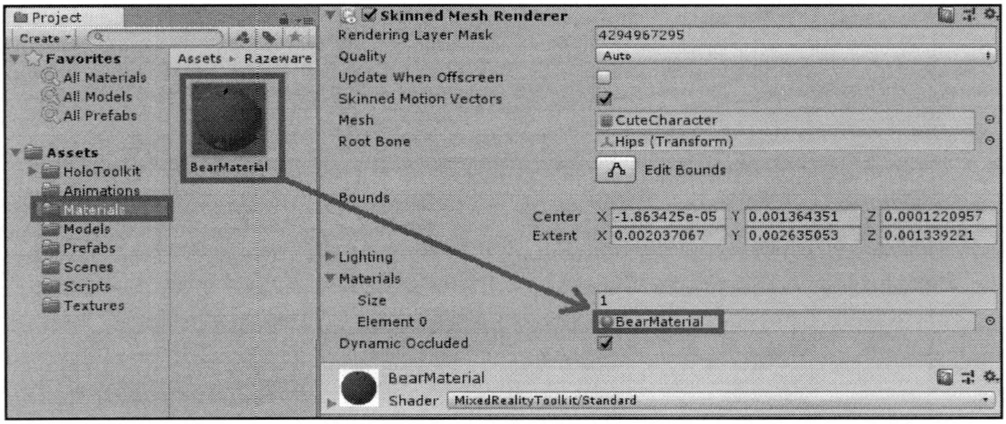

Your hierarchy and view should look like the following image.

Create a new **Animator Controller** in the **Razeware/Animations** folder and name it **PetAnimatorController**. In this chapter's project, this controller will make the character wave when you approach it.

Double click **PetAnimatorController** to open the Animator view. Right click on the background, select **Create State ▸ Empty** to create a new state and name it **Idle**. Now create a second new state and name it **Wave**. In the **Idle** state, change **Motion** to **Armature|Idle**. In the **Wave** state, set **Motion** to **Armature|Wave**.

Transition conditions determine when the animator controller state engine should switch to a different animation for the model. Next, you'll need to set a condition to cause transitions to occur between animator states. These conditions can then be controlled from a script.

Click the **Parameters** tab on the left-side of the **Animator** window. Click the **+** button to add a new **Int** parameter named **CurrentState**.

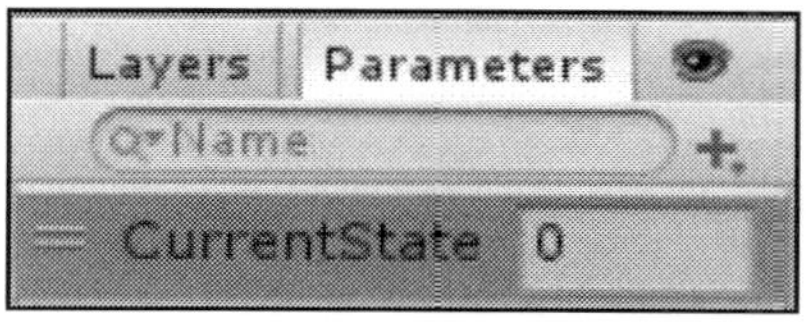

Transitions control how Unity switches between animation states. Transition conditions tell the animator controller state engine when to transition between animations based on certain conditions.

Add a new transition by right-clicking on **Idle** and choosing **Make Transition**. Drag the line to the **Wave** state to connect the transition. Next, create another transition from **Wave** back to **Idle**.

Finally, create a self-transition by creating a transition from **Idle** back onto itself. In the **Idle ▸ Wave** and **Wave ▸ Idle** transitions, uncheck **Has Exit Time**. Disabling the exit time allows the animation to instantly break to transition to the other animation state.

Click on the **Idle ▸ Wave** transition and add a new condition with **CurrentState**, **Equals** and **1**. As you might have guessed, the transition will now only activate if the **CurrentState** parameter's value is **1**.

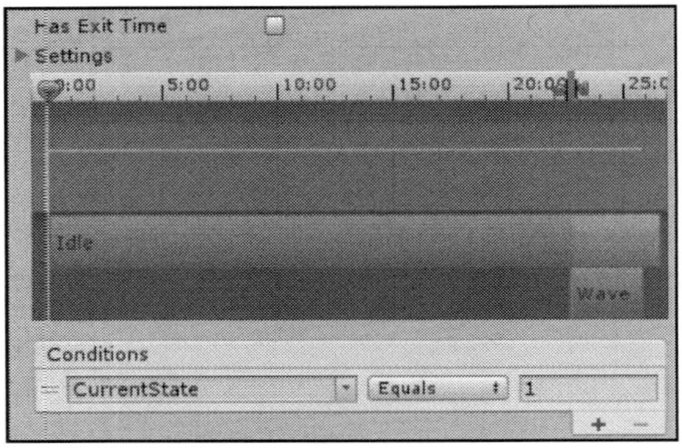

Next, for the **Wave ▸ Idle** transition, add a condition setting **CurrentState** as **NotEqual** to **1**. Lastly, add self-transitions for the **Idle ▸ Idle** transition with a condition that requires **CurrentState**, **Equals** and **0** and **Wave ▸ Wave** with **CurrentState**, **Equals** and **1**.

Your animation transitions should now look something like this:

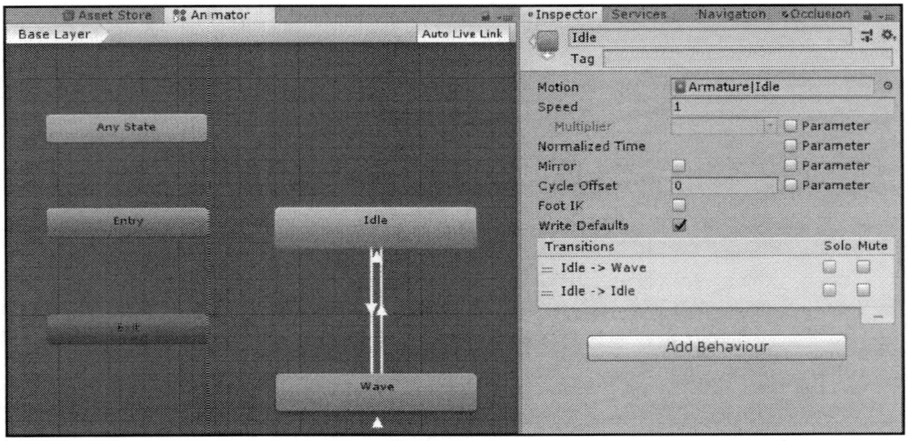

Open the stubbed C# script **Razeware\Scripts\WaveNearby.cs** in a code editor.

This script is a Monobehaviour which will be attached to the **BearModel** to check it's distance to the **MixedRealityCamera** (your headset). When the **HelloDistance** is less than 1.5 meters, the **CurrentState** parameter of the **PetAnimator** value causes the animation states to transition to waving.

```
public class WaveNearby : MonoBehaviour
{
    // Wave when camera (headset) is within 1.5 meters
    public float helloDistance = 1.5f;

    private const int IDLE = 0;
    private const int WAVING = 1;

    //...
}
```

Within the **Start()** method hook up the GameObjects and Animators.

```
private GameObject myHeadset;
private Animator myAnimator;

// 1. At Start we find the headset and a character animator.
void Start()
{
    // Find the camera for the user's headset.
    myHeadset = GameObject.Find("MixedRealityCamera") as
GameObject;

    // Animator is a component on the GameObject of this script.
    myAnimator = GetComponent<Animator>();
}
```

Use the **Update()** method to check when the user's headset is nearby the model and then set the animator condition causing a waving animation.

```
// 2. Update will transition to waving when player is nearby.
void Update()
{
    int layer = 0; // Base Layer
    AnimatorStateInfo stateInfo =
        myAnimator.GetCurrentAnimatorStateInfo(layer);

    float distance =
Vector3.Distance(myHeadset.transform.position,
        gameObject.transform.position);

    if (distance < helloDistance)
    {
```

```
            myAnimator.SetInteger("CurrentState", WAVING);
        }
        else
        {
            myAnimator.SetInteger("CurrentState", IDLE);
        }
    }
```

Save the script and return to the editor. Select **BearModel** and set **PetAnimatorController** as the **Controller** for the **Animator** component. Next, add a **Wave Nearby** component to **BearModel** and drag **Pet** to the **Prefabs** folder to save the completed prefab.

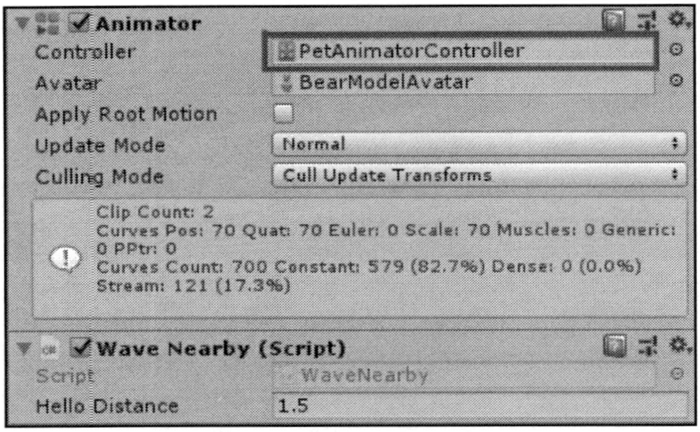

Finally, select **MixedRealityCameraParent**'s child **MixedRealityCamera** and in the **Mixed Reality Camera Manager**, change the **Transparent Display Settings** for **Near Clip** to **0.3** to prevent premature clipping of the model.

Pat yourself on the back because you just built your animated character!

Build and launch on the HoloLens

You're now ready to try your project on the HoloLens.Select **File ▸ Build Settings** and make sure the Platform is set to **Universal Windows Platform**. Next, verify that the **Target Device** is set to **HoloLens**. Click the **Add Open Scenes** button to include the open scene in the build.

Finally, click the **Build** button and choose a location to save the compiled build to.

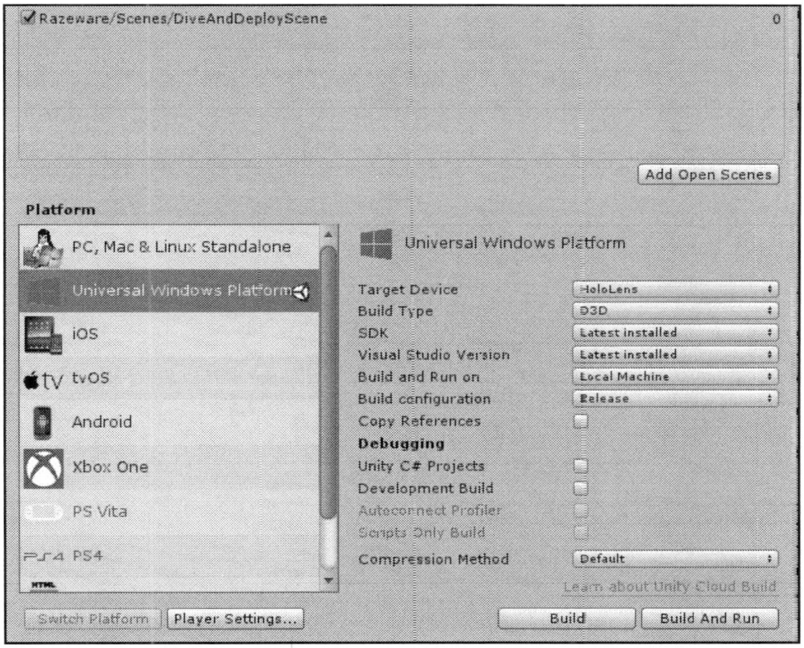

After Unity successfully builds the project, the folder that contains project will open up. Notice there's an .sln file in there; double-click that file to open it as a Visual Studio solution.

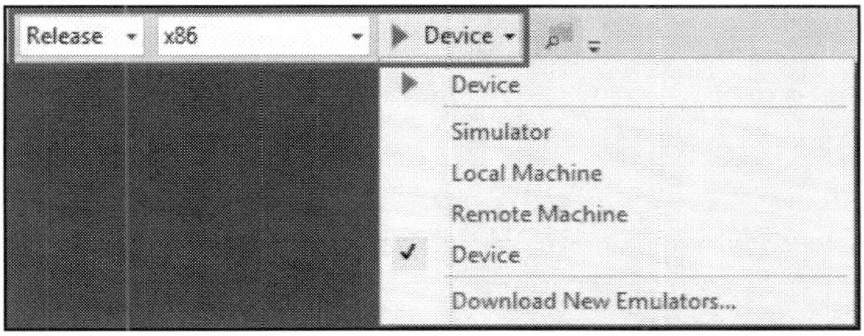

With Visual Studio 2017 open and the newly built solution loaded, configure the project in **Release** mode and use **x86** as the architecture in the top toolbar of the solution view.

> **Note**: When building a final application package to submit to the app store, you are required to target **Master** instead of **Release**.

You can deploy to the HoloLens using either a WiFi connection or a USB cable. The general recommendation is that you deploy via USB as this is much faster than WiFi, so that's what you'll do here.

Connect a USB cable from the HoloLens to your PC, and choose **Device** from the drop-down menu in Visual Studio. Next, choose **Build ▸ Build Solution**.

If there are no errors, you can move on to deploying to the HoloLens by selecting **Build ▸ Deploy Solution**. When deploying, make sure the HoloLens is powered on to allow the PC to connect to it and deploy your application.

Run the application on the HoloLens by clicking on button with the green arrow named **Device** and choose **Continue Debugging** at the prompt.

Now, you will see the default Splash screen of the Unity logo. Moments later, your virtual pet loads in the room in front of you. When you walk closer, the wave animation activates so your pet nods and waves 'Hello!'

Setting the icons

An extra step for you to complete is to add an icon for the application. Create a new folder named **Razeware/Textures/Icons**, and copy the five example icons from **starter / icons** folder into the new folder. Select all five icons in the Project window, and set their **Texture Type** to **Sprite (2D and UI)**.

Next, select **Build Settings ▸ Player Settings** to open the player settings. Under the **Icon** tab, find the **Scale 200%** entry, and for each icon size, set the matching **VirtualPet-Icon XX by XX** texture. You must match the exact dimensions for the images or Visual Studio will fail to build the application.

2D UWP Windows applications also display a flat window when in standby. A background can be set via the **Splash Image** tab and **Windows** section. Set the icon for the **Scale 200%** field to the **VirtualPet-Splash** image. You have now customized the icons to provide positive impressions for your application.

Where to go from here?

Congratulations! You've deployed your HoloLens application!

Being able to visualize a model on the HoloLens is the first step to creating more exciting applications. In this simple project you have learned how to include the Mixed Reality Toolkit in your Unity project and quickly setup a Mixed Reality project for the HoloLens. You learned how use the MRTK Standard Shader for creating efficient Materials for the HoloLens and how to setup a basic animated character.

In the next chapter you will make this character come to life and walk the spatial meshes that describe the real world.

Chapter 22: Navigating Around HoloLens Spatial Maps

Matt Larson

Augmented reality at its best creates fresh interactions that feel magical. In this chapter, you'll spark that feeling when your character walks over the real surfaces of your room.

Unity provides **NavAgents** that are an advanced engine for navigating a character through a complex environment of obstacles and finding a short path through to a destination. Typically, these work on static, pre-baked **NavMesh** data.

The starter package contains NavMeshComponents (https://github.com/Unity-Technologies/NavMeshComponents) that dynamically create your Unity navigation data from the HoloLens spatial maps.

In this chapter, you'll add the spatial mapping of the environment, and enable the character to walk across the scanned data.

Note: If you're using the Hololens simulator software on your Windows PC along with this project, you may find that launching the game in the Unity editor also launches the **Mixed Reality Portal** software and shows the game there too.

Simulator users can disable the virtual headset in the Simulator software so the game runs only in the Unity Editor Game Window. By doing so, you can avoid some odd issues with the Mixed Reality Portal Simulator.

If you are using the Simulator, disable the Headset in the Mixed Reality Portal simulator **Developer Settings** before continuing.

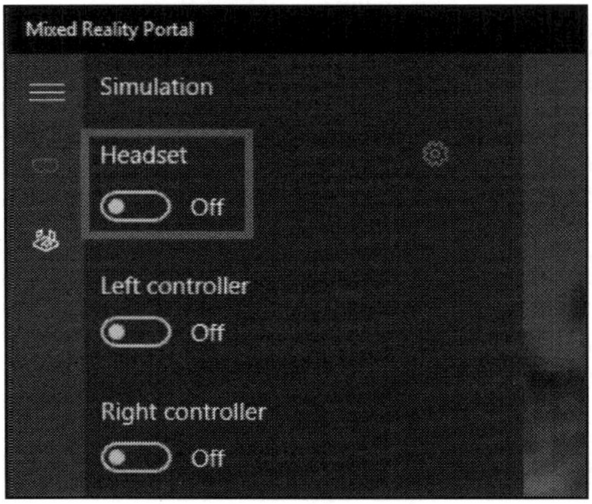

HoloLens Spatial Mapping

Spatial mapping is a mechanism for accessing the advanced sensor information that the HoloLens provides. Unity receives this information as meshes of 3D surfaces. As the application is running, new meshes may be added, or existing meshes may be updated with new information. When you connect to the Windows Device Portal, you can see the scanning being done by the HoloLens.

Begin by opening the **starter** project found in the materials folder for this chapter in Unity.

> **Note**: The starter project for this chapter picks up from the previous chapter but contains additional menu assets, so you don't need to worry about imports.

If you haven't already enabled the Device Portal on the Hololens, turn on your HoloLens, gaze at the **Settings** tile and **air-tap** to open. Select the **Update**, **For Developers** and enable the **Device Portal**.

Find your IP address for the device under **Settings > Network & Internet > Wi-Fi > Advanced Options**. Then, on another computer, open a web-browser and navigate to "https://<YOUR_HOLOLENS_IP_ADDRESS>".

After the device portal loads, select the **3D View** menu item to see the meshes being scanned by the device. Choose **Update** under Spatial mapping to refresh the scan.

After building a reasonably complete room scan, select **Save** to store the mapping as an .obj file. Alternatively, you can use the **FakeSpatialMesh.fbx** model inside the project's **Razeware \ Models** folder for testing within the Unity editor.

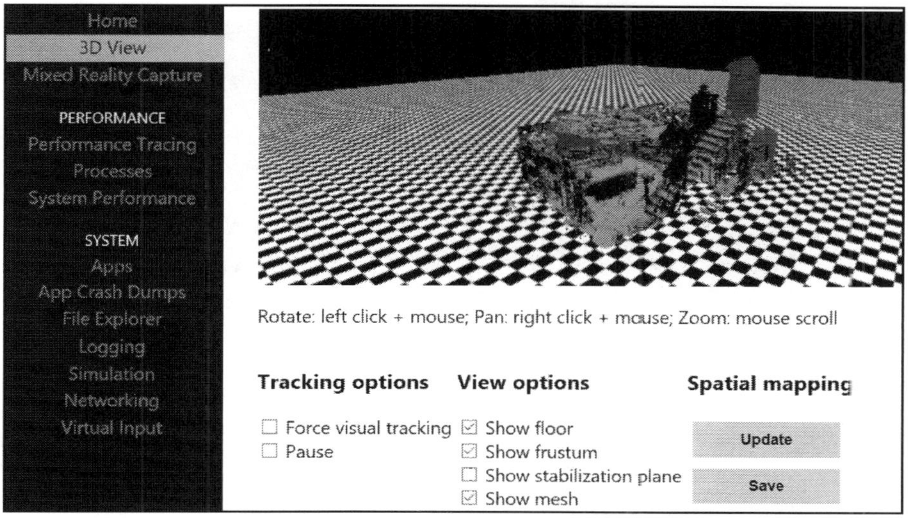

Configure the project for the spatial mapping capability

Begin by opening the **CreateHolographicUI** scene inside of the **Razeware \ Scenes** folder, which contains a basic **MixedRealityCamera** setup, but no models.

Select **File > Build Settings** in the top menu and set the project build settings to use **Universal Windows Platform**. Also, set **Target Device** to **HoloLens**.

Click **Add Open Scenes** to ensure the **CreateHolographicUI** scene gets added to the build settings. Finally, click **Switch Platform** to ensure the build settings are applied.

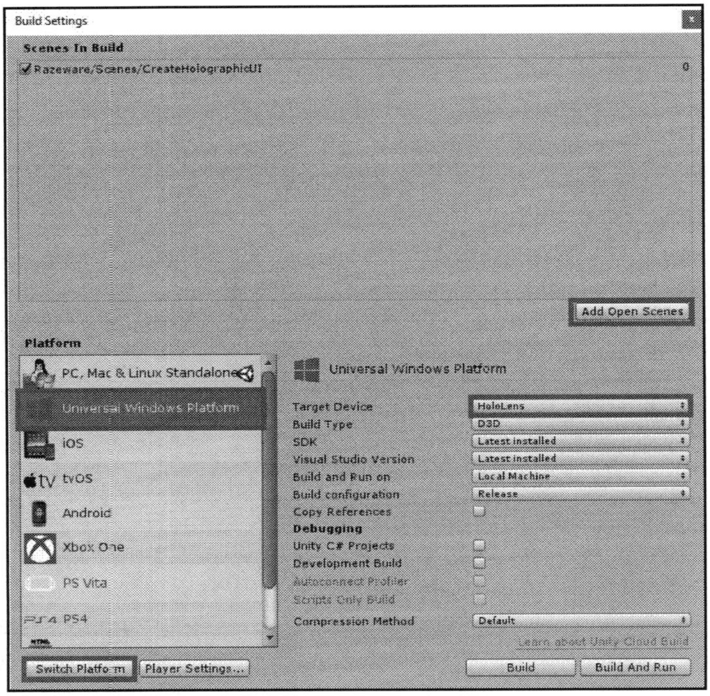

With the Build Settings window still open, select **Player Settings > Settings for Universal Windows Platform > Publishing Settings > Capabilities**. Enable the **SpatialPerception** capability to allow the application to query spatial mapping data.

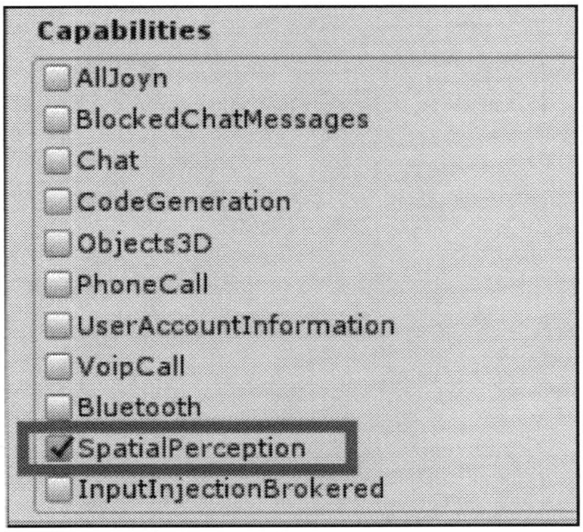

Adding Spatial Mapping to your project

Drag the **SpatialMapping** prefab from the **HoloToolkit \ SpatialMapping \ Prefabs** folder into the Hierarchy.**SpatialMapping** will activate the HoloLens spatial mapping abilities and provide mesh data representing the rough scans of the room.

Select **SpatialMapping**, and in the Inspector, find the component named **Object Surface Observer**. Set the **Room Model** field to the **FakeSpatialMesh.fbx** model or import and set a custom FBX room model to act as a mock room scan when testing within the Unity editor.

Spatial mapping can be configured to change the resolution and scanning rate in the **Spatial Mapping Observer** component. For now, leave the default values unchanged. The meshes will be visually displayed with a wireframe material, but this can be replaced with custom materials for specialized scanning effects.

Replace the **Surface Material** in the **Spatial Mapping Manager** component with the Occlusion material found in the **Assets \ HoloToolkit \ SpatialMapping \ Materials** folder to activate occlusion of virtual objects by real-world obstacles like walls and floors.

Create a new empty GameObject named **EditorOnlyRoomModel** in the root of the Hierarchy that will render the **FakeSpatialMesh.fbx** only within the Unity editor.

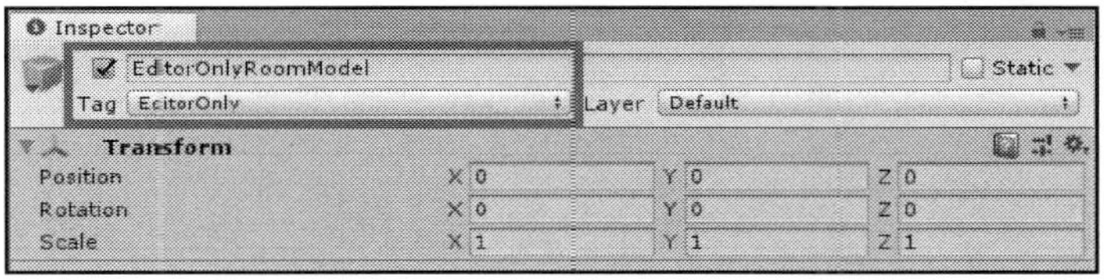

Assign this new GameObject the **EditorOnly** tag to disable it when running on the HoloLens. Add the **FakeSpatialMesh.fbx** (or your own custom created model) as a child of **EditorOnlyRoomModel**, and change its Material to **FlatMaterial** to give it a blue color. Make sure the **FakeSpatialMesh**'s position and rotation are set to **(X:0, Y:0, Z:0)**.

Now the scene will render the testing spatial mesh while running in the Unity Editor (the room will be positioned behind the camera).

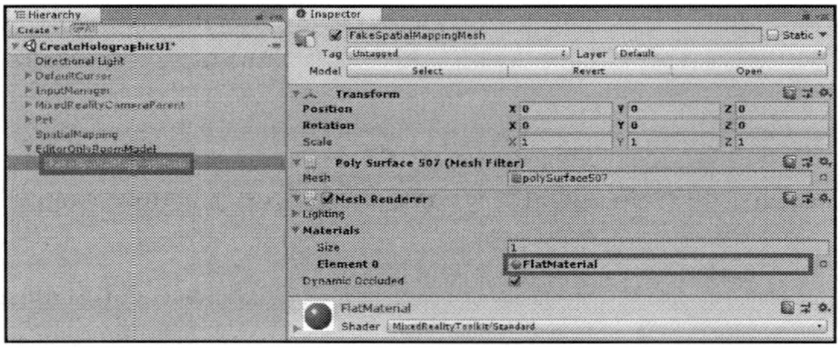

Placing the Pet on a Spatial Mesh

If you don't have a **Pet** GameObject already in the Hierarchy, drag a **Razeware \ Prefabs \ Pet** prefab into the scene.

Create an empty child GameObject named **Placeable** under **Pet** and select it. Add a **Box Collider** component that covers the pet with a **Size** of **X:0.2, Y:0.3, Z:0.2** and the **Center** placed at **X:0, Y:0.15, Z:0**.

Add the MRTK solver component named **TapToPlace** to **Placeable**. Because **Placeable** is a child and you want to be placing is parent, **Pet**, enable the **Place Parent on Tap** checkbox on the **Tap To Place** component and set **Pet** as its **Parent Game Object**. Finally, disable **Allow Mesh Visualization** to keep the spatial mapping occlusion from being toggled.

Your **Tap To Place** component will look like this once done:

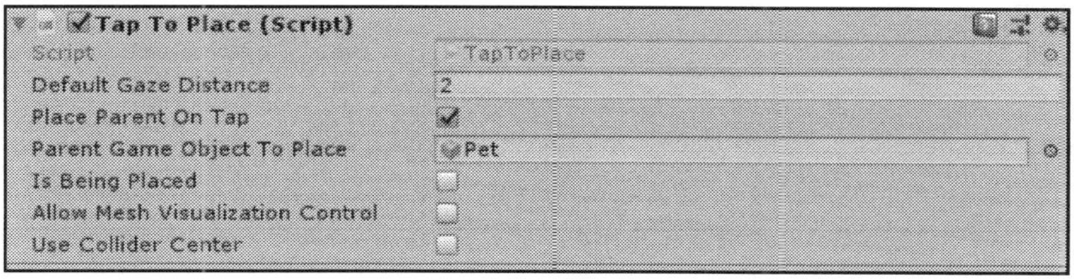

Run the scene in the editor and try tapping on the bear character in the scene to start moving it around the visible surfaces.

When you build and deploy this on the HoloLens after scanning the room, you will be able to place your pet on any surfaces of the real world!

Rename **Pet** to **MoveablePet** and drag it into the **Razeware \ Prefabs** folder to turn it into a prefab. After this, remove **MoveablePet** from the Hierarchy for now.

Building a menu

The player shouldn't start directly by placing the character but should be greeted by a friendly application menu.

You'll build a menu that can respond to the HoloLens **air-tap** gestures to start the game.

Unlike a desktop application, you should not overlay the menus as flat projections because Terminator-style heads-up-displays break all feelings of immersion.

Drag the **VirtualPetTitle** prefab from the **Assets \ Razeware \ Prefabs** into the root of the Hierarchy to start building the basic title menu.

VR and AR user interfaces should avoid locking menus to the camera projection, but this begs the question: how do you make sure that when you can look in any direction, you'll find the menu?

Luckily, the Mixed Reality ToolKit provides a helpful mechanism to solve this problem via a script that keeps objects within the viewing frustum.

Add a MRTK component named **Tagalong** to **VirtualPetTitle**.When a player turns their head enough that the objects leave the viewing frustum, this component pulls the objects back into view.

Another mechanic to increase the visibility of the menu is facing it towards the view no matter how your head turns.

Attach a **Billboard** component to **VirtualPetTitle** to make its children keep their relative orientation towards the user.

As you may have noticed, the **Tagalong** component automatically adds a **BoxCollider**, and its size is enormous! Change its **Size** to **(X:0.4, Y:0.3, Z:0.0)** to only cover the menu objects.

Doing so prevents the **BoxCollider** from blocking any of the buttons you'll add inside its volume. **VirtualPetTitle** will now look like this:

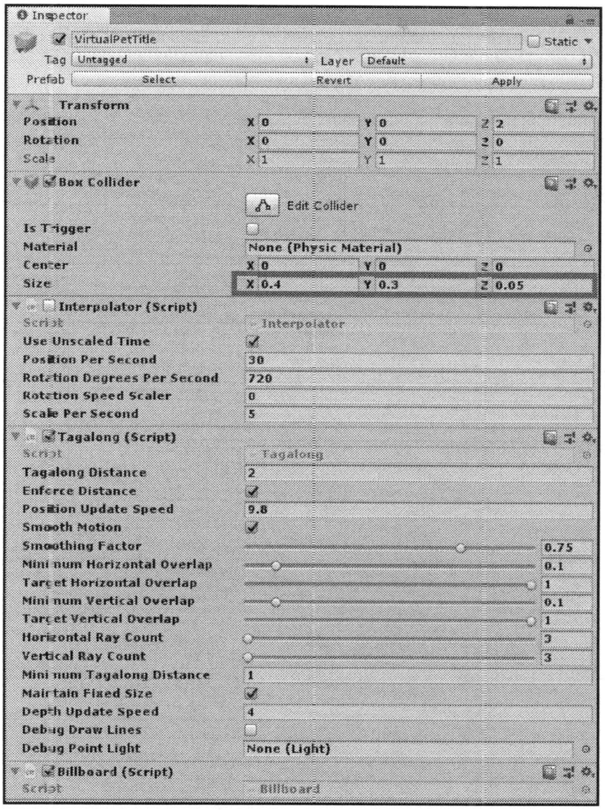

Creating buttons

You'll now add several buttons to the menu for the player to interact with.

Start by creating a new empty GameObject named **ButtonCollection** as a child of **VirtualPetTitle**. This object will hold all of the buttons you'll create and will provide an easy way to organize the buttons.

Create another empty GameObject, name it **Button** and make it a child of **ButtonCollection**. Drag a **MeshButton** prefab from the **Assets \ HoloToolkit \ UX \ Prefabs \ Buttons** folder on top of it to parent it and rename it to **NewButton**.

A **MeshButton** can create buttons out of any 3D mesh data.

Note: There's an example **Button** prefab inside the **Prefabs** folder with coloring styles and text already configured; you can use these to skip the button configuration steps below.

Replace the Mesh in the **Mesh Filter** with the **NameTagMesh** mesh and set the scale for **NewButton** to **(X:1, Y:1, Z:1)**.

In the **Compound Button Mesh** component, set the profile to a preconfigured **Razeware / Misc / ButtonMeshProfile**.

The button mesh profile provides color values for different states. A single profile can provide a complex, shared configuration to many UI buttons that determine the color, translation, or scale of the button during states of interaction:

- **Observation**: The default state.
- **ObservationTargeted**: Triggers when a gaze focuses on the button.
- **Targeted**: This is in effect when an air-tap begins.
- **Pressed**: Triggers when the button has been clicked.

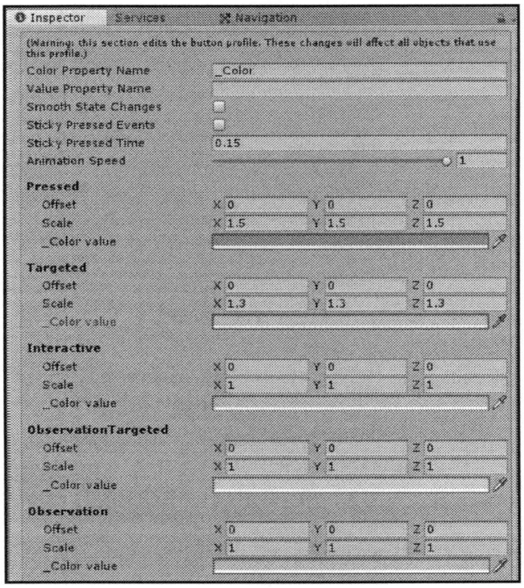

Next, drag **NewButton** both to the **Target Transform** slot and the **Renderer** slot. **NewButton** will now look like this in the Inspector:

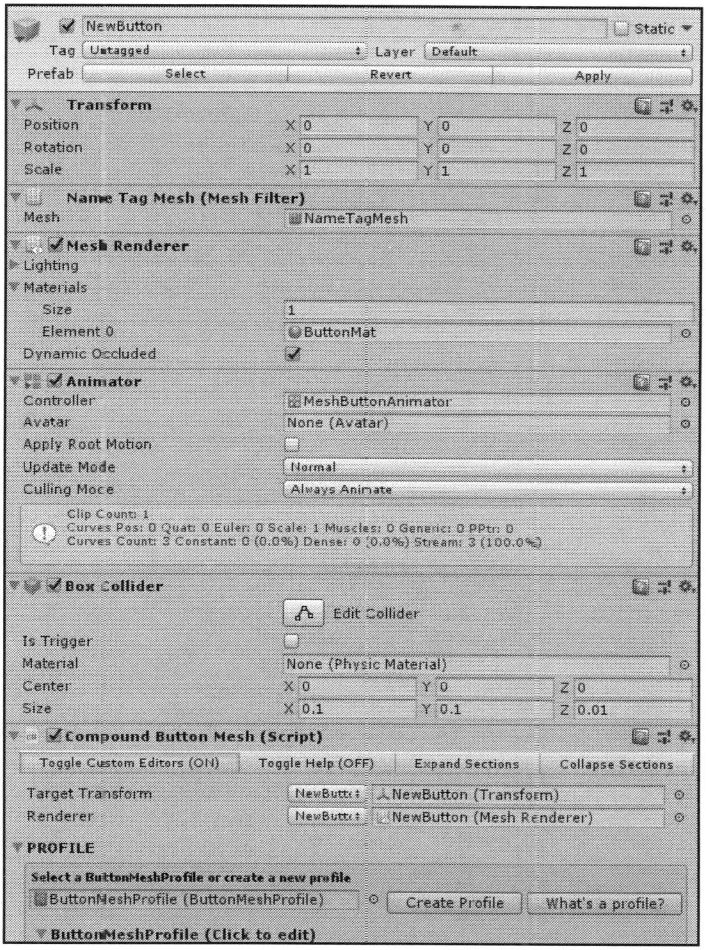

Adjust the **Box Collider** component on **NewButton** so that it only covers the mesh for this object using a **Size** of **(X:0.1, Y:0.1, Z:0.01)**.

Another companion script called **CompoundButton** is needed to enable a basic button functionality with the **CompoundButtonMesh**.

Add a **CompoundButton** component to **NewButton** and assign **NewButton** to **Target Transform** and set **NewButton** as the **Renderer** as was done for the **CompoundButtonMesh** component before.

Finally, you will add a 3D text label to the button:

Locate the **3DTextPrefab** prefab inside **Assets \ HoloToolkit \ UX \ Prefabs** folder and drag it into the Hierarchy as a child of **NewButton**.

Select **3DTextPrefab** and decrease its **Font Size** to **40** to better fit the button size. Change **Text** to **New**, set the **Font Style** to **Bold** and change **Color** to black for better contrast.

Creating a button required a lot of custom configuration, so drag the **NewButton** to the **Assets \ Razeware \ Prefabs** folder to turn it into a prefab — this way you can use this to make additional buttons quickly in the future.

To put your new button prefab to good use, make a second button. To do this, create another empty GameObject called **Button** as a child of **ButtonCollection**. Next, drag a copy of the **NewButton** prefab as a child of the new **Button** you just created.

Rename the new **NewButton** instance to **LoadButton** and change the text in its child **3DTextPrefab** to **Load**. The buttons will be now overlap, but don't worry about that, as you will soon use the **ObjectCollection** component to neatly organize the buttons in your menu.

Here's what the **VirtualPetTitle** scene hierarchy will now look like:

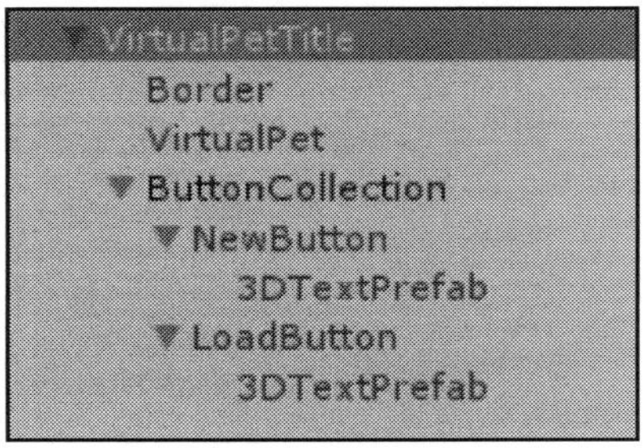

ObjectCollections

The **ObjectCollection** component is an excellent feature of MRTK that provides a quick and easy organization for buttons and UI elements. It works similarly to the **Grid** component used to create a table structure for 2D user interfaces, but in a 3D space.

Attach an **ObjectCollection** component to **ButtonCollection** and change its position to **(X:0, Y:-0.2, Z:0)** to put the buttons below the menu frame. Now, in the **ObjectCollection** component, set the following:

- **Rows**: 1
- **Cell Width**: 0.15

- **Cell Height**: 0.15
- **Orient Type**: Face Origin

Next, click the **Update Collection** button on the **Object Collection** component to organize the **ButtonCollection**.

You can experiment with different row/column layouts and the **Surface Type**. For example, if instead you change **Surface Type** to cylinder and set the radius to **0.25**, then click **Update Collection**, the buttons will align as if wrapped around an invisible cylinder.

Creating a menu controller script

MRTK provides a mechanism for quickly wiring and responding to button events with the **InteractionReceiver** script. You'll now build out a menu system by extending this script.

Open the stubbed C# script named **Razeware / Scripts / MenuController.cs** which extends from the **InteractionReceiver** parent class. The important method to handle interactions is call `InputDown`:

```
    protected override void InputDown(GameObject obj,
InputEventData eventData)
    {
        eventData.Use();

        // 1 The button you will use in this scene.
        if ("NewButton".Equals(obj.name))
        {
            // Place a character and exit the menu.
            PlaceCharacter();
            Destroy(gameObject, 0.2f);
        }
    }
```

Fill in the `PlaceCharacter` method of **MenuController.cs** as follows:

```
    // 2 Instantiate a character in front of the camera.
    private void PlaceCharacter()
    {
        GameObject character = Instantiate(placeCharacter, new
Vector3(0, 0, 2), Quaternion.identity);

        // Move the character into the gaze of the camera
        Vector3 hmdPosition = Camera.main.transform.position;
        Vector3 hmdDirection = Camera.main.transform.forward;
        character.transform.position = hmdPosition +
hmdDirection * 2f;
    }
```

1. `InputDown` will check if the input being responded to was with a GameObject named "NewButton". In that case, it begins placing a character in the scene and hides the menu.

2. `PlaceCharacter` instantiates the pet prefab ahead of the user's view to be placed in the scene.

Save the script and return to the editor.Attach a **MenuController** component to **VirtualPetTitle** and drag the **MoveablePet** prefab from the **Prefabs** folder onto the **Place Character** slot. This will instantiate it in the scene upon air-tapping the **New Game** button.

Next, drag both **NewButton** and **LoadButton** onto the **Interactables** slot to wire clicking on a button to activating the **InputDown** method of the **MenuController** component.

Your **Menu Controller** will now look like this:

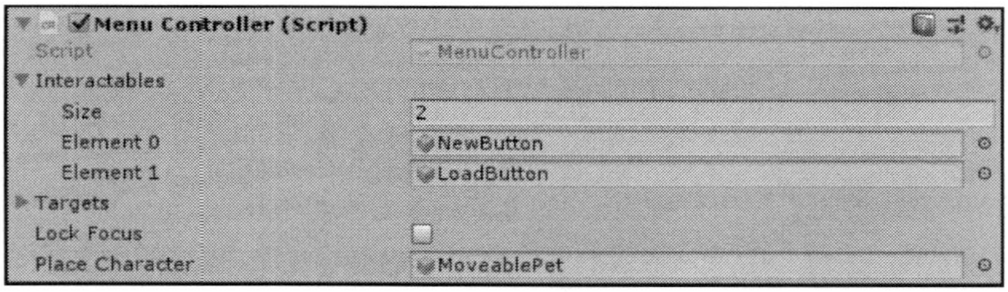

Run the scene in Unity. You'll see an interactive menu, try air-tapping on the **New** button and the menu will exit and you'll be able to place the bear in the scene.

In a later chapter, you'll hook up the **Load** button to load the game from a saved state.

Creating a dynamic runtime NavMesh

In Unity, characters can find paths across game surfaces by use of static **NavMeshes** that are baked into the scene before playing. Since the floor, table and furniture meshes are provided when the HoloLens scans the room, you cannot bake the NavMeshes before play. You'll tackle this limitation next.

Create an empty GameObject, name it **LocalNavMeshBuilder** and add a **LocalNavMeshBuilder** component. The **LocalNavMeshBuilder** will dynamically create NavMesh(es) for any of the 3D meshes tagged with a **NavMeshSourceTag** tag.

You'll handle tagging of meshes by creating a script that automatically adds the **NavMeshSourceTag** tag on any created and modified meshes of the **SpatialMapping** GameObject.

Open the stubbed C# script named **Razeware / Scripts / SpatialMappingNavMesh.cs** in a code editor and fill in the Awake method:

```
    // 1 Awake will add event handlers for the
spatialMappingSources
    private void Awake()
    {
        SpatialMappingSource[] spatialMappingSources =
```

```
gameObject.GetComponents<SpatialMappingSource>();

        foreach (var source in spatialMappingSources)
        {
            source.SurfaceAdded +=
SpatialMappingSourceSurfaceAdded;
            source.SurfaceUpdated +=
SpatialMappingSourceSurfaceUpdated;
        }
    }
```

Fill in the **SpatialMappingNavMesh.cs** callback `SpatialMappingSourceSurfaceAdded` as described here:

```
    // 2 Event handler for when a SpatialMapping mesh is added
    private void SpatialMappingSourceSurfaceAdded(object sender,
DataEventArgs<SpatialMappingSource.SurfaceObject> dataEvent)
    {
        dataEvent.Data.Object.AddComponent<NavMeshSourceTag>();
    }
```

Now fill the callback for updates in **SpatialMappingNavMesh.cs**:

```
    // 3 Event handler for when a SpatialMapping mesh is updated
    private void SpatialMappingSourceSurfaceUpdated(object
sender, DataEventArgs<SpatialMappingSource.SurfaceUpdate>
dataEvent)
    {
        NavMeshSourceTag navMeshSourceTag =
dataEvent.Data.New.Object.GetComponent<NavMeshSourceTag>();

        if (navMeshSourceTag == null)
        {

dataEvent.Data.New.Object.AddComponent<NavMeshSourceTag>();
        }
    }
}
```

1. `Awake` adds callbacks to the **SpatialMappingSource** instances for when new surfaces are added, or surfaces are updated.
2. The callback `SpatialMappingSourceSurfaceAdded` adds a **NavMeshSourceTag** to any newly created spatial meshes added to the scene.
3. The callback `SpatialMappingSourceSurfaceUpdated` checks if the mesh has a **NavMeshSourceTag** but otherwise adds a **NavMeshSourceTag** if missing.

Attach this script to **SpatialMapping** and it will now automatically tag the spatial meshes with **NavMeshSourceTag** at runtime. This tag will identify the meshes so that they contribute to the **NavMesh** of the scene.

Unity NavMesh Agents

Unity provides an advanced engine for navigating a character through a complex environment of obstacles and finding a short path through to a destination.

Now that NavMeshes are being built in the scene, you need to set up a **NavMeshAgent** that can explore the spatial mapping data.

Drag a **MoveablePet** prefab from the **Prefabs** folder into the Hierarchy and add a **NavMeshAgent** component to **BearModel** (nested under **MoveablePet**).

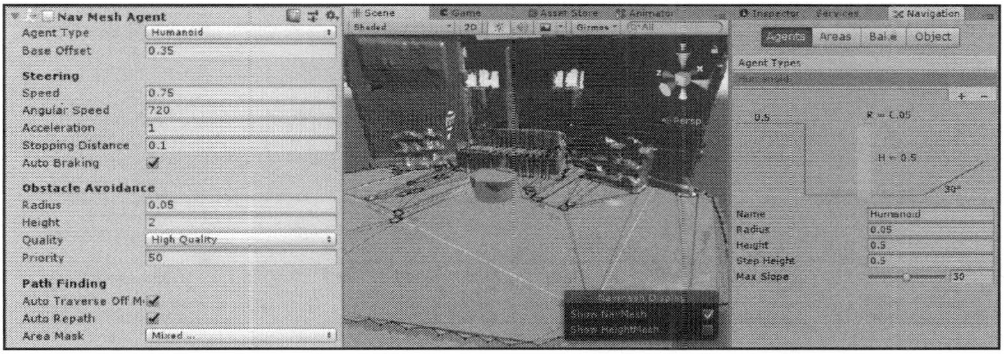

On the **NavMeshAgent** component in the Inspector, set the agent's **Radius** to **0.05** to create a small pet shape in the **Obstacle Avoidance** section.

Increase the **Angular Speed** to **720** for faster turning, set **Acceleration** to **1** and change **Speed** to **0.75** with a **Stopping Distance** of **0.1**.

Select the **Window->AI->Navigation** menu item to open the **Navigation** tab. Click the **Agents** button to see the configuration for an agent (default is `Humanoid`).

Set the agent's **Radius** to **0.05** to make the NavAgent engine find paths matching its smaller size of a pet.

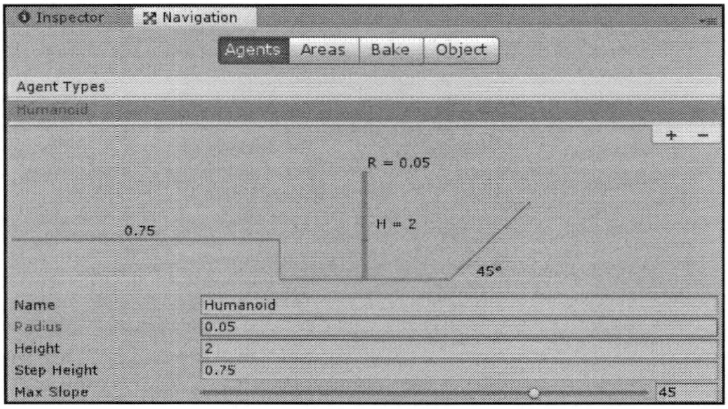

Run the scene and select the **Navigation** window. Change from **Game** at the **Scene** view to see that NavMeshes are been created over surfaces in the scene.The view should appear as below:

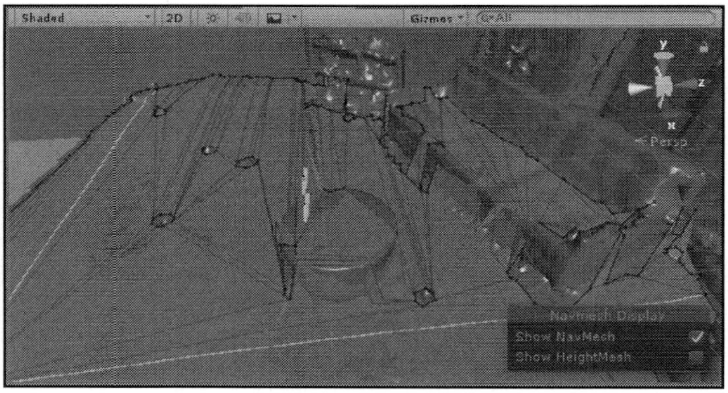

Tap-to-move NavMeshAgents

Now you have a configured **NavMeshAgent** and **NavMesh**, but how do you direct the character to move in the scene?

You will create a **MonoBehaviour** to attach to the **BearModel** that directs the character toward a location obtained by the gaze.

Open the stubbed C# script **Razeware \ Scripts \ TapToMove.cs** in your favorite code editor and start by filling in the `Awake()` method:

```
    // 1 Wire in the NavMeshAgent, and LineRenderer for the path
visualization
    public void Awake()
    {
        agent = gameObject.GetComponent<NavMeshAgent>();
        lineRenderer = gameObject.GetComponent<LineRenderer>();
        lineRenderer.positionCount = 0;
    }
```

Next fill in the `SetDestination` method of **TapToMove.cs**:

```
    // 2 Set a destination
    public void SetDestination(Ray ray)
    {
        if (agent.isActiveAndEnabled)
        {
            if (Physics.Raycast(ray.origin, ray.direction, out
hitInfo, maxDistance))
            {
                if (agent.isOnNavMesh)
                {
                    agent.destination = hitInfo.point;
                }
                else
                {
                    agent.Warp(hitInfo.point);
                }
            }
        }
        CreatePath();
    }
```

Continuing, fill the `OnInputClicked` method of **TapToPlace.cs**:

```
    // 3 Handle air tapping to find Physics.Raycast hit for
HoloLens.
    public void OnInputClicked(InputClickedEventData eventData)
    {
        // Don't intercept other events from
IInputClickHandlers.
        if
(eventData.selectedObject.GetComponent<IInputClickHandler>() !=
null) return;

        Transform cameraTransform = CameraCache.Main.transform;
        Ray ray = new Ray(cameraTransform.position,
cameraTransform.forward);
        SetDestination(ray);
```

```
        eventData.Use();
    }
```

Add the code for `CreatePath` next in **TapToPlace.cs**:

```
    // 4 Visualize the agents path with the line renderer.
    private void CreatePath()
    {
        NavMeshPath path = new NavMeshPath();
        NavMesh.CalculatePath(agent.transform.position,
agent.destination, NavMesh.AllAreas, path);
        Vector3[] positions = path.corners;

        lineRenderer.positionCount = positions.Length;
        for (int i = 0; i < positions.Length; i++)
        {
            lineRenderer.SetPosition(i, positions[i]);
        }
    }
```

Finally, fill the `SetEnabled` method of **TapToPlace.cs**:

```
    // 5 Call when ready to use the NavAgent.
    public void SetEnabled(bool enable)
    {
        active = enable;

        // Enable the NavMeshAgent component.
        if (active)
        {
            if (agent != null)
            {
                agent.enabled = true;

InputManager.Instance.PushFallbackInputHandler(gameObject);
            }
        }
        else
        {
            if (agent != null)
            {
                agent.enabled = false;
            }
        }
    }
```

In summary:

1. `Awake()` wires in attached components such as the `NavMeshAgent` and `LineRenderer`.
2. `SetDestination` converts a RayCast hit into a destination position for the NavAgent controlling the Pet. If the Pet ever falls off the NavMesh, the use of `Warp(hitInfo.point)` will position the Pet back on the NavMesh. The fallback to `Warp` makes the navigation resilient to unstable dynamic mesh data of spatial meshes.
3. The pet will navigate with a modal input and needs to handle Air-Tap input via the `OnInputClicked` method of the `IInputClickHandler` interface. In this case, the camera direction is given as a Ray to the `SetDestination` method and the event is consumed with `eventData.Use()`.
4. The `CreatePath` method converts the current path calculated by the NavMeshAgent and fills an array of points for the **LineRenderer** component to draw the path in the world.
5. The `SetEnabled` method provides a way to enable a NavAgent when ready to move around. The **TapToMove** script uses modal input that would conflict with **TapToPlace** so **TapToMove** and the **NavAgent** must only become activated after placing the bear in the world.

Save the script and return to the editor.

The starter project provides the **Razeware \ Scripts \ IActivatable.cs** script which provided the interface `IActivatable` which describes activatable components like the **TapToPlace** component above.

```
public interface IActivatable
{

    /* Call to activate a GameObject's functions.
    * @param : active (true/false)
    */
    void SetEnabled(bool active);
}
```

Now that the basics for scripting **TapToMove** are complete:

Attach a **LineRenderer** and a **TapToMove** component to the **BearModel**. Set the LineRenderer's **Width** to **0.1**.

The **LineRenderer** will visualize the path the bear is going to take to your tap position.

Open the stubbed C# script named **Razeware \ Scripts \ PlaceThenMove.cs** in the **Scripts** folder.

PlaceThenMove with inherit from **TapToPlace** but override the `OnInputClicked` method to enable `IActivatable` components after the prefab is placed.

Fill in the `Start` method:

```
    // 1.
    void Start()
    {
        base.Start();
        if (IsBeingPlaced)
        {
            currentState = states.placeMode;
        }
    }
```

Next, edit the **PlaceThenMove** `Update` method:

```
    // 2
    void Update()
    {
        base.Update();
    }
```

Finally, finish the **PlaceThenMove** `OnInputClicked` method:

```
    // 3
    public override void OnInputClicked(InputClickedEventData 
eventData)
    {

        if (currentState == states.start)
        {
            base.OnInputClicked(eventData);
            currentState = states.placeMode;
        }
        else if (currentState == states.placeMode)
        {
            base.OnInputClicked(eventData);
            currentState = states.moveMode;
            GameObject placeable = ParentGameObjectToPlace ? 
ParentGameObjectToPlace : gameObject;

            // Enable IActivatable(s) after GameObject is placed on 
a surface.
            foreach (IActivatable agent in 
placeable.GetComponentsInChildren(typeof(IActivatable)))
            {
                agent.SetEnabled(true);
            }
        }
    }
```

1. `Start` initiates the class in a "placeMode" state.
2. `Update` simply calls the **TapToPlace** Update method.
3. The `OnInputClicked` method overrides the original method from **TapToPlace**. Now, when in "placeMode", the object will be placed and then any **IActivatable** components will be enabled. This allows the modal input of the Pet's **TapToMove** component to activate after placing is completed.

Select **Placeable** (nested inside **MoveablePet**) and replace the **TapToPlace** component with your new **PlaceThenMove** component.

Like you did before, check the **Place Parent on Tap** checkbox and assign **MoveablePet** to the **Parent Game Object To Place** slot.

Finally, disable **Allow Mesh Visualization Control**. Here is how **Placeable** will now look in the Inspector:

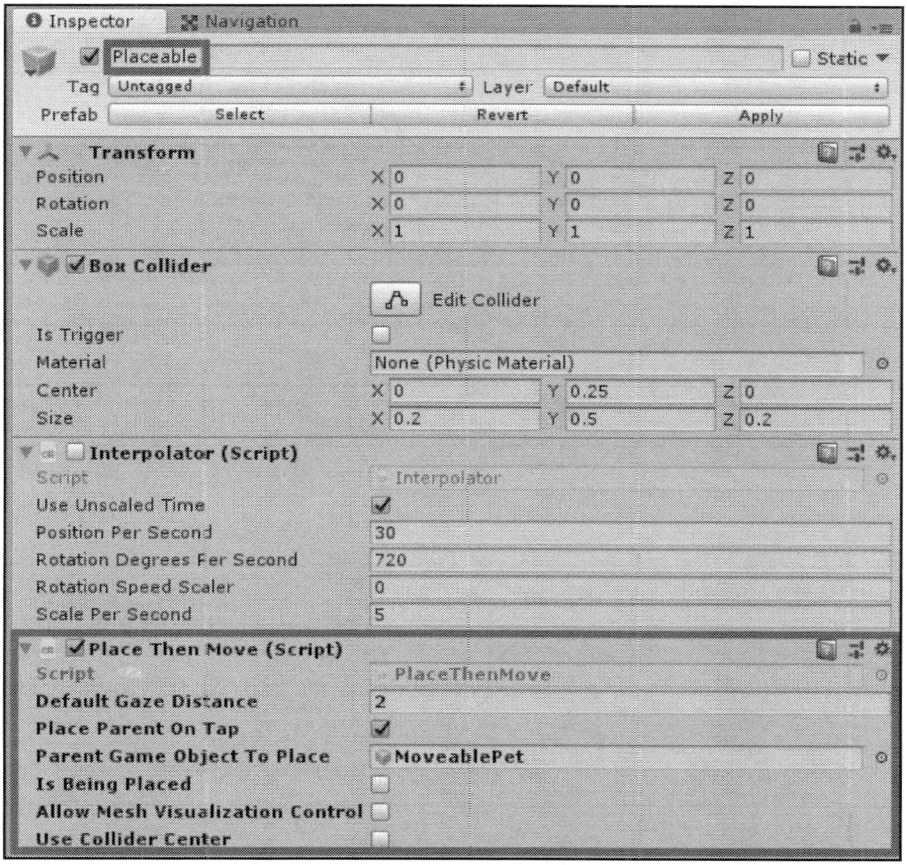

Disable the **NavMeshAgent** component on **BearModel**, select **MoveablePet** and update its prefab by clicking **Apply** at the top of the Inspector.

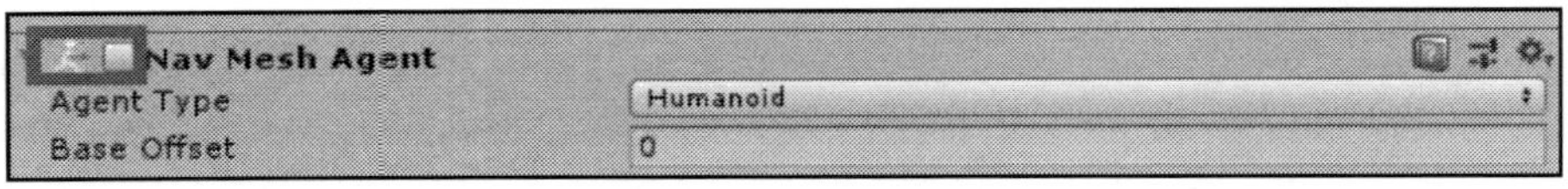

Run the scene to test things out. When clicking **NewButton**, you get a bear that's placeable. Air-taps now direct the character to move to different positions in the room.

Animating the character's walk

The last piece of polish you need to add is to animate the character and provide a text message to clarify that the character needs to be placed to start the game.

Remove the **WaveNearby** component from **BearModel**. You'll now replace this with more complex animations, and you'll handle this by changing animation states based on the **NavMeshAgent** component.

Open the stubbed C# script **Razeware / Scripts / AnimationController.cs** in a code editor and complete the `Start()` method:

```
    void Start()
    {
        anim = GetComponent<Animator>();
        agent = GetComponent<UnityEngine.AI.NavMeshAgent>();
        agent.updatePosition = false;
    }
```

`Start` will hook in components to the script, and also disable the automatic update of positions by the NavAgent.

Next, fill in the `Update()` method for **AnimationController.cs**:

```
    void Update()
    {
        Vector3 worldDeltaPosition = agent.nextPosition -
transform.position;
        float distance = worldDeltaPosition.magnitude;

        // 1. Map 'worldDeltaPosition' to local space
        float dx = Vector3.Dot(transform.right,
worldDeltaPosition);
        float dy = Vector3.Dot(transform.forward,
worldDeltaPosition);
        Vector2 deltaPosition = new Vector2(dx, dy);

        // 2. Low-pass filter the deltaMove
        float smooth = Mathf.Min(1.0f, Time.deltaTime / 0.15f);
        smoothDeltaPosition = Vector2.Lerp(smoothDeltaPosition,
deltaPosition, smooth);

        // 3. Update velocity if time advances
        if (Time.deltaTime > 1e-5f)
        {
            velocity = smoothDeltaPosition / Time.deltaTime;
        }

        // 4. Determine whether animation is 'Idle' or 'Walk'
        bool shouldMove = velocity.magnitude > 0.05f &&
agent.remainingDistance > 0.001f;
        if (shouldMove && !walking)
        {
            walking = true;
            SetState((int)CurrentState.Walk);
        }

        if (!shouldMove && walking)
        {
            walking = false;
            SetState((int)CurrentState.Idle);
```

```
        }

        // 5. LookAt turns head in the walking direction before
the body.
        LookAt lookAt = GetComponent<LookAt>();
        if (lookAt)
        {
            lookAt.lookAtTargetPosition = agent.steeringTarget +
transform.forward;
        }
    }
```

1. The method obtains the next position from the NavAgent.
2. The movement is smooth over time.
3. The current velocity is calculated.
4. Velocity and distance to the destination determine whether to animate the Pet as a 'Walk' or 'Idle' animation state.
5. The head can turn in the walking direction before the body to achieve a better animation effect.

Lastly, fill in the `SetState` and `OnAnimatorMove` methods:

```
    // 1. Cause transitions in the Animator state machine.
    public void SetState(int state)
    {
        anim.SetInteger("CurrentState", state);
    }

    // 2. Update the GameObject(s) position.
    void OnAnimatorMove()
    {
        transform.position = agent.nextPosition;
    }
}
```

1. The Animator state machine transitions based on the `CurrentState` variable which is set here.
2. `OnAnimatorMove` updates transform's position each frame, but after the animations have been evaluated.

Save this script and return to the editor.

A more advanced animation should also move the character's head toward the target before the character starts moving in that direction. The script below uses the `OnAnimatorIK` method to rotate the bone controlling the head of the character smoothly in the direction of `lookAtTargetPosition`.

Open the stubbed C# script named **Razeware / Scripts / LookAt.cs** and complete the `Start` method:

```
    void Start()
    {
        if (!head)
        {
            Debug.LogError("No head transform - LookAt disabled");
            enabled = false;
            return;
        }
        // 1. Get the animator component and set look direction.
        animator = GetComponent<Animator>();
        lookAtTargetPosition = head.position + transform.forward;
        lookAtPosition = lookAtTargetPosition;
    }
```

1. The `Start` method obtains the `Animator` component, and gets an initial look direction.

Now, fill in the `OnAnimatorIK` method in **LookAt.cs**:

```
    // 1.
    void OnAnimatorIK(int layerIndex)
    {
        // 2. Head will rotate to look in general direction at
  same height.
        lookAtTargetPosition.y = head.position.y;
        float lookAtTargetWeight = looking ? 1.0f : 0.0f;

        Vector3 curDir = lookAtPosition - head.position;
        Vector3 futDir = lookAtTargetPosition - head.position;

        // 3. Update the current direction
        curDir = Vector3.RotateTowards(curDir, futDir, 6.28f *
  Time.deltaTime, float.PositiveInfinity);
        lookAtPosition = head.position + curDir;

        // 4. Set the look weight and position.
        float blendTime = lookAtTargetWeight > lookAtWeight ?
  lookAtHeatTime : lookAtCoolTime;
        lookAtWeight = Mathf.MoveTowards(lookAtWeight,
  lookAtTargetWeight, Time.deltaTime / blendTime);
        animator.SetLookAtWeight(lookAtWeight, 0.2f, 0.5f, 0.7f,
  0.5f);
        animator.SetLookAtPosition(lookAtPosition);
    }
  }
```

1. `OnAnimatorIK()` is called by the Animator Component immediately before it updates its internal IK system.
2. The script finds a point in a general direction of the target.
3. `lookAtPosition` will be a point in the direction of the target.
4. The `animator` LookAtWeight and LookAtPosition are both set.

Save the script and return to the editor.Attach the new **Animation Controller** and **LookAt** components to **BearModel**. Set the character's bone controlling the head in the **LookAt** component's **Head** field to the **Head** bone. You'll find this within the armature of **BearModel**. Again, update the **MoveablePet** prefab by clicking the Apply button.

> **Note**: The `OnAnimatorIK` method requires that you enable **IK Pass** for your animator layer in the Animator for the **Animator Controller**. This functionality requires Unity Pro since Unity 2018.1.

Enable **IK Pass** if you have Unity Pro on the **Base Layer** of your Animation Controller **PetAnimator** using the **Animator** window.

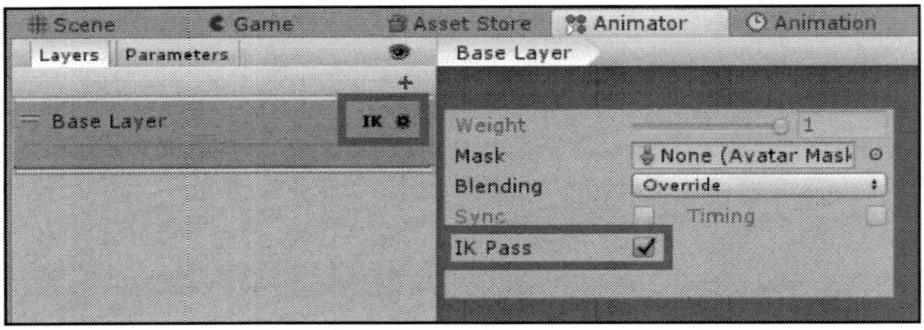

Add a new **Walk** state to **PetAnimator** and set its animation to **Armature|Walk**.

Make transitions from **Idle** to **Walk** and a self-transition from **Walk** to **Walk**. Add a condition for these transitions that requires **CurrentState equals 2**.

Finally, add a return transition **Walk** to **Idle** with a condition **CurrentState not equal to 2**.

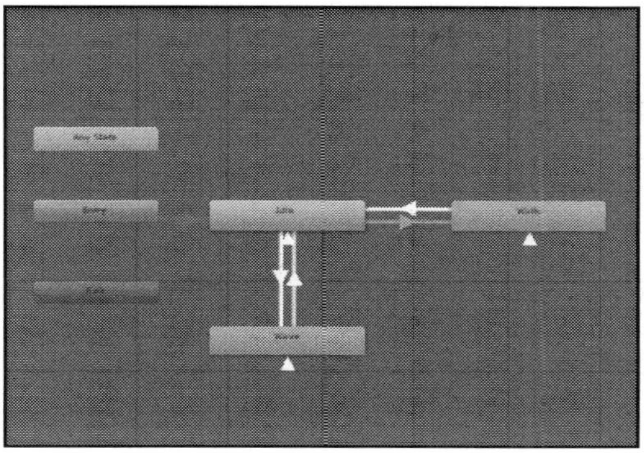

The final Animator graph should look like the above. After adding the additional transitions, it is now possible to transition from `Idle` animations to either a `Wave` or a `Walk` animation for the pet. Additional animations for the pet would each be provided by adding other states and transitions.

Providing a fading text message hint

It would be helpful to provide a hint to the player after starting a new game indicating that they need to place the bear in the room. You'll do this next using a custom script and prefab.

Open the stubbed C# script **Razeware / Scripts / FadeAndRemove.cs** and complete the `Start()` method:

```
void Start()
{
    // 1. fade via a coroutine + destroy with a delay.
    Destroy(gameObject, DelayBeforeFade + FadeTime);
    // 2. start a coroutine.
    StartCoroutine(Fade());
}
```

1. `Start` will set the attached GameObject to be destroyed after a time delay.
2. `StartCoroutine` will initiate a coroutine function. Coroutine functions can break a task over many frames. Here it is used to start a `Fade()` task that changes an alpha transparency value.

Now, add an `IEnumerator Fade()` method to define the coroutine in **FadeAndRemove.cs**:

```
    // 1.  Define the IEnumerator coroutine.
    IEnumerator Fade()
    {
        while (timer < DelayBeforeFade)
        {
            timer += Time.deltaTime;
            // 2. Pause here to carry on next frame.
            yield return null;
        }

        CanvasGroup group = GetComponent<CanvasGroup>();
        while (group.alpha > 0)
        {
            group.alpha -= Time.deltaTime / FadeTime;
            // 2. Pause here to carry on next frame.
            yield return null;
        }
    }
```

1. A coroutine a function of IEnumerator return type.
2. A coroutine pauses at the `yield` statement and continues at the next frame. This iterator gradually fades out the `CanvasGroup` over time.

Save the script and return to the editor.Drag the **HintCanvas** prefab from the **Assets \ Razeware \ Prefabs** folder onto **MoveablePet** to parent an instance of it. Attach the new **Fade And Remove** component to **HintCanvas** and update the **MoveablePet** prefab with the changes by clicking the Apply button

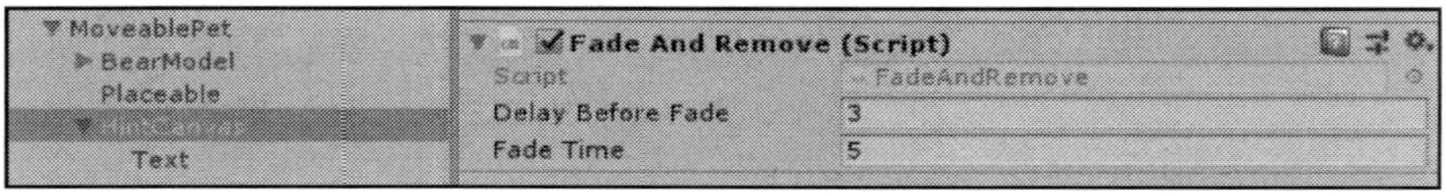

Play the scene a final time to test out the changes.At this point, you have a starting menu with buttons to make a bear appear and be placed on spatial mesh data. You also now have mixed reality and the ability to create dynamic interactions with the world.

The bear will navigate over any objects in the room such as floors, couches and tables with your Air-Tap gestures. Well done!

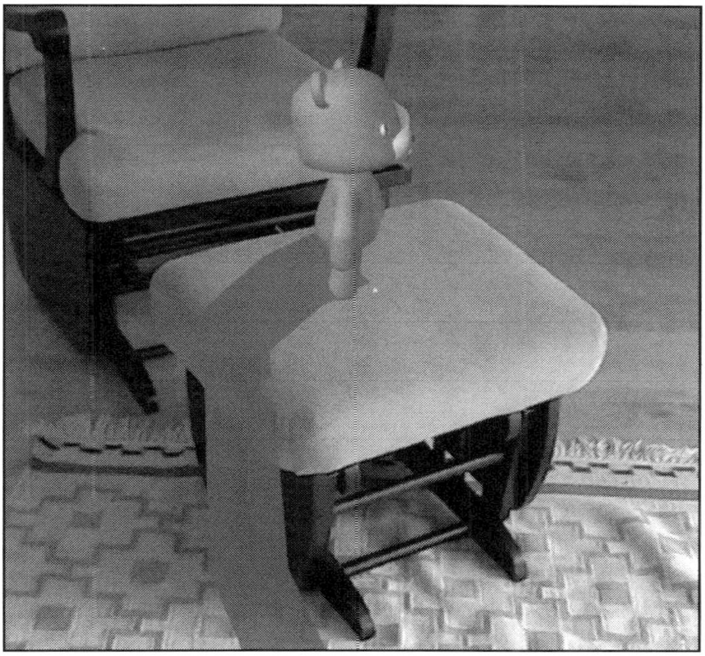

Where to go from here?

You've made great progress and can make a character walk across your room! In the next chapter you will learn how to persist objects in a save game and use spatial anchors to tie objects to their real-world locations. You will also learn about some more tools from the Mixed Reality Toolkit to quickly create menu(s) and modify objects.

Chapter 23: Persisting Real-World Locations on the HoloLens

Matt Larson

In the previous two chapters you learned how to setup a basic HoloLens project, animate a character, and make this character walk over spatial meshes of real surfaces in the room. Let's continue by adding additional objects for the Pet, exploring saving data, and working with spatial anchors.

Spatial anchors

Mixed reality requires game objects that can spatially co-exist with the real world. Since you can't fully control the environment of your game due to unpredictable configurations of furniture, room shapes and size, you'll need different mechanisms for building a game. In this chapter, you'll learn how to dynamically place virtual objects and get them to keep their locations in the real world when saving and loading a game.

Open the starter project for this chapter in Unity.The project continues building the Virtual Pet application. There are some new prefabs in the **Razeware \ Prefabs \ Extras** folder along with stubbed C# scripts for the MonoBehaviours you'll be working with in this chapter. You'll also find some new scripts in the **Razeware \ Scripts \ Persistence** folder.

Open the **PersistingLocations** scene to start your project. To start off, switch to the **Universal Windows Platform / HoloLens** Target Device in **Build Settings**.

More toys for your pet

Your pet needs things in its world — like bowls, beds and a house — and the player should be able to add these dynamically. The prefab objects you'll use are located in the **Razeware \ Prefabs \ Extras** folder. For each object, you'll need a menu, a 3D model and a button. You'll start with the menu.

Create an empty GameObject in the Hierarchy named **HoverMenu**. Next, create another empty GameObject named **CreateButton** and add it as a child of **HoverMenu**.

Open the **Razeware \ Scripts \ Persistence \ CreateButton** script, open it in a code editor and add the following method:

```
public void OnInputClicked(InputClickedEventData eventData)
{
   if (PrefabToCreate)
   {
      GameObject SceneRoot =
GameObject.FindObjectOfType<SceneRoot>().gameObject;
      GameObject obj = GameObject.Instantiate(PrefabToCreate,
SceneRoot.transform);

      GameObject bear =
GameObject.FindObjectOfType<NavMeshAgent>().gameObject;
      obj.transform.position = bear.transform.position +
bear.transform.forward * 0.25f;
   }
   eventData.Use();
}
```

This simple handler instantiates the **PrefabToCreate** directly in front of the pet.

Save the script and return to the editor. Add a **CreateButton** component to the **CreateButton** in the Hierarchy.Next, drag the **Bed** prefab from the **Razeware \ Prefabs \ Extras** folder into the **Prefab To Create** slot of **CreateButton**.

Now add a **BoxCollider** to the **CreateButton** and set its **Size** to **(X:0.1, Y:0.1, Z:0.1)**. Drag another **Bed** prefab from the **Razeware \ Prefabs \ Extras** folder onto **CreateButton** to parent an instance.

This is what **CreateButton** should look like in the Inspector:

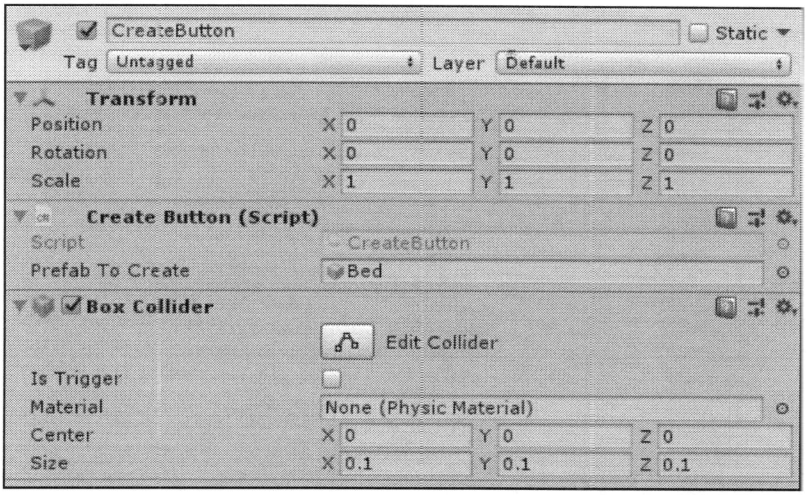

Duplicate the **CreateButton** under **HoverMenu** and replace its **Prefab To Create** with **FoodBowl**. Delete its child **Bed** and drag a **FoodBowl** prefab from the **Razeware \ Prefabs \ Extras** folder in its place.

Repeat the steps above to make buttons for the following other items: **Camera**, **WaterBowl** and **House**.

To make the models fit within the confines of their **BoxCollider**, select the children of each **CreateButton** and set their scale to **(X:0.25, Y:0.25, Z:0.25)**.

All of the icons are still stacked on top of each other. In the parent **HoverMenu**, add an **ObjectCollection** component and set the following properties:

- **Layout Type**: Column Then Row
- **Rows**: 2
- **Cell Width**: 0.15
- **Cell Height**: 0.15

Click **Update Collection** to organize all of the GameObjects neatly in the menu.

Next, you'll add a button to save the game in the **HoverMenu**.

Drag a **Button** prefab from the **Razeware \ Prefabs** folder on top of **HoverMenu** and rename its child **NewButton** to **SaveButton**. Next, change the **3DTextPrefab**'s **Text** value to **Save**.

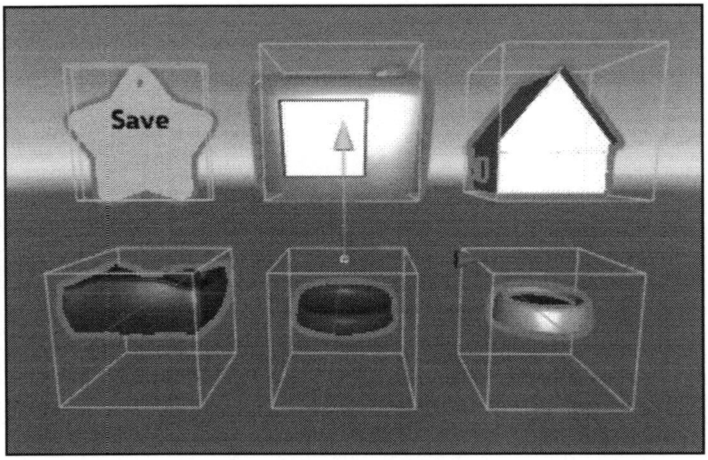

Add a **SaveButtonHandler** component to the **SaveButton** . You'll connect this behavior when it's needed for the saving system.Next, add a **Billboard** component to **HoverMenu** and save **HoverMenu** as a prefab inside the **Razeware \ Prefabs** folder. When you're done, remove the **HoverMenu** instance from the Hierarchy.

The collection of menu items will now look like this:

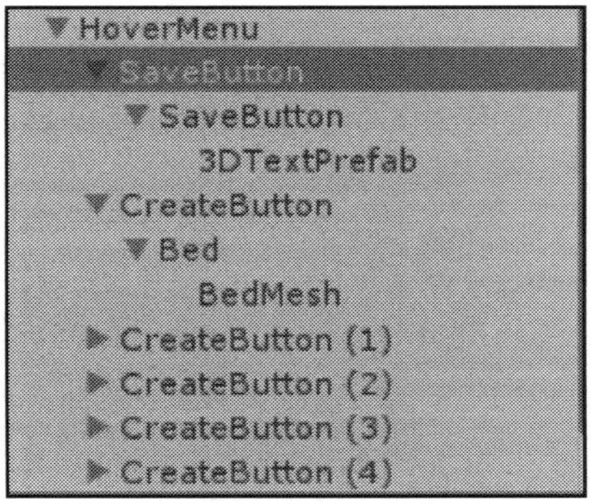

Add the hover menu to your pet

You'll make the menu appear when the user focuses their gaze on the **Pet** during the game, to do this, you'll need to edit the **FocusMenu** script. Open the **FocusMenu** script in the **Razeware \ Scripts \ Persistence** folder and and implement the class body:

```
// 1. Add these data members
[Tooltip("Set the prefab to be shown.")]
public GameObject Menu;
[Tooltip("Set the offset position.")]
public Vector3 Offset;

[Tooltip("Delay before showing.")]
public float ShowDuration = 1f;
[Tooltip("Delay before hiding.")]
public float HideDuration = 5f;

private bool haveFocus = false;
private float timer = 0f;
private GameObject menu;
```

Add the code to the Start() method to instantiate the **Menu** prefab.

```
// 2. Use this for initialization
void Start()
{
   menu = Instantiate(Menu, gameObject.transform);
   menu.transform.localPosition = Offset;
   ShowOrHideMenu(false);
}
```

Add code to Update() to track when to show or hide the **menu** GameObject. The `ShowOrHideMenu()` method will change whether the GameObject **menu** is active.

```
// 3. Update used to track when to show/hide
void Update()
{
   timer += Time.deltaTime;

   if (haveFocus && timer > ShowDuration)
   {
      ShowOrHideMenu(true);
   }

   if (!haveFocus && timer > HideDuration)
   {
      ShowOrHideMenu(false);
   }
}
```

```
// 4. Change if menu is visible
public void ShowOrHideMenu(bool show)
{
    if (menu && menu.active != show)
    {
        menu.active = show;
    }
}
```

Most importantly, you must implement the `OnFocusEnter()` and `OnFocusExit()` methods as required by the MRTK `IFocusable` interface. These methods show or hide the **menu** GameObject after exceeding a duration.

```
// When user's gaze is on this GameObject
public void OnFocusEnter()
{
    timer = 0f;
    haveFocus = true;
}

// When user's gaze leaves this GameObject
public void OnFocusExit()
{
    timer = 0f;
    haveFocus = false;
}
```

Save the script and return to the editor. Add a **MoveablePet** prefab from the **Prefabs** folder to the Hierarchy. Attach a **FocusMenu** component to **MoveablePet**'s child **BearModel**.

To make the menu appear above the head of the character, set the **Menu** field to point to the **HoverMenu** prefab, and change **Offset** to **(X:0, Y:0.5, Z:0)**. Now add a **Capsule Collider** and set the following values:

- **Radius**: 0.1
- **Height**: 0.3
- **Center**: (X:0, Y:0.2, Z:0)

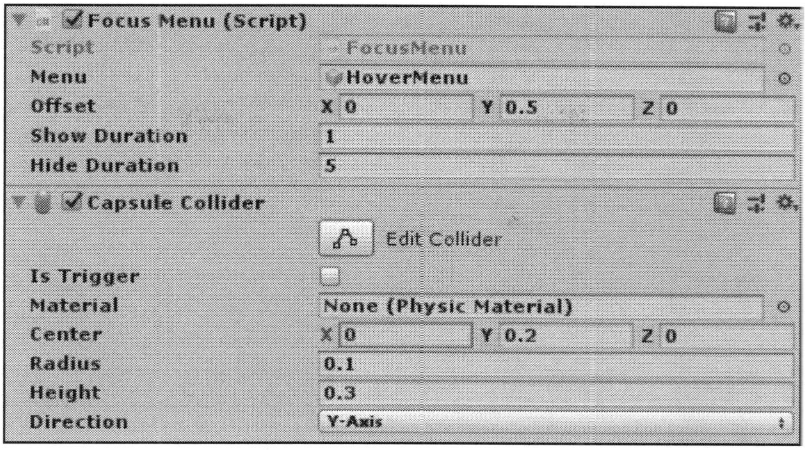

Apply the changes to the **MoveablePet** prefab again and remove it from the scene.

Create an empty GameObject named **SceneRoot**, reset its Transform and attach a **SceneRoot** component to it. **SceneRoot** acts as a container for objects the user dynamically adds to keep the scene hierarchy clean.

Play the scene and start a new game. Upon directly gazing on the pet, the **HoverMenu** appears at its head.

You can now dynamically place objects anywhere on the floor where the pet can walk. The pet can walk on and interact with these objects because every GameObject with a **MeshRenderer** also has a **NavMeshSourceTag** component that signals to the **LocalNavMeshBuilder** that these should be part of the **NavMesh** for the character to walk on and around.

Spatial anchors and saving

The HoloLens uses **spatial anchors** to describe a point in the world to track. Each spatial anchor has a local coordinate system that provides the real-world locations to attached GameObjects. You'll combine the built-in **WorldAnchorStore** to save object anchors and the common XML data format to persist the objects are in the scene and their locations.

The easiest method for saving on the Universal Windows Platform is to serialize to an XML file with the built-in **XmlSerializer**.

Note: To **serialize** means to arrange data objects in a serial format. This can be plain text, JSON, XML or even binary. Usually, the resulting data is then saved to a storage device to be read later on and converted to data objects again — this is called **deserialization**.

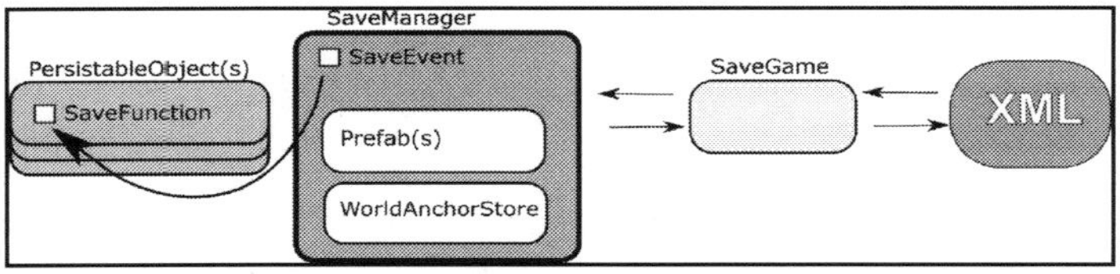

Open the **Razeware \ Scripts \ Persistence \ SaveGame.cs** script in a code editor and complete the `PrefabState` class:

```
// 1. Annotations on the class
[System.Serializable]
[XmlRoot("prefabState")]
public class PrefabState
{
   // 2. Matching prefab tag
   [XmlElement("prefabTag")]
   public string prefabTag = "";
   // 3. Local Position/Rotations.
   [XmlElement("position")]
   public Vector3 position = new Vector3(0, 0, 0);
   [XmlElement("rotation")]
   public Quaternion rotation = new Quaternion();
   // 4. Unique ID.
   [XmlElement("id")]
   public int id = 0;
}
```

1. The `PrefabState` class can be serialized to XML for saving data. The annotations at the top of the class declare it to be serializable, and give the XML entry the root name 'prefabState'.
2. `prefabTag` is a text field that is used to match against an existing Prefab in the the Assets folder by name.
3. An object will keep position in the world by a **WorldAnchor**. The `rotation` field provides additional pose information, and the `position` field provides a location when spatial anchoring is not available (such as testing in the Unity Editor).
4. `id` provides a simple id for each individual savable object.

The annotations above variables describe how the data will be named in the XML file.

In the same file, complete the `SaveGame` class, which mainly contains a list of the `PrefabState`:

```
public class SaveGame
{
    // 1. Data members
    public string AppAnchorPrefix = "VirtualPet_";
    public List<PrefabState> SaveableObjects = new
List<PrefabState>();
    private int id = 0;

    // 2. Auto-increment a unique id.
    public int GetUniqueId()
    {
       return id++;
    }
}
```

1. `SaveGame` itself is quite basic, and only needs a `List` of `PrefabState` that will be saved to disk, or read from disk.
2. `GetUniqueId()` will provide an incremented unique id for any new saveable object.

Save this script and return to the editor.

The SaveManager

Open the **SaveManager** script in the **Razeware \ Scripts \ Persistence** folder in a code editor. To reduce the complexity to find and call **SaveManager**, this class derives from the Mixed Reality Toolkit helper **Singleton** class. The **Singleton** class ensures that only one instance of the **SaveManager** can exist in a scene.

Additionally, any other script can directly call methods such as **New()**, **Save()**, or **Load()** from the **SaveManager** by directly using the **SaveManager.Instance**. **Instance** is a static variable which will always be guaranteed to hold the one unique instance of the **SaveManager** class that is present.

When `Save` is called, a `SaveEvent` occurs and each **PersistentObject** generates a serializable record for the XML document.

Spatial anchors are stored in the **WorldAnchorStore**, a managed data store that abstracts and holds the spatial anchor information for the HoloLens. This allows you to persist GameObjects in real-world positions.

At the top of the `SaveManager` class, add these variables:

```
// 1. Prefab list
public List<GameObject> SaveablePrefabs;

// 2. All active saveable objects will be children
private GameObject SceneRoot;

// 3. Any saveable GameObject provides a SaveDelegate callback
function
public delegate void SaveDelegate(object sender, EventArgs
args);
public event SaveDelegate SaveEvent;

// 4. Save game and an anchor store where data is persisted.
public SaveGame Game;
public WorldAnchorStore Store = null;
private string saveGameName;
```

1. The `SaveablePrefabs` is populated with prefabs that you can save and reload into the scene under `SceneRoot`. This is managed by drag-n-dropping Prefabs into the field in the Unity Editor.

2. The `SceneRoot` is the parent GameObject in the scene containing saveable GameObjects to keep the scene hierarchy organized.

3. The `SaveDelegate` is a C# delegate for creating callback functions. Any saveable object will subscribe to the `SaveEvent` by adding their `SaveDelegate` method.

4. There will be only one active `SaveGame` and `WorldAnchorStore`, and a save event will trigger the collection of data into these objects and then serialization.

The `WorldAnchorStore` must be initialized asynchronously during the `Awake()`, to be ready when saving is needed. Fill in the `Awake()` and `StoreLoaded` methods as below:

```
void Awake ()
{
   saveGameName = Application.persistentDataPath + "/
gamesave.save";
   Debug.Log("Will save to " + saveGameName);

   SceneRoot =
GameObject.FindObjectOfType<SceneRoot>().gameObject;

   // 1. Need to prepare the WorldAnchorStore
   WorldAnchorStore.GetAsync(StoreLoaded);
}

private void
StoreLoaded(UnityEngine.XR.WSA.Persistence.WorldAnchorStore
store)
{
    // 2. Keep the readied store
    this.Store = store;
}
```

1. The `WorldAnchorStore` is created asynchronously.
2. When the store is available it will be set to the local member `Store` during `StoreLoaded`

During `Awake`, the `SaveManager` object needs to ready `WorldAnchorStore`. `WorldAnchorStore` is loaded asynchronously and is available when its needed later to load or save spatial anchors.

For testing saving in the editor, fill in the `Update()` method of `SaveManager` as below:

```
void Update ()
{
   // 1. For testing in editor
   if (Input.GetKeyDown(KeyCode.P))
   {
      Save();
   }
   if (Input.GetKeyDown(KeyCode.L))
   {
      Load();
   }
   if (Input.GetKeyDown(KeyCode.N))
   {
      New();
   }
}
```

1. 'Input.GetKeyDown(..)' provides the hotkeys (P, L, and N) which can be used to test saving, loading and clearing the scene in the editor. Each will trigger respective method of `SaveManager`.

Within **SaveManager**, implement the `New()` method:

```
public void New()
{
   // 1. Clear data
   Game = new SaveGame();
   InstantiateState(false);
   Debug.Log("New Game");
}
```

1. `New` clears the `SaveGame` object and starts a clear state.

Next implement `Save()` in **SaveManager**:

```
// Save the game.
public void Save()
{
   // 1 Create empty save game data.
   Game = new SaveGame();

   // 2 Fire off event to have all objects add save data.
   if (SaveEvent != null)
   {
      SaveEvent(null, null);
   }
   // 3 Serialize
   XmlSerializer serializer = new
XmlSerializer(typeof(SaveGame));

   File.Delete(saveGameName);
   FileStream stream = new FileStream(saveGameName,
FileMode.OpenOrCreate);

   serializer.Serialize(stream, Game);
   stream.Dispose();
   Debug.Log("Game Saved");
}
```

1. `Save` creates an empty `SaveGame` object.
2. Then it fires off a `SaveEvent` to collect all of the serializable data into the `SaveGame` object.
3. Next the **XmlSerializer** writes the collected data to disk.

Finally, in **SaveManager**, implement the `Load()` method:

```
// Load the game.
public void Load()
{
   if (File.Exists(saveGameName))
   {
       // 1 - ceserialize the save game information.
       XmlSerializer serializer = new
XmlSerializer(typeof(SaveGame));
       FileStream stream = File.Open(saveGameName,
FileMode.Open);
       Game = serializer.Deserialize(stream) as SaveGame;
       stream.Dispose();

       // 2 - any setup after loading data.
       InstantiateState(true);

       // 3 - restart the any objects
       foreach (Transform child in SceneRoot.transform)
       {
          GameObject go = child.gameObject;
          IActivatable activate =
go.GetComponent(typeof(IActivatable)) as IActivatable;
          if (activate != null)
          {
             activate.SetEnabled(true);
          }
       }
       Debug.Log("Game Loaded");
   }
}
```

Appropriately, `Load` does the opposite of `Save`:

1. If a save game exists, `XmlSerializer` deserializes the data file back into a `SaveGame` with the descriptive information about the objects in the scene.
2. `InstantiateState` makes the GameObjects in the scene.
3. If any GameObjects need to be activated, they can be restarted here.

In **SaveManager** fill in the `Cleanup` method to `Destroy` any present GameObjects.

```
// 1 Clear all from the SceneRoot.
public void Cleanup()
{
   foreach (Transform child in SceneRoot.transform)
   {
      GameObject.Destroy(child.gameObject);
   }
}
```

Finally, in **SaveManager** fill in `InstantiateState` with code to recreate GameObject(s) in the Scene:

```
public void InstantiateState(bool restoreAnchors)
{
   // 1.
   Cleanup();

   // 2. Convert from PrefabState -> Prefabs.
   foreach (PrefabState p in Game.SaveableObjects)
   {
      GameObject prefab = null;
      foreach (GameObject go in SaveablePrefabs)
      {
         PersistentObject info =
go.GetComponent<PersistentObject>();
         if (info)
         {
            if (info.PrefabTag == p.prefabTag)
            {
               // 3. Instantiate in the scene
               prefab = GameObject.Instantiate(go);
               break;
            }
         }
      }

      if (prefab)
      {
         // 4. Set local position/rotation
         prefab.transform.position = p.position;
         prefab.transform.rotation = p.rotation;

         // 5. Try to restore a world anchor.
         if (restoreAnchors && Store != null)
         {
            String storeId = Game.AppAnchorPrefix + p.id;
            bool haveAnchor = this.Store.Load(storeId, prefab);
            if (haveAnchor)
            {
               Debug.Log("Added previous spatial anchor");
            }
         }

         // 6. Set the parent only after restoring the
WorldAnchor.
         prefab.transform.SetParent(SceneRoot.transform, true);
         Debug.Log(prefab.name + " restored to the scene.");
      }
   }
}
```

`InstantiateState` does much of the heavy lifting to convert `PrefabState` entries back to instantiate matching prefabs.

1. Existing objects are removed from the `SceneRoot`.
2. Each `PrefabState` will get matched up with a Prefab, if possible.
3. When a Prefab is matches, it is Instantiated in the scene.
4. The local position/rotation are set for the GameObject.
5. If a WorldAnchor existed for this `PrefabState` id, it is possible to restore it back to the same real-world anchored position.
6. The GameObject can be parented under `SceneRoot`, but this should happen after setting the WorldAnchor for the GameObject, or an incorrect transform occurs.

Create a new empty GameObject in the Hierarchy, name it **SaveManager** and add a **SaveManager** component to it.

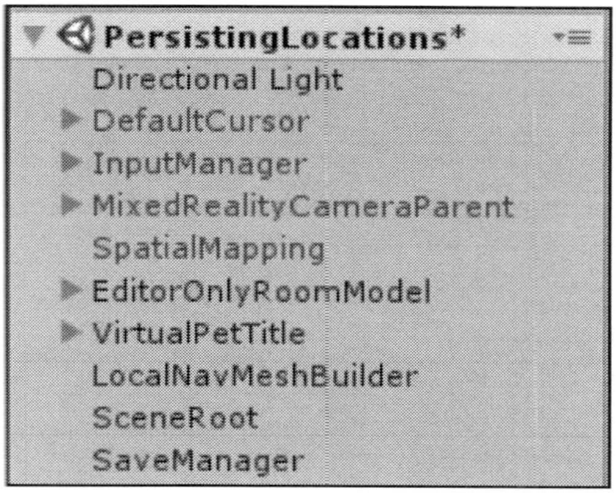

In the Inspector, drag each of the prefabs from the **Razeware \ Prefabs \ Extras** folder onto the **Saveable Prefabs** list.

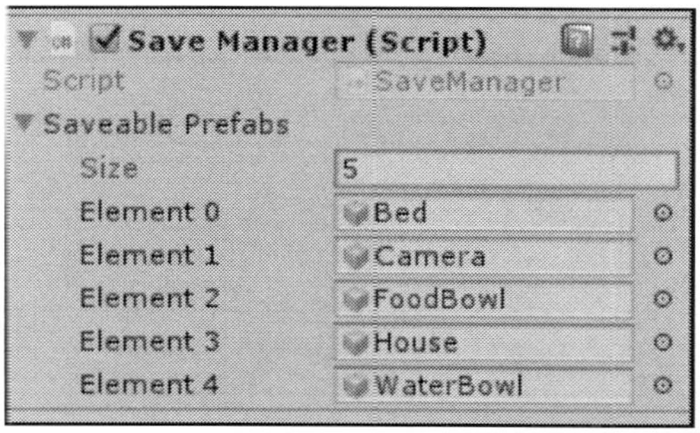

Making a PersistentObject

Open **Razeware \ Scripts \ Persistence \ PersistentObject.cs** in a code editor and complete the `Start` method:

```
void Start()
{
    // Register this object as a saveable object.
    SaveManager.Instance.SaveEvent += SaveFunction;
}
```

Here, the **PersistentObject** registers a callback **SaveFunction**. The **SaveFunction** method gets called when a **SaveEvent** is fired from the **SaveManager**.

Then, finish the `OnDestroy` method of **PersistentObject.cs**:

```
void OnDestroy()
{
    if (SaveManager.Instance != null)
    {
        SaveManager.Instance.SaveEvent -= SaveFunction;
    }
}
```

The same method needs to be unregistered when the GameObject is destroyed.

Now, fill in the implementation for `SaveFunction` of **PersistentObject.cs**:

```
public void SaveFunction(object sender, EventArgs args)
{
    PrefabState ps = new PrefabState();
    ps.prefabTag = PrefabTag;
    ps.position = gameObject.transform.position;
    ps.rotation = gameObject.transform.rotation;
    ps.id = SaveManager.Instance.Game.GetUniqueId();
    SaveManager.Instance.Game.SaveableObjects.Add(ps);

    // 1. Save a spatial anchor, if possible.
    WorldAnchorStore store = SaveManager.Instance.Store;
    if (store != null)
    {
        Debug.Log("Begin saving World Anchor for " +
gameObject.name);
        // 2. Get an existing anchor or add a new one.
        WorldAnchor anchor =
gameObject.GetComponent(typeof(WorldAnchor)) as WorldAnchor;
        if (anchor == null)
        {
            anchor = gameObject.AddComponent(typeof(WorldAnchor))
as WorldAnchor;
```

```
        }
        // 3. Save this position to restore later.
        if (anchor != null && anchor.isLocated)
        {
            String storeId =
SaveManager.Instance.Game.AppAnchorPrefix + ps.id;
            if (store.Delete(storeId))
            {
                Debug.Log("Deleted old World Anchor for " +
gameObject.name);
            }
            if (store.Save(storeId, anchor))
            {
                Debug.Log("World Anchor Saved for " +
gameObject.name);
             }
        }
    }
    Debug.Log(gameObject.name + " added to save game");
}
```

1. Checks if the WorldAnchorStore is ready (available on HoloLens, unavailable in the Unity Editor).
2. When a GameObject is being saved, it needs to have a **WorldAnchor** as a component to match it to a real-world position. If it doesn't already have one, adding a new **WorldAnchor** will establish the position.
3. A **WorldAnchor** is stored with a identifying id. If this id already exists it will not be overwritten, so you must delete the pre-existing **WorldAnchor** id.

In `SaveFunction`, a `PrefabState` object is built that describes the position and rotation in the scene, the type of prefab it is and a unique ID. If a `WorldAnchorStore` is ready, it checks if the GameObject needs a `WorldAnchor`; if so, it creates one and attaches this to the GameObject. Following this, the method stores this `WorldAnchor` object in the `WorldAnchorStore` using `store.Save(id, anchor)`. Save the script and return to the editor.

Making toys persistent objects

Select all of the prefabs in the **Razeware \ Prefabs \ Extras** folder attach a **Persistent Object** component to all of them. Next, select each prefab individually, and fill in the **Prefab Tag** field for the **Persistent Object** with a unique and valid name like "Bed", "WaterBowl" and so on depending on the prefab.

This tag is used to find the correct prefab to match what's stored in the **PrefabState** XML entry.

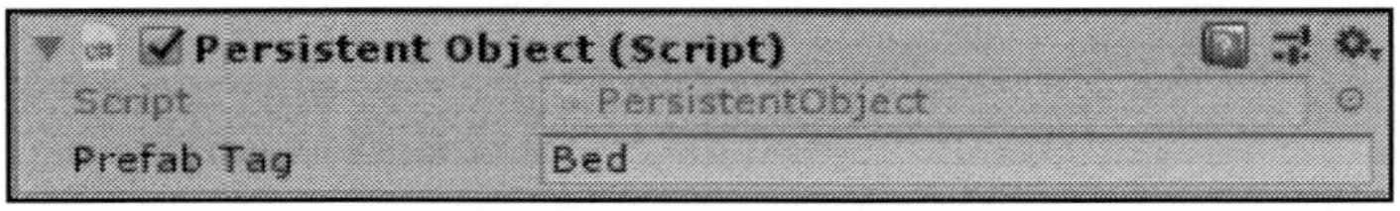

Hook in the save button

Finish by hooking in the button for the hovering menu to call the `Save` method.

Open the **SaveButtonHandler** script in the **Razeware \ Scripts \ Persistence** folder and implement the method for `OnInputClicked`:

```
public void OnInputClicked(InputClickedEventData eventData)
{
    SaveManager.Instance.Save();
    eventData.Use();
}
```

`OnInputClicked` handles input events such as air-taps, and the implementation in **SaveButtonHandler** now hooks back to call `SaveManager.Instance.Save()`, triggering the saving of our scene's state.

Save the script and return to the editor.

Update the start menu

Next, you'll also need to update the title menu.

Open the **MenuController** script in the **Razeware \ Scripts** folder in a code editor and replace the `InputDown` method to hook in the `SaveManager`'s for `New` and `Load` methods:

```
protected override void InputDown(GameObject obj, InputEventData
eventData)
{
    bool needCharacter = false;

    // 1 The button you will use in this scene.
    if ("NewButton".Equals(obj.name))
    {
        SaveManager.Instance.New();
        needCharacter = true;
```

```
    }

    // 2 Implement other button responses here.
    if ("LoadButton".Equals(obj.name))
    {
        SaveManager.Instance.Load();
        needCharacter = true;
    }

    // 3 Start placing character.
    if (needCharacter)
    {
        GameObject SceneRoot =
GameObject.FincObjectOfType<SceneRoot>().gameObject;
        GameObject character = Instantiate(placeCharacter,
SceneRoot.transform);
        // Move the character into the gaze of the camera
        Vector3 hmdPosition = Camera.main.transform.position;
        Vector3 hmdDirection = Camera.main.transform.forward;
        character.transform.position = hmdPosition + hmdDirection
* 2f;
    }

    eventData.Use();
    // Exit menu - give 0.2 sec. time for button animations.
    Destroy(gameObject, 0.2f);
}
```

1. Replace the original `New` method to hook in the **SaveManager**.
2. Add the `Load` method that also calls **SaveManager**.
3. Both save and load begin with manually placing the pet in the scene.

Save the script and return to the editor.It's now possible to load a saved game directly from the starting menu.

Start the scene, and start a new game. Gaze on the pet to display the menu. After adding several objects, **Save**, stop and restart the app. Then choose **Load** and all of the objects reappear in their same locations.

> **Note**: When running on the HoloLens, restoring **WorldAnchors** to objects keeps the real-world locations of the last save, regardless of the orientation of the user's headset when they started the application.

Adding the bounding box rig and AppBar

Suppose you want to remove an object from the scene or make fine adjustments — you can create your own solution of course, but there's a much simpler way included with the MRTK.

The Mixed Reality Toolkit includes a **Bounding Box Rig** component, which provides manipulation controls and an **AppBar** with options to hide, adjust and remove the attached GameObject from the scene.

Select all of the prefabs in the **Prefabs \ Extras** folder and add a **Bounding Box Rig** component to all of them. In the Inspector, point the **Bounding Box Prefab** slot to the **BoundingBoxBasic** prefab located in the **Assets \ HoloToolkit \ UX \ Prefabs \ BoundingBoxes \ BoundingBoxBasic** folder.

Play the scene now and gaze on the pet to open the menu. After placing an object they will now have a hovering **AppBar** in front of the GameObject.

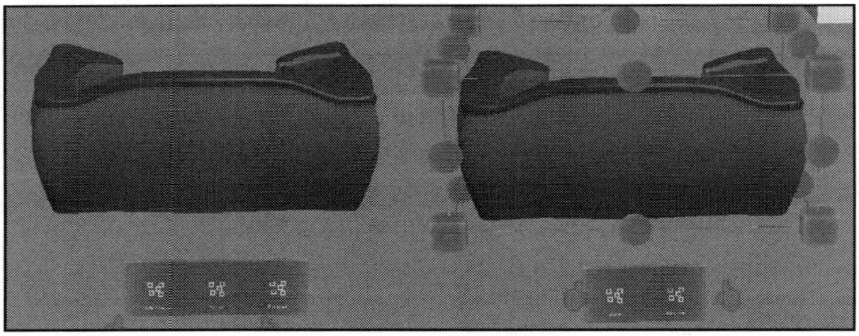

The image above shows an **AppBar** in front of one of the pet's toys. Gaze on the icon for **Adjust** and *Air-tap* to start adjusting. A bounding box rig wraps the object, which can rotate, scale and adjust the object in the scene.

Where to go from here?

Congratulations, your pet can now build a home and surround it with objects! Each object is anchored in the real world and will persist in this location using a save game and world anchor store.

In the next chapter, you'll hook up each of these GameObjects with actions and animations for the pet to finish a fully interactive experience.

Chapter 24: Mixing Media

Matt Larson

You already created the UI with the Mixed Reality Toolkit, read spatial mapping data, created a NavAgent that walks across spatial maps, added character animations in Unity, and saved spatial anchoring data.

In this chapter, you'll bring the game to life by adding complex character animations and media including voice commands, spatial audio and camera.

Are you ready to explore the unique interactions possible for augmented reality?

Getting started

In this final chapter, you'll add animation actions that let the bear interact with items. You'll work with HoloLens media like microphone input, spatial 3D audio, and the HoloLens front-facing color camera. Finally, you'll learn how to hide objects behind surfaces using an occlusion effect, and you'll create shaders for your own unique effects on spatial meshes.

The starter project continues from where the previous chapter left off. However, it includes additional sound and music samples in **Razeware / Audio**, as well as an updated animation controller found inside **Razeware / Animations / PetAnimatorController** that includes all of the character animations in the state machine. It also contains stubbed C# scripts for each of the code blocks you'll work on in this chapter.

Start by opening the starter project **HoloLensMedia** and the **Media** scene in the **Razeware / Scenes** folder.

Note: When opening this project for the first time, select **Mixed Reality Toolkit > Configure > Apply Mixed Reality Project settings** from the top menu and select **Apply**. This configures Unity to simulate the HoloLens when running the scene.

Complex Character Animations

You'll start by adding more animations to allow the bear to work with each object. Using a **TargetObject** component, you'll label all of the placeable GameObjects from the previous chapter so the player can select the object, move the bear to the object, perform an action and resolve the action.

You can add the **Razeware / Scripts / Game / TargetObject.cs** MonoBehaviour provided in the starter project to GameObjects to label them with a `TargetType`:

```
public class TargetObject : MonoBehaviour
{
  public enum TargetType { Food, Water, Bed, Points };
  public TargetType Target;
}
```

Select the prefabs in the **Razeware / Prefabs / Extras** folder that contain a **MeshFilter**.

Add a **TargetType** and a **MeshCollider** component to each of the children **FoodBowl**, **BedMesh** and **WaterBowl**.

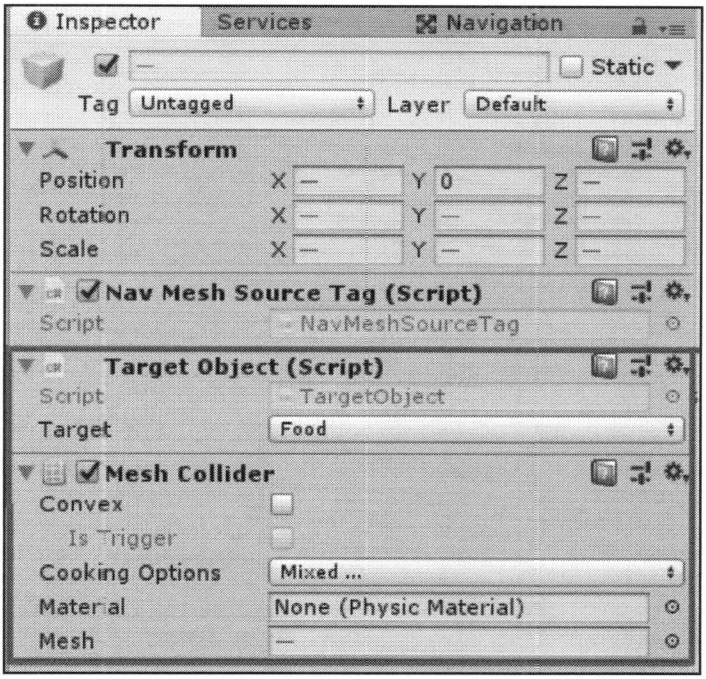

Individually set the **Target** field to match the prefab so that the FoodBowl **Target Object** is set as **Target : Food**, Bed is set as **Target : Bed** and WaterBowl is set as **Target : Water**.

Adapting the character to interact with these objects requires a behavior to know when the character is walking to an object, has reached an object, started an action and resolved an action. The following state diagram gives two examples:

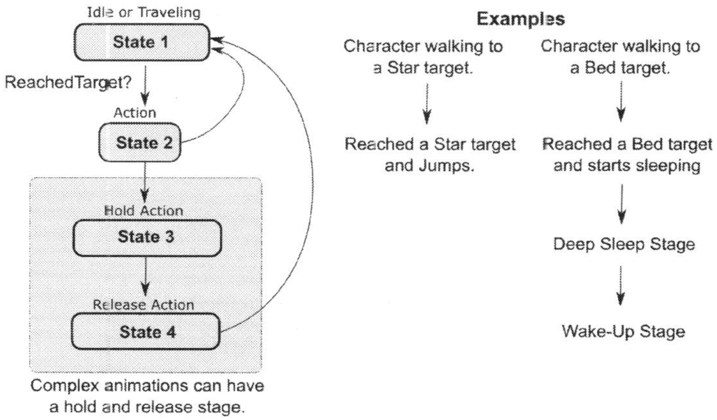

It's time to examine how to make a sleeping bear. First, you need the bear to walk to the bed, yawn and settle in. Next, it can enter a deep sleep until the player wakes it. While sleeping, the bear cannot move — unless, of course, you want a sleep-walking bear! Using three scripts included with this chapter, you can extend and create state machines to build these behaviors yourself.

The MonoBehaviour scripts **GameState.cs**, **StateTransition.cs** and **AbstractStateMachine.cs**, are located in **Razeware / Scripts / StateMachine**. These are helper scripts you'll use to build a generic state machine inside a **MonoBehaviour**. These scripts are not covered in depth in this tutorial. However, you'll use them to create your state machine **PetState**.

In summary, you can build a state machine **MonoBehaviour** by inheriting from `AbstractStateMachine` and setting a `CurrentState` as the starting `GameState`.

Between each `GameState` are `StateTransition` instances that can define when it's possible to transition to another state.

You'll start by building the **PetState** state machine. Open the stubbed C# script **Razeware / Scripts / Game / PetState.cs** and populate `Start()`:

```
void Start()
{
    // 1. define the states
    GameState canMove = new GameState("canMove", EnterCanMove);
    GameState action = new GameState("action", EnterAction);
    GameState holdAction = new GameState("holdAction",
EnterHold);
    GameState releaseAction = new GameState("releaseAction",
EnterRelease);

    // 2. add transitions
    canMove.AddTransition(new StateTransition(() =>
IsAtTarget(), action));

    action.AddTransition(new StateTransition(() => CanExit &&
CanHold(), holdAction));
    action.AddTransition(new StateTransition(() => CanExit && !
CanHold(), canMove));

    holdAction.AddTransition(new StateTransition(() => CanExit,
releaseAction));

    releaseAction.AddTransition(new StateTransition(() =>
CanExit, canMove));

    // 3. set the first state and action
    CurrentState = canMove;
    CurrentAction = ActionType.Navigating;
}
```

Here's how this code works:

1. **PetState** `Start()` defines states that match the behaviors such as jumping or sleeping. When you construct each **GameState**, you provide it with a name and a callback function (ex. `canMove` and `EnterCanMove`). Upon entering a state, the callback function triggers and can play animations, sounds or other content
2. Transitions determine when the state machine can enter a different state. In `Start()`, several transitions are created, and each has a C# delegate function that checks if criteria that allows a state to transition are met. The second parameter describes a destination state that it can transition to.
3. The `CurrentState` is set as `canMove` to initialize the state machine. The `CurrentAction` value is also set to an enum value and provides information that other scripts can use to know what animation to display based on what the character is doing.

The `AbstractStateMachine` checks transitions during `Update()`. If it's necessary to add logic to an `Update()` method, then it's necessary to call the `base.Update()` to ensure the `AbstractStateMachine` updates.

Fill in the first transition check, `IsAtTarget()`, of **PetState.cs**:

```
bool IsAtTarget()
{
    // 1.
    if (Target && Vector3.Distance(Target.transform.position,
gameObject.transform.position) < 0.2f)
    {
        return true;
    }
    return false;
}
```

`IsAtTarget` checks if the Pet arrives within a range of the **Target** GameObject.

Fill in the second transition check, `CanHold()`, of **PetState.cs**:

```
bool CanHold()
{
    // 1.
    if (CurrentAction == ActionType.Sleep)
    {
        return true;
    }
    return false;
}
```

CanHold is only true for the sleep animations which enter a hold state for deep sleep. All other animations perform once and then return the character to a movement state immediately.

Next, fill in `EnterCanMove()` of **PetState.cs**:

```
void EnterCanMove()
{
    // 1
    Target = null;
    CurrentAction = ActionType.Navigating;
    CanExit = false;
}
```

Entering the `CanMove` state clears any targets and sets the action to navigating, allowing the pet to move.

Fill in `EnterAction()` of **PetState.cs**:

```
void EnterAction()
{
    // 1.
    if (Target.GetComponent<TargetObject>().Target ==
TargetObject.TargetType.Bed)
    {
        CurrentAction = ActionType.Sleep;
        StartCoroutine(ExitAfterTime(3.6f));
    }
    // 2.
    if (Target.GetComponent<TargetObject>().Target ==
TargetObject.TargetType.Food)
    {
        float animTime = 7.7f;
        CurrentAction = ActionType.Eat;
        StartCoroutine(ExitAfterTime(animTime));

        GameObject hand = GameObject.Find("Hand.R");
        GameObject kibble = Instantiate(Kibble);
        if (hand && kibble)
        {
            kibble.transform.SetParent(hand.transform);
            kibble.transform.localPosition = new Vector3(0, 0,
0);
            Destroy(kibble, animTime/2);
        }
    }
    // 3.
    if (Target.GetComponent<TargetObject>().Target ==
TargetObject.TargetType.Water)
    {
        CurrentAction = ActionType.Drink;
```

```
        StartCoroutine(ExitAfterTime(7.7f));
    }
    // 4.
    if (Target.GetComponent<TargetObject>().Target ==
TargetObject.TargetType.Points)
    {
        Destroy(Target, 0.5f);
        CurrentAction = ActionType.Jump;
        StartCoroutine(ExitAfterTime(1.9f));
    }
}
```

Here's a closer look at how this works:

1. The sleep action starts the `ActionType.Sleep` enum action type which animates the bear lying down in the bed.
2. The eating action makes some pet food appear in the hand of the bear and starts the eating animation.
3. The drink action shows the bear bent over for a drink.
4. The bear can jump to celebrate earning a point.

`EnterAction` is all you need for most actions, but this is only the first step for multi-step actions like sleeping. Sleeping also uses the hold and release actions for animations.

Fill in `EnterHold()` of **PetState.cs**:

```
void EnterHold()
{
    CanExit = false;
}
```

By setting the `CanExit` boolean to `false`, `EnterHold` creates a state that pauses the state machine until user action allows the state to exit and wakes up the bear.

Fill in `EnterRelease()` of **PetState.cs**:

```
void EnterRelease()
{
    CanExit = false;
    if(CurrentAction == ActionType.Sleep)
    {
        // 1.
        CurrentAction = ActionType.None;
        StartCoroutine(ExitAfterTime(8f));
    }
}
```

`EnterRelease` resolves the sleeping state, and pauses the state machine until the waking animation has time to complete.

Now fill in the `ExitAfterTime` coroutine of **PetState.cs**:

```
IEnumerator ExitAfterTime(float time)
{
    // 1.
    yield return new WaitForSeconds(time);
    CanExit = true;
}
```

`ExitAfterTime` is a coroutine method and the `yield` statement here allows a timer delay that can delay actions a specified number of seconds without blocking the main thread. At the end of the delay, `CanExit` is set to true, allowing states to exit.

Save all of your changes to **PetState.cs** and return to the editor.**PetState** needs to hook into the **AnimationController** to update animations. You created **AnimationController.cs** in **Chapter 22: Create a Holographic User Interface** to transition idle and walking animations. Now it needs to trigger all of the action animations.

Open **Razeware / Scripts / AnimationController.cs** and complete `Start()`:

```
void Start()
{
    anim = GetComponent<Animator>();
    agent = GetComponent<UnityEngine.AI.NavMeshAgent>();
    // 1
    state = GetComponent<PetState>();
    // Don't update position automatically, happens during
OnAnimator.
    agent.updatePosition = false;
}
```

This connects the `state` to a **PetState** component on the GameObject to which this script is attached.

Now, fill in `Update()` inside **AnimationController.cs** to describe the new animation states:

```
void Update()
{
    // 1
    if (state && state.CurrentAction !=
PetState.ActionType.Navigating)
    {
        walking = false;
        switch (state.CurrentAction) {
```

```
                case PetState.ActionType.Drink :
                case PetState.ActionType.Eat:
                    SetState((int)CurrentState.Eat);
                    break;
                case PetState.ActionType.Jump:
                    SetState((int)CurrentState.Jump);
                    break;
                case PetState.ActionType.Wave:
                    SetState((int)CurrentState.Wave);
                    break;
                case PetState.ActionType.Sleep:
                    SetState((int)CurrentState.Sleep);
                    break;
                default:
                    SetState((int)CurrentState.Idle);
                    break;
            }
        }
        // 2
        else {
            AnimateMove();
        }
    }
```

Here's what this does:

1. This switch/case block now changes the **PetAnimator** to the correct animation state based on **PetState**.
2. The default state still toggles between an idle or walking animation for when the **PetState** is `canMove`.

Whew! After all of that script work, switch back to the Unity editor. Drag the **Razeware / Prefabs / MoveablePet** prefab into the Hierarchy.

Find the child **BearModel** and add **Pet State** as a component to this **BearModel**.

Drag the **Razeware / Prefabs / Extra / Kibble** prefab into the **Kibble** field from **Pet State** to provide a food item to spawn when eating.

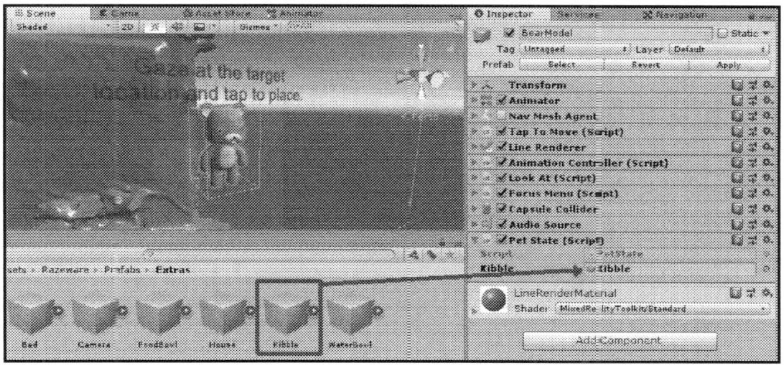

Save the **MoveablePet** as the **Razeware / Prefabs / MoveablePet** prefab by clicking the **Apply** button on **MoveablePet** in the Inspector.

Next, delete **MoveablePet** from the Hierarchy.

There is one more step before you can experience these actions. You'll need to set the target object for the **PetState** by making updates to the **TapToMove** script from **Chapter 22 : Create a Holographic User Interface**

Setting a TargetObject with TapToMove

You created the **TapToMove** script in an earlier chapter to provide a modal **IInputClickHandler** to direct the pet via *Air-Tap* gestures. You need to modify this script to set the **TargetObject** when the player *Air-taps* on an object.

Open **Razeware / Scripts / TapToMove.cs** and add additional logic for `OnInputClicked()`:

```
public void OnInputClicked(InputClickedEventData eventData)
{
    // 1
    if
(eventData.selectedObject.GetComponent<IInputClickHandler>() !=
null) return;

    // 2
    PetState state = GetComponent<PetState>();
    if (state.CurrentState.Name == "holdAction")
    {
        state.CanExit = true;
        eventData.Use();
        return;
    }

    // 3
    if (eventData.selectedObject.GetComponent<TargetObject>() !=
null)
    {
        TargetObject t =
eventData.selectedObject.GetComponent<TargetObject>();
        state.Target = t.gameObject;
    }

    Transform cameraTransform = CameraCache.Main.transform;
    Ray ray = new Ray(cameraTransform.position,
```

```
cameraTransform.forward);
    SetDestination(ray);

    eventData.Use();
}
```

Here's the code breakdown:

1. Prevent the modal input handler from intercepting click events that would hit other `IInputClickHandlers`.
2. Get the **PetState** component and check if it's currently in a `holdAction` state. If so, the air-tap can break out of whatever looping action is happening.
3. Otherwise, if the air-tap has selected an object with the **TargetObject** component, establish a target for the **PetState**.

Now save the **TapToMove** script and return to the editor.

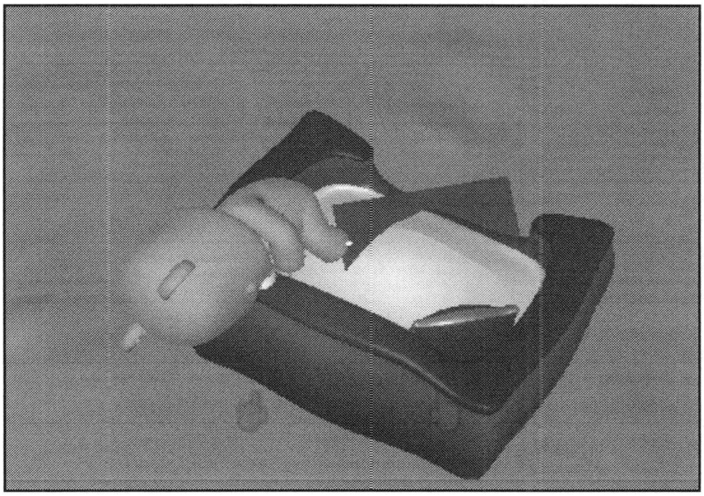

Drag and drop the **Bed** prefab into the Hierarchy so you'll have something to test with. Position it somewhere in the middle of the scene so you can find it easily.

Now play the scene. When you target the bed, the bear walks to the bed and falls into a deep sleep — other actions like eating and drinking trigger when selecting the food bowl and water bowl. You can add these to the scene if you'd like to try it out.

Adding voice commands

In addition to controlling an app using gestures like the *Air-Tap*, it's also possible to add voice interactions. Keywords and phrases are recognizable from microphone input via **KeywordRecognizer**.

You'll implement an action named `GoThere` and hook this into phrase recognition to respond to verbal commands like "Go There!" or "Come Here!".

Open **Razeware / Scripts / TapToMove.cs** and populate `GoThere()`:

```
public void GoThere(bool there)
{
    Transform cameraTransform = CameraCache.Main.transform;
    Ray ray;
    if (there)
    {
        // 1
        ray = new Ray(cameraTransform.position,
cameraTransform.forward);
    } else
    {
        // 2
        Vector3 origin = cameraTransform.position +
cameraTransform.forward * 0.25f;
        Vector3 direction = Vector3.down;
        ray = new Ray(origin, direction);
    }
    SetDestination(ray);
}
```

This is what this piece of code does:

1. `GoThere` handles a command to go to the current gaze position — like the current Air-Tap navigation point.
2. Or it directs the character to a position directly in front of the player's real-world location.

Razeware / Scripts / Media / PetKeywordRecognizer.cs describes these data members:

```
// 1. KeywordRecognizer and KeywordAction
private KeywordRecognizer keywordRecognizer;
private delegate void KeywordAction(PhraseRecognizedEventArgs
args);
private Dictionary<string, KeywordAction> keywordCollection;

// 2. GoThereEvent to respond to "Go There" or "Come Here"
public delegate void GoThereDelegate(bool there);
public event GoThereDelegate GoThereEvent;
```

Here's how this works:

1. The `KeywordRecognizer` is a built-in component that can perform basic speech recognition to match voice input to provided text phrases.
2. A `KeywordAction` is a delegate function that's called when a matching phrase is recognized. Phrases and their callback functions are provided via the dictionary `keywordCollection`.

Open **Razeware / Scripts / TapToMove.cs** again and populate `Start()` and `OnDestroy()` to subscribe and unsubscribe to and from the `GoThereEvent` event:

```
public void Start()
{
    if (PetKeywordRecognizer.Instance != null)
    {
        // 1.
        PetKeywordRecognizer.Instance.GoThereEvent += GoThere;
    }
}

public void OnDestroy()
{
    if (PetKeywordRecognizer.Instance != null)
    {
        // 2.
        PetKeywordRecognizer.Instance.GoThereEvent -= GoThere;
    }
}
```

Here's the breakdown:

1. Adding to the `PetKeywordRecognizer.Instance.GoThereEvent` during `Start()` subscribes to the event.
2. Subtracting from the `PetKeywordRecognizer.Instance.GoThereEvent` during `OnDestroy()` unsubscribes before the GameObject is destroyed.

Now, you'll set up the **PetKeywordRecognizer** to handle speech:

`Start()` needs to initialize and configure the `KeywordRecognizer`. Populate `Start()` of **PetKeywordRecognizer.cs** as follows:

```
void Start()
{
    keywordCollection = new Dictionary<string, KeywordAction>();

    // 1. voice commands are added to the dictionary
    keywordCollection.Add("Go there", OnGoThere);
    keywordCollection.Add("Come here", OnComeHere);
```

```
    // 2. KeywordRecognizer is created
    keywordRecognizer = new
KeywordRecognizer(keywordCollection.Keys.ToArray());
    keywordRecognizer.OnPhraseRecognized +=
KeywordRecognizer_OnPhraseRecognized;
    keywordRecognizer.Start();
}
```

Here's how it works:

1. The `Dictionary` mapping `string` to `KeywordAction` is created, and two phrases are added: "Go there" and "Come here". When a user says these phrases at any time during the game, it triggers their callback functions `OnGoThere` and `OnComeHere`.
2. The `KeywordRecognizer` is constructed, then a callback function is added to event producer `OnPhraseRecognized` to direct the appropriate **KeywordAction** to occur.

Complete `KeywordRecognizer_OnPhraseRecognized()` of **PetKeywordRecognizer.cs**:

```
private void
KeywordRecognizer_OnPhraseRecognized(PhraseRecognizedEventArgs
args)
{
    KeywordAction keywordAction;
    if (keywordCollection.TryGetValue(args.text, out
keywordAction))
    {
        keywordAction.Invoke(args);
    }
}
```

Whenever the **KeywordRecognizer** recognizes a phrase, it passes the text of the phrase as an argument in the variable `args.text`. `TryGetValue(args.text, out keywordAction)` attempts to get a value for a key from the dictionary, and if successful, the `KeywordAction` value is invoked to launch the callback function.

Implement `OnGoThere(..)` and `OnComeHere(..)` of **PetKeywordRecognizer.cs**:

```
// 1
void OnGoThere(PhraseRecognizedEventArgs prea)
{
    if (GoThereEvent != null)
    {
        GoThereEvent(true);
    }
}

// 2
void OnComeHere(PhraseRecognizedEventArgs prea)
```

```
{
    if (GoThereEvent != null)
    {
        GoThereEvent(false);
    }
}
```

This first method sends an event to go to a gaze point. The second method sends an event to return to the user's feet.

Save **PetKeywordRecognizer.cs** and switch back to Unity for some more editor work.

Create an empty GameObject in the Hierarchy, name it **SpeechManager** and add a **Pet Keyword Recognizer** component.

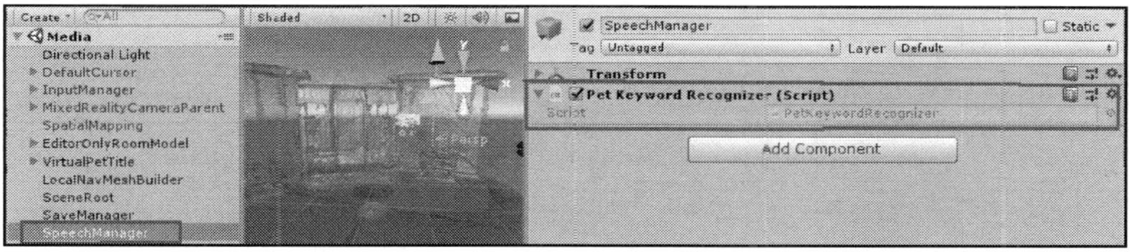

Before the **SpeechManager** can work, you need to enable the microphone capability to allow the HoloLens application access to the microphone input.

Select **Mixed Reality Toolkit > Configure > Apply UWP Capability Settings** in the top menu, enable the **Microphone** capability and click **Apply**.

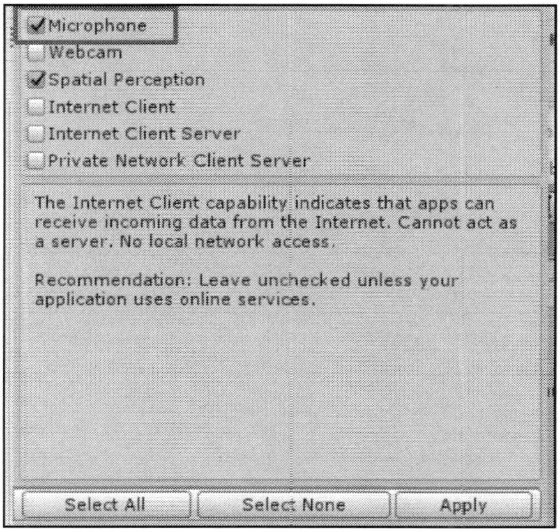

At this point, if you deploy the application to the HoloLens, the voice commands allow you to navigate the pet, in addition to the air-tap gestures. Nice!

Next up, you'll explore the HoloLens photo camera and **PhotoCapture** features.

PhotoCapture

On the HoloLens, you can record in-game photos and movies via the **PhotoCapture** API.

> **Note**: A recent bug introduced in Unity 2018.2.x (1076629) prevents the HoloLens from taking photos via **PhotoCapture**. Unity has a fix to be added to 2018.2 and 2018.3 series, but you can use the known working version of 2018.1.8f1 until this is available.

Open **Razeware / Scripts / Media / PhotoTaker.cs** and populate `Start()`:

```
void Start()
{
    cameraResolution =
PhotoCapture.SupportedResolutions.OrderByDescending((res) =>
res.width * res.height).First();
    if (takePhotoOnStart)
    {
        TakePicture();
    }
}
```

`Start` selects the best camera resolution and can initiate a photo capture.

Now fill in `TakePicture()` in the **PhotoTaker.cs** script:

```
public void TakePicture()
{
    // Set the first parameter true to include holograms.
    PhotoCapture.CreateAsync(true, OnPhotoCaptureCreated);
}
```

`TakePicture()` asynchronously creates the **PhotoCapture** object which activates the callback `OnPhotoCaptureCreated` when ready.

Next, complete `OnPhotoCaptureCreated` in **PhotoTaker.cs**:

```
void OnPhotoCaptureCreated(PhotoCapture captureObject)
{
    photoCaptureObject = captureObject;

    CameraParameters c = new CameraParameters();
    // 1. Use full opacity to get a mixed image.
    c.hologramOpacity = 1.0f;
    // 2. Set width, height, and a pixel format.
    c.cameraResolutionWidth = cameraResolution.width;
    c.cameraResolutionHeight = cameraResolution.height;
    c.pixelFormat = CapturePixelFormat.BGRA32;
    // 3. Hook in the next async callback
    photoCaptureObject.StartPhotoModeAsync(c,
OnStartPhotoCapture);
}
```

Here's how it works:

1. `OnPhotoCaptureCreated` sets the Holograms to render as fully opaque.
2. It then sets the resolution for the photo and pixel format based on current camera settings.
3. Finally, it asynchronously starts photo mode, hooking in the `OnStartPhotoCapture` callback.

Fill in `OnStartPhotoCapture` of **PhotoTaker.cs**:

```
void OnStartPhotoCapture(PhotoCapture.PhotoCaptureResult result)
{
    if (result.success)
    {
        if (renderToTexture)
        {
            // 1

photoCaptureObject.TakePhotoAsync(OnCapturedPhotoToMemory);
        } else
        {
            // 2
            string filename = string.Format(@"CapturedImage{0}
_n.jpg", Time.time);
            string filePath =
System.IO.Path.Combine(Application.persistentDataPath,
filename);
            photoCaptureObject.TakePhotoAsync(filePath,
PhotoCaptureFileOutputFormat.JPG, OnCapturedPhotoToDisk);
        }
    }
}
```

Here's what happens:

1. Rendering to a texture hooks in `OnCapturedPhotoToMemory`.
2. Rendering to a fill sets up a filename and writes the image to a file via `TakePhotoAsync`.

Next, fill in `OnCapturedPhotoToDisk` of **PhotoTaker.cs**:

```
void OnCapturedPhotoToDisk(PhotoCapture.PhotoCaptureResult
result)
{
    photoCaptureObject.StopPhotoModeAsync(OnStoppedPhotoMode);
}
```

Saving to a texture memory displays the photo by applying the texture to a material.

Fill in `OnCapturedPhotoToMemory` of **PhotoTaker.cs** with:

```
void OnCapturedPhotoToMemory(PhotoCapture.PhotoCaptureResult
result, PhotoCaptureFrame photoCaptureFrame)
{
    // 1 Copy the raw image data into the target texture
    Texture2D targetTexture = new
Texture2D(cameraResolution.width, cameraResolution.height);
    photoCaptureFrame.UploadImageDataToTexture(targetTexture);

    // 2 Create a GameObject to which the texture can be applied
    GameObject photo = Instantiate(Photo);
    Renderer quadRenderer = photo.GetComponent<Renderer>() as
Renderer;
    quadRenderer.material = new
Material(Shader.Find("MixedRealityToolkit/Standard"));

    // 3 Set its position to be in front of the camera view.
    Transform camera = CameraCache.Main.transform;
    photo.transform.position = camera.position + camera.forward
* 1f;
    photo.transform.rotation =
Quaternion.LookRotation(camera.forward);
    quadRenderer.material.SetTexture("_MainTex", targetTexture);

    // 4 Deactivate the camera
    photoCaptureObject.StopPhotoModeAsync(OnStoppedPhotoMode);
}
```

Here's how it works:

1. The image data is copied to a Texture2D.
2. Instantiate a **Photo** prefab and create a new material to hold the texture.

3. Move the photo ahead of the camera view and set the texture on a quad renderer.
4. Deactivate the camera.

Fill in the clean-up code in `OnStoppedPhotoMode` in **PhotoTaker.cs**:

```
void OnStoppedPhotoMode(PhotoCapture.PhotoCaptureResult result)
{
    photoCaptureObject.Dispose();
    photoCaptureObject = null;
    Destroy(this);
}
```

Regardless of the destination for the photo, clean-up is needed to reclaim memory. `OnStoppedPhotoMode` disposes of the **PhotoCapture** instance and destroys the attached GameObject.

Save the script and return to the editor.

Taking photos in the game

Add a new **3D Object > Quad** to the Hierarchy and rename this to **Photo**.Set **Photo**'s scale to **(X:0.5 Y:0.5 Z:0.5)** in the Inspector.

Add a **Bounding Box Rig** component to **Photo** and point the **AppBar Prefab** field to the **HoloToolkit / UX / Prefabs / AppBar / AppBar.prefab** prefab.

Now set the **Bounding Box Prefab** field to the **HoloToolkit / UX / Prefabs / BoundingBoxes / BoundingBoxBasic.prefab** prefab.

The bounding box rig and app bar provide basic controls to change scale, rotate and remove photos (see **Chapter 23 Build an immersive experience with sound and state** for more information).

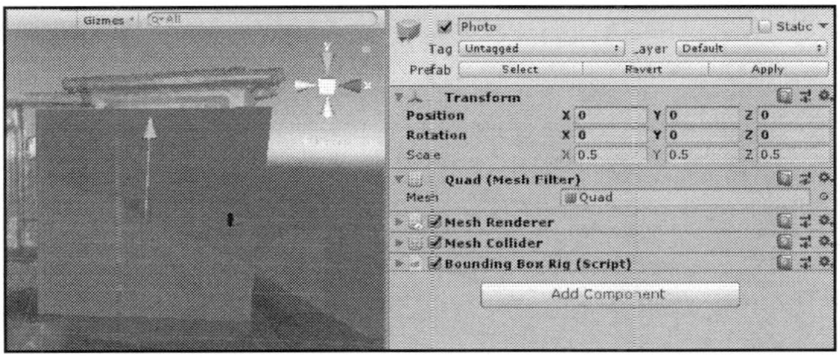

Save **Photo** as a prefab inside **Razeware / Prefabs** and remove this GameObject from the scene.

Create a new empty GameObject in the Hierarchy, name it **PhotoTaker** and add a **Photo Taker** component.Now drag **Razeware / Prefabs / Photo** into the `Photo` field to provide the GameObject to be created in the scene.

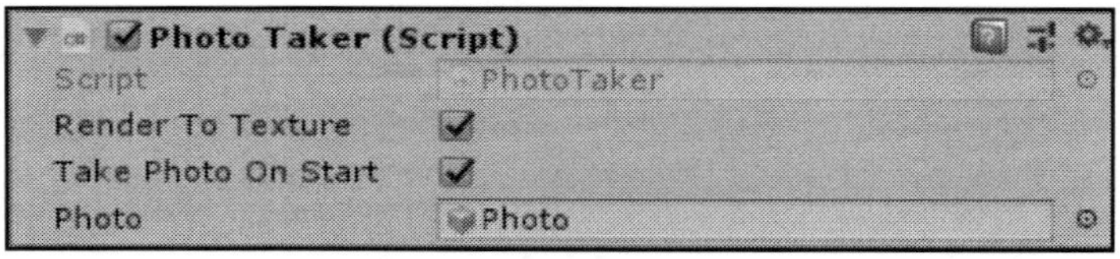

Save **PhotoTaker** as a prefab in **Razeware / Prefabs** and remove this from the scene as well.

Now, as a way to hook in the photo-taking feature, find **Razeware / Prefabs / HoverMenu**, expand the prefab and select the button containing a camera mesh:

In the Inspector, change the **Create Button** component's field **Prefab to Create** value to the newly created **Razeware / Prefabs / PhotoTaker** prefab.

You'll need to enable a UWP capability to use the HoloLens camera. Choose the menu item **Mixed Reality Toolkit > Configure > Apply UWP Capability Settings** and enable the **Webcam** capability, then click **Apply**.

If you're on a computer with a webcam, you can now test the **PhotoTaker** by running the scene in the Unity editor. Otherwise, you can deploy the application to the HoloLens to test.

Place the pet, gaze on the pet to open the menu and click on the camera button.

Unity takes a photo and maps the image as a texture onto a **Photo** GameObject that appears in the world ahead of the user's view.

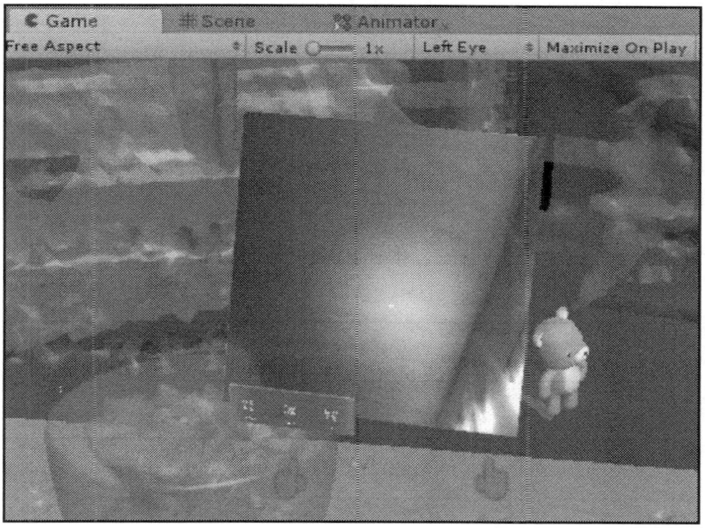

Hidden World Effects

A novel effect that you can make with augmented reality is to create *holes* in the real-world that let you see hidden virtual objects underneath. This is demonstrated by the **Roboraid** application for the HoloLens where laser shots blasted holes in the wall to reveal bricks and pipes.

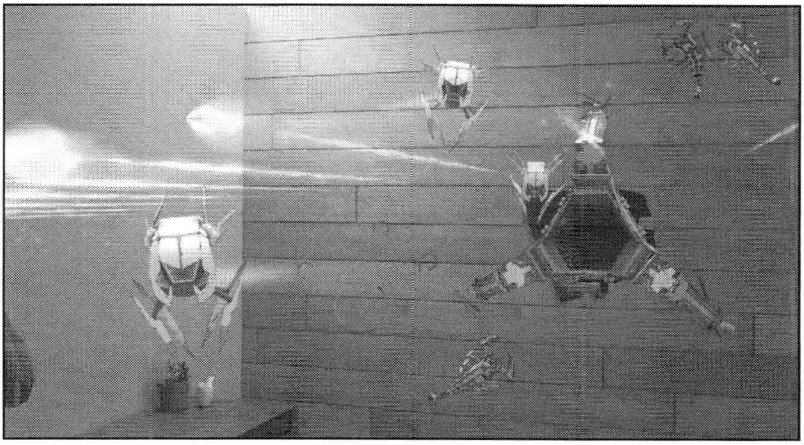

The key to creating this illusion is to allow a view through a hole to hidden geometry while other angles should block the view. An occluding box can create this effect, and the provided **Hole** mesh is an example of a pinhole box.

Make an empty GameObject in the Hierarchy named **HiddenItem** and set its position to **(X:0, Y:0, Z:2.0)**. Drag the **Razeware / Models / Hole** model as a child underneath **HiddenItem**.

The **Hole** is a box with a circle cutout in one face. Reset the Transform component for **Hole** and then set the scale to **(X:0.15, Y:0.15, Z:0.15)**.

Find the **Animator** component of **Hole** and set the **Controller** field to the **Razeware / Animations / HoleAnimator**.

Drag **Razeware / Models / NameTag** as a child of **Hole** and name this **StarPoint**. Set the scale to **(X:1, Y:1, Z:1)**. Set the position to **(X:0, Y:-0.05, Z:0)**. Set the Material for **StarPoint** to **Razeware / Materials / ButtonMat**.

Create a **Plane** named **Floor** as a child of **HiddenItem**. To fit the plane within the box at the base, in the Inspector, set the scale to **(X:0.04, Y:0.04, Z:0.04)** and the position to **(X:0, Y:-0.125, Z:0)**.

Set the Material for **Floor** to **RazeWare / Materials / FloorMaterial** to make the plane display a pipes-and-rafters texture that enhances the illusion of seeing into the floor.

Right now, the scene looks like this:

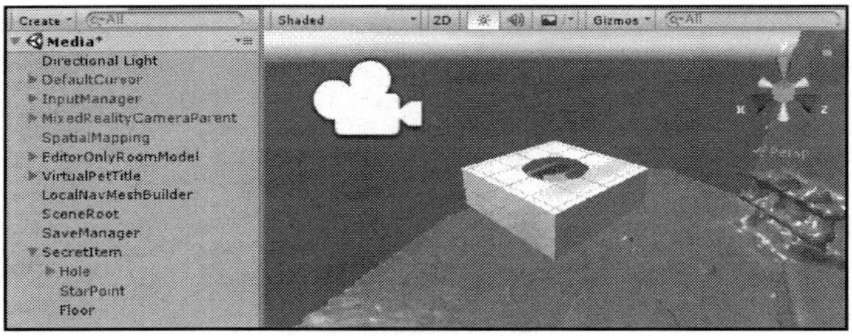

Time to make the box turn invisible! For this magic trick, you need to use the shader from the MRTK library named **WindowOcclusion**.

Create a material and name it **Razeware / Materials / WindowOcclusionMat**. Change the **Shader** field using the Inspector to **MixedRealityToolkit / WindowOcclusion**.

Find **HiddenItem / Hole / Hole** and set its material to the newly created **Razeware / Materials / WindowOcclusionMat**. The **WindowOcclusion** shader does not draw visible pixels, but it does write to the memory called the depth stencil. This causes other objects to avoid drawing if they exist behind the location of the wall, effectively occluding it.

This is a similar material to the **Occlusion** material applied on the spatial map meshes (See **Chapter 23: Build an Immersive Experience With Sound and State**). However, **WindowOcclusion** is designed to interact better with closer objects.

After applying this material, the box looks like this:

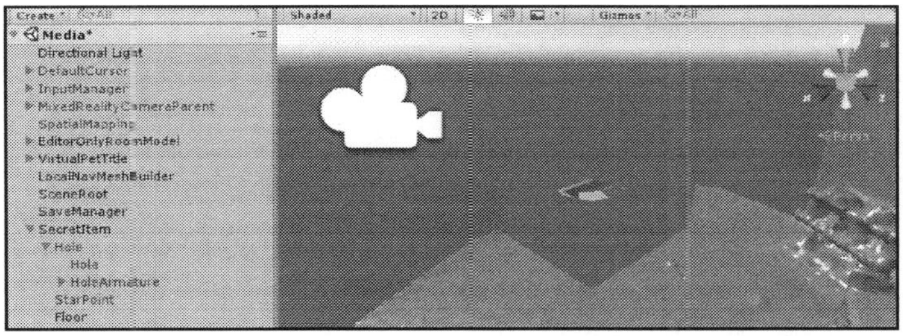

Now, you'll create the **HiddenItem** script that responds when the pet nears the hole in the floor.

Open the stubbed **Razeware / Scripts / Game / HiddenItem.cs** and populate `Start()`:

```
void Start()
{
    animator = Hole.GetComponent<Animator>();
    animator.SetBool("IsOpen", false);
    SetupShader();
}
```

`Start()` obtains the animator from the child **Hole** for animating the hole opening. `SetupShader()` is described later.

Next, fill in `Update` of **HiddenItem.cs**:

```
void Update ()
{
    Radius += Time.deltaTime;
    if (Time.time > NextTime)
    {
        NextTime = Time.time + Interval;

        // 1. Update the shader.
        UpdateShader();

        // 2. Restart ping when exceed a radius.
        if (Radius > MaxRadius)
        {
            Radius = MinRadius;
            PlaySound(PulseSound);
        }
    }
}
```

Here's how it works:

1. The method updates a visual effect via the `UpdateShader()` call. `UpdateShader` is described further on.
2. The method plays a spatial sound at the location of the **HiddenItem** and resets the `Radius` when it exceeds the `MaxRadius`. This creates a sonar ping effect. `PlaySound` is described further on as well.

Detecting when the player finds the **HiddenItem** happens when the pet collides with a **BoxCollider** of the **HiddenItem**. This is checked during the `OnTriggerEnter(..)` method of **HiddenItem.cs**:

```
void OnTriggerEnter(Collider other)
{
    IsEntered = true;
    animator.SetBool("IsOpen", true);

    StartCoroutine(CoinJump());
}
```

`OnTriggerEnter` is called when a collision triggers the method. It sets the state `IsEntered` to `true` so that you can recognize that an object was found, which triggers a coin jump effect (by way of invoking a Coroutine).

Attach **Razeware / Scripts / Game / HiddenItem.cs** as a component to **HiddenItem**. Set the field **Coin** to **StarPoint** and set the field **Hole** to the top-level **Hole** (i.e. the parent **Hole** GameObject).

You'll also need to set the field references for:

- **Sonar Pulse Mat**: Use **Razeware / Materials / SonarPulseMat.mat**.
- **Pulse Sound**: Use **Razeware / Audio / SonarPulse.wav**.
- **Coin Sound**: Use **Razeware / Audio / CoinBling.wav**.

After attaching the **HiddenItem** component, locate the **BoxCollider** in the Inspector and enable the field **IsTrigger**.

When the **MoveablePet** enters the collider of the **HiddenItem**, it activates `OnTriggerEnter` and opens the hole mesh animator.

Select the **HiddenItem**, and in the Inspector, change the **Layer** field to **IgnoreRaycast** to allow raycasts to select positions within the boundary of the collider of **HiddenItem**. Select **Yes, change children** when prompted about changing the Layer for child objects too.

Save **HiddenItem** as a prefab inside **Razeware / Prefabs / HiddenItem** and remove it from the scene Hierarchy.

Note: By default, the camera clears the screen with a skybox, which does not clear the **WindowOcclusion** area when running in the Unity editor. Select the **MixedRealityCameraParent / MixedRealityCamera** and change the **Opaque Display Settings** to set **Clear Flags:Color** to clear as a solid black color, matching the **Transparent Display Settings** that renders without issue on the HoloLens.

To trigger the collider of **HiddenItem**, the **MoveablePet** needs to have a GameObject with both a **Collider** and a **RigidBody**.

Bring **MoveablePet** back into the Hierarchy view (drag and drop the **MoveablePet.prefab** prefab back into the scene) and add an empty GameObject as a child named **MoveablePet / BearModel / RigidColliderChild**.

Adjust the scale of **RigidColliderChild** to **(X:0.1, Y:0.1, Z:01)** and add a **RigidBody** and a **BoxCollider** component.

On the **RigidBody**, enable **IsKinematic**. The requirement to include a **RigidBody** is to satisfy the rules of Unity collider triggers which requires one of the two collider objects to contain a **RigidBody**.

Save **MoveablePet** as a prefab in **Razeware / Prefabs / MoveablePet** (just click **Apply** in the Inspector for **MoveablePet** and remove it from the scene.

Making hidden objects appear

In the game *RoboRaid*, objects randomly appear on different walls, and the player has to react to spatial audio and visual clues to find the objects before it's too late. You'll create a similar game flow here where objects will spawn in random floor locations, and the bear needs to discover the hidden object in time to score a point.

The **HiddenState** MonoBehaviour will describe the game flow of making objects appear and finding them.

Spawning objects in the room

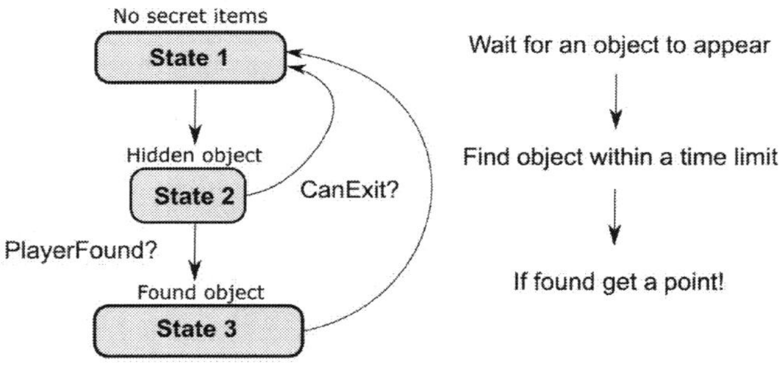

You'll use the **HiddenState** MonoBehaviour to describe the state machine; it will be responsible for creating and destroying hidden objects in the scene.

Open **Razeware / Scripts / Game / HiddenState.cs** and populate `Start()`:

```
public void Start()
{
    // 1. States
    GameState ready = new GameState("ready", EnterReady);
    GameState hidden = new GameState("hidden", EnterHidden);
    GameState found = new GameState("found", EnterFound);

    // 2. Transitions
    ready.AddTransition(new StateTransition(() => CanExit,
```

```
hidden));
        // 3. IsTriggered
        hidden.AddTransition(new StateTransition(() =>
IsTriggered(), found));
        hidden.AddTransition(new StateTransition(() => CanExit,
ready));
        found.AddTransition(new StateTransition(() => CanExit,
ready));

        // 4. Start the state machine.
        SetCurrentState(ready);
        SetEnabled(true);
    }
```

Here's how it works:

1. Create the `GameState`.
2. Add the `StateTransition` between states to the `StateMachine`. Most states have a transition checking `CanExit` that allows exits after a time limit.
3. `IsTriggered()` checks the **Collider** trigger on the hidden object.
4. Set the starting state, enable the state machine and trigger `EnterReady()` to begin.

Next, fill in two helper methods of **HiddenState.cs**:

```
void StartExitTimer(int seconds)
{
    // 1
    if (Timer != null)
    {
        StopCoroutine(Timer);
    }
    // 2
    Timer = WaitToExit(seconds);
    StartCoroutine(Timer);
}

IEnumerator WaitToExit(int seconds)
{
    // 3
    yield return new WaitForSeconds(seconds);
    // 4
    CanExit = true;
}
```

Here's what they do:

1. `StartExitTimer(..)` enables a timer to exit the current state. First, it cancels any existing timer.
2. Next, it obtains an IEnumerator coroutine that acts as a timer for `seconds`.
3. The coroutine yields for the number of seconds.
4. Finally, it sets the `CanExit` value to `true`.

Fill in `EnterReady()` of **HiddenState.cs**:

```
void EnterReady()
{
    Destroy(HiddenGameObject);
    CanExit = false;
    StartExitTimer(5);
}
```

`EnterReady()` first destroys any existing **HiddenGameObject**, then it sets a timer to exit the state after five seconds to move from the ready to the hidden state.

Fill in `EnterHidden()` of **HiddenState.cs**:

```
void EnterHidden()
{
    // 1
    CanExit = false;
    StartExitTimer(15);

    // 2
    Vector3 navPt;
    if (RandomNavPoint(gameObject.transform.position,
SpawnRadiusToPlayer, out navPt))
    {
        GameObject SceneRoot =
GameObject.FindObjectOfType<SceneRoot>().gameObject;
        HiddenGameObject = Instantiate(HiddenItemPrefab);
        HiddenGameObject.transform.position = navPt;
        HiddenGameObject.transform.parent = SceneRoot.transform;
    }
}
```

Here's what's happening:

1. Again, `EnterHidden()` can exit the state after waiting 15 seconds.
2. However, it also picks a new random location on the NavMesh; if successful, it creates a `HiddenItem` at this location.

Now fill in `EnterFound()` of **HiddenState.cs**:

```
void EnterFound()
{
    CanExit = false;
    StartExitTimer(5);
}
```

The found state delays five seconds then returns to the ready state.Next, fill in `IsTriggered()` of **HiddenState.cs**:

```
bool IsTriggered()
{
    if (HiddenGameObject)
    {
        HiddenItem item =
HiddenGameObject.GetComponent<HiddenItem>();
        if (item)
        {
            return item.IsEntered;
        }
    }
    return false;
}
```

This method checks the **HiddenItem** MonoBehaviour that checks when the pet crosses a boundary box around the **HiddenItem**. The value of `item.IsEntered` is returned (`true` or `false`), otherwise `false` is returned.

Now fill in `RandomNavPoint(..)` of **HiddenState.cs** with the following:

```
public static bool RandomNavPoint(Vector3 origin, float
distance, out Vector3 location)
{
    int layermask = -1;
    Vector3 randomDirection =
UnityEngine.Random.insideUnitSphere * distance;
    randomDirection += origin;

    NavMeshHit navHit;
    NavMesh.SamplePosition(randomDirection, out navHit,
distance, layermask);
    location = navHit.position;
    return (navHit.distance < distance);
}
```

This method attempts to find a random point within a unit sphere of distance that exists on the NavMesh. If successful, it returns the real-world position of the point.

Save **HiddenState.cs**.

Back in the editor, create an empty GameObject named **HiddenItemSource**. Attach **Razeware / Scripts / Game / HiddenState.cs** to **HiddenItemSource**.

Set the field **Hidden Item Prefab** to **Razeware / Prefabs / HiddenItem** you previously created.

Save **HiddenItemSource** as **Razeware / Prefabs / HiddenItemSource**.

Move the **HiddenItemSource** in the Hierarchy to be a child of the **MixedRealityCameraParent / MixedRealityCamera** GameObject.

The **HiddenItemSource** now spawns **HiddenItem** objects in locations near the player's real-world position. Give it a try!

Spatial sound

How will the player know where to look for the **HiddenItems**? The first clue will be spatial sound providing 3D audio effects originating from the location of the **HiddenItem**.

First off, configure your project to support Microsoft Spatial Audio by selecting **Edit > Project Settings > Audio** in the top menu.Next, select the drop-down field **Spatializer Plugin** and change its value to **MS HRTF Spatializer**. This is the spatial audio plugin used with the Microsoft HoloLens.

Now drag **Razeware / Prefabs / HiddenItem** back into the Hierarchy, select it and add an **Audio Source**.

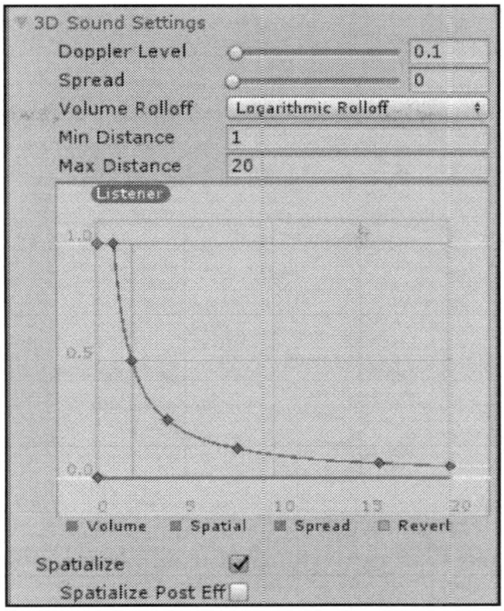

In the **AudioSource** component, enable the **Spatialize** option at the bottom of the **AudioSource** component properties. Set **Doppler Level** to **0.1** to lessen the Doppler pitch change effects. Set **Volume Rolloff** to **Logarithmic Rolloff** and then set **Max Distance** to **20**.

Open **Razeware / Scripts / Game / HiddenItem.cs** and fill in `PlaySound()`:

```
void PlaySound(AudioClip clip)
{
    AudioSource source = GetComponent<AudioSource>();
    if (source && clip)
    {
        source.PlayOneShot(clip);
    }
}
```

Now the **HiddenItem** is configured to emit a spatial sound. Update the **HiddenItem** prefab to ensure your latest changes are reflected in the prefab, and remove the edited **HiddenItem** from the scene Hierarchy.

Next, add some looping background music. This does not require spatial localization.

Find **MixedRealityCameraParent/MixedRealityCamera** and add an **AudioSource** component to it. Set the **AudioClip** field to the **Razeware/Audio/WanderingBackgroundMusic** audio clip and check the **Loop** box to have this music act as a continuous background soundtrack.

By attaching the sound to the camera, it follows the current location of the player as they move around the room.

Shader effect

Finally, you can add a visual effect to complement the 3D audio.

The starter project includes a **sonar tap** shader that draws on the surface of a mesh when a sphere intersects with the mesh. This can provide interesting spatial mesh effects, especially if you dynamically update the location of the sphere and the radius of the sphere.

You'll use this to provide a visual pulse that spreads over real surfaces to help find the hidden object.

Select **SpatialMapping** in the Hierarchy, look in the Inspector and find the **Spatial Mapping Manager** component. Here, change the field **Surface Material** to **Razeware / Materials / SonarPulseMat.mat**. This switches from the occlusion shader to one that displays visual pulses on the world objects.

Open **Razeware / Scripts / Game / HiddenItem.cs** in your IDE and fill in `SetupShader()`:

```
void SetupShader()
{
    SonarPulseMat.SetVector("_Center", transform.position);
    SonarPulseMat.SetInt("_UseWireframe", 0);
    SonarPulseMat.SetFloat("_PulseWidth", 0.1f);
}
```

Update the `UpdateShader()` method too:

```
void UpdateShader()
{
    if (SonarPulseMat)
    {
        // 1
        float Intensity = Mathf.Max(1.0f - Radius / 2f, 0.0f);
        // 2
        SonarPulseMat.SetFloat("_Radius", Radius);
        SonarPulseMat.SetVector("_PulseColor", new
Vector4(Intensity, Intensity, Intensity, -1));
    }
}
```

Here's how it works:

1. The `Intensity` is a color value that can go from white to black, depending on how far the `Radius` value is from the center point.
2. To cause an interesting shader effect here on the spatial mesh, you alter the **SonarPulseMat** Material parameters `_Radius` and `_PulseColor` using the current value of `Radius`, which increases with time.

Run the game scene one more time:

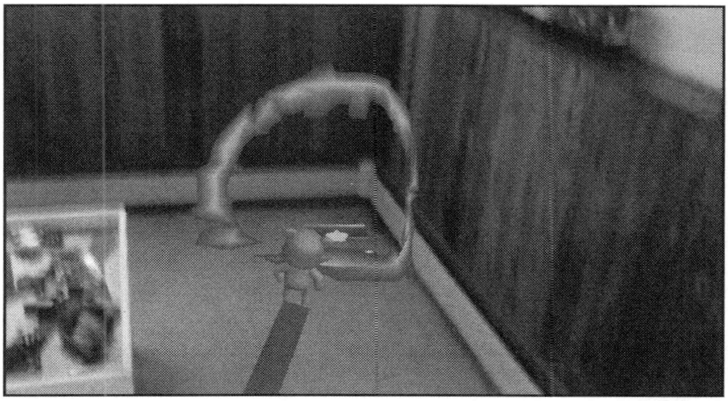

Now, when a **HiddenItem** appears, the updating parameters of **SonarPulseMat** create ripples over the meshes that describe the room surfaces.

The visual pulses match the spatial audio, and the player sees these to identify the source that is the hidden item.

Conclusion

This chapter introduced a variety of media you can use in HoloLens games including music, spatial audio effects, voice recognition and camera use.

The HoloLens chapters introduced many of the features of building applications in Unity that realize the abilities of the Microsoft HoloLens sensors for spatial mapping, gestures, microphone and camera inputs.

The completed projects show how you can utilize navigation to create games where characters that can walk across real-world surfaces.

Where to go from here?

You can extend the final project to create character-based projects for the Microsoft HoloLens. For example, you can:

1. Add a spatial **AudioSource** on your pet and play the **AudioClips** from **Razeware / Audio** for each action such as eating and sleeping with the **Razeware / Scripts / Game / PetState.cs** state machine.
2. Save your point score by adding a field to the **SaveGame** class to describe how many points you have found.
3. Customize the game by adding more 3D objects from the Unity Asset Store. Or replace the pet character with your own character and create your own **Animator**.
4. Use other shaders for the Material that is applied via the **SpatialMapping** GameObject. Can you create other interesting effects?

That's it! You're now ready to venture into the world of VR and AR and create your own amazing projects.

Conclusion

Congratulations! You've completed your deep dive into Virtual and Augmented Reality. The knowledge and skills you've gained throughout these chapters will help you in creating new games and experiences for all to enjoy.

The world of VR and AR is still young and constantly evolving, we hope that this book has been useful to you as a guide for your first steps into this amazing tech and will prove to be a valuable resource in your future projects.

And, remember, if you want to further your general understanding of Unity after working through *Unity AR & VR by Tutorials*, we suggest you read *Unity Games by Tutorials*, available on our online store:

- https://store.raywenderlich.com/products/unity-games-by-tutorials

If you have any questions or comments as you work through this book, please stop by our forums at http://forums.raywenderlich.com and look for the particular forum category for this book.

Thank you again for purchasing this book. Your continued support is what makes the tutorials, books, videos, conferences and other things we do at raywenderlich.com possible, and we truly appreciate it!

Wishing you all the best in your continued adventures,

– The *Unity AR & VR by Tutorials* team

Appendix A: VR Glossary

Eric Van de Kerckhove

Active presence: Also known as hand presence or tomato presence. A state of immersion achieved by using a handheld tool/device (peripheral) in VR. The brain intuitively accepts any object that replaces the hand as if it was part of the player's body. **Examples**: Replacing a virtual hand with an object, pressing a button, flipping a switch, pulling a lever.

Cockpit: A virtual anchor that is fixed to the player to help ground them in the virtual world. Research shows that this can help to avoid virtual reality sickness symptoms. **Examples**: Fighter jet cockpit, train cabin, car seat.

Duck test: The informal name for testing whether or not a player has reached a state of presence and immersion by monitoring their behavior when threatened by a virtual object. **Examples**: Does the player duck if an ax swings toward their head? Does the player move sideways to avoid virtual people and objects? Does the player avoid contact with walls, desks and other objects in their path?

Emotional presence: An immersive state that evokes an emotional response from the player. Much like in the real world, this can be stimulated by music, colors, symbols, words and a whole spectrum of other things. **Examples**: Empathy, joy, sadness, anger.

Eye tracking: The ability for a head-mounted display (HMD) to read the direction of the player's eyes. As technology evolves, this will become a standard for the future generations of VR. **Examples**: Tobii VR, FOVE.

Field of view: The field of view (or FOV) is the visible area a player can see in an HMD, expressed in degrees. The average human has a FOV of ~200 degrees, which means you can see objects to the immediate left and right and also ~20 degrees behind you. The first generation of both the HTC Vive and Oculus Rift in comparison allow ~100 degrees.

Flow: A mental state where a person is so engrossed in performing an activity that they forget about the world around them and can focus their full attention on the activity. This state can occur while doing just about anything that requires a high level of attention in an environment with minimal distractions. **Examples**: Playing video games, watching a movie, experiencing VR, playing an instrument.

Haptics: Haptics simulate the sense of touch through the sensation of pressure and/or vibration. Common ways to introduce haptics include rumble motors or actuators. **Examples**: Gamepad with rumble, Plexus gloves, HTC Vive controller, HoloSuit.

Head tracking: A type of motion sensing that allows head-mounted displays to monitor the position and orientation of the player's head through tracking. Positional tracking often requires extra hardware like infrared cameras placed around the player to work accurately enough to allow for room scale VR. **Examples**: Oculus Rift, HTC Vive.

Head mounted display: Commonly abbreviated to HMD. A headset or a helmet with small screens and lenses in front of each eye on which images can be shown at a high frame rate. An HMD occludes the outside world and immerses the user in a virtual reality environment. This is in contrast with an optical head-mounted display (OHMD), which projects images on a reflective, see-through surface. **Examples**: Oculus Rift, HTC Vive.

Immersion: Immersion in the context of VR is the perception of being physically present in a virtual world. This perception is created by surrounding the player with images, sounds and interactions that cause stimulation and a feeling of presence.

Latency: The delay between an action and a response. High latency causes symptoms of motion sickness and drastically lowers immersion. **Examples**: Frame drops, freezes, hitches, jarring movement.

Locomotion: Movement within a virtual environment. This can be done in all sorts of ways, some more immersive than others. **Examples**: Teleporting, arm swinging, riding a vehicle, climbing, swinging from a grappling hook.

Occlusion: The hiding of an object behind another object. Occlusion culling disables all objects occluded by another. Frustum culling, on the other hand, only disables all objects outside of the frustum (the pyramid-shaped render area) of the camera. **Examples**: Wall, tree, mountain, house.

Peripheral: A real-world device that enhances a VR experience, lets the player interact more tangibly with the virtual world and strongly increases immersion. **Examples**: Gloves, shoes, controllers, weapons.

Player: Also known as user or experiencer. The person inside the virtual reality world who is playing, interacting or witnessing the VR experience. **Examples**: You and everyone else playing or experiencing VR.

Positional audio: Sounds and music that are placed inside of a virtual world and react based on where the player is looking. **Examples**: Voice of NPC can only be heard when looking at its direction, music starts playing when looking at a sunset.

Presence: The feeling of being a part of a virtual world and ignoring any real-world distractions and limitations. **Examples that increase presence**: An NPC talking to you, the sound of your footsteps as you move, allowing interaction with all objects in some way.

Room scale: Allowing players to move freely within a room-sized environment while experiencing VR. Real world movements are mirrored in the virtual world, creating a state of presence. **Examples**: HTC Vive, Oculus Rift.

Virtual Reality: Often abbreviated to VR. Virtual reality places the player in virtual surroundings, occluding their view in all directions, either in interactive form or inside of a video. **Examples**: Oculus Rift, Google Cardboard, Google Daydream, HTC Vive.

Virtual Reality sickness: Also known as motion sickness or simulation sickness. The feeling of discomfort caused by experiencing virtual reality. Symptoms can include headache, nausea, vomiting, drowsiness and disorientation. This is a significant barrier for many people who wish to engage in VR.**Causes**: Taking away the control from the player, fast movement, fast rotation, low frame rate, free falling, mapping the player's movement to a joystick/touchpad.

Appendix B: AR Glossary

Jimmy Alamparambil

Accelerometer: A sensor that detects linear acceleration of a mobile device, usually packaged in an IMU with a gyroscope.

Anchors: Objects whose positions and orientations in the real world can be used to attach virtual objects. These anchors can move as the device gets a better understanding of the real-world environment.**Examples**: Plane anchors, image anchors, face anchors, object anchors.

Augmented reality (AR): Augmented reality augments the real world by overlaying it with virtual content. AR can be used in games and applications and is commonly used with mobile devices or HMDs.**Examples**: ARKit, ARCore, Windows Mixed Reality, Hololens, Magic Leap.

Camera intrinsics: The physical characteristics of the image sensor in a camera. These parameters, which includes focal length, optical center and aspect ratio, can be used with computer vision to analyze viewable objects.

Computer vision: A branch of science that examines images and sequences of images to discover more about the real-world environment from which those images were captured. Research in this field is used in AR, but also in other fields like artificial intelligence, machine learning, robotics, autonomous vehicles and surveillance.

Eye-tracking or gaze tracking: The detection by an AR SDK used to determine which direction the user is looking. This information can be used to find out how the user wants to interact with the system.**Examples**: Looking at a real-world object through an HMD gives you more information about that object, presented as a virtual UI projected on top of the object.

Face-tracking: The detection by an AR SDK used to determine the position and orientation of the user's face. Using this information, you can augment the user's face with virtual objects like ornaments, masks and other enhancements. It can also provide input to the system by detection of landmarks and expressions on the face that can be used to interact with virtual objects.**Examples**: ARKit Face Tracking, Pinscreen, Visage SDK.

Feature point: A point that's distinguishable in shape or texture and whose real-world position is determined by combining computer vision algorithms and motion sensor data on AR devices.

Field of view (FOV): A parameter of the camera that determines how much of a scene is observable from a certain position.

Gesture: A non-verbal communication through the body, usually performed with the head or hands. These movements can be tracked and mirrored by a motion-sensing camera or a touchscreen to perform interactions.**Examples**: Dragging, pinching, pointing, nodding.

Gyroscope: A sensor that detects rotation of a mobile device, usually packaged in an IMU with an accelerometer.

Hand-tracking: Detection by an AR SDK used to determine the position and orientation of the user's hand, including the pose and location of the fingers. This can be used as input into the system for gestures, or direct manipulation of virtual objects in the AR experience.**Examples**: LeapMotion.

Handheld AR: Augmented reality that is experienced through a display window, usually implemented via a mobile device. The display window typically shows the video footage — as seen from the device's camera — while using virtual objects rendered by the mobile device to augment the scene.**Examples**: ARKit, ARCore, Vuforia.

Head-mounted display (HMD): A device that's worn on the user's head and provides a display. For AR, the display is typically see-through, so the wearer can see the real-world environment while also seeing the virtual objects provided by the augmented reality.**Examples**: Hololens, Magic Leap, "Sword of Damocles" device.

Hit test: The process of finding points in the real world that are the result of raycasting through the AR camera and colliding against detected planes, point clouds or other anchors.

Image tracking: Detection by an AR SDK to determine the presence of specific images and their position and orientation in the real world. This can be used to provide an anchor for placing virtual objects.**Examples**: ARKit, ARCore, Vuforia.

Immersion: A measure of how believable an experience is based on the reaction of the person experiencing it. In AR, this translates to how well the virtual objects fit into the real-world environment, and how the user perceives this interaction.

Inertial Measurement Unit or IMU: A sensor found on mobile devices that can detect 1) linear acceleration using an accelerometer and 2) orientation of the device using a gyroscope. It's typically used in combination with computer vision algorithms to detect feature points and enable world-tracking.

Light estimation: A feature of an AR platform that gives an estimation of the amount of light in the real-world environment. This estimation provides parameters that can enhance the rendering of virtual objects, so they're more immersive.**Examples**: Ambient light estimate, Directional light estimate, Environment probe.

Multiplayer AR: A multiplayer experience where all of the players share the same AR experience in the same real-world environment.

Object tracking: Detection by an AR SDK to determine the presence of a pre-scanned 3D object in the real-world environment. This can be used as an anchor for virtual object attachment.

Plane detection: An algorithm used for finding flat surfaces based on the presence of feature points. These planes can expand as more feature points are detected, and they can be used to place virtual content.

Room mapping: Generating meshes out of the walls, floors, ceilings and the contents of a room so that virtual objects can occlude against real objects. With room mapping, you can also have your virtual objects interact with the real-world environment using physics.

Sensor fusion: The procedure of using computer vision algorithms and IMU data to provide an algorithm that drastically reduces world-tracking errors.

Visual Inertial Odometry or VIO: A name for the mechanism of using computer vision and IMU together to carry out world-tracking. *Visual* denotes using camera images; *Inertial* denotes using IMU data; and *Odometry* denotes measuring movement or distance.

Virtual objects: Objects that are rendered by the graphics engine in a mobile device or computer. These objects can be superimposed on footage of the real-world environment to make it appear as if they exist in the real world.**Examples**: Sphere with gold material, plane with transparency, onscreen button.

World tracking: A significant feature of augmented reality that accurately determines the position and orientation of an AR device in the real world.

Made in United States
Orlando, FL
10 November 2026

90498876R00302